rphan
nie
TRAVEL GAME
for two three or four players
LOOKIE, SANDY! THERE GOES A LEAPIN' LIZARD-
ARF!
HAROLD GRAY
LICENSED BY
S ARTISTS SYNDICATE
COPYRIGHT BY
MILTON BRADLEY CO., SPRINGFIELD, MASS., U. S. A
D1601863

THE COMPLETE

VOLUME THREE:

AND A BLIND MAN SHALL LEAD THEM

DAILY AND SUNDAY COMICS 1929-1931

FEATURING

THE INCREDIBLE TRIALS AND TRIBULATIONS OF

THE KID WITH A HEART OF GOLD AND A QUICK LEFT HOOK

Other Books in
The Library of American
Comics

Terry and the Pirates
by Milton Caniff, vols. 1-6

Dick Tracy
by Chester Gould, vols. 1-7

Scorchy Smith and
the Art of Noel Sickles

Little Orphan Annie
by Harold Gray, vols. 1-2

Volume Three in
The Complete Little Orphan Annie

And a Blind Man Shall Lead Them

Daily and Sunday Comics 1929–1931

by

Harold Gray

The Library of American Comics

IDW Publishing
San Diego, California

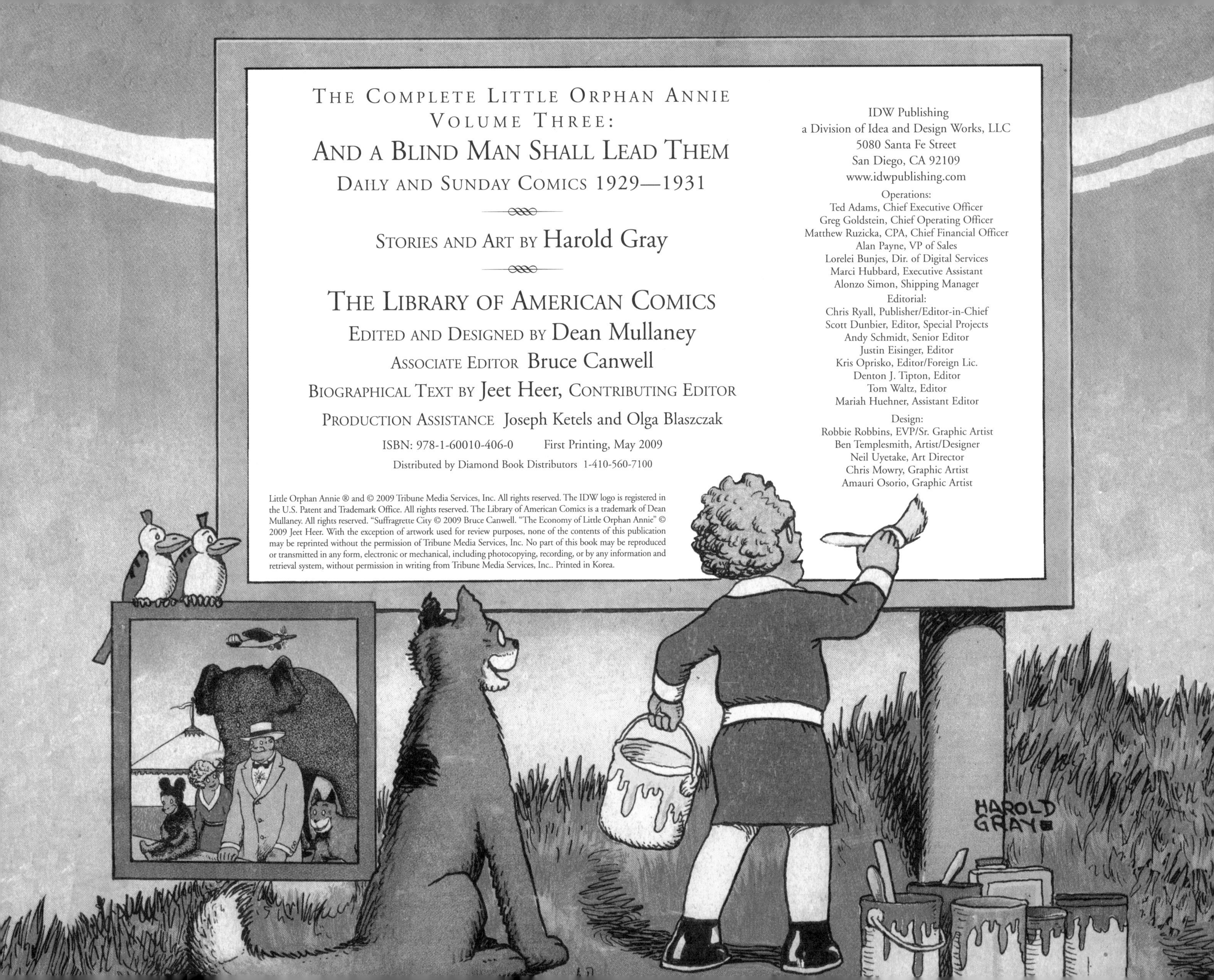

The Complete Little Orphan Annie
Volume Three:
And a Blind Man Shall Lead Them
Daily and Sunday Comics 1929—1931

Stories and Art by Harold Gray

The Library of American Comics

Edited and Designed by Dean Mullaney

Associate Editor Bruce Canwell

Biographical Text by Jeet Heer, Contributing Editor

Production Assistance Joseph Ketels and Olga Blaszczak

ISBN: 978-1-60010-406-0 First Printing, May 2009

Distributed by Diamond Book Distributors 1-410-560-7100

IDW Publishing
a Division of Idea and Design Works, LLC
5080 Santa Fe Street
San Diego, CA 92109
www.idwpublishing.com

HAROLD GRAY

Suffragette City

by Bruce Canwell

By the early 21st Century, though skirmishes remained to be fought, the major battles in the American woman's struggle for emancipation had been won. Women candidates ran for high elective office at the local, state, and federal levels. Female athletes triumphed at the Olympics, on Indy Car race tracks, and in their own professional Women's National Basketball Association. A sound could be heard ringing throughout the fifty states—the sound of glass ceilings being shattered.

A noticeable figure in the march to women's equality, however, is often neglected. For the average 21st Century American, the name *Little Orphan Annie* does not evoke images of a female trail blazer—instead, "Daddy" Warbucks's adopted daughter is often viewed as a nostalgic footnote to a bygone era. This perception is primarily fueled by the *Annie* stage play and its John Huston film adaptation in which handfuls of the comic's broad tapestry were sliced away, leaving intact only Harold Gray's pluckiest, most upbeat, "can-do" thematic threads. That is hardly a criticism—American-style self-reliance is, after all, the strip's linchpin. Yet by embracing *Annie* over *Little Orphan Annie*, by reducing the comic strip's source material to the head of a thematic pin, the "pee-pul" have allowed Annie's place in the long march toward what was once called Women's Liberation to become sadly obscured.

Annie did not secure her position as a female role model by being swiftest in any race: several child stars illuminated the landscape of popular fiction before her debut in 1924. The Rover Boys originally appeared in 1899; their popularity drove an early 20th Century market for series novels featuring such youthful protagonists as the Bobbsey Twins and Tom Swift. Child heroes in the comics predated their prose brethren: Richard Outcault's beloved Yellow Kid bowed in 1895 and was followed by mischievous Buster Brown in 1902. Rudolph Dirks introduced the *Katzenjammer Kids* to the pages of Hearst's *New York Journal* late in 1897, while Edwina Dumm's *Cap Stubbs and Tippie*—still fondly remembered by many—first hit newspaper pages in 1918.

Nor does Annie rightly stake a claim to being the first female headliner in newspaper comics, though arguably she is the first *superstar* in that field of competition. Grace Gebbie brightened the pages of the *Philadelphia Press* with *Dolly Drake* as early as 1900. A decade later, under her married name, Grace Wiederseim placed *Dottie Dimple*, working together with her sister, Margaret Hays. By 1915, divorced and remarried as Grace Drayton (the name under which she created the iconic Campbell Soup Kids), this prolific talent produced a new comics heroine whose name, "Dolly Dimples," was appropriated from her previous characters.

Following Grace Drayton by three years, Alfred Earle Hayward created the first ongoing syndicated comic starring a woman and featuring a predominantly female setting. The Ledger Syndicate began distributing Hayward's *Somebody's Stenog* to its clients on December 16, 1918. The 1920 strip, *Winnie Winkle, the Breadwinner*, was approved by Captain Joe Patterson—ramrod of the Chicago Tribune New York News Syndicate—after cartoonist Martin Branner agreed to increase the pathos by giving Winnie the responsibility of providing financial support to her two elderly parents. Four months later, at the start of 1921, King Features Syndicate released Russell Westover's *Tillie the Toiler*. *Tillie* went on to boast the distinction of featuring the first professional comic strip work by Alex (*Flash Gordon*, *Rip Kirby*) Raymond, who grew up in Westover's neighborhood and signed on as the artist's assistant in 1929. For its part, King Features would seek to reprise *Tillie*'s success in 1924 (months before *Little Orphan Annie*'s first appearance) with Chic Young's pre-*Blondie* strip, *Dumb Dora*.

If the marketplace into which Annie was born had its share of young protagonists, women protagonists, and young women protagonists, what qualities set the little chatterbox apart from her competition? What made Annie a standout where the Women's Movement is concerned? The answers are tied partly to the type of character Harold Gray invented, partly to the types of conflicts and situations he created for her.

By giving his heroine uncommon pragmatism and scrappiness, Gray made his orphan stand out from other 1920s female characters. Annie possessed abundant "street smarts" more than a half-century before the term had been coined, and in situations where intelligence would not win the day, she doubled her fists and roughhoused with the best of them. Even in the midst of the carefree "flapper era," a fighting-mad female was a novelty. Whether they recognized it or not, readers of Harold Gray's January 5, 1925 strip were seeing a new type of heroine in action as Annie rescued Sandy by literally stomping a bully-boy's face into the ground while snarling, "I'll give you a job—go pick the cinders outa yer pan!"

The flexibility Gray built into his series concept surely helped many a female reader to imagine possibilities beyond humdrum domesticity. The needs of her mother and father kept Winnie Winkle close to home, Tillie (the Toiler) Jones pursued her career primarily inside the offices of clothier J. Simpkins, but Annie was positioned to go anywhere, do anything, interact with anyone. She was equally at home in "Daddy's" mansion or on the Silos' farm, spieling the bally at the circus or shipwrecked on a desert isle, catching thieves or working as a newspaper hawker.

The early 1920s were the right time for an activist female protagonist like Annie. When Harold Gray's strip debuted, American women had held the legal right to vote for only four years: it was 1920 when the Nineteenth Amendment to the U.S. Constitution was ratified. In the United Kingdom, although women over the age of thirty had been enfranchised since 1918, it would take another full decade before women over twenty-one years of age received voting rights. Think of the adventures Annie experienced in the years between 1924 and 1928 as her British sisters waited for legal suffrage!

Women were playing a growing role in the warp and woof of society and Annie had achieved great success on the comics pages, yet the floodgates did not open for savvy, scrappy female series stars. Popular culture seemed more comfortable with the idea of active-and-intelligent heroines than with active-and-pugnacious ones. By 1930, the teen-sleuthing formula of the *Hardy Boys* (whose series had launched three years earlier) was married to *Little Orphan Annie*'s female-protagonist concept. The result was the *Nancy Drew* mysteries, sixteen of which were published in the character's first decade of existence. Nancy possessed a clear-headedness familiar to *Little Orphan Annie* readers; she was, however, significantly older and more decorous than Annie.

A resistance to activist women was not limited to fiction, but occurred in real life, as well. Katharine Hepburn arrived on the silver screen in 1932, starring in fifteen films and winning her first Academy Award prior to 1940. She played tomboy Jo March in 1933's *Little Women* and high-octane socialite Susan Vance in Howard Hawks's delightful 1938 romp, *Bringing Up Baby*. That same year, however, Hepburn was dubbed "box office poison" in a poll of cinema owners. Her intellectual, tart-tongued personality, "shocking" preference for pants and men's suits, and anti-Hollywood/anti-movie-star approach (she snubbed the press and often refused to sign autographs) were heavily criticized at the time. Of course, those same qualities would eventually help turn her into a motion picture icon, ranked in 1999 by the American Film Institute as the pre-eminent female star in the history of U.S. film.

There was significant resistance throughout the 1930s to the idea of the "fightin' female," yet the concept gained the occasional toehold. Patricia Savage did not headline her own series, but she was the sole recurring female in the *Doc Savage* pulps, debuting in the eleventh supersaga, 1934's "Brand of the Werewolf." Doc's bronze-skinned cousin could be seen as Annie, fully grown. In his 1973 "biography," *Doc Savage—His Apocalyptic Life*, author Philip Jose Farmer praises Pat: "[She] doesn't just stand around and wait to be rescued, as so many heroines of fiction and the movies did and still do...She is a 'metallic tigress,' and her small right fist swings with the timing and precision of a trained boxer's...Pat won't take anything from anybody, even if it endangers her own life."

Since Pat was Doc's blood relative, the question of sex in the *Savage* pulps was neutralized at the outset. The same held true for *Little Orphan Annie* throughout the series's run. Annie's perpetual prepubescence, combined with the total absence of sexuality displayed by the adult characters in Harold Gray's cast, played a significant role in the strip's sustained popularity. Anyone could look around the neighborhood and see the dusty faces of pig-tailed tomboys. Annie was their totem: feisty and precocious, ready to befriend the friendless and defend the defenseless, facing trouble head-on, yet ready to collapse and have a good cry in "Daddy's" arms once the worst was over. Children lived vicariously through her exploits; adults were reassured by them, because while the real-life tomboys eventually grew into young women, brides, and mothers, Annie was unchanging—forever young, forever resolute—and thus, forever comforting.

Little Orphan Annie may not have offered readers much in the way of romance, but the red-haired adventuress who joined Annie in the newspapers on June 30, 1940 took care of that department. Dale Messick's glamorous "news hen," Brenda Starr, was a no-nonsense heroine ready to travel the world in pursuit of a story, often enjoying a steamy love affair in the process.

The next year, editorial decree brought radio character Margo Lane into *The Shadow*'s pulps; the magazine's letters page was quickly filled with outcries from male readers. "I am against the Margo Lane business very much. I never liked snooping women in magazines and this instance is no exception."..."I guess I was a bit hard on Margo, but if I never read about her again, it'll be soon enough." Miss Lane remained a presence in the *Shadow* novels until they ceased publication in 1949, but her acceptance by the pulp audience was grudging at best.

The same year Margo took her print bows, female costumed heroines first appeared in comic strips and comic books, bringing an element of kinkiness along with them. Tarpe Mills sold her feline heroine, Miss Fury, to the Bell Syndicate, and Wonder Woman was a red-white-and-blue thunderbolt on the cover of January, 1941's *Sensation Comics* #1. The early adventures of Diana, the Amazon princess, contained a subtext of bondage and dominance—"I like to *submit*, to be *told* what to do!"—while *Miss Fury* featured whips, lingerie shots that scandalized several newspaper editors, and a villainess whose forehead was marked with the Nazi swastika by a white-hot branding iron. Such titillation was unheard of in the world of Annie and "Daddy" Warbucks!

But the cat was out of the bag—literally, in the case of the panther-suited Miss Fury—and the "kink quotient" continued to establish itself in popular culture. By the 1960s, American audiences were treated to a modern heroine from across the ocean, as Diana Rigg brought Mrs. Emma Peel of *The Avengers* to life on television screens from coast to coast. Amateur sleuth and scientist, former corporate leader, adept armed and unarmed combatant, possessor of a unique feline beauty, Mrs. Peel was regularly attired in black leather combat outfits. She once described herself as "thoroughly emancipated," and she backed up her words by tossing men about during the action scenes in every episode. U.S. audiences went crazy for her. Still, one of her costumes was deemed too risqué for prime time—the spiked collar, ebon corset, and knee-high boots she wore as "the Queen of Sin" in *A Touch of Brimstone* caused that episode to be banned from U.S. airwaves in 1966. Fourteen years later, comic book audiences would see a reprise of that daring ensemble: artist John Byrne used it as the template for Jean Grey's "Black Queen" outfit in *Uncanny X-Men* # 132-134.

By the time those *X-Men* issues were published, the floodgates were well and truly opened for a full range of commanding female headliners: Stephen King and Sissy Spacek's Carrie, Charlie's Angels, Ms. Marvel, Norma Rae, Ripley from the *Alien* films. They would be joined over time by the likes of Punky Brewster, Emily the Strange, Thelma & Louise, Dora the Explorer, Neil Gaiman's Coraline, and many, many more.

Today, fictional female headliners can be young girls or adult women. They can be smart, funny, vulnerable, sexy, bold, and brassy. Each of them is a branch on a tree grown tall, wild, and vivid with the passage of time, a tree anchored by and nourished from the root that sprouted on August 5, 1924, the day Little Orphan Annie first scrubbed floors at Miss Asthma's orphanage, working her way into our lives and into our hearts.

LEAPIN' LIZARDS HERE COMES BARBARA

Harold Gray drawing Little Orphan Annie, early 1930s.

THE ECONOMY OF LITTLE ORPHAN ANNIE

BY Jeet Heer

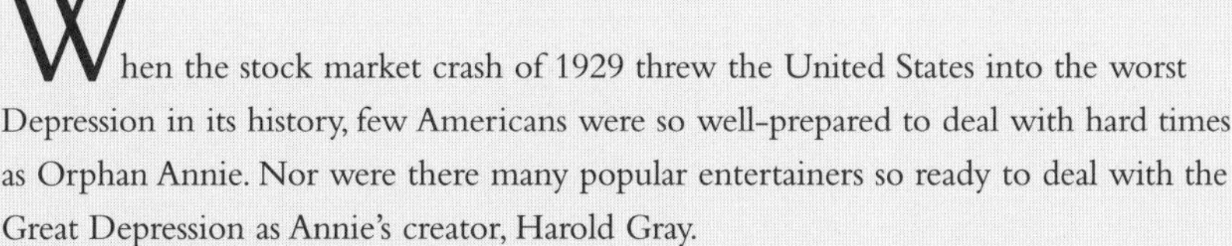

When the stock market crash of 1929 threw the United States into the worst Depression in its history, few Americans were so well-prepared to deal with hard times as Orphan Annie. Nor were there many popular entertainers so ready to deal with the Great Depression as Annie's creator, Harold Gray.

As we've seen in the first two volumes of the series, Annie's life isn't so much a "rags to riches" story as an endless adventure with the heroine struggling in poverty for protracted periods, with a few fleeting moments of comfort when she is in the care of her wealthy adopted father, "Daddy" Warbucks. From her earliest days subsisting on mush and milk at a rundown orphanage, Annie leads a precarious existence, shadowed by poverty at every step. In her first adventures, she rides the rails like a hobo, scrounges around for coal on the railway tracks to get some much-needed fuel, works as a waitress at a dingy dive, and often fends off landlords looking for rent or mortgage payments. The 1920s were no frivolous Jazz Age party for Annie, but a grim time when she and her friends had to fight to survive. In the 1930s, when belts became tighter and breadlines longer, Annie didn't have to adjust her way of life since she already knew the world of subsistence living all too well.

On August 11, 1928, Herbert Hoover, Secretary of Commerce and soon to be President, proudly declared: "We in America today are nearer to the final triumph over poverty than ever before in the history of any land. The poorhouse is vanishing from among us. We have not yet reached the goal, but, given a chance to go forward with the policies of the last eight years, we shall soon with the help of God be in sight of the day when poverty will be banished from this nation." If Annie heard those words she would likely have snorted, since she and many of her friends had to constantly worry about the poorhouse (which is where, indeed, Annie ends up briefly in early 1930).

Throughout the 1920s, cartoonist Harold Gray took issue with the self-celebratory smugness of Hoover-types who were willing to relegate poverty to the status of a fast-diminishing problem. On the Sunday page of December 26, 1926, Annie and Warbucks are enjoying dinner at a fancy restaurant when they overhear a fatuous young man (complete with a fancy cigarette holder) say, "You know, really, I am sick of this sob stuff. At Christmas the papers are depressing with all this rubbish about suffering among the poor. Lazy beggars. Work and they wouldn't be poor. As a matter of fact there is practically no suffering any more. It's the bunk."

Annie is quick to give this conceited toff the stern rebuff he deserves. "Say: listen windy," she tells him, "You're outa yer head, see? I hate to start a row in a swell joint like this but every time I hear a dumb Isaac like you tootin' I lose my temper. Whaddyuh mean 'th' bunk'? Whaddyuh mean 'No sufferin'. Huh? Just 'cause you're

STAGE BROADWAY SCREEN

VARIETY

PRICE 25¢

NEW YORK, WEDNESDAY, OCTOBER 30, 1929

VOL. XCVII. No. 3 88 PAGES

WALL ST. LAYS AN EGG

Going Dumb Is Deadly to Hostess In Her Serious Dance Hall Profesh

A hostess at Roseland has her problems. The paid steppers consider their work a definite profession calling for specialized technique and high-power salesmanship.

"You see, you gotta sell your personality," said one. "Each one of we girls has our own clientele to cater to. It's just like selling dresses

Hunk on Winchell

When the Walter Winchells moved into 204 West 55th street, late last week, June, that's Mrs. Winchell, selected a special room as Walter's exclusive sleep den for his late

DROP IN STOCKS ROPES SHOWMEN

Many Weep and Call Off Christmas Orders — Legit Shows Hit

MERGERS HALTED

Kidding Kissers in Talkers Burns Up Fans of Screen's Best Lovers

Talker Crashes Olympus

Paris, Oct. 29.

Fox "Follies" and the Fox Movietone newsreel are running this week in Athens, Greece, the first sound pictures

Boys who used to whistle and girls who used to giggle when love scenes were flashed on the screen are in action again. A couple of years ago they began to take the love stuff seriously and desisted but the talkers are reviving the ha ha for film osculators.

Heavy loving lovers of silent

LEFT: *The famous* Variety *headline by Claude Binyon, reporting on "Black Tuesday," the disastrous 16,000,000-share day on the stock market.*

eatin' regular, an' go blind everytime yuh see some poor guy that's down and out, yuh think everything's rosey, do yuh?" Berated by Annie, the formerly self-satisfied young man quickly flees the restaurant.

In popular memory, the Twenties are fondly recollected as a period of national prosperity, when a fast-rising stock market and easy credit allowed millions of Americans to enjoy for the first time the middle class comforts of car and home ownership. There is a measure of truth to this sunny picture, but the economy of the 1920s had many dark clouds that were ignored at the time and often forgotten since.

Not everyone shared in the general prosperity. For farmers, those were hard years, when falling prices and tighter competition from Europe led to much lower incomes than they enjoyed in the early 20th century.

◆ ◆ ◆

For many working class Americans, the 1920s were a time of struggle, not luxury. The conflict between Capital and Labor—which had first become a national issue with industrialization at the end of the 19th century—intensified in the 1920s. With friends of big business like Calvin Coolidge and Herbert Hoover in power, labor had a hard time calling attention to the fact that the rising productivity of the country wasn't matched by rising wages. Unions were on the defensive, and wages just barely kept above inflation.

The easy money that funded the speakeasy parties of the 1920s was sometimes purely fictitious. Charles Ponzi (whose name became memorialized in the phrase "Ponzi scheme") was only the most notorious of the many con men who lured investors with promises of quick wealth. Warm and inviting Florida was ground zero for a wildly overblown housing bubble and the widespread fraudulent sale of swampland as "waterfront property." Reputable brokers encouraged cash-strapped citizens to buy stocks on margin (they'd be foolish not to, since everyone knows stocks can only go up…). The New York Stock Exchange started to resemble a giant casino rather than a sober house of investment. In many ways, the 1920s were not unlike early years of the 21st century, with speculative growth creating a false picture of prosperity.

The dark side of the 1920s economy is worth lingering over because all of these problems, often ignored or pooh-poohed by mainstream journalists and high-ranking government officials, were amply discussed in an unexpected place: the comic strip section of any newspaper that carried *Little Orphan Annie*. In 1929, readers of Annie

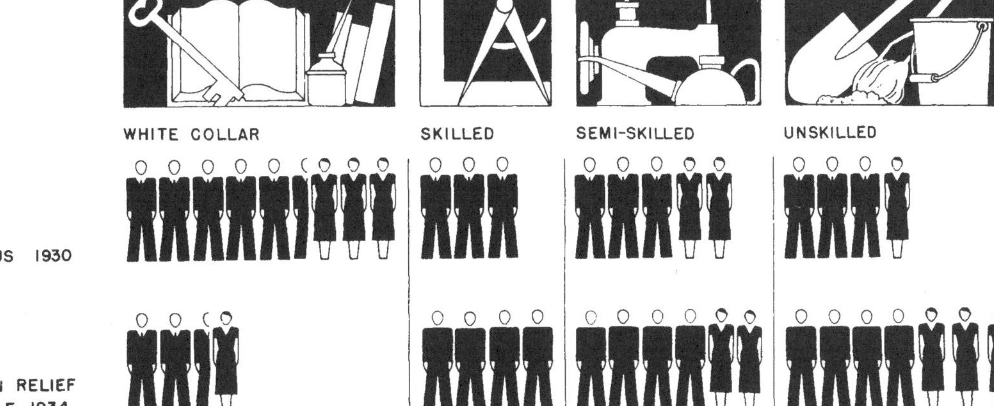
SOCIO-ECONOMIC DISTRIBUTION OF TOTAL AND RELIEF WORKERS
AF-1549, W. P. A.
WHITE COLLAR
SKILLED
SEMI-SKILLED
UNSKILLED
CENSUS 1930
URBAN RELIEF SAMPLE 1934

LEFT AND BELOW: A *1934 study by President Roosevelt's Works Progress Administration, comparing those gainfully employed in 1930—the first year of the Depression—with citizens on public relief in 1934. Manual laborers and factory workers, those classified as semi-skilled and unskilled, were hardest hit. It was discovered that the average period of time out of work from the last job at the usual occupation was thirty months for men and twenty months for women.*

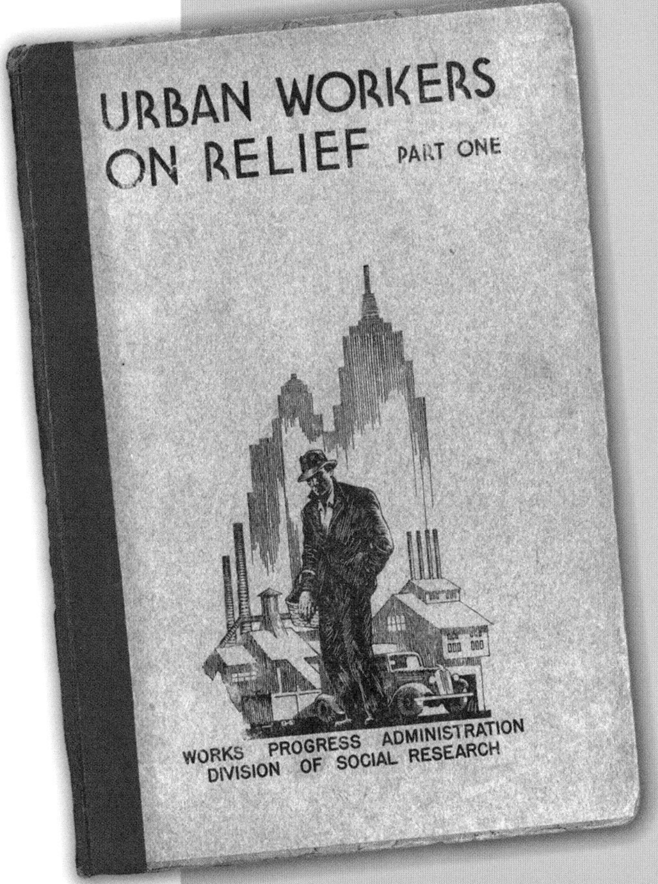
URBAN WORKERS ON RELIEF PART ONE
WORKS PROGRESS ADMINISTRATION
DIVISION OF SOCIAL RESEARCH

heard Byron Silo cogently complain about the tough lot of farmers; later readers witnessed the difficulty Monk Dooley, a hardworking cab driver, had in supporting his family on his meager income; and finally, readers saw the story of old John Blunder, a banker whose reckless stock market speculation nearly destroys the savings of a whole town. (The Blunder sequence, as seen at the end of the last volume, featured a run on a bank, and is especially prescient, foretelling the crisis of 1933 when President Franklin Roosevelt was forced to call a banking "holiday"—forcing banks to temporarily close their doors until the public's immediate panic subsided.) As Annie says about the troubles of the Monk family, "I betcha, Sandy, mighty few folks realize how close to th' edge most poor folks really are all th' time. Even poor folks don't re'lize till somethin' happens."

Harold Gray is often unfairly dismissed as a simple-minded conservative who endlessly recycled bromides about the greatness of the free market. The sociologist and comics scholar Arthur Asa Berger, in his 1973 book *The Comic-Stripped American*, once characterized *Little Orphan Annie* as "a legacy of the Coolidge era." Gray was a conservative Republican but his worldview was quite distinct from someone like Coolidge, a complacent celebrator of the status quo who believed that "the business of America is business." Unlike Coolidge (or Coolidge's successor, Herbert Hoover), Gray was alert to social problems. His cartooning was informed by a reporter's instinct to find out what was happening in the world. Everywhere in *Orphan Annie* we see evidence of a cartoonist who has his eyes open and is paying attention to how people live and work.

Gray's interest in social problems served him well in the 1920s, when it gave *Annie* an abrasive grittiness lacking in other strips. But it was the 1930s, when stories of poverty suddenly took on a new resonance and urgency, that allowed Gray's plebeian realism to become part of the national conversation. When it was no

Tuesday, March 10

Saturday, April 11

Friday, October 2

longer possible to ignore poverty, the struggles of Annie no longer seemed fanciful adventures; they now seemed closer to a newspaper headline than an outgrowth of Victorian fiction. During the Great Depression, Annie would become much more popular than ever before, as well as the source of real political controversy, as Senators and Congressmen debated whether the strip offered a fair picture of the world.

The late-1929 Blunder episode also demonstrates the new level of care with which Gray told his stories. In the early *Annie* strips, characters were often introduced in a haphazard fashion, and plot meandered from week to week with little sense of an overall direction. The Blunder episode, however, was as carefully plotted as a mystery story or a three-act drama: Gray brings Annie into Blunderville, introduces her over a few weeks to the key players of the drama (the poor widow Mrs. Twinkle, the cold-blooded rich banker and his kind son, the adventurer Jack Pepper, Judge Tort, and the railway agent Ed Barker who has his life savings in the bank). All these characters will eventually play a necessary role in the unfolding story, so their distinctive personalities are sharply defined. From the start, there is foreshadowing from the start of the generational conflict that will be the major theme of the story, which plays out before our eyes crisply and convincingly.

With the resolution of the Blunder storyline, Gray is quick to set the stage for the next drama, which opens this volume. Again, Gray's care in construction is evident: certain characters who would hamper the action are quickly taken off stage. While Annie's life in Blunderville seems at first unusually placid, there are hints of the trouble to come.

Clearly by 1929, Gray was becoming a much more thoughtful craftsman in terms

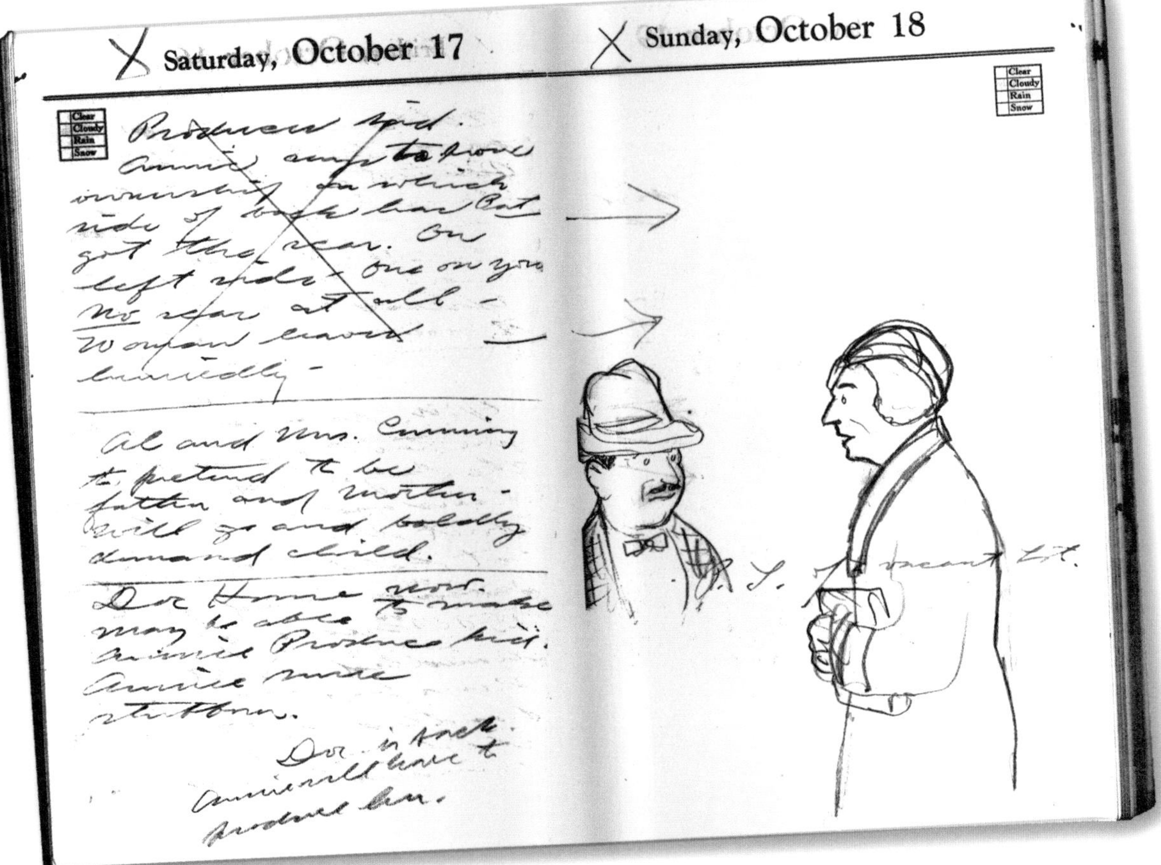
Saturday, October 17
Clear
Cloudy
Rain
Snow
Sunday, October 18
Clear
Cloudy
Rain
Snow

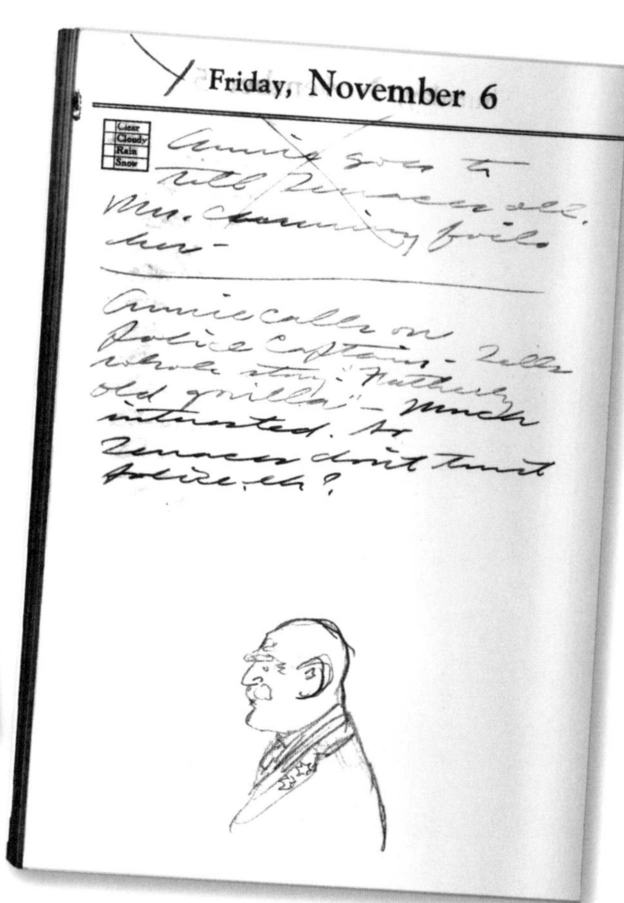
Friday, November 6
Clear
Cloudy
Rain
Snow

of plotting. Why the change? A few factors seem to be at work. One is personal. As we noted last volume, Gray married Helen Winifred Frost on July 17, 1929. The new Mrs. Gray took an active interest in the comic strip and became a collaborator of sorts with her husband. Having a second set of eyes looking over his shoulders may have made Gray more mindful in his approach to narrative.

The year of Gray's marriage also seems to have coincided with a new compositional method that the cartoonist adopted. So far as we can tell, 1929 is the first year Gray used a diary to plot out his storyline. From then on, he would annually buy a diary and jot down, day by day, bits of dialogue and plot points. The diary method—which was also used by Frank King for his work on *Gasoline Alley*—seems perfectly suited for a cartoonist doing a daily strip: it allowed Gray to plot out far in advance each story, and to think about each day as a building block in a much larger narrative edifice. (King was using the diary method in the mid 1920s; since the two men were colleagues for the same newspaper syndicate, it is possible that King passed along the method to Gray.)

As Gray's stories became more tightly plotted, they also became more experimental and ambitious. In early 1930, for the first and only time, he tries to introduce some romance into Annie's life, with her schoolmate Itchy Jones developing a

BOTH PAGES: *Examples of Harold Gray's method of plotting* Little Orphan Annie, *in the form of daily entries in a diary, sometimes including sketches of the characters. All these examples are from the 1931 stories in this volume, including the key October 17 sequence in which Al and Mrs. Cunning claim to be little Pat's parents.*

ABOVE: *Contemporary caricature of President Calvin Coolidge by "Cesare." The question mark cards dropping from the President's hands reflect the belief that "concerning most problems which confronted his Administration he had not the slightest notion."*

ABOVE RIGHT: *People warily watching the rising tide of the Mississippi River during the great flood of 1927.*

crush on the young orphan. This tale of puppy love, written and drawn while the Gray's marriage was still basking in the warmth of its honeymoon phase, might have been influenced by the cartoonist's personal life. Certainly Itchy, shown to be a gawky country boy sometimes snubbed by the town kids, a dreamer who likes to make his own dolls and model houses, a lonely only child who spends much of his time reading adult books, resembles the young Gray as he described himself in autobiographical accounts.

Although the adults in *Annie*, including "Daddy" Warbucks, would occasionally fall in love, after Itchy Jones, Gray never again allowed a hint of romance into Annie's life, although he received regular entreaties from readers who wanted the prepubescent waif to grow into a teenager and have boyfriends. But perhaps these letters, and the brief experiment with Itchy, made Gray aware of the dangers of allowing Annie to grow up. An essential conceit of the strip is that Annie remains unchanging: not just her age but her personality and worldview are fixed and firm. If Annie grew up, she'd stop being Annie. So Gray must have decided the Itchy gambit was too risky to try again.

Gray's loftier goals can also be seen in the literary models he more explicitly echoed. As we saw in Volume Two, right from the start Gray used Dickens and other Victorian writers to supply him with characters, themes, and narrative techniques. In 1929, we see two stories that boldly resemble literary classics: Annie's time on the raft calls to mind *Huckleberry Finn*, while her adventures on a deserted island rework *Robinson Crusoe*. By using these familiar plotlines, Gray was calling attention to how novelistic his storytelling was becoming.

Gray also made a small but intriguing allusion to a more popular work of literature on November 25, 1930, when we discover that one of Warbucks's butlers is named Geeves, a near-namesake of the P.G. Wodehouse valet Jeeves, the gentleman's gentleman who serves Bertie Wooster. On at least two other occasions Gray borrowed names from the Jeeves/Wooster stories, evidence that the cartoonist was undoubtedly a Wodehouse reader.

The flood story of May 1930 in this present volume was taken not just from literature but also deliberately echoed a recent national tragedy. Readers at the time would have recalled the great Mississippi flood of 1927, when the levee system broke. The flood killed 246 people in seven states. Gray reshaped the then-familiar story of the flood and turned it into a Depression era parable about how poor people can come together to overcome adversity. As Annie reflects, "Folks here have lost most ever'thing. But I never knew folks who were any more generous. Guess people who've had bad luck are most always a little bigger-hearted. They know what it feels like to be up against it."

Gray wasn't alone in seeing the Mississippi flood in populist terms. In the early days of the flood, President Coolidge ignored repeated pleas to provide aid and make an appearance. In response to the indifference of the government, the humorist and "cowboy philosopher" Will Rogers organized relief efforts that raised more than $100,000 for the victims of the natural disaster, and wryly commented that Coolidge was waiting with "the hope that those needing relief will perhaps have conveniently died in the meantime."

As the literary critic Michael Denning noted in his 1998 book, *The Cultural Front*, narratives about floods and other natural disasters were popular in the 1930s precisely because they contained a message of how communities can come together to overcome seemingly insurmountable problems. Gray's message is clear: just as Americans overcame the flood, they can withstand the economic crisis. His use of a flood storyline in 1930 is as pointed as someone making a film about Hurricane Katrina in 2009.

The full extent of Gray's novelistic ambitions became evident in 1931, when for the first time we have an Annie adventure that takes up nearly a full year. This adventure shows Warbucks losing his fortune, forcing both the former millionaire and his adopted daughter to endure the brunt of the Depression. "Daddy" had been impoverished once before, in 1925, but there is a world of difference between the two storylines: in the first tale, Warbucks, although momentarily shell-shocked, quickly recovers and even in poverty never loses his characteristic single-minded determination. In 1931, by contrast, "Daddy" is whipped with the full lash of poverty: temporarily homeless until he finds lodging in a run-down rooming house in the "bum part of town." He's forced to take manual jobs, made to depend on Annie, and is ultimately reduced to beggary. Day after day, everything that gives Warbucks pride—including his health—is taken away from him. This tale of a man beset and besieged is as relentless as the Book of Job.

The humiliation of Warbucks has a humanizing effect. No longer the confident, blustery captain of industry, he comes to terms with his own limits. "I always said any man who had his health and his two hands could get work if he wanted to work," Warbucks reflects. "Huh! What a sap I was. I have no union card and no trade. I can't even be a janitor or a street-cleaner."

Certainly many readers in 1931 who lost their jobs or watched their loved ones sink into poverty and despair would have related to the tale of Warbucks and Annie. Gray is particularly insightful on the gender dynamics of the Depression: social workers at the time noticed that men who lost their work suffered a particular anguish when they felt that they were letting down their kids and failing in their role as breadwinners, a situation mirrored in the Annie/Warbucks relationship. "Has it come to this?" Annie's guardian wonders, referring to himself. "Warbucks practically supported by a little girl?"

The very length of the 1931 story surely owes something to the Depression. In the 1920s, Annie could overcome each new problem in a few months, but the Depression presented a new challenge. It seemed to go on forever, with no end in sight. In this new era, Gray's stories also took on a longer duration; there were no simple solutions anymore and every problem required a long time horizon.

Even before 1931 Gray was bringing the Great Depression into his comic strip. There is a particularly shocking panel in late 1930 showing kids picking through a garbage can. But in the 1931 storyline, with its epic length and complexity, Gray is taking on the Depression on a large scale.

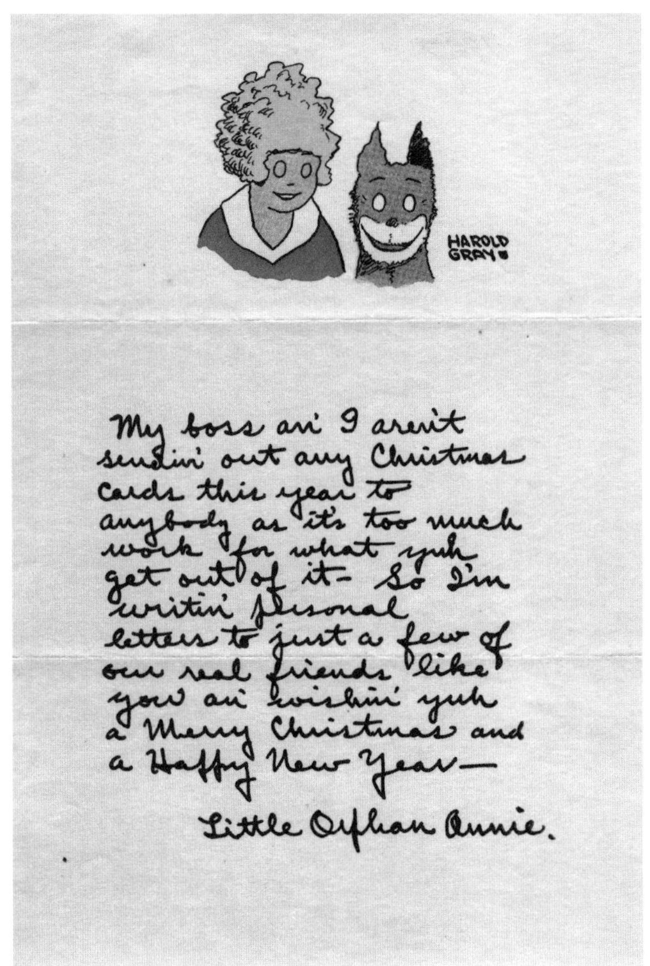

HAROLD GRAY

My boss an' I aren't sendin' out any Christmas cards this year to anybody as it's too much work for what yuh get out of it— So I'm writin' personal letters to just a few of our real friends like you an' wishin' yuh a Merry Christmas and a Happy New Year—

Little Orphan Annie.

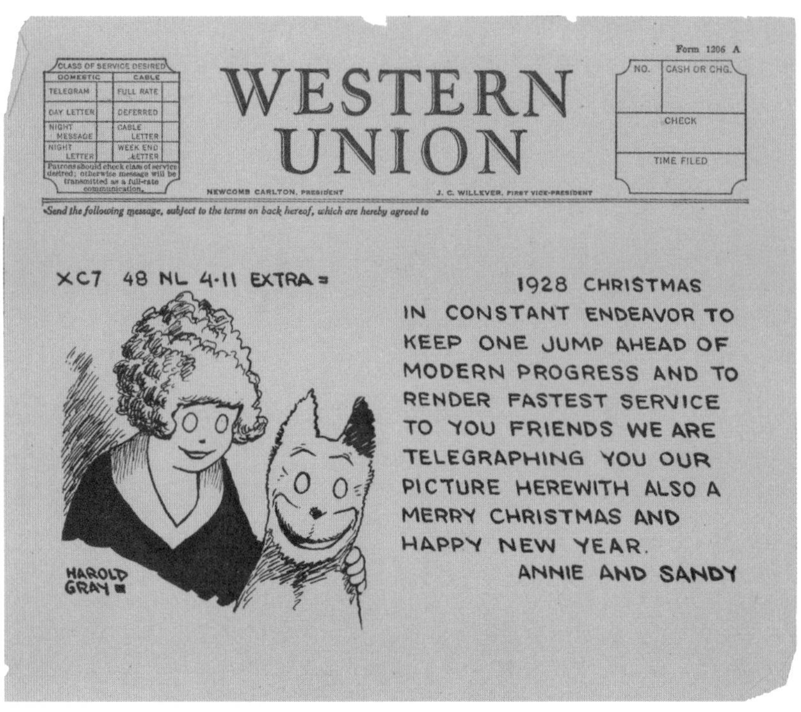

HAROLD GRAY

WESTERN UNION

Form 1206 A

Send the following message, subject to the terms on back hereof, which are hereby agreed to

XC7 48 NL 4-11 EXTRA

1928 CHRISTMAS
IN CONSTANT ENDEAVOR TO KEEP ONE JUMP AHEAD OF MODERN PROGRESS AND TO RENDER FASTEST SERVICE TO YOU FRIENDS WE ARE TELEGRAPHING YOU OUR PICTURE HEREWITH ALSO A MERRY CHRISTMAS AND HAPPY NEW YEAR.
ANNIE AND SANDY

FROM LEFT TO RIGHT: *Harold Gray's Christmas cards from 1927, 1928, 1929, 1930, and 1931.*

For Annie, of course, poverty is just a return to the old neighborhood. As always, she's good at making friends, and finds fellowship with her landlady, Maw Green, and Jake, who runs a local grocery store. Annie's new companions belong to the working poor: they don't have much money and the surroundings are grubby and seedy, but they hold fast to their dignity and pride.

The neighborhood is also distinctly ethnic in flavor, an example of the melting pot ethos of Annie's world. Shoppers at Jake's store include Mrs. Glotz and Mrs. Goldblatt. Although his religion is never explicitly identified, Jake himself is clearly Jewish-American, with a slight Yiddish inflection in his speech and a habit of wearing his hat indoors. Maw Green is Irish-American, as can be seen not just by her last name but also her odd Celtic turn of phrase.

Gray's habit of dealing with ethnicity is to provide clues about his characters background but not be explicit in labelling them with a group identity. Thus, when a foundling is introduced into the strip, the characters show their backgrounds by the names they want to give to the kid. Annie, who has no specific background, likes the name "Cleopatra" (another powerful woman). Maw Green is initially uneasy with the name Cleopatra but warms up when she realizes it can be shortened to the Celtic-sounding "Pat." Jake is willing to live with Pat, although his preference was for the Hebrew favorite, Rebecca. Just two years previous, Annie had been under the care of an Irish-American couple, Nora and Monk Dooley.

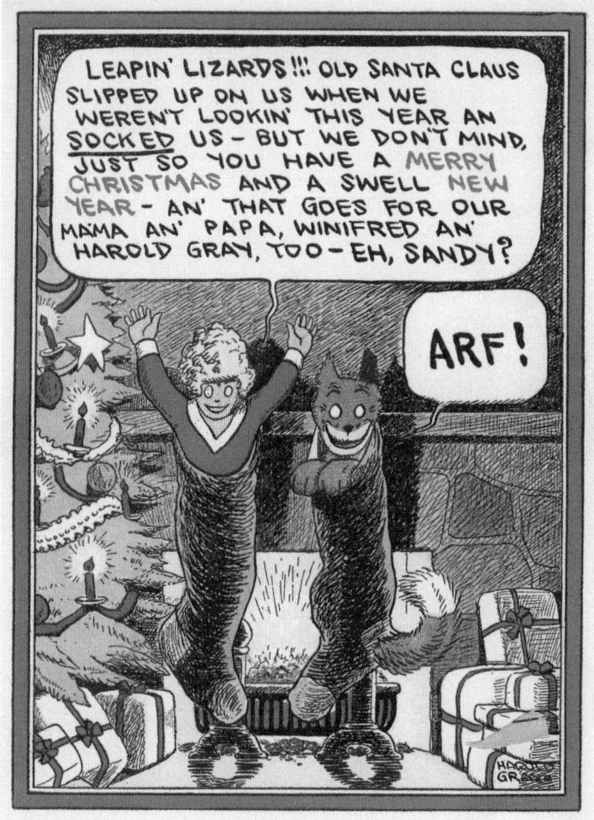
LEAPIN' LIZARDS!!! OLD SANTA CLAUS SLIPPED UP ON US WHEN WE WEREN'T LOOKIN' THIS YEAR AN SOCKED US - BUT WE DON'T MIND, JUST SO YOU HAVE A MERRY CHRISTMAS AND A SWELL NEW YEAR - AN' THAT GOES FOR OUR MAMA AN' PAPA, WINIFRED AN' HAROLD GRAY, TOO - EH, SANDY?
ARF!

HAROLD AND WINIFRED GRAY REQUEST US TO SAY, IF YER MERRIEST CHRISTMAS AND HAPPIEST NEW YEAR, TIED TO TH' END O' THIS TAG, DON'T ARRIVE IN PERFECT CONDITION, PLEASE ADVISE AT ONCE, BY WIRE OR CABLE, PREPAID-
ARF!
XMAS
HAROLD GRAY

A Merry Christmas
IS·ABOUT·ALL·WINIFRED·AND·HAROLD ARE·GIVIN'·AWAY·THIS·YEAR····YOU SEE·THEY·WENT·AN·BOUGHT·A·HOME FOR·THEMSELVES·INSTEAD···BUT WE'RE·HOPIN'·SANTA·HAS LAID·OFF·O'·REAL ESTATE·AND·IS ABLE·TO TREAT·YOU REAL·SWELL
120·N·HIGHLAND·AV. CROTON·ON·HUDSON NEW YORK

Ethnicity was a controversial issue in Harold Gray's era. The terrorism of the Ku Klux Klan was fueled by the paranoid complaint that Anglo-Saxon Americans were being inundated by immigrants from southern and Eastern Europe. On a higher plane, groups like the Daughters of the American Revolution tried to hold on to notions that "older" Americans were the natural rulers of the country, while immigrants like Jake and Maw Green needed to be kept out of the best clubs. In 1928, Al Smith lost the presidency in part because of anti-Catholic bigotry. (In future years, Smith was one of the very few Democratic politicians that Gray would quote with approval. Metropolitan, street-smart, tolerant, an opponent of Prohibition, and a believer in charity but opposed to expanding the welfare state, Smith had many qualities that Gray could admire.) Throughout the run of *Annie*, Gray consistently waged war against ethnic snobbery by showing that good Americans could come from anywhere in the world.

Jake the store owner, who soon hires Annie, allows Gray to offer his own solutions to the Great Depression. Working together, Annie and Jake spruce up the store and learn the value of advertising. They are helped by another old friend of Annie's, Mr. Walsh, the circulation manager of a big city newspaper, last seen in 1928. Aside from being a typical Gray homily on the virtues of hard work in overcoming adversity, the sequence with Jake's store is also a subtle plug on behalf of the comic strip's true friends, newspapers. As a daily cartoonist and lifelong newspaper employee, Gray often took the time to sing the praises of the press, in this case arguing that advertising could solve the Depression. While his solution might have been limited and faulty, it does show his loyalty to the institutions that nurtured his career.

The subplot about Jake's grocery story allows Gray to demonstrate his skill at portraying the mundane and everyday. As Annie and Jake clean the store, stock the shelves, and hire employees, we get to see the daily operations of an ordinary small business. Gray's love of portraying daily life in all its ordinariness owes something to

Clare Briggs, a cartoonist who found glory in the quotidian. Like Briggs, Gray had a Midwestern respect for the routine entities of life, the hard factual things and creatures that furnish existence.

Briggs's influence can also be seen in *Private Life of* __, the "bottom strip" that Gray introduced to the *Annie* Sunday page in 1931. Each week, Gray would follow a common, unobtrusive, easy to ignore object or creature: a lump of coal, a snowman, a groundhog. In a few panels he would give these easy to ignore things the dignity of a biography. The strip was clearly inspired by Briggs's earlier series *What a __ Thinks About,* where the blank space could be a dog, a horse, or an ironing board. Briggs, a giant of Midwestern cartooning, had died in early 1930, so perhaps Gray was of a mind to pay a small tribute to a former mentor.

Over the years, Gray had to deal with letters from readers who complained that *Annie* wasn't funny the way a comic strip should be, but rather presented dark and grim stories. Some of these letters were printed in "The Voice of the People," a regular column offering reader opinions, sometimes anonymously, that ran in both the *Chicago Tribune* and the *New York Daily News* (the flagship papers carrying *Annie*). Using Annie as a mouthpiece, Gray took the opportunity to respond to these critiques. "I like to read 'The Voice of the People,'" Annie says over breakfast one morning. "I always wondered what this guy 'Anonymous' looks like. Here he's got a roast for my favorite funny. He claims it's too sad. Yeah. And if it was just a stale gag each day this same bird would be yammering that it isn't true to life. Shux. Life isn't all funny. Yuh get sick of a bird who's always trying to be funny. But why try to please a bird named 'Anonymous'?"

Gray was in a good position to scorn his critics, whether they were anonymous or not. Already a success in the 1920s, *Annie*'s increasing popularity in the 1930s is remarkable, and owed much to the way Gray took his already existing characters and threw them into the maelstrom of the Great Depression. In the early 1930s, conservative politicians lost public favor because their response to the Depression seemed inadequate; all they were offering were lectures on how the economy was fundamentally strong and things would soon improve if the poor just pulled themselves up by their bootstraps.

Gray shared in some of these ideas, but unlike the politicians, he didn't view poverty from afar. His characters endured the same hardships that millions of readers were also facing. Although Gray was politically opposed to Franklin Roosevelt, the cartoonist offered an allegory that resembled the message of the Democratic politician who would win the presidency in 1932. Just as Roosevelt overcame polio through sheer will power to become president, "Daddy" Warbucks also overcomes his own physical affliction to regain his empire. Gray truly caught the tempo of the 1930s in a way that no other cartoonist did, and this made *Annie* beloved by millions.

Wonder What a Public Drinking Fountain Thinks About

I'M HAVING AN AWFUL BUSY SUMMER, I'M SO POPULAR··· IT DIDN'T USED TO BE LIKE THIS
I SURE DO MEET A FUNNY BUNCH OF PEOPLE···· LAMP THIS ONE FOR INSTANCE··· IT'S A GOOD THING I'M NOT TICKLISH·
THIS GUY HAS AN AWFUL THIRST···WHY THE POOR THING IS PARCHED···· HE MAKES A SIPPING NOISE LIKE A HORSE-- THE FISH!
I WISH PEOPLE LIKE THIS WOULDN'T GET SO CLOSE···· THIS BIRD MUST HAVE HAD A BIG NIGHT
NOW— HERE'S THE KIND OF FOLKS I LOVE TO SERVE··· THIS KID IS ONE OF MY MOST APPRECIATIVE PATRONS ··· HE SIMPLY WALLOWS IN ME-
THIS TYPE COMES AT ME WITH A DO OR DIE EXPRESSION··· A FACE LIKE A DRIED LEMON···· I'LL BE GLAD WHEN SHE'S THROUGH-
HERE'S ANOTHER HANG OVER.... OTTO IS A HARD WORKING GUY AND TO HIM I'M ONLY A FIRE EX- TINGUISHER··· THAT'S RIGHT GET IT ALL OVER YOUR FACE-
WELL IT'S ABOUT TIME SOMETHING LIKE THIS CAME ALONG···· I THINK I'M ENTITLED TO SOME REWARD---
BRIGGS

OPPOSITE and the FOLLOWING TWO PAGES: Private Life of __ *was a "bottom strip" introduced on the first Sunday in 1931. It continued until the final Sunday page of 1932, after which Maw Green—introduced in this volume—became the star of the feature. The "bottom strip" was necessitated by a change in Gray's Sunday page format. Prior to 1931, the full- and tab-sized Sundays contained a (usually) throwaway header panel that newspapers running the strip as a half page would omit. By deleting the header and incorporating the logo into the first panel (see page 178), Gray's Sunday layout could easily be reformatted according to each newspaper's needs. The bottom strip took the space previously used by the header.*

ABOVE: *An example of Clare Briggs's* What a __ Thinks About *series, which clearly influenced Gray's bottom strip.*

Private Life of A SNOWMAN

TALK ABOUT GETTING A START IN THE WORLD! I CAN FEEL MYSELF GETTING BIGGER EVERY SECOND-

JIM-MIE!
I'M COMIN, MOM-

OH, MOLLIE- ISN'T HE CUTE?
HE'S THE MOST HANDSOME THING-
"CUTE"- "HANDSOME" HEH! HEH! HEH!

GREAT SCOTT!!! THERE COMES THAT TOUGH KID FROM NEXT DOOR- THAT'S SURE BAD LUCK-

I KNEW IT- BUT THERE'S NOTHING I CAN DO- YOU CAN'T DODGE FATE-

WELL, IT COULD HAVE BEEN WORSE- AND HERE COMES THE SUN- EVERYTHING WILL BE BRIGHT NOW-

IT MAY BE SUNSHINE FOR SOME, BUT IT'S THE END FOR ME- STILL, I'VE NO KICK- I'VE HAD MY FLING- I HAD 'EM ALL LOOKIN' AT ME IN MY DAY- I'VE HAD MY HARD KNOCKS, TOO- BUT I DIDN'T FLINCH-
HAROLD GRAY

A LITTLE HOPE, AN HOUR OF GLORY, A FEW SCARS, AND A LITTLE TIME FOR REFLECTION- AFTER ALL, WHAT ELSE IS THERE? I'VE SEEN EVERYTHING-
Reg. U. S. Pat. Off., Copyright, 1931, by The Chicago Tribune

Bottom strip, January 11, 1931.

Private Life of a Potato

I WAS THE BIGGEST AND HANDSOMEST POTATO ON OUR VINE-

I'D LIKE TO TELL YOU WHAT STATE I GREW UP IN, BUT OTHER STATES WOULD GET JEALOUS, SO MY PAST MUST REMAIN A MYSTERY-

ALL I CAN SAY OF MY ANCESTRY IS THAT I AM OF IRISH DESCENT- SOME FOLKS EVEN CALL ME AN IRISH LEMON-

BUT SPEAKING OF RACES AND NATIONALITIES-
TO MARKET

I WAS RAISED BY A NORWEGIAN, DUG BY A DANE AND SOLD TO A SCOTCH GROCER-

BOUGHT FROM HIM BY A GERMAN RESTAURANT OWNER AND BAKED BY A FRENCH CHEF-

SERVED BY AN ITALIAN WAITER-

TO A SPANIARD IN A BOHEMIAN RESTAURANT-
HAROLD GRAY

AND NOW HERE COMES A SWISS BUS-BOY TO CLEAR AWAY WHAT'S LEFT OF ME- HEIGH, HO- BUT, NO MATTER WHERE WE COME FROM, WE'RE ALL GOOD AMERICANS NOW-
Reg. U. S. Pat. Off.; Copyright, 1931, by The Chicago Tribune.

Bottom strip, March 1, 1931.

Private Life of a House

STONE ON STONE MY FOUNDATION WAS LAID - AND THERE WAS A DEEP CELLAR - NOW-DAYS THEY'D CALL IT A BASEMENT -

THEN ALL OF ME ABOVE GROUND WAS CAREFULLY BUILT OF LUMBER, HAULED FROM THE SAW-MILL THIRTY MILES AWAY -

AT LAST I WAS FINISHED AND IN MOVED MY FIRST OWNERS - A YOUNG COUPLE - THEY DIDN'T HAVE MUCH, PERHAPS, BUT THEY WERE HAPPY -

YEARS PASSED AND THE PATTER OF LITTLE FEET BECAME ALMOST A PART OF ME -

HEIGH HO - A HUNDRED AND FIFTY YEARS - CHILDREN GREW UP, MARRIED, GREW OLD AND DIED - THE UNALTERING CYCLE -

JOY - TRAGEDY - WORK AND REST - LOVE AND DISSENSION, ALL BENEATH MY ROOF - SUCCESS AND FAILURE - THE EBB AND FLOW OF LIFE -

WARS AND PESTILENCE HAVE PASSED OVER AND THROUGH ME AND LEFT THEIR SCARS - STORMS HAVE COME, BUT I WAS BUILT TO STAND -

STILL, TIME AND THE ELEMENTS WILL NOT BE DENIED - THE FIELDS ABOUT ME ARE WORN OUT NOW - LAST YEAR I WAS DESERTED - MY ROOF SAGS - SOON I'LL SINK BACK INTO THE DUST -

MY WINDOWS ARE BROKEN - EMPTY EYES - BUT THE SIGHTS THEY'VE SEEN - AYE, AND THE SIGHTS THEY YET MAY WITNESS - WHO CAN TELL?
HAROLD GRAY
Reg. U.S. Pat. Off.; Copyright, 1931, by The Chicago Tribune.

Bottom strip, March 15, 1931.

Private Life of a Hat

MY FIRST OWNER WASN'T MUCH TO LOOK AT, WITH HIS SILLY LITTLE MOUSTACHE -

BUT HE HAD DOUGH - HE PAID TWENTY DOLLARS FOR ME - AND HE SURE TOOK ME ON SOME SWELL TRIPS - CHECK GIRLS SURE TREATED ME WITH RESPECT -

BUT HE'D SIT OUT ON THE OBSERVATION PLATFORM WITH THE CINDERS AND SOOT FALLING ON ME LIKE RAIN TILL I GOT TIRED OF IT ALL -

I'D HARDLY LIT BESIDE THE TRACKS WHEN A SMALL BOY PICKED ME UP - OF COURSE I WAS TOO BIG FOR HIM, BUT HE WAS A SMART YOUNGSTER -

HE TOOK ME STRAIGHT TO THE HOTEL IN HIS LITTLE TOWN AND SOLD ME TO A TRAVELING MAN FOR A DOLLAR -

IT WAS A BLOW TO MY PRIDE TO BE SOLD FOR ONLY A DOLLAR, BUT MY NEW OWNER KNEW MY VALUE AND TOOK GOOD CARE OF ME - BUT AT LAST THE INEVITABLE HAPPENED -

NO HAT CAN COME BACK, AFTER TANGLING WITH A TRUCK ON A MUDDY STREET - IF I'D BEEN A DERBY I GUESS IT WOULD HAVE BEEN WORSE - BUT IT COULDN'T HAVE BEEN MUCH WORSE - I FIGURED MY END HAD COME -

STILL, AS BATTERED AS I WAS I WAS TO LEARN THERE WAS ANOTHER HAT WORSE OFF THAN I - LIFE HAD BEEN CRUEL TO ME, BUT CLASS WILL TELL - MY CROWN WAS MUDDY, BUT UN TORN - A TRAMP SIZED ME UP AT A GLANCE -

SOUTH IN THE WINTER - NORTH IN SUMMER - A BIRD OF PASSAGE - I HAVE MY SCARS AND MY MEMORIES - A BROKEN-DOWN ARISTOCRAT - BUT AT LEAST I WAS AN ARISTOCRAT ONCE -
HAROLD GRAY
Reg. U.S. Pat. Off., Copyright, 1931, by The Chicago Tribune.

Bottom strip, March 22, 1931.

Private Life of an Acorn

"GREAT OAKS FROM LITTLE ACORNS GROW"- AT LEAST THAT'S WHAT THEY SAY-

WHEN I FINALLY FELL FROM THE OLD OAK ON WHICH I GREW I THOUGHT IT WAS AS SIMPLE AS THAT- HOW LITTLE I KNEW-

I HAD HARDLY LIT AMONG THE AUTUMN LEAVES, WHEN I NOTICED A BIG SQUIRREL- THE MONSTER WAS EATING OTHER ACORNS, JUST LIKE ME-

I TRIED TO BURROW DOWN OUT OF SIGHT BUT IT WAS NO USE- HE HAD SEEN ME AND I SEEMED DOOMED-

BUT WHILE HE WAS IN THE ACT OF CARRYING ME TO HIS NEST IN A HOLLOW TREE, A DOG APPEARED-

THAT SQUIRREL WAS SO MAD HE STARTED CHATTERING AT THE DOG AND DROPPED ME-

I LIT ON A HARD, BARE SPOT AND BOUNCED AND ROLLED DOWN A LONG HILL AND UNDER A FINE PILE OF LEAVES WELL OUT OF SIGHT-

IT WAS QUIET HERE AND DARK TOO, BUT I'D SEEN PLENTY TO LAST ME FOR A LONG WHILE- I'D FOUND THAT LIFE DOESN'T ALWAYS WORK OUT LIKE THE POETS SAY- NOT BY A LONG SHOT- IT WAS QUIET- GUESS I FELL ASLEEP-

AND HERE IT IS SPRING- I'M NOT AN ACORN ANY MORE- I'M AN OAK NOW- COURSE I'M NOT A "GREAT" OAK YET- THAT WILL TAKE A HUNDRED YEARS OR MORE- BUT I'M ON MY WAY-
HAROLD GRAY
Reg. U. S. Pat. Off.; Copyright, 1931, by The Chicago Tribune.

Bottom strip, April 5, 1931.

Private Life of a Base Ball

I WASN'T THE FIRST BALL OF THE SEASON, THROWN IN BY THE PRESIDENT- NOT EVEN A' MAYOR PUT ME INTO THE GAME-

I WAS JUST ANOTHER NEW BALL- AROUND THE INFIELD I WENT TO TAKE THE SHINE OFF MY COVER-

THEN THE PITCHER HAD ME- HE SURE KNEW HOW TO GRIP A BALL, AND WHAT A WING HE HAD- TWICE I WHISTLED OVER FOR CALLED STRIKES-

THEN, UP I CAME AGAIN- BUT BEFORE I WAS HALF WAY IN I KNEW I WAS IN FOR IT- THAT BATTER'S EYE WAS ON ME- I FELT AS BIG AS A HOUSE-

WHACK!!! WHAT A RIDE- NOW I KNOW HOW A BULLET FEELS-

CRASH!!! THROUGH THE WINDSHIELD OF A PARKED CAR- BOUNCE! UNDER ANOTHER CAR-

BEAT IT, JIMMY- HERE COMES DE COP-
I'VE GOT IT-
THE KIDS HEARD ME LIGHT AND WERE AFTER ME LIKE A FLASH-

JIMMY GOT ME AND LIT OUT- HIS PAL FAKED A FALL AND THE COP WENT SPRAWLING OR HE'D HAVE HAD ME-
HAROLD GRAY

SO HERE I AM- NO LONGER JUST ANOTHER NEW BALL, BUT THE BALL- IF I'M LOST THE GAME STOPS- I LIKE IT HERE IN ASH-CAN ALLEY- I'M A BIG SHOT HERE-
Reg. U. S. Pat. Off.; Copyright, 1931, by The Chicago Tribune.

Bottom strip, June 14, 1931.

The Continuing Story of Little Orphan Annie (so far)

ARF!

After being rescued by "Daddy" from the clutches of the crooked banker, Mr. Mack, the intrepid duo — with Sandy in tow, of course — return to the city.

But no sooner are they swimming in the luxury of a five-star hotel than "Daddy" must yet again leave on business. Within short order, the hotel evicts our little heroine, and she finds shelter with the poor Mrs. Pewter and her brood of children, selling newspapers to pay her way.

When Mrs. Pewter meets with a terrible accident, Annie becomes mother to the brood, and to help nurse her back to health, takes the clan to the small town of Mayfair and the hospitality of Mr. and Mrs. Wells.

The ever-industrious Annie gets a job as a waitress, overhears a plot to rob the train, and through her best efforts, the holdup gang is caught.

"DADDY"
WARBUCKS

But, wait — they break jail and capture Annie for ransom!

Never fear — dear Annie escapes, and ends up, of all places, back at the the "Home" with Miss Asthma!

MISS
ASTHMA

Meanwhile, "Daddy" has returned and is on an all-out search for his girl. High and low, over hill and under dale, he searches, to no avail. In utter desperation, he hopes to find some

MONK & NORA DOOLEY

clue in Annie's adoption records at the Home. But when he gets there, the building is a blazing inferno. Annie has saved all the children, but is stuck inside!

You don't think she's gonna die, do you? Oh no — she jumps out the window in the nick of time, is found by "Daddy," and all is well.

Annie goes to stay with Mr. and Mrs. Silo on the farm, and "Daddy" buys a new plane so he can quickly go back and forth to the city.

But good times seem never to last long. Warbucks's business rival, Foxpaw, has the plane sabotaged and "Daddy" lies near death for weeks!

Will he survive? The doctors don't think so, but they don't know Oliver Warbucks. Survive he does, and he and Annie return to their hotel suite in the city so he can wreak his revenge on Foxpaw.

But Annie gets lost (are you surprised?), and takes up with cab driver Monk Dooley and his wife. She goes to school, and for the first time in her life, gets a best friend—Ellen. It's all so normal, except that Ellen's stepmother abandons her, Monk and his wife take the girl in, and then Monk's cab gets wrecked.

The family's strapped without income, so selfless Annie sneaks out in the middle of the night to hit the long and winding road.

JACK PEPPER

She wanders into the appropriately-named town of Blunderville. There, she moves in with the widow Twinkle and tries another stretch at a formal education…

…and makes a bunch of new friends, including crusty Jack Pepper, an ol' pal of "Daddy" Warbucks, the wise Judge Tort, and the town's bankers: mean John Blunder the elder, and good-hearted John Blunder the younger.

When the elder plays fast and loose with the bank's money, it's the younger who must pay. Until Annie and Jack Pepper save the day!

That's what happened in Volume Two.

Annie's still in Blunderville, so sit back, turn the page, and see what happens next…

TH' BIG DUMMY----
"MAY I CARRY YER BOOKS?"
DO I LOOK WEAK OR
SOMETHIN'? TH' POOR
SAP MUST BE GOIN'
SQUIRRELLY-

CHAPTER ONE

THE SEVEN-YEAR ITCHY

IN WHICH ANNIE

LEARNS THAT FUN CAN BE
HAD AT A TEDDY BEAR'S PICNIC

FINDS THAT SHE HAS
A NOT-SO-SECRET ADMIRER

AND THAT UNBENOWNST TO HER,
"DADDY" IS WATCHING OVER
HER FROM A DISTANCE...

G-BYE, MRS. TWINKLE- I'M STARTIN' FOR SCHOOL-
GOOD-BYE, ANNIE- DON'T FORGET TO STOP AT THE STORE FOR THE SUGAR ON YOUR WAY HOME TO LUNCH-
EARLY AN' LATE MRS. TWINKLE KEEPS AT IT- SEWIN'- SEWIN'- SEWIN'- COURSE SHE MAKES A LIVIN' AT IT- BUT SHE SURE EARNS EVERY CENT SHE MAKES-
CHRISTMAS THINGS IN TH' WINDOWS - GEE- THEY SURE LOOK SWELL- BUT HOW CAN I BUY ANY CHRISTMAS PRESENTS THIS YEAR- AFTER SPENDIN' ALL MY DOUGH FOR THAT SEWIN' MACHINE FOR MRS. TWINKLE-
XMAS SEALS
I'M GLAD I DID IT, BUT, JUST TH' SAME, THIS IS NO TIME O' YEAR TO BE BUSTED- WOW- TH' LAST BELL- I'VE SURE GOTTA HURRY OR I'LL BE LATE FOR SCHOOL-
DING! DONG!
HAROLD GRAY
Reg. U. S. Pat. Off.; Copyright, 1929, by The Chicago Tribune.
"BOY WANTED"- HUH- WHY DOES IT HAVE TO BE A BOY? BOYS ARE MOSTLY AWFUL LAZY- I CAN DO MORE WORK AN' A BETTER JOB THAN ANY BOY I EVER KNEW- AND I'VE GOTTA EARN SOME CHRISTMAS MONEY-
BOY WANTED
LISTEN, MR. SELLERS - I'M NOT SCARED O' WORK - I NEED TH' JOB AN' I'LL SHOW YUH I CAN HELP YUH LOTS MORE'N ANY BOY-
I'VE WORKED IN STORES BEFORE - I REMEMBER WHAT I'M TOLD TO DO AND I DO IT- CAN'T YUH JUST GIVE ME A CHANCE?
WELL, I GUESS IT DOESN'T HAVE TO BE A BOY - NEVER THOUGHT O' HIRING A GIRL- I NEED SOMEBODY EXTRA TILL CHRISTMAS- I'LL GIVE YOU A TRIAL- IF YOU CAN MAKE GOOD THE JOB'S YOURS-
THANKS!
HAROLD GRAY
Reg. U. S. Pat. Off.; Copyright, 1929, by The Chicago Tribune.
YOU'RE TAKING HOLD FINE, ANNIE- THE JOB'S YOURS TILL CHRISTMAS-
SAY, MR. SELLERS, HOW MUCH YUH GOIN' TO PAY ME FOR WORKIN' HERE AFTER SCHOOL AND ALL DAY SATURDAYS?
WHY, ANNIE- I RECKON THAT'LL BE WORTH ABOUT THREE DOLLARS A WEEK-
I GOT FIVE A WEEK BACK IN TH' CITY-
YES- BUT THIS ISN'T THE CITY- THIS IS BLUNDERVILLE- EVERYTHING'S CHEAPER HERE-
GUESS YOU'RE RIGHT- MONEY DOES HAVE TO GO FARTHER OUT HERE THAN IT DOES IN TH' CITY-
OH, WELL- THREE BUCKS A WEEK ISN'T BAD- I'M MIGHTY GLAD TO GET IT- BUT I FIGGERED THERE'S NEVER ANY HARM IN ASKIN' FOR MORE-
HAROLD GRAY
Reg. U. S. Pat. Off.; Copyright, 1929, by The Chicago Tribune.

December 9–11, 1929

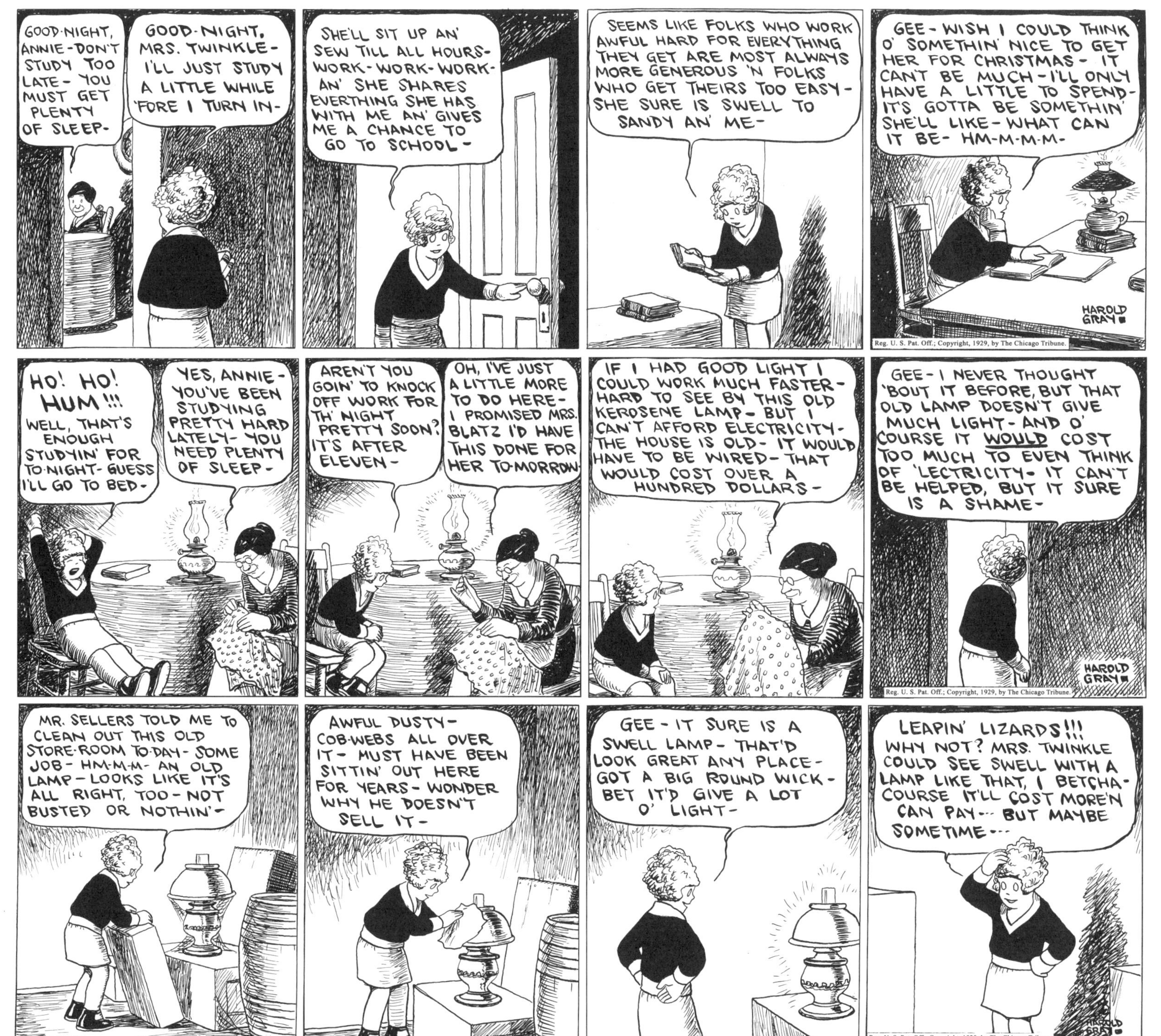
GOOD-NIGHT, ANNIE-DON'T STUDY TOO LATE- YOU MUST GET PLENTY OF SLEEP-
GOOD-NIGHT, MRS. TWINKLE- I'LL JUST STUDY A LITTLE WHILE 'FORE I TURN IN-
SHE'LL SIT UP AN' SEW TILL ALL HOURS- WORK-WORK-WORK- AN' SHE SHARES EVERTHING SHE HAS WITH ME AN' GIVES ME A CHANCE TO GO TO SCHOOL-
SEEMS LIKE FOLKS WHO WORK AWFUL HARD FOR EVERYTHING THEY GET ARE MOST ALWAYS MORE GENEROUS 'N FOLKS WHO GET THEIRS TOO EASY- SHE SURE IS SWELL TO SANDY AN' ME-
GEE- WISH I COULD THINK O' SOMETHIN' NICE TO GET HER FOR CHRISTMAS- IT CAN'T BE MUCH-I'LL ONLY HAVE A LITTLE TO SPEND- IT'S GOTTA BE SOMETHIN' SHE'LL LIKE- WHAT CAN IT BE- HM-M-M-M-
HAROLD GRAY
Reg. U. S. Pat. Off.; Copyright, 1929, by The Chicago Tribune.
HO! HO! HUM!!! WELL, THAT'S ENOUGH STUDYIN' FOR TO-NIGHT- GUESS I'LL GO TO BED-
YES, ANNIE- YOU'VE BEEN STUDYING PRETTY HARD LATELY- YOU NEED PLENTY OF SLEEP-
AREN'T YOU GOIN' TO KNOCK OFF WORK FOR TH' NIGHT PRETTY SOON? IT'S AFTER ELEVEN-
OH, I'VE JUST A LITTLE MORE TO DO HERE- I PROMISED MRS. BLATZ I'D HAVE THIS DONE FOR HER TO-MORROW-
IF I HAD GOOD LIGHT I COULD WORK MUCH FASTER- HARD TO SEE BY THIS OLD KEROSENE LAMP- BUT I CAN'T AFFORD ELECTRICITY- THE HOUSE IS OLD- IT WOULD HAVE TO BE WIRED- THAT WOULD COST OVER A HUNDRED DOLLARS-
GEE- I NEVER THOUGHT 'BOUT IT BEFORE, BUT THAT OLD LAMP DOESN'T GIVE MUCH LIGHT- AND O' COURSE IT WOULD COST TOO MUCH TO EVEN THINK OF 'LECTRICITY- IT CAN'T BE HELPED, BUT IT SURE IS A SHAME-
HAROLD GRAY
Reg. U. S. Pat. Off.; Copyright, 1929, by The Chicago Tribune.
MR. SELLERS TOLD ME TO CLEAN OUT THIS OLD STORE-ROOM TO-DAY- SOME JOB- HM-M-M- AN OLD LAMP- LOOKS LIKE IT'S ALL RIGHT, TOO- NOT BUSTED OR NOTHIN'-
AWFUL DUSTY- COB-WEBS ALL OVER IT- MUST HAVE BEEN SITTIN' OUT HERE FOR YEARS- WONDER WHY HE DOESN'T SELL IT-
GEE- IT SURE IS A SWELL LAMP- THAT'D LOOK GREAT ANY PLACE- GOT A BIG ROUND WICK- BET IT'D GIVE A LOT O' LIGHT-
LEAPIN' LIZARDS!!! WHY NOT? MRS. TWINKLE COULD SEE SWELL WITH A LAMP LIKE THAT, I BETCHA- COURSE IT'LL COST MORE'N I CAN PAY--- BUT MAYBE SOMETIME---
HAROLD GRAY
Reg. U. S. Pat. Off.; Copyright, 1929, by The Chicago Tribune.

December 12–14, 1929

MR. SELLERS SAYS THAT LAMP USED TO BE $11.00 BUT MOST EVER'BODY IN TOWN HAS 'LECTRICITY- SAYS HE'D BE LUCKY TO GET FIVE BUCKS FOR IT- I'M GOIN' TO BUY IT FOR MRS. TWINKLE FOR CHRISTMAS- SHE'LL LIKE THAT-
YES, MRS HORSELAF- I THINK I HAVE A FEW OF THEM LEFT OUT HERE IN THE STORE-ROOM-
LEAPIN' LIZARDS! WHAT A SAP I WAS TO SHINE UP THAT LAMP AN' LEAVE IT SITTIN' RIGHT OUT IN PLAIN SIGHT- IT'D BE JUST LIKE MRS. HORSELAF TO GET STUCK ON MY LAMP AN' BUY IT-
COURSE IT ISN'T REALLY MY LAMP YET- BUT IT'S GOIN' TO BE SOON AS I EARN ENOUGH DOUGH TO PAY FOR IT - GEE-
HAROLD GRAY
Reg. U. S. Pat. Off.; Copyright, 1929, by The Chicago Tribune.
WELL, ANNIE- YOU WENT TO WORK HERE IN THE STORE A WEEK AGO TO-DAY- HERE'S THE SALARY I PROMISED YOU FOR THE WEEK- THREE DOLLARS-
THANKS-
I DIDN'T SAY ANYTHING BEFORE 'CAUSE I DIDN'T HAVE ANY DOUGH- BUT I WANT TO BUY THAT LAMP IN TH' STORE-ROOM THAT YOU SAID YOU'D BE GLAD TO GET FIVE BUCKS FOR- HERE'S TWO-FIFTY AND I'LL GIVE YUH THE OTHER TWO-FIFTY OUTA NEXT WEEK'S PAY- HOW'S THAT?
NOW DON'T TELL ANYBODY ELSE WHO YUH SOLD IT TO, PLEASE, WILL YUH, MR. SELLERS?
NO-NO- TRUST ME- I WON'T TELL A SOUL-
SOLD
WELL, I'LL BE KICKED BY A MULE- BUYING IT FOR OLD WIDOW TWINKLE FOR CHRISTMAS- GENEROUS LITTLE SCAMP- YUH DON'T SEE MANY KIDS AS THOUGHTFUL AS THAT THESE DAYS-
HAROLD GRAY
Reg. U. S. Pat. Off.; Copyright, 1929, by The Chicago Tribune.
GEE- I CAN HARDLY HELP TELLIN' MRS. TWINKLE WHAT I'M GETTIN' HER FOR CHRISTMAS- I WONDER IF SHE'D LIKE SOMETHIN' ELSE BETTER-
SAY, MRS. TWINKLE- WHAT WOULD YUH LIKE ME TO GIVE YOU FOR CHRISTMAS?
OH, ANNIE- DON'T THINK OF GIVING ME A THING-
BUT I'M WORKIN', YOU KNOW- I'LL HAVE A LITTLE DOUGH TO SPEND-
NO-NO- I CAN'T THINK OF A THING I NEED, ANNIE- AND ANYWAY, DIDN'T YOU GIVE ME THAT WONDERFUL SEWING MACHINE? THAT'S GIFT ENOUGH FOR TEN CHRISTMASES-
SHUX! JUST TH' SAME, IT MADE HER FEEL GOOD TO KNOW I WAS THINKIN' OF HER- AN' I BET SHE'LL LIKE THAT SWELL LAMP- GEE- WHO WOULDN'T?
HAROLD GRAY
Reg. U. S. Pat. Off.; Copyright, 1929, by The Chicago Tribune.

December 16–18, 1929

MR. SELLERS SURE IS A NICE GUY TO WORK FOR- COURSE HE ONLY PAYS ME THREE DOLLARS A WEEK FOR AFTER SCHOOL AN' SATURDAYS-
BUT I'D RATHER WORK FOR HIM AT THREE BUCKS A WEEK, THAN FOR LOTS OF BIRDS I'VE KNOWN AT FIVE A WEEK-
TO-MORROW'LL BE TH' LAST DAY O' SCHOOL TILL AFTER CHRISTMAS VACATION- THERE'LL BE PLENTY TO KEEP ME BUSY HERE TILL CHRISTMAS- BUT AFTER THAT I'LL BE OUT OF A JOB AGAIN-
OH, WELL- I'VE BEEN LUCKY TO HAVE THIS JOB EVEN FOR TWO WEEKS WHEN I NEED CHRISTMAS MONEY SO BAD-
HAROLD GRAY
Reg. U. S. Pat. Off.; Copyright, 1929, by The Chicago Tribune.
OF COURSE, MRS. FROSTBITE, YOU CAN 'PRECIATE A SWELL PITCHER- I DON'T HAVE TO TELL YOU HOW NICE THAT WOULD LOOK IN YOUR BE'UTIFUL HOME-
HM-M-M- YES-YES- TO BE SURE- IT REALLY IS CHARMING- I'LL TAKE IT-
YES, AS YOU SAY, FLOOR LAMPS OF THAT STYLE ARE QUITE POPULAR THIS SEASON- I WILL TAKE THAT ONE-
YESSUM- I'LL HAVE IT SENT RIGHT OUT- AND WE HAVE SOME VERY FINE DRESSER SETS I KNOW YOU WOULD LIKE- RIGHT OVER HERE-
WHAT!!! NOT MRS. FROSTBITE? YOU DIDN'T SELL HER ANYTHING, DID YOU? HOW DID YOU DO IT?
SURE- THERE'S HER MONEY FOR TH' STUFF- ONE PITCHER- ONE FLOOR LAMP ONE DRESSER SET- ONE SET OF DISHES- THREE VASES- LE'SSEE- THERE WAS SOMETHIN' ELSE-
GREAT SCOTT- I ONLY LEFT HER TO WATCH THE STORE WHILE I STEPPED OUT FOR A MINUTE- FIGURED SHE WAS TOO YOUNG TO WAIT ON FOLKS AND OLD MRS. FROSTBITE!!! BEEN IN HERE A HUNDRED TIMES BUT NEVER'D BUY A THING FROM ME- HM-M-M- THAT GIRL'S GOT SENSE-
HAROLD GRAY
Reg. U. S. Pat. Off.; Copyright, 1929, by The Chicago Tribune.
I CAN'T GET OVER THE WAY THAT YOUNGSTER TOOK HOLD WHEN I WAS OUT AND SOLD ALL THAT STUFF TO MRS. FROSTBITE- DOG-GONE IT- I LIKE THAT KID- SHE'S GOT COMMON SENSE- DON'T WANT TO SPOIL HER, BUT I'D LIKE TO DO SOMETHING FOR HER-
THANKS, MR. SELLERS-
HERE, ANNIE- YOU CAN TAKE THE LAMP NOW- AND HERE'S THE FIFTY CENTS YOU'LL HAVE EARNED NEXT TUESDAY- FIGURE YOU MIGHT WANT TO DO SOME CHRISTMAS SHOPPING EARLY-
GEE- PAID ME IN ADVANCE AN' LET ME TAKE TH' LAMP- HE'S SURE A REG'LAR GUY- NOW HOW TH' DICKENS AM I GOIN' TO WRAP THIS UP SO ANY-BODY WHO SEES IT WON'T KNOW WHAT IT IS?
NIX, SANDY- NO NOISE, NOW- I'VE GOTTA SNEAK THIS THING IN TH' BACK WAY AN' HIDE IT SOME PLACE WHERE MRS. TWINKLE WON'T FIND IT- THAT'S GOIN' TO BE SOME JOB-
HAROLD GRAY
Reg. U. S. Pat. Off.; Copyright, 1929, by The Chicago Tribune.

December 19–21, 1929

ONE THING NICE 'BOUT LIVIN' OUT HERE IN A LITTLE COUNTRY TOWN- WE CAN HAVE A NICE CHRISTMAS TREE JUST BY GOIN' OUT AN' CUTTIN' IT DOWN-
AN' IT'S NOT ONE THAT'S BEEN IN SOME STORE TILL IT'S WHISKERS ARE ALL COMIN' OUT- GEE- WONDER IF I'LL GET ANYTHING FOR CHRISTMAS THIS YEAR- SANTA CLAUS IS AN AWFUL BUSY GUY-
AN' IT'S NOT LIKE I HAD FOLKS TO GO TO TH' FRONT FOR ME- COURSE I WROTE HIM A LETTER, BUT HE GETS THOUSANDS AN' THOUSANDS O' LETTERS FROM KIDS-
OH, WELL- I DON'T REALLY NEED ANYTHING- I'M LOTS BETTER OFF THAN A LOT O' POOR KIDS I'VE KNOWN- BUT IT WOULD BE NICE IF HE'D GIVE ME SOME LITTLE THING- I'D JUST LIKE TO FEEL I'M REMEMBERED-
HAROLD GRAY
Reg. U. S. Pat. Off.; Copyright, 1929, by The Chicago Tribune.
MRS. TWINKLE'S IN BED AN' I'M S'POSED TO BE- BUT HOW CAN I GO TO BED EARLY ON CHRISTMAS EVE? 'SIDES I'VE GOT THINGS TO DO-
MOST LIKELY I WON'T GET ANYTHING IN MY STOCKINGS, BUT AT LEAST I'VE HUNG 'EM UP- AN' TH' TREE IS ALL DEC'RATED- NOW TO PUT MRS. TWINKLE'S PRESENT UNDER TH' TREE-
GEE- I'LL BET SHE'LL BE S'PRISED- I GOT SOME SWELL RIBBON FROM MR. SELLERS AND A "MERRY CHRISTMAS" CARD TO PUT ON IT-
THERE- GEE, SANDY- DOESN'T THAT LOOK CHRISTMASY? NOW LET'S HURRY TO BED, SO SANTY CLAUS'LL HAVE A CHANCE IF HE IS COMIN' HERE-
MERRY CHRISTMAS ANNIE
HAROLD GRAY
Reg. U. S. Pat. Off.; Copyright, 1929, by The Chicago Tribune.
HUH? WHERE AM I? WHY, THIS IS CHRISTMAS- NOT DAYLIGHT YET- SLEIGH-BELLS!!! MAYBE THAT'S SANTA CLAUS!!!
TINKLE TINKLE TINKLE
WHAT'S THAT? SOMETHIN' SCRATCHIN' AT TH' DOOR- MAYBE A CAT----
SCRATCH SCRATCH SCRATCH
LEAPIN' LIZARDS!!! WHAT---- WHO---- HOW---- ???
WHEE!!! LOOK WHAT SANTA CLAUS BROUGHT ME - A REAL LIVE LITTLE BEAR!
?
HAROLD GRAY
Reg. U. S. Pat. Off.; Copyright, 1929, by The Chicago Tribune.

December 23–25, 1929

OH, ANNIE- IT'S A BEAUTIFUL LAMP- AND IT WILL MAKE MY WORK SO MUCH EASIER- YOU'RE SO DEAR AND THOUGHTFUL AND KIND TO ME-
SHUX- THAT'S NOTHIN'- JUST THINK WHAT I GOT FROM SANTA CLAUS- A REAL LIVE BABY BEAR- I'VE NAMED HIM WILLIE- ISN'T THAT A CUTE NAME?
WELL, IT WAS A GREAT CHRISTMAS, EH, SANDY?
ARF!
SO YUH SORTA LIKE SUGAR, DO YUH, WILLIE? LICK IT UP CLEAN- GEE, YOU'RE SURE A FRIENDLY LITTLE FELLA- JUST WAIT TILL TH' KIDS HEAR ABOUT YOU-
?
HAROLD GRAY
Reg. U. S. Pat. Off.; Copyright, 1929, by The Chicago Tribune.
WHAT? A REAL LIVE BEAR? YUH SAY ANNIE GOT IT FOR CHRISTMAS?
YES, SIR- JOE SEWELL SAW IT HISSELF- C'MON- LET'S GO UP TO HER HOUSE-
GEE-
AIN'T HE CUTE?
A REAL BEAR-
YES, SIREE- SANTA CLAUS BROUGHT HIM TO ME EARLY CHRISTMAS MORNING-
YOU'LL HAVE TO S'CUSE LITTLE WILLIE- COURSE HE'S PRETTY TIRED YET FROM HIS LONG TRIP ALL TH' WAY HERE WITH SANTY FROM TH' NORTH POLE- BUT HE'LL BE RESTED UP IN A DAY OR SO-
GEE- JUST LOOK AT HIM, SANDY- CURLED UP IN HIS BOX AND SOUND ASLEEP- POOR LITTLE FELLA- ALL TUCKERED OUT-
HAROLD GRAY
Reg. U. S. Pat. Off.; Copyright, 1929, by The Chicago Tribune.
HE MOST LIKELY JUST HAPPENED ALONG- THAT SANTA CLAUS STUFF IS TH' BUNK-
IS THAT SO? WELL, IF YOU'RE SO BLAMED WISE, MAYBE YUH CAN TELL WHY I HEARD SLEIGH-BELLS JUST AT TH' SAME TIME HE STARTED SCRATCHIN' AT TH' DOOR-
AND WITH 365 DAYS IN TH' YEAR TO PICK FROM, WHY DID HE HAVE TO COME ON CHRISTMAS DAY, IF SANTA CLAUS DIDN'T BRING HIM- I S'POSE THAT JUST HAPPENED TOO, EH?
HUH!
GEE- I GUESS MAYBE ANNIE'S RIGHT, AT THAT-
SURE- IT MUST HAVE BEEN SANTA CLAUS-
YEAH-
HAROLD GRAY
Reg. U. S. Pat. Off.; Copyright, 1929, by The Chicago Tribune.

December 26–28, 1929

THE SEVEN-YEAR ITCHY

JUST LOOK AT TH' LITTLE RASCAL - PICKS UP NEW TRICKS IN NO TIME -
I'VE HEARD BEARS ARE LIKE THAT - START THEM YOUNG ENOUGH AND THEY CAN LEARN ALL SORTS OF TRICKS -
SANDY!!! WHAT'S TH' BIG IDEA? WE KNOW YUH CAN DANCE -
SANDY WANTS TO BE PART OF THE SHOW, TOO - JUST LIKE A CHILD -
AW - DON'T BE SILLY, SANDY - ACT YER AGE AN' QUIT SHOWIN' OFF -
DON'T BE HARD ON HIM, ANNIE - HE JUST WANTS A LITTLE APPLAUSE, TOO -
ALL RIGHT, NOW, WILLIE - SIT UP - THAT'S TH' STUFF - NOW SHAKE HANDS - COME ON - I'LL SHOW YUH HOW - SHAKE HANDS -
?
HAROLD GRAY
Reg. U. S. Pat. Off.; Copyright, 1929, by The Chicago Tribune.
HEY! LAY OFF O' WILLIE - HE NEVER DID ANYTHING TO YOU -
TH' IDEA! JEALOUS! POOR LITTLE WILLIE - TH' CUTE LITTLE GUY - TRYIN' TO GO ALONG AN' BE FRIENDLY AN' YOU PICK ON HIM - YOU OUGHTA LOVE HIM -
DON'TCHA SEE, SANDY? THERE'S NOTHIN' TO BE JEALOUS 'BOUT - YOU SHOULD FIGGER WILLIE'S JUST LIKE YER LITTLE BROTHER -
HAROLD GRAY
Reg. U. S. Pat. Off.; Copyright, 1929, by The Chicago Tribune.
THERE Y'ARE, WILLIE - EVER'THING YUH LIKE - AND MOLASSES ALL OVER IT TOO -
NIX - I CAN'T TRUST YOU IN TH' SAME ROOM WITH WILLIE - HERE'S YOUR SUPPER, SANDY - IT'S JUST AS GOOD AS WILLIE'S -
HEIGH-HO - NEW YEAR'S DAY - ANOTHER YEAR GONE - AND WHAT A YEAR! GEE - JUST A BIG BUST!!!
BUT WHY LOOK BACK? THERE'S NOTHIN' YUH CAN DO TO FIX WHAT'S HAPPENED IN TH' PAST - IT'S TH' FUTURE YUH'VE GOTTA WATCH - AND, B'LIEVE ME, THIS YEAR'S GOIN' TO BE DIFFERENT -
HAROLD GRAY
Reg. U. S. Pat. Off.; Copyright, 1930, by The Chicago Tribune.

December 30, 1929–
January 1, 1930

GEE- MR. SELLERS SENT WORD HE WANTS TO SEE ME AT TH' STORE- WONDER WHAT HE WANTS TO TALK TO ME ABOUT-
DID YOU WANT TO SEE ME, MR. SELLERS?
YES, ANNIE- I'VE BEEN DOING SOME THINKING- FIGGER I CAN USE SOME HELP AROUND HERE, IF IT'S THE RIGHT KIND OF HELP-
I NEED SOMEBODY WHO WILL KEEP THINGS DUSTED- MAKE THE STORE INVITING AND WAIT ON PEOPLE- YOU SHOWED YOU CAN DO THAT-
TIME WAS WHEN I THOUGHT I COULD RUN THIS PLACE ALONE- BUT I'M NOT SO SPRY AS I USED TO BE- WHAT DO YOU SAY? WILL YOU HELP ME OUT AFTER-NOONS AND SATURDAYS?
SURE- THANKS!
HAROLD GRAY
Reg. U. S. Pat. Off.; Copyright, 1930, by The Chicago Tribune.
WHY, WILLIE- A WHOLE SACK O' GUM DROPS- AND YOU MEAN TO SAY YOU WON'T EAT THE LAST ONE?
ULP!
SHUX! WHAT'LL I DO WITH THIS LAST GUM-DROP?
YOU LIKE GUM-DROPS, DON'T YOU, SANDY? HERE- YOU CAN HAVE IT- WILLIE DOESN'T WANT IT-
HAROLD GRAY
Reg. U. S. Pat. Off.; Copyright, 1930, by The Chicago Tribune.
NOW I CAN'T STAY HERE AN' WATCH THESE COOKIES ALL TH' TIME- BUT YOU KNOW, SANDY, COOKIES ARE NOT FOR LITTLE DOGGIES- STAY OUT OF 'EM, 'LESS YUH WANT A PADDLIN- SEE?
HEY- ANYBODY AT THOSE COOKIES? IF THERE IS I'LL SURE WHALE TH' STUFFIN' OUT OF 'M-
Reg. U. S. Pat. Off.; Copyright, 1930, by The Chicago Tribune.
OH, MRS. TWINKLE- JUST COME AN' SEE WHAT LITTLE WILLIE'S GONE AN' DONE- YOU WOULDN'T B'LIEVE IT- IT'S TH' CUTEST TRICK-
HAROLD GRAY

January 2–4, 1930

GEE, THAT BUNCH O' KIDS HAVE BEEN TAGGIN' AFTER ME EVER SINCE I LEFT TH' HOUSE -
THEY JUST STAY 'BOUT SO FAR BEHIND ALL TH' TIME - BUT EVERY TIME I TURN A CORNER THEY TURN TOO - MUST BE SOME REASON FOR IT.
WELL, I'LL JUST WAIT HERE, 'FORE I GO INTO TH' STORE, AN' SEE WHAT THEY'VE BEEN FOLLOWIN' ME FOR -
LEAPIN' LIZARDS!!! LITTLE WILLIE!!! HOW IN THE WORLD DID YOU GET OUT OF TH' HOUSE?
HAROLD GRAY
Reg. U. S. Pat. Off.; Copyright, 1930, by The Chicago Tribune.
LEAPIN' LIZARDS! WILLIE!!! YOU HERE AGAIN?
I LOCKED HIM IN TH' HOUSE WHEN I LEFT- BUT HERE HE IS- WHAT'LL WE DO WITH HIM? I CAN'T HAVE HIM HERE IN THE STORE - HE'LL BE INTO EVERYTHING -
HM-MM- THE SHOW-WINDOW'S EMPTY - PUT HIM IN THERE TILL YOU GO HOME -
THAT'S A GOOD IDEA- HE CAN'T GET OUT OF THERE AND WE'LL KNOW WHERE HE IS.
HA-HA- LOOK, MR. SELLERS- PLATE GLASS IS A NEW ONE ON WILLIE-
MY- MY- JUST LOOK AT THOSE KIDS AROUND THAT WINDOW - NEVER HAD SO MANY PEOPLE IN FRONT OF MY STORE BEFORE -
Reg. U. S. Pat. Off.; Copyright, 1930, by The Chicago Tribune.
HAROLD GRAY
HELLO, WILLIE! HAVIN' A GOOD TIME? THAT'S TH' STUFF - PLAY WITH TH' BALL FOR TH' PEOPLE - ALWAYS GIVE TH' PUBLIC A SHOW -
SURE WAS NICE O' MR. SELLERS TO LET ME BRING WILLIE TO TH' STORE AN' STAY IN TH' WINDOW EVERY DAY- WILLIE HAS A PICNIC AND IT SURE BRINGS PEOPLE TO TH' STORE -
HM-M-M-- WONDER WHAT AILS MR. SELLERS- BEEN JUST SITTIN' THERE LIKE THAT FOR AN HOUR-
IT'S ALL RIGHT, ANNIE, FOR WILLIE TO DRAW FOLKS TO THE STORE - HE GETS 'EM HERE, BUT THEY STOP OUT IN FRONT - CUSTOMERS ON THE OUTSIDE DON'T BUY GOODS - WHAT WE NEED IS CUSTOMERS ON THE INSIDE -
HAROLD GRAY
Reg. U. S. Pat. Off.; Copyright, 1930, by The Chicago Tribune.

January 6–8, 1930

WHEN I LEFT WILLIE AT TH' STORE THIS MORNING MR. SELLERS WAS MAKIN' A LITTLE PEN FOR HIM BY TH' BACK COUNTER- FIGGERED FOLKS WILL COME INSIDE TH' STORE TO SEE HIM-
GEE- IT SURE MUST HAVE WORKED ALL RIGHT- JUST LOOK AT THAT GANG O' KIDS CROWDIN' IN TH' FRONT DOOR-
RAL STORE
I WISH SOMEBODY'D GIVE ME A BEAR FOR CHRISTMAS SOME TIME-
HOW LONG WILL IT BE BEFORE HE GROWS UP TO BE A REAL BIG BEAR?
I WOULDN'T BE 'FRAID TO POKE A LITTLE BEAR LIKE THAT-
I'M GOIN' TO BRING HIM SOME CANDY TO-MORROW-
JUST LOOK AT TH' LITTLE RASCAL SIT UP-
WELL, MY PLAN WORKED FINE, ANNIE- NEVER HAD SUCH A CROWD IN MY STORE BEFORE-
WILLIE SURE PACKS 'EM IN- WE OUGHTA DO LOTS MORE BUSINESS FROM NOW ON-
HAROLD GRAY
Reg. U. S. Pat. Off.; Copyright, 1930, by The Chicago Tribune.
WE'VE GOT THE CROWD, ALL RIGHT- LOOK AT 'EM OVER THERE CROWDING AROUND THAT BEAR- BUT MOST OF THEM ARE YOUNGSTERS- JUST COME IN TO LOAF- DON'T SPEND A CENT-
WHAT'S THE USE OF GETTING A BIG CROWD IN THE PLACE IF THEY'RE THE PEOPLE WHO DON'T BUY ANYTHING? ANSWER THAT, IF YOU CAN-
GEE- THAT'S SO- MOST ALL KIDS- AND THIS IS A GENERAL STORE- ABOUT EVER'THING GROWN FOLKS COULD WANT- BUT GROWN FOLKS HAVE SEEN BEARS- NO NEW GROWN FOLKS COME IN HERE-
HAROLD GRAY
THERE'S SOMETHIN' CAN BE DONE 'BOUT IT, BUT I'M DOG-GONED IF I KNOW WHAT?
NEITHER DO I, ANNIE- IT'S A PROBLEM- I ADMIT I'M STUMPED-
Reg. U. S. Pat. Off.; Copyright, 1930, by The Chicago Tribune.
I'VE GOT IT! I'VE GOT IT!
GOT WHAT? MEASELS, OR SUTHIN'?
NO! I'VE FIGGERED OUT WHAT WE CAN DO- WHAT WE'VE GOT TO SELL IS ALL FOR GROWN-UPS- BUT TH' CROWD WE GET IN TH' STORE IS MOSTLY KIDS- WELL- WHY NOT HAVE THINGS TO SELL THAT KIDS WILL BUY?
BY JINGO!!! ANNIE, YOU'VE HIT THE NAIL RIGHT ON THE HEAD- PUT IN A LINE OF STUFF FOR CHILDREN- LET'S SEE, NOW- WHAT ALL WILL WE HAVE TO ORDER?
LITTLE JARS O' HONEY- MAPLE SUGAR- CANDY- LOLLY-POPS- THEY'LL BUY THAT STUFF TO FEED WILLIE- AN' WE CAN HAVE SCHOOL THINGS- TABLETS- PENCILS- COLORED CRAYONS- WATER-COLORS- AN' WE CAN PUT IN SOME CHEAP TOYS- SOME BRIGHT AN' FLASHY STUFF-
I'LL 'PHONE THIS ORDER AND WE'LL HAVE THE STUFF MONDAY-
HAROLD GRAY
Reg. U. S. Pat. Off.; Copyright, 1930, by The Chicago Tribune.

January 9–11, 1930

GEE- ALL THAT NEW LINE O' CANDY AN' THINGS KIDS BUY OUGHTA BE AT TH' STORE BY NOW- I'VE GOTTA GET THERE EARLY AND HELP MR. SELLERS UNPACK-
WE'LL PUT ALL THIS STUFF ON A SPECIAL COUNTER AND I'M GOING TO TURN IT ALL OVER TO YOU, ANNIE-
WOW- A COUNTER THAT I CAN RUN JUST LIKE IT WAS MY OWN LITTLE STORE-
LOOK, MR. SELLERS- I CAN HARDLY SEE OVER THIS COUNTER. WHAT'LL WE DO 'BOUT THIS?
HM-M-M- LET'S SEE, NOW-
THERE- DO THOSE BOARDS RAISE YOU UP HIGH ENOUGH?
GEE- MAKES ME FEEL LIKE I'D GROWN UP ALL OF A SUDDEN-
HAROLD GRAY
Reg. U. S. Pat. Off.; Copyright, 1930, by The Chicago Tribune.
HE WANTS A PENNY'S WORTH O' GUM-DROPS AN' I WANT A NICKEL'S WORTH O' PEA-NUTS FOR LITTLE WILLIE-
LOOK AT HIM GOBBLE UP THOSE MARSHMALLOWS
HERE, WILLIE- SEE HOW YUH LIKE THIS ALL-DAY SUCKER-
OH, BOY- ARE WE DOIN' A SWELL BUSINESS!!! EVER SINCE SCHOOL LET OUT TH' KIDS HAVE BEEN BUYIN' AN' BUYIN' THINGS TO FEED WILLIE-
OH, HELLO, SANDY- KNEW IT WAS QUITTIN' TIME SO YOU CAME DOWN TO THE STORE TO WALK HOME WITH ME, EH? JUST WAIT TILL I GET WILLIE-
GEE, SANDY- YUH OUGHTA SEE TH' WAY TH' KIDS FEED WILLIE CANDY AN' THINGS- WILLIE'S SURE POP'LAR WITH EVER'BODY-
HAROLD GRAY
Reg. U. S. Pat. Off.; Copyright, 1930, by The Chicago Tribune.
C'MON, WILLIE- WE'RE CLOSIN' UP TH' STORE- IT'S TIME TO GO HOME-
HERE, WILLIE- HERE'S A SWELL CHOC'LATE-COVERED NUT FOR YUH- WHY, WILLIE!!! DON'TCHA WANT IT? NEVER SAW YOU TURN DOWN CANDY BEFORE-
OH, THE YOUNGSTERS HAVE BEEN STUFFING HIM WITH CANDY AND NUTS AND HONEY FOR THREE DAYS- MOST LIKELY HE'S JUST BEGINNING TO GET FILLED UP-
GUESS YOU'RE RIGHT, MR. SELLERS- TH' KIDS SURE HAVE BEEN NICE TO WILLIE-
HE'S SO FULL HE CAN HARDLY WALK-
HAROLD GRAY
Reg. U. S. Pat. Off.; Copyright, 1930, by The Chicago Tribune.

January 13–15, 1930

SOMETHIN' WRONG WITH LITTLE WILLIE - I COULD HARDLY GET HIM DOWN HERE - HE WANTED TO LIE DOWN ALL TH' TIME -
JUST LOOK, WILLIE - A PERFECTLY GORG'OUS, GREEN ALL-DAY SUCKER - TH' KIND YOU LIKE BEST -
?
LEAPIN' LIZARDS! CAN YUH BEAT IT? RUNS LIKE I'D POINTED A GUN AT HIM -
?
OW!
HAROLD GRAY
Reg. U. S. Pat. Off.; Copyright, 1930, by The Chicago Tribune.
OH, DOCTOR SCALPEL - I KNOW YOU JUST DOCTOR FOLKS, BUT WON'T YOU PLEASE COME IN AN' LOOK AT LITTLE WILLIE? HE'S AWFUL SICK -
HE WAS GREAT TILL JUST A COUPLE O' DAYS AGO - THEN HE HAD PAINS AND WOULDN'T EAT - 'FORE THAT HE ATE EVER'THING -
SO HE ATE EVERYTHING, DID HE? HM-M-M--- I CAN BELIEVE IT -
LITTLE PEOPLE OR LITTLE BEARS - WHEN THEY'RE SICK THERE'S NOTHING SO GOOD AS CASTOR OIL -
GLUG! GLUG!
O-O-O-OH! CASTOR OIL - POOR LITTLE WILLIE! I KNOW JUST HOW HE FEELS -
NOW, WHEN HE GETS TO FEELING BETTER, GIVE HIM GOOD, PLAIN FOOD - BUT NO MORE STUFFING HIM WITH CANDY -
O. K. DOCTOR - AND THANKS A LOT -
HAROLD GRAY
Reg. U. S. Pat. Off.; Copyright, 1930, by The Chicago Tribune.
WELL, THAT CASTOR OIL HELPED WILLIE A HEAP - HE'S LOTS BETTER TO-DAY, BUT I'M DOG-GONED IF I'M GOIN' TO LET HIM GET SICK AGAIN, IF I CAN HELP IT -
THERE - THAT OUGHTA DO TH' TRICK -
"DO NOT FEED THE ANIMAL"
BUT, ANNIE - IF THE YOUNGSTERS CAN'T FEED CANDY AND NUTS TO WILLIE THEY WON'T BUY NEARLY SO MUCH - IT WILL HURT BUSINESS -
YEAH? I S'POSE IT WOULDN'T HURT BUSINESS ANY TO LET 'EM KEEP ON STUFFIN' HIM TILL HE BUSTED!!! A LIVE BEAR, EVEN IF YUH MUSTN'T FEED HIM, IS LOTS BETTER'N NO BEAR AT ALL - THINK IT OVER -
HAROLD GRAY
Reg. U. S. Pat. Off.; Copyright, 1930, by The Chicago Tribune.

January 16–18, 1930

DOG GONE IT- I JUST CAN'T SEEM TO GET MY HISTRY LESSON GOOD ENOUGH TO SATISFY TH' TEACHER- AN' 'RITHMETIC AN' G'OGRAPHY AN' SPELLIN' ALL SEEM TO GET TOUGHER EVERY DAY-
WELL, WELL, ANNIE- I'M GLAD TO SEE YOU ARE PURSUING YOUR STUDIES-
YESSUM- I'M SURE PURSUIN' 'EM, ALL RIGHT-
AT LEAST I ALWAYS SEEM TO BE WAY BEHIND-
?
HAROLD GRAY
Reg. U. S. Pat. Off.; Copyright, 1930, by The Chicago Tribune.
NOPE- NO MAIL IN TH' BOX TO-DAY- DIDN'T THINK THERE WOULD BE- OH, WELL-
SAY, ANNIE- DO YOU KNOW IF OLD JACK PEPPER IS IN TOWN? GOT A LETTER HERE FOR HIM-
HE'S BEEN IN TH' CITY FOR A FEW DAYS, BUT I HEARD HE'S COMIN' HOME TO-MORROW-
RECKON I'D BETTER HOLD THIS LETTER TILL HE COMES IN- LOOKS IMPORTANT- LOTTA FOREIGN STAMPS- SAYS "SINGAPORE" ON IT IN ONE PLACE- SURE CAME A RIGHT SMART WAYS-
GEE!
SINGAPORE- I'M GONNA LOOK THAT UP IN MY G'OGRAPHY- THAT'S ONE O' TH' PLACES "DADDY" USED TO TALK ABOUT- WONDER WHERE "DADDY" IS NOW, ANYWAY-
HAROLD GRAY
Reg. U. S. Pat. Off.; Copyright, 1930, by The Chicago Tribune.
POST O
GOOD MORNING, MR. PEPPER- I SEE YOU GOT YOUR LETTER-
HELLO, ANNIE- YES, THANKS- I GOT IT, ALL RIGHT-
AREN'T YUH GOIN' TO OPEN IT AN' SEE WHO IT'S FROM AN' WHAT IT SAYS?
OH, IT'S BEEN ON THE WAY FOR A MONTH OR MORE- A FEW MINUTES NOW WON'T MAKE MUCH DIFFERENCE-
SHUX- SOME FOLKS NEVER GET 'CITED 'BOUT ANYTHING- WHY, NO TELLIN' WHAT MIGHT BE IN A LETTER LIKE THAT-
Reg. U. S. Pat. Off.; Copyright, 1930, by The Chicago Tribune.
HAROLD GRAY

January 20–22, 1930

ALL, RIGHT. HUANG - I WON'T NEED ANYTHING MORE TO-NIGHT -
VELLY GOOD, MR. JACK -
WELL, WELL - IT'S FROM WARBUCKS - THE OLD RASCAL - WRITTEN NEARLY THREE MONTHS AGO AND STARTED BY NATIVE MESSENGER - FINALLY MAILED AT SINGAPORE IT'S A WONDER IT EVER REACHED ME AT ALL - LET'S SEE WHAT HE SAYS -
HE'S WELL, BUT WILL HAVE TO STAY ON THE JOB THERE FOR SOME TIME - AND HE WANTS ME TO TRY TO LOCATE LITTLE ANNIE AND SEE THAT SHE IS BEING TAKEN CARE OF PROPERLY AND LOOK OUT FOR HER TILL HE RETURNS - CAN YOU BEAT THAT?
LITTLE ANNIE - HE THINKS SHE'S STILL IN THE CITY WHERE HE LEFT HER - AND HERE SHE IS IN BLUNDERVILLE IMAGINE SUCH A COINCIDENCE - IN A NOVEL IT WOULD BE THOUGHT TOO IMPOSSIBLE - YET HERE IT IS -
HAROLD GRAY
Reg. U. S. Pat. Off.; Copyright, 1930, by The Chicago Tribune.
GEE, MR. PEPPER MUST WANT TO SEE ME 'BOUT SOMETHIN' 'PORTANT OR HE WOULDN'T HAVE SENT HUANG AFTER ME -
HELLO, ANNIE - GLAD TO SEE YOU - COME RIGHT IN -
HELLO, MR. PEPPER -
YOU WERE RIGHT - THAT LETTER WAS IMPORTANT - IT WAS FROM YOUR "DADDY" WARBUCKS AND IT WAS ALL ABOUT YOU -
"DADDY?" WHERE IS HE? IS HE COMING BACK SOON? IS HE ALL RIGHT?
HAROLD GRAY
HE'S FINE, ANNIE - BUT I FEAR HE WON'T BE BACK FOR SOME TIME - HE WANTED ME TO LOOK FOR YOU - OUT OF OVER A HUNDRED MILLION PEOPLE THAT MIGHT HAVE BEEN QUITE A JOB - BUT HERE WE ARE IN THE SAME LITTLE TOWN - AND THEY SAY THERE'S NO SUCH THING AS LUCK -
WHO SAYS SO?
Reg. U. S. Pat. Off.; Copyright, 1930, by The Chicago Tribune.
WARBUCKS HAS ASKED ME TO LOOK OUT FOR LITTLE ANNIE TILL HE GETS BACK - THAT'S A BIG RESPONSIBILITY FOR AN OLD COOT LIKE ME - I WANT TO DO WHAT'S BEST FOR HER -
I COULD GIVE HER MONEY, FINE CLOTHES, PRIVATE SCHOOL - BUT SHE'LL BE HAPPIER WITH MRS. TWINKLE - AND AS FOR THE WORK SHE DOES, ANY YOUNGSTER HER AGE IS BETTER OFF IF THINGS DON'T COME TOO EASY -
GEE, IT'S GOOD TO KNOW "DADDY'S" O. K. - I'LL HAVE A LOT TO TELL HIM WHEN I SEE HIM - WHY, HE'S NEVER SEEN LITTLE WILLIE, HERE - WISH HE'D COME BACK SOON -
'CORDIN' TO THAT LETTER "DADDY" WON'T BE HOME FOR A LONG, LONG TIME - WELL, WE'LL SURE BE MIGHTY GLAD TO SEE HIM WHEN HE DOES COME BACK - EH, SANDY?
ARF!
HAROLD GRAY
Reg. U. S. Pat. Off.; Copyright, 1930, by The Chicago Tribune.

January 23–25, 1930

THERE'S THAT GOOFY ITCHY JONES - WONDER WHAT HE'S WAITIN' THERE ON TH' CORNER FOR - WHY DOESN'T HE GO ON HOME?
HELLO, ITCHY -
HELLO, ANNIE - C-C-CAN I ---- I MEAN MAY I ---- CARRY YER B-B-BOOKS?
NAW - I CAN CARRY 'EM, O.K. I'M NOT CRIPPLED - AN' PUT ON YER CAP, 'FORE YUH CATCH COLD -
?
TH' BIG DUMMY ---- "MAY I CARRY YER BOOKS?" DO I LOOK WEAK OR SOMETHIN'? TH' POOR SAP MUST BE GOIN' SQUIRRELLY -
HAROLD GRAY
Reg. U. S. Pat. Off.; Copyright, 1930, by The Chicago Tribune.
ANNIE - WHAT CITY IS THE CAPITOL OF SOUTH CAROLINA?
SOUTH CAROLINA? ER --- ER --- ULP ---
COLUMBIA!
COLUMBIA!
I HEARD YOU, YOUNG MAN - YOU MARCH RIGHT INTO THE PRINCIPAL'S OFFICE THIS INSTANT - DO YOU HEAR?
YESSUM -
WHACK! OUCH! WHACK WOW! WHACK
WE WILL NOW PROCEED WITH THE RECITATION -
GEE - POOR ITCHY -
HAROLD GRAY
Reg. U. S. Pat. Off.; Copyright, 1930, by The Chicago Tribune.
GEE, ITCHY - I'M AWFUL SORRY YUH GOT A LICKIN' FOR HELPIN' ME IN REC'TATION YESTERDAY -
SHUX - THAT'S ALL RIGHT - TH' OLD PRINC'PAL WASN'T STRONG 'NUFF TO WHALE ME VERY HARD -
GWAN! IF HE DIDN'T WHALE YUH HARD WHY DIDJA HOLLER SO LOUD?
AW, I WASN'T HOLLERIN' - I WAS LAUGHIN' AT TH' OLD GUY -
GEE - I'LL BET IT MADE HIM AWFUL MAD WHEN YUH LAUGHED AT HIM -
I HOPE T' TELL YUH IT DID - HE SOCKED ME SO HARD HE BUSTED HIS RULER -
GEE! AND YUH DIDN'T BAWL, EVEN THEN?
NAW - I HAVEN'T BAWLED SINCE I WAS JUST A KID -
HAROLD GRAY
Reg. U. S. Pat. Off.; Copyright, 1930, by The Chicago Tribune.

January 27–29, 1930

HELLO, ITCHY- I THOUGHT YOU ALWAYS WENT UP MAPLE STREET TO SCHOOL-
AW, ER- WELL, I JUST HAPPENED TO GO THIS WAY TO-DAY-
LISTEN TO THOSE FRESH KIDS-
HEY! LOOKIE!..
ITCHY AN' ANNIE!..
YA-A-A-A-A...
ANNIE AND ITCHY JONES
ANNIE AND ITCHY-
HAW--HAW..
ARE YUH SCARED? AREN'T YUH GOIN' TO DO ANYTHING ABOUT IT?
AW, I DON'T CARE- DO YOU?
YA-A-A-A- ITCHY'S GOT A GIRL- ITCHY'S GOT A GIRL-
YUH DOG GONED SMARTY- YOU'D BETTER BUTTON YER LIP- SEE?
YA-A-A-A! WHO'S GOIN' TO MAKE ME- ITCHY'S SCARED TO FIGHT-
HAROLD GRAY
Reg. U. S. Pat. Off.; Copyright, 1930, by The Chicago Tribune.
YUH BIG BULLY-
THERE! THAT'LL COOL YUH OFF!
HAW-HAW! RIGHT IN A MUD PUDDLE-
YOU--- YOU---- YOU!!!
?
PUSH HER, WILL YUH? I'LL TEACH YUH!
HOW D'YUH LIKE IT? HAVE YUH HAD ENOUGH? YOU 'POLIGIZE TO HER--- LOUDER-
NO! YES! OW!!! GLUG-GLUG- I 'POLGIZE- BLUB!
HAROLD GRAY
Reg. U. S. Pat. Off.; Copyright, 1930, by The Chicago Tribune.
GEE- WHAT A BEATIN' ITCHY JONES GAVE THAT SMART SKID HAMMER- AND ITCHY NEVER HAD A FIGHT BEFORE- BUT WHEN SKID SHOVED ME INTO THAT MUD PUDDLE ITCHY SURE TORE INTO HIM-
EVER'BODY'S BEEN SCARED O' SKID- BUT ITCHY SURE CUT HIM DOWN- THERE'S ITCHY NOW-
GEE, ITCHY- THANKS FOR HELPIN' ME OUT- I NEVER KNEW YOU COULD FIGHT LIKE THAT-
AW, SHUX- NEITHER DID I- GUESS I JUST HAD TO DO IT-
HUH! WHAT ON EARTH IS TH' MATTER WITH HIM TO RUN LIKE THAT? HIS FACE IS AS RED AS A TOMATO- GOOFIEST GUY I EVER SAW-
HAROLD GRAY
Reg. U. S. Pat. Off.; Copyright, 1930, by The Chicago Tribune.

January 30–
February 1, 1930

BEGINNING TO-MORROW, ANY PUPIL WHO IS TARDY WILL HAVE TO REMAIN HALF AN HOUR AFTER SCHOOL-
GEE- HALF AN HOUR IS A LONG TIME-
YEAH- ANY TIME'S A LONG TIME TO HAVE TO STAY AFTER SCHOOL-
AN' WORKIN' AT TH' STORE 'FORE AN' AFTER SCHOOL, LIKE I AM, I CAN'T 'FORD TO GET KEPT LATE- BLAMED OLD RULE!
I'M HARDLY EVER TARDY- BUT FROM NOW ON I DON'T DARE BE TARDY EVEN ONCE-
HAROLD GRAY
Reg. U. S. Pat. Off.; Copyright, 1930, by The Chicago Tribune.
GOOD GRIEF- THERE'S THAT GOOFY ITCHY JONES WAITIN' UP AT TH' CORNER TO WALK TO SCHOOL WITH ME- THANK GOODNESS- HERE'S GUSSIE SNIPP- I'LL WALK WITH HER-
HELLO, GUSSIE- HOW ARE YUH? GOIN' TO SCHOOL?
HELLO, ANNIE- TRYIN' TO DODGE THAT AWFUL ITCHY JONES, EH? I DON'T BLAME YOU-
OF ALL TH' BIG, DUMB YOKELS, HE'S THE PRIZE WINNER- DIDJA EVER NOTICE HOW HIS EARS STICK OUT?
TH' MEAN LITTLE CAT- WHAT RIGHT HAS SHE TO KNOCK POOR ITCHY- HE CAN'T HELP HIS EARS- AN' ANYWAY, HE'S NOT SO BAD-
HAROLD GRAY
Reg. U. S. Pat. Off.; Copyright, 1930, by The Chicago Tribune.
LEAPIN' LIZARDS! THERE GOES TH' LAST BELL- I'M TARDY AN' I'LL HAVE TO STAY AFTER SCHOOL-
BONG! BONG! BONG!
OH, BOY! WHAT A BREAK- TEACHER'S OUT O' TH' ROOM AN' DIDN'T CATCH ME COMIN' IN LATE-
WELL, CHILDREN- I'M GLAD TO SEE YOU ARE ALL HERE ON TIME THIS MORNING-
WE WEREN'T ALL HERE ON TIME- ANNIE WAS LATE-
GUSSIE SNIPP-
IS THAT TRUE, ANNIE?
HAROLD GRAY
Reg. U. S. Pat. Off.; Copyright, 1930, by The Chicago Tribune.

February 3–5, 1930

WHEN WAS THE BATTLE OF BUNKER HILL? HM-M... ER... LET ME SEE....
ER... WAS IT TH' EIGHTEENTH OF APRIL, '75?
NO!
THAT WILL DO, ANNIE- YOU MAY SIT DOWN- AND I WILL LET SOME ONE RECITE WHO HAS STUDIED THE LESSON- GUSSIE, YOU MAY ANSWER THE QUESTION-
THE BATTLE OF BUNKER HILL WAS FOUGHT ON JUNE SEVENTEENTH, 1775-
I'M GLAD TO SEE SOME ONE HAS PREPARED THEIR LESSON-
HAROLD GRAY
Reg. U. S. Pat. Off.; Copyright, 1930, by The Chicago Tribune.
POOR ITCHIE- HE SEEMS SORTA LONESOME- GUESS I'LL WAIT AND WALK HOME WITH HIM-
?
OH, ITCHIE- YOU'RE GOING THE SAME WAY- WOULD YOU MIND CARRYING MY BOOKS? THEY'RE SO HEAVY-
?
YOU DON'T MIND WALKING DOWN THE STREET WITH ME, DO YOU, ITCHIE? TEE-HEE-HEE- YOUR FACE IS SO RED-
HUH! WONDER IF SHE THINKS I CARE- SHE'S WELCOME TO TH' BIG DUMMY-
HAROLD GRAY
Reg. U. S. Pat. Off.; Copyright, 1930, by The Chicago Tribune.
I HEARD GUSSIE TATTLE ON YOU WHEN YOU WERE TARDY- AND I SAW HER CHEATIN', TOO- SHE LOOKED IN HER BOOK DURIN' REC'TATION-
SHE'S A MEAN LITTLE CROOK- I DIDN'T WANT TO WALK HOME WITH HER YESTERDAY- BUT SHE ASKED ME TO CARRY HER BOOKS-
WHAT COULD I DO?
HAW! HAW! HAW! WHY TELL ME ABOUT IT? IT'S NOTHIN' TO ME- HAW! HAW! HAW!
SO THAT GUSSIE SNIPP CHEATS HUH- BUT IF YUH TOLD ON HER YUH'D BE JUST AS BAD A TATTLE-TALE AS SHE IS- COURSE I DON'T GIVE THREE WHOOPS 'BOUT HER WALKIN' HOME WITH ITCHY- BUT A CROOK LIKE SHE IS OUGHTA GET WHAT'S COMIN' TO HER-
HAROLD GRAY
Reg. U. S. Pat. Off.; Copyright, 1930, by The Chicago Tribune.

February 6–8, 1930

THAT DOG-GONED GUSSIE SNIPP- CHEAT- CHEAT- CHEAT- BUT SHE NEVER GETS CAUGHT-
COPIES EVERYTHING I WRITE- BUT TEACHER THINKS SHE'S A LITTLE ANGEL- AND WHAT CAN I DO?
GUSSIE TOLD ON VIRGINIA FOR WHISPERIN' AN' GIN GOT KEPT AFTER SCHOOL-
HUH- I S'POSE GUSSIE NEVER WHISPERS- OR CHEATS OR PUTS GUM ON SEATS OR NOTHIN'-
BUT YUH CAN'T TELL ON HER- IT'S LIKE THROWIN' MUD ON SOMEBODY TO TATTLE ON 'EM- YUH FIX THEM ALL RIGHT, BUT YUH GET JUST ABOUT AS DIRTY YERSELF DOIN' IT-
HAROLD GRAY
Reg. U. S. Pat. Off.; Copyright, 1930, by The Chicago Tribune.
ALL RIGHT, CHILDREN- YOU MAY HAND IN YOUR PAPERS, NOW-
CLASS IS DISMISSED- ANNIE AND GUSSIE WILL REMAIN-
THIS IS VERY STRANGE- BOTH OF YOU MADE THE SAME MISTAKES- IT IS VERY EVIDENT SOMEONE HAS BEEN COPYING- ANNIE- WHAT HAVE YOU TO SAY FOR YOURSELF?
YUH'D THINK TEACHER'D HAVE SENSE ENOUGH TO FIGGER OUT WHO COPIED- BUT I CAN'T SNITCH AN' GUSSIE LIES OUT OF IT- HER DAD'S ON TH' SCHOOL BOARD- THAT MAKES HER PERFECT- LEAPIN' LIZARDS!!! HOW YUH GOIN' TO BEAT A GAME LIKE THAT?
HAROLD GRAY
Reg. U. S. Pat. Off.; Copyright, 1930, by The Chicago Tribune.
LINCOLN SURE MUST HAVE BEEN A MIGHTY SMART MAN- EH, ITCHY?
YEAH-
BUT HE NEVER HAD TO WASTE A LOT O' HIS TIME GOIN' TO SCHOOL-
AW, I GUESS HE DIDN'T GET TO BE PRES'DENT JUST 'CAUSE HE NEVER WENT TO SCHOOL- HE GOT TO BE PRES'DENT IN SPITE OF IT-
IF HE'D HAD A CHANCE TO GO TO SCHOOL THERE'S NO TELLIN' HOW GREAT HE MIGHT HAVE GOT TO BE-
HAROLD GRAY
Reg. U. S. Pat. Off.; Copyright, 1930, by The Chicago Tribune.

February 10–12, 1930
THE SEVEN-YEAR ITCHY

WHY, GUSSIE- WHAT WAS THE MATTER? LESS THAN HALF YOUR ANSWERS WERE CORRECT- I COULD ONLY GIVE YOU FORTY-FIVE-
45
SAY- WE WERE ALL WRONG ON OVER HALF OF THE QUESTIONS-
YEAH? WHADDYUH MEAN WE WERE ALL WRONG?
LOOK IT OVER- 98 TWO OFF FOR NEATNESS 'CAUSE I ERASED SO MUCH-
OH, BOY! DID SHE STEP INTO THAT ONE! SHE DIDN'T SEE ME CHANGE MY ANSWERS AFTER SHE'D COPIED THE PHONEY ONES I'D PUT DOWN FIRST-
98
HAROLD GRAY
Reg. U. S. Pat. Off.; Copyright, 1930, by The Chicago Tribune.
WHAT'S THAT YER PUTTIN' ON ANNIE'S DESK?
YOU KEEP YOUR HANDS OFF- 'TISN'T FOR YOU-
WHEW! ALMOST TARDY AGAIN- GEE- WONDER WHY EVER'BODY'S SO QUIET- TEACHER'S NOT IN TH' ROOM-
SH!
HERE SHE COMES-
ANNIE
WHAT'S THIS? "TO MY VAL-----" WHY! IT'S---IT'S A VALENTINE FOR ME!
DIDJA SEE IT?
GEE!
HEY- ANNIE- LET'S SEE IT-
LOOK AT ITCHY BLUSH-
IT'S GOT HEARTS ALL OVER IT-
AW, ANNIE- SHOW IT TO US 'FORE TEACHER COMES IN-
HAROLD GRAY
Reg. U. S. Pat. Off.; Copyright, 1930, by The Chicago Tribune.
SAY, ITCHY- THAT WAS AN AWFUL PRETTY VALENTINE YUH GAVE ME YESTERDAY- I DIDN'T GET A CHANCE TO THANK YUH BEFORE-
AW, SHUX- IT WASN'T NOTHIN'-
DIDJA MEAN ALL IT SAID? YOU KNOW- 'BOUT ALWAYS BEIN' TRUE-BLUE- AN' THAT ABOUT ER--ER- LOVE? DIDJA?
ER---ER--- ULP! SURE- THAT IS---
NOW WHAT MADE HIM GET ALL RED IN TH' FACE AN' DIG OUT LIKE THAT? SHUX- GUYS ARE ALL ALIKE, I GUESS- GOOFY-
HAROLD GRAY
Reg. U. S. Pat. Off.; Copyright, 1930, by The Chicago Tribune

February 13–15, 1930
THE SEVEN-YEAR ITCHY

NOW, CHILDREN - IT'S TO BE A WASHINGTON'S BIRTHDAY PARTY AT MY HOUSE NEXT SATURDAY AFTERNOON - AND REMEMBER - YOU ARE ALL INVITED -
WHEE! WE'LL SURE BE THERE -
GEE!
GEE - A REAL PARTY - AN' IT'S TH' FIRST ONE I'VE BEEN 'VITED TO SINCE I CAME TO BLUNDERVILLE -
WHADDYUH THINK, SANDY? I'M 'VITED TO A SWELL, BIG PARTY NEXT SATURDAY AT TEACHER'S HOUSE -
Reg. U. S. Pat. Off.; Copyright, 1930, by The Chicago Tribune.
OH, MRS. TWINKLE - I'M 'VITED TO A PARTY - TH' WHOLE CLASS IS GOIN' -
MY, ANNIE - THAT WILL BE VERY NICE INDEED -
HAROLD GRAY
GEE, I CAN HARDLY WAIT TILL SATURDAY - I BETCHA WE'LL HAVE ICE CREAM AN' CAKE AN' JUST LOTS O' SWELL EATS - AN' GAMES ---
OH, JUST WAIT TILL YOU GIRLS SEE MY NEW DRESS - YELLOW VOILE ----
MY MOM'S MAKIN' ME A PINK TAFFETA WITH RUFFLES AN' EVER'THING -
I'M GETTIN' A NEW GREEN CRÊPE-DE-CHINE WITH FANCY COLLAR -
?
THERE'S THAT ORPHAN KID - I HOPE SHE DOESN'T 'SPECT TO COME TO TH' PARTY IN THAT OLD SWEATER -
SHE HASN'T ANY CLOTHES FOR PARTIES -
AW -- SHE WON'T BE THERE -
SH-H-H - SHE'LL HEAR YOU -
AW - I DIDN'T KNOW YUH HAD TO BE ALL DRESSED UP SPECIAL TO GO TO A LITTLE OLD PARTY - AW - I DON'T CARE - IF I DON'T GO NOBODY'LL MISS ME -
HAROLD GRAY
Reg. U. S. Pat. Off.; Copyright, 1930, by The Chicago Tribune.
WELL, ANNIE - I PRESUME YOU'RE ALL EXCITED ABOUT GOING TO THE PARTY SATURDAY -
AW, I DUNNO - I DON'T THINK I'LL GO -
WELL, I PRESUME IT'S ALL RIGHT IF YOU DON'T CARE TO GO - BUT I'D THINK YOU'D ENJOY A PARTY -
ULP -
THERE - THERE - ANNIE - YOU JUST TELL ME ALL ABOUT IT - WHAT'S THE MATTER?
AW, NOTHIN'S TH' MATTER - THERE'S NOTHIN' TO TELL - YOU WOULDN'T UNDERSTAND -
HAROLD GRAY
Reg. U. S. Pat. Off.; Copyright, 1930, by The Chicago Tribune.

February 17–19, 1930

G-BYE-
GOOD-BYE, ANNIE - RUN ALONG NOW OR YOU'LL BE LATE FOR SCHOOL -
SNIFF-SNIFF- SHE THINKS I DON'T UNDERSTAND - MY-MY.. IT'S BEEN MANY A YEAR BUT I HAVEN'T FORGOTTEN- I JUST DIDN'T THINK - A PARTY AND NO NEW DRESS- AND SHE'S TOO BRAVE TO TELL ME -
THERE - THAT OUGHT TO DO - IT'S MUCH FINER MATERIAL THAN ONE CAN BUY TO-DAY - AND WITH THAT OLD IRISH LACE- HM-M-M--- AND SHE MUST HAVE A COAT-
AH - I KNOW - THAT BROAD-CLOTH COAT I HAD YEARS AGO IS GOOD - AND THAT OLD MINK MUFF - I CAN USE THAT-
HAROLD GRAY
Reg. U. S. Pat. Off.; Copyright, 1930, by The Chicago Tribune.
AW, SHUX- I'D 'MOST FORGOT I'M AN ORPHAN KID TILL THIS PARTY CAME ALONG - GUESS I'LL BE TH' ONLY KID IN CLASS THAT WON'T BE THERE-
OH, ANNIE- PLEASE COME IN HERE A MINUTE-
YESSUM-
ANNIE- I'VE BEEN THINKING IT ALL OVER AND I CAN'T SEE ANY REASON WHY YOU SHOULDN'T GO TO THE PARTY AND HAVE A GOOD TIME -
OH! A DRESS FOR ME!!!
YES, ANNIE - TRY IT ON - I HOPE IT FITS - BUT WE STILL HAVE TIME FOR ANY LITTLE ALTERATIONS -
OH-OH-OH! IT'S PERFECTLY BEAUTIFUL!
I HOPED YOU'D LIKE IT, ANNIE -
HAROLD GRAY
Reg. U. S. Pat. Off.: Copyright, 1930, by The Chicago Tribune
OH, BOY - ARE SOME O' TH' SMART KIDS IN THIS TOWN GOIN' TO GET A S'PRISE!
HELLO, TEACHER-
WHY, ANNIE - COME IN - WHAT A GORGEOUS COAT-
GEE- LOOK-
IT'S ANNIE!
DID YOU EVER SEE SUCH A WONDERFUL DRESS? WHERE DO YOU S'POSE SHE GOT A DRESS LIKE THAT?
AND HER COAT - IT'S GOT REAL MINK TRIMMING -
HAROLD GRAY
WELL, ANNIE - HOW WAS THE PARTY? DID YOU HAVE A GOOD TIME?
OH - IT WAS WONDERFUL - EVER'BODY WAS SWELL - AND THEY WERE CRAZY 'BOUT MY COAT AND DRESS - GEE! YOU SURE WERE GOOD TO ME -
Reg. U. S. Pat. Off. Copyright, 1930, by The Chicago Tribune

February 20–22, 1930

WHAT'S TH' IDEA, ITCHY? GOIN' IN FOR DOLLS, ARE YUH? I THOUGHT YOU WERE TOO OLD FOR THAT STUFF -
WHAT ARE YUH GOIN' TO DO WITH IT WHEN YUH GET IT DONE? TOO SMALL FOR A DOG HOUSE -
AW, GEE - I DUNNO - I SORTA THOUGHT.......
HAW! HAW! HAW! ITCHY JONES PLAYS WITH DOLLS - THAT'S A CORKER - WAIT'LL TH' KIDS HEAR THAT ONE -
AW-ANNIE - YOU WOULDN'T -
HAROLD GRAY
Reg. U. S. Pat. Off.; Copyright, 1930, by The Chicago Tribune.
I HADN'T OUGHTA HAVE KIDDED POOR ITCHIE 'BOUT THAT DOLL HOUSE HE'S MAKIN' - HE'S STILL JUST A KID AN' IF HE GETS FUN OUT O' SUCH THINGS...
HELLO, ANNIE -
HELLO, ITCHIE - H'ARE YUH?
SAY, ITCHY - I DIDN'T MEAN TO KID YUH 'BOUT MAKIN' A DOLL HOUSE - BUT, GEE WHIZ - DO YOU REALLY GET A KICK OUT O' KID STUFF LIKE THAT?
Reg. U. S. Pat. Off.; Copyright, 1930, by The Chicago Tribune.
SOMETHIN' QUEER 'BOUT THAT - HE SEEMS O. K. MOST WAYS - BUT A BOY PLAYIN' WITH A DOLL HOUSE - HM-M-M-M-
HAROLD GRAY
NOW WHO'S THAT KNOCKIN' ON OUR DOOR DO YUH S'POSE?
RAP! RAP! RAP!
HERE, ANNIE - I MADE THIS FOR YOU, BUT I GUESS YOU DON'T CARE MUCH FOR DOLL HOUSES AFTER ALL -
OH, ITCHY - I DO TOO - I LOVE IT -
BUT WHY DO ALL THIS FOR ME, ITCHY?
AW, I DUNNO - MAKE BELIEVE IT'S FOR YOUR BIRTHDAY -
BIRTHDAY! GEE - WHY NOT? IT MIGHT BE, AT THAT - LEAPIN' LIZARDS - OTHER KIDS HAVE BIRTHDAYS -
HAROLD GRAY
Reg. U. S. Pat. Off.; Copyright, 1930, by The Chicago Tribune.

February 24–26, 1930

WHAT A PERFECT DREAM OF A DOLL HOUSE - TWO FLOORS AN' TH' FRONT ALL OPENS UP -
AN' THERE'S SWELL FURNITURE IN EVERY ROOM - ITCHY JONES SURE KNOWS HOW TO MAKE TH' NICEST THINGS - THINK O' HIM DOIN' ALL THIS JUST FOR ME -
COURSE I S'POSE I'M TOO BIG FOR DOLLS - BUT I DUNNO - GUESS I'LL NEVER BE TOO BIG TO LIKE SUCH THINGS - JUST NEVER HAD MUCH TIME FOR DOLLS BEFORE -
I FEEL LIKE A PLUGGED NICKEL EVERY TIME I THINK HOW I KIDDED POOR ITCHY 'BOUT MAKIN' A DOLL HOUSE - AN' ALL TH' TIME HE WAS DOIN' IT JUST FOR ME - GEE -
HAROLD GRAY
Reg. U. S. Pat. Off.; Copyright, 1930, by The Chicago Tribune.
BY THE WAY, ANNIE - I HAVE SOMETHING HERE THAT YOU CAN HAVE IF YOU CARE FOR IT -
A DOLLY!
YES, ANNIE - IT'S NOT AN EXPENSIVE DOLL - BUT I MADE NEW CLOTHES FOR HER -
OH - SHE'S A PERFECT DARLING - AND WHAT GORGEOUS CLOTHES -
I HOPED YOU'D LIKE IT, ANNIE -
Reg. U. S. Pat. Off.; Copyright, 1930, by The Chicago Tribune.
WHEN I WAS REAL LITTLE I HAD EMILY MARIE - BUT I LOST HER - AND I'VE ALWAYS WANTED A REAL NICE DOLLIE - BUT I NEVER THOUGHT I'D HAVE ONE - GEE - I'M A LUCKY GIRL -
HAROLD GRAY
I HEAR SOME ONE AT THE FRONT DOOR, ANNIE - I WONDER IF YOU'D GO AND SEE WHO IT IS -
SURE, MRS. TWINKLE -
HM-M-M--- MRS. TWINKLE LOOKED SORTA FUNNY - WONDER IF SHE KNOWS WHO IT IS -
S'PRISE!
S'PRISE!
S'PRISE, ANNIE -
S'PRISE!
S'PRISE!
OH! A PARTY FOR ME - THE FIRST ONE I EVER HAD - AND YOU KNEW IT ALL THE TIME -
WELL, ANNIE - I GUESS YOU DESERVE A PARTY IF ANY LITTLE GIRL EVER DID -
HAROLD GRAY
Reg. U. S. Pat. Off.; Copyright, 1930, by The Chicago Tribune.

February 27–
March 1, 1930

G-OGRAPHY! I THINK THIS IS MY FAVORITE STUDY- IT'S ALMOST LIKE REALLY TRAVELIN'- AFRICA-- INDIA-- CHINA- TH' SOUTH SEA ISLANDS-- GEE-
THINK O' "DADDY" WARBUCKS- HE'S REALLY BEEN TO ALL THOSE PLACES AN' SEEN 'EM- HE GOT HIS G'OGRAPHY ON TH' HOOF- THAT'S TH' REAL WAY TO KNOW TH' WORLD- BUT IF YUH CAN'T GO TO PLACES TH' NEXT BEST THING IS TO READ 'BOUT 'EM.
AN' THIS G'OGRAPHY BOOK HAS LOTS AN' LOTS O' PITCHERS-- BR-R-R-R-- JUST LOOK AT THOSE HEAD-HUNTERS- BUT "DADDY" SAYS THEY'RE NOT BAD GUYS IF YUH KNOW 'EM- HE CAN HAVE MY SHARE OF 'EM-
GEE- I WONDER WHERE "DADDY" IS NOW- YUH SORTA FORGET MOST FOLKS WHEN THEY'RE AWAY FOR A LONG TIME- BUT WE'LL NEVER FORGET "DADDY", WILL WE, SANDY?
ARF!
HAROLD GRAY
Reg. U. S. Pat. Off.; Copyright, 1930, by The Chicago Tribune.
WELL, I'M GETTING ABOUT FED UP WITH THIS JOB- HAVEN'T SEEN A WHITE MAN FOR MONTHS-
BUT I'M THROUGH OUT HERE- TO-MORROW WE'LL PACK UP AND START THE LONG TRIP BACK TO CIVILIZATION-
TO-MORROW WE TAKE LONG WALK- GET ME? AND WE'LL WALK FOR LOTS OF TO-MORROWS- BY AND BY BIG VILLAGE- MANY WHITE MEN- SEE?
OH, BOY- IT SURE WILL BE GREAT TO GET BACK HOME- POOR LITTLE ANNIE- I SUPPOSE IT'S NOT SURPRISING I HAVEN'T HEARD FROM HER OUT IN THIS JUNGLE-
Reg. U. S. Pat. Off.; Copyright, 1930, by The Chicago Tribune.
HAROLD GRAY
WHAT'S THAT? OH, YOU SAY SOME ONE IS RUNNING OUR WAY-
YEP- THERE HE IS- A NATIVE RUNNER- AND HE'S SURE MAKING GOOD TIME-
AH- NOW WHAT'S THIS? IT MUST BE IMPORTANT- IT'S PROBABLY BAD NEWS- THAT ALWAYS TRAVELS FASTEST-
I KNEW IT- WELL, THIS KNOCKS ALL MY PLANS INTO A COCKED HAT- THIS MEANS ANOTHER MONTH IN THE JUNGLE, OR I'LL LOSE ALL I'VE GAINED-
HAROLD GRAY
Reg. U. S. Pat. Off.; Copyright, 1930, by The Chicago Tribune.

March 3–5, 1930

IF I WAS ONLY SURE THAT ANNIE IS ALL RIGHT- BUT I'VE BEEN OUT OF TOUCH WITH THE WORLD FOR MONTHS- ANYTHING MAY HAVE HAPPENED-
IF I QUIT NOW AND GO HOME I'LL LOSE, WHEN BY STAYING ON HERE I COULD WIN- THE WORLD WILL CALL ME A QUITTER-

AND I'M SICK OF THIS LIFE- NEVER SAFE TO MOVE A FOOT UN-ARMED- I DON'T MIND DANGER- BEEN USED TO IT FOR YEARS-

BUT THE LONELINESS- THE MONOTONY- I THOUGHT THIS JOB WAS DONE- THAT I HAD CLEANED UP OUT HERE AND COULD GO HOME-

AND NOW THIS MESSAGE- QUIT NOW AND THE WHOLE ENTERPRISE WILL COLLAPSE- BUT I CAN'T GO ON UNTIL I KNOW THAT ANNIE IS O. K.
HAROLD GRAY

BUT ISN'T ANNIE'S WELFARE WORTH MORE TO ME THAN ALL THE MONEY IN THE WORLD? YES!

MY MIND'S MADE UP- I'LL NOT WAIT ANOTHER MINUTE- HEY!!! SNAP OUT OF IT!

WE'RE PULLING OUT- GET A MOVE ON, THERE- THOSE CASES WON'T BURN YUH- PICK 'EM UP-
HAROLD GRAY

WHAT? ANOTHER RUNNER- I'M GETTING MORE LETTERS LATELY THAN A MOVIE HERO-

GREAT SCOTT! THIS IS A SURPRISE- A LETTER FROM OLD JACK PEPPER- TRUST THAT OLD CAMPAIGNER TO KNOW HOW AND WHERE TO FIND ME- AND THIS IS ALL ABOUT ANNIE-

SHE'S FINE AND HAPPY AND HEALTHY- GOING TO SCHOOL NOW- SANDY TOO IS WELL- OH, BOY- DOES THAT MAKE ME FEEL GOOD! NOW I CAN GO ON AND FINISH MY JOB OUT HERE WITH A CLEAR CONSCIENCE-

TURN AROUND, BOYS- WE'RE GOING BACK- AND WE'LL FINISH THE JOB HERE IF IT TAKES SIX MONTHS- NOTHING CAN STOP ME NOW-
HAROLD GRAY

March 6–8, 1930

OH, LOOKIE- THERE GOES JUDGE TORT-
GEE- THEY'RE TAKIN' HIM TO TH' TRAIN-
YEP- THEY SAY HE'S GOIN' ON A LONG TRIP-
YEAH- HE'S GOIN' TO TRAVEL FOR HIS HEALTH- MAYBE HE'LL NEVER COME BACK TO BLUNDERVILLE, THEY SAY-
MY MOM SAYS HE'S SOLD HIS HOUSE TO SOME FOLKS FROM TH' CITY-
UH-HUH- I HEARD THAT, TOO- WONDER WHO THEY ARE-
THERE'S HIS HOUSE- ALL TH' SHADES PULLED DOWN TIGHT-
GEE- IT'S FUNNY HOW EASY YUH CAN SPOT AN EMPTY HOUSE- SOMETHIN' SORTA LONESOME AND SPOOKY 'BOUT IT- POOR OLD JUDGE- HE WAS A GOOD FRIEND O' MINE-
HAROLD GRAY
Reg. U. S. Pat. Off.; Copyright, 1930, by The Chicago Tribune.
WELL, SANDY, WE WON'T SEE OLD JUDGE TORT 'ROUND HERE ANY MORE, I GUESS- SOLD OUT AND GONE- WE'RE GOIN' TO MISS HIM A LOT-
FINEST HOUSE IN TOWN- BUT WHAT GOOD IS A SWELL HOUSE IF NO-BODY LIVES IN IT? ALL TH' SHADES DRAWN JUST LIKE IT HAD SHUT ITS EYES AND GONE TO SLEEP-
SOMETHIN' 'BOUT A VACANT HOUSE THAT ALWAYS SORTA GIVES ME TH' CREEPS-
WONDER HOW SOON THOSE FOLKS FROM TH' CITY WILL BE MOVIN' IN- THEY MUST BE RICH TO BUY A PLACE AS BIG AS THAT-
HAROLD GRAY
Reg. U. S. Pat. Off.; Copyright, 1930, by The Chicago Tribune.
LOOK OUT- JUMP!
WHY DON'TCHA TOOT YER HORN?
HONK! HONK! HONK!
GEE WHIZ, ANNIE!!! THAT'S TH' NEW FOLKS THAT BOUGHT TH' TORT PLACE-
YEAH- MUST BE- THEY'VE SURE GOT A SWELL CAR AN' THEY LET TH' KID DRIVE IT-
Reg. U. S. Pat. Off.; Copyright, 1930, by The Chicago Tribune.
GEE, ANNIE- ISN'T HE GRAND?
AW, HE'S STUCK ON HIMSELF- I HATE A GUY THAT STRUTS- AN' HE'S TOO YOUNG TO DRIVE A CAR-
HAROLD GRAY

March 10–12, 1930
THE SEVEN-YEAR ITCHY

WELL, WELL, WILLIE- WHO LET YOU OUT O' YOUR CAGE-
HE'S GETTING SO BIG- HE WAS CLIMBING OUT- I THOUGHT A CHAIN WOULD DO BETTER-
LE'SSEE, NOW- I MUSTN'T MAKE ANY MISTAKES IN THIS ORDER-
YOU DON'T SAY--- FOR THE OLD TORT PLACE?
YES SIR, SELLERS- THEY PAID SPOT CASH- EVERY DIME- THEY'RE MOVING IN SATURDAY-
Reg. U. S. Pat. Off.; Copyright, 1930, by The Chicago Tribune.
SPOT CASH!!! BY CRACKY- THEY MUST HAVE A LOT OF MONEY-
MONEY! HAH! DID YOU SEE THAT CAR O' THEIRS? FINEST CAR I EVER SAW- OH, THEY'RE RICH, ALL RIGHT-
HAROLD GRAY
I HEAR YOU SAW THE NEW PEOPLE THAT ARE MOVIN' INTO THE OLD TORT PLACE-
YES- I JUST HAPPENED TO BE A'LOOKIN' OUT OF THE WINDOW WHEN THEY DROVE IN NEXT DOOR-
FILCH IS THEIR NAME- YOU CAN TELL THEY'RE FROM THE CITY, ALL RIGHT- HE HAD ON SPATS- AND SHE WAS DRESSED BEAUTIFUL- SORTA FAT, SHE IS, AND GOES 'ROUND WITH HER NOSE IN THE AIR-
ANY CHILDREN?
ONE BOY IS ALL, SO FAR AS I COULD SEE- BUT THE SAINTS KNOW ONE LIKE HIM WOULD BE MORE'N PLENTY FOR ME- SMUG LITTLE IMP AND DRIVIN' THE CAR, HE WAS-
WELL, FOR JUST TAKIN' ONE LITTLE PEEK SHE DIDN'T MISS MUCH-
HAROLD GRAY
Reg. U. S. Pat. Off.; Copyright, 1930, by The Chicago Tribune.
OH, LOOKIE- TH' NEW FOLKS ARE MOVIN' IN ALL RIGHT-
YEAH- THEIR NAME IS FILCH AN' THEY'RE AWFUL RICH, I HEAR- WE'LL JUST WALK BY-
I CERTAINLY WOULD BE 'SHAMED TO STAND AN' RUBBER LIKE THOSE KIDS-
YES- SOME KIDS DON'T HAVE ANY MANNERS AT ALL- JUST STAND AND STARE-
OH, GOLLY! JUST LOOK AT THAT GORGEOUS DIVAN-
LEAPIN' LIZARDS!!! IT SURE IS A KNOCK-OUT- AN' LOOK AT THAT GRAND PIANO-
GEE- AND THEY'VE GOT A 'LECTRIC WASHIN' MACHINE-
OH, BOY! AND DO YOU SEE THAT SCRUMPTIOUS RADIO- THAT'S WHAT I CALL CLASS-
HAROLD GRAY
Reg. U. S. Pat. Off.; Copyright, 1930, by The Chicago Tribune.

March 13–15, 1930

THE 17TH O' MARCH - WHY, THIS IS ST. PATRICK'S DAY - BUT THERE'LL BE NO PARADES AN' GRAND FIGHTS IN THIS TOWN - HARDLY ANY IRISH HEREABOUTS AT ALL - OH, WELL - THE IRISH ARE A HOT-HEADED LOT ANYWAY -
RED-HEAD! RED-HEAD!
CARROT TOP! CARROT TOP!
BRICK TOP! BRICK TOP!
FIRE! FIRE!
RED HEAD, IS IT? I'LL RED HEAD YUH!!!
LOOK OUT!
SHE'S GOT A BRICK!
SHE'LL THROW IT TOO -
YOU KNOW HOW RED-HEADS ARE WHEN THEY'RE MAD -
Reg. U. S. Pat. Off.; Copyright, 1930, by The Chicago Tribune.
DOG GONE IT - I CAN'T HELP IT - WHEN FOLKS MAKE FUN O' MY RED HAIR I JUST GO ALL TO PIECES!
HAROLD GRAY
OH, HERE COMES EDGAR FILCH WHOSE FOLKS BOUGHT TH' OLD TORT PLACE - WE'LL GET A GOOD LOOK AT HIM -
HM-M-M - THAT MUST BE THE ORPHAN KID I HEARD ABOUT - SHE'S FROM TH' CITY ALL RIGHT - ANYBODY COULD SEE SHE'S DIFFERENT FROM THE YOKELS IN THIS BURG -
Reg. U. S. Pat. Off.; Copyright, 1930, by The Chicago Tribune.
I'D HAVE SPOKEN TO HIM, BUT HE'S SNUBBED ALL TH' OTHER KIDS - I'M NOT GOIN' TO GIVE HIM A CHANCE TO SNUB ME - TH' LITTLE STUCK-UP - NO SIR, SANDY - I DON'T LIKE THAT GUY -
HAROLD GRAY
ANYTHING ELSE TO-DAY?
NOPE - THAT'S ALL -
HERE Y'ARE THAT'LL BE JUST FORTY CENTS -
O. K. TAKE IT OUTA THIS DOLLAR -
HEY - YOU SHORT-CHANGED ME - YOU SAID FORTY CENTS AND YOU'VE KEPT FIFTY-FIVE CENTS -
Reg. U. S. Pat. Off.; Copyright, 1930, by The Chicago Tribune.
UH-HUH! SURE - THE EXTRA FIFTEEN CENTS WAS FOR TH' GUM-DROPS YUH SWIPED AN' STUCK IN YER POCKET, WHILE MY BACK WAS TURNED - DIDJA THINK THIS WAS A GIFT SHOP?
HAROLD GRAY

March 17–19, 1930

WHEW! I'D BETTER SNAP OUT OF IT OR I'LL BE LATE FOR SCHOOL - THAT EDGAR FILCH IS STARTIN' TO SCHOOL TO-DAY - HOPE HE ISN'T IN MY CLASS -
GEE - WONDER WHAT'S TH' 'CITEMENT - ALL TH' KIDS STANDIN' AROUND IN TH' HALL WAITIN' FOR TH' LAST BELL -
UM-M-M - ISN'T HE GRAND?
HE'S TRAVELED EVERY-WHERE -
OH, YES - WE RAN OVER TO LONDON LAST SUMMER - AND OF COURSE WE SPENT THE WINTER IN BERMUDA - I DARE SAY NONE OF YOU HAVE EVER TRAVELED MUCH -
HUH! AS IF ANYBODY CARED WHERE HE'S BEEN - HE SURE DIDN'T LEARN MANY GOOD MANNERS TRAVELIN' - BUT THOSE POOR SAPS THINK HE'S GREAT - BEATS ALL WHAT A BRAGGER CAN GET AWAY WITH -
HAROLD GRAY
Reg. U. S. Pat. Off.; Copyright, 1930, by The Chicago Tribune.
SO THIS IS THE BEAR I'VE HEARD 'EM TALKIN' ABOUT - THEY SAY HE DOES TRICKS - LET'S SEE SOME OF 'EM -
THAT'S TH' STUFF, WILLIE - HEP! HEP! TEEDLE DEE DEE! TEEDLE DUM DUM!
SHUX - ANY BEAR CAN DANCE - I THOUGHT HE KNEW SOME REAL TRICKS -
NEVER YOU MIND, WILLIE - YOU DANCED SWELL - AN' YOU'RE YOUNG YET - WHEN YOU'RE AS OLD AS THAT SMART ALECK YOU'LL KNOW TEN TIMES AS MUCH AS HE DOES, I BETCHA -
HAROLD GRAY
Reg. U. S. Pat. Off.; Copyright, 1930, by The Chicago Tribune.
THAT'S IT, WILLIE - THAT'S TH' STUFF - COME ON, NOW - ALL BY YOUR SELF -
OVER YOU GO - WHEE! 'AT A BOY -
YES SIR - A PERFECT SOMERSAULT - EH, SANDY?
ARF!
Reg. U. S. Pat. Off.; Copyright, 1930, by The Chicago Tribune.
YESSIR, WILLIE - YOU'RE GETTIN' BETTER EVERY DAY - COURSE AN EDGE'CATION TAKES TIME - BUT YOU'RE SMART - SOME DAY YOU'LL BE TH' BEST P'FORMIN' BEAR IN TH' WORLD -
HAROLD GRAY

March 20–22, 1930

DID YOU GIRLS SEE THE PER-FECT-LY GOR-GEOUS DRESS MRS. FILCH WAS WEARING AT CHURCH YESTERDAY?
THE FILCHES ARE PERFECTLY LOVELY PEOPLE- SO DEMOCRATIC IN SPITE OF ALL THEIR MONEY-
YES, INDEED- MY JOHN SAYS MR. FILCH HAS TAKEN HOLD IN COMMUNITY AFFAIRS- MR. FILCH SAYS HE'S GOING TO ORGANIZE A BUSINESS MEN'S CLUB-
MR. FILCH SAYS IF YOU HAVE PUSH YOU DON'T NEED PULL TO SUCCEED-
MY HENRY SAYS THAT MR. FILCH IS A MARVELOUS BUSINESS MAN-
HUH! BUSINESS MAN! HOW DO THEY KNOW HOW HE GOT HIS DOUGH? BUT HE'S GOT IT- AN' THAT MAKES HIM O.K. MOST FOLKS SEEM TO FIGGER-
HAROLD GRAY
Reg. U. S. Pat. Off.; Copyright, 1930, by The Chicago Tribune.
NOW, THEN- HOW MUCH AM I OFFERED FOR THIS BEAUTIFUL, GREEN GUM-DROP ALL COVERED WITH SUGAR? GOING.....GOING....
ARF!
BOUF!
TELL ME, ANNIE- WHAT DO YOU HEAR ABOUT THESE NEW PEOPLE WHO HAVE BOUGHT THE OLD TORT PLACE?
WHO? TH' FILCHES? AW, I DUNNO- THEIR KID'S NAME IS EDGAR- HE'S NOT SO MUCH- BUT I GUESS THEY HAVE A LOT O' DOUGH- FOLKS SAY SO, ANYWAY- AN' EVER'BODY SAYS THEY'RE FINE PEOPLE-
HM-M-M- OH, YES- I SEE- THEY GIVE THE IMPRESSION OF BEING WEALTHY- AND OF COURSE THEY COME FROM THE CITY- IT'S ODD HOW QUICKLY PEOPLE OF APPARENT WEALTH ARE WELCOMED TO ANY COMMUNITY AND NO QUESTIONS ASKED-
YEP-
HAROLD GRAY
Reg. U. S. Pat. Off.; Copyright, 1930, by The Chicago Tribune.
'FRAID I DIDN'T DO SO WELL ON THAT EXAM- I'M GOIN' TO WAIT TILL I'M ALONE 'FORE I LOOK AN' SEE WHAT GRADE TEACHER GAVE ME-
LEAPIN' LIZARDS!!! 97- THAT'S DOG-GONED NEAR PERFECT- I HAVEN'T HAD ANYTHING LOWER'N 90 FOR OVER A MONTH NOW- AN' EVER'THING'S GETTIN' LOTS EASIER-
GEE- WON'T "DADDY" BE PROUD O' ME WHEN HE COMES BACK AN' I SHOW HIM TH' GRADES I'VE MADE IN SCHOOL- AN' I'VE GOT A SWELL HOME WITH MRS. TWINKLE- AN' A JOB AT TH' STORE-
ARF! ARF!
AN' SANDY AN' LITTLE WILLIE- YEP- I'M SURE A MIGHTY, MIGHTY LUCKY KID-
HAROLD GRAY
Reg. U. S. Pat. Off.; Copyright, 1930, by The Chicago Tribune.

March 24–26, 1930

SO THEY HAVEN'T FORGOTTEN OLD JACK PEPPER- THAT'S GRATIFYING- BUT TO BE AWAY FOR A MONTH OR MORE- HM-M-M---- OF COURSE I COULD USE THE MONEY IT WOULD MEAN-
AND ANNIE SEEMS TO BE GETTING ALONG ALL RIGHT WITHOUT ME- STILL, I'M HERE IF SHE SHOULD NEED A FRIEND- AND WARBUCKS ASKED ME TO LOOK OUT FOR HER-
GOOD OLD WARBUCKS- MANY'S THE TIGHT PLACE WE'VE BEEN IN AND OUT OF TO-GETHER- IF ANNIE WERE IN ANY DANGER I'D STAY, OF COURSE-
BUT WHAT HARM COULD POSSIBLY COME TO HER HERE IN BLUNDERVILLE? AND I'LL BE BACK IN A MONTH, OR A BIT OVER PERHAPS- SHE'S SAFE - I'LL GO-
HAROLD GRAY
Reg. U. S. Pat. Off.; Copyright, 1930, by The Chicago Tribune.
OF COURSE, MRS. TWINKLE, I'D NEVER THINK OF GOING- BUT ANNIE IS SAFE WITH YOU- AND ANYTHING I CAN DO TO HELP-----
THANK YOU, MR. PEPPER- BUT WE HAVE EVERY-THING TO MAKE US COMFORTABLE-
HELLO, MR. PEPPER-
HELLO, ANNIE- I JUST DROPPED IN TO TELL YOU I'M GOING AWAY FOR A MONTH OR SO-
BUT I'LL BE BACK SOON- THINK YOU'LL BE ALL RIGHT EVERY WAY?
SORRY YOU'RE GOIN' AWAY, MR. PEPPER- SURE, I'LL BE FINE- MRS. TWINKLE IS SWELL TO ME AN' EVER'THING IS GREAT-
NO WONDER WARBUCKS THINKS SO MUCH OF THAT LITTLE TYKE- IF I'D EVER HAD A DAUGHTER I'D HAVE WANTED HER TO BE JUST LIKE ANNIE-
HAROLD GRAY
Reg. U. S. Pat. Off.; Copyright, 1930, by The Chicago Tribune.
GOOD-BYE, ANNIE- NOW TAKE GOOD CARE OF YOURSELF TILL I GET BACK-
GOOD-BYE, MR. PEPPER- GOOD LUCK-
GOOD-BYE!
GEE, I HATE TO SEE OLD JACK PEPPER PULLIN' OUT- HE'S A SWELL GUY-
FIRST IT WAS OLD JUDGE TORT- NOW JACK PEPPER- I HAVEN'T ANY REAL SURE FRIENDS THAT I CAN COUNT ON IN THIS TOWN ANY MORE, 'CEPT MRS. TWINKLE, O' COURSE- BUT NOTHIN'S GOIN' TO HAPPEN-
THERE GOES THAT EDGAR FILCH- EVERY WHERE I LOOK LATELY I SEE THAT GUY- HE'S ALL OVER TH' PLACE LIKE A RASH-
HAROLD GRAY
Reg. U. S. Pat. Off.; Copyright, 1930, by The Chicago Tribune.

March 27–29, 1930
THE SEVEN-YEAR ITCHY

HA-HA-HA- I SAID I'D GET EVEN WITH HER- AND THE BEST PART OF IT IS SHE'LL NEVER HAVE A CHANCE TO EVEN GUESS HOW IT REALLY HAPPENED- I'LL FIX HER!!!

CHAPTER TWO

THE FRAME, THE FARM, AND THE FLOOD

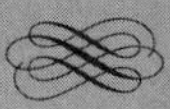

IN WHICH ANNIE

DISCOVERS THAT WEALTH AND TRUSTWORTHINESS ARE NOT SYNONYMOUS

IS WHISKED AWAY TO THE COUNTY POOR FARM

AND RIDES THE RISING TIDE...

THERE'S THAT ORPHAN KID WALKIN' WITH THAT BIG YOKEL- SHE'S DIFFERENT FROM THE RUBES IN THIS TOWN- SHE'S CLASS- I CAN PICK 'EM-
YEAH- SHE DOESN'T KNOW IT YET, BUT SHE'S GOING TO BE MY GIRL- I ALWAYS GET WHAT I GO AFTER- THEY ALL FALL FOR ME-
GEE, WHAT A SWELL CAR- THAT EDGAR FILCH SURE IS A LUCKY STIFF- HE HAS ABOUT EVERYTHING-
YEAH- BUT WHAT GOOD DOES IT DO HIM? HE'S STUCK-UP- THINKS HE'S BETTER'N OTHER FOLKS CAUSE HE'S GOT MONEY-
WELL, MOST GIRLS ARE CRAZY 'BOUT ANY FELLER THAT'S GOT A SWELL CAR AN' DRESSES FLASHY AND HAS MONEY-
YEAH? WELL, I'VE SEEN TOO MANY LITTLE WISE GUYS LIKE EDGAR- HE'S NO BIG SENSATION IN MY LIFE-
HAROLD GRAY
Reg. U. S. Pat. Off.; Copyright, 1930, by The Chicago Tribune.
C'MON, ANNIE- DITCH THAT BUNCH AND I'LL WALK HOME WITH YOU-
OH, GEE- MY BERET- I WONDER IF I LEFT IT IN THE CLOAK ROOM-
WHY, ANNIE DIDN'T WEAR ANY HAT TO SCHOOL TO-DAY, DID SHE?
NO- I DON'T THINK SO- BUT WHY DID SHE SEND HIM BACK INTO THE SCHOOL HOUSE?
LOOK- ANNIE'S DIGGIN' OUT FOR HOME AN' NOT WAITIN' FOR HIM-
SHE SENT HIM BACK ON PURPOSE SO SHE COULD DITCH HIM-
GEE- 'MAGINE THROWIN' DOWN A RICH FELLA LIKE EDGAR-
Reg. U. S. Pat. Off.; Copyright, 1930, by The Chicago Tribune.
HAW! HAW! HAW! WHERE'S ANNIE'S BERET THAT SHE DIDN'T WEAR TO-DAY?
YAH-H-H! APRIL FOOL!
SHE WAS GIVIN' YUH TH' RAZZ-BERRIES!
APRIL FOOL!
HAROLD GRAY
THOUGHT YUH WERE AWFUL SMART, RUNNIN' OFF AN' LEAVIN' ME FLAT YESTERDAY, DIDN'T YUH? TRIED TO MAKE A SAP O' ME-
NAW- I WAS TOO LATE FOR THAT-
LEMME TELL YOU SOMETHIN'- I'LL NEVER GIVE YOU A CHANCE TO WALK HOME WITH ME AGAIN-
GEE! NOW THAT'S TOO BAD- THAT'S JUST GOIN' TO BREAK ME ALL UP-
HELLO, ITCHY- GOIN' MY WAY?
I THINK EDGAR FILCH IS SO FUNNY- DON'T YOU?
HAROLD GRAY
Reg. U. S. Pat. Off.; Copyright, 1930, by The Chicago Tribune.

March 31–
April 2, 1930

THAT LITTLE RED-HEADED ORPHAN THINKS SHE CAN MAKE ME LOOK SILLY, DOES SHE? HUH! HERE COMES ITCHY JONES- HE'S THE ONLY GUY IN TOWN WHO'LL GO WITH HER- I'LL BREAK THAT UP- I'LL SHOW HER!
LISTEN, YOU! I SEE YOU WALKIN' WITH ANNIE- WELL, DON'T DO IT ANY MORE OR YOU'LL WISH YOU HADN'T-
IF SHE FIGGERS SHE'S TOO SWELLED UP TO WALK WITH ME SHE'LL DO HER WALKIN' ALONE- SEE? YOU KEEP AWAY FROM HER IF YOU DON'T WANT TO GET HURT- THAT'S ALL-
Reg. U. S. Pat. Off.; Copyright, 1930, by The Chicago Tribune.
DOG GONE! WHAT DID I DO? WHAT'S HE SO MAD AT ME FOR? I DON'T WANT TO FIGHT WITH HIM- BUT, GEE WHIZ- HE CAN'T TALK TO ME LIKE THAT- AND ABOUT ANNIE, TOO-
HAROLD GRAY
YUH WON'T FIGHT, EH? YELLOW, ARE YUH? SCARED TO FIGHT-
AW, I JUST DON'T WANT TO FIGHT- I'M NOT MAD- THAT'S ALL-
ITCHY! LOOK OUT!!!
'TACK A GUY FROM BEHIND WHEN HE'S NOT LOOKIN', WILL YUH? I'LL TEACH YUH, YUH LITTLE SNEAK!
OW! LEGGO MY HAIR!
THERE, NOW! GET UP AN' GIT, 'FORE I LOSE MY TEMPER AN' TAKE A GOOD BELT AT YUH-
HAROLD GRAY
Reg. U. S. Pat. Off.; Copyright, 1930, by The Chicago Tribune.
GEE- MAYBE I SOCKED EDGAR HARDER'N I OUGHTA YESTERDAY- BUT HIM JUMPIN' ON ITCHY FROM BEHIND MADE ME AWFUL MAD FOR A MINUTE-
OH, YOU'RE GOIN' TO PAY- YOU'LL SEE- YOU AND THAT BIG YOKEL GOT THE BEST OF ME YESTERDAY- BUT IT TOOK TWO OF YOU TO DO IT-
WHADDYUH MEAN TWO OF US? ITCHY DIDN'T TOUCH YUH- I GAVE YUH ALL YUH GOT, AN' I CAN DO IT AGAIN ANY TIME ANY PLACE FOR MONEY, MARBLES OR CHALK- SEE? SIC 'EM, SANDY-
GR-R!
HAROLD GRAY
I'LL GET EVEN WITH THAT DAME IF IT'S THE LAST THING I EVER DO- SHE CAN'T GET THE BEST OF ME- I'LL FIX HER!!!
Reg. U. S. Pat. Off.; Copyright, 1930, by The Chicago Tribune.

April 3–5, 1930

HERE, ANNIE- I HAD ANOTHER KEY MADE FOR THE FRONT DOOR- DON'T LOSE IT NOW-
I WANT YOU TO OPEN UP MORNINGS- IT WILL MEAN GETTING UP A LITTLE EARLIER, BUT YOU'RE YOUNG AND WON'T MIND IT-
AND I'LL LET YOU OFF EARLY EVENINGS TO MAKE UP FOR IT- RUN ALONG, NOW, SO YOU WON'T OVERSLEEP-
YES SIR, MR. SELLERS-
Reg. U. S. Pat. Off.; Copyright, 1930, by The Chicago Tribune.
HAROLD GRAY
LEAPIN' LIZARDS!!! A TEN DOLLAR BILL- WHOEVER DROPPED THAT SURE BROUGHT ME GOOD LUCK-
AH-HA! SHE PICKED IT UP ALL RIGHT- THEN LOOKED ALL AROUND TO SEE IF ANYBODY WAS WATCHIN' AND HID IT IN HER DRESS- GOOD- SHE'LL NOT SAY A WORD ABOUT IT OR SPEND IT FOR A DAY OR TWO- THAT WILL BE LONG ENOUGH FOR ME-
IT WOULD BE WORTH A HUNDRED DOLLARS TO GET EVEN WITH HER- MY PLANS ARE WORKING OUT PERFECT- NOW FOR THE NEXT MOVE- THEN LET HER TRY TO EXPLAIN WHERE SHE GOT THAT TEN DOLLARS-
HA-HA-HA- I SAID I'D GET EVEN WITH HER- AND THE BEST PART OF IT IS SHE'LL NEVER HAVE A CHANCE TO EVEN GUESS HOW IT REALLY HAPPENED- I'LL FIX HER!!!
HAROLD GRAY
Reg. U. S. Pat. Off.; Copyright, 1930, by The Chicago Tribune.
WHAT A CINCH- A HAIR-PIN WOULD HAVE OPENED THAT FRONT DOOR- NO CHANCE OF GETTING CAUGHT- EVERYBODY GOES TO BED AT TEN O'CLOCK IN THIS BURG-
FUNNY DREAM I HAD LAST NIGHT 'BOUT EDGAR FILCH- HA-HA! OH, WELL- THAT WAS JUST A DREAM-
HAROLD GRAY
LEAPIN' LIZARDS!!! NOT A CENT- MR. SELLERS MAY HAVE TAKEN ALL TH' MONEY HOME WITH HIM LAST NIGHT- AND YET--------
Reg. U. S. Pat. Off.; Copyright, 1930, by The Chicago Tribune.

April 7–9, 1930

SO YOU HAD A KEY TO THE STORE, EH?
YES, SIR - IT WAS MY JOB TO OPEN UP THE STORE IN THE MORNING -
THERE WAS ABOUT TEN DOLLARS TAKEN FROM THE TILL - WHAT DO YOU KNOW ABOUT THAT?
ER - I DON'T KNOW ABOUT THAT - BUT HERE'S A TEN DOLLAR BILL -
AH-HA!!! WHERE DID YOU GET THAT TEN DOLLARS?
I FOUND IT -
HA! HA! FOUND IT, EH? THAT'S A LIKELY STORY - FOUND IT IN THE TILL, PERHAPS - WELL, SELLERS, I GUESS WE DON'T HAVE TO LOOK ANY FARTHER FOR THE THIEF -
HAROLD GRAY
Reg. U. S. Pat. Off.; Copyright, 1930, by The Chicago Tribune.
WE BOTH KNOW YOU DIDN'T TAKE THE MONEY, ANNIE - SO DON'T WORRY - RIGHT WILL PREVAIL - THEY CAN'T CONVICT YOU FOR SOMETHING YOU DIDN'T DO -
YESSUM, MRS. TWINKLE - I S'POSE YOU'RE RIGHT -
BUT, GEE WHIZ - EVER'BODY IN TOWN THINKS I DID IT - AN' THEY'RE NOT EVEN TRYIN' TO FIND OUT WHO TH' ROBBER REALLY WAS - I'M SAME AS 'RESTED - GOTTA STAY HERE IN TH' HOUSE TILL THEY WANT ME -
IF JUDGE TORT OR OLD JACK PEPPER WERE ONLY HERE - THEY'D HELP ME OUT - BUT THEY'RE BOTH GONE - COURSE MRS. TWINKLE IS ON OUR SIDE •
Reg. U. S. Pat. Off.; Copyright, 1930, by The Chicago Tribune.
BUT SHE FIGGERS IF YER INNOCENT YUH DON'T HAVE TO PROVE IT - THAT'S A NICE WAY TO LOOK AT IT - "RIGHT WILL PREVAIL" - MAYBE - BUT NOT WITHOUT A GOOD HARD SCRAP MOST ALWAYS -
HAROLD GRAY
THE LOSS WAS NOTHING - I CAN'T UNDERSTAND IT AT ALL - I WON'T PROSECUTE ANNIE - IN SPITE OF THE EVIDENCE I CAN'T BELIEVE SHE DID IT - SHE'S AN HONEST GIRL -
HONEST - HA! HA! AFTER HER ROBBING HIM - AND HE CALLS HER HONEST!
I ALWAYS SAID THERE'S NO GOOD IN THESE ORPHANS FROM THE SLUMS - POTENTIAL CRIMINALS, I CALLS 'EM -
QUITE RIGHT -
AH - GOOD MORNING, MR. FILCH - WHAT DO YOU THINK OF THE ROBBERY?
A SHOCKING THING - I HATE TO BELIEVE IT OF A POOR CHILD - BUT THERE'S NO DOUBT, I FEAR - MY EDGAR SAW HER RUNNING FROM THE STORE THAT NIGHT HE TELLS ME -
HAROLD GRAY
I SUPPOSE WE SHOULDN'T BLAME THE CHILD - BUT SOMETHING SHOULD BE DONE AS A MORAL LESSON -
YES, INDEED - THE CHILD IS A MENACE - SHE SHOULD BE PUNISHED AS A LESSON TO OTHERS -
YES INDEED
Reg. U. S. Pat. Off.; Copyright, 1930, by The Chicago Tribune.

April 10–12, 1930
THE FRAME, THE FARM, AND THE FLOOD

WELL, MRS. TWINKLE - IT'S BEEN DECIDED AND I CAME TO TELL YOU - ANNIE'S TO GO TO THE COUNTY POOR FARM -
WHAT, MR. SELLERS? THE COUNTY FARM! WHOSE IDEA WAS THAT, - I'D LIKE TO KNOW -
WELL, MR. FILCH SAID HIS SON SAW ANNIE RUN FROM THE STORE THAT NIGHT - I SAID IT LOOKED FUNNY - WHAT WAS HE DOING AROUND THE STORE - BUT EVERYBODY SAID OF COURSE EDGAR COULDN'T HAVE BEEN IN IT - NO REASON TO STEAL WITH ALL HIS MONEY -
SAY - THAT'S AN IDEA - WHAT WAS EDGAR DOIN' AROUND TH' STORE? HE SAID HE'D GET ME INTO TROUBLE - GEE - NOW I WONDER IF HE IS BACK O' THIS -
OH, DEAR! OH, DEAR! THE COUNTY FARM - WHAT SHALL WE DO?
Reg. U. S. Pat. Off.; Copyright, 1930, by The Chicago Tribune.
SHUX, MRS. TWINKLE - IT'S NOT SO BAD OUT THERE, I HEAR - AND THEY'LL SOON FIND OUT I DIDN'T DO IT AND LET ME OUT -
OH, ANNIE - IF THERE WAS ONLY SOME WAY I COULD HELP YOU - BUT THEY ARE ALL AGAINST US, IT SEEMS -
HAROLD GRAY
MORNIN - I'M BERT YELP FROM TH' COUNTY FARM - JUST CAME TO SAY IF ANNIE'LL GIT HER THINGS TOGETHER AN' BE READY I'LL PICK HER UP ON MY WAY HOME TO-MORROW - DON'T WANTA RUSH HER -
MORNIN', MR. FILCH - I JUST SEEN THE WIDDER AN' FIXED IT TO TAKE ANNIE TO TH' FARM TO-MORROW -
AH, FINE, YELP - FINE - A SAD CASE - BUT IT'S THE BEST THING FOR THE COMMUNITY - AND SHE'S TOO YOUNG FOR JAIL -
EVEN THOUGH SHE'S AN ORPHAN I HATED TO BELIEVE IT OF HER - BUT THERE'S NOT A SHADOW OF DOUBT AS TO HER GUILT - OH, NOT A SHADOW - WHY, MY SON, EDGAR, SAW HER SNEAK AWAY FROM THE STORE LATE THAT NIGHT - IT'S A CLEAR CASE -
GUILTY, MY EYE - EDGAR'S A SLICK ONE, THE LITTLE RASCAL - WHEN HE GOES OUT TO GET SOME ONE, HE GETS 'EM - TAKES AFTER HIS OLD MAN - BUT HE CAN'T FOOL ME - HE FRAMED THAT ORPHAN BRAT - HA-HA! WHAT A BOY -
HAROLD GRAY
Reg. U. S. Pat. Off.; Copyright, 1930, by The Chicago Tribune.
DON'T YOU WORRY, MRS. TWINKLE - I'LL BE ALL RIGHT - AN' I CAN COME AN' VISIT YOU OFTEN -
GOOD-BYE, ANNIE -
C'MON, SANDY - HOP IN - THERE'S LOTS O' ROOM - WILLIE CAN SIT ON MY LAP -
NO! CAN'T HAVE NO DOGS OR BEARS -
THE COUNTY DON'T PAY ME TO FEED NO VARMINTS -
OH!
HAROLD GRAY
Reg. U. S. Pat. Off.; Copyright, 1930, by The Chicago Tribune.

April 14–16, 1930

THIEF OR NO THIEF, THAT KID'S STARTIN' OUT LIKE A WORKER- SHE'S MADE ALL TH' BEDS- SWEPT- WASHED TH' DISHES AN' NOW SHE'S OUT CHURNIN'-
WELL, YOUNG LADY, YOU'LL GIT ALONG FINE IF YER WILLIN' TO PITCH IN- I'VE ALWAYS HELD AS HOW GOOD, HARD WORK NEVER HURT ANYBODY- KEEP IT UP, ANNIE-
AH-H-H! THIS IS THE LIFE- FIRST CHANCE I'VE HAD TO SIT DOWN AND DRAW A LONG BREATH FOR MONTHS- IF THAT KID KEEPS ON SHE'S GOIN' TO SPOIL ME-
ALMANAC
HAROLD GRAY
Reg. U. S. Pat. Off.; Copyright, 1930, by The Chicago Tribune.
WHEW- WHAT A MESS O' DIRTY DISHES- BUT THEY WON'T TAKE LONG IF I DIG RIGHT IN- THERE SURE IS PLENTY TO DO IN THIS PLACE-
AND I SEEM TO BE TH' ONLY ONE WORKIN' AROUND HERE- BUT, OUTSIDE O' MR. AND MRS. YELP, ALL TH' OTHER FOLKS HERE AT TH' POOR FARM ARE REAL OLD- NO KIDS HERE AT ALL RIGHT NOW, 'CEPT ME-
THAT'S RIGHT- GLAD TO SEE A GIRL WHO ISN'T SCARED O' DISH-WATER- YOU KEEP THAT UP AND WE'RE GOING TO GET ALONG GREAT-
IT SURE DOES A SOUL GOOD TO SEE ONE GIRL WHO ISN'T LAZY AND WHO KNOWS HOW TO PITCH IN AND DO A DAY'S WORK-
HAROLD GRAY
Reg. U. S. Pat. Off.; Copyright, 1930, by The Chicago Tribune.
POOR OLD SANDY- I HOPE HE'S NOT SO LONESOME AS I AM- I WOULDN'T MIND IT HERE SO MUCH IF HE AN' WILLIE COULD BE HERE TOO- BUT I GUESS THEY'LL BE ALL RIGHT WITH MRS. TWINKLE-
HEY!!! WHERE YOU GOING?
ER- WHY, I WAS JUST LOOKING FOR ANNIE- THAT'S ALL-
I THOUGHT SO- SHE'S BUSY- WHAT DO YOU WANT OF HER?
WELL, I THOUGHT MAYBE I'D GET HER TO HELP ME WITH THE CHORES-
OH, YOU THOUGHT THAT, DID YOU? YOU BIG, LAZY WHELP- AS IF THE POOR CHILD DIDN'T HAVE ENOUGH TO DO- YOU'LL DO YOUR OWN CHORES- ME SLAVING MYSELF INTO AN EARLY GRAVE AND YOU WANT TO STEAL THE FIRST HELP I'VE HAD FOR YEARS- GIT!
HAROLD GRAY
Reg. U. S. Pat. Off.; Copyright, 1930, by The Chicago Tribune.

April 17–19, 1930

WELL, WELL- ALL DONE MILKIN' SO SOON?
YEP- IT DOESN'T TAKE VERY LONG WHEN YUH KEEP RIGHT AT IT-
GEE, HE'S LAZY- BUT I DON'T MIND DOIN' HIS WORK- BOTH HE AND MRS. YELP ARE ALWAYS PRAISIN' ME FOR TH' WAY I CAN PITCH IN AN' GET THINGS DONE-
S'POSE IT'S MOSTLY BALONEY- BUT IT MAKES YUH FEEL GOOD TO KNOW YOUR WORK IS 'PRECIATED- THIS POOR FARM ISN'T BAD- IT COULD BE LOTS WORSE-
Reg. U. S. Pat. Off.; Copyright, 1930, by The Chicago Tribune.
AN-NIE! TIME TO START GETTIN' SUPPER-
YESSUM, MRS. YELP- I'M COMIN'-
HAROLD GRAY
STEADY, NOW, MR. BASCOM- TAKE IT EASY- JUST LEAN ON ME- I WON'T LET YUH SLIP-
NOW AIN'T THAT SWEET? ALWAYS FINDING SOME WAY TO HELP SOMEBODY- I WANT BERT TO SEE THIS IF HE'S NOT TOO BUSY- HEY, BERT- C'ME HERE A SECOND-
WONDER WHERE HE WENT- HE WAS RIGHT HERE A MINUTE AGO- WHY TH'-----
Z-Z-Z
Z-Z-Z
Reg. U. S. Pat. Off.; Copyright, 1930, by The Chicago Tribune.
HEY! WHAT'S THE IDEA? WORK TO DO AT THE BARN AND YOU SLEEPIN'-
WASN'T SLEEPIN'- JUST THINKIN'- GOTTA PLAN MY WORK, AIN'T I?
HAROLD GRAY
HERE Y'ARE, TOMMY- PRETTY SOFT FOR YOU- ALL TH' MILK YOU CAN DRINK AN' NO DOGS TO CHASE YOU-
YOU'RE BETTER NATURED THAN MOST CATS- WHY, I EVEN B'LIEVE YOU AN' SANDY'D GET ALONG FINE-
GEE- WHAT I'D GIVE TO SEE SANDY AN' WILLIE- BUT I GUESS THEY MUST BE ALL RIGHT-
Reg. U. S. Pat. Off.; Copyright, 1930, by The Chicago Tribune.
MRS. TWINKLE LIKES 'EM- SHE'LL SEE TO IT THAT THEY HAVE A SWELL HOME TILL I CAN HAVE 'EM AGAIN-
HAROLD GRAY

April 21–23, 1930

HEARD SOME NEWS IN TOWN - FARMERS FROM OVER WEST O' HERE HAVE BEEN LOSIN' SHEEP -
STRAY DOGS HAVE BEEN KILLIN' 'EM - THREE OR FOUR EVERY NIGHT, THEY SAY -
THEY'RE SURE PRETTY MAD ABOUT IT - I ALWAYS SAID DOGS CAN'T BE TRUSTED -
NO! SANDY'D NEVER KILL A SHEEP - BUT THAT DON'T MEAN ANYTHING - FOLKS PROVED I STOLE THAT MONEY, WHEN I DIDN'T - GUESS THEY COULD PROVE SANDY KILLED SHEEP TH' SAME WAY - GEE -
HAROLD GRAY
Reg. U. S. Pat. Off.; Copyright, 1930, by The Chicago Tribune.
THERE'S TH' SHERIFF - WONDER WHAT HE'S COMIN' IN HERE FOR - HE'S GOIN' OUT TO SEE MR. YELP 'BOUT SOMETHIN'
I'M OUT PASSIN' THE WORD, YELP - THIS SHEEP-KILLIN' HAS GOT TO BE STOPPED - GOT TO GET RID O' ALL STRAY DOGS -
STARTIN' TO-NIGHT, ALL TH' FARMERS IN THESE PARTS ARE GOIN' OUT HUNTIN' - WE'RE GOIN' TO SHOOT EVERY STRAY DOG IN THIS COUNTY -
GOOD IDEE, SHERIFF -
OH-H-H! WHAT IF POOR SANDY GOES OUT TO-NIGHT? SOMEBODY'LL GET HIM SURE - HE'S NOT A BAD DOG, BUT NO ONE WOULD STOP TO ASK - IF HE'S SEEN HE'LL BE SHOT -
HAROLD GRAY
Reg. U. S. Pat. Off.; Copyright, 1930, by The Chicago Tribune.
I HEARD MR. YELP SAY THERE'S FARMERS OUT WITH GUNS TO-NIGHT WATCHIN' EVERY ROAD - POOR SANDY - IF HE TRIES TO COME OUT TO SEE ME THEY'LL GET HIM SURE -
AND THERE'S NO WAY I CAN WARN HIM - HE WON'T KNOW HIS DANGER TILL IT'S TOO LATE - HE'S SO FRIENDLY AN' TRUSTFUL -
I HOPE HE DOESN'T TRY TO COME OUT HERE TO-NIGHT - BUT IF HE DOESN'T, HOW AM I GOIN' TO KNOW THAT HE DIDN'T START? THIS IS AWFUL -
HAROLD GRAY
AN-NIE! WHERE ARE YOU? YOU AIN'T FINISHED TH' DISHES YET -
YESSUM, MRS. YELP - COMIN' - (OH, IT ISN'T FAIR - IT ISN'T FAIR!)
Reg. U. S. Pat. Off.; Copyright, 1930, by The Chicago Tribune.

April 24–26, 1930

Little Orphan Annie

NOW DON'T BE GONE LONG, SANDY- UNDERSTAND?
ARF!
HAROLD GRAY

NOW IS MY CHANCE, WHILE NO ONE IS LOOKING- I MUST SLIP OUT TO THE FENCE AND WARN POOR SANDY-

ALL THE FARMERS ARE OUT TO-NIGHT WITH GUNS AND THEY'RE GOING TO SHOOT EVERY DOG THEY SEE, JUST BECAUSE SOME DOG HAS BEEN KILLIN' SHEEP-

SANDY'D NEVER HURT A SHEEP- BUT THEY'LL SHOOT HIM IF THEY SEE HIM-AND HE'LL BE COMIN' TO SEE ME NOW- OH, IF HE COULD ONLY KNOW TH' DANGER!

BANG!

BANG!

DIDJER HIT HIM, JOSH? WHAT DID HE LOOK LIKE?
NOPE- MISSED HIM, CONSARN IT- BUT HE'S HIDIN' RIGHT IN HERE SOME PLACE-

THERE HE IS!
WHERE?

YEOW!
BOOM!

YOU ADDLE-PATED, PIN-HEADED IDJIT!!! I'LL HAVE TH' LAW ON YOU FER THIS!

OH, SANDY! SANDY! I HEARD TH' SHOOTIN' AND I WAS SO 'FRAID THEY'D SEEN YOU- HOW CAN I EVER MAKE YOU UNDERSTAND? YOU SO TRUSTIN' AND FRIENDLY- HOW CAN I WARN YOU?

LEAPIN' LIZARDS!!! LOOK AT HIM- HE'S STAYIN' IN TH' SHADOWS- HE SEEMS TO KNOW IT'S NOT SAFE FOR HIM 'ROUND HERE ANY MORE- HE MUSTA UNDERSTOOD WHAT I WAS TELLIN' HIM- YESSIR- HE'S SMART-
Reg. U. S. Pat. Off., Copyright, 1930, by The Chicago Tribune

April 27, 1930

WHAT ON EARTH ARE YOU A-LOOKIN' AT?
SH-H-H!!! I'M WATCHIN' ANNIE- SHE'S AWFUL UNEASY ABOUT SOMETHIN'-
I KETCHED HER TWICE OUT LOOKIN' THROUGH TH' FENCE- WE'VE GOTTA KEEP AN EYE ON HER- IT'D BE A FINE NOTE IF SHE'D UP AN' RUN AWAY, AN' HER THE WORKER SHE IS- AND WE'D LOSE THE COUNTY PAY FOR HER KEEP, TOO-
WELL, WELL, ANNIE- STILL WORKIN'- BETTER QUIT FOR TO NIGHT I RECKON, AND GET TO BED- YOU MUST GET YOUR REST-
OH, I'M ALMOST DONE, MRS. YELP- DON'T WAIT UP FOR ME-
Reg. U. S. Pat. Off.; Copyright, 1930, by The Chicago Tribune.
NO SIREE- I NEVER WAS ONE TO LET ANYBODY OVERDO JUST 'CAUSE THEY WAS WILLIN'- I'M A-GOIN' TO SEE YOU SAFE IN BED-
AW- I'M NOT A BIT SLEEPY, HONEST-
HAROLD GRAY
GOOD-NIGHT, ANNIE- SLEEP TIGHT-
GOOD NIGHT, MRS. YELP-
LOCKED IN-
CLICK!
JUST LIKE BEIN' IN JAIL- CAN'T EVEN GO TO TH' FENCE TO WAIT FOR SANDY ANY MORE, BUT WHAT MRS. YELP IS TAGGIN' RIGHT ALONG- I THOUGHT I'D LET HER GO TO BED, AN' THEN I'D SLIP OUT-
Reg. U. S. Pat. Off.; Copyright, 1930, by The Chicago Tribune.
BUT NOW SHE'S LOCKED TH' DOOR- AN' ALL TH' FARMERS OUT WITH GUNS SHOOTIN' STRAY DOGS- OH- OH- OH!!! BOO! HOO! HOO!!! I CAN'T STAND THIS- I'VE GOTTA DO SOMETHIN'-
HAROLD GRAY
IF I'M LUCKY I MAY GET DOWN THAT TREE WITHOUT BREAKIN' MY NECK-
THEN THERE'S ONLY THAT FENCE TO CLIMB- THAT'S EASY- BUT IT'S TOO LATE TO START TO NIGHT- I COULDN'T COVER ENOUGH DISTANCE 'FORE DAYLIGHT- AN' I DON'T WANTA MAKE A MESS O' THIS-
LESSEE, NOW- THAT'S ABOUT EVER'THING I'VE GOT- I'LL WEAR MY SWEATER- AN' I'LL SLIP A LITTLE GRUB OUTA TH' KITCHEN TO-MORROW-
COURSE I COULD MAKE A BREAK FOR IT TO-NIGHT- BUT I FIGGER A LITTLE TIME SPENT IN PLANNIN' THINGS OUT CAREFUL SAVES A HEAP O' TIME AN' TROUBLE LATER-
HAROLD GRAY
Reg. U. S. Pat. Off.; Copyright, 1930, by The Chicago Tribune.

April 28–30, 1930

TH BUNDLE HARDLY MADE A SOUND WHEN I DROPPED IT- NOW, FOR TH' TOUGH PART-
LEAPIN' LIZARDS! MRS. YELP-
SHE'S BEEN WAITIN' THERE ALL TH' TIME TO NAIL ME IF I TRIED TO 'SCAPE- AN' I NEVER GUESSED- WHEW! S'POSIN' SHE HADN'T BEEN SO SOUND ASLEEP-
IT'S MOON LIGHT- I'M GOIN' TO HIT OUT STRAIGHT ACROSS TH' FIELDS FOR TOWN- DASSEN'T USE TH' ROAD- SOME BUSYBODY'D BE SURE TO SEE ME-
HAROLD GRAY
Reg. U. S. Pat. Off.; Copyright, 1930, by The Chicago Tribune.
THAT'S MRS. TWINKLE'S HOUSE- IT'S SURE STILL- BUT IF THEY'VE MISSED ME AT TH' FARM THEY'LL BE LAYIN' FOR ME HERE- I DASSEN'T GO NEAR- I'LL JUST TRY ONE WHISTLE AND SEE WHAT HAPPENS-
SH-H-H- HERE COMES SOMETHIN' THROUGH TH' BUSHES- CAN IT BE? YES- IT IS!!!
SANDY!!! WILLIE!!! BOTH SAFE AND SOUND- AND THEY'LL NEVER GET US SEPARATED AGAIN- NEVER!
BOUF!
ARF!
Reg. U. S. Pat. Off.; Copyright, 1930, by The Chicago Tribune.
HAROLD GRAY
I SAY, SHERIFF, YELP HERE JUST TELLS ME THAT ORPHAN, ANNIE, ESCAPED FROM THE COUNTY FARM LAST NIGHT- FOR THE GOOD OF THE COMMUNITY SHE SHOULD BE LOCATED AND SENT BACK THERE AT ONCE-
AS A CITIZEN I WILL OFFER A REWARD OF FIFTY DOLLARS FOR HER CAPTURE-
FIFTY DOLLARS! I'LL CALL UP TH' TOWNS 'ROUND HERE- SHE WON'T GET FAR, MR. FILCH- FOR FIFTY DOLLARS I'LL CATCH HER MYSELF-
WHILE, FROM SHADOW TO SHADOW, THREE DARKER SHADOWS FLIT SILENTLY OVER HILL AND DALE-
THOSE GUYS ARE HUNTIN' STRAY DOGS- BUT WE MUSTN'T LET 'EM SEE US-
WELL, WE'RE MILES AN' MILES FROM BLUNDERVILLE, BUT I DON'T FEEL SAFE YET- WE'LL HIDE SOME PLACE WHEN DAY-LIGHT COMES AN' GO ON TO-MORROW NIGHT-
Reg. U. S. Pat. Off.; Copyright, 1930, by The Chicago Tribune.
HAROLD GRAY

May 1–3, 1930

Little Orphan Annie
HATE
CRUELTY
HUNGER
THE POOR-HOUSE
YES, SIR- THAT'S A MIGHTY, MIGHTY PRETTY SUNRISE-
HOPE

LEAPIN' LIZARDS! HERE COMES A CAR- NO TELLIN' WHO IT IS - I DON'T THINK THEY'D BOTHER TO FOLLOW ME FROM TH' COUNTY POOR FARM- BUT YUH NEVER CAN TELL-

NO USE TAKIN' ANY SILLY CHANCES- QUICK! UNDER TH' BRIDGE TILL THAT CAR GOES BY-

HAVEN'T SEEN A LITTLE GIRL GO BY HERE, HAVE YUH? RUN AWAY FROM TH' FARM- AND NOW THERE'S A REWARD OUT FER HER-
NOPE- SHE HAIN'T PASSED HERE- BEEN WATCHIN' FER STRAY DOGS ALL NIGHT- I'D 'A' SEEN HER-

WELL, SHE CAN'T GIT FUR- I'VE GOT TH' RIVER BRIDGE WATCHED-
HOW BIG'S TH' R'WARD?

WHEW! IF WE'D GONE ANOTHER STEP ON THAT ROAD WE'D HAVE BEEN GRABBED-

NOW THERE'S A REWARD OUT FOR ME- AN' IF THEY SEE YOU, SANDY, THEY'LL SHOOT YOU- THE ROADS AREN'T SAFE- WE'LL FOLLOW THIS DRY CREEK- NOT SO LIABLE TO MEET FOLKS-

THE RIVER! WE'VE GOTTA GET ACROSS- BUT HOW? IF WE HADN'T HEARD 'EM TALKIN' WE'D HAVE WALKED RIGHT INTO TROUBLE AT TH' BRIDGE-

GEE- IT'S NOT MUCH OF A BOAT, BUT IT'S BETTER'N NOTHIN'- C'MON, YOU GUYS- NO TIME NOW TO BE CAREFUL-

WE'VE FLOATED MORE'N A MILE DOWN-STREAM, BUT WE'RE ALMOST ACROSS AN' NOBODY'S SEEN US- IF WE ONLY HAD SOMETHIN' TO EAT NOW, I'D FEEL SWELL-

WHAT LUCK! LOOK! A LUNCH BOX IN TH' BOAT AND IT'S FULL O' SANDWICHES AND THERE'S A BOTTLE O' COFFEE- IT WAS UNDER TH' SEAT ALL TH' TIME-

COURSE IT ISN'T OURS, BUT I GUESS WE NEED IT MORE'N ANYBODY ELSE, RIGHT NOW- AN' IT ISN'T OUR BOAT, EITHER- BUT WE JUST BORROWED THAT- TH' OWNER WOULDN'T MIND, IF HE KNEW WHAT A TOUGH SPOT WE'RE IN-

THERE, NOW- I FEEL A HEAP BETTER- NOTHIN' LIKE A GOOD, SQUARE MEAL TO PEP YUH UP AN' MAKE EVER'THING LOOK LOTS BRIGHTER- EH, BOYS?
ARF!
BOUF!

May 4, 1930

WELL, WE GOT ACROSS TH' RIVER WITHOUT BEIN' SEEN- MOST LIKELY WE'RE SAFE ENOUGH NOW- WHAT'S THAT PAPER OVER THERE ON THAT TREE?
REWARD !!! AN' IT'S FOR FIFTY BUCKS TO ANYBODY WHO BRINGS ME BACK TO TH' COUNTY FARM-
REWARD
CAN YUH BEAT THAT? YUH'D THINK I WAS A BIG CROOK! GEE WHIZ! WHY CAN'T THEY LET ME ALONE? I NEVER THOUGHT THEY'D CHASE ME THIS FAR-
JUST SHOWS YUH HOW LOW DOWN AN' MEAN SOME FOLKS CAN BE FOR A FEW DOLLARS- C'MON, BOYS- IT'S TH' WOODS FOR US FOR A WHILE LONGER-
HAROLD GRAY
Reg. U. S. Pat. Off.; Copyright, 1930, by The Chicago Tribune.
Z-Z-Z-Z-Z N-N-N-N
C'MON, SANDY- CRAWL OUT O' TH' HAY- IT'S TIME WE WERE ON TH' HOOF AGAIN- MOON'S UP- IT'LL BE A SWELL NIGHT TO TRAVEL-
UM-M- I CAN SMELL SUPPER COOKIN'- BUT I'M SCARED TO GO DOWN AN' ASK FOR A HANDOUT- THEY MIGHT HAVE SEEN ONE O' THOSE REWARD NOTICES AN' GRAB ME-
AN' THERE'S A LITTLE GRUB IN TH' PACK YET- I'D RATHER EAT STALE BREAD FOR A DAY OR TWO, THAN RUN TH' CHANCE O' EATIN' POOR-HOUSE GRUB FOR YEARS-
HAROLD GRAY
Reg. U. S. Pat. Off.; Copyright, 1930, by The Chicago Tribune.
WE COULD MAKE LOTS BETTER TIME IN TH' OPEN, BUT WE'D BE LOTS EASIER TO SEE, TOO, IF ANYBODY WAS LOOKIN'- NOPE- WE'LL STICK TO TH' WOODS-
GEE- ANOTHER RIVER- AN' IT'S BIGGER'N TH' LAST ONE WE CROSSED-
BUT WE DON'T HAVE TO CROSS THIS ONE- THERE'S ALWAYS WOODS ALONG A RIVER- AN' A RIVER ALWAYS GOES SOME PLACE-
WE'LL JUST FOLLOW ALONG DOWN-STREAM- EVERY STEP THIS WAY TAKES US FARTHER FROM THAT POOR-FARM.
HAROLD GRAY
Reg. U. S. Pat. Off.; Copyright, 1930, by The Chicago Tribune.

May 5–7, 1930

BOUF!
HEY! KEEP AWAY FROM ME- LOOK OUT!!! HELP! HELP! SANDY!!
RUN HIM OUTA GAS - HE THOUGHT I WAS ALONE AN' WAS FIXIN' TO BITE ME-
YI!
MUST BE GETTIN' AWAY FROM TH' NEIGHBORHOOD WHERE TH' FARMERS WERE SHOOTIN' STRAY DOGS OR THAT MUTT WOULDN'T BE OUT- THAT'S A GOOD SIGN-
YI! YI! YI!
HAROLD GRAY
Reg. U. S. Pat. Off.; Copyright, 1930, by The Chicago Tribune.
THERE'S A NICE LOOKIN' TOWN- I S'POSE IT'D BE SAFE TO BE SEEN NOW- BUT I HATE TO TAKE A CHANCE TILL I HAVE TO-
I S'POSE WE COULD MAKE BETTER TIME IF WE'D MAKE A RAFT OR FIND AN OLD BOAT- IT'D BE LOTS EASIER'N HOOFIN' IT THROUGH TH' WOODS, TOO-
LEAPIN' LIZARDS! JUST 'MAGINE WHERE WE'D BE IF WE WENT OVER A DAM LIKE THAT IN A BOAT- WALKIN' MAY BE SLOW AN' HARD, BUT IT'S SAFE-
AN' LOOK AT THOSE ROCKS AN' WHIRL-POOLS - NO, SIR- DRY LAND FOR ME- TOO MUCH WATER SCARES ME-
HAROLD GRAY
Reg. U. S. Pat. Off.; Copyright, 1930, by The Chicago Tribune.
YOU GUYS THINK YOU'RE HUNGRY- OW-W-W-W!!! YOU CATCH A RABBIT OR SOMETHIN' 'MOST EVERY DAY- ALL I CATCH IS A STUMMICK-ACHE-
IF I HAD A BELT I COULD PULL IT UP- I'VE GOTTA STOP SOME PLACE SOON AN' TRY TO GET SOMETHIN TO EAT- GEE, I COULD EAT A RUBBER BOOT AN' LIKE IT-
PLANTIN' CORN- I COULD ASK THAT FARMER 'BOUT A JOB, BUT HE'D THINK IT FUNNY, ME COMIN' OUT O' TH' WOODS - HE'D ASK TOO MANY QUESTIONS
WE'VE COME A LONG WAY- MAYBE IT'D BE SAFE TO TRY THIS TOWN- SAFE OR NOT, I CAN'T HOLD OUT MUCH LONGER 'LESS I HAVE FOOD-
Reg. U. S. Pat. Off.; Copyright, 1930, by The Chicago Tribune.

May 8–10, 1930

Little Orphan Annie
?
A MOTHER LOVES YUH ALWAYS, NO MATTER HOW BAD YUH ARE- GEE! IT MUST BE SWELL TO HAVE A REAL MOTHER, LIKE OTHER KIDS-
HAROLD GRAY

NICE LOOKIN' LITTLE TOWN- WONDER IF IT'S SAFE TO LET FOLKS SEE US- WE'RE A LONG WAY FROM BLUNDERVILLE- THEY WOULDN'T HAVE CHASED US THIS FAR-

UM-YUM-M-M! JUST LOOK AT TH' SWELL CAKES AN' PIES AN' THINGS IN THAT WINDOW- BUT HOW ARE WE GOIN' TO BUY ANYTHING TO EAT? WE'RE BROKE-

A TAME BEAR, EH? DOES HE KNOW ANY GOOD TRICKS?
SURE HE KNOWS GOOD TRICKS- HE'S A SMART BEAR- WANTA SEE HIM P'FORM? C'MON, WILLIE- DANCE!

HAW! HAW! THEY'RE GOOD-
GOOD ENOUGH TO BE IN A CIRCUS-
THAT'S TH' STUFF, BOYS- HEP- HEP- HEP- HOW'S THAT, FOLKS?

O-OO- STOP THE CAR- WE MUST SEE THIS- A LITTLE GIRL WITH A PERFORMING BEAR- ISN'T THAT QUAINT?
RICH TOURISTS-

HERE, LITTLE GIRL- I ENJOYED YOUR SHOW SO MUCH-
WAL, I'M DURNED- GIVIN' HER FIVE DOLLARS-
OH, GEE! THANKS, LADY-

FIVE BUCKS! C'MON, BOYS- SHOW'S OVER- HERE'S WHERE WE BUY OURSELVES SOME GROCERIES-

HM-M-M- SEEMS AS HOW THERE'S SOMETHIN' F'MILIAR 'BOUT THAT GIRL- WHERE HAVE I SEEN HER BEFORE? LET ME THINK-

NOW TO GET OUT O' TOWN WHERE THERE'S LOTS O' ROOM AN' WE'LL EAT- WHAT'S THAT BIRD LOOKIN' AT ME LIKE THAT FOR? GEE- HE'S A CONSTABLE-
?

NOW I REMEMBER- I GOT A WARNIN' FROM BLUNDERVILLE TO BE ON TH' LOOKOUT FOR THAT GIRL- DESCRIPTION TALLIES PERFECT- YES SIREE- THERE'S A REWARD OUT FOR HER-

C'MON, BOYS SHE WENT THIS WAY AND SHE CAN'T HAVE GOT FUR-

DOG GONE- THEY'RE HOT ON OUR TRAIL AGAIN- BUT THEY'LL NEVER FIGGER ON US GOIN' TH' OTHER WAY- WE'RE SAFE FOR TO-NIGHT- AND WE'VE GOT GRUB, AN' A LITTLE MONEY NOW- THINGS MIGHT BE LOTS WORSE-

May 11, 1930

WELL, WE SURE HAD ONE GOOD BREAK YESTERDAY - GOT A SQUARE MEAL AN' A LITTLE DOUGH - BUT WE ALMOST GOT NABBED BY GOIN' INTO THAT TOWN - BUT LET 'EM CHASE US -
WE KNOW NOW THAT THERE'S A REWARD OUT FOR US AND WE WON'T TAKE A CHANCE LIKE THAT AGAIN - GEE - IT'S STARTIN' TO RAIN -
OH, WELL - LET IT RAIN - WE'LL BE DRY HERE IN THIS OLD HOLLOW TREE - AND WE'RE PERFECTLY SAFE IN THESE WOODS -
LEAPIN' LIZARDS! KEEP BACK - THERE'S THAT CONSTABLE STILL LOOKIN' FOR US - BEATS ALL WHAT SOME BIRDS WILL DO TO GET A LITTLE FIFTY DOLLAR REWARD - I HOPE HE GETS WET THROUGH -
HAROLD GRAY
Reg. U. S. Pat. Off.; Copyright, 1930, by The Chicago Tribune.
AN' THEY TALK ABOUT JUSTICE ALWAYS COMIN' OUT ON TOP IN TH' END - MAYBE SO - BUT I'M HERE TO SAY IT'S A LONG TIME IN COMIN' AND MIGHTY TOUGH IN TH' MEANTIME FOR HONEST FOLKS SOME TIME -
SH-H-H--- HOLD EVERYTHING! BACK, SANDY - I HEAR SOMEBODY COMIN' AND THEY'VE GOT A LANTERN -
I TELL YUH, BOYS, THAT KID ISN'T FAR FROM HERE - SCATTER OUT -
WHEW - THAT WAS A CLOSE ONE - ISN'T THAT CONSTABLE EVER GOIN' TO GET TIRED AN' GIVE UP CHASIN' US? THEY MUST HAVE SEEN OUR TRACKS -
HAROLD GRAY
Reg. U. S. Pat. Off.; Copyright, 1930, by The Chicago Tribune.
GEE - THEY'RE ALL THROUGH TH' WOODS BEHIND US - I'M 'FRAID WE'RE CORNERED UNLESS WE CAN CROSS TH' RIVER -
WOW - LOOK AT IT - IT'S BEEN RAININ' SO MUCH TH' WATER'S WAY OVER TH' BANKS - NOT A CHANCE TO GET ACROSS -
AN' WE'RE OUT ON A POINT WITH THAT CONSTABLE AN' A LOT O' HIS CROWD CLOSIN' IN FROM BEHIND AN' LOOKIN' UNDER EVERY BUSH -
C'MON - IF WE CAN FIND SOME PLACE TO HIDE AN' KEEP OUT O' SIGHT TILL IT GETS DARK WE MAY HAVE A CHANCE TO SLIP PAST 'EM -
HAROLD GRAY
Reg. U. S. Pat. Off.; Copyright, 1930, by The Chicago Tribune.

May 12–14, 1930

WE'RE CAUGHT- THEY SEE US- THERE'S NO WAY OUT-
THERE SHE IS- GRAB 'ER-
CLOSE IN- LOOK OUT FOR THAT DOG-
SH-H- WHAT'S THAT? SORT OF A HISSIN' SOUND- AND IT'S GETTIN' LOUDER-
PS-S-S-T- LISTEN- WHAT'S THAT NOISE- IT SOUNDS LIKE WATER- LISTEN!!!
RUN! RUN! GET TO HIGH GROUND! TH' DAM'S GONE OUT!!! RUN, OR WE'LL ALL BE DROWNED!!!
SUFFERIN' SUNFISH!
? ?
YEOW!
OW!
HAROLD GRAY
Reg. U. S. Pat. Off.; Copyright, 1930, by The Chicago Tribune.
OH- OH!!! IF I CAN ONLY GET ONTO THIS OLD BARN-DOOR- BET I'VE SWALLOWED TEN GALLONS O' WATER-
LUCKY I CAN SWIM- BUT EVEN A CORK'D HAVE A TOUGH TIME STAYIN' O' TOP O' THAT FLOOD- OH! WHAT'S BECOME O' POOR SANDY AN' WILLIE? SANDY!!!
COME ON BOYS- JUST A LITTLE MORE AND I CAN REACH YOU-
'AT A BOY- EASY GOES IT NOW OR WE'LL ALL BE IN TH' DRINK-
HAROLD GRAY
Reg. U. S. Pat. Off.; Copyright, 1930, by The Chicago Tribune.
WELL, HERE WE ARE- TH' SUN'S SHININ'- I'M ABOUT DRY- TH' RIVER'S NOT SO ROUGH TODAY- BUT, GOLLY! WHAT A LOT O' WATER-
NOTHIN' ELSE IN SIGHT BUT TH' TOPS O' TREES- BUT WE'RE STILL FLOATIN'- I FISHED OUT THIS BOX FOR A SEAT, I HUNG ONTO MY BUNDLE AN' WE'RE ALL TOGETHER-
THERE GOES SOMEBODY'S HOUSE WONDER WHERE TH' FOLKS ARE WHO USED TO LIVE IN IT- GUESS WE'RE LUCKY TO BE WHERE WE ARE-
BUT LUCKY OR NOT THERE'S NO USE WORRYIN'- NOTHIN' WE CAN DO 'CEPT JUST FLOAT- AT TH' RATE WE'RE GOIN' WE'RE BOUND TO GET SOME PLACE 'FORE VERY LONG-
HAROLD GRAY
Reg. U. S. Pat. Off.; Copyright, 1930, by The Chicago Tribune.

May 15–17, 1930

Little Orphan Annie
DO YOU MEAN TO SAY YOU CALL THIS A FLOOD? HAW! HAW! HAW! WHERE I COME FROM THIS WOULDN'T BE MORE THAN A HEAVY DEW—
ARK - No 1 -
HAROLD GRAY

LEAPIN' LIZARDS!!! WHAT A FLOOD— WHY, THIS RIVER MUST BE FIVE MILES WIDE— NO SHORE ANYWHERE— LIKE BEIN' ON TH' OCEAN.

LOOKIE- THERE GOES A HOUSE WITH A COUPLE O' CHICKENS RIDIN' ON IT- EVERYWHERE YUH LOOK THERE'S SOMETHIN' FLOATIN'- NOTHIN' STANDIN' STILL-

WHAT'S T-T-THAT? ALL LONG ARMS AN' THINGS WAVIN' OUT O' TH' WATER- IT'S MAKIN' FOR US!!! IT'S A M-M-MONSTER!

OH, IT'S TH' ROOTS OF A FLOATIN' TREE- IT'S GOIN' TO HIT US-

YI-I-I-!!! WE'RE SINKIN'— HANG ON!

OW!!!

DOG GONE IT!!! NOW IT'S TH' OTHER END THAT'S GOIN' DOWN-

WHEW!!! WELL, I'M STILL IN TH' MIDDLE O' THIS RAFT- AN' WE'RE STILL FLOATIN'- BUT SANDY!!! WILLIE!!! GONE!

OH, SANDY - SANDY!!! I THOUGHT I'D NEVER SEE YOU AGAIN- BOY!!! THAT SURE WAS A CLOSE ONE - AND THERE'S WILLIE-

WHAT WAS THE MATTER WITH YOU GUYS? WHY DIDN'T YOU STICK TIGHT, LIKE I DID? WHY, I DIDN'T EVEN GET MY FEET WET- THAT'S A GOOD ONE ON YOU TWO BIRDS -HA-HA!

?

May 18, 1930

WHAT A BUM BREAK- WATER FOR MILES AND US FLOATIN' NOBODY KNOWS WHERE- AND HUNGRY!
AND JUST A LITTLE WHILE AGO I WAS SITTIN' PRETTY- HAD A SWELL HOME WITH MRS. TWINKLE, A GOOD JOB, AND WAS GOIN' TO SCHOOL- THEN, BAM!!!
I KNOW BLAMED WELL THAT LITTLE EDGAR FILCH GOT ME INTO ALL THAT TROUBLE- IF IT HADN'T BEEN FOR HIM---- OH, WELL- NO USE BEIN' TOO SORE AT HIM RIGHT NOW-
NOTHIN' I COULD DO 'BOUT IT NOW IF I WANTED TO- I KNOW I'M HONEST- AND GUYS LIKE THAT GET WHAT'S COMIN' TO 'EM, SOONER OR LATER- WHY WORRY 'BOUT IT?
HAROLD GRAY
Reg. U. S. Pat. Off.; Copyright, 1930, by The Chicago Tribune.
LOOKIE- THERE'S A LOT O' FOLKS ON THAT SHORE- BUT WE CAN'T GET TO 'EM-
SHUX! CAN'T EVEN SEE 'EM ANY MORE PAST THAT ISLAND-
THERE'S A MOTOR BOAT- BUT HE DOESN'T SEE US- AND THAT GUY COULDN'T HEAR IT THUNDER WITH THAT ENGINE GOIN'-
THERE HE GOES- WELL, IT'S NICE TO SEE SOMEBODY FOR A CHANGE, ANYWAY- MAYBE WE'LL COME TO A TOWN 'FORE LONG-
PUT! PUT! PUT!
HAROLD GRAY
Reg. U. S. Pat. Off.; Copyright, 1930, by The Chicago Tribune.
GOIN' TO BE NIGHT 'FORE LONG- IF I COULD JUST FASTEN THIS RAFT TO THIS ISLAND SOME WAY TILL MORNING---
I'M SCARED TO GO FLOATIN' AT NIGHT- NEVER KNOW WHAT YOU'RE GOIN' TO BUMP INTO IN TH' DARK-
YI!!! I'M SLIPPIN'-
SHUX!
HAROLD GRAY
Reg. U. S. Pat. Off.; Copyright, 1930, by The Chicago Tribune.

May 19–21, 1930

HEY! HAVE YUH GOT A ROPE YUH COULD THROW US?
WHY- IT'S A LITTLE GIRL AND A DOG AND A-- A-- A BEAR!
TH' CURRENT'S BRINGIN' 'EM IN-SHORE- C'MON, BOYS- WE CAN REACH 'EM IN A MINUTE-
AH-H-H! THERE WE ARE- A PERFECT LANDING- EH, YOUNG LADY?
WELL, WELL- NOW WHAT'S YOUR NAME AND WHERE DID YOU COME FROM?
MY NAME'S ANNIE AND WE'VE FLOATED FOR HUNDREDS O' MILES- AND WE HAVEN'T HAD A BITE TO EAT FOR DAYS-
HAROLD GRAY
Reg. U. S. Pat. Off.; Copyright, 1930, by The Chicago Tribune.
WOW! AM I TIRED! HARDLY DARED TO SHUT MY EYES ON THAT RAFT- AND WEREN'T THOSE BEANS SWELL? AND TH' CORN-BREAD AND 'LASSUS-
LE'SSEE- THIS IS MY COT- SO MANY FOLKS HAVE BEEN FLOODED OUT O' THEIR HOMES THEY'VE PUT UP TENTS IN THIS TOWN FOR 'EM-
MIGHTY LITTLE GRUB IN THIS TOWN- FOLKS HERE HAVE LOST MOST EVER'THING- BUT I NEVER KNEW FOLKS WHO WERE ANY MORE GENEROUS- GUESS PEOPLE WHO'VE HAD BAD LUCK ARE MOST ALWAYS A LITTLE BIGGER-HEARTED- THEY KNOW HOW IT FEELS TO BE UP AGAINST IT-
HAROLD GRAY
Reg. U. S. Pat. Off.; Copyright, 1930, by The Chicago Tribune.
Z-Z-Z-Z!
Z-Z-Z-Z-Z-
Z-Z-Z-Z-Z-
Z-Z-Z-Z
HERE, ANNIE- HERE'S TWO BUCKETS OF HOT COFFEE FOR THE MEN ON THE LEVEE- THINK YOU CAN HANDLE THEM?
YESSUM-
GEE- I'M SURE TIRED- IT'S WAY AFTER MIDNIGHT- WONDER WHEN THEY QUIT WORK AROUND HERE AND GO TO BED-
HERE, BOYS- GUESS WE CAN TAKE TIME FOR A CUP OF HOT COFFEE- BUT MAKE IT SNAPPY- THE RIVER'S RISING AGAIN-
LEAPIN' LIZARDS! GUESS IF THEY CAN KEEP WORKIN' LIKE THAT DAY AN' NIGHT AN' NOT KICK, I CAN KEEP GOIN' A WHILE YET-
HAROLD GRAY
Reg. U. S. Pat. Off.; Copyright, 1930, by The Chicago Tribune.

May 22–24, 1930

Little Orphan Annie
YESSIR- THERE'S A ZAMPLE OF HONEST ADVERTISING-
RUNNING WATER IN EVERY ROOM
HOTEL

SHUX! I CAN'T SLEEP- GUESS I'LL GET UP AND TAKE A WALK-

JUST LISTEN TO THAT RIVER- IT MAKES ME NERVOUS-

WATER AS FAR AS YUH CAN SEE- COURSE THIS LEVEE'S STRONG, AND THERE'S GUARDS WATCHIN' ALL TH' TIME- BUT WHAT IF TH' LEVEE SHOULD BREAK?

THE WATER WOULD BE FORTY FEET DEEP IN THIS TOWN- HOW DO THEY KNOW TH' LEVEE WON'T BREAK HERE WITH ALL THAT WATER PUSHIN' ON THE OTHER SIDE?

BUT NOBODY SEEMS TO WORRY- 'CEPT FOR THOSE GUARDS UP ON THE LEVEE, EVERYBODY DOWN HERE IN TOWN IS SOUND ASLEEP-

NO USE GOIN' ANY FARTHER THIS WAY- THAT ROAD LEADS OFF THROUGH THE WOODS TO THE BACK COUNTRY- NO DANGER FROM THAT WAY, I S'POSE-

S'POSE I'M SILLY, BUT I DON'T FEEL SAFE HERE ON LOW GROUND- LET'S GO BACK TO THE LEVEE- SH-H-H-- DO YOU HEAR WATER SORTA SWISHIN' AND GURGLIN'?

YI-I-I-I! IT IS WATER! AN' IT'S COMIN' IN FROM BEHIND US- SOMETHING'S BUSTED BACK OF US AND IT'S COMIN' UP A FOOT A MINUTE- RUN!!!

RUN FOR YER LIVES!!! WAKE UP!!! RUN FOR TH' LEVEE! RUN! RUN! RUN!!!

GO ON, SANDY- I'LL MAKE IT ALL RIGHT- WE'RE THE LAST ONES AND WE'RE ALMOST THERE-

THE WHOLE TOWN IS UNDER WATER-
YES- WE WERE WARNED JUST IN TIME-
THAT LITTLE GIRL SAVED US ALL-
ALL SAFE- NOT A SOUL MISSING

WE ALL OWE OUR LIVES TO YOU, ANNIE- WITHOUT YOUR WARNING WE ALL WOULD HAVE BEEN DROWNED- HOW CAN WE THANK YOU?
AW, SHUX- THAT'S ALL RIGHT-

May 25, 1930

LEAPIN' LIZARDS! FOLKS HERE HAD MIGHTY LITTLE BEFORE THIS FLOOD- NOW THEY'VE GOT NOTHIN' AT ALL SINCE TH' WATER BUSTED THROUGH-
IT'S TOUGH- AFTER WORKIN' SO HARD TO SAVE TH' LEVEE, TOO- JUST 'CAUSE IT WENT AN' BUSTED WAY OFF SOME PLACE MILES AWAY FOLKS HERE BLAMED NEAR GOT DROWNED-
HEY, MOM- LOOKIE- THERE'S TH' BEAR AN' TH' LITTLE GIRL WHO SAVED OUR LIVES-
SHUX! JUST CAUSE I SAW TH' WATER FIRST AN' HOLLERED THEY FIGGER I SAVED THEIR LIVES- WHO WOULDN'T HAVE HOLLERED- I WAS SCARED SILLY- BUT AT THAT THEY ALL GOT OUT ALIVE- THAT'S THE MAIN THING-
HAROLD GRAY
Reg. U. S. Pat. Off.; Copyright, 1930, by The Chicago Tribune.
THERE GOES THE OLD GENERAL SYLVESTER LOADED TO THE LIMIT- NO ROOM FOR ANY MORE PASSENGERS-
NO USE HAILING- 'TWOULDN'T BE SAFE FOR ANY BOAT TO GET TOO CLOSE TO THE LEVEE NOW- WE'RE WELL ENOUGH HERE FOR THE PRESENT-
GEE- MAYBE WE ARE O. K. HERE ON THIS LEVEE LIKE THEY SAY, BUT I'D FEEL A HEAP SAFER ON THAT BOAT-
BOATS MOST ALWAYS STAY ON TOP O' TH' WATER- BUT S'POSIN' TH' RIVER'D RISE ANOTHER FOOT OR SO THIS LEVEE'D BE MIGHTY LITTLE GOOD TO US-
HAROLD GRAY
Reg. U. S. Pat. Off.; Copyright, 1930, by The Chicago Tribune.
NO USE STAYIN' IN ONE PLACE- THEY SAY THIS LEVEE RUNS FOR MILES LIKE THIS- MIGHT AS WELL MOVE ALONG-
GEE- HERE'S A LOW SPOT- OR MAYBE TH' RIVER'S COMIN' UP SOME MORE- BUT THERE'S NOTHIN' WE CAN DO 'BOUT IT-
NOBODY CAN DO MUCH NOW, 'CEPT WAIT- WATER ON BOTH SIDES- JUST A NARROW ROAD ALONG TH' TOP OF TH' LEVEE-
HAROLD GRAY
ALL TH' BOATS YUH SEE ARE LOADED FULL- FOLKS ON TH' LEVEE JUST SIT- LOST EVER'THING- MIGHTY LITTLE TO EAT- POOR AS WE ARE WE'RE AS WELL OFF AS ANYBODY HEREABOUTS- EH, SANDY?
ARF!
Reg. U. S. Pat. Off.; Copyright, 1930, by The Chicago Tribune.

May 26–28, 1930

THAT'S TH' STUFF-
SHOW 'EM HOW
YOU CAN STEP-
TUM--- TUM---
TIDDY-DUM-DUM-
WHADDYUH SAY, BOYS?
I CLAIM THAT'S A BLAMED
GOOD SHOW- JUST WHAT WE
NEEDED TO CHEER US UP- HOW
ABOUT A LITTLE COLLECTION
FOR THE YOUNGSTER?
JUST A SMALL TOKEN OF OUR APPRECIATION, LITTLE GIRL-
AW, GEE- I COULDN'T TAKE MONEY FROM YOU FOLKS- YOU'VE LOST YER HOMES AN' EVER'THING- BUT IF YUH COULD SPARE US A LITTLE SOMETHIN' TO EAT---- WE'RE NOT FUSSY---- COLD CORN BREAD- ANYTHING-
Reg. U. S. Pat. Off.; Copyright, 1930, by The Chicago Tribune.
HEAR THAT? WELL, I RECKON WE SURE CAN FIX UP SOME SORT OF A MEAL FOR A LITTLE LADY WHO IS AS THOUGHTFUL AND GENEROUS AS THAT- EH, BOYS?
YES SIREE!
YOU BET-
HAROLD GRAY
DOG GONED RAIN- AS IF THERE WASN'T ENOUGH WATER HERE NOW- GEE! THERE'S AN OLD PIECE O' CANVAS-
HM-M-M-M! IT LOOKS LIKE IT MIGHT DO- ANYTHING'S BETTER'N BEIN' RAINED ON-
AH- JUST LIKE A TENT- GUESS MAYBE THIS ISN'T NICE AND COZY- WE'LL JUST SIT HERE TILL IT STOPS-
LEAPIN' LIZARDS! I FORGOT THAT WATER MIGHT RUN ALONG TH' GROUND- BR-R-R-R!!!
HAROLD GRAY
Reg. U. S. Pat. Off.; Copyright, 1930, by The Chicago Tribune.
WELL, IT'S QUIT RAININ'- BUT WITH SO MUCH WATER TH' LEVEE'S PLUMB SOAKED FULL AND SORTA JIGGLES LIKE JELLY WHEN YUH WALK ON IT-
LEAPIN' LIZARDS!
WOW! DID YOU SEE THAT? JUST MELTED AWAY- LUCKY WE WEREN'T STANDIN' RIGHT THERE-
C'MON, BOYS- LET'S GET OUT O' HERE- HURRY! BUT, FOR TH' LOVE O' MIKE, WALK SOFT!!!
HAROLD GRAY
Reg. U. S. Pat. Off.; Copyright, 1930, by The Chicago Tribune.

May 29–31, 1930

Little Orphan Annie
LEAPIN' LIZARDS!!! I BET FOLKS WHO LIVE IN A DESERT ALL THEIR LIVES NEVER REALIZE HOW LUCKY THEY ARE - EH, SANDY?
ARF!
HAROLD GRAY
SINCE TH' WATER BUSTED THROUGH AN' FLOODED TH' TOWN LAST SUNDAY WE'VE HAD NO PLACE TO GO, 'CEPT UP AN' DOWN ON TH' LEVEE -
NOW TH' LEVEE'S SO SOAKED FULL O' WATER IT SHAKES JUST LIKE JELLY WHEN YUH WALK - LOOK OUT!!!
LEAPIN' LIZARDS!!! IT JUST MELTED AWAY LIKE A LUMP O' BROWN SUGAR IN HOT COFFEE - LET'S GET AWAY FROM HERE, QUICK -
GOTTA TELL FOLKS 'BOUT THIS ----- OH-H-H!!! STOP, SANDY - KEEP BACK -
COME AWAY - IT'S TOO WIDE TO JUMP, AN' NO TELLIN' WHEN SOME MORE WILL CAVE IN -
NOW WE ARE IN A PICKLE FOR SURE - LEFT HERE ON JUST THIS LITTLE CHUNK O' DIRT THAT'S GETTIN' SMALLER ALL TH' TIME - AN' WHEN IT DOES WASH AWAY WE HAVEN'T ONE CHANCE IN A MILLION -
OH-OH-OH!!! WE'RE DONE FOR - POOR WILLIE - POOR SANDY - I NEVER MEANT TO GET YOU INTO A MESS LIKE THIS - ONLY A FEW MINUTES MORE AT THIS RATE AND WE'LL ALL BE DONE FOR -
WHEW! WHAT'S THAT? WHY, IT'S A STEAM BOAT WHISTLIN' -
BOOO!!
HELP! HELP! HELP!!! OH, BOY - LOOKIE! THEY SEE US AN' ARE COMIN' OUR WAY -
SUFFERIN' SUNFISH!!! HURRY! HURRY! I CAN FEEL TH' GROUND MOVIN' UNDER US - ANY SECOND NOW WE MAY BE WASHED AWAY -
WHEW! SAVED - BUT THAT'S CUTTIN' IT A LOT TOO FINE TO SUIT ME -
YES, SIREE - A SECOND LONGER AND WE'D HAVE BEEN TOO LATE -

June 1, 1930

WHEW - THIS RIVER BOAT SURE PICKED US UP JUST IN TIME - THE LEVEE IS ALL GONE -
NOT A BIT OF DRY LAND IN SIGHT ANYWHERE - JUST A FEW TREE-TOPS - WE SURE ARE LUCKY TO BE ALIVE AN' KICKIN' -
WHILE INTO A DISTANT PORT STEAMS A LINER FROM FAR AWAY - BUT WHAT HAS THIS TO DO WITH LITTLE ANNIE? WE SHALL SEE -
HAROLD GRAY
WELL, MR. WARBUCKS - WE'LL BE AT THE PIER IN FIVE MINUTES - GOOD-BYE AND I HOPE YOU FIND THE LITTLE GIRL WELL AND HAPPY -
THANKS, CAPTAIN - I HAVEN'T TOLD HER I'M COMING - I WANT TO SURPRISE HER -
Reg. U. S. Pat. Off.; Copyright, 1930, by The Chicago Tribune.
SURE BEATS ANYTHING O' TH' KIND I EVER SAW -
YESSIR - THEM ANIMALS SURE KIN ACT -
FASTER, WILLIE - SANDY'S BEATIN' YUH - WATCH 'EM, FOLKS - THEY ROLL THEIR OWN -
WOW! DID WE CLEAN UP! FOLKS ON THIS RIVER BOAT SURE ARE GENEROUS - BET WE COULD MAKE A GOOD LIVIN' JUST RIDIN' UP AN' DOWN TH' RIVER ALL TH' TIME GIVIN' SHOWS -
WHILE IN THE MEANTIME "DADDY" WARBUCKS SPEEDS TOWARD BLUNDERVILLE AND DISAPPOINTMENT -
BLUNDERVILLE - THERE IT IS - THINK YOU CAN LAND ME THERE TO MORROW?
I AM SURE I CAN -
WHAT IF THERE IS NO LANDING FIELD WHEN WE GET THERE?
OH, WE'LL ARRIVE IN DAYLIGHT - IT WILL BE SIMPLE ENOUGH TO LAND IN SOME FIELD NEAR THE TOWN -
HAROLD GRAY
Reg. U. S. Pat. Off.; Copyright, 1930, by The Chicago Tribune.
ONE THING - FOLKS ON THIS BOAT DON'T ASK US A LOT O' SILLY QUESTIONS OR BOTHER US OR PAY ANY 'TENTION TO US AT ALL, 'LESS WE PUT ON A SHOW OR SOMETHIN' -
GUESS THEY'VE ALL GOT PLENTY OF THEIR OWN TROUBLES TO WORRY 'BOUT WITHOUT MIXIN' INTO OURS - IT'S SURE NICE TO MEET FOLKS THAT MIND THEIR OWN BUSINESS -
AND IN THE MEANTIME WARBUCKS SWOOPS DOWN ON BLUNDERVILLE LITTLE GUESSING THAT ANNIE HAS VANISHED, NO ONE KNOWS WHITHER -
HERE WE ARE - THAT'S BLUNDERVILLE - NOW WHERE CAN WE LAND?
THERE'S A BIG OPEN FIELD -
WON'T ANNIE BE SURPRISED WHEN I WALK IN ON HER? MAYBE SHE'S SEEN THE PLANE ALREADY AND GUESSED - SHE'S MIGHTY SHREWD - BOY! IT WILL BE GREAT TO SEE HER AGAIN -
HAROLD GRAY
Reg. U. S. Pat. Off.; Copyright, 1930, by The Chicago Tribune.

June 2–4, 1930

C'MON, YOU GUYS- EVERBODY'S UP IN FRONT- WE'RE COMIN' TO A TOWN AND WE'LL ALL GO ASHORE- I HEARD 'EM TALKIN' 'BOUT IT- WON'T IT BE GREAT TO GET REAL DIRT UNDER OUR FEET AGAIN-
WOW- THAT IS A CITY, TOO- JUST LOOK AT TH' SPIRES AN' SMOKE AN' EVER'THING- WELL, WE CAN'T GET THERE ANY TOO SOON TO SUIT ME-
WHILE, BACK IN BLUNDERVILLE, "DADDY" WARBUCKS IS HEARING FROM OLD JACK PEPPER, OF ANNIE'S SHAMEFUL PERSECUTION
AND THAT'S ALL I KNOW, WARBUCKS- I WAS AWAY AT THE TIME OR IT COULD NEVER HAVE HAPPENED- WHEN I RETURNED ANNIE HAD DISAPPEARED-
WELL, PEPPER, YOU'VE GIVEN ME A PRETTY CLEAR IDEA OF WHAT HAPPENED- I THINK I KNOW JUST ABOUT HOW SHE WAS FRAMED AND WHO DID IT- WHO IS THIS BIRD, FILCH? I THINK I'M GOING TO ENJOY MEETING HIM AND HIS SON, EDGAR, VERY MUCH-
HAROLD GRAY
Reg. U. S. Pat. Off.; Copyright, 1930, by The Chicago Tribune.
SO YOU'RE THE ILL-BRED LITTLE BABOON THAT FRAMED ANNIE, EH? WELL, THIS SURE IS A PLEASURE-
HERE !!! TAKE YOUR HANDS OFF MY BOY OR I'LL....
WAH!
AH- AND NOW FOR YOU--- WHY, IF IT ISN'T SLIMY SAM- BEEN YEARS SINCE I'VE SEEN YOU-
WARBUCKS!!! BUT--- BUT I THOUGHT YOU WERE IN CHINA---
SO YOU'RE THE SHERIFF- WELL, WELL- WHAT A SLEUTH- YOU EARN YOUR SALARY BY HELPING PIN A CRIME ON AN INNOCENT LITTLE GIRL, AND PAL AROUND WITH FILCH, ALIAS SLIMY SAM HERE- THERE'S BEEN A FIVE THOUSAND REWARD OUT FOR HIM FOR YEARS- COLLECT IT-
OH, MR. WARBUCKS- I'VE BEEN SO WORRIED- BUT NO ONE WOULD LISTEN TO ME- WHERE CAN ANNIE HAVE GONE?
DON'T YOU WORRY, MRS. TWINKLE- YOU WERE A REAL FRIEND TO ANNIE- WE'LL FIND HER, I PROMISE YOU THAT-
HAROLD GRAY
Reg. U. S. Pat. Off.; Copyright, 1930, by The Chicago Tribune.
MY, WHAT A LOT O' PEOPLE IN THIS TOWN- ALL TH' FOLKS WHO'VE BEEN FLOODED OUT O' THEIR HOMES FOR MILES ARE HERE- I HARDLY KNOW WHERE TO GO-
BUT WE'VE GOT A LITTLE MONEY- I GUESS TH' FIRST THING TO DO IS EAT- THEN MAYBE WE'LL GET AN IDEA- HEY, MISTER- GOT ANY HOT DOGS?
HAMBU
WHILE FAR AWAY, UP THE FLOODED RIVER, WARBUCKS TAKES UP THE UNCERTAIN TRAIL-
ALL RIGHT, BOYS- WE'VE GOT A GOOD BOAT AND PLENTY OF GAS- LET'S GO-
YESSIR, MR. WARBUCKS- I'VE BEEN ON THIS OLD RIVER EVER SINCE I KIN REMEMBER- NOT A NOOK OR CRANNIE ON EITHER SHORE THAT I DON'T KNOW BY DAY OR NIGHT-
GOOD- YOU'RE THE MAN I WANT- WE'LL COMB EVERY INCH OF THE SHORES- BOUND TO FIND SOME TRACE OF HER BEFORE LONG-
HAROLD GRAY
Reg. U. S. Pat. Off.; Copyright, 1930, by The Chicago Tribune.

June 5–7, 1930

Little Orphan Annie
NOW REMEMBER SANDY- CALL ME EARLY IN THE MORNIN'-
HAROLD GRAY

ARF! ARF!

WELL, WELL- G'MORNIN', BOYS- TIME TO GET UP, EH? YOU'RE SURE A SWELL ALARM CLOCK, SANDY- DON'T HAVE TO WIND YOU UP OR NOTHIN'-

HEIGH-HO! ANOTHER DAY- WELL, I HAD A GOOD ROOM LAST NIGHT- NOW TO FIND BREAKFAST-

WHEN THAT STEAMER BROUGHT US HERE I FIGGERED WE WERE ALL SET- BUT WHAT CHANCE HAVE WE GOT WITH HUNDREDS O' FOLKS OUT O' WORK IN THIS TOWN NOW? BUT WE'VE GOTTA MAKE DOUGH IF WE S'PECT TO EAT-

HO! HO! LOOKIE, HERE, MATES-
HM-M-M! A WHOLE CROWD O' GUYS STANDIN' AROUND HERE ON TH' WATERFRONT WAITIN' TO START LOADIN' BOATS- HM-M-M-

GEN'MEN- WITH YOUR KIND 'TENTION I WILL HAVE THESE TWO WILD ANIMALS P'FORM FOR YOU TRICKS WHICH I BET YOU NEVER SAW BEFORE-

'AT A BOY, WILLIE- GO TO IT, SANDY- TH' ACKER-BATIC BEAR AN' TH' DANCIN' DOG- BUT IF ONE O' YOU GEN'MEN WILL KINDLY LEND ME A BOTTLE O' POP I GUARANTEE TO STARTLE YOU ALL-

THERE YOU ARE- WITH NOTHIN' BUT HIS TEETH HE OPENS TH' BOTTLE- WATCH HIM CLOSELY, GEN'MEN-

HAW-HAW! THAT'S GOOD-
DOGGONED IF HE AIN'T DRINKIN' IT DOWN LIKE AN OLD-TIMER-
YESSIR, FELLERS- THAT'S SURE A REAL SMART BEAR-

HOW'S THAT FOR A TRICK? LET'S GIVE TH' LITTLE BEAR A GREAT BIG HAND-

OH, I THANK YOU! WILLIE THANKS YOU! SANDY THANKS YOU! WE ALL THANK YOU!!!

C'MON, SANDY- C'MON, WILLIE- I SEE A SWELL LUNCH WAGON- WITH YOUR TALENT AN' MY BRAINS WE'LL NEVER HAVE TO GO HUNGRY-

June 8, 1930

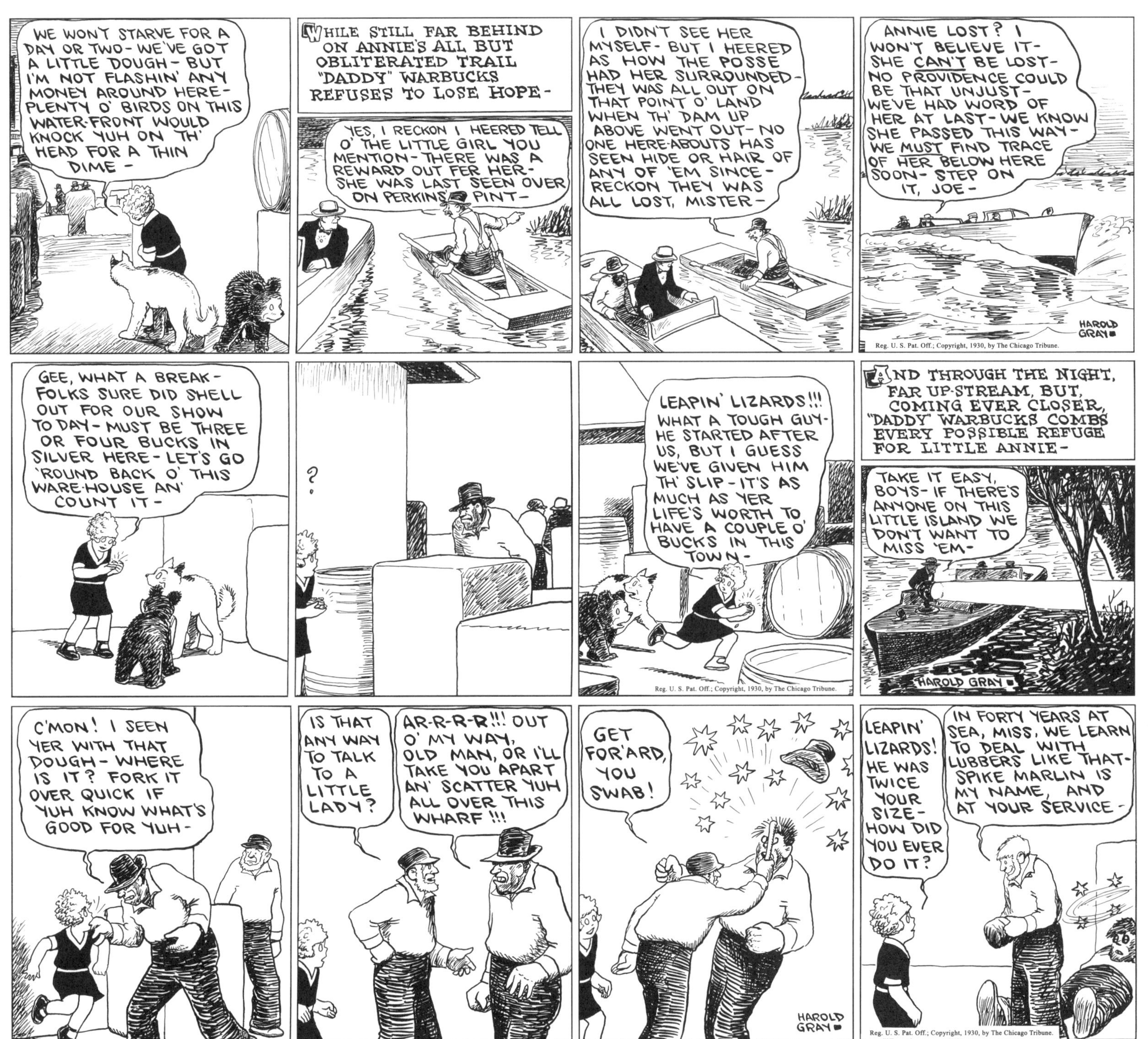
WE WON'T STARVE FOR A DAY OR TWO- WE'VE GOT A LITTLE DOUGH- BUT I'M NOT FLASHIN' ANY MONEY AROUND HERE- PLENTY O' BIRDS ON THIS WATER-FRONT WOULD KNOCK YUH ON TH' HEAD FOR A THIN DIME-
WHILE STILL FAR BEHIND ON ANNIE'S ALL BUT OBLITERATED TRAIL "DADDY" WARBUCKS REFUSES TO LOSE HOPE-
YES, I RECKON I HEERED TELL O' THE LITTLE GIRL YOU MENTION- THERE WAS A REWARD OUT FER HER- SHE WAS LAST SEEN OVER ON PERKINS' PINT-
I DIDN'T SEE HER MYSELF- BUT I HEERED AS HOW THE POSSE HAD HER SURROUNDED- THEY WAS ALL OUT ON THAT POINT O' LAND WHEN TH' DAM UP ABOVE WENT OUT- NO ONE HERE-ABOUTS HAS SEEN HIDE OR HAIR OF ANY OF 'EM SINCE- RECKON THEY WAS ALL LOST, MISTER-
ANNIE LOST? I WON'T BELIEVE IT- SHE CAN'T BE LOST- NO PROVIDENCE COULD BE THAT UNJUST- WE'VE HAD WORD OF HER AT LAST- WE KNOW SHE PASSED THIS WAY- WE MUST FIND TRACE OF HER BELOW HERE SOON- STEP ON IT, JOE-
HAROLD GRAY
Reg. U. S. Pat. Off.; Copyright, 1930, by The Chicago Tribune.
GEE, WHAT A BREAK- FOLKS SURE DID SHELL OUT FOR OUR SHOW TO DAY- MUST BE THREE OR FOUR BUCKS IN SILVER HERE- LET'S GO 'ROUND BACK O' THIS WARE-HOUSE AN' COUNT IT-
?
LEAPIN' LIZARDS!!! WHAT A TOUGH GUY- HE STARTED AFTER US, BUT I GUESS WE'VE GIVEN HIM TH' SLIP- IT'S AS MUCH AS YER LIFE'S WORTH TO HAVE A COUPLE O' BUCKS IN THIS TOWN-
Reg. U. S. Pat. Off.; Copyright, 1930, by The Chicago Tribune.
AND THROUGH THE NIGHT, FAR UP-STREAM, BUT, COMING EVER CLOSER, "DADDY" WARBUCKS COMBS EVERY POSSIBLE REFUGE FOR LITTLE ANNIE-
TAKE IT EASY, BOYS- IF THERE'S ANYONE ON THIS LITTLE ISLAND WE DON'T WANT TO MISS 'EM-
HAROLD GRAY
C'MON! I SEEN YER WITH THAT DOUGH- WHERE IS IT? FORK IT OVER QUICK IF YUH KNOW WHAT'S GOOD FOR YUH-
IS THAT ANY WAY TO TALK TO A LITTLE LADY?
AR-R-R-R!!! OUT O' MY WAY, OLD MAN, OR I'LL TAKE YOU APART AN' SCATTER YUH ALL OVER THIS WHARF!!!
GET FOR'ARD, YOU SWAB!
HAROLD GRAY
LEAPIN' LIZARDS! HE WAS TWICE YOUR SIZE- HOW DID YOU EVER DO IT?
IN FORTY YEARS AT SEA, MISS, WE LEARN TO DEAL WITH LUBBERS LIKE THAT- SPIKE MARLIN IS MY NAME, AND AT YOUR SERVICE-
Reg. U. S. Pat. Off.; Copyright, 1930, by The Chicago Tribune.

June 9–11, 1930

AYE, ANNIE- YOU'VE HAD AN EVENTFUL LIFE - THAT YOU HAVE - AND NOW FOR MY STORY, THOUGH IT'S NOT MUCH- FORTY YEARS ON THE SEVEN SEAS - WRECKED ON THE CHINA COAST - FIT WITH PIRATES - BEEN TO EVERY CORNER OF THE WORLD, I HAVE, AND GOIN' AGAIN-

GOT MY OWN LITTLE CRAFT, NOW, AND I'M THE MASTER AND CREW AS WELL- NONE O' THESE NEW-FANGLED AFFAIRS WITH AN ENGINE SMELLIN' TO HEAVEN NEITHER, BUT A TIGHT LITTLE SAILIN' VESSEL, NOT TOO LITTLE AN' NOT TOO BIG-

WHILE SLOWLY, BUT STEADILY, CLOSER AND CLOSER, "DADDY" WARBUCKS APPROACHES THE END OF THE TRAIL-

YES - A LITTLE GIRL WITH A DOG AND A TRAINED BEAR-

YEP- SHE WAS ON THE LEVEE ABOVE HERE WHEN IT WENT OUT- BUT SOME SAY A STEAMER PICKED HER UP- WE DON'T KNOW AS TO THAT-

THAT WAS TEN DAYS AGO- BUT RIVER STEAMERS ARE SLOW AND THERE ARE FEW LANDING PLACES NOW- WE'RE BOUND TO OVERTAKE HER SOON - FASTER, JOE - OPEN UP-

HAROLD GRAY

YESSIR, ANNIE, THIS IS A SOUND LITTLE CRAFT- WITH PROPER HANDLING IT'LL TAKE ONE ANYWHERE IN ANY WEATHER-

AROUND THE WORLD, IF YOU LIKE- BUT WHAT I SAY IS, THIS TOWN IS NO FIT PLACE FOR A YOUNGSTER- I'LL TAKE YOU OUT OF THIS RIVER AND LAND YOU AT SOME PORT WHERE THE BACK COUNTRY ISN'T ALL AWASH AND WHERE YOU CAN GET WORD TO YOUR FRIENDS-

WHILE WARBUCKS, ONLY A NIGHT'S JOURNEY AWAY, RACES DOWN ON THE CITY WHERE HE KNOWS LITTLE ANNIE IS BOUND TO BE-

I'M CERTAIN, NOW, THAT ANNIE HAS COME THROUGH THIS FLOOD ALIVE - SHE MUST HAVE BEEN PICKED UP BY THAT STEAMER-

IF SO WE'LL FIND HER WHEN WE LAND IN THE MORNING - IT'S A BIG CITY, AND MUST BE CROWDED WITH REFUGEES - NO PLACE FOR A CHILD - BUT, ONCE THERE, WE'LL LOCATE HER IN SHORT ORDER-

HAROLD GRAY

AYE, IT'S GREAT TO BE ON THE OPEN WATER WITH A FRESH WIND A-BEAM - AND IT'S A RELIEF TO BE OUT OF THAT DIRTY, SMOKEY, SMELLY CITY - BETTER WHEN IT'S OUT OF SIGHT—

YOU MIGHT GO BELOW, ANNIE, AND HAVE A LOOK AROUND- YOU'LL FIND IT'S A NICE, ROOMY CABIN AND ALL SHIP-SHAPE-

C'MON, SANDY- AN' YOU TOO, WILLIE- WE'LL GO DOWN-STAIRS AN' HAVE A LOOK- GEE- THIS IS JUST LIKE A ROOM IN A HOUSE-

A LITTLE SAIL-BOAT- JUST LEFT THE CITY AND IS PUTTING OUT DOWN THE RIVER TO THE SEA- FUNNY IF ANNIE WERE ABOARD-

WHAT DID YOU MAKE OUT THROUGH THE GLASSES, MR. WARBUCKS? ANY SIGN OF THE LITTLE GIRL OR THE DOG?

NOPE- JUST AN ORDINARY SAIL-BOAT WITH AN OLD CODGER AT THE WHEEL- NO ONE ELSE ABOARD, FAR AS I CAN SEE- WELL, WE'RE ALMOST THERE

HAROLD GRAY

June 12–14, 1930

QUICK, ANNIE- LIE DOWN FLAT AND GRAB HOLD OF A GOOD, STOUT TREE - AND NO MATTER WHAT HAPPENS HANG ON - HERE IT COMES -

CHAPTER THREE

SHIP-WRECKED

IN WHICH ANNIE

FINDS THAT THERE'S WATER, WATER EVERYWHERE

LEARNS MORE WAYS TO PLAY WITH COCONUTS THAN SHE EVER THOUGHT POSSIBLE

AND IS THE OBJECT OF A TIRELESS SEARCH AND RESCUE OPERATION...

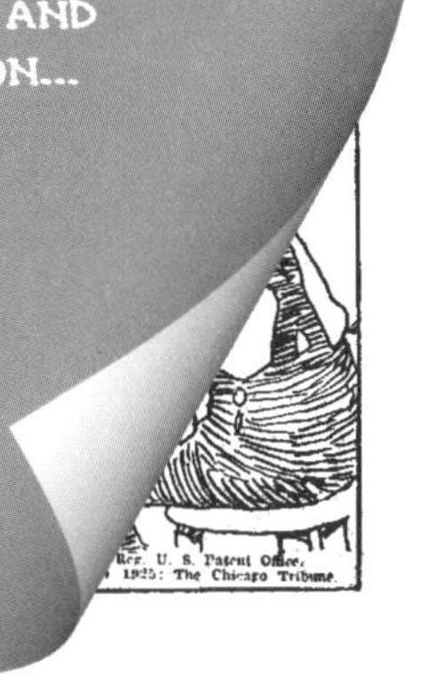

Little Orphan Annie
HAROLD GRAY
YESSIR- FOGS IS BAD, ANNIE- BUT EVEN LINERS HAS TO GO SO SLOW IN THICK WEATHER WE'VE GOT PLENTY O' TIME TO KEEP CLEAR IF WE KEEP A SHARP LOOKOUT-

YOU'LL FIND COFFEE AND BEANS AND ALL THE OTHER TACKLE BELOW IN THE GALLEY-
AYE, AYE, CAP'N MARLIN-

LEAPIN' LIZARDS!!! SOME KITCHEN- STOVE, ICE BOX, DISHES, POTS AN' PANS- ALL IN A LITTLE PLACE NO BIGGER'N A CLOSET- AN' YET IT'S ALL FIGGERED OUT SO SMART THERE'S PLENTY O' ROOM- I'LL SURE SHOW TH' CAP'N WHETHER OR NOT I'M A GOOD COOK- NOW WHERE'S TH' CAN-OPENER?

TALK ABOUT LUCK- THERE WE WERE STUCK IN THAT TOUGH TOWN- NO WAY TO GET OUT- AN' ALONG COMES CAP'N SPIKE MARLIN AN' OFFERS TO TAKE US AWAY ON HIS BOAT FOR NOTHIN'- HE'S SURE A SWELL OLD GUY-

HEY, CAP'N- DINNER'S READY- BUT YUH'LL HAVE TO COME AN' GET IT- I'LL BREAK MY NECK IF I TRY TO CARRY IT UP THERE ON DECK-

AYE, ANNIE- YOU'RE AN ABLE HAND WITH VICTUALS, AND NO MISTAKE- I THINK I'LL APPOINT YOU FIRST MATE O' THIS 'ERE VESSEL-

YOU'RE A BRIGHT 'UN- A LITTLE PRACTICE AND YOU CAN STEER AS GOOD AS ANY IN FAIR WEATHER-

HAVING YOU ABOARD WILL BE A BIG HELP- IT'S SHORT-HANDED I'VE BEEN ALL ALONE ON MANY A VOYAGE, AND LONESOME AS SIN, TOO-

IF YOU'D DECIDE TO STAY YOU'D LEARN TO LIKE THE SEA- BUT I'LL LAY TO MY BARGAIN- THAT I WILL-

THAT TOWN WHERE I FOUND YOU WAS NO RIGHT PLACE FOR A YOUNG UN- COULDN'T LEAVE YOU THERE- IT WASN'T FITTIN'-

SO I PROMISED TO TAKE YOU TO SOME PORT WHERE THE BACK COUNTRY WASN'T ALL A-WASH- A PLACE AS HAD DRY LAND 'ROUND IT-

WHERE YOU COULD GO AN' COME AS YOU PLEASED AND GET WORD TO YOUR FRIENDS- THAT WAS MY PROMISE AND OLD SPIKE MARLIN NEVER WENT BACK ON HIS WORD-

BUT WHAT FINER LIFE THAN THE OPEN SEA IN A SOUND CRAFT? NO DIRTY CITIES FOR OLD SPIKE MARLIN, OR FOR A GRAND-DAUGHTER O' MINE, IF I HAD ONE- BUT, THINK IT OVER-

June 15, 1930

THIS SURE IS A SOFT LIFE- A SNUG LITTLE HOME- TH' WHOLE OCEAN FOR A FRONT YARD- AND NO GRASS TO CUT-
AYE, ANNIE- PLENTY OF PROVISIONS- A TIGHT LITTLE CRAFT- A FAIR BREEZE AND A SUMMER SEA- THAT'S AS NEAR TO HEAVEN AS I EVER HOPE TO GET- WHO COULD ASK FOR MORE?
WHILE WARBUCKS COMBS THE WATERFRONT IN A FRANTIC EFFORT TO LOCATE LITTLE ANNIE-
SHE'S BEEN SEEN HERE- I'VE FOUND OUT THAT MUCH- BUT WHERE IS SHE NOW?
Reg. U. S. Pat. Off.; Copyright, 1930, by The Chicago Tribune.
WHEW- WHAT A DIVE- SOME ONE ON THIS WATER-FRONT MUST KNOW WHERE SHE IS- BUT HOW CAN I MAKE THEM TALK? THAT'S THE QUESTION-
HAROLD GRAY
GEE- I SURE FEEL LAZY- JUST LOOK AT ALL THOSE FUNNY LOOKIN' FISH WAY DOWN THERE- I NEVER KNEW THERE WERE SO MANY COLORS- YUH CAN SEE DOWN HUNDREDS O' FEET, TH' WATER'S SO CLEAR-
WHILE "DADDY" AT LAST PICKS UP ANNIE'S TRAIL ONCE MORE-
THIS GENT WILL PAY A HUNDRED DOLLARS TO ANY BIRD WHO TELLS HIM WHERE TH' RED-HEADED KID WENT- AND NO QUESTIONS ASKED-
YEAH, I SEEN HER, ALL RIGHT- WAS JUST PASSIN' TH' TIME O' DAY WIT' HER WHEN THIS GANG ATTACKS ME- PIRATES THEY WAS, I'LL BE BOUND- SEE WOT THEY DONE TO ME? A WHOLE GANG OF 'EM- AND THEY TOOK TH' KID WITH 'EM- WENT ON A SAILIN' BOAT-
HAROLD GRAY
HM-M-M- OF COURSE MOST OF HIS YARN IS THE BUNK- BUT I CAN BELIEVE PART OF IT- BY GEORGE- I'LL BET SHE WAS ON THAT VERY SAIL BOAT THAT I SAW GOING OUT TO SEA AS WE LANDED HERE-
Reg. U. S. Pat. Off.; Copyright, 1930, by The Chicago Tribune.
GEE- THIS SURE IS THE LIFE- WOULDN'T "DADDY" WARBUCKS BE S'PRISED IF HE KNEW I COULD SAIL A BOAT LIKE THIS?
ONCE MORE ON ANNIE'S TRAIL WARBUCKS LOSES NO TIME IN TAKING UP THE PURSUIT-
THERE SHE IS, MR. WARBUCKS- YOU'LL FIND HER THE FASTEST CRAFT OF HER SIZE AFLOAT-
I'M LUCKY TO FIND THIS YACHT FOR SALE- NOW LET'S HAVE A LOOK AT THE ENGINES- IF ALL IS O. K. I'LL TAKE HER AND BE OFF AT ONCE-
HERE'S MY CHECK, CAPTAIN- SEND THIS TO YOUR OWNER- FROM NOW ON YOU AND THE CREW ARE WORKING FOR ME- SEE THAT WE ARE READY TO SAIL BY DAY-LIGHT TOMORROW MORNING-
YES SIR, MR. WARBUCKS
HAROLD GRAY
Reg. U. S. Pat. Off.; Copyright, 1930, by The Chicago Tribune.

June 16–18, 1930

HM-M-M--- AYE - IT'S FINE WEATHER - TOO FINE, IF YOU ASK ME - IT CAN'T LAST - THERE'S FOUL WEATHER AHEAD - MARK MY WORDS -
IS THERE ANY DANGER?
DANGER? HO! HO! NOT IN A SOUND CRAFT LIKE THIS - WHY, WE COULD RIDE OUT THE WORST TYPHOON ANY SAILOR-MAN EVER HEARD TELL OF - YES SIR-E-E - WHY, I CAN REMEMBER ONE VOYAGE IN THE CHINA SEA---------
WHILE FIVE DAYS AFTER ANNIE'S DEPARTURE WARBUCKS SETS FORTH IN HIS FAST YACHT TO COMB THE SEAS FOR HER -
BUT HOW DO WE KNOW WHICH WAY SHE WILL GO?
WE DON'T - BUT WE CAN MAKE A CLOSE GUESS -
WE KNOW THE WINDS AND CURRENTS - IF I'M NOT MISTAKEN THAT SAIL-BOAT WILL TAKE THE EASIEST WAY - WE'LL FOLLOW THAT COURSE - WE'RE ONLY FIVE DAYS BEHIND - WITH OUR SPEED WE SHOULD OVERTAKE THEM IN A COUPLE OF DAYS AT MOST -
HAROLD GRAY
Reg. U. S. Pat. Off.; Copyright, 1930, by The Chicago Tribune.
NOT A BREATH OF AIR - AND THE BAROMETER IS FALLING A MILE A MINUTE - THERE'S A BIG STORM ON THE WAY SURE -
BUT NO USE WORRYING - IF IT'S COMING, IT'S COMING, AND FRETTING CAN'T STOP IT - LET IT COME - I NEVER YET SAW THE STORM I COULDN'T LICK -
GEE - WE HAVEN'T MOVED AN INCH ALL DAY - SAY - LOOK - THERE'S A LITTLE CLOUD OVER THERE -
AYE - THAT'S A STORM CLOUD, AND NO MISTAKE - IT'LL BE AN HOUR OR MORE BEFORE IT GETS HERE - WE'D BETTER BE GETTIN' TH' CANVAS IN - IF I'M NOT MISTAKEN WE'RE IN FOR A BLOW -
Reg. U. S. Pat. Off.; Copyright, 1930, by The Chicago Tribune.
WHILE CLOSER AND CLOSER-------
NOT A BREATH OF AIR - THAT SAIL-BOAT MUST BE BECALMED - IF WE CAN ONLY REACH IT BEFORE THE STORM HITS -
HAROLD GRAY
I PUT SANDY AN' WILLIE DOWN IN TH' CABIN AND SHUT TH' HATCH - WHAT DO YUH WANT ME TO DO?
GOOD - THEY'LL BE SAFE DOWN THERE - YOU'D BE BETTER OFF THERE, TOO - BUT IT'S TOO LATE TO TRY TO GET THERE NOW - HANG ON!
A TYPHOON - IN FORTY YEARS AT SEA I'VE NEVER SEEN IT WORSE - MANY A GALLANT SHIP WILL FOUNDER THIS DAY - BUT WE'LL RIDE THIS OUT - I'VE NEVER LOST A CRAFT YET -
WHILE ALMOST WITHIN SIGHT OF THE LITTLE SAIL-BOAT, THE GREAT YACHT FEELS THE FURY OF THE STORM -
HAROLD GRAY
NO LITTLE SAIL-BOAT COULD LAST FIVE MINUTES IN THIS SEA, MR. WARBUCKS - SHALL WE TURN FOR PORT AND RUN FOR IT?
NONSENSE, YOU LUBBER - AND LEAVE HER TO DROWN? NO! ANNIE'D NEVER GIVE UP LIKE THAT - AND I'LL NOT QUIT HER - FULL SPEED AHEAD -
Reg. U. S. Pat. Off.; Copyright, 1930, by The Chicago Tribune.

June 19–21, 1930

Little Orphan Annie
HAROLD GRAY
LISTEN - IT'S GOIN' TO BLOW SOMETHIN' FIERCE - YOU GUYS BETTER GO BELOW - THAT'S THE CAP'N'S ORDERS -
LEAPIN' LIZARDS! ARE WE GOIN' TO SINK?
WELL, NOW, ANNIE, YOU'VE GOT ME THERE - WE'VE GOT A SOUND LITTLE CRAFT -
BUT, MAN AND BOY, I'VE SAILED THE SEAS FOR FIFTY YEARS AND NEVER SEEN A WORSE STORM - NO SIR - NOT EVEN IN THE CHINA SEA -
GREAT CAESAR'S SUSPENDERS! A SHARK!!! AND HE'S LOOKIN' RIGHT AT ME!
CAP'N - THERE'S A LOT O' SHARKS ALL AROUND US - GREAT BIG MEAN LOOKIN' ONES - WHAT ARE THEY FOLLOWIN' US FOR?
WELL, I RECKON THEY'RE BETTIN' WE WON'T RIDE OUT THIS GALE - BUT WE'LL FOOL 'EM, IF IT DOESN'T GET ANY WORSE'N THIS -
LOOK AT TH' BAROMETER CAP'N - IT LOOKS AWFUL FUNNY -
AYE, AYE - IT'S DROPPED TO NOTHIN' AT ALL - THAT MEANS WE'RE IN FOR IT NOW AND NO MISTAKE -
OW!!! WHAT'S THAT BIG BLACK CLOUD? IT'S COMIN' RIGHT FOR US -
OH! OH! IT'S GETTIN' DARK -
HANG ON, ANNIE! IT'S A TYPHOON!
HELP ME HOLD THE WHEEL, ANNIE -
AYE-AYE, CAP'N -
WE'RE ON THE ROCKS!
NO! WE'VE MISSED 'EM SO FAR -
IT MUST HAVE BEEN A REEF - WE'RE OVER IT WITHOUT A SCRATCH -
BUT WE'VE LOST OUR MAST AND RIGGING - WE'RE HELPLESS.
WELL, WE'RE STILL FLOATIN' - AND TH' STORM CAN'T GET ANY WORSE -

June 22, 1930
SHIPWRECKED

MAST AND RIGGING GONE- OUR RUDDER CARRIED AWAY- WE'RE AT THE MERCY OF THE SEA, ANNIE-
BUT DON'T YOU BE SKEERED, ANNIE- OLD SPIKE MARLIN'S NEVER LET THE SEA BLUFF HIM YET- COURSE WE MAY GO DOWN- BUT THEN AGIN, WE AIN'T SUNK YET- THAT'S SOMETHIN', AIN'T IT?
WHILE, NOW VERY NEAR, INDEED, BUT HIDDEN BY THE ALL-OBSCURING STORM, "DADDY" WARBUCKS FORGES DOGGEDLY EVER CLOSER-
I TELL YOU, MR. WARBUCKS, IT'S NO USE- NO SAILING BOAT COULD POSSIBLY BE AFLOAT ANY LONGER IN THIS STORM-
WHY, IT'S ALL WE CAN DO TO KEEP THIS MODERN VESSEL AFLOAT- OUR FORE-HOLD IS LEAKING BADLY.....
WHAT OF IT? LET IT LEAK- GOT PUMPS, HAVEN'T WE? USE 'EM- I'M NOT QUITTING TILL WE FIND HER- GET THAT THROUGH YOUR THICK HEAD-
HAROLD GRAY
Reg. U. S. Pat. Off.; Copyright, 1930, by The Chicago Tribune.
BREAKERS! WITH OUR MAST AND RUDDER GONE WE HAVEN'T A CHANCE TO KEEP CLEAR OF THOSE ROCKS!
WOW!
HANG ON, ANNIE! HANG ON!
WHILE LESS THAN A MILE BEHIND, IN THE BLINDING STORM, WITH GIANT MOTORS STRAINING AT TOPMOST SPEED, THE POWERFUL YACHT SWERVES TO AVOID THE MURDEROUS SHOALS-
HAROLD GRAY
EVEN WITH OUR POWERFUL MOTORS IT'S A MIRACLE WE EVER AVOIDED THAT ROCKY REEF- NO TELLING WHERE WE ARE- OUR CHARTS ARE USELESS IN THIS STORM-
OF COURSE I'M AN OLD FOOL- BUT SOMEHOW I FEEL ANNIE IS VERY NEAR-
Reg. U. S. Pat. Off.; Copyright, 1930, by The Chicago Tribune.
GEE- YUH'D NEVER KNOW THERE'D BEEN A STORM IN HERE.
NO SIR- PEACEFUL AS A LITTLE POND- THAT REEF WE SCRAPED OVER KEEPS THE BREAKERS OUT OF THIS LITTLE HARBOR-
WHEE! TH' WATER'S JUST AS WARM- C'MON, YOU GUYS- HAVEN'T YOU HAD ENOUGH BOAT RIDIN' FOR A WHILE?
LEAPIN' LIZARDS!!! DIDJA EVER SEE TREES SO GREEN? WONDER WHERE TH' NEAREST TOWN IS-
I CALCULATE THIS IS AN ISLAND- MAYBE THERE'S FOLKS ON IT AND THEN AGAIN MAYBE THERE AIN'T- BUT WE'LL CRUISE AROUND AND SEE WHAT'S WHAT-
WHILE FAR AWAY, AND EVER FARTHER, "DADDY" COMBS THE STILL RESTLESS, BUT EMPTY SEA-
NOT A SIGN OF HER- NOT A SAIL- NOT EVEN A BIT OF FLOATING WRECKAGE- NOTHING- BUT WE'LL KEEP LOOKING-
HAROLD GRAY
Reg. U. S. Pat. Off.; Copyright, 1930, by The Chicago Tribune.

June 23–25, 1930

GEE, IT SURE IS QUIET HERE, AND PRETTY, TOO, WITH ALL THESE PALM TREES- LIKE PITCHERS YUH SEE IN TH MOVIES -
WELL, I'LL BE A SARDINE! WE ARE ON AN ISLAND - WATER FAR AS YUH CAN SEE-
RIGHT YOU ARE, ANNIE - A TROPICAL ISLAND AND NOT ANOTHER SOUL ON IT SO FAR AS I CAN MAKE OUT- NO SIGN OF A HOUSE OR TENT-
SEE ANYTHING, CAP'N? ANY LAND ANYWHERE, OR A SHIP, MAYBE?
NOPE- JUST WATER, FAR AS I CAN SEE- NOT A SAIL OR EVEN A BIT OF SMOKE- GUESS WE'RE STUCK HERE FOR A SPELL-
WHILE ONLY A LITTLE BEYOND THE RANGE OF OLD SPIKE MARLIN'S SPY-GLASS "DADDY'S" YACHT GOES ON THE AIMLESS QUEST, FARTHER AND FARTHER AWAY-
HAROLD GRAY
Reg. U. S. Pat. Off.; Copyright, 1930, by The Chicago Tribune.
THAT REEF SURE DID PLAY THE OLD NED WITH OUR VESSEL - LUCKY WE WERE DRIVING SO FAST OR WE'D NEVER HAVE MADE SHALLOW WATER-
BUT SHE'S A SOUND VESSEL YET- A FEW PLANKS AND SHE'LL BE TIGHT AS EVER- WE HAVE TOOLS- WHY, I COULD MAKE PLANKS TO DO THE BUSINESS OUT OF TREES ON THIS ISLAND- I COULD BUILD A WHOLE BOAT COMPLETE IF I HAD TO-
YES SIR, ANNIE- THERE'S MIGHTY FEW THINGS SPIKE MARLIN CAN'T DO- I REMEMBER ONE TIME I WAS ON A BIG OLD WINDJAMMER ------
LISTEN TO HIM- OLD WINDJAMMER IS RIGHT!
DOWN-HEARTED, AND ALMOST DISCOURAGED, POOR "DADDY" WARBUCKS FIGHTS OFF THE SPECTRE OF DESPAIR-
OF COURSE SHE IS SAFE- BUT HOW COULD A SAIL BOAT EVER LAST OUT SUCH A TERRIFIC STORM?
HAROLD GRAY
Reg. U. S. Pat. Off.; Copyright, 1930, by The Chicago Tribune.
NOPE-NOTHING BUT WATER- IT'S PLAIN ENOUGH THIS ISLAND IS FAR OFF THE BEATEN PATH, AS YOU MIGHT SAY- BUT SOME CRAFT MUST PASS HERE BEFORE MANY DAYS-
BUT IF THEY DO PASS HOW WILL THEY KNOW WE'RE HERE?
THAT'S SO, ANNIE- WE MUST HOIST A DISTRESS SIGNAL ON THAT HILL WHERE IT CAN BE SEEN FOR MILES OUT TO SEA- AND WE CAN KEEP A GOOD BRIGHT FIRE GOIN' NIGHTS-
AT LAST "DADDY" IS FORCED TO REALIZE THAT SOMEHOW, SOMEWHERE, HE HAS MISSED CONNECTION WITH LITTLE ANNIE- STILL HE WILL NOT GIVE UP-
THE CAPTAIN'S RIGHT- THE YACHT IS BADLY CRIPPLED- WE MUST PUT IN FOR REPAIRS-
ALL RIGHT, CAPTAIN- PUT INTO THE NEAREST PORT WHERE WE CAN MAKE REPAIRS- AND WHILE YOU'RE AT THAT I WILL SCOUR THE COAST- SHE MAY HAVE LANDED- I'LL NOT BELIEVE SHE CAN BE LOST FOREVER-
YES SIR-
HAROLD GRAY
Reg. U. S. Pat. Off.; Copyright, 1930, by The Chicago Tribune.

June 26–28, 1930

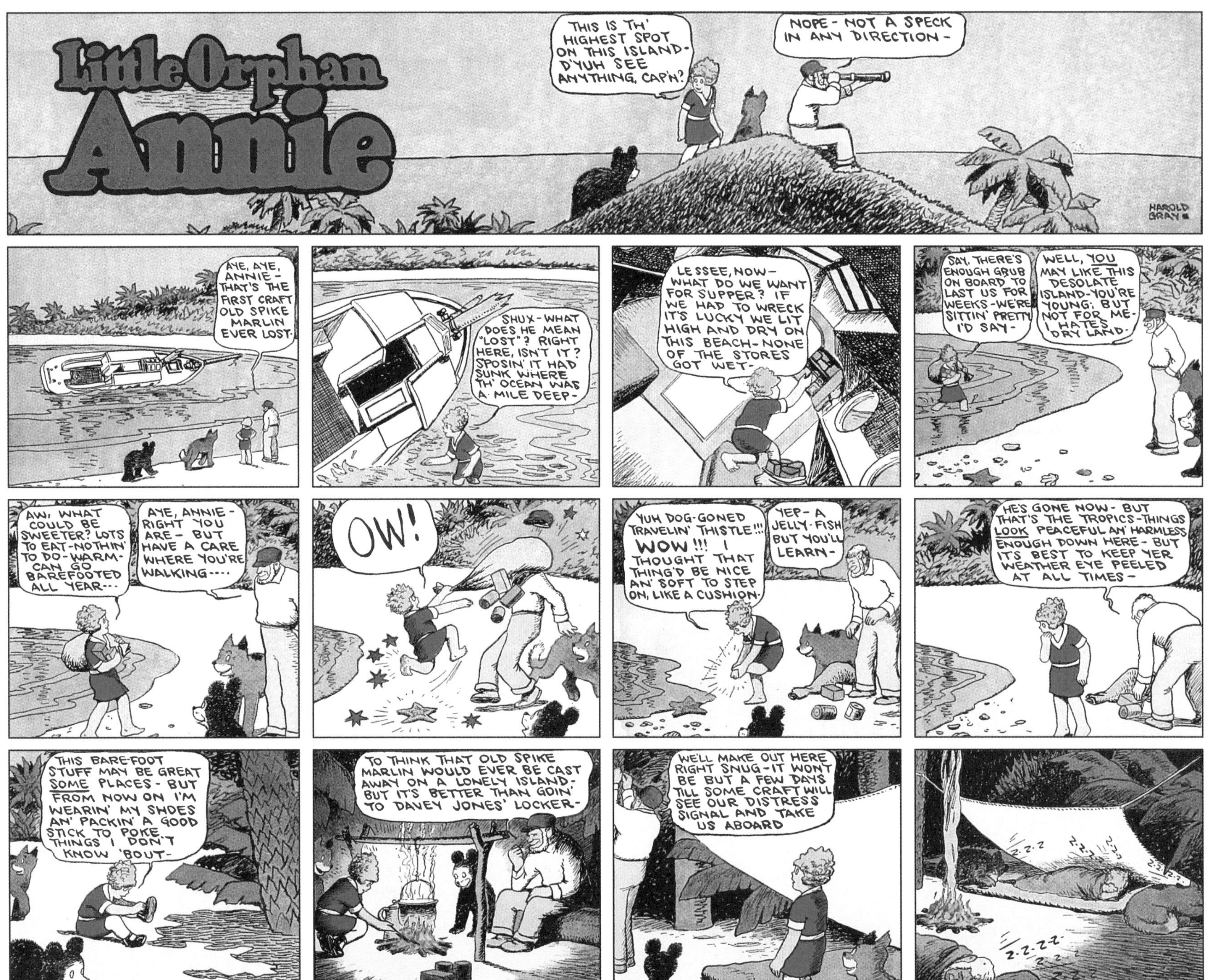
Little Orphan Annie
THIS IS TH' HIGHEST SPOT ON THIS ISLAND- D'YUH SEE ANYTHING, CAP'N?
NOPE - NOT A SPECK IN ANY DIRECTION -
HAROLD GRAY
AYE, AYE, ANNIE - THAT'S THE FIRST CRAFT OLD SPIKE MARLIN EVER LOST.
SHUX - WHAT DOES HE MEAN "LOST"? RIGHT HERE, ISN'T IT? SPOSIN' IT HAD SUNK WHERE TH' OCEAN WAS A MILE DEEP-
LESSEE, NOW - WHAT DO WE WANT FOR SUPPER? IF WE HAD TO WRECK IT'S LUCKY WE LIT HIGH AND DRY ON THIS BEACH - NONE OF THE STORES GOT WET-
SAY, THERE'S ENOUGH GRUB ON BOARD TO LAST US FOR WEEKS - WE'RE SITTIN' PRETTY I'D SAY-
WELL, YOU MAY LIKE THIS DESOLATE ISLAND - YOU'RE YOUNG; BUT NOT FOR ME - I HATES DRY LAND-
AW, WHAT COULD BE SWEETER? LOTS TO EAT - NOTHIN' TO DO - WARM - CAN GO BAREFOOTED ALL YEAR---
AYE, ANNIE - RIGHT YOU ARE - BUT HAVE A CARE WHERE YOU'RE WALKING----
OW!
YUH DOG-GONED TRAVELIN' THISTLE!!! WOW!!! I THOUGHT THAT THING'D BE NICE AN' SOFT TO STEP ON, LIKE A CUSHION.
YEP - A JELLY-FISH BUT YOU'LL LEARN-
HE'S GONE NOW - BUT THAT'S THE TROPICS - THINGS LOOK PEACEFUL AN' HARMLESS ENOUGH DOWN HERE - BUT IT'S BEST TO KEEP YER WEATHER EYE PEELED AT ALL TIMES -
THIS BARE-FOOT STUFF MAY BE GREAT SOME PLACES - BUT FROM NOW ON I'M WEARIN' MY SHOES AN' PACKIN' A GOOD STICK TO POKE THINGS I DON'T KNOW 'BOUT-
TO THINK THAT OLD SPIKE MARLIN WOULD EVER BE CAST AWAY ON A LONELY ISLAND - BUT IT'S BETTER THAN GOIN' TO DAVEY JONES' LOCKER-
WE'LL MAKE OUT HERE RIGHT SNUG - IT WON'T BE BUT A FEW DAYS TILL SOME CRAFT WILL SEE OUR DISTRESS SIGNAL AND TAKE US ABOARD
Z-Z-Z
Z-Z-Z-Z-

June 29, 1930
SHIPWRECKED

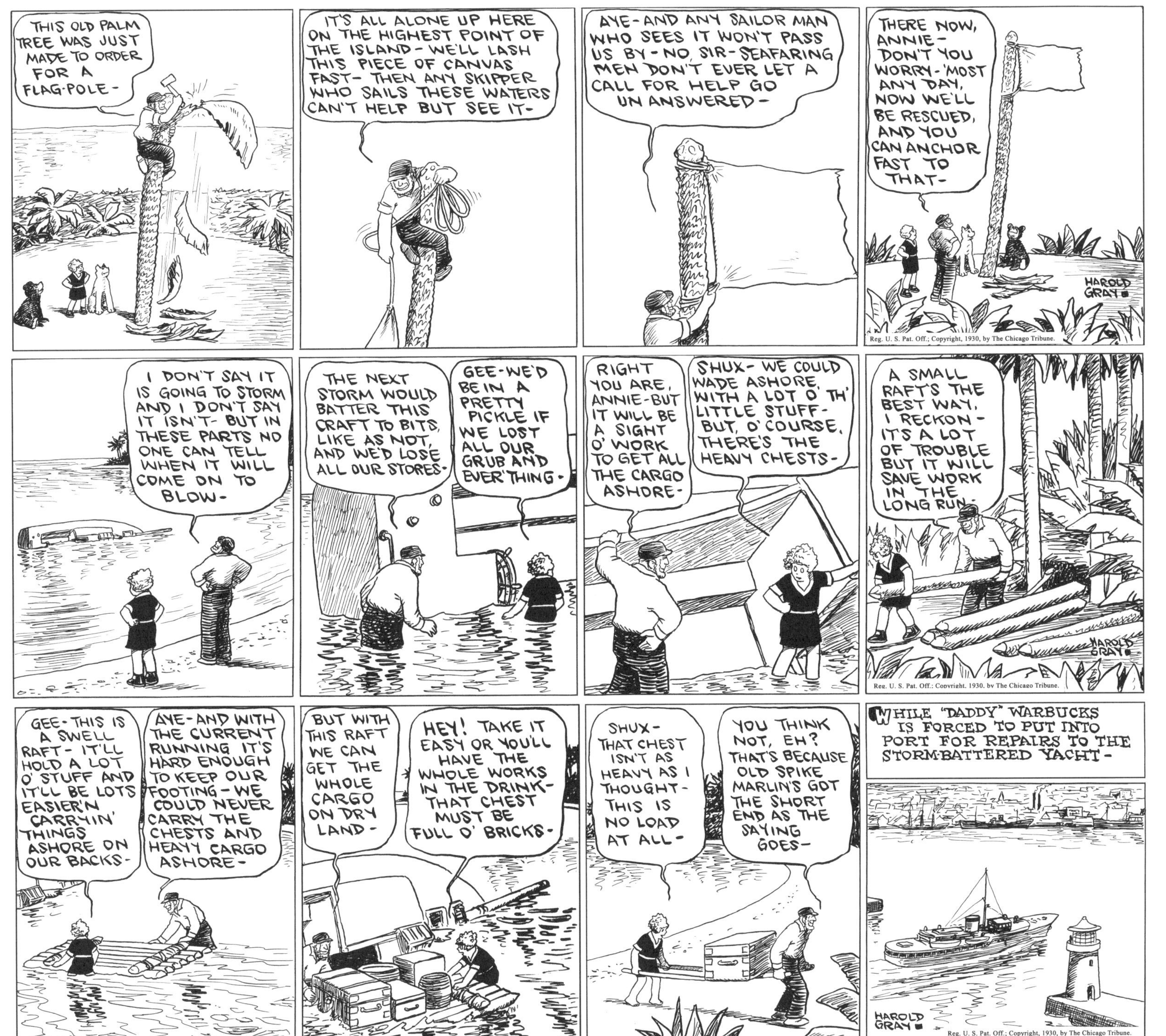
THIS OLD PALM TREE WAS JUST MADE TO ORDER FOR A FLAG-POLE-
IT'S ALL ALONE UP HERE ON THE HIGHEST POINT OF THE ISLAND - WE'LL LASH THIS PIECE OF CANVAS FAST- THEN ANY SKIPPER WHO SAILS THESE WATERS CAN'T HELP BUT SEE IT-
AYE- AND ANY SAILOR MAN WHO SEES IT WON'T PASS US BY - NO, SIR - SEAFARING MEN DON'T EVER LET A CALL FOR HELP GO UNANSWERED -
THERE NOW, ANNIE - DON'T YOU WORRY- 'MOST ANY DAY, NOW WE'LL BE RESCUED, AND YOU CAN ANCHOR FAST TO THAT-
HAROLD GRAY
Reg. U. S. Pat. Off.; Copyright, 1930, by The Chicago Tribune.
I DON'T SAY IT IS GOING TO STORM AND I DON'T SAY IT ISN'T- BUT IN THESE PARTS NO ONE CAN TELL WHEN IT WILL COME ON TO BLOW-
THE NEXT STORM WOULD BATTER THIS CRAFT TO BITS, LIKE AS NOT, AND WE'D LOSE ALL OUR STORES-
GEE- WE'D BE IN A PRETTY PICKLE IF WE LOST ALL OUR GRUB AND EVER'THING-
RIGHT YOU ARE, ANNIE- BUT IT WILL BE A SIGHT O' WORK TO GET ALL THE CARGO ASHORE-
SHUX- WE COULD WADE ASHORE WITH A LOT O' TH' LITTLE STUFF- BUT, O' COURSE, THERE'S THE HEAVY CHESTS-
A SMALL RAFT'S THE BEST WAY, I RECKON- IT'S A LOT OF TROUBLE BUT IT WILL SAVE WORK IN THE LONG RUN-
HAROLD GRAY
Reg. U. S. Pat. Off.; Copyright, 1930, by The Chicago Tribune.
GEE- THIS IS A SWELL RAFT- IT'LL HOLD A LOT O' STUFF AND IT'LL BE LOTS EASIER'N CARRYIN' THINGS ASHORE ON OUR BACKS-
AYE- AND WITH THE CURRENT RUNNING IT'S HARD ENOUGH TO KEEP OUR FOOTING- WE COULD NEVER CARRY THE CHESTS AND HEAVY CARGO ASHORE-
BUT WITH THIS RAFT WE CAN GET THE WHOLE CARGO ON DRY LAND-
HEY! TAKE IT EASY OR YOU'LL HAVE THE WHOLE WORKS IN THE DRINK- THAT CHEST MUST BE FULL O' BRICKS-
SHUX- THAT CHEST ISN'T AS HEAVY AS I THOUGHT- THIS IS NO LOAD AT ALL-
YOU THINK NOT, EH? THAT'S BECAUSE OLD SPIKE MARLIN'S GOT THE SHORT END AS THE SAYING GOES-
WHILE "DADDY" WARBUCKS IS FORCED TO PUT INTO PORT FOR REPAIRS TO THE STORM-BATTERED YACHT-
HAROLD GRAY
Reg. U. S. Pat. Off.; Copyright, 1930, by The Chicago Tribune.

June 30–
July 2, 1930

LEAPIN' LIZARDS! THIS IS ABOUT TH' TENTH LOAD WE'VE TAKEN ASHORE-
AYE-AYE-ANNIE- AND THERE'S PLENTY MORE TO GO ASHORE IF THE WEATHER HOLDS FAIR LONG ENOUGH-
GEE- I NEVER KNEW A LITTLE BOAT LIKE THAT COULD HOLD SO MUCH STUFF-
SEA FARING FOLK LEARN TO STOW AWAY A LOT IN A LITTLE SPACE- EVERY INCH COUNTS ABOARD SHIP-
ASHORE WARBUCKS PREPARES TO CARRY ON, IN SPITE OF BAD NEWS-
THE YACHT WILL REQUIRE TEN DAYS IN DRY-DOCK AT THE VERY LEAST, MR. WARBUCKS-
VERY WELL, CAPTAIN- BUT HURRY REPAIRS ALL YOU CAN-
TO THE HOTEL- THE MEN I SENT FOR SHOULD BE THERE BY NOW- I HAVE A THOUSAND THINGS TO DO AS SOON AS POSSIBLE- NO TELLING WHAT A FEW MINUTES' DELAY MAY MEAN-
HAROLD GRAY
Reg. U. S. Pat. Off.; Copyright, 1930, by The Chicago Tribune.
FUNNY- I'VE LOST ALL TRACK O' WHAT DATE THIS IS- NOW LET'S SEE- WE STARTED OUT IN TH' BOAT ON A SATURDAY- I CAN REMEMBER THAT- BUT WHAT DAY OF THE MONTH?
HM-M-M- THAT WAS JUNE 14TH- I REMEMBER THAT-
THEN JUST A WEEK LATER TH' STORM HIT US- THAT LASTED THREE DAYS- AND WE'VE BEEN HERE- ---LET'S SEE--- WHY, THIS MUST BE- YES--- IT IS- IT'S THE FOURTH OF JULY!!!
WELL, I'LL BE A FLOUNDER- SO IT IS-
BUT DATES MEAN NOTHING TO WARBUCKS IN HIS RELENTLESS SEARCH FOR LITTLE ANNIE-
YOUR JOB IS TO SCATTER UP AND DOWN THE COAST- SHE MUST HAVE COME ASHORE AT SOME POINT- THERE'LL BE A FORTUNE FOR THE ONE OF YOU WHO FINDS HER- GET BUSY-
NOW WE'LL HAVE OUR OWN BROADCASTING STATION WORKING IN A FEW DAYS- IN THE MEANTIME I'VE ARRANGED FOR TIME ON THE AIR EVERY DAY AND NIGHT- YOU'RE IN CHARGE OF THE RADIO END OF THIS SEARCH- GO TO IT-
HAROLD GRAY
Reg. U. S. Pat. Off.; Copyright, 1930, by The Chicago Tribune.
IT SEEMS TO ME IT'S TAKIN' US A DOG-GONED LONG TIME TO GET RESCUED- DON'T ANY SHIPS EVER GO BY HERE? WE'VE BEEN HERE TEN DAYS ALREADY-
WE'RE SITTIN' PRETTY, IN A WAY- PLENTY TO EAT- ALL TH' STUFF OUT O' TH' BOAT SAFE ON SHORE- EVEN IF A BIG STORM CAME ALONG NOW WE'D BE O. K. S'POSE WE'VE GOT A LOT TO BE THANKFUL FOR-
STILL, I DON'T WANT TO STAY ON THIS ISLAND TH' REST O' MY LIFE- WONDER IF THERE'S ANY WILD ANIMALS HERE- LEAPIN' LIZARDS!!! I NEVER THOUGHT O' THAT BEFORE-
WHILE, AT HIS NEWLY-ESTABLISHED HEADQUARTERS, WARBUCKS HOPEFULLY AWAITS WORD OF ANNIE FROM HIS ARMY OF SEARCHERS-
THE WHOLE COAST-LINE IS BEING GONE OVER WITH A FINE TOOTH COMB- WHY, EVEN A PIECE OF SEA-WEED COULDN'T HAVE BEEN WASHED ASHORE WITHOUT SOME OF MY MEN KNOWING IT BY NOW- I'M BOUND TO HAVE WORD OF ANNIE SOON-
HAROLD GRAY
Reg. U. S. Pat. Off.; Copyright, 1930, by The Chicago Tribune.

July 3–5, 1930

Little Orphan Annie
HEY, CAP'N- YUH WANTED TURTLE SOUP, DIDN'T YUH? WELL, THEN, GRAB THIS ROPE AND HELP A BIT-
HAROLD GRAY

GEE WHIZ! WE'VE BEEN STUCK ON THIS ISLAND FOR OVER A WEEK AND HAVEN'T SEEN A BOAT OR EVEN A LITTLE SMOKE WAY OFF OR NOTHIN'-

IT'S JUST A LITTLE ISLAND AND THERE DOESN'T SEEM TO BE ANYBODY HERE BUT US- STILL, YUH'D THINK A BOAT WOULD GO BY HERE SOME TIME-

BUT NO-BODY EVER SEEMS TO PASS THIS WAY- HM-M-M- NOW I WONDER WHAT SANDY'S FOUND- I'D BETTER GO OVER AND HAVE A LOOK-

JUST AN OLD EMPTY BOTTLE- STILL, THAT'S SORTA FUNNY- WE HAVEN'T THROWN AWAY ANY BOTTLES LIKE THAT- WHERE COULD IT HAVE COME FROM-

IT'S CORKED UP TIGHT- IT MIGHT HAVE FLOATED A LONG, LONG WAY- I'VE HEARD O' BOTTLES FLOATIN' FOR THOUSANDS O' MILES-

WE'LL SHOW THIS TO OLD CAP'N MARLIN- MAYBE HE CAN TELL US WHERE IT MIGHT HAVE COME FROM- HE'S A PRETTY SMART BIRD-

IT'S NOT SO MUCH WHERE IT'S FLOATED FROM, BUT WHERE WOULD IT BE LIKELY TO FLOAT TO-
GEE- THAT'S RIGHT, TOO- I NEVER THOUGHT O' THAT- WHERE WOULD IT FLOAT TO?

I'LL PUT DOWN OUR BEARIN'S SO'S ANY SEA-FARIN' MAN WILL KNOW WHERE TO LOOK FOR US- AND OUR NAMES AND A BIT MORE-
GEE- THEN IF SOMEBODY FINDS THAT LETTER IN TH' BOTTLE THEY'LL COME AND GET US-

RIGHT YOU ARE, ANNIE- IF THEY FIND THIS BOTTLE- AND WHEN THEY FIND IT- BUT HOW LONG IT'LL BE BEFORE IT'S PICKED UP THERE'S NO TELLIN'-
BUT SOMEBODY'S ALMOST SURE TO FIND IT SOME TIME AREN'T THEY?

AYE- SOME TIME- BUT THERE'S CASES ON RECORD O' SUCH MESSAGES BEIN' FOUND TWENTY YEARS AND MORE AFTER THEY WERE SENT- WE'LL HOPE THIS ONE MAKES A FASTER JOURNEY- NOW THERE'S A CURRENT OFF THIS POINT SETS IN FOR THE MAINLAND, I FIGGER-

SO THERE GOES OUR LITTLE MESSENGER, ALL CORKED TIGHT AND SHIP-SHAPE- WATCH IT CLOSE NOW, ANNIE-

CAN YOU MAKE IT OUT? IS IT HOLDING THE PROPER COURSE?
AYE, AYE, CAP'N- I SEE IT- AND IT SURE IS GOIN' JUST TH' WAY YOU SAID IT WOULD- SEE IT, SANDY?
ARF!

July 6, 1930

YESSIR, ANNIE - SOMEBODY'S CERTAIN SURE TO PICK UP THAT MESSAGE OF OURS SOON - I WROTE IT CLEAR AND I SEALED THE CORK IN THE BOTTLE SO IT WON'T GET SPOILED -
AN' TH' CURRENT CARRIED IT AWAY FROM THE ISLAND -
NARY A SAIL OR A BIT OF SMOKE SO FAR AS I CAN SEE - WELL, I RECKON IT'S A BIT TOO SOON TO EXPECT AN ANSWER TO THAT BOTTLED MESSAGE -
GEE - I S'POSE IT MIGHT BE A LONG TIME 'FORE ANYBODY FINDS IT -
IS IT TRUE THAT BOTTLES WITH MESSAGES IN 'EM HAVE BEEN KNOWN TO FLOAT FOR YEARS 'FORE THEY WERE FOUND?
AYE - FOR MANY YEARS - TILL LONG AFTER THE FOLKS AS WROTE THE MESSAGES HAD PASSED ON AND BEEN FORGOTTEN - BUT WE'LL HOPE FOR BETTER LUCK -
MEANWHILE THE FRAGILE BOTTLE, WITH ITS PRECIOUS CARGO, BOBS UP AND DOWN, UP AND DOWN, ON THE RESTLESS SURFACE OF THE VAST AND LONELY SEA -
HAROLD GRAY
Reg. U. S. Pat. Off.; Copyright, 1930, by The Chicago Tribune.
THIS CAN'T BE A VERY BIG ISLAND - WE CAN SEE IT ALL FROM TH' TOP OF THE HILL -
AYE - I GRANT WE CAN SEE THE WHOLE ISLAND FROM THERE - BUT ALL WE SEE IS THE TOPS OF THE TREES. WHAT I AIM TO EXPLORE IS WHAT'S UNDER THOSE TREES -
MIGHT BE WILD ANIMALS OR EVEN CANNIBALS ON THIS ISLAND - IF SO WE WANT TO SEE THEM FIRST - I'VE GOT MY OLD PISTOL - YOU HANG ONTO THAT HATCHET -
WHY DO WE HAVE TO CARRY ALL THIS STUFF - FRYIN' PAN AND ALL - WE'LL BE CLEAR ACROSS AND BACK IN A COUPLE O' HOURS -
DON'T YOU FOOL YOURSELF - WALKIN' THROUGH JUNGLE TAKES A HEAP O' TIME -
I DON'T LIKE IT - IT'S TOO BLAMED QUIET - I FEEL LIKE WE'RE BEING WATCHED -
AW - WHAT IF WE ARE BEIN' WATCHED? I DON'T MIND - I'M NOT BASHFUL -
HAROLD GRAY
Reg. U. S. Pat. Off.; Copyright, 1930, by The Chicago Tribune.
GEE - I SURE SLEPT LIKE A LOG - THIS CAMPIN' OUT IS GREAT STUFF -
SLEEP! I HARDLY GOT A WINK ALL NIGHT - KEPT HEARIN' THINGS MOVIN' IN THE JUNGLE -
SH-H-! WHAT WAS THAT? SOMETHIN' SURE MADE THAT NOISE - BUT WE HAVEN'T SEEN A THING -
GOLLY - I FEEL SORTA NERVOUS - I COULD SWEAR I SEE EYES IN THE SHADOWS
AYE - I CAN FEEL THINGS MOVIN' ALL ABOUT US - BUT WHAT SORT O' THINGS? AND PALM LEAVES MOVE - BUT YUH NEVER SEE WHAT MOVES 'EM -
IF ANNIE AND CAP'N MARLIN ARE NERVOUS, FANCY THE EXCITEMENT OF THE LITTLE FOREST FOLK, AS THEY SPY FEARFULLY ON THESE STRANGERS IN THEIR MIDST -
HAROLD GRAY
Reg. U. S. Pat. Off.; Copyright, 1930, by The Chicago Tribune.

WHEE!
LOOKIE! TURTLES!
AYE- THEY'LL COME IN HANDY FOR SOUP AND MEAT, LATER ON-
AND THERE'S FINE FISHING TO BE HAD RIGHT FROM THE SHORE- AND WE HAVE GRAPES AND COCOANUTS AND BANANAS- WE CAN'T STARVE-
GEE- I'M GLAD WE'RE OUT OF TH' JUNGLE- LET'S GO BACK BY TH' BEACH- I DON'T CARE IF IT IS FARTHER THAT WAY-
HAROLD GRAY
WHILE THE LITTLE BOTTLE, WITH ITS CALL FOR HELP, DRIFTS AIMLESSLY, A MATTER OF INTEREST ONLY TO THE FISH-
Reg. U. S. Pat. Off.; Copyright, 1930, by The Chicago Tribune.
OH, DO BE CAREFUL! I CAN HEAR IT MOVIN' AROUND-
SH-H-H-H- YOU CLIMB THAT TREE WHERE YOU'LL BE SAFE WHILE I DO A LITTLE SCOUTIN'- OLD SPIKE MARLIN CAN TAKE CARE OF HIMSELF IN ANY PORT-
YI!
BA-A-A!
BAM!
WHY, IT'S A BILLY-GOAT!
Reg. U. S. Pat. Off.; Copyright, 1930, by The Chicago Tribune.
HEH! HEH! HEH! DID YOU SEE HIM RUN? I JUST BANGED AWAY TO SKEER HIM- HEH! HEH! HEH! IF YOU COULD HAVE SEEN THE LOOK ON HIS FACE-
YEAH? HERE'S YER CAP AND TH' PISTOL-
HAROLD GRAY
GEE, IT SURE IS GOOD TO GET BACK HOME AGAIN- BUT I'M GLAD WE S'PLORED TH' ISLAND- I FEEL A LOT SAFER NOW-
AYE- WE KNOW NOW THAT WE'RE THE ONLY HUMANS HERE- AND THERE'S PLENTY TO EAT, EVEN IF WE SHOULD RUN OUT OF SHIP'S RATIONS-
HERE, SANDY! HERE, WILLIE! COME AN' GET IT-
SAY; DO YUH S'POSE THAT GOAT WE SAW YESTERDAY IS A TAME ONE SOMEBODY LEFT HERE-
NO- MOST LIKELY THERE ARE A LOT OF WILD GOATS ON THIS ISLAND- WE MIGHT CATCH SOME AND TAME THEM-
AYE- THEN WE COULD HAVE REAL GOAT'S MILK FOR OUR COFFEE- AND GOAT MEAT IS BETTER'N NO MEAT AT ALL- AYE, ANNIE, WE'VE BEEN SET DOWN IN A LAND O' PLENTY, AND NO MISTAKE-
HAROLD GRAY
Reg. U. S. Pat. Off.; Copyright, 1930, by The Chicago Tribune.

July 10–12, 1930

Little Orphan Annie
HAROLD GRAY
LEAPIN' LIZARDS!!! JUST LOOK AT TH' LITTLE IMP- I'D LIKE TO BE HERE TO SEE THE FUN WHEN THOSE TWO BOZOS WAKE UP- BUT THEY MIGHT BLAME ME- C'MON, SANDY-
EEK!
BOUF! BOUF!
YEOW!
EEK!
EEK!
YI-I-I
AR-R-R!
E-YAH! E-YAH!
I KNEW IT- WILLIE'S BEEN PICKIN' ON TH' MONKEYS AGAIN, AND AFTER ALL I'VE TOLD HIM-
OUCH!
HEY! LOOK OUT WHO YER SOCKIN' WITH THOSE COCOA-NUTS, WILL YUH? I DIDN'T DO ANYTHING TO YOU-
WELL, I HOPE YOU'RE SATISFIED- THAT JUST GOES TO SHOW YUH, TROUBLE IS ONE THING YUH CAN ALWAYS FIND WITHOUT MORE'N HALF LOOKIN' FOR IT-

July 13, 1930

DOGGONE THOSE MONKEYS! ALL OVER TH' PLACE AND INTO EVER'THING-
SHOO! GET OUT! BEAT IT! SCAT!!! ON YER WAY!
THEY'RE GETTING USED TO US NOW AND ARE BEGINNING TO GET FRIENDLY.
FRIENDLY! HUH- THEY'RE A BUNCH O' BURGLARS- AN' LOOK HOW BIG THEY ARE-
AYE- THEY ARE A BIT BIGGER THAN MOST IN THESE PARTS- I CAL'LATE LIKE AS NOT THEY'RE SOME AS GOT AWAY FROM A CIRCUS SHIP- BUT MONKEYS ARE HARMLESS IF YOU TREAT 'EM KIND-
HAROLD GRAY
Reg. U. S. Pat. Off.; Copyright, 1930, by The Chicago Tribune.
TH' NERVE O' THAT LITTLE IMP- STANDIN' UP AND ARGUIN' WITH WILLIE- BUT WILLIE'S BIG ENOUGH TO SETTLE HIM-
BOUF!
ICKIE ICK ICK!
LEAPIN' LIZARDS!!! TRYIN' TO RUN US OUT OF OUR OWN CAMP- I'LL SETTLE THAT GUY IN A HURRY-
AR-R-R-R!! CHEEEEE!!! CHEET-CHEET-CHEET!!
WHAT ARE WE GOIN' TO DO, CAP'N? LOOK AT THAT BIG BOZO- HE'S GOT ME BLUFFED- EVEN SANDY'S SCARED- AT LEAST HE WON'T DO A THING TO HELP-
HAROLD GRAY
Reg. U. S. Pat. Off.; Copyright, 1930, by The Chicago Tribune.
THERE'S THAT BIG BULLY- NOW WHAT'S HE UP TO?
GREAT SCOTT! WHAT A NERVE-
AN' WILLIE STANDS FOR IT- 'MAGINE THAT? STILL I DON'T BLAME HIM MUCH-
YUH'D THINK SANDY WOULD GET SORE- BUT HE DOESN'T SEEM TO CARE WHAT TH' BIG BABOON DOES- WONDER IF SANDY'S GETTIN' YELLOW- GEE! I'M GETTIN' SCARED O' THOSE MONKS-
HAROLD GRAY
Reg. U. S. Pat. Off.; Copyright, 1930, by The Chicago Tribune.

July 14–16, 1930

HEY! LEGGO O' THAT- I TELL YUH THAT'S MY COCOANUT- WHO D'YUH THINK YOU ARE?
BR-R-R!
LEAPIN' LIZARDS! SANDY!!! DO BE CAREFUL!
GR-R-R!!!
OOP!
GREAT SCOTT- HE'S WHALIN' TH' STUFFIN' OUTA THAT BIG BULLY- AN' I THOUGHT SANDY WAS SCARED O' HIM.
YEOW!
SANDY- YOU DARLIN'- YOU JUST COULDN'T STAND BY AND SEE ANYBODY PICK ON ME, COULDJA?
ARF!
HAROLD GRAY
Reg. U. S. Pat. Off.; Copyright, 1930, by The Chicago Tribune
HM-M-M--- NOT A SOUND- HAVEN'T KNOWN IT TO BE SO QUIET 'ROUND HERE FOR DAYS- NOT SINCE THOSE MONKEYS STARTED VISITIN' US-
POOR WILLIE- HE'S SURE CATCHIN' UP ON HIS BACK SLEEP- HASN'T DARED SHUT HIS EYES FOR DAYS- NEVER KNEW WHAT TH' MONKS WOULD BE UP TO NEXT-
AN' CAP'N MARLIN'S TAKIN' A NAP, TOO- BUT THEN HE CAN SLEEP NO MATTER WHAT HAPPENS-
HEIGH-HO! GUESS I'LL GRAB A FEW WINKS MYSELF- YESSIR, SANDY- YOU SURE TAUGHT THAT BIG BULLY A LESSON YESTERDAY- I'LL BET HE WON'T FORGET FOR A WHILE- NOT TILL HIS TAIL GETS WELL ANYWAY-
HAROLD GRAY
Reg. U. S. Pat. Off.; Copyright, 1930, by The Chicago Tribune.
BACK AGAIN- JUST LOOK AT THAT LITTLE SHRIMP- I'D YELL AT HIM, BUT THAT BIG BULLY'S WITH HIM-
E-E-EK!
SUFFERIN' SUNFISH!!! HE'S WHALIN' TH' LITTLE GUY FOR STEALIN'-
ICKITY BLICK BLICK!
YI-I-I!
WELL, BIG BOY- YOU SURE HAVE CHANGED A LOT- FIGGER IT'S HEALTHIER TO BE GOOD, EH?
EEK!
AFTER DAYS AND DAYS THE LITTLE BOTTLE STILL DRIFTS BUT AT LAST IT IS CARRYING ITS MESSAGE OF DISTRESS INTO BUSIER WATERS WHERE IT MAY BE PICKED UP ALMOST ANY TIME-
HAROLD GRAY
Reg. U. S. Pat. Off.; Copyright, 1930, by The Chicago Tribune.

July 17–19, 1930

Little Orphan Annie
HAROLD GRAY
THANKS, BOYS-

WELL, WHADDYUH KNOW 'BOUT THAT? THE LITTLE RASCAL WANTS TO PLAY WITH YOU- GO ON- THROW IT BACK TO HIM-

THAT'S TH' STUFF, WILLIE- SHOW 'EM YOU KNOW A COUPLE O' TRICKS YOURSELF-

SO YOU WANTA GO AND PLAY WITH YOUR NEW FRIENDS, EH? THEY MIGHT SHOW YOU A LOT O' NEW TRICKS - GO AHEAD-

GEE, SANDY- ISN'T THAT CUTE- WILLIE'LL HAVE THE TIME OF HIS LIFE-

COURSE THOSE MONKEYS AREN'T JUST OUR KIND- BUT, SHUX- WHAT IF WILLIE DOES PLAY WITH 'EM- HE'S A GOOD LITTLE BEAR- THEY CAN'T DO HIM ANY HARM-

THEY'RE JUST LIKE LOTS O' KIDS- MAYBE IF THEY LIKE WILLIE THEY'LL GIVE HIM PRESENTS TO BRING HOME- GEE- NO TELLIN' WHAT THEY MIGHT GIVE HIM-

HEY! LOOKIE! WHY, IT'S WILLIE!!! HE'S COMIN' BACK- WHAT ON EARTH IS TH' MATTER WITH HIM?
?

WILLIE! WHAT'S HAPPENED? ARE YUH HURT? DIDJA EAT SOMETHIN'?

WHAT TH'---- CAN IT BE? YES! IT IS--

SOMETHIN' IS BITIN' ME!
OW-W-W--

IT ALL COMES O' YOU HANGIN' OUT WITH THOSE BLAMED MONKEYS- I SAID, MAYBE THEY'D GIVE YUH SOMETHIN' TO BRING HOME- THEY SURE DID!
Reg. U. S. Pat. Off.: Copyright, 1930, by The Chicago Tribune

IF I EVER CATCH YOU PLAYIN' WITH THOSE MONKEYS AGAIN I'LL TAN YUH TILL YER HIDE SMOKES- THAT JUST PROVES YOU CAN'T BE TOO CAREFUL O' TH' CROWD YOU HANG OUT WITH-

July 20, 1930

SAY, CAP'N- WHEN ARE YOU GOIN' TO GET AT FIXIN' THE BOAT LIKE YOU SAID YOU WOULD?
I'M FIGGERIN' ON IT RIGHT NOW- GOTTA PLAN A BIG JOB LIKE THAT- CAN'T BE TOO CAREFUL- HAVE TO LAY A COURSE BEFORE YOU CAN FOLLOW IT-
FIGGERIN'!!! BLAH! HE'S JUST PLAIN LAZY-ALL TH' FIGGERIN' HE'S DONE LATELY IS FIGGER HOW HE CAN DODGE WORK-
BUT WARBUCKS IS NOT RESTING- ONCE MORE ABOARD HIS YACHT HE IS MAKING A SYSTEMATIC SEARCH OF EVERY CHARTED ISLAND IN THESE WATERS-
THERE ARE HUNDREDS OF LITTLE ISLANDS- SHE MIGHT BE ON ANY ONE OF THEM-
HAROLD GRAY
Reg. U. S. Pat. Off.; Copyright, 1930, by The Chicago Tribune.
HM-M-M-- THAT'S A BAD HOLE- BUT THEN, ON THE OTHER HAND, IT COULD BE WORSE, AS YOU MIGHT SAY-
CAN YOU FIX IT ALL RIGHT, CAP'N?
WELL, MAYBE I CAN, AND THEN AGAIN, MAYBE I CAN'T- IT ALL DEPENDS- IF ANYBODY CAN DO IT I RECKON, I CAN-
WHAT'S SO TOUGH ABOUT THAT JOB?
WELL, I'LL TELL YOU- IF I HAD THE PLANKS IT WOULD BE EASY ENOUGH- COURSE THERE'S TREES ON THE ISLAND- AND WE HAVE TOOLS- WE COULD MAKE PLANKS OF A SORT-
BUT WOOD FOR THAT JOB HAS TO BE JUST A CERTAIN KIND- NOW THE QUESTION IS, ARE THERE ANY SUCH-LIKE TREES ON THIS ISLAND? WE'LL HAVE TO LOOK INTO THAT-
HAROLD GRAY
Reg. U. S. Pat. Off.; Copyright, 1930, by The Chicago Tribune.
SAY- WHEN ARE YOU GOIN' TO START LOOKIN' FOR A TREE MADE OUTA TH' RIGHT KIND O' WOOD TO USE FOR FIXIN' TH' BOAT-
HO-O-O-- HUM!!! THERE'S NO TIME LIKE TH' PRESENT, AS I ALWAYS SEZ-
THERE'S A FINE TREE- AYE, A NOBLE SPECIMAN- BUT IT WON'T DO FOR OUR PURPOSE- HAVEN'T SEEN JUST THE RIGHT KIND YET-
BUT WE'LL KEEP LOOKIN'- WHEN OLD SPIKE MARLIN STARTS A JOB HE NEVER QUITS TILL IT'S DONE, NO MATTER HOW LONG IT TAKES-
DOES IT ALWAYS TAKE YOU A LONG TIME?
HAROLD GRAY
Reg. U. S. Pat. Off.; Copyright, 1930, by The Chicago Tribune.

July 21–23, 1930

ANNIE - I'VE FOUND IT - JUST THE TREE WE NEED - THERE'LL BE PLANKS ENOUGH IN IT TO MAKE THE OLD BOAT GOOD AS NEW -
YEAH? NO FOOLIN'?
WHILE THE LITTLE BOTTLE, WITH ITS MESSAGE, FLOATS ON AND ON, A PLAYTHING OF THE BOUNDLESS DEEP-
LOOK, JOE - A DIRTY OLD BOTTLE - AT FIRST I THOUGHT THERE WAS A PAPER OR SOMETHIN' INSIDE IT -
AW, YER SEEIN' THINGS, CHUCK - JUST AN OLD BOTTLE - LOTS OF 'EM FLOATIN' HERE-ABOUTS THESE DAYS -
HAROLD GRAY
Reg. U. S. Pat. Off.; Copyright, 1930, by The Chicago Tribune.
LEAPIN' LIZARDS!!! WONDER IF HE'S GOT A TOUCH O' SLEEPIN' SICKNESS OR SOMETHIN - I NEVER SAW SUCH A GUY FOR RESTIN' HIMSELF -
Z-Z-Z
HE WAS GOIN' TO START CUTTIN' UP THAT TREE THIS MORNIN' - BUT HE SAID TH' AXE NEEDED SHARPENIN' AND WE HAVEN'T ANY GRIND-STONE -
HEY!!! WAKE UP!!!
THAT WHET-STONE MAY TAKE A LOT O' ELBOW GREASE, BUT YOU'RE ALL RESTED NOW AN' WON'T MIND THAT -
RIGHT YOU ARE, ANNIE - MAKE THE BEST OF WHAT YOU HAVE - THAT'S WHAT I'VE ALWAYS HELD -
HAROLD GRAY
Reg. U. S. Pat. Off.; Copyright, 1930, by The Chicago Tribune.
WELL, SUPPER'S 'MOST READY - GUESS I'LL GO SEE HOW OLD CAP'N MARLIN IS GETTIN' ALONG - HE OUGHTA BE GOOD AND HUNGRY AFTER WORKIN' ALL DAY -
HE TOOK HIS AXE AN' STARTED OUT THIS MORNIN' - HE MUST HAVE THAT TREE ALL CUT UP AND 'MOST ALL MADE INTO PLANKS BY NOW - HE'S A GOOD WORKER WHEN HE STARTS -
LEAPIN' LIZARDS!!! SOUND ASLEEP - AND HE HASN'T EVEN STARTED -
Z-Z-Z
WHILE THE LITTLE BOTTLE FLOATS ACROSS THE COURSE OF COASTWISE STEAMERS AND EVER NEARER TO THE SHORE -
LOOK, MAMA - THERE'S A BOTTLE - MAYBE IT'S GOT A MESSAGE IN IT LIKE IN THE STORIES -
NONSENSE - WHAT WILL YOU BE IMAGINING NEXT?
HAROLD GRAY
Reg. U. S. Pat. Off.; Copyright, 1930, by The Chicago Tribune.

July 24–26, 1930

Little Orphan Annie
HERE'S A STICKER, ANNIE- WHAT'S THE DIFFERENCE BETWEEN CROQUET AND POLO?
GAGS
HORSES! HORSES!
HAROLD GRAY
HM-M-M- NOW I'VE GOTTA GET THIS BAG FULL O' COCOANUTS- THERE ARE PLENTY UP IN THOSE TREES-
BUT IT'S TOO AWFUL HOT TO GO CLIMBIN' TREES TO DAY- THERE MUST BE SOME EASIER WAY- JUST LOOK AT THOSE MONKEYS CLIMB, WILL YUH? IT'S PLAY FOR THEM-
CHIT-CHIT-CHIT!!!
YI!
AW, PIPE DOWN- WHO YOU CHATTERIN' AT?
WOW! THAT SURE GOT A RISE OUT OF 'EM-
BOP!
LEAPIN' LIZARDS! THAT'S SERVICE FOR YUH- THOSE BABIES SURE MAKE DELIVERIES IN A HURRY-
WELL, I GUESS TH' SHOOTIN' IS OVER- NOT A SIGN O' THOSE MONKEYS ANY MORE-
OH, BOY- THEY'VE TOSSED ME ENOUGH COCOANUTS TO FILL THREE BAGS- IT WOULD HAVE TAKEN ME AN HOUR TO PICK THAT MANY-
WHEE!!! WHY, TH' LITTLE RASCALS- THEY WERE FOOLIN' ME THAT TIME-
WONDER HOW MANY MORE COCOANUTS THERE ARE UP THERE, ANYWAY-
SOCK!
YA-A-A-H!!! HM-M-M--- WELL, IF THEY HAD ANY MORE AMMUNITION THAT'D START IT COMIN' MY WAY SOON ENOUGH-
NO WONDER THEY CALL SO MANY FOLKS MONKEYS- KID 'EM ALONG RIGHT AND YOU CAN GET 'EM TO DO ALL YOUR HARD JOBS FOR YOU-
YESSIR- THAT JUST GOES TO SHOW YUH- IF YUH USE YER HEAD YOU CAN 'MOST ALWAYS SAVE YERSELF A HEAP OF WORK-
Reg. U. S. Pat. Off.; Copyright, 1930, by The Chicago Tribune.

July 27, 1930

YESSIR, ANNIE - TRAININ' TELLS - WHEN I WAS A YOUNG SWAB I WORKED IN THE SHIP-YARDS AT BATH -
BATH - GEE, THAT MUST HAVE BEEN A NICE CLEAN PLACE TO WORK -
MANY'S THE FINE SHIP WE BUILT IN THOSE DAYS - SAILIN' VESSELS THEY WAS - SOME OF 'EM IS STILL AFLOAT -
WELL, CAP'N - I WILL SAY YOU KNOW YER BUSINESS - NOT MANY GUYS COULD TURN OUT SWELL PLANKS LIKE THAT WITH JUST A TREE AND AN AXE -
DIDN'T TAKE YUH VERY LONG, EITHER, WHEN YUH FINALLY GOT STARTED -
AYE - WHEN YOU START A JOB DON'T STOP TILL YOU FINISH IT - THAT'S ALWAYS BEEN MY SAILIN' ORDERS -
AT LAST THE LITTLE BOTTLE, WITH ITS PRECIOUS MESSAGE, HAS REACHED THE MAINLAND, BUT, ALL UNNOTICED, IT RESTS ON A DESERTED BEACH -
HAROLD GRAY
Reg. U. S. Pat. Off.; Copyright, 1930, by The Chicago Tribune.
ONE MORE VOYAGE AND WE'LL HAVE ALL THOSE PLANKS DOWN ON THE SHORE - THEN IT WILL BE EASY TO FLOAT 'EM OUT TO WHERE WE NEED 'EM -
ONCE WE GET THE OLD BOAT AFLOAT IT WILL BE EASY TO FIT A NEW MAST - AND THERE'S EXTRA SAILS IN THE HOLD FOR'ARD -
WELL, THIS ISLAND ISN'T SUCH A BAD PLACE - PLENTY TO EAT HERE - AN' MIGHTY RESTFUL - IT COULD HAVE BEEN LOTS WORSE -
BUT, JUST TH' SAME, I'LL BE MIGHTY GLAD TO GET AWAY FROM HERE AND ON OUR WAY -
AYE - IT'S A SNUG LITTLE COVE - BUT ANY PLACE THAT'S TOO QUIET GETS MIGHTY TIRESOME AFTER A WHILE
HM-M - SORTA CLOUDIN' UP - LITTLE LATE TO START A BIG JOB LIKE THAT TO DAY - WE'LL LAY TO TILL MORNING AND GET AN EARLY START -
GEE - I HOPE IT DOESN'T STORM - IT LOOKS PRETTY BLACK WAY OUT THERE IN THE SOUTH WEST -
HAROLD GRAY
Reg. U. S. Pat. Off.; Copyright, 1930, by The Chicago Tribune.
LEAPIN' LIZARDS! CAP'N!!! COME QUICK! LOOK - IT'S A STORM AND IT'S SURE A'COMIN' -
COME ON, ANNIE - RUN - BACK INTO THE WOODS - A TIDAL WAVE WOULD SWEEP THAT BEACH CLEAN AS A WHISTLE -
QUICK, ANNIE - LIE DOWN FLAT AND GRAB HOLD OF A GOOD, STOUT TREE - AND NO MATTER WHAT HAPPENS HANG ON - HERE IT COMES -
HAROLD GRAY
Reg. U. S. Pat. Off.; Copyright, 1930, by The Chicago Tribune.

July 28–30, 1930

WOW!!! THAT SURE WAS A HUMDINGER OF A STORM- BUT YOU'D NEVER GUESS IT- LOOK HOW SMOOTH THE WATER IS-
AYE-QUIET AN' PEACEFUL AS A LITTLE LAKE- BUT WHERE IS OUR BOAT- MAYBE IT WAS WASHED OUT TO SEA-
HERE IT IS, CAP'N- ER, THAT IS HERE'S PART OF IT- ALL BUSTED INTO A THOUSAND PIECES-
GEE- I GUESS THAT JUST ABOUT ENDS OUR IDEA O' TAKIN' ANY BOAT RIDE AWAY FROM HERE FOR A WHILE-
AYE- WE'RE STUCK HARD AND FAST HERE ON THE ISLAND NOW AND NO MISTAKE-
WHILE, ON A DISTANT SHORE, A FAINT ECHO OF THE STORM DISLODGES THE LITTLE BOTTLE AND SENDS IT ONCE MORE ON ITS AIMLESS WAY-
HAROLD GRAY
Reg. U. S. Pat. Off.; Copyright, 1930, by The Chicago Tribune.
WELL, MAYBE WE CAN USE THESE BOARDS FOR SOMETHIN'- THEY'RE WORTH SAVIN', ANYWAY-
AYE- WE MIGHT USE THIS LUMBER TO BUILD A HOUSE LATER ON-
A HOUSE? SAY- THAT'S A GOOD IDEA- THINK YOU COULD BUILD A HOUSE?
AYE- THERE'S FEW THINGS OLD SPIKE MARLIN CAN'T DO WITH A GOOD SET OF TOOLS-
LUCKY WE BROUGHT ALL TH' TOOLS AN' THINGS ASHORE WHERE THEY'RE SAFE 'FORE THAT STORM OR WE SURE WOULD BE UP AGAINST IT-
BUT THERE'S NO HURRY ABOUT STARTIN' A HOUSE- A SHIP MAY COME ALONG AND RESCUE US ALMOST ANY DAY-
YEAH? WELL, IF ANY SHIP IS GOIN' TO RESCUE US IT'S SURE TAKIN' IT'S TIME GETTIN' HERE-
HAROLD GRAY
Reg. U. S. Pat. Off.; Copyright, 1930, by The Chicago Tribune.
FAR FROM THE ISLAND THE LITTLE BOTTLE DRIFTS PAST A CITY WATER-FRONT, POWERLESS TO AVOID THE DANGERS THAT THREATEN TO SILENCE THE MESSAGE IT BEARS FOREVER-
HEY, YOU GUYS- IF YER SUCH SWELL SHOTS LET'S SEE WHO'S FIRST TO SOCK THAT OLD BOTTLE OUT THERE-
AW, YOU'RE PUNK- WATCH THIS ONE- THIS'LL HIT IT SURE-
YOU MISSED IT A MILE- JUST WAIT'LL I GET TH' RANGE-
SHUX- ALMOST GOT IT THAT TIME-
AH, YOU'RE ALL BUM SHOTS- OH, WELL- WHAT'LL WE THROW AT NOW?
HAROLD GRAY
Reg. U. S. Pat. Off.; Copyright, 1930, by The Chicago Tribune.

July 31–
August 2, 1930
SHIPWRECKED

Little Orphan Annie
ALL OUR DRINKIN' GLASSES GOT BROKEN EXCEPT THAT ONE OLD GOBLET-
NO FOOLIN'- IS THAT A GOBLET? AND I ALWAYS THOUGHT A GOBLET WAS WHAT THEY CALLED A SAILOR'S LITTLE BOY-
HAROLD GRAY
GEE, I WISH THERE WAS A GOOD MOVIE TO GO TO - AND A NICE, COLD ICE-CREAM SODA WOULDN'T GO SO BAD EITHER- THIS ISLAND SURE IS A DEAD PLACE- NO KIDS TO PLAY WITH- NOTHIN' TO DO-
STILL, I S'POSE IT COULD BE LOTS WORSE- I'VE BEEN IN PLACES WHERE THERE WAS A HEAP O' HARD WORK TO DO - AN' LOTS O' KIDS CAN'T PLAY FIVE MINUTES WITHOUT GETTIN' SORE 'BOUT SOMETHIN'-
THERE'S NO SQUAWKIN' RADIO NEXT DOOR HERE TO DRIVE YUH NUTTY- AN' YUH DON'T HAVE TO RISK YER LIFE DODGIN' TRUCKS EVERY TIME YUH TAKE A WALK-
WE'VE GOT PLENTY TO EAT- AND TH' WEATHER IS SWELL- AND WE'RE NOT PESTERED WITH A LOT O' BUSY-BODIES TELLIN' US HOW TO RUN OUR BUSINESS-
HEIGH-HO- AND YUH CAN SLEEP AS LATE AS YUH WANT TO, AND TAKE A NAP ANY OLD TIME-
?
Z-Z
NOW WHAT'S WILLIE GONE AND GOT INTO?
E-YOW!
GREAT SCOTT! WHAT'S TH' MATTER, WILLIE? COME OUT O' THERE-
GEE- A LITTLE TURTLE-
WELL, I TOLD YUH TO STAY OUT O' TH' WATER, DIDN'T I?
THAT'S WHAT YUH GET FOR NOT MINDING- LUCKY IT WAS ONLY A LITTLE TURTLE AND NOT A SHARK- EH, SANDY?
ARF!
AR-R-R!
LEAPIN' LIZARDS! YUH DON'T HAVE TO GET SORE AT US 'BOUT IT-
HE'LL GET OVER IT- JUST LIKE A LOT O' FOLKS- GET INTO TROUBLE DOIN' WHAT THEY KNOW IS WRONG AND IN STEAD O' BLAMIN' THEMSELVES THEY GET SORE AT EVER'BODY IN SIGHT-

August 3, 1930

NO USE TRYING TO FISH FROM A BEACH LIKE THIS - WHAT WE NEED IS A BOAT -
MAYBE WE COULD MAKE A RAFT -
HM-M-M--- YES, I RECKON A RAFT MIGHT FILL THE BILL - HERE'S SOME LIKELY TREES AND HANDY TO THE SHORE -
YOU WAIT HERE - I'LL RUN AND GET THE AXE -
S'POSE WE COULD HAVE WAITED TILL TO-MORROW, BUT I KNOW YOU ALWAYS WANT TO GET RIGHT AT ANY BIG JOB THAT COMES ALONG -
STILL IGNORED, THE LITTLE BOTTLE DRIFTS IN AND OUT AMONG THE SHIPS AND PIERS - WILL IT'S MESSAGE NEVER BE PICKED UP?
HAROLD GRAY
Reg. U. S. Pat. Off.; Copyright, 1930, by The Chicago Tribune.
WE'LL HAVE A SEA-GOING CRAFT HERE YET -
GEE - MAYBE WE COULD GET AWAY FROM THE ISLAND ON THIS RAFT -
AYE, WE COULD GET AWAY ALL RIGHT, BUT WE'D NEVER MAKE THE MAINLAND - A RAFT LIKE THIS IS STAUNCH ENOUGH FOR QUIET WATER, BUT HEAVY SEAS WOULD TEAR IT INTO A HUNDRED PIECES IN NO TIME -
BUT STILL THE UNRELENTING SEARCH GOES ON, FOR TO WARBUCKS THERE IS NO SUCH WORD AS "QUIT" -
WHAT MORE CAN WE DO, MR. WARBUCKS? WE'VE FOLLOWED EVERY CLEW - NOT A TRACE OF HER ANYWHERE -
HERE'S WHAT WE CAN DO - SEE THAT CHART? THERE ARE THOUSANDS OF SMALL ISLANDS ALL MARKED - WE'LL MAKE A SYSTEMATIC SEARCH OF EVERY ONE OF THE ISLANDS ON THAT CHART, NO MATTER HOW SMALL IT IS -
HAROLD GRAY
Reg. U. S. Pat. Off.; Copyright, 1930, by The Chicago Tribune.
WE'LL MAKE A SAILOR OUT OF YOU YET - I USED TO BE AS SPRY AS YOU BE - HAVE YOU GOT THAT LINE MADE FAST?
AYE, AYE, CAP'N -
GEE, CAP'N - YOU SURE ARE HANDY WITH A NEEDLE - I DIDN'T KNOW YOU COULD SEW LIKE THAT -
A GOOD SAILOR HAS TO KNOW HOW TO DO JUST ABOUT EVERYTHING - I RECKON I COULD BUILD A FULL-RIGGED SHIP SINGLE-HANDED IF I HAD THE TIME AND THE MAKINGS -
CAUGHT IN A CURRENT THE LITTLE BOTTLE ONCE MORE STARTS OUT TO SEA TO BE NEARLY RUN DOWN BY WARBUCKS' YACHT, BUT IS UNNOTICED BY ANYONE ON BOARD -
HAROLD GRAY
Reg. U. S. Pat. Off.; Copyright, 1930, by The Chicago Tribune.

August 4–6, 1930

SHE DOESN'T HANDLE LIKE A YACHT EXACTLY, BUT, ON THE OTHER HAND, I RECKON SHE'LL SERVE OUR PURPOSE-
IT'D BE PRETTY HARD TO TIP THIS THING OVER, ANYWAY-
THE WIND'S COMING ON TO BLOW- WE'D BETTER BE GETTING BACK- STAND BY TO GO ABOUT-
ARE WE COMING INTO THE CREEK ALL RIGHT, ANNIE?
A LITTLE MORE TO STARBOARD, CAP'N-
WHILE ON AND ON THE LITTLE BOTTLE FLOATS, THROUGH A FISHING FLEET UNNOTICED, AND ON AND ON-
HAROLD GRAY
Reg. U. S. Pat. Off.; Copyright, 1930, by The Chicago Tribune.
WELL, WE'VE GOT ENOUGH FOR ONE DAY- BETTER WEIGH ANCHOR AND PUT FOR HOME BEFORE THE TIDE STARTS OUT-
HEY! I'VE GOT ANOTHER BITE, I THINK-
LEAPIN' LIZARDS! IT MUST BE A WHALE!!!
WHALE NOTHIN'- NO WHALE EVER MOVED THAT FAST- HANG ON, ANNIE-
IT'S A GIANT SWORDFISH!
WHEW! LOOKS TO ME MORE LIKE A SEA-GOIN' SCISSOR-BILL-
HAROLD GRAY
Reg. U. S. Pat. Off.; Copyright, 1930, by The Chicago Tribune.
AYE, ANNIE- THERE'S NOTHIN' BETTER'N FRESH FISH FRIED OVER A CAMP FIRE-
FRESH FISH! FRESH FISH!
W-WH-WHO'S T-T-TH-THERE?
LOOK OUT, SANDY- KEEP BACK!
WHY, IT'S A PARROT!
HA! HA! HA! HA! HA! FRESH FISH!!!
HAROLD GRAY
Reg. U. S. Pat. Off.; Copyright, 1930, by The Chicago Tribune.

August 7–9, 1930

Little Orphan Annie
HAROLD GRAY
GO ON, YUH BLANKETY BLANK SO-AN'-SO-YUH LOP-EARED !!.—!!!
ARRR!
NIX, SANDY! NIX! DON'T MIND DEACON - TH' POOR LITTLE INNOCENT DOESN'T REALIZE WHAT HE'S SAYING -
LEAPIN' LIZARDS! CLEANED UP EVERY BIT O' YER DINNER LIKE A GOOD BOY - C'MON, DEACON - I'LL LIFT YUH UP ON TH' SWELL PERCH CAP'N MARLIN MADE FOR YUH -
NOW YOU'RE A SMART FELLOW - AND YOU'RE OLD ENOUGH TO TALK - SAY ANNIE! GO ON - ANNIE! ANNIE! ANNIE! YOU CAN SAY THAT -
TRY "DADDY WARBUCKS" - MAYBE THAT'S TOO MUCH TO START - WARBUCKS! WARBUCKS! WARBUCKS! LEARN THAT MUCH FIRST -
SAY, YOU SON OF A SEA-COOK! YOU PAY ATTENTION TO ME WHEN I'M TALKIN' TO YOU -
?
OH; YER GOIN' TO SULK NOW, ARE YUH? TOO LAZY TO EVEN TRY TO TALK FOR ME -
BLAH! WHAT A MESS O' HORSH-RADISH YOU TURNED OUT TO BE - YOU GIVE ME A PAIN IN TH' NECK - YOU'LL NEVER LEARN TO TALK -
PAIN IN TH' NECK!!! PAIN IN TH' NECK - BLAH! BLAH! BLAH! HA-HA-HA-HA-HA!!! SON-OF-A SEA-COOK! SON-OF-A-SEA-COOK!
HEY! CUT THAT OUT - STOP IT, I SAY -
LEAPIN' LIZARDS! LEAPIN' LIZARDS!
NO! NO! NO! YOU MUST NEVER SAY THOSE WORDS AGAIN - NOT EVER - SEE?
AWK!
WHAT CAN YUH DO WITH A GUY LIKE THAT? JUST LIKE A KID - PICK UP EVERY WORD THEY SHOULDN'T - CAN'T BLAME 'EM - DON'T KNOW ANY BETTER -
BUT DEACON IS GOIN' TO LEARN BETTER - HE'S GOIN' TO BE DIFFERENT - HE'S SMART - HE'S LEARNED HIS LESSON - I'LL BET YOU NEVER HEAR HIM SPILL ANOTHER WORD OF SLANG - - - -
?
HORSE-RADISH!
Reg. U. S. Pat. Off.; Copyright, 1930, by The Chicago Tribune.

August 10, 1930

LISTEN- YOUR NAME IS "DEACON"- NOW YOU'VE GOTTA GET SO YOU CAN SAY IT- SEE?
NO-NO! NOTHING LIKE THAT, DEACON- DEACON! IT'S EASY- JUST TRY IT- DEACON!
BLURK!
?
?
HEY- WHAT'S TH' MATTER? YOU GUYS AREN'T WALKIN' OUT ON US, ARE YUH?
HAROLD GRAY
Reg. U. S. Pat. Off.; Copyright, 1930, by The Chicago Tribune.
I WON'T BE GONE BUT A MINUTE, DEACON- JUST SIT THERE TILL I GET BACK-
AWK!
ICK!
ICK!
ICK!
LEAPIN' LIZARDS! WHAT ON EARTH EVER HAPPENED TO YOU? IF SANDY AND WILLIE WERE HERE I'D SUSPECT THEM O' THIS-
HAROLD GRAY
Reg. U. S. Pat. Off.; Copyright, 1930, by The Chicago Tribune.
AYE- HE BE SMART ENOUGH, I DON'T DOUBT- BUT HE'S LIKE MOST PARROTS- OBSTINATE-
BLAH!
THE CAP'N THINKS YER A BUST- AND SANDY AND WILLIE ARE JEALOUS OF YUH- BUT NEVER YOU MIND, DEACON- I'M FOR YUH AND I'M GOIN' TO TEACH YUH TO TALK SWELL- COME ON, NOW- FOR ME- SAY, DEACON-
SAY! IS THAT ANY WAY TO ACT? YOU'VE GOT A NERVE, TURNIN' YER BACK ON ME WHEN I'M TALKIN' TO YUH-
ALL RIGHT FOR YOU! BE DUMB ALL YER LIFE AN' SEE IF I CARE-
HAROLD GRAY
Reg. U. S. Pat. Off.; Copyright, 1930, by The Chicago Tribune.

August 11–13, 1930

HEY! GET AWAY FROM THERE, YOU GUYS!
SURE - I KNOW - YOU'RE JUST KEEPIN' DEACON COMPANY SO HE WON'T GET LONESOME - BUT IF HE FALLS OFF THAT SWING WHERE YOU CAN GET AT HIM, GOOD NIGHT!
DOG-GONED IF I KNOW WHY I SHOULD BE WORRYIN' 'BOUT YOU GETTIN' A FEW FEATHERS KNOCKED OUT - YOU WON'T TALK FOR ME - YOU WON'T EVEN TRY -
HAROLD GRAY
Reg. U. S. Pat. Off.; Copyright, 1930, by The Chicago Tribune.
? ?
ARF!
BOUF!
AWK!
LAY TO, YOU FLEA-BITTEN SON-OF-A-SEA-COOK!!! I'LL BATTEN YER HATCH WITH A BELAYIN' PIN---
? ?
RUN, YOU SWABS!!! HA! HA! HA! HA! HA!
Reg. U. S. Pat. Off.; Copyright, 1930, by The Chicago Tribune.
HAROLD GRAY
C'MON, YOU GUYS! I GOT A JOB FOR YUH -
?
GREAT CAESAR'S SUSPENDERS! SANDY AN' WILLIE OUT ON TH' SAND-BAR DIGGIN' OYSTERS AN' GIVIN' 'EM TO DEACON - AN' ONLY DAY 'FORE YESTERDAY THEY WERE TRYIN' TO BREAK HIS NECK - HE'S SURE GOT THEIR GOAT - BUT HOW?
HAROLD GRAY
Reg. U. S. Pat. Off.; Copyright, 1930, by The Chicago Tribune.

August 14–16, 1930
SHIPWRECKED

Little Orphan Annie
ANY MORE FRESH CRACKS OUTA YOU AND I'M GOIN' TO MAKE YOU INTO A SWELL PIE-
SAYS YOU!
HAROLD GRAY

LEAPIN' LIZARDS!!! OUR CALENDAR- NOT A MARK ON IT FOR DAYS AND DAYS-

CAP'N MARLIN WAS GOIN' TO PUT A MARK EVERY DAY SO WE'D ALWAYS KNOW JUST WHAT DAY IT WAS- I S'POSED HE'D BEEN TAKIN' CARE OF IT-

NOW WE ARE IN A PICKLE- DOG GONE THAT OLD GEEZER- HE'S GOT NOTHIN' TO DO BUT SIT IN TH' SHADE- I'M GOIN' TO TELL HIM A FEW THINGS-

NOW YOU'VE GONE AN' GOT US INTO A SWELL MESS- WHAT WAS TH' IDEA O' FORGETTIN' TO MARK TH' DAYS ON OUR CALENDAR? NOW HOW DO WE KNOW WHAT DAY IT IS?

CAN'T TELL SUNDAYS OR HOLIDAYS FROM ANY OTHER DAY- CAN'T EVEN TELL HOW LONG WE'VE BEEN HERE-
BATTEN MY HATCHES!!! I PLUMB FORGOT ALL ABOUT THE CALENDAR- SO MANY OTHER THINGS ON MY CHART- BEEN TOO BUSY-

TOO BUSY!!! TOO BUSY!!! HA-HA-HA-HA-HA!

SAY- TH' DEACON'S NOT SO DUMB- SOME TIMES I THINK HE'S RIGHT SMART-
SMART!!! BAH! SMART-ALECK, I'D SAY-

COME TO THINK OF IT, I CAN'T SEE WHY A CALENDAR IS SO BLAMED 'PORTANT TO US, ANYWAY- WE HAVEN'T ANY DATES TO KEEP- WE'RE NOT GOIN' ANYWHERE-

WHEN-EVER WE WANT A HOLIDAY WE CAN GO AHEAD AND HAVE ONE WITHOUT HAVIN' TO WAIT TILL SOME OLD CALENDAR SAYS IT'S TH' RIGHT TIME- NEVER THOUGHT O' THAT BEFORE-

MOST FOLKS HAVE TO WAIT A WHOLE WEEK JUST FOR SATURDAY AFTERNOON AND SUNDAY TO COME SO THEY CAN GO FISHIN' OR PICNICIN'- WE CAN MAKE EVERY DAY A DAY OFF, IF WE WANT TO-

THIS HAVIN' CERTAIN DAYS FOR EVERYTHING IS A LOT O' HORSE-RADISH- S'POSE EVER'BODY THREW AWAY THEIR CALENDARS- S'POSE DAYS WEREN'T NAMED- OR MONTHS- HOW'S THAT FOR AN IDEA?

HORSE-RADISH!!!
Reg. U. S. Pat. Off., Copyright, 1930, by The Chicago Tribune.

August 17, 1930

NOPE- NOT A SPECK ANY WHERE- LOOKS LIKE WE MIGHT BE MAROONED ON THIS ISLAND FOR YEARS-
GEE, IT'S SURE FUNNY NOBODY EVER EVEN COMES NEAR THIS PLACE-
COURSE WE CAN MAKE OUT ALL RIGHT- PLENTY HERE TO EAT, SUCH AS IT IS- BUT I TELL YUH ONE THING WE NEED IF WE'RE GOIN' TO STAY HERE MUCH LONGER- THAT'S A HOUSE-
RIGHT YOU BE, ANNIE- THE RAINY SEASON WILL BE HERE BEFORE LONG- WE'VE GOT ENOUGH LUMBER TO BUILD A GOOD HOUSE, TOO- WE SAVED ALMOST ALL THE BOAT- AND WE HAVE TOOLS AND PLENTY OF TIME-
WHILE THE LITTLE BOTTLE FLOATS UN NOTICED ALMOST UNDER THE NOSE OF JOHNNIE SCROD, FISHERMAN-
HAROLD GRAY
Reg. U. S. Pat. Off.; Copyright, 1930, by The Chicago Tribune.
NOW THERE'D BE A SWELL PLACE FOR OUR HOUSE- TH' TREES'D SHADE IT- IT'S HIGH ENOUGH TO BE SAFE FROM TH' OCEAN- AND IT'S CLOSE TO TH' SPRING.
NOW HERE'S MY IDEA- WE DON'T WANT A BIG HOUSE- AND TH' SAND IS CLEAN AND WILL MAKE A SWELL FLOOR- ALL WE NEED IS WALLS AND A ROOF-
AH HA! HOME, SWEET HOME!!!
AT LAST THE LITTLE BOTTLE, WITH IT'S PRECIOUS MESSAGE, CATCHES THE EYE OF A FISHERMAN-
?
HUH! JUST ANOTHER O' THEM BLAMED EMPTY BOTTLES- PIECE O' PAPER IN THAT ONE- BUT I'VE GOT NO USE FOR ANY PAPER-
HAROLD GRAY
Reg. U. S. Pat. Off.; Copyright, 1930, by The Chicago Tribune.
YESSIR- THERE OUGHTA BE EVER'THING WE NEED IN THAT PILE- MIGHT AS WELL START CARRYIN' TH' BOARDS UP WHERE WE NEED 'EM-
I BETCHA, CAP'N, WE HAVE A SWELL SHACK 'FORE WE GET DONE- THERE'S PLENTY O' LUMBER HERE AN' YOU'RE A DOG-GONED GOOD CARPENTER-
AYE, ANNIE- IF IT CAN BE DONE WITH TOOLS I RECKON OLD SPIKE MARLIN IS THE MAN TO DO IT- ALWAYS BEEN HANDY THAT WAY-
AND THUS THE LITTLE BOTTLE ENDS ITS AIMLESS WANDERING- HOW WILL JOHNNIE SCROD REACT TO IT'S VITAL MESSAGE?
THAT BLAMED BOTTLE HAS BEEN HANGIN' AROUND MY BOAT FOR TWO DAYS- MIGHT USE IT FOR SOMETHIN'-
HM-M-M-- YEP- THERE'S A PAPER IN IT WITH WRITIN' ON IT- CAN'T SEE IT VERY WELL WITHOUT TAKIN' IT OUT- I'LL TAKE IT HOME AN' LET ELLA LOOK AT IT-
HAROLD GRAY
Reg. U. S. Pat. Off.; Copyright, 1930, by The Chicago Tribune.

August 18–20, 1930

WONDER WHERE THAT S. O. S. OF OURS IN THE BOTTLE HAS FLOATED TO BY THIS TIME- MUSTA GONE A LONG WAY BY NOW
GEE- I'D 'MOST FORGOTTEN 'BOUT THAT BOTTLE-
AND HERE AT LAST WE SEE JOHNNIE SCROD BRINGING HOME THE PRECIOUS BOTTLE, STILL UNOPENED-
ELLA'S FUNNY- SHE'LL GIT A BIG KICK OUTA THIS-
FOUND THAT FLOATIN' OFF TH' PINT- LOOK- THERE'S A PAPER IN THERE WITH WRITIN' ALL OVER IT-
YEAH- GEE- THAT'S CUTE, AIN'T IT- WONDER WHERE IT CAME FROM- BET IT SAYS SOMETHING AWFUL IMPORTANT-
SURE WISHT I COULD READ-
YEAH- SO DO I-
HAROLD GRAY
Reg. U. S. Pat. Off.; Copyright, 1930, by The Chicago Tribune.
RUN AND GET ME SOME MORE NAILS, WILL YOU PLEASE, ANNIE?
GEE- THIS IS SURE GOIN' TO BE SOME SHACK!
SOME SHACK, EH?
WELL, WE'VE DONE A PRETTY GOOD DAY'S WORK- BY TO MORROW NIGHT WE'LL HAVE THE ROOF ON-
WITH A GOOD ROOF OVER US WE WON'T CARE HOW HARD IT RAINS- C'MON- LET'S KNOCK OFF NOW AND HAVE SUPPER- WHADDYUH SAY?
FATE, OH UNKIND FATE! WHAT HAS ANNIE EVER DONE TO YOU THAT YOU SHOULD THUS SILENCE HER CALL FOR HELP?
AW, SOMEBODY AS KIN READ WILL COME ALONG SOME DAY- SET IT THERE ON THE SHELF FOR NOW-
LOOKS NICE UP THERE, DON'T IT- SORTA MYSTERIOUS LIKE- NO TELLIN' WHERE IT CAME FROM, OR WHO WRIT IT, OR NOTHIN'-
HAROLD GRAY
Reg. U. S. Pat. Off.; Copyright, 1930, by The Chicago Tribune.
THERE- THAT'LL JUST FINISH THIS ROOF ALL TIGHT AND SNUG-
HOT DAWG! YESSIR, THAT'S GOIN' TO BE SOME HOUSE!
QUIETLY ON THE SHELF THE LITTLE BOTTLE SITS, UNABLE TO CRY ALOUD, HELPLESS TO DELIVER IT'S MESSAGE-
THERE'S THAT BOTTLE- ELLA'S GOT A CRAZY IDEE IT'S IMPORTANT- DON'T KNOW WHY-
JUST AN ORDINARY BOTTLE- STILL, THAT WRITIN' MIGHT SAY 'MOST ANYTHING- I DUNNO- I'LL HAVE TO GET SOME FELLER AS KIN READ TO LOOK AT IT- ELLA'LL NEVER BE SATISFIED TILL I DO-
HAROLD GRAY
Reg. U. S. Pat. Off.; Copyright, 1930, by The Chicago Tribune.

August 21–23, 1930

Little Orphan Annie
HEY, CAP'N! LOOKIE! I'VE GOT TH' MAKIN'S OF A SWELL FISH FRY -
HAROLD GRAY

YEAH - THAT'S A SWELL HOUSE, ALL RIGHT - BUT, GREAT SCOTT - NO WINDOWS? ANY REAL HOUSE HAS GOTTA HAVE WINDOWS -
HM-M- THAT'S RIGHT -

LEAPIN' LIZARDS!!! CAN'T LEAVE JUST HOLES IN TH' WALL - COURSE LIGHT WOULD COME IN ALL RIGHT, BUT SO WOULD RAIN AND SKEETERS AND 'MOST ANYTHING -

HM-M-M - THERE'S TH' SKY-LIGHT FROM TH' BOAT - NOW I BETCHA THERE'S SOME WAY WE COULD USE THAT - TH' GLASS ISN'T BUSTED AT ALL -

HEY, SANDY - YOU RUN BACK AND GET CAP'N MARLIN AND BRING HIM HERE QUICK AS YUH CAN -

GEE - I DUNNO JUST HOW WE'RE GOIN' TO USE THIS, BUT TH' CAP'N IS PRETTY HANDY - HE'LL FIGGER IT OUT -

SEE? THERE'S TH' SKY-LIGHT - THERE OUGHTA BE SOME WAY O' MAKIN' WINDOWS OUTA THAT -
AYE-AYE, ANNIE - RIGHT YOU ARE, AND NO MISTAKE -

CAREFUL, ANNIE - DON'T DROP THAT - WE CAN'T GET ANY OTHER -
SAY - WHOSE IDEA WAS THIS, ANYWAY? D'YUH THINK I'M GOIN' TO BUST THIS IF I CAN HELP IT?

GEE - TH' CAP'N SURE TOLD TH' TRUTH WHEN HE SAID HE WAS A SWELL CARPENTER -

SAY, YOU'RE FULL OF IDEAS, TOO, AREN'T YOU, CAP'N - I'D NEVER HAVE THOUGHT OF A PORCH -
THESE BAMBOO POLES ARE LIGHT AND STRONG - THEY'LL MAKE A SOLID FRAME -

HEY - DON'T PULL IT TOO TIGHT OR YOU'LL RIP IT -
THERE - NOW WE'LL BE SNUG AND SHIP-SHAPE NO MATTER WHAT HAPPENS -

LOOK AT TH' DEACON - HE SURE HAS IT SOFT - WONDER WHAT HE THINKS 'BOUT ALL THIS BUILDIN' -
AHOY THERE, DEACON - HOW'S THIS FOR A SNUG PORT?

PRETTY SOFT!!! PRETTY SOFT!!! HA-HA-HA-HA -
HAW-HAW!! CHECK AND DOUBLE CHECK!
AYE, AYE -

August 24, 1930

WELL, ANNIE- HOW'S THAT FOR A HOUSE?
GEE, CAP'N- IT SURE IS A PEACH-
NOW WE'LL CARRY IN THE CHESTS AND THE REST OF OUR STUFF AND WE'LL BE DONE-
WHADDYUH MEAN, "DONE"? I'M GOIN' TO HAVE TO HAVE A BUNCH O' CUP-BOARDS AN' SHELVES- AN' WE NEED A TABLE RIGHT AWAY, TOO-
WHILE STILL THE LITTLE BOTTLE SITS, IT'S MESSAGE STILL UNTOLD-
SAY, JOHNNIE- WHEN ARE YUH GOIN' TO GIT THAT PAPER READ?
OH, I'LL GIT SOME FELLER AS KIN READ TO LOOK AT IT SOME DAY-
NOT JUST SOME FELLER- THAT PAPER MIGHT BE AWFUL IMPORTANT- YOU GIT A FELLER AS IS HONEST, ELSE HOW'LL YOU KNOW IF HE'S REALLY TELLIN' YOU WHAT IT SAYS?
HAROLD GRAY
Reg. U. S. Pat. Off.; Copyright, 1930, by The Chicago Tribune.
THAT'S A MIGHTY SWELL FENCE- BUT DO YUH THINK IT'LL BE STRONG ENOUGH TO HOLD GOATS?
AYE- IT'LL BE STRONG ENOUGH, IF WE CAN ONLY CATCH THE GOATS-
WILD GOATS ARE MIGHTY SHY O' PEOPLE- BUT IT'S A SMALL ISLAND- WE OUGHT TO BE ABLE TO CATCH A FEW-
GEE- THEN WE CAN HAVE MILK AN' BUTTER AN' CHEESE JUST LIKE A REG'LAR FARM-
WHILE JOHNNIE SCROD REFUSES TO BECOME EXCITED OVER WHAT THE PAPER IN THE BOTTLE MAY HAVE TO TELL-
DURNED IF I DON'T ALMOST WISHT I'D NEVER TAKEN THAT BOTTLE HOME- ELLA WON'T GIVE ME A MINUTE'S REST- TALKS ABOUT IT ALL TH' TIME-
NOBODY 'ROUND HERE AS READS- COURSE I COULD TAKE THAT PAPER 'ROUND TH' PINT TO TH' STORE- FELLER THERE COULD READ IT- BUT WHAT'S HER HURRY? I'VE GOT WORK TO DO- IT'LL KEEP-
HAROLD GRAY
Reg. U. S. Pat. Off.; Copyright, 1930, by The Chicago Tribune.
YIPPEY! YIPPEY! YIPPEY! KEEP 'EM BUNCHED- THEY'RE HEADED STRAIGHT FOR TH' GATE IN TH' PEN-
STEADY, NOW- IF ONE OF 'EM GOES IN THEY'LL ALL FOLLOW HIM AN' WE'LL HAVE 'EM-
STOP 'EM, SANDY- AW, SHUX!!! WHADDYUH WANTA LET 'EM GET AWAY FOR? AN' AFTER ALL TH' TROUBLE WE HAD GETTIN' 'EM THIS FAR-
YIPE
THE LITTLE BOTTLE THAT WILL BOB NO MORE
OH, MY HEAVENLY STARS! IT SLIPPED-
HAROLD GRAY
Reg. U. S. Pat. Off.; Copyright, 1930, by The Chicago Tribune.

August 25–27, 1930

THERE'S THOSE GOATS NOW- BUT YUH CAN'T GET ANYWHERE NEAR 'EM- THEY'RE TOO BLAMED CAGEY-
YEAH - I KNEW IT - TOOK ONE LOOK AT ME AN' LIT OUT A HUNDRED MILES AN HOUR- I'M THEIR FRIEND, BUT HOW YUH GOIN' TO SELL AN IDEA LIKE THAT TO A WILD GOAT?
AND NOW TO GET BACK TO THE BOTTLE AND IT'S MESSAGE -
HEY, ELLA- WHAT DIDJA DO WITH THAT BOTTLE?
OH, I MEANT TO TELL YUH ABOUT THAT- IT DROPPED AND BUSTED- BUT I SAVED TH' PAPER WITH THE WRITIN' ON IT- I GOT IT PUT AWAY-
HAROLD GRAY
Reg. U. S. Pat. Off.; Copyright, 1930, by The Chicago Tribune.
DON'T WAKE ME UP- IS IT? YESSIR- IT IS - A LITTLE BABY GOAT!
AH! GOT HIM!
BAA!
COURSE HE'S JUST A LITTLE FELLER. BUT MOST BIG BUSINESSES HAVE STARTED SMALL THEY SAY- I MAY BE WRONG, BUT IF MY IDEA WORKS OUT I BET I GET A HERD O' GOATS 'FORE LONG- WE'LL SEE-
FIRST THE BOTTLE GOES CRASH--- NOW WHAT HAS BECOME OF THE PAPER?
JOHNNIE WANTS TO TAKE THAT PAPER TO TOWN TO GIT IT READ - NOW WHERE DID I PUT IT? I REMEMBER PUTTIN' IT AWAY REAL CAREFUL- LET ME THINK-
HAROLD GRAY
Reg. U. S. Pat. Off.; Copyright, 1930, by The Chicago Tribune.
BAA-A!
THERE!!! NOW I'VE GOT 'EM WHERE I WANT 'EM-A LITTLE KIND TREATMENT NOW AN' THEY'LL BE TAME IN NO TIME-
BA-AA-
BA-A-A
AND IN THE MEANTIME THE MESSAGE OF DISTRESS SEEMS WELL ON THE ROAD TO OBLIVION-
WELL, I AIN'T A'GOIN' TO WAIT ALL DAY- WHERE DIDJA PUT IT?
AIN'T I A'LOOKIN' FOR IT? I'LL FIND IT- GIMME TIME-
AIN'T THAT A MAN FOR YUH? JUST 'CAUSE I CAN'T LAY MY HANDS ON THAT PAPER RIGHT OFF, AWAY HE GOES WITHOUT IT- NO TELLIN' NOW WHEN WE'LL GIT IT READ, IF EVER-
HAROLD GRAY
Reg. U. S. Pat. Off.; Copyright, 1930, by The Chicago Tribune.

August 28–30, 1930

Little Orphan Annie

HEY- LOOK BEHIND YUH!
WHERE?
HAROLD GRAY

AH HA! AH HA! GOOD MORNING! GOOD MORNING! GOOD MORNING!
MORNIN' YERSELF, DEACON - YOU SURE ARE GETTIN' TO TALK SWELL-

WELL, GUESS I MIGHT AS WELL GO AN' DO TH' MILKIN'- SINCE WE CAUGHT THOSE GOATS AN' GOT TH' GARDEN PLANTED WE'RE GETTIN' TO HAVE QUITE A COUNTRY ESTATE-

SHOO!!! DOG GONED BIRDS! DIG UP TH' SEEDS FASTER'N YUH CAN PLANT 'EM-

I'VE TOLD HIM AN' TOLD HIM TO PUT UP THAT SCARE-CROW - OH, WELL- I'LL 'TEND TO IT MYSELF- GOTTA DO TH' MILKIN' FIRST-

LEAPIN' LIZARDS!!! TH' GOATS HAVE BUSTED OUT- I KNEW THEY WOULD- THERE WAS A WEAK SPOT IN TH' FENCE THERE YESTERDAY-

I TOLD HIM 'BOUT THAT, TOO, AN' HE SAID HE'D FIX IT RIGHT AWAY- HE'S TOO LAZY TO BREATHE- I'M SURE GOIN' TO FEED HIM A STRIP O' MY MIND 'BOUT THIS- AN' AFTER ALL TH' TROUBLE WE HAD CATCHIN' THOSE GOATS!

SOUND ASLEEP AGAIN- WELL, BY JOSHUA, I'VE GOT AN ALARM CLOCK I'LL BET WILL WAKE HIM UP FOR ALL DAY-

THESE HORNETS WORKED A WEEK BUILDIN' THIS- GOTTA BE QUICK, NOW- IT'S TOO HOT TO HANDLE CARELESS- JUST ONE FUMBLE AND WE'D ALL BE AWFUL SORRY-

THERE, SLEEPIN' BEAUTY- SEE IF YUH CAN SNORE THROUGH THAT!!!

YI!

WHY, CAP'N- YOU'RE UP EARLY- TAKIN' YER MORNIN' PLUNGE ALREADY? THAT'S FINE- LOTS TO DO TO-DAY- TH' GOATS ARE OUT- GOTTA FIX TH' FENCE- I BROUGHT YUH THE AXE-

YESSIR, CAP'N- IT SURE WAS LUCKY YOU HAPPENIN' TO WAKE UP SO EARLY WHEN THERE'S SO MUCH TO DO- I'LL STAY RIGHT HERE TILL YUH GET IT DONE- .... AN' HELP YUH-

August 31, 1930
SHIPWRECKED

AFTER ALL TH' TROUBLE WE HAD CATCHIN' THOSE GOATS TO HAVE 'EM BUST LOOSE RIGHT AWAY-
THEY'LL BE HARDER THAN EVER TO CATCH NOW AFTER THIS-
AYE- BUT IF YOU DO CATCH THEM AGAIN THEY WON'T BREAK THROUGH THIS FENCE, I WARRANT YOU-
WHILE FAR AWAY JOHNNIE SCROD, PEACEFULLY DOZING AND HEEDLESS OF FOG HORNS, IS NEARLY RUN DOWN BY A LARGE YACHT-
HEY!
WATCH WHERE YER GOIN'- YUH ✱!!! !!!!!✱!!
BUTTON YOUR LIP- CAN'T YOU HEAR A FOG HORN? ARE YOU ASLEEP?
HAROLD GRAY
Reg. U. S. Pat. Off.; Copyright, 1930, by The Chicago Tribune.
SH-H-H-- THERE'S THAT LITTLE GOAT NOW- IF I CAN ONLY CATCH HIM AGAIN-
SHUX!
BA-A-A-A!
ALREADY WARBUCKS HAS FORGOTTEN THE FISHERMAN HIS YACHT NEARLY HIT IN THE FOG- IF HE COULD ONLY KNOW THAT THAT MAN, JOHN SCROD, COULD GIVE HIM THE KEY TO HIS PUZZLE-
LET'S SEE, NOW- ONLY A FEW PLACES LEFT TO LOOK-
ONLY A FEW MORE ISLANDS AND WE'LL HAVE SWEPT THESE WATERS CLEAN- FUNNY WE'VE PICKED UP NO TRACE OF HER THUS FAR- THAT BOAT MUST HAVE COME ASHORE SOME PLACE- WELL, I'LL KEEP ON LOOKING- I WON'T GIVE UP-
HAROLD GRAY
Reg. U. S. Pat. Off.; Copyright, 1930, by The Chicago Tribune.
?
BAA!
NICE, BILLY- NICE NANNY- COME, BILLY- COME, NANNY- THAT'S A GOOD GOAT- DON'T BE SCARED- I JUST WANTA PET YUH-
DOG GONE THEIR HIDES! THEY'RE FAST AS LIGHTNIN' AND NOT EVEN A GOOD SIZED TAIL TO GRAB HOLD OF-
HUMPH! I'LL NEVER GET TO FIRST BASE THAT WAY- THEY'LL COME RIGHT UP TO ME BUT THEY WON'T LET ME TOUCH 'EM- STILL, AS LONG AS THEY'RE THAT FRIENDLY THERE MUST BE SOME WAY TO FOOL 'EM-
HAROLD GRAY
Reg. U. S. Pat. Off.; Copyright, 1930, by The Chicago Tribune.

September 1–3, 1930

GOT A NEW LINE FOR YUH, DEACON - YOU LEARN THIS AND I'LL SURE SEE THAT YOU AREN'T SORRY -
COME, NANNY! COME, BILLY! TRY IT NOW, DEACON - COME, BILLY!
BLAH!
ALL RIGHT FOR YOU - IF YER GOIN' TO GET BULL-HEADED I CAN SEE WHERE WE'RE GOIN' TO HAVE A SWELL PARROT-PIE MIGHTY SOON - WHERE'S THAT BIG KETTLE?
COME, BILLY!!! COME, NANNY!!!
?
HAROLD GRAY
Reg. U. S. Pat. Off.; Copyright, 1930, by The Chicago Tribune.
I KNOW IT'S TOUGH, DEACON - BUT YOU HADN'T OUGHTA HAVE TO STAY HERE LONG IF YUH HOLLER LIKE I SAID -
THAT OUGHTA BRING 'EM OUT - SH-H-H-H - I HEAR 'EM COMIN' NOW -
COME, BILLY - COME, NANNY!
? ? ?
HERE, NANNY! HERE, BILLY!
SHUX - THEY JUST COME AND LISTEN BUT WON'T COME OUTA TH' BUSHES - THEY SURE ARE GETTIN' HARD TO FOOL - S'PICIOUS - THAT'S WHAT THEY ARE -
HAROLD GRAY
Reg. U. S. Pat. Off.; Copyright, 1930, by The Chicago Tribune.
HERE, NANNY - HERE, BILLY -
THERE! THAT TRICK WORKED OUT AFTER ALL -
MA-A-A!
NOW BLAT YER HEAD OFF - TH' LOUDER TH' BETTER - YOU'LL HAVE LOTS O' COMPANY IN HERE 'FORE LONG -
GOOD WORK, DEACON - YUH KEPT HIS 'TENTION SO I COULD SLIP UP BEHIND HIM - SORRY IT TOOK SO LONG - YOU MUST BE AWFUL TIRED -
AW, BLAH! PAIN IN TH' NECK! !!! !!
HAROLD GRAY
Reg. U. S. Pat. Off.; Copyright, 1930, by The Chicago Tribune.

September 4–6, 1930

Little Orphan Annie
HAROLD GRAY
WELL, I S'POSE LOTS O' KIDS WOULD BE GLAD TO TRADE PLACES WITH ME TO KEEP FROM GOIN' BACK TO SCHOOL - GEE- I'D SURE SWAP PLACES WITH ANY KID THAT DUMB, AND NO QUESTIONS ASKED -

YI!

OW-W-W--- RIGHT ON MY THUMB !!!

HOLD STILL NOW, CAP'N- I KNOW IT HURTS, BUT THIS'LL FIX IT UP IN NO TIME-
JUST MY LUCK- SEEMS LIKE EVERYTHING GOES WRONG FOR ME- ALWAYS BEEN THAT WAY-

YESSIR- I'VE SURE HAD MORE'N MY SHARE OF BAD LUCK IN MY LIFETIME-

BLAH !! - BAD LUCK! ALWAYS PUTTIN' UP A SQUAWK ABOUT SOMETHIN'- S'POSE HE NEVER STOPS TO COUNT TH' GOOD BREAKS HE'S HAD- WHY, HE'S LUCKY TO BE ALIVE-

GEE- WHEN I THINK O' TH' GOOD LUCK I'VE HAD !!! EVEN TH' ORPHAN "HOME" COULD HAVE BEEN WORSE- AND DIDN'T TH' "HOME" BURN DOWN?

AND WHEN TH' BANK ROBBERS CAUGHT ME I GOT AWAY, DIDN'T I?

AND JUST THINK O' ALL TH' FRIENDS I'VE MADE- TH' SILOS, TH' FLINTS, MRS. PEWTER, TH' DOOLEYS, MRS. TWINKLE, AND TH' BEST OF 'EM ALL IS "DADDY" WARBUCKS- HAVIN' FRIENDS LIKE THAT SURE IS A GOOD BREAK-

AND HEALTH- COURSE I'VE HAD ACCIDENTS, SAME AS MOST FOLKS- BUT I'VE GOT ALL MY ARMS AN' LEGS AN' I FEEL LIKE A MILLION BUCKS-

AND JUST TAKE THIS LAST TRIP- I COULD HAVE GOT DROWNED EASY AS NOT-

BUT HERE WE ARE, SAFE AN' SOUND, ON THIS ISLAND- NICE CLIMATE- PLENTY TO EAT- NOTHIN' MUCH TO DO- NO SANCT'MONIOUS OLD BUSY-BODIES TRYIN' TO RUN OUR BUSINESS FOR US- WHAT IF EVER'THING ISN'T JUST ZACTLY PERFECT?

NO SIR- 'STEAD O' ALWAYS CRABBIN' ABOUT HOW MUCH BAD LUCK THEY'VE HAD, WHY CAN'T FOLKS GO AROUND BRAGGIN' A LITTLE AN' SAY "I'VE SURE HAD MY SHARE O' GOOD LUCK IN THIS WORLD"-
Reg. U. S. Pat. Off.; Copyright, 1930, by The Chicago Tribune.

September 7, 1930

TH' CAP'N'S BEEN JUST SITTIN' THERE LIKE THAT EVER SINCE HE GOT UP - ACTS LIKE HE DOESN'T FEEL SO GOOD -
I WOULDN'T SAY HE'S JUST LAZY, BUT, JUST TH' SAME, IT'S PRETTY EASY TO FEEL A LITTLE SICK WHEN YUH THINK O' ALL THERE IS TO DO AN' HOW HOT IT IS - CAN'T BLAME HIM FOR STALLIN' A LITTLE -
HERE'S YER DINNER, CAP'N -
RECKON I WON'T EAT ANYTHING RIGHT NOW, ANNIE - I FEEL A LEETLE BIT UNDER THE WEATHER -
LEAPIN' LIZARDS! HE NEVER TURNED DOWN FOOD BEFORE - HE MUST BE A LITTLE SICK, AFTER ALL -
HAROLD GRAY
Reg. U. S. Pat. Off.; Copyright, 1930, by The Chicago Tribune.
GEE - TH' CAP'N DIDN'T EAT A THING ALL DAY YESTERDAY, AND HERE IT IS NOON AND HE'S STILL IN BED - SOMETHIN' SURE IS WRONG WITH HIM -
HOW YUH FEELIN' TO DAY, CAP'N? BETTER?
NO, ANNIE - CAN'T SAY AS I BE ANY BETTER - RECKON THE HEAT OR SOMETHING SORTA GOT THE BEST O' ME -
WELL, YOU JUST TAKE IT EASY - BUT KEEP COVERED UP - I THINK YOU HAVE JUST A LITTLE FEVER -
HAROLD GRAY
LITTLE FEVER! HE'S RED HOT - AND I DON'T KNOW A DOG-GONED THING I CAN DO 'BOUT IT - OH, WELL - A GOOD REST AND HE'LL BE O. K., I GUESS -
Reg. U. S. Pat. Off.; Copyright, 1930, by The Chicago Tribune.
HERE, CAP'N - TRY THIS - IT'S A LIME JUICE DRINK - I MADE FOR YOU - IT'S AS COLD AS I COULD MAKE IT WITHOUT ICE - YOU'LL LIKE THIS -
HE DRANK THAT AND ASKED FOR MORE - WELL, WE'VE GOT PLENTY O' LIMES AND PLENTY O' GOOD, COLD SPRING-WATER - I'LL MAKE A BIG PITCHER FULL AND PUT IT RIGHT BY HIS BED -
HERE Y'ARE, CAP'N - ANY TIME YUH WANT IT -
GEE, WHIZ - IF WE ONLY HAD A DOCTOR - BUT I DON'T KNOW WHAT TO DO - HE'S HOTTER'N A 4-11 FIRE - 'CEPT FOR YOU TWO GUYS HE'S TH' ONLY FRIEND I'VE GOT ANY MORE -
HAROLD GRAY

September 8–10, 1930

THIS SPRING WATER IS ALMOST ICE COLD- IF I COULD ONLY KEEP IT THAT WAY- BUT HOW CAN YUH WITHOUT ICE?
GOTTA KEEP COLD TOWELS ON TH' CAP'N'S HEAD- HE RESTS LOTS EASIER AN' IT KEEPS HIS FEVER DOWN A LITTLE- HE SURE IS AWFUL SICK-
ASLEEP- HE DOESN'T KNOW WHAT'S GOIN' ON AT ALL MOST O' TH' TIME TO DAY- GEE- WHAT IF I'D LOSE TH' CAP'N- WHAT'D I DO THEN?
AW, THAT'S SELFISH- I'D GET BY SOME WAY- I ALWAYS HAVE- BUT WE'VE GOTTA PULL HIM THROUGH- HE'S TOO SWELL A GUY TO LET DOWN- HE NEEDS STRENGTH- MAYBE I CAN GET HIM TO TAKE SOME SOUP TO NIGHT-
HAROLD GRAY
Reg. U. S. Pat. Off.; Copyright, 1930, by The Chicago Tribune.
YO-HO-HO! AND A BOTTLE O' RUM!!!
ALL HANDS ON DECK- LEAVE GO THE MAIN SHEET YOU —!—!!! LUBBERS!
NOW, NOW, CAP'N- STEADY- YOU'LL BE ALL RIGHT- EASY, NOW- EVER'THING'S GOIN' TO BE O.K.
Reg. U. S. Pat. Off.; Copyright, 1930, by The Chicago Tribune
WHOOPS IT UP ONE MINUTE AND OUT COLD TH' NEXT- HE'S GETTIN' WORSE EVERY SECOND- WHAT CAN I DO, SANDY? WHAT CAN I DO?
HAROLD GRAY
OH, ANNIE!
YES, CAP'N- GEE, I DIDN'T KNOW HE WAS AWAKE-
WHAT TIME IS IT, ANNIE?
OH, IT'S EARLY YET- TH' SUN'S ONLY BEEN UP A LITTLE WHILE-
GEE- YOU'RE SURE LOTS BETTER TO DAY-
AYE- GUESS I'VE BEEN A LITTLE OUT OF MY HEAD- HOPE I DIDN'T SAY ANYTHING I SHOULDN'T- SAILOR MEN TALK PRETTY ROUGH SOME TIMES-
NAW- YOU WERE O.K. BUT I SURE WAS SCARED- YOU HAD AN AWFUL FEVER-
NEVER WORRY OVER ME, ANNIE- OLD SPIKE MARLIN IS TOO TOUGH AN OLD SALT TO BE LICKED BY A LITTLE FEVER-
HAROLD GRAY
Reg. U. S. Pat. Off.; Copyright, 1930, by The Chicago Tribune.

September 11–13, 1930

Little Orphan Annie

LEAPIN' LIZARDS!!! HAVE I CHANGED THAT MUCH JUST FROM LIVIN' ON THIS ISLAND FOR A COUPLE O' MONTHS?

HAROLD GRAY

THERE - THAT DRESS SURE NEEDED WASHIN' - BUT I'VE GOT IT GOOD AND CLEAN AT LAST - I'LL JUST PUT IT HERE ON THIS BUSH IN THE SUN TO DRY WHILE I GO FOR A LITTLE SWIM -

OH, BOY - IS THIS SWELL!!! MUSTN'T GO OUT TOO FAR OR I'LL HAVE A FLOCK O' SHARKS AFTER ME - BUT HERE NEAR THE SHORE I'M SAFE ENOUGH -

SANDY WAS SOUND ASLEEP WHEN I LEFT THE HOUSE - HE'LL HAVE A FIT WHEN HE WAKES UP AND FINDS I'M GONE - I CAN JUST SEE HIM LOOKIN' ALL OVER FOR ME NOW -

ARF!

EEK!
YIPE!

AR-R-R!!!
OOPIE!

E-YEOW!

R-R-R!
YI-
YI-
YI-

RIGHT ON TH' BUSH WHERE I LEFT IT, ALL NICE AND DRY - IT SURE DOES FEEL GOOD TO GET INTO CLEAN CLOTHES -

WELL - SO YOU FINALLY WOKE UP AND CAME TO FIND ME - YOU DON'T KNOW TH' HALF OF IT - HERE I'VE WASHED MY DRESS AND I'VE BEEN FOR A SWIM - YOU SURE MISSED A LOT, ALL RIGHT -

September 14, 1930

TH' CAP'N SURE IS COMIN' BACK FAST- GOT HIS APPETITE BACK ALL RIGHT- SAYS HE WANTS COCOANUT MILK TO DRINK NOW-
AH! I SEE YOU FOUND SOME NICE RIPE COCOANUTS- THAT'S THE TICKET-
HEY! WHAT'S THIS? SITTIN' UP? YOU'D BETTER TAKE IT EASY FOR A WHILE YET-
OH, I FEEL ALMOST AS HALE AND HEARTY AS I EVER DID- I'LL BE GETTING UP SOON-
YEAH? WELL, YOU'VE BEEN MIGHTY SICK- YOU CAN'T EXPECT TO BE ALL WELL IN A DAY-
THERE Y'ARE- HOW DOES THAT TASTE?
AH-H-H!!! NOTHING LIKE COCOANUT MILK FOR WHAT AILS YOU- I FEEL STRONGER EVERY MINUTE-
HAROLD GRAY
Reg. U. S. Pat. Off.; Copyright, 1930, by The Chicago Tribune.
THERE - SOUND ASLEEP AT LAST- HE NEEDS THE REST- HE'S BETTER, BUT HE'S AWFUL WEAK YET-
GEE, I'M TIRED- BUT I'VE GOT TOO MUCH TO DO TO EVEN THINK OF TAKIN' A NAP NOW-
HAVEN'T HAD HARDLY A WINK OF SLEEP FOR A WEEK- BUT I'LL HAVE LOTS O' TIME TO CATCH UP MY REST, NOW THAT TH' CAP'N IS COMIN' AROUND O. K.
Reg. U. S. Pat. Off.; Copyright, 1930, by The Chicago Tribune.
SHUX! I'M YOUNG AN' STRONG- WHAT IF I DO FEEL TIRED RIGHT NOW- ONE GOOD NIGHT'S REST AND I'LL BE FRESH AS A DAISY-
HAROLD GRAY
AH, THAT'S IT, ANNIE- THE MEDICINE CHEST- I KNEW IT WAS AROUND SOME PLACE-
GEE- I DIDN'T KNOW WE HAD ANY MEDICINE- WHY DIDN'T YOU TELL ME BEFORE?
GUESS I SORTA FORGOT IT MYSELF- OUT OF MY HEAD, AS IT WERE- GOTTA GO EASY WITH IT, ANYWAY- CAN'T GET ANY MORE WHEN THIS RUNS OUT- NO DRUG STORES HEREABOUTS-
ONE OR TWO GOOD DOSES WILL CHASE WHAT'S LEFT OF THIS FEVER OUT OF MY SYSTEM IN NO TIME-
I TASTED IT- GEE- IT'S AWFUL STUFF- I BETCHA I'D ALMOST RATHER HAVE A FEVER THAN TAKE MUCH O' THIS-
MEDICINE- GEE- DRUG STORES ARE SO HANDY MOST FOLKS NEVER RE'LIZE HOW 'PORTANT THEY ARE- GUESS YUH HAVE TO MISS SOMETHIN' REAL BAD 'FORE YUH REALLY 'PRECIATE IT-
HAROLD GRAY
Reg. U. S. Pat. Off.; Copyright, 1930 by The Chicago Tribune.

September 15–17, 1930

WHEW!!! I DIDN'T RE'LIZE IT WAS GETTIN' SO LATE- JUST LOOK WHERE THE SUN IS- I'D BETTER HURRY-
IT'S TIME FOR TH' CAP'N'S MEDICINE- HE'LL NEVER TAKE IT IF I DON'T FIX IT FOR HIM- GEE, HOW HE HATES IT-
HERE Y'ARE, CAP'N - A NICE, BIG GLASS FULL- HOLD YER NOSE AN' YUH'LL HARDLY TASTE IT AT ALL-
THANKS, ANNIE- BUT I REALLY DON'T THINK I NEED IT-
BR-R-R- OOF! THAT'S TERRIBLE SLOP!!!
HAW! HAW! HAW! GEE, WHAT A FACE! IT SURE MUST BE GOOD FOR YOU TO MAKE YOU LOOK LIKE THAT-
HAROLD GRAY
Reg. U. S. Pat. Off.; Copyright, 1930, by The Chicago Tribune.
OH, I CAN WALK ALL RIGHT ALONE, ANNIE- I FEEL FINE TO DAY-
SURE- I KNOW- BUT I'LL JUST STICK CLOSE, IN CASE-
THERE- HOW'S THAT? PRETTY GOOD TO GET OUT IN THE OPEN AGAIN, EH?
AYE! I'LL GET MY STRENGTH BACK FAST NOW THAT I CAN GET ABOUT ON MY OWN POWER-
HE'S AWFUL WOBBLY ON HIS PINS- BUT HE'S UP AN' AROUND- I'LL JUST FIX HIS BED UP- HE'LL BE TIRED OUT QUICK TH' FIRST TIME OR TWO-
AT THAT I BET HE CAN'T GET AS TIRED AS I AM - COURSE I MUSTN'T LET HIM KNOW HOW ALL IN I AM- I'LL GET A CHANCE TO SLEEP IN A DAY OR TWO- GOT TO GET HIM ALL WELL FIRST
HAROLD GRAY
Reg. U. S. Pat. Off.; Copyright, 1930, by The Chicago Tribune.
GEE- TH' CAP'N SURE IS GETTIN' HIS STRENGTH BACK FAST- THERE HE GOES FOR A REAL WALK ALL ALONE- GUESS HE'S ABOUT WELL AGAIN NOW ALL RIGHT-
OOOH! GEE, I FEEL AWFUL FUNNY INSIDE- MUST BE SOMETHIN' I ATE- BEEN FEELIN' THIS WAY FOR A COUPLE O' DAYS- OH, WELL- A GOOD SLEEP AND I'LL BE O. K.-
OW!!! THERE GOES THAT HEADACHE AGAIN- I NEVER HAVE HEADACHES- MUST BE TH' HEAT OR SOMETHIN'- WISH I COULD LIE DOWN FOR A WHILE-
BUT I'VE GOTTA GET DINNER READY FIRST- THEN I'M GOIN' TO TURN IN AND SLEEP FOR A WEEK- I SURE AM SO-
HAROLD GRAY
Reg. U. S. Pat. Off.; Copyright, 1930, by The Chicago Tribune.

September 18–20, 1930

Little Orphan Annie

NOW, SANDY-
WHADDYUH SAY?
ARF!
HAROLD GRAY

WELL, TH' CAP'N HAD A LITTLE TOUCH O' M'LERIA, OR JUNGLE FEVER, OR SOMETHIN'- DON'T KNOW JUST WHAT IT WAS, BUT HE SURE WAS SICK- BUT HE'S ON HIS PINS AGAIN NOW-

WELL, TH' FISH WE CAUGHT YESTERDAY ARE O. K.- I JUST WANTED TO BE SURE THEY WERE STILL HERE-

COURSE I COULD CATCH SOME MORE IF I HAD TO, BUT I DON'T FEEL SO BLAMED GOOD TO DAY- SORTA DOPEY- BUT I CAN'T 'FORD TO GET SICK- GOTTA KEEP GOIN'-

LEAPIN' LIZARDS!!! I SURE FEEL DIZZY- AND HOT ALL OVER-

MUST BE TH' HEAT- GET IN TH' SHADE AND I'LL BE ALL RIGHT- GOLLY, I CAN HARDLY WALK- AND NOW I FEEL COLD ALL OVER- BR-R-R-R!!!
?
?

SOMETHIN'S WRONG WITH ME- EVER'THING'S GOIN' AROUND LIKE A TOP- I'LL JUST SIT HERE FOR A MINUTE-

BELAY, THERE, SANDY- WELL, JAM MY WINDLASS! WHAT'S UP? WANT ME TO FOLLOW YOU, EH?

OH, I FEEL TERRIBLE- ALL HOT AN' COLD- AN' EVER'THING LOOKS FUNNY- I DON'T KNOW WHICH WAY IS HOME- SANDY- WILLIE- CAP'N----

EASY, NOW- DON'T YOU WORRY- OLD SPIKE MARLIN IS RIGHT HERE ON DECK-
OH, OH- EVER'THING IS GETTIN' BLACK- I'M FALLING, FALLING---

THE POOR LITTLE LAMB- WORKING AS HARD AS SHE HAS IN THIS TERRIBLE HEAT- SHE'S ALL TUCKERED OUT-

HM-M-M-- PULSE LIKE A TRIP-HAMMER- A RAGING FEVER- THIS IS A CASE FOR A DOCTOR- WELL, I RECKON IT'S UP TO OLD SPIKE TO DO THE BEST HE CAN-
POOR ANNIE! POOR ANNIE!

September 21, 1930

AW, I DON'T FEEL SO BAD - JUST SORTA DIZZY - I'M GOIN' TO GET UP - MOVE AROUND A LITTLE AND I'LL BE O. K.
IT'S A TOUCH OF FEVER, ANNIE - AND IT'S NOT SAFE TO TAKE ANY CHANCES WITH JUNGLE FEVER - HERE'S SOME MEDICINE I FIXED FOR YOU -
AR-R-R-R!!! BRRRRR-R-R--!!! COURSE I KNOW IT'S GOOD FOR ME, BUT OO-O-O-O!!!
THERE! NOW YOU JUST LIE DOWN AND KEEP COVERED UP - TRY TO GO TO SLEEP - REST AND PROPER CARE AND YOU MAY BE UP IN A DAY OR TWO -
HAROLD GRAY
Reg. U. S. Pat. Off.; Copyright, 1930, by The Chicago Tribune.
ANNIE'S FEVER IS GOING UP EVERY MINUTE - AND THE RAINY SEASON WILL BE HERE ANY TIME NOW - WE'LL HAVE TO HAVE A FIRE THEN TO KEEP THE SHACK DRY -
SHE MOST LIKELY NEVER WOULD HAVE COME DOWN WITH FEVER IF IT HADN'T BEEN FOR HER WEARING HERSELF OUT NURSING ME - SHE HARDLY GOT A WINK OF SLEEP FOR OVER A WEEK -
IF SHE HADN'T STUCK ON THE JOB AND LOOKED OUT FOR ME THIS OLD SAILOR WOULDN'T BE HERE NOW - AYE, SHE SAVED MY LIFE, AND THAT'S A FACT -
AND NOW BECAUSE SHE'S ALL WORN OUT SHE CATCHES IT - PRETTY POOR PAY, I CALLS IT - BUT WE'LL PULL HER THROUGH -
HAROLD GRAY
Reg. U. S. Pat. Off.; Copyright, 1930, by The Chicago Tribune.
GEE, CAP'N - I'M MAKIN' YOU A LOT O' BOTHER - IT SURE IS SWELL O' YOU TO GO TO ALL THIS FUSS OVER ME -
HUH! NO MORE THAN YOU DID FOR ME, OR HALF AS MUCH -
YOU STOOD BY WHEN OLD SPIKE MARLIN WAS ON THE REEFS - HERE - SWALLOW THIS -
OH, GEE - THAT LOOKS AWFUL GOOD, BUT HONEST, CAP'N, I COULDN'T EAT A THING RIGHT NOW -
A LITTLE DINNER WOULD BE GOOD FOR YOU, ANNIE - IT'D GIVE YOU STRENGTH -
ASLEEP - WELL, MAYBE IT'S BEST - FEED A COLD AND STARVE A FEVER, THEY SAY - AND SHE HAS HER MEDICINE - BUT I DON'T LIKE HER COLOR - SHE'S A MIGHTY SICK YOUNGUN -
HAROLD GRAY
Reg. U. S. Pat. Off.; Copyright, 1930, by The Chicago Tribune.

September 22–24, 1930

RAIN! RAIN! RAIN! WELL, IT WAS BOUND TO COME - AND WHEN IT STARTS TO RAIN IN THESE PARTS IT POURS FOR DAYS AND WEEKS -
WE'VE GOT DRY WOOD AND A TIGHT HOUSE - BUT DAMPNESS WILL CREEP IN, AND DAMPNESS IS BAD FOR FEVER -

AYE, THIS WILL BE BAD FOR ANNIE - WHY COULDN'T THE RAIN HAVE HELD OFF A LITTLE LONGER?
HAROLD GRAY
Reg. U. S. Pat. Off.; Copyright, 1930, by The Chicago Tribune.

ANNIE'S WORSE TO DAY - I KNEW SHE WOULD BE WITH THIS RAIN AND DAMPNESS EVERYWHERE - IT WAS BOUND TO RUN HER FEVER UP -

THANK GOODNESS WE HAVE MEDICINE - AND THE SPRING-WATER IS PURE, BUT I'LL BOIL EVERY DROP OF IT WE USE AND TAKE NO CHANCES -

HERE, ANNIE - TRY THIS - HOW DO YOU FEEL? ARE YOU RESTED AFTER YOUR NIGHT'S SLEEP?

SOUND ASLEEP AGAIN - SHE TOOK HER MEDICINE, BUT I DOUBT IF SHE KNEW IT - SHE'S GOT AS BAD A CASE AS I EVER SAW IN FORTY YEARS IN THE TROPICS - THE CRISIS MUST COME SOON -
HAROLD GRAY
Reg. U. S. Pat. Off.; Copyright, 1930, by The Chicago Tribune.

RAGING FEVER - PULSE LIKE A TRIP-HAMMER - THIS CAN'T KEEP UP LIKE THIS MUCH LONGER - SHE MUST SHOW SOME CHANGE SOON -

WHILE FAR AWAY, IN A LAZY FISHING TOWN, ONE OF WARBUCK'S ARMY OF SEARCHERS AT LAST STUMBLES ACROSS A FAINT BUT INTERESTING CLEW -
HEH! HEH! HEH! FELLER NAMED JOHNNIE SCROD - QUEER CARD - SEEMS HE PICKED UP A BOTTLE WITH A PAPER IN IT -

CAIN'T READ - NEITHER CAN HIS WOMAN - WELL SIR - THEY FIGGERED MAYBE THIS 'ERE PAPER WAS A MESSAGE - BUT WHEN THEY COME TO HAVIN' IT READ SHE'D MISLAID IT - FRIEND O' MINE GOT THE STORY FROM A MATE O' HIS WAY UP TH' COAST - MOST LIKELY TH' WHOLE THING'S JUST A YARN -

YARN OR NO YARN, WARBUCKS WILL WANT TO HEAR OF THIS - NO TELEGRAPH HERE - QUICKEST WAY IS TO CHARTER A BOAT - NO SPEED BOATS HERE - HAVE TO TAKE ANY BOAT I CAN GET -
HAROLD GRAY
Reg. U. S. Pat. Off.; Copyright, 1930, by The Chicago Tribune.

September 25–27, 1930
SHIPWRECKED

Little Orphan Annie

HAROLD GRAY

'LO, DOC! HOW'S TH' PATIENT?

WELL, HER FEVER'S A TRIFLE LOWER THIS MORNING AND SHE'S GETTING A LITTLE SLEEP - POOR LITTLE LAMB -
POOR ANNIE!

RAIN - RAIN - RAIN - THE TROPICS ARE NO PLACE FOR WHITE FOLKS IN THE RAINY SEASON - BUT HERE WE ARE AND HERE WE HAVE TO STAY, SEEMS LIKE, RAIN OR NO RAIN -

ONE THING - WE SAVED THE MEDICINE CHEST FROM THE BOAT - ALL THAT CAN BE DONE FOR HER IS BEING DONE - GOOD OLD SANDY - I KNOW YOU WANT TO HELP BUT THERE'S MIGHTY LITTLE ANY OF US CAN DO -

YOU NEVER KNOW WHEN SICKNESS IS GOING TO STRIKE - YOU SELDOM NOTICE ANY WARNIN' SIGNS - MOST GENERALLY YOU'RE FEELIN' YER BEST JUST BEFORE YOU RUN SMACK INTO IT -

WHEN YER WELL YOU NEVER FIGGER ON GETTIN' SICK, EITHER - THAT'S WHY FOLKS MOST GENERALLY ARE SO UN-PREPARED -

STILL ASLEEP - THAT'S GOOD - THE MORE REST SHE GETS THE BETTER - HER FEVER'LL BE STARTIN' UP AGAIN IN AN HOUR -

NO MATTER HOW PURE WATER IS IN THE TROPICS IT'S BEST TO BILE IT FUST OFF -

WELL, AS LONG AS ANNIE GETS HER MEDICINE REGULAR SHE'S GOT A FIGHTIN' CHANCE - HM-M-M - THAT BOTTLE'S PLUMB EMPTY - BEEN USING IT PRETTY FAST THIS LAST WEEK -

BUT THAT'S ALL RIGHT - GOT PLENTY MORE IN THE MEDICINE CHEST - THERE'S ANOTHER FULL BOTTLE IN HERE - ENOUGH TO LAST HER A MONTH -

SHE'LL MOST LIKELY BE WELL AGAIN 'FORE IT'S ANYWHERE NEAR USED UP - WITHOUT MEDICINE NOW SHE'D BE A GONER IN NO TIME - BUT OLD SPIKE NEVER FORGETS TO KEEP A FULL STORE OF MEDICINES -

GREAT SONS O' NEPTUNE!!! IT'S NEARLY EMPTY - I REMEMBER NOW - I FORGOT TO FILL THAT BOTTLE LAST TIME I WAS IN PORT -

ONLY ENOUGH TO LAST A COUPLE OF DAYS, AT THE RATE WE'VE BEEN GOING - THE TURNING POINT MUST COME SOON OR WE'LL BE HELPLESS, SANDY - HELPLESS!

September 28, 1930

WHAT A FOOL I WAS TO LET MY MEDICINE RUN LOW - SHOULD HAVE CHECKED THAT UP WHEN I WAS IN PORT LAST - NOW WE'RE NEARLY OUT -
ENOUGH TO LAST NEARLY A WEEK IF I'M CAREFUL - BUT WILL THAT SAVE HER? SHE MUST CHANGE FOR THE BETTER SOON - WITHOUT MEDICINE SHE WON'T HAVE A CHANCE -
WHILE WARBUCKS' OPERATIVE NO. 738 SEEKS FRANTICALLY FOR SOME MEANS OF CARRYING NEWS OF THE BOTTLE TO WARBUCKS.
HUH - WELL, THAT'S NO RACING BOAT, BUT I GUESS IT'S ABOUT MY ONLY HOPE - ALL RIGHT - HOP IN AND LET'S BE ON OUR WAY -
SHE'S NOT SO FAST AND SHE'S NOISY, BUT SHE'LL GIT US THERE IN A DAY OR TWO -
A DAY OR TWO! GREAT SCOTT! WHAT I'D GIVE FOR A PLANE - BUT ON THIS BENIGHTED COAST I'M LUCKY TO FIND EVEN THIS -
CHUG! CHUG! CHUG!
HAROLD GRAY
Reg. U. S. Pat. Off.; Copyright, 1930, by The Chicago Tribune.
OH, WILL RESCUE NEVER COME? I DON'T CARE FOR MYSELF - BUT EVERY DAY THE MEDICINE IS RUNNING LOWER AND NO CHANCE TO GET MORE - IF HELP DOESN'T COME SOON IT WILL DO NO GOOD -
WHILE EVEN THE RUMOR OF THE BOTTLE AND IT'S UNKNOWN MESSAGE SEEMS DESTINED TO BE A LONG TIME IN REACHING WARBUCKS -
WELL, IT LOOKS LIKE WE'RE STUCK AND NO TELLIN' WHEN WE'LL GET PICKED UP IN THESE WATERS -
STUCK!!! WHAT'S WRONG WITH THE ENGINE?
ENGINE'S ALL RIGHT - SHE'S JUST OUT O' GAS - CAME AWAY SO QUICK I PLUMB FORGOT TO FILL THE TANK - THAT'S A GOOD ONE ON ME - HA! HA! HA!
OUT OF GAS, EH? HAW! HAW! HAW! FIFTY MILES FROM SHORE WHERE BOATS HARDLY EVER PASS - ISN'T THAT FUNNY!!!
YOU BLITHERING IDIOT!!!
HAROLD GRAY
Reg. U. S. Pat. Off.; Copyright, 1930, by The Chicago Tribune.
YOU'D THINK I FORGOT TO FILL UP WITH GAS ON PURPOSE - I'M GETTIN' JUST AS WET AND HUNGRY AS YOU ARE, AIN'T I?
AW, ONE MORE CRACK LIKE THAT OUTA YOU AND I'LL HEAVE YOU OVERBOARD ON THE END OF A ROPE AND MAKE YOU TOW US - WE HAVEN'T MOVED FOR TWENTY FOUR HOURS -
HEY! LOOK! A SHARK!
YEAH!!! THAT'S NICE - NOW WE'VE GOT COMPANY ANYWAY - HERE COMES ANOTHER ONE -
ISN'T IT EVER GOIN' TO QUIT RAINING? CAN'T EVEN SMOKE - BETTER FIND TH' BUCKET BEFORE IT GETS DARK - GOING TO HAVE TO START BAILING SOON IF WE EXPECT TO FOOL THOSE SHARKS -
HAROLD GRAY
Reg. U. S. Pat. Off.; Copyright, 1930, by The Chicago Tribune.

September 29–October 1, 1930

GUESS IT'S MORNING, BUT WITH THIS RAIN YOU CAN'T SEE FIFTY FEET- SH-H-H- LISTEN! WHAT'S THAT NOISE?

HEY!
LOOK OUT!

MAN OVERBOARD! MAN OVERBOARD!
BONG! BONG! BONG!
CRASH!
HAROLD GRAY

HAW! HAW! OLD DAVEY JONES HISSELF FISHED RIGHT OUT O' TH' SEA- AN' TELLIN' ME I GOTTA TURN MY TUG AROUND AN' MAKE A BLOOMIN' TAXICAB OUTA HER FOR YOU- HAW! HAW!
LAUGH ALL YOU LIKE- BUT I'M TELLIN' YOU THIS IS IMPORTANT-
THAT'S RIGHT!
Reg. U. S. Pat. Off.; Copyright, 1930, by The Chicago Tribune.

FOR THE LAST TIME I'M TELLIN' YOU, NO!!! I DON'T CHANGE MY COURSE FOR ANYBODY- YOUR BOSS! WHAT DO I CARE FOR HIM? WHO IS YOUR BOSS, ANYWAY?
HIS NAME IS WARBUCKS!

WARBUCKS!!! YOU DUMB LUBBER! WHY DIDN'T YOU SAY SO? THAT'S DIFFERENT-

YOU'LL BE WELL PAID-

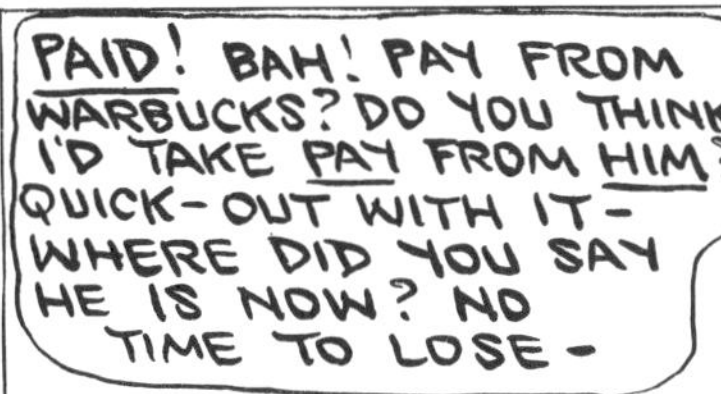
PAID! BAH! PAY FROM WARBUCKS? DO YOU THINK I'D TAKE PAY FROM HIM? QUICK- OUT WITH IT- WHERE DID YOU SAY HE IS NOW? NO TIME TO LOSE-

HERE- GIMME THAT WHEEL AN' GET BELOW AND HELP SHOVEL COAL- WE'RE GOIN' BACK AND I WANT THAT BOILER RED HOT ALL THE WAY- GIT!
HAROLD GRAY
Reg. U. S. Pat. Off.; Copyright, 1930, by The Chicago Tribune.

THAT TUG, SIR- IT'S SIGNALING US- I DIDN'T KNOW IF I SHOULD BOTHER TO TELL YOU, SIR- IT MET US AS WE LEFT THE HARBOR-
STOP AT ONCE- SEE WHAT THEY WANT-

HERE'S SOMETHIN' I FISHED OUT O' TH' OCEAN- SAYS YOU WANTED TO SEE HIM, SO HERE HE IS-
WELL, THAT'S SURE A FAVOR I WON'T FORGET, SKIPPER-

OF COURSE, IT'S JUST A RUMOR, MR. WARBUCKS- BUT I THOUGHT YOU SHOULD KNOW AT ONCE- I DIDN'T INVESTIGATE AS I FIGURED IT WOULD SAVE TIME IF YOU WENT YOURSELF-
RIGHT- YOU SAY THERE'S TALK OF A MESSAGE IN A BOTTLE HAVING BEEN PICKED UP-

HM-M-M- FROM WHAT YOU HEARD, THIS MAN SCROD MUST LIVE RIGHT ALONG HERE- WE CAN MAKE THAT BY MONDAY- IT'S WORTH CHECKING UP-
YES- THEY SAY HE AND HIS WIFE HAVE A LITTLE SHACK JUST AROUND THAT POINT-
HAROLD GRAY
Reg. U. S. Pat. Off.; Copyright, 1930, by The Chicago Tribune.

October 2–4, 1930

Little Orphan Annie
HAROLD GRAY
At last a vague rumor, concerning a bottle, said to have contained a message, reaches "Daddy" Warbucks and he sets out at once to investigate- Will he find the message? Will he find the island? And, if he does, will he arrive in time?

EMPTY- I MADE THAT MEDICINE LAST AS LONG AS POSSIBLE, BUT THERE'S NOT A GRAIN LEFT- AND POOR ANNIE IS GROWING WEAKER EVERY HOUR- WEAKER AND WEAKER-
AW, DON'T YOU WORRY, CAP'N-

I THOUGHT YOU WERE ASLEEP- OLD SPIKE WAS SORTA TALKIN' TO HIMSELF-
I KNOW - TH' MEDICINE'S GONE - BUT IT WAS AWFUL-TASTIN' STUFF ANYWAY - AND IT'S QUIT RAININ'- AND I DON'T THINK I FEEL QUITE SO ALL ON FIRE AS I DID -

AYE - YOUR FEVER IS A LEETLE LOWER- I GRANT YOU THAT-
SURE- I'M LOTS BETTER-AN' ANYWAY WE'LL BE RESCUED 'FORE LONG- JUST LOOK HOW LONG WE'VE BEEN HERE ON THIS ISLAND - SOMEBODY'S GOTTA FIND US 'MOST ANY TIME NOW -

ASLEEP AGAIN- HER FEVER WILL START UP IN A FEW MINUTES, AND NO MEDICINE THIS TIME- FOR THE FIRST TIME IN MY LIFE I GUESS I'M LICKED-

ARE YUH GOIN' TO QUIT? ARE YUH GOIN' TO QUIT?
WHO? ME?

NO, BY JUPITER! I MAY BE HELPLESS, BUT NO SWAB CAN SAY OLD SPIKE MARLIN EVER QUIT-

SUPPOSIN' SOME CRAFT WERE IN SIGHT THIS MINUTE AND PASSED US BY FOR LACK OF A LOOK-OUT TO HAIL HER AND BRING HER TO-

OF COURSE IT'S HER FEVER - BUT THERE'S SENSE TO HER TALK- WE CAN'T BE LEFT HERE FOREVER -

BUT RESCUE MUST COME SOON IF IT'S TO HELP LITTLE ANNIE - WITHOUT MEDICINE, HOURS NOW MAY MEAN EVERYTHING -

OF COURSE THIS FAIR WEATHER WILL HELP HER SOME - BUT I KNOW TROPIC FEVER- SHE CAN'T BEAT IT ALONE -

NOTHING IN SIGHT - I'M JUST A TOUGH OLD SALT- NEVER DID MUCH PRAYIN'- DO YOU RECKON A PRAYER FROM ME WOULD HELP ANY -
ARF!

I DON'T COUNT- IT'S NOT FOR ME I'M ASKIN' IT- BUT FOR THE SWEETEST LITTLE GIRL IN THE WORLD - ANY KIND OF A SHIP- BUT MAKE IT COME QUICK!
Reg. U. S. Pat. Off.; Copyright, 1930, by The Chicago Tribune.

October 5, 1930

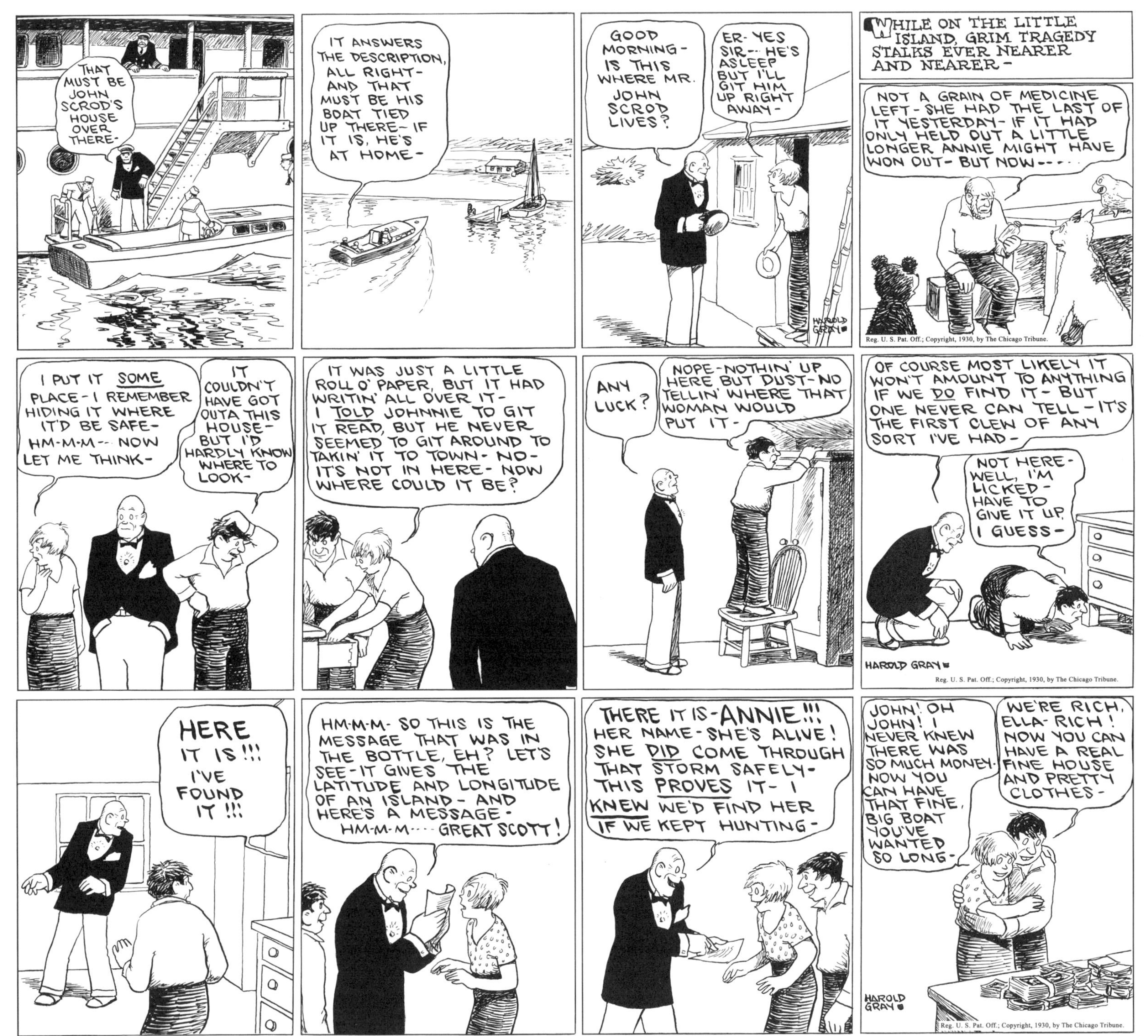

THAT MUST BE JOHN SCROD'S HOUSE OVER THERE-
IT ANSWERS THE DESCRIPTION, ALL RIGHT- AND THAT MUST BE HIS BOAT TIED UP THERE- IF IT IS, HE'S AT HOME-
GOOD MORNING- IS THIS WHERE MR. JOHN SCROD LIVES?
ER- YES SIR-- HE'S ASLEEP BUT I'LL GIT HIM UP RIGHT AWAY-
HAROLD GRAY
WHILE ON THE LITTLE ISLAND, GRIM TRAGEDY STALKS EVER NEARER AND NEARER-
NOT A GRAIN OF MEDICINE LEFT- SHE HAD THE LAST OF IT YESTERDAY- IF IT HAD ONLY HELD OUT A LITTLE LONGER ANNIE MIGHT HAVE WON OUT- BUT NOW----
Reg. U. S. Pat. Off.; Copyright, 1930, by The Chicago Tribune.
I PUT IT SOME PLACE- I REMEMBER HIDING IT WHERE IT'D BE SAFE- HM-M-M-- NOW LET ME THINK-
IT COULDN'T HAVE GOT OUTA THIS HOUSE- BUT I'D HARDLY KNOW WHERE TO LOOK-
IT WAS JUST A LITTLE ROLL O' PAPER, BUT IT HAD WRITIN' ALL OVER IT- I TOLD JOHNNIE TO GIT IT READ, BUT HE NEVER SEEMED TO GIT AROUND TO TAKIN' IT TO TOWN- NO- IT'S NOT IN HERE- NOW WHERE COULD IT BE?
ANY LUCK?
NOPE- NOTHIN' UP HERE BUT DUST- NO TELLIN' WHERE THAT WOMAN WOULD PUT IT-
OF COURSE MOST LIKELY IT WON'T AMOUNT TO ANYTHING IF WE DO FIND IT- BUT ONE NEVER CAN TELL- IT'S THE FIRST CLEW OF ANY SORT I'VE HAD-
NOT HERE- WELL, I'M LICKED- HAVE TO GIVE IT UP, I GUESS-
HAROLD GRAY
Reg. U. S. Pat. Off.; Copyright, 1930, by The Chicago Tribune.
HERE IT IS!!! I'VE FOUND IT!!!
HM-M-M- SO THIS IS THE MESSAGE THAT WAS IN THE BOTTLE, EH? LET'S SEE- IT GIVES THE LATITUDE AND LONGITUDE OF AN ISLAND- AND HERE'S A MESSAGE- HM-M-M---- GREAT SCOTT!
THERE IT IS- ANNIE!!! HER NAME- SHE'S ALIVE! SHE DID COME THROUGH THAT STORM SAFELY- THIS PROVES IT- I KNEW WE'D FIND HER IF WE KEPT HUNTING-
JOHN! OH JOHN! I NEVER KNEW THERE WAS SO MUCH MONEY- NOW YOU CAN HAVE THAT FINE, BIG BOAT YOU'VE WANTED SO LONG-
WE'RE RICH, ELLA- RICH! NOW YOU CAN HAVE A REAL FINE HOUSE AND PRETTY CLOTHES-
HAROLD GRAY
Reg. U. S. Pat. Off.; Copyright, 1930, by The Chicago Tribune.

October 6–8, 1930

WHAT DID I TELL YOU, CAPTAIN? I SAID ANNIE WAS ALIVE - THAT MESSAGE PROVES IT-
HM-M-M - YES - IT SEEMS TO - BUT - THESE BEARINGS - THEY DON'T SOUND RIGHT TO ME-

YES - I THOUGHT SO - RIGHT THERE IS WHERE THE BEARINGS IN THIS MESSAGE PLACE THE ISLAND - SEE FOR YOURSELF, MR. WARBUCKS - NOT EVEN A SPECK OF LAND AT THAT POINT OR FOR A HUNDRED MILES - NOTHING - OPEN WATER -

WHOEVER WROTE THIS MADE A MISTAKE - OR ELSE THIS IS A FAKE MESSAGE GOTTEN UP BY SOME ONE WHO FIGURED YOU'D PAY WELL FOR IT - THAT'S REASONABLE - AT ANY RATE THESE DIRECTIONS CAN'T HELP US -

YOU MAY BE RIGHT - BUT I'M BULL-HEADED - IF IT'S A FAKE MESSAGE I'LL SQUARE THAT LATER - NOW WE'RE GOING TO THE SPOT THAT THOSE BEARINGS CALL FOR - SEE? AND WE'RE GOING AT FULL SPEED -
HAROLD GRAY

I'M TELLING YOU, MR. WARBUCKS, YOU'LL FIND NO LAND THERE -
YEAH? WELL, IT WON'T HURT TO LOOK - I'VE GOT TO BE SHOWN - THAT MESSAGE LOOKED TOO GENUINE FOR ME TO IGNORE IT -

THE MORE I THINK ABOUT IT THE MORE I AM CONVINCED IT WAS THE WORK OF CROOKS - PLENTY OF PEOPLE KNEW OF YOUR SEARCH FOR THE LITTLE GIRL - IT WOULD HAVE BEEN EASY TO FAKE SUCH A MESSAGE - I FEEL THIS IS A WILD GOOSE CHASE -

SAY! ARE YOU GOING TO KEEP HARPING ON THAT FOREVER? DON'T YOU SUPPOSE I THOUGHT OF THAT? THAT MESSAGE MAY BE THE BUNK - BUT MY HUNCH IS IT'S ON THE LEVEL - ANYWAY IT'S WORTH CHECKING UP ON -

AS IF I WASN'T SCARED ENOUGH WITHOUT THAT OLD WALRUS RUBBING IT IN - THERE CAN'T BE ANY ISLAND THERE - BUT STILL I BELIEVE THAT MESSAGE IS GENUINE - WE'LL KNOW MIGHTY SOON, NOW, ANYWAY -
HAROLD GRAY

WITH GIANT MOTORS RACING AT TOP SPEED THE GREAT YACHT IS RUSHING ON--- ---TO WHAT? WAS OLD SPIKE MARLIN'S RECKONING WRONG? WILL "DADDY" FIND THE ISLAND OR ONLY EMPTY SEA?

THERE!!! NO ISLAND, EH? WHADDYUH CALL THAT? NOW WHO'S CRAZY?
I CAN HARDLY BELIEVE IT. IT'S NOT ON THE CHART - I CAN'T UNDERSTAND IT AT ALL -

UNCHARTED - THAT'S WHY, IN ALL OUR SEARCHING, WE NEVER FOUND IT -
IT'S SURROUNDED BY MEAN LOOKING REEFS - HAVE TO WAIT TILL MORNING TO LAND - THEN FOR A BIG SURPRISE FOR ANNIE -

WHILE LITTLE ANNIE SINKS LOWER AND LOWER - HAS WARBUCKS REACHED THE END OF THE TRAIL TOO LATE?
HER STRENGTH IS GOING - SHE CAN'T HOLD OUT MUCH LONGER - AND I AM HELPLESS! HELPLESS!
HAROLD GRAY

Little Orphan Annie
HAROLD GRAY
DADDY - DADDY - HERE I AM - DON'T YOU SEE ME? OH, IT'S HOT HERE - HOT - HOT - HOT - BUT YOU'LL TAKE ME WHERE IT'S COOL - I KNEW YOU'D COME -
DELIRIOUS! THE POOR LITTLE ANGEL - IF HELP DOESN'T COME SOON SHE HASN'T A CHANCE -
POOR ANNIE - WITH THE MEDICINE GONE HER FEVER IS MOUNTING STEADILY - OLD SPIKE MARLIN MUST STAND BY HELPLESS THOUGH HE WOULD GLADLY GIVE HIS LIFE IF IT WOULD SAVE HER

THAT MESSAGE IN THE BOTTLE WAS RIGHT - THERE'S A LITTLE ISLAND - IT WASN'T ON THE CHART - NO WONDER WE NEVER FOUND IT - BUT WE'VE BEEN ALL AROUND IT - NOT A SIGN OF LIFE - AND IT'S A TREACHEROUS COAST TO TRY TO LAND ON -

THERE CAN'T BE A SOUL ON THAT ISLAND, MR. WARBUCKS - LOOK AT THOSE REEFS - ANY BOAT WOULD BE SMASHED TO BITS BEFORE IT WAS NEAR THE SHORE -
HM-M-M MAYBE YOU'RE RIGHT - I'LL HAVE ONE MORE LOOK -

WHILE IN THE MEANTIME, SANDY, WORN OUT BY HIS CEASELESS VIGIL AT ANNIE'S BEDSIDE, TROTS DOWN TO THE BEACH, HELPLESS, DEFEATED AND FOR FORLORN.

DO HIS EYES DECEIVE HIM? IS IT A MIRAGE? NO! HE KNOWS IT IS A BOAT - AND A BOAT MEANS HELP FOR ANNIE -
ARF! ARF! ARF!

LOOK! THERE'S SANDY! ANNIE CAN'T BE FAR AWAY - WE'VE FOUND HER -

COME ON, BOYS, SNAP INTO IT - GET THAT BOAT IN THE WATER - REEFS OR NO REEFS, I'M GOING ASHORE -

GIVE 'ER TH' GUN, BOYS - IT'S ONLY A REEF - IF SHE COMES APART WE CAN SWIM IN FROM HERE EASY ENOUGH -

SANDY!
ARF!

WHERE IS SHE, SANDY? QUICK!!! WHERE IS SHE? TAKE ME TO HER -

STEP ON IT, SANDY - BOY - WILL I BE GLAD TO SEE LITTLE ANNIE AGAIN!!!

WARBUCKS! IT MUST BE WARBUCKS - AM I DREAMING?
GREAT SCOTT! FEVER! AM I TOO LATE?

QUICK! TO THE YACHT - GET THE DOCTOR - NURSES - MEDICINE - GIT - WHAT ARE YOU STANDING THERE FOR? IT'S LIFE AND DEATH - GO!!!

October 12, 1930
SHIPWRECKED

THIS SHACK IS FAR FROM BEING A HOSPITAL, BUT WE MUST DO OUR BEST TO TRANSFORM IT INTO ONE - SHE'S VERY WEAK - TO TRY TO MOVE HER NOW WOULD BE FATAL -
YES SIR, DOCTOR -
I NEVER EXPECTED TO FIND LITTLE ANNIE LIKE THIS - I HAD THE DOCTOR AND NURSE ABOARD JUST IN CASE - LUCKY I DID - WISH HE'D COME OUT AND TELL US HOW SHE REALLY IS -
HERE'S A LIST OF THINGS WE NEED FROM THE YACHT AT ONCE - ONE OF THE SAILORS CAN GET THEM FOR ME -
I'LL GO MYSELF - I WOULDN'T TRUST THAT JOB TO ANY ONE ELSE - THEY'D FORGET SOMETHING -
HEY! WHERE ARE YOU GOING, MARLIN?
I'M GOING WITH YOU - I KNOW THE CHANNEL THROUGH THOSE REEFS - THINK I'M GOING TO RISK HAVING ANYTHING GO WRONG WHEN IT'S FOR LITTLE ANNIE?
HAROLD GRAY
Reg. U. S. Pat. Off.; Copyright, 1930, by The Chicago Tribune.
HOW IS SHE THIS MORNING, DOCTOR? DOES SHE SHOW ANY IMPROVEMENT?
WELL, I'D LIKE TO SAY SHE IS BETTER, MR. WARBUCKS, BUT TO TELL THE TRUTH, SHE SHOWS NO CHANGE SO FAR -
BUT SHE IS NO WORSE - SHE IS JUST HOLDING HER OWN - SHE WAS VERY, VERY NEAR THE END - WE ARRIVED BARELY IN TIME - - - I HOPE - WE ARE DOING ALL THAT CAN BE DONE - THE NEXT FEW HOURS SHOULD TELL IF WE ARE IN TIME -
WHAT A CHEERFUL BIRD THAT GUY IS - STILL HE TELLS THE TRUTH - DOESN'T TRY TO KID ME ALONG - AND HE'S THE BEST DOC I KNOW OF AND A WONDER ON FEVER - WHY, OH WHY, COULDN'T WE HAVE FOUND HER LONG AGO?
WELL, SANDY, YOU HEARD WHAT THE DOC SAID - THINGS LOOK MIGHTY BLACK - BUT SHE'S A FIGHTER, SANDY, AND FROM NOW ON SHE'LL GET THE BREAKS - THIS SURE IS A FUNNY WORLD - EH, SANDY?
ARF!
HAROLD GRAY
Reg. U. S. Pat. Off.; Copyright, 1930, by The Chicago Tribune.
HERE WE SIT, TWO ABLE-BODIED MEN, LIKE TWO BUMPS ON A LOG, UNABLE TO DO A THING TO HELP -
AYE - I'M HELPLESS - BUT YOU BROUGHT HER A DOCTOR AND A NURSE AND MEDICINES, YOU'VE DONE YOUR PART -
ROT - AND IF IT HADN'T BEEN FOR YOU TAKING CARE OF HER AND NURSING HER AS YOU DID EVEN AFTER THE MEDICINE GAVE OUT, ALL THE DOCTORS IN THE WORLD WOULD HAVE ARRIVED TOO LATE - IF SHE GETS WELL SHE'LL HAVE YOU TO THANK - NOT ME -
DIDN'T SHE SAVE MY LIFE WHEN I WAS OUT OF MY HEAD FOR DAYS WITH FEVER? SHE'S AS DEAR AS ANY DAUGHTER COULD BE - BUT I FAILED - NOW IT'S UP TO YOU -
NOBODY'S FAILED YET - DON'T SAY THAT WORD SPIKE - SHE'S GOT TO GET WELL!
Reg. U. S. Pat. Off.; Copyright, 1930, by The Chicago Tribune.
HOLD YOURSELF TO GETHER - SHE'LL PULL THROUGH YET - I KNOW HOW YOU FEEL - I FEEL THE SAME WAY MYSELF - GUESS WE'RE JUST A COUPLE OF LONELY OLD SOULS WHO HAVE BEEN WARMED BY THE SAME RAY OF SUNSHINE -
HAROLD GRAY

October 13–15, 1930

ARF!
?
HELLO, SANDY!!! WHAT'S UP NOW? SOMETHING YOU WANT TO SHOW ME, EH?
ARF!
WELL, AS I LIVE! WANT ME TO MEET WILLIE, EH? HEARD ABOUT YOU, WILLIE, FROM CAPTAIN MARLIN - HOW ARE YOU? SURE GLAD TO MEET YOU -
BOUF!
Reg. U. S. Pat. Off.; Copyright, 1930, by The Chicago Tribune.
SPIKE TELLS ME YOU'RE QUITE A FELLOW - SAYS YOU'VE BEEN WITH ANNIE FOR A LONG TIME - WELL, SIR, ANY FRIEND OF HERS IS A PAL OF MINE, AND DON'T YOU FORGET IT -
HAROLD GRAY
I'LL GO CRAZY IN ANOTHER MINUTE IF THAT DOCTOR DOESN'T COME OUT AND TELL ME HOW SHE IS -
LISTEN, DOCTOR - SHE'D BE A LOT BETTER OFF ON THE YACHT AWAY FROM THIS FEVER-SOAKED ISLAND -
YES - BUT UNTIL SHE SHOWS A CHANGE FOR THE BETTER, TO MOVE HER WOULD BE FATAL -
I EXPECT A CHANGE SOON - WHAT IT WILL BE IS IMPOSSIBLE TO FORETELL - ALL WE CAN DO NOW IS WAIT AND HOPE -
Reg. U. S. Pat. Off.; Copyright, 1930, by The Chicago Tribune.
WAIT AND HOPE ! OF COURSE I KNOW HE'S DOING ALL THAT CAN BE DONE - BUT THAT DOESN'T MAKE WAITING MUCH EASIER - WE'RE SO HELPLESS ! HELPLESS !!!
HAROLD GRAY
DOC SAYS SHE'S A LITTLE BETTER!
GREAT JUPITER! AT LAST!
HEY - STEP ON IT, YOU LUBBERS - THERE'S WORK TO BE DONE - ARE YOU GOING TO BE ALL DAY GETTING THAT BOAT ASHORE?
WE'RE TAKING ANNIE ABOARD THE YACHT IN THE MORNING - THE LAUNCH MUST BE IN PERFECT SHAPE - THERE MUST BE NO SLIPS - AND HER CABIN MUST BE READY TO THE LAST DETAIL -
HAROLD GRAY
THE DEAR LITTLE TYKE - IF WE CAN ONLY GET HER ONTO THE YACHT SAFELY - BUT YOU LEAVE THAT TO YOUR OLD "DADDY" - AT LAST I'VE FOUND SOME WAY TO HELP -
Reg. U. S. Pat. Off.; Copyright, 1930, by The Chicago Tribune.

October 16–18, 1930

Little Orphan Annie
SURROUND HIM, MEN! SHOOT HIM IN HIS TRACKS!!! HA! HA! HA!
PIRATES!!! IF I CAN ONLY GET TO THE BOAT- OH, WHY DID I EVER COME ASHORE ALONE?
HAROLD GRAY

SHE SEEMS A TRIFLE STRONGER TO-DAY- BUT IF WE ARE TO MOVE HER TO THE YACHT AT ALL IT MUST BE AT ONCE- SHE'LL HAVE A CHANCE THERE-
RIGHT YOU ARE, DOCTOR- THE YACHT IS CLEAN AND AIRY- NOT LIKE THIS FEVER-SOAKED ISLAND-

MARLIN-DO YOU THINK YOU KNOW THE CHANNEL THROUGH THE REEFS WELL ENOUGH TO PILOT OUR LAUNCH OUT TO THE YACHT WITHOUT ACCIDENT?
IF IT'S ANNIE IS TO BE TAKEN SAFELY ABOARD OLD SPIKE MARLIN IS YOUR MAN FOR THE JOB- NONE OF YOUR LUBBERLY CREW OF SWABS CAN STEER HER BOAT WHILE I'M AROUND, SIR-

IN HER CONDITION THE LEAST MISHAP WOULD BE FATAL- BUT IT'S OUR ONLY CHANCE- THE POOR LITTLE TYKE- IT'S WELL SHE DOESN'T KNOW-

THERE'S A BUNK MADE UP BELOW IN THE CABIN FOR ANNIE- SHE'LL BE SNUG AND DRY THERE-
GOOD FOR YOU, MARLIN- SHE'S IN YOUR HANDS NOW- IT'S UP TO YOU-

HERE COMES THE REEF- THERE'S ONLY A NARROW, CROOKED PASSAGE AND A TREACHEROUS CURRENT- STEADY- HERE WE GO....

AH!!! SO FAR SO GOOD- IN FORTY YEARS AT SEA I'VE NEVER SEEN A WICKEDER BIT OF WATER-

GOOD WORK, MARLIN- I DON'T KNOW HOW YOU DID IT, BUT YOU BROUGHT US THROUGH WITH LESS THAN AN INCH TO SPARE, AND NOT A SCRATCH-

STAND BY, YOU SWABS! IF YOU LET 'ER BUMP I'LL BASH IN TH' HATCH OF EVERY ONE OF YOU LUBBERS-

HER ROOM IS ALL READY, SIR-
GOOD-

THERE- OFF THAT PLAGUE-INFESTED ISLAND AT LAST- IF IT ONLY ISN'T TOO LATE-

YOU'LL HAVE TO GET OUT NOW, MR. WARBUCKS- SHE MUST HAVE ABSOLUTE QUIET- I'LL TELL YOU OF ANY CHANGE-
O.K. DOCTOR- YOU KNOW BEST- YOU'RE THE BOSS ON THIS SHIP NOW-

POOR OLD SANDY- GUESS YOU'RE AS SCARED AS I AM- BUT THEN WE TWO KNOW BETTER THAN ANY-ONE ELSE HOW DEAR SHE IS- BUT SHE WILL PULL THROUGH- SHE MUST GET WELL-
ARF!
POOR ANNIE-

October 19, 1930

YES, SHE STOOD THE TRIP ABOARD BETTER THAN I FEARED SHE WOULD-
HOW IS SHE, DOC.? DO YOU THINK SHE'S ANY BETTER? CAN I SEE HER TO-DAY?
NO-NO- YOU MISUNDERSTAND - SHE'S WORSE, IF ANYTHING- IT WILL TAKE SEVERAL DAYS TO OVERCOME THE EFFECTS OF MOVING HER- BUT WE ARE ANCHORED IN QUIET WATER AND THERE MUST BE ABSOLUTE SILENCE- NOTHING TO DISTURB HER-
I SAY, MR. WARBUCKS, HOW SOON SHALL WE BE STARTING BACK? I CAN HAVE THE YACHT IN MOTION IN FIVE MINUTES-
HAROLD GRAY
NIX- THAT WOULD DISTURB ANNIE- WE'VE GOTTA KEEP HER QUIET- IT'S DOC'S ORDERS- NOT A SOUND ON THIS BOAT TILL HE SAYS THE WORD-
YES SIR-
Reg. U. S. Pat. Off.; Copyright, 1930, by The Chicago Tribune.
HAW! HAW! HAW!!! THAT'S A GOOD ONE! HAW! HAW! HAW!
HEY! WHERE D'YUH THINK YOU ARE? ANOTHER HORSE LAUGH LIKE THAT OUTA YOU BIRDS AND OVER-BOARD YOU GO- THE SHARKS AROUND HERE ARE CRAZY ABOUT LOUD GUYS LIKE YOU-
GET FOR'ARD - AND TIP-TOE! IF THERE'S ANOTHER SOUND ON THIS BOAT I'LL QUIET THE YOKEL THAT MAKES IT SO HE'LL STAY QUIET- SEE?
Reg. U. S. Pat. Off.; Copyright, 1930, by The Chicago Tribune.
NOW I WONDER WHERE SANDY AND WILLIE WENT- THEY WERE HERE JUST A MINUTE AGO-
HAROLD GRAY
HM-M--M! PRETTY WEAK- BUT STILL IT MIGHT BE WORSE, I SUPPOSE- HM-M-M----
HER CASE IS PECULIAR- WE NEED CERTAIN MEDICINES WHICH I COULD NOT FORESEE- THERE'S NO WAY TO GET THEM NOW, FOR TO TRY TO TAKE HER TO THE MAINLAND WOULD BE TOO LONG AND ROUGH A JOURNEY-
THAT'S EASY- HEY, SPARKS! GET THIS MESSAGE OFF AT ONCE- DOC'LL TELL YOU WHAT HE NEEDS-
RADIO
YOU'VE GOT THE NAMES OF ALL THAT STUFF DOC. NEEDS- NOW GET HOLD OF BUGS BALLARD AND GIVE HIM OUR BEARINGS AND TELL HIM IT'S A MATTER OF LIFE AND DEATH-
HAROLD GRAY
Reg. U. S. Pat. Off.; Copyright, 1930, by The Chicago Tribune.

October 20–22, 1930

?
HOW IS SHE TO-DAY, NURSE? TEMPERATURE DOWN A BIT, EH?
OF COURSE IT'S ALWAYS A BIT LOWER IN THE MORNING - BUT HER CHART SHOWS NO CHANGE - SHE'S HOLDING HER OWN - THAT'S ALL I CAN SAY -
HOLDING HER OWN! GREAT SCOTT! THAT BURNING FEVER ALL THE TIME — NOBODY CAN STAND THAT BEYOND A CERTAIN POINT -
Reg. U. S. Pat. Off.; Copyright, 1930, by The Chicago Tribune.
A DAY OR TWO MORE AT THIS RATE, AND THEN------ WON'T THAT MEDICINE EVER COME?
HAROLD GRAY
THAT'S BUGS, ALL RIGHT - LOOK AT HIM COME - I KNEW HE'D NOT LET US DOWN -
ALL RIGHT, BOYS - THROW HIM A LINE - HURRY - AND BE CAREFUL OF THAT CASE HE'S CARRYING -
HELLO, MR. WARBUCKS - DIDJA THINK I WAS NEVER COMING?
GREAT WORK, BUGS - I KNEW YOU'D MAKE GOOD - THAT'S WHY I CALLED ON YOU -
Reg. U. S. Pat. Off.; Copyright, 1930, by The Chicago Tribune.
AH - HERE WE ARE - A SMALL BOTTLE, BUT A VERY POWERFUL DRUG - IF THIS DOESN'T WORK NOTHING WILL - BUT WE SHALL SEE -
HAROLD GRAY
ANNIE! ANNIE! YOU REMEMBER YOUR OLD "DADDY", DON'T YOU?
SURE - HELLO, "DADDY" - WHERE AM I? HOW'D I GET HERE? GEE - I'M SO SLEEPY ---
YOU MUST COME AWAY NOW, MR. WARBUCKS - SHE'S GONE TO SLEEP - BUT IT'S A HEALTHY SLEEP THIS TIME - THE FEVER IS PRACTICALLY GONE -
SHE'S DECIDEDLY BETTER, BUT SHE MUST STILL HAVE PERFECT QUIET - IT WOULD BE VERY EASY FOR HER TO HAVE A RELAPSE -
SHE KNEW ME - DID YOU HEAR HER CALL ME "DADDY"? DOC, YOU'RE A WONDER -
HAROLD GRAY
SHE'S BETTER! SHE'S GOING TO GET WELL, BOYS - DO YOU UNDERSTAND? SHE'S GOING TO GET WELL!!!
ARF!
BOUF!
Reg. U. S. Pat. Off.; Copyright, 1930, by The Chicago Tribune.

October 23–25, 1930

Little Orphan Annie
HAROLD GRAY

SILENCE
'LO, ANNIE !!! HOW'S TH' KID?
HEY! GIT AWAY FROM THERE, YOU SQUAWKIN' IDIOT- CAN'T YOU READ ENGLISH?

IT'S BEEN A WEEK TO DAY SINCE WE BROUGHT ANNIE ABOARD THE YACHT- THE DOCTOR SAYS SHE SEEMS A LITTLE STRONGER, BUT SHE IS STILL MIGHTY WEAK-

DOC. PROMISED IF SHE WAKES UP TO DAY HE MIGHT LET ME SEE HER FOR A MINUTE- SHE HASN'T RECOGNIZED ME YET- BEEN TOO LOW TO KNOW OR CARE WHERE SHE IS-

ALL RIGHT, WARBUCKS- YOU MAY SEE HER FOR ONE MINUTE BUT NO LONGER-
FINE - DO YOU THINK SHE'LL KNOW ME, DOCTOR?

WELL, IT'S HARD TO SAY- IF SHE DOES, SEEING YOU MAY HELP TO GIVE HER NEW HOPE AND STRENGTH-

"DADDY!" IS IT REALLY YOU? I KNEW YOU'D FIND ME BUT IT TOOK SO LONG-
YES- IT DID TAKE A LONG TIME, BUT EVERYTHING'S ALL RIGHT NOW-

IS THERE ANYTHING YOU'D LIKE, ANNIE?
I'D LIKE TO SEE SANDY AN' WILLIE- WHERE ARE THEY?

OH, THEY DIDN'T DARE COME IN HERE TODAY- IT WAS ALL I COULD DO TO GET THE DOCTOR TO LET ME IN TO SEE YOU-

ARF!
BOUF!
SANDY! WILLIE!

TIME'S UP!!! OUT YOU GO, ALL OF YOU- MY, MY!!! HOW DID YOU TWO RASCALS EVER GET IN HERE?

HA! HA! IF ANNIE COULD SEE ANY VISITORS YOU TWO WEREN'T GOING TO BE LEFT OUT, WERE YOU?
ARF!
BOUF!

October 26, 1930

NOW LISTEN, YOU BIRDS- DOC SAYS WE CAN SEE HER FOR JUST A MINUTE- BUT WE MUST BE VERY CAREFUL NOT TO EXCITE HER-
HERE ARE SOME OLD FRIENDS TO SEE YOU, ANNIE-
ARF!
BOUF!
SANDY! WILLIE! IT SURE IS SWELL O' YOU TO COME TO SEE ME-
COME ALONG, NOW-WE MUSTN'T STAY ANY LONGER TODAY-
HAROLD GRAY
WELL, IT'S PRETTY GOOD TO SEE ANNIE GETTING ALONG SO MUCH BETTER, EH, BOYS?
BOUF!
ARF!
Reg. U. S. Pat. Off.; Copyright, 1930, by The Chicago Tribune.
AYE - FOR FORTY YEARS AN' MORE I'VE BEEN A SEA-FARIN' MAN - I GRANT YOU HAVE A REAL, TRIM CRAFT HERE - BUT FOR ME, GIVE OLD SPIKE MARLIN A GOOD SAILIN' VESSEL - EVERY TIME - BUT I'M GETTIN' OLD - TIMES HAVE CHANGED, I RECKON-
POOR OLD CODGER- COURAGE AND A HEART OF GOLD - AND EVERYTHING HE HAD IN THE WORLD WAS LOST WHEN THAT SAIL-BOAT OF HIS BROKE UP ON THE BEACH- BUT HE SAVED ANNIE'S LIFE-
HE SAVED HER FROM THOSE WATER-FRONT THUGS, THEN FROM THAT WRECK- AND HE HELD BACK THE FEVER TILL HELP CAME - I OWE HIM MORE THAN I CAN EVER PAY-
SOMETHING MUST BE DONE FOR HIM- BUT YOU CAN'T PAY A CHAP LIKE SPIKE MARLIN - HE'S TOO BIG AND REAL A MAN - MONEY WON'T DO - BUT HE MUST BE TAKEN CARE OF IN SOME WAY - LET ME THINK-
HAROLD GRAY
Reg. U. S. Pat. Off.; Copyright, 1930, by The Chicago Tribune.
IF SPIKE HAD A FORTUNE HE'D NOT KEEP IT A YEAR- SAILORS ARE ROTTEN BUSINESS MEN- NO- AND HE'D NOT ACCEPT MONEY ANYWAY- BUT I'VE GOT TO BE SURE HE'S MADE COMFORTABLE AND HAPPY FOR LIFE-
I'VE GOT IT- A TRUST FUND- I'LL FIX IT SO HE'LL ALWAYS HAVE A COMFORTABLE LIVING IN SPITE OF ANYTHING HE CAN DO- AND I'LL DO IT NOW- HE WON'T BE ABLE TO REFUSE THIS-
I'LL HAVE THE FINEST, SNUGGEST LITTLE SAILING BOAT HE EVER SAW READY FOR HIM TO STEP ABOARD- HE'LL NEVER BE HAPPY ASHORE FOR LONG- AND THERE'LL BE A HOUSE OVERLOOKING THE OPEN SEA- AN OBSERVATION TOWER ON IT, TOO- ALL FURNISHED LIKE A SHIP'S CABIN-
AND A TRUST FUND ARRANGED SO HE'LL BE LOOKED OUT FOR AS LONG AS HE LIVES AND NO MATTER WHERE HE GOES- THERE, NOW- THAT COVERS THE GROUND, I GUESS- NOW TO RADIO THIS TO MY ATTORNEYS AND HAVE IT MADE AIR-TIGHT-
HAROLD GRAY
Reg. U. S. Pat. Off.; Copyright, 1930, by The Chicago Tribune.

October 27–29, 1930

YO! HO! HO! AND A BOTTLE O' POP!!! WHOOPIE!
GREAT SCOTT! WHO'S DOING THAT? AND ANNIE TAKING HER NAP!!!
BLOW TH' MAN DOWN! BATTEN YOUR HATCH YOU !!!!—!!! LUBBERS!!!
AR-R-R-
URP!
Reg. U. S. Pat. Off.; Copyright, 1930, by The Chicago Tribune.
WOW! YOU'RE SURE A GUY OF ACTION, WILLIE- BUT THAT'S ENOUGH- I THINK DEACON HAS THE IDEA NOW-
ULP!
HAROLD GRAY
WELL, DOC., HOW SOON CAN WE GET STARTED HOME?
WELL, SHE SEEMS MUCH STRONGER- I BELIEVE WE MIGHT START ANY TIME NOW-
HEY! CAPTAIN! WE'RE OFF- DOC. SAYS ANNIE'S A LOT BETTER- WE CAN START THE MOTORS ANY TIME- LET'S GO!!!
HOW SOON CAN YOU HAVE THE YACHT MOVING, CAPTAIN?
HOW SOON? IN FIVE MINUTES- WE CAN'T GET AWAY FROM HERE ANY TOO SOON TO SUIT ME-
HAROLD GRAY
HOMEWARD BOUND AT LAST- TAKE YOUR LAST LOOK AT THE ISLAND, BOYS, AND THANK YOUR STARS YOU'LL NEVER SEE THAT FEVER-SOAKED PLACE AGAIN-
Reg. U. S. Pat. Off.; Copyright, 1930, by The Chicago Tribune.
WE'VE GOT A CHAIR FIXED UP FOR YOU ON THE AFTER DECK OUT OF THE WIND-
GEE- IT'S SWELL TO GET OUT DOORS AGAIN-
THERE- ARE YOU SURE YOU'RE PERFECTLY WARM AND SNUG NOW? FEEL ALL RIGHT?
THIS IS GREAT-
?
NOTHING MORE YOU CAN THINK OF? IF THERE IS JUST MENTION IT, AND WE'LL GET IT-
Reg. U. S. Pat. Off.; Copyright, 1930, by The Chicago Tribune.
GREAT SCOTT! THE FINAL TOUCH- A MAGAZINE FOR ME TO READ TO ANNIE, EH? SANDY, YOU THINK OF EVERYTHING-
HAROLD GRAY

October 30–
November 1, 1930

Little Orphan Annie
HAROLD GRAY
THEY TOLD ME NOT TO TRY TO GET OUT O THIS CHAIR— BUT HERE I GO!
NIX! NIX! YOU DO, AN' I'LL HOLLER FOR TH' DOCTOR!

GEE, IT'S SURE SWELL TO BE ABLE TO SIT OUT ON DECK— WONDER HOW SOON TH' DOC. WILL LET ME WALK—
OH, IT WON'T BE LONG NOW— BUT YOU'RE STILL MIGHTY WEAK— YOU MUST TAKE IT EASY FOR A WHILE YET—

LUNCHEON, MISS ANNIE— IS THERE ANYTHING SPECIAL YOU'D LIKE ME TO BRING YOU?
YES— EVERYTHING! I CAN'T THINK OF A THING TO EAT THAT I DON'T WANT— SAY— IS THAT REAL CHICKEN? YOU WOULDN'T FOOL ME?

YESSIR, "DADDY", YOUR COOK SURE KNOWS HIS BUSINESS— HOW LONG WILL IT BE TILL THE NEXT MEAL?
GOOD FOOD AND PLENTY OF IT WILL MAKE YOU FIT AS A FIDDLE IN SHORT ORDER—

AH-H-H-! THAT WAS SOME MEAL— BOY! DO I FEEL GREAT! DON'T SEEM LIKE I'D EVER BEEN SICK— I COULD GO TO SLEEP NOW WITHOUT HALF TRYIN'— BUT I DON'T NEED ANY MORE SLEEP—

BEEN SLEEPIN' FOR WEEKS— WHAT I WANT NOW IS EXERCISE— THEY ALL SAY I'M TOO WEAK— WHAT DO THEY KNOW 'BOUT IT? NOT A SOUL IN SIGHT—

NOW'S MY CHANCE— I'LL SHOW 'EM WHO'S WEAK!

SHUX! I FEEL SWELL— STEADY AS A ROCK— THAT DOC WAS CUCKOO WHEN HE SAID I COULDN'T WALK FOR A WEEK YET—

ER--- WHAT TH--- TH' BOAT MUST BE SORTA ROLLIN', I GUESS—

OH, I'M ALL RIGHT— HONEST— JUST A LITTLE SHAKEY— HAVEN'T GOT MY SEA LEGS YET--

THANKS, WILLIE— I'LL BE ALL RIGHT IN A MINUTE—

WHAT'S UP, SANDY? WHERE IS SHE?
ARF! ARF!

MY, MY, ANNIE! DIDN'T THE DOCTOR SAY YOU'RE TOO WEAK TO WALK YET?
YEAH— THAT'S WHAT HE SAID— BUT HOW DID I KNOW HE WAS RIGHT TILL I TRIED?

November 2, 1930

GEE, I GET AWFUL TIRED O' JUST SITTIN' AROUND - DOC SAYS I'M STILL TOO WEAK TO WALK, BUT WHAT DOES HE KNOW 'BOUT IT? I FEEL SWELL-
COURSE I'LL BE A LITTLE WOBBLY ON MY PINS AT FIRST, I S'POSE - BUT HOW AM I EVER GOIN' TO GET STRONG IF I DON'T EXERCISE?
WHO-OO-PIE!!! I SURE DO FEEL FUNNY - MY LEGS FEEL JUST LIKE THEY WERE MADE O' RUBBER-
HA! HA! HA! RUBBER LEGS!!!
?
?
Reg. U. S. Pat. Off.; Copyright, 1930, by The Chicago Tribune.
I'M STILL PRETTY SHAKY - BUT IF I HANG ONTO SOMETHIN' I'M ALL RIGHT - JUST LIKE A BABY LEARNIN' TO WALK-
HEY! JUST WHAT'S GOING ON AROUND HERE?
O-OH! YOU SCARED ME-
WALKING, EH? WELL, A LITTLE OF THAT GOES A LONG WAY - YOU'VE HAD ENOUGH FOR ONE DAY, YOUNG LADY-
HAROLD GRAY
I THOUGHT SO - ALL TIRED OUT - BUT DON'T WORRY - A LITTLE MORE EACH DAY AND YOU'LL BE GOOD AS NEW IN NO TIME - THAT IS, IF YOU DON'T OVERDO-
Reg. U. S. Pat. Off.; Copyright, 1930, by The Chicago Tribune.
GEE, NURSE - WHAT A PRETTY DRESS - WHERE DID IT COME FROM?
OH, MR. WARBUCKS BOUGHT IT FOR YOU - HE WAS SURE WE'D FIND YOU, SO HE GOT A WHOLE OUTFIT FOR YOU, BEFORE WE STARTED OUT ON THE YACHT-
HE THOUGHT OF EVERY THING - BROUGHT THE DOCTOR AND ME ALONG IN CASE WE SHOULD BE NEEDED, TOO - ALL THE REST GAVE UP FINDING YOU MONTHS AGO - BUT NOT MR. WARBUCKS - HERE - JUST LOOK IN THIS TRUNK AND THERE ARE MANY OTHERS ALL FULL OF THINGS FOR YOU - DIDN'T HE TELL YOU?
OH, "DADDY"-
SMACK!!!
SMACK!!!
HAROLD GRAY
WHAT TH---? THE LITTLE IMP - NOW WHY DO YOU SUPPOSE SHE DID THAT? BUT THEY SAY THERE'S NO FIGURING WOMEN - I SUPPOSE THAT GOES FOR THAT LITTLE LADY, TOO-
Reg. U. S. Pat. Off.; Copyright, 1930, by The Chicago Tribune.

November 3–5, 1930

SHIPWRECKED

WELL, DOCTOR- WHAT DO YOU THINK OF THE PATIENT?
PRACTICALLY WELL, MR. WARBUCKS- JUST A MATTER OF TIME NOW- TAKE A LOOK AT HER-
HM-M-M-- PLAYING SHUFFLE-BOARD, EH?
I DIDN'T KNOW WHAT IT WAS CALLED, BUT IT'S A SWELL GAME- WANT TO PLAY?
NOT JUST NOW- BY THE WAY, WE'LL BE GETTING HOME BEFORE MANY MORE DAYS-
OH, GEE- THEN WE'LL HAVE TO GET OFF THIS YACHT- I COULD BE HAPPY JUST RIDIN' LIKE THIS FOREVER-
HAROLD GRAY
Reg. U. S. Pat. Off.: Copyright, 1930, by The Chicago Tribune.
SANDY! WHAT IN THE WORLD ARE YOU SO EXCITED 'BOUT?
WHY, IT'S A LIGHT - AND IT'S WINKIN'- IT DOESN'T LOOK LIKE IT'S MOVING- IT MUST BE ON LAND-
ARF!
GEE- WE'D BETTER TELL "DADDY" 'BOUT THIS-
HAROLD GRAY
HEY-THERE'S A LIGHT WAY OFF OVER THERE AN' IT KEEPS GOIN' OUT AN' THEN LIGHTIN' UP AGAIN-
YES- THAT'S A BEACON ON THE MAINLAND- WE'RE GETTING BACK TO CIVILIZATION NOW, ANNIE-
Reg. U. S. Pat. Off.; Copyright, 1930, by The Chicago Tribune.
NOW WHAT'S UP, ANNIE?
COME QUICK, "DADDY"- IT'S RIGHT OFF OUR PORT BOW AS TH' CAP'N SAYS-
HURRY- IT'S GOIN' TO BEAT TH' BAND, TOO, BUT WE'RE PASSIN' IT LIKE NOTHIN'- LOOK- THERE IT IS- SEE TH' SMOKE-
GEE- IT'S A BIG LINER, ISN'T IT, "DADDY"?
YEP!
THAT'S THE FIRST BIG OCEAN LINER I EVER SAW- WHERE DID IT COME FROM AND WHERE IS IT GOING?
IT'S COME FROM ACROSS THE OCEAN AND GOING WHERE WE'RE GOING- WE'RE IN THE TRADE LANES- FROM NOW ON YOU'LL SEE ALL SORTS OF CRAFT-
HAROLD GRAY
Reg. U. S. Pat. Off.; Copyright, 1930, by The Chicago Tribune.

November 6–8, 1930

Little Orphan
Annie

SAILING-- SAILING-- OVER THE BOUNDING MAIN--
ARF! ARF! ARF!
BOUF! BOUF!
HAROLD GRAY

GEE, IT'S SURE SWELL TO BE ABLE TO BE UP AN' DRESSED AN' COME TO TH' TABLE FOR MEALS- SOME TIMES I 'MOST FORGET I'VE BEEN SICK-
YES, ANNIE- IT'S SWELL FOR A LOT OF PEOPLE BESIDES YOURSELF- BUT YOU WANT TO TAKE IT EASY- YOU'RE BOUND TO BE A LITTLE WEAK YET-

YOU SURE HAVE A PEACH OF A BOAT HERE, DADDY- IF I DIDN'T LOOK OUT TH' WINDOW AN' SEE TH' WATER GOIN' BY I'D THINK I WAS IN A SWELL HOUSE-

IT'S PRETTY ROUGH TO DAY- LOOK OUT!!!

NIX- I'M O.K.- HONEST- EVERYTHING TIPPED, BUT I FORGOT TO TIP TOO- THAT'S ALL- I WON'T GET FOOLED AGAIN-

I TELL YOU WHAT- YOU RUN AND PUT ON A COAT AND I'LL TAKE YOU UP TO THE PILOT HOUSE AND SHOW YOU HOW WE RUN THE YACHT-
WILL YOU, HONEST? GEE-

LOOK AT HER GO- WONDERFUL HOW QUICKLY YOUNGSTERS RECOVER FROM A SIEGE OF ILLNESS- YOUTH- YOUTH- YOUTH-

ALL SET, DADDY- HERE I AM- LET'S GO-

HANG ON TIGHT, NOW- DON'T SLIP-

GEE- WOULDN'T A LOT O' KIDS I KNOW BE POP-EYED WITH JEALOUSY IF THEY COULD ONLY SEE ME NOW-

SEE THAT BIG LINER, ANNIE? LOOK CLOSE AND YOU CAN MAKE OUT THE PEOPLE ON DECK- AND THERE TO THE LEFT IS A FRUIT BOAT- SEE? THE WHITE ONE-

EVERYWHERE YUH LOOK THERE'S SHIPS- I BET I CAN SEE FIFTY IF I LOOK CAREFUL- WE MUST BE GETTIN' CLOSE TO A BIG TOWN-
RIGHT YOU ARE, ANNIE- WE'LL BE IN PORT IN A COUPLE OF DAYS-

WE'LL SOON BE HOME AGAIN, AND TO STAY THIS TIME, ANNIE- THEY'LL NEVER GET YOU AWAY FROM ME AGAIN- FROM NOW ON WHEN I GO YOU GO, TOO-

November 9, 1930

WELL, ANNIE, DO YOU SEE ANYTHING THROUGH THE GLASSES?
ONLY A COUPLE O' LITTLE FISHIN' BOATS AN' A FREIGHTER - TOO BLAMED COLD FOR FOLKS TO GO BOAT-RIDIN' IF THEY CAN HELP IT, I GUESS -
YES - WE'RE GETTING UP NORTH NOW - NOT MUCH LIKE THE CLIMATE ON THAT ISLAND -
NO - BUT I LIKE IT NICE AND SNAPPY LIKE THIS - THIS KIND OF WEATHER PUTS PEP IN YUH -
STILL, THERE'S NO USE FREEZIN' YER EARS OFF - LET'S GO INSIDE TILL I GET THAWED OUT -
WELL, ONLY A FEW MORE DAYS AND WE'LL BE HOME -
THAT'LL BE GREAT - BUT I COULD BE HAPPY RIGHT HERE ON THIS YACHT TH' REST O' MY LIFE, I BETCHA -
HAROLD GRAY
Reg. U. S. Pat. Off.; Copyright, 1930, by The Chicago Tribune.
NOT MUCH FOR THE LOG TO-DAY - HM-M-M - NOVEMBER ELEVENTH - JUST TWELVE YEARS AGO TO-DAY - HOW TIME FLIES - IT SEEMS ONLY YESTERDAY -
TWELVE YEARS - THE WORLD EXHAUSTED AND TIRED OF KILLING - THE WAR, THAT HAD SEEMED SO IMPOSSIBLE TILL IT BEGAN, AT AN END - AND YET IT CAME AS WARS HAVE ALWAYS COME -
NOW THEY SAY WE'LL NEVER HAVE ANOTHER - TWELVE YEARS - YOUNGSTERS OF ANNIE'S AGE GROW UP IN TWELVE YEARS - THE WAR WAS GLORIOUS TO YOUNGSTERS -
NOW THOSE YOUNGSTERS ARE YOUNG MEN AND WOMEN - WAR IS NOT SO TERRIBLE TO THEM - HUMAN NATURE DOESN'T CHANGE - WHO WAS IT SAID, "ETERNAL VIGILANCE IS THE PRICE OF PEACE."? WELL, HE SURE SAID A MOUTH FUL -
HAROLD GRAY
Reg. U. S. Pat. Off.; Copyright, 1930, by The Chicago Tribune.
WITH LONELY SEAS AND TREACHEROUS TROPIC ISLANDS FAR BEHIND, THE YACHT COMES AT LAST INTO BUSY WATERS AND VERY NEAR TO THE JOURNEY'S END -
SHIPS FROM EVERY PORT PASS HERE - SEE, ANNIE, THAT ONE IS BOUND FOR CHINA - AND THERE IS A GREAT LINER FROM ENGLAND -
GEE, "DADDY" - I FEEL ALL FIDGETY - ISN'T IT EXCITING TO BE GETTING BACK WHERE THERE'S SO MUCH GOING ON?
YES, ANNIE - NO MATTER HOW MANY TIMES ONE DOES IT THERE IS ALWAYS A THRILL IN COMING HOME -
GEE, SANDY - WE'RE GETTIN' RIGHT INTO TH' MIDDLE O' THINGS - DON'T YUH GET A KICK OUTA COMIN' BACK TO TH' BIG TOWN AGAIN WHERE THERE'S ALWAYS 'CITEMENT?
ARF!
HAROLD GRAY
Reg. U. S. Pat. Off.; Copyright, 1930, by The Chicago Tribune.

November 10–12, 1930

SAY, "DADDY"- WHAT'S TH' MATTER? THERE'S SOMETHING WRONG- I CAN TELL-
WHAT'S THAT? "WRONG"?
HAROLD GRAY

CHAPTER FOUR

BUSTED!

IN WHICH ANNIE

ENJOYS THE HIGH -- AND DRY -- LIFE ON "DADDY'S" ESTATE

GIVES EJU-CATION YET ANOTHER TRY

AND REALIZES THAT WHEN THE CHIPS ARE DOWN, SHE AND "DADDY" HAVE NO ONE TO RELY ON EXCEPT ONE ANOTHER...

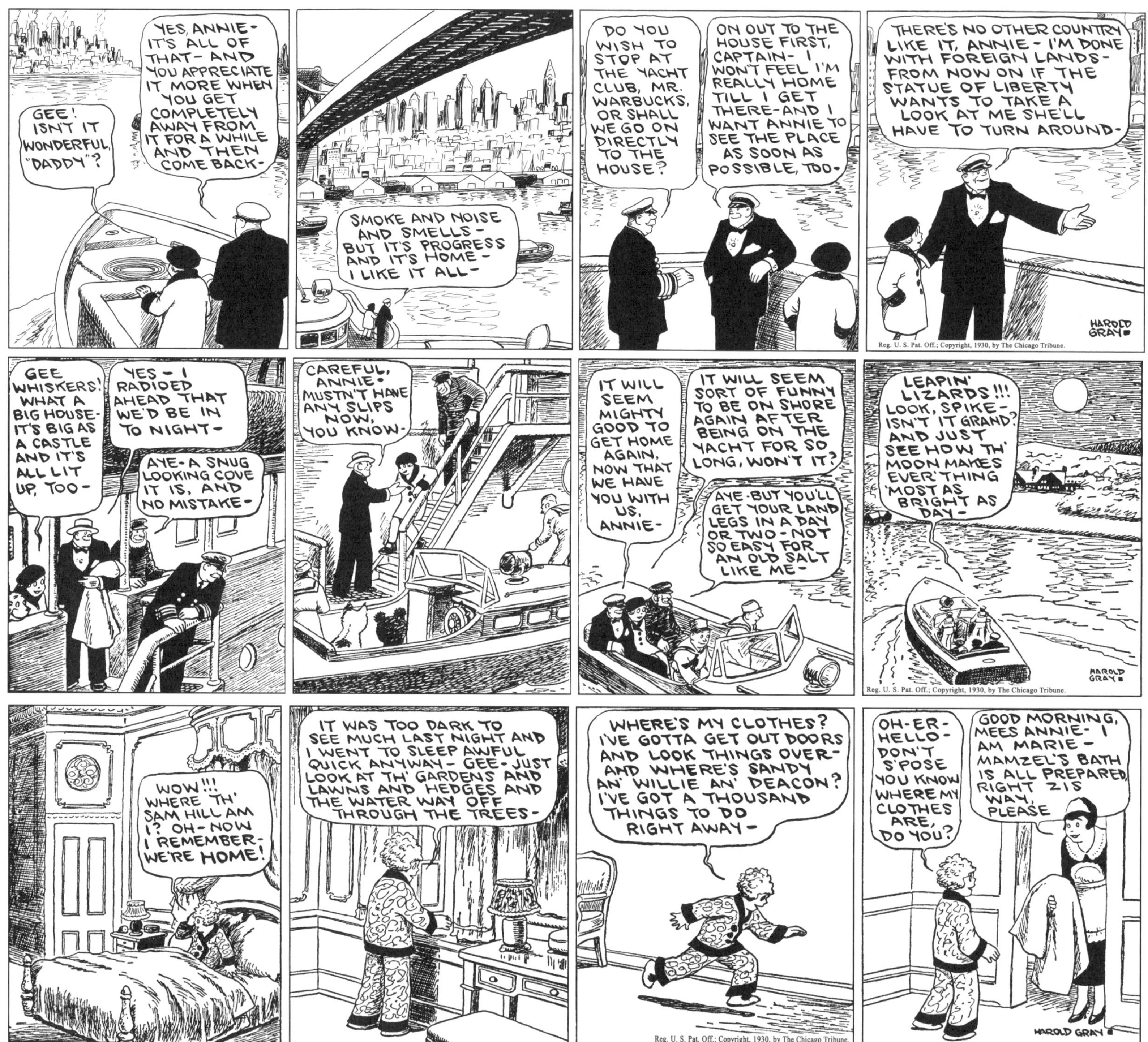
GEE! ISN'T IT WONDERFUL, "DADDY"?
YES, ANNIE- IT'S ALL OF THAT- AND YOU APPRECIATE IT MORE WHEN YOU GET COMPLETELY AWAY FROM IT FOR A WHILE AND THEN COME BACK-
SMOKE AND NOISE AND SMELLS- BUT IT'S PROGRESS AND IT'S HOME- I LIKE IT ALL-
DO YOU WISH TO STOP AT THE YACHT CLUB, MR. WARBUCKS, OR SHALL WE GO ON DIRECTLY TO THE HOUSE?
ON OUT TO THE HOUSE FIRST, CAPTAIN- I WON'T FEEL I'M REALLY HOME TILL I GET THERE-AND I WANT ANNIE TO SEE THE PLACE AS SOON AS POSSIBLE, TOO-
THERE'S NO OTHER COUNTRY LIKE IT, ANNIE- I'M DONE WITH FOREIGN LANDS- FROM NOW ON IF THE STATUE OF LIBERTY WANTS TO TAKE A LOOK AT ME SHE'LL HAVE TO TURN AROUND-
HAROLD GRAY
Reg. U. S. Pat. Off.; Copyright, 1930, by The Chicago Tribune.
GEE WHISKERS! WHAT A BIG HOUSE- IT'S BIG AS A CASTLE AND IT'S ALL LIT UP, TOO-
YES- I RADIOED AHEAD THAT WE'D BE IN TO NIGHT-
AYE- A SNUG LOOKING COVE IT IS, AND NO MISTAKE-
CAREFUL, ANNIE- MUSTN'T HAVE ANY SLIPS NOW, YOU KNOW-
IT WILL SEEM MIGHTY GOOD TO GET HOME AGAIN, NOW THAT WE HAVE YOU WITH US, ANNIE-
IT WILL SEEM SORT OF FUNNY TO BE ON SHORE AGAIN AFTER BEING ON THE YACHT FOR SO LONG, WON'T IT?
AYE- BUT YOU'LL GET YOUR LAND LEGS IN A DAY OR TWO- NOT SO EASY FOR AN OLD SALT LIKE ME-
LEAPIN' LIZARDS!!! LOOK, SPIKE- ISN'T IT GRAND? AND JUST SEE HOW TH' MOON MAKES EVER'THING 'MOST AS BRIGHT AS DAY-
HAROLD GRAY
Reg. U. S. Pat. Off.; Copyright, 1930, by The Chicago Tribune.
WOW!!! WHERE TH' SAM HILL AM I? OH- NOW I REMEMBER- WE'RE HOME!
IT WAS TOO DARK TO SEE MUCH LAST NIGHT AND I WENT TO SLEEP AWFUL QUICK ANYWAY- GEE- JUST LOOK AT TH' GARDENS AND LAWNS AND HEDGES AND THE WATER WAY OFF THROUGH THE TREES-
WHERE'S MY CLOTHES? I'VE GOTTA GET OUT DOORS AND LOOK THINGS OVER- AND WHERE'S SANDY AN' WILLIE AN' DEACON? I'VE GOT A THOUSAND THINGS TO DO RIGHT AWAY-
Reg. U. S. Pat. Off.; Copyright, 1930, by The Chicago Tribune.
OH- ER- HELLO- DON'T S'POSE YOU KNOW WHERE MY CLOTHES ARE, DO YOU?
GOOD MORNING, MEES ANNIE- I AM MARIE- MAMZEL'S BATH IS ALL PREPARED, RIGHT ZIS WAY, PLEASE
HAROLD GRAY

November 13–15, 1930

Little Orphan Annie
WELL, NO MATTER HOW MUCH "DADDY" PAID FOR THIS PLACE HE GOT A BARGAIN -
SOME SHACK! SOME SHACK!
HAROLD GRAY

RUN ALONG, ANNIE, AND LOOK OVER THE PLACE - I BOUGHT IT IN A HURRY - DON'T KNOW WHAT ALL WE HAVE HERE MYSELF -
SANDY AN' I WILL SORTA SNOOP AROUND AND GIVE IT THE ONCE OVER -

LEAPIN' LIZARDS! JUST LOOK AT THAT FLOWER GARDEN - ACRES AN' ACRES - AND THOUSANDS OF DIFFERENT KINDS OF FLOWERS -

AN' HERE IT'S JUST LIKE BEIN' IN TH' WOODS - BIG OLD TREES FAR AS YUH CAN SEE - I SURE LIKE LOTS O' TREES ON A PLACE -

GEE - AND DOWN HERE IS THE OCEAN - "DADDY" SURE HAS A WHOPPIN' BIG PLACE - WAY OUT THERE IS HIS YACHT - HE HAS EVER'THING -

THERE'S ONE OF HIS CARS - GOT A DOZEN OTHER CARS - AN' HORSES TO RIDE, TOO - WHAT A LAYOUT -

OH, HELLO, WILLIE - I WONDERED WHERE YOU WERE - COME ALONG - WE'RE LOOKIN' OVER TH' PLACE -

TAKE A MONTH TO SEE THIS HOUSE RIGHT - MUST BE FIFTY BED-ROOMS - THIS IS "DADDY'S" OFFICE - I DON'T SEE HOW ANY BODY CAN WORK IN A PLACE THIS SWELL - AN' THERE'S DRAWIN' ROOMS AN' SITTIN' ROOMS AN' CARD ROOMS, AN' A BILLIARD ROOM -- AN' --

OH, HELLO - SAY, WHERE IS THE SWIMMIN POOL AN' TH' CONSERVATORY? ARE THEY OUT THIS WAY?
ALLOW ME TO SHOW YOU TO THEM, MISS -

NOW WHERE DID WILLIE GO? HERE A MINUTE AGO - PLAYIN' HIDE AND SEEK AS USUAL I SUPPOSE -
SHE'S GOING TO BE A BALLY NUISANCE - AND THAT GRUBBY DOG! BAH! WHAT WILL THE MARSTER BE BRINGING HOME NEXT?

OH, THERE HE IS -
YI!
BOUF!

MY HEAVENLY STARS!!! A BEAR! HELP! HELP!

GEE, HE'S SURE A SPRY OLD CODGER - DIDN'T THINK AT FIRST THAT I WAS GOIN' TO LIKE HIM - TOO STIFF - BUT YOU TOOK TH' STARCH OUT O' HIM IN A HURRY, WILLIE - HE MAY GIVE US A LOT O' LAUGHS YET, EH BOYS?
ARF!
BOUF!

November 16, 1930
BUSTED!

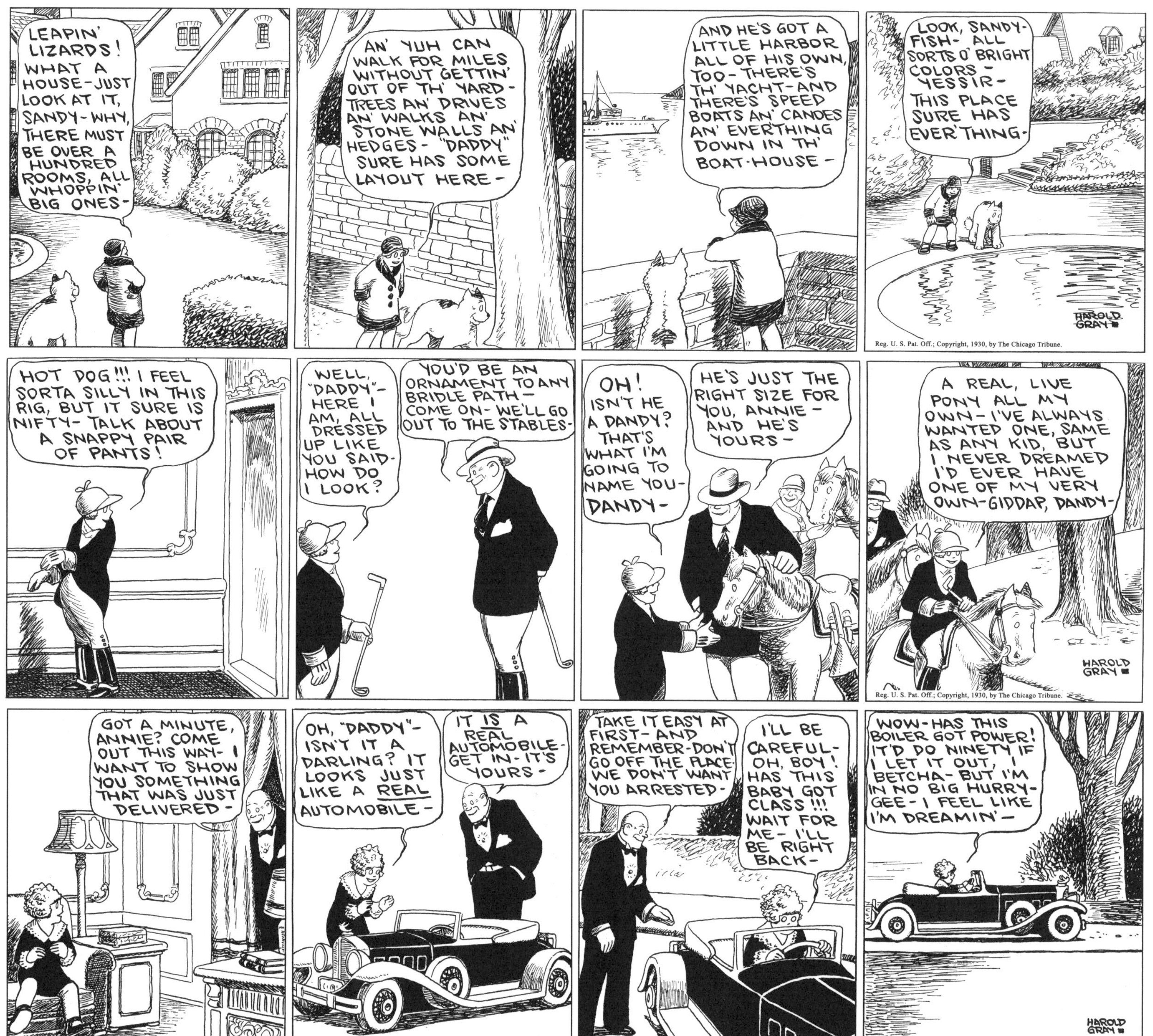
LEAPIN' LIZARDS! WHAT A HOUSE-JUST LOOK AT IT, SANDY-WHY, THERE MUST BE OVER A HUNDRED ROOMS, ALL WHOPPIN' BIG ONES-
AN' YUH CAN WALK FOR MILES WITHOUT GETTIN' OUT OF TH' YARD-TREES AN' DRIVES AN' WALKS AN' STONE WALLS AN' HEDGES-"DADDY" SURE HAS SOME LAYOUT HERE-
AND HE'S GOT A LITTLE HARBOR ALL OF HIS OWN, TOO-THERE'S TH' YACHT-AND THERE'S SPEED BOATS AN' CANOES AN' EVERTHING DOWN IN TH' BOAT-HOUSE-
LOOK, SANDY-FISH-ALL SORTS O' BRIGHT COLORS-YESSIR-THIS PLACE SURE HAS EVER'THING-
HAROLD GRAY
Reg. U. S. Pat. Off.; Copyright, 1930, by The Chicago Tribune.
HOT DOG!!! I FEEL SORTA SILLY IN THIS RIG, BUT IT SURE IS NIFTY-TALK ABOUT A SNAPPY PAIR OF PANTS!
WELL, "DADDY"-HERE I AM, ALL DRESSED UP LIKE YOU SAID-HOW DO I LOOK?
YOU'D BE AN ORNAMENT TO ANY BRIDLE PATH-COME ON-WE'LL GO OUT TO THE STABLES-
OH! ISN'T HE A DANDY? THAT'S WHAT I'M GOING TO NAME YOU-DANDY-
HE'S JUST THE RIGHT SIZE FOR YOU, ANNIE-AND HE'S YOURS-
A REAL, LIVE PONY ALL MY OWN-I'VE ALWAYS WANTED ONE, SAME AS ANY KID, BUT I NEVER DREAMED I'D EVER HAVE ONE OF MY VERY OWN-GIDDAP, DANDY-
HAROLD GRAY
Reg. U. S. Pat. Off.; Copyright, 1930, by The Chicago Tribune.
GOT A MINUTE, ANNIE? COME OUT THIS WAY-I WANT TO SHOW YOU SOMETHING THAT WAS JUST DELIVERED-
OH, "DADDY"-ISN'T IT A DARLING? IT LOOKS JUST LIKE A REAL AUTOMOBILE-
IT IS A REAL AUTOMOBILE-GET IN-IT'S YOURS-
TAKE IT EASY AT FIRST-AND REMEMBER-DON'T GO OFF THE PLACE-WE DON'T WANT YOU ARRESTED-
I'LL BE CAREFUL-OH, BOY! HAS THIS BABY GOT CLASS!!! WAIT FOR ME-I'LL BE RIGHT BACK-
WOW-HAS THIS BOILER GOT POWER! IT'D DO NINETY IF I LET IT OUT, I BETCHA-BUT I'M IN NO BIG HURRY-GEE-I FEEL LIKE I'M DREAMIN'-
HAROLD GRAY
Reg. U. S. Pat. Off.; Copyright, 1930, by The Chicago Tribune.

November 17–19, 1930

DOG GONE IT! I LIKE TO BE ALONE ONCE IN A WHILE - EVERY PLACE I GO SOME SERVANT FOLLOWS ME - IT'S DRIVIN' ME CHITTERY - EVERY TIME I LOOK OVER MY SHOULDER, THERE'S THAT BUTLER - HE'S HARDER TO LOSE THAN MY SHADOW - I'LL JUST DUCK THROUGH THIS DOOR ---
HOT DOG!!! A SWIMMIN' POOL - I DIDN'T KNOW 'BOUT THIS BEFORE GEE!
LUCKY I LOST THAT BUTLER - NOW IS MY CHANCE FOR A SWIM BEFORE ANYBODY MISSES ME - SERVANTS ARE ALL RIGHT, BUT THEY GET TO BE A NUISANCE AT TIMES ---
HAROLD GRAY
AHEM --- ER -- BEG PARDON, MISS ANNIE - BUT HERE IS YOUR BATHING COSTUME -
? ? ? ? ? ?
Reg. U. S. Pat. Off.; Copyright, 1930, by The Chicago Tribune.
HM-M-M -- NOW I WONDER WHERE THAT SPIRAL STAIR GOES TO - HAVE TO LOOK INTO THIS -
UP AN' UP AN' UP - I MUST COME TO THE TOP BEFORE LONG -
GEE - I SURE AM UP IN THE WORLD NOW - IT'S TAKEN ME A WEEK TO FIND THIS TOWER - BUT THIS HOUSE IS BIG AS A CASTLE - TAKE A YEAR TO REALLY KNOW YER WAY ALL OVER IT -
WOW - WHAT A VIEW - BUT ALL TH' LAND YUH CAN SEE FROM HERE BELONGS TO "DADDY" - WHAT A HOUSE AND YARD FOR ONE GUY TO OWN -
HAROLD GRAY
Reg. U. S. Pat. Off.; Copyright, 1930, by The Chicago Tribune.
GEE, I DON'T KNOW WHERE I'M GOIN' TO FIND ROOM FOR ANOTHER BITE, "DADDY" -
OH, THERE'S STILL THE DESSERT, ANNIE - YOU CAN'T QUIT YET -
CHOC'LATE CAKE AN' ICE CREAM!!! WELL, I GUESS MAYBE I CAN EAT A LITTLE MORE - I'LL TRY -
AN' JUST THINK - ONLY A LITTLE WHILE AGO I WAS LIVIN' IN A SHACK AN' EATIN' COCOA-NUTS AN' FISH - IT SEEMS AGES AGO, NOW -
HERE I AM, SAFE AND SOUND, LIVING IN A CASTLE JUST LIKE A PRINCESS - GEE, "DADDY", IT'S ALL LIKE A WONDERFUL DREAM, AND YOU MADE IT COME TRUE -
HAROLD GRAY
Reg. U. S. Pat. Off.; Copyright, 1930, by The Chicago Tribune.

November 20–22, 1930

Little Orphan Annie
JUST LOOK AT THAT SAP - IF HE'D LOOKED AT A CALENDAR HE'D KNOW THIS IS A BUM TIME FOR HIM TO GO STRUTTIN' AROUND LIKE THAT WITHOUT AN IRON VEST -
HAROLD GRAY

LEAPIN' LIZARDS! DID YOU RE'LIZE, "DADDY" THAT IT'S A LONG TIME SINCE I'VE SEEN MY OLD FRIENDS -
RIGHT YOU ARE, ANNIE - WE'LL HAVE TO DOPE OUT SOME SPECIAL WAY TO CELEBRATE -

I HAVE IT - WHY NOT INVITE ALL YOUR OLD FRIENDS FOR A BIG BLOWOUT HERE? YOU KNOW - THE SILOS AND ALL THE REST -
GEE, "DADDY" - THAT'S TH' BEST IDEA YOU COULD HAVE HAD -

THERE'S HARDLY TIME TO WRITE - SIT DOWN HERE AT MY DESK - THERE ARE THE TELEGRAPH BLANKS - GO TO IT, ANNIE - IT'S YOUR PARTY - YOU MAKE ALL THE ARRANGEMENTS -

THE SILOS - THE FLINTS - MRS. PEWTER AND TH' KIDS - THE DOOLEYS - MRS. TWINKLE - JUDGE TORT - OLD JACK PEPPER - GEE - I MUSTN'T GET EXCITED AND FORGET ANYBODY -

HERE Y'ARE CHARLEY - WILL YOU PLEASE SEE THAT THESE GET GOING RIGHT AWAY?
QUITE SO, MISS ANNIE, THANK YOU KINDLY -

NOW THEN FOR TH' MOST PORTANT PART O' THIS FEAST - I'M HUNGRY ALREADY JUST THINKIN' 'BOUT IT - ARMAND AN' I HAVE GOT TO HAVE A LONG TALK -

GEE - WHAT A SWELL KITCHEN - HELLO, ARMAND - ARE YUH AWFUL BUSY? I'VE GOT SOMETHIN' AWFUL 'PORTANT TO TALK TO YOU 'BOUT -

AH - MEES ANN-EE - ZIS IS ZE HONOR - EET IS ABOUT ZE CELEBRATION DINNER, EES EET NOT? EET MUST BE ZE MOST SUPERB OF REPASTS -

ZE HORS D'OEUVRES, ZE SOUP - ZE SALAD - LEAVE ALL ZAT TO ARMAND - NOW LET US SEE - WHAT IS MEES ANN-EE'S PLAISIR -

WELL, FOR ONE THING, TURKEY, WITH CHESTNUT STUFFIN' AN' CRANBERRY SAUCE - AND PUNKIN PIE! I'M A SUCKER FOR PUNKIN PIE -

GEE, ARMAND'S A PEACH - HE LIKES TH' SAME THINGS I LIKE - THAT'S GOIN' TO BE TH' SWELLEST MEAL ANYBODY EVER DUG INTO - AN' HAVIN' ALL MY FRIENDS IS GOIN' TO MAKE IT TWICE AS GOOD -

GEE, DADDY, IT'S GREAT TO BE RICH ENOUGH TO HAVE EVER'THING YUH WANT -
YES - BUT IT'S GREATER WHEN YOU USE YOUR WEALTH TO MAKE OTHERS HAPPY, AS YOU DO, ANNIE -
Reg. U. S. Pat. Off.; Copyright, 1930, by The Chicago Tribune.

November 23, 1930

OH, BOY! ARE WE GOIN' TO BUST LOOSE WITH A REAL BLOWOUT NEXT THURSDAY - TH' SILOS ARE COMIN', AN' MRS. TWINKLE AN' OLD JACK PEPPER AN' EVER'BODY -

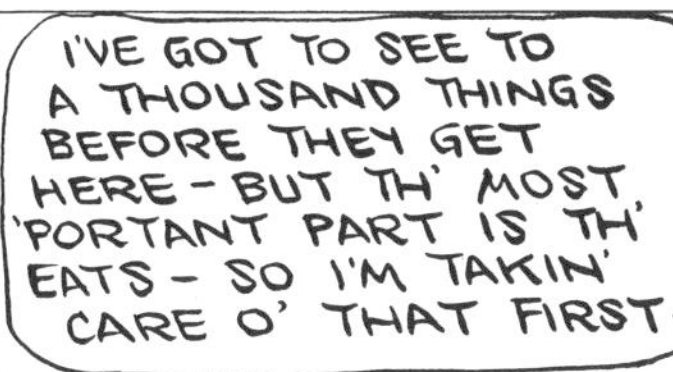
I'VE GOT TO SEE TO A THOUSAND THINGS BEFORE THEY GET HERE - BUT TH' MOST 'PORTANT PART IS TH' EATS - SO I'M TAKIN' CARE O' THAT FIRST -

WELL, ARMAND, WHADDYUH SAY? DIDJA SEE TO GETTIN' TH' TURKEYS AN' TH' MINCE MEAT I SPOKE TO YOU ABOUT?
AH, MEES ANN-EE - ALL WILL BE AS YOU WISH EET -

THERE ARE ZE TURKEYS AN' ZE CRANBERRY SAUCE - AND, AH, MAM'ZELL - HERE IS ZE STUFFING, AS YOU CALL EET, WITH ZE SAGE, AND ZE CHESTNUTS - AND ZE PUMPKIN AND ZE MINCE PIES -
GEE!
HAROLD GRAY
Reg. U. S. Pat. Off.; Copyright, 1930, by The Chicago Tribune.

AUTUMN LEAVES TO DEC'RATE TH' HALLS - JACK FROST SURE KNOWS HIS COLORS, ALL RIGHT -

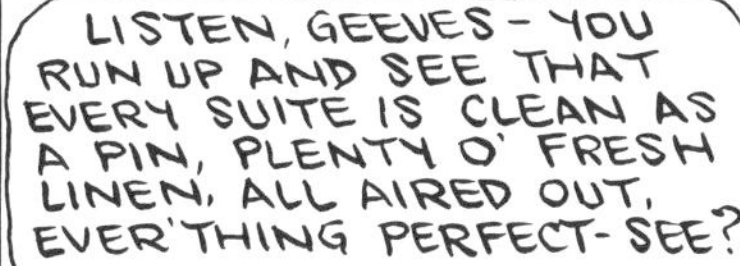
LISTEN, GEEVES - YOU RUN UP AND SEE THAT EVERY SUITE IS CLEAN AS A PIN, PLENTY O' FRESH LINEN, ALL AIRED OUT, EVER'THING PERFECT - SEE?

NOW WE WANT LOTS O' FLOWERS IN EVERY ROOM WHEN TH' FOLKS GET HERE - I'M LEAVIN' ALL THAT UP TO YOU, AUGUST -
TRUST ME, MISS ANNIE - YOU WILL SEE EVERYWHERE SUCH FLOWERS AS NO BODY EVER SAW BEFORE -

GEE, IT'S GETTIN' LATE - GOT A DOZEN THINGS TO SEE TO YET - BUT WE'LL HAVE TH' HOUSE IN SHAPE WHEN THEY GET HERE IF WE HURRY -
HAROLD GRAY
Reg. U. S. Pat. Off.; Copyright, 1930, by The Chicago Tribune.

HURRY, "DADDY"! HERE COMES THEIR TRAIN -

HERE THEY ARE - HELLO MRS. SILO - HELLO MR. SILO -

MY - MY - IT'S GOOD TO SEE YOU AGAIN, ANNIE - I THOUGHT THE TRAIN WOULD NEVER GET HERE -
HURRY - WE'VE GOT TH' CAR RIGHT HERE AN' WE'LL GET OUT TO TH' PLACE IN NO TIME -

WE'VE BEEN SO WORRIED ABOUT YOU, ANNIE - WE HADN'T HEARD FROM YOU FOR MONTHS - THEN WE GOT YOUR TELEGRAM -
OH, BOY! HAVE I GOT A LOT TO TELL YOU!!!
HAROLD GRAY
Reg. U. S. Pat. Off.; Copyright, 1930, by The Chicago Tribune.

November 24–26, 1930

WELL, I SURE HAVE A HEAP TO BE THANKFUL FOR - GOT MY HEALTH AN' PLENTY TO EAT, BUT, BEST OF ALL, I'VE GOT ALL YOU FRIENDS RIGHT HERE WHERE I CAN LOOK AT YUH -

GEE - I NEVER THOUGHT I'D QUIT IN TH' MIDDLE OF A PIECE OF MINCE PIE - BUT IT'S MY SECOND PIECE - AN' AFTER ALL TH' TURKEY AN STUFFIN' AND EVER'THING I GUESS I'VE HAD ENOUGH -

AH - THERE SHE IS, FAST ASLEEP - I WONDERED WHERE SHE DISAPPEARED TO RIGHT AFTER DINNER -
Z-Z-Z-Z
Z-Z-Z!
HAROLD GRAY
Reg. U. S. Pat. Off.; Copyright, 1930, by The Chicago Tribune.

WELL, SPIKE, NO MATTER HOW MUCH BAD LUCK WE MAY HAVE, I GUESS WE MOST ALWAYS HAVE A LOT TO BE THANKFUL FOR IF WE STOP TO FIGURE UP -
AYE - AND SOMETHING A LOT MORE WORTH-WHILE THAN ALL THE WEALTH IN THE WORLD IS THE LOVE OF A SWEET LITTLE YOUNGSTER LIKE ANNIE - EH, WARBUCKS?

WHEW - I SURE STUFFED MYSELF TIGHTER'N A DRUM YESTERDAY - AFTER EATIN' AN' EATIN' I REMEMBER LYIN' DOWN ON A SOFA, JUST FOR A MINUTE - AN' THAT'S ALL I REMEMBER -

BUT IT WAS A SWELL FEED, AND I FEEL GREAT THIS MORNIN', ONLY A LITTLE HUNGRY FOR BREAKFAST - GEE - I BET EVER'BODY'S UP - I GOTTA HURRY -

MR. SILO WILL WANT TO SEE MY PONY AND ALL TH' SADDLE HORSES - AND MRS. SILO AN' MRS. TWINKLE WILL WANT TO SEE TH' HOUSE AN' GARDENS - I'LL WANT TO SHOW 'EM AROUND -

THERE THEY ARE NOW ALL READY TO GO IN TO BREAKFAST - I'M JUST IN TIME - MORNIN', FOLKS !!! I'LL BE RIGHT DOWN -
HAROLD GRAY
Reg. U. S. Pat. Off.; Copyright, 1930, by The Chicago Tribune.

GOOD BYE, FOLKS - COME AGAIN REAL SOON -
GOOD BYE, ANNIE - DON'T FORGET TO WRITE -

WELL, IT WAS MIGHTY NICE TO SEE THEM ALL AGAIN, EH, ANNIE?
YOU BETCHA - AN' I THINK THEY HAD A GOOD TIME, TOO - I HOPE WE CAN HAVE 'EM ALL TO OUR PLACE AGAIN 'FORE LONG -

WE SURE CAN, ANNIE - THEY'RE MIGHTY WELCOME ANY TIME -
GEE, IT'S GREAT TO HAVE A LOT O' MONEY AND A SWELL BIG HOME SO YOU CAN HAVE LOTS AN' LOTS OF YER REAL FRIENDS FOR COMPANY -
HAROLD GRAY

I WISH THEY COULD HAVE STAYED LONGER, BUT THEY'RE ALL PRETTY BUSY AN' HAVE TO HURRY HOME - BUT IT WAS GREAT TO SEE 'EM EVEN FOR A LITTLE WHILE - COURSE I COULD NEVER FORGET TH' SILOS AN' TH' REST, BUT SEEIN' YER FRIENDS NOW AN' THEN ALWAYS MAKES 'EM SEEM CLOSER -
Reg. U. S. Pat. Off.; Copyright, 1930, by The Chicago Tribune.

Little Orphan Annie
MALICIOUS GOSSIP
LOOK OUT, SANDY! THOSE THINGS GET BIGGER EVERY SECOND AND THERE'S NO STOPPIN' 'EM, ONCE THEY GET GOIN'- AN' IF YUH EVER GET TANGLED UP WITH ONE OF 'EM, YOU'RE A GONER-
HAROLD GRAY

YOU WAIT HERE IN THE LOBBY, ANNIE, WHILE I MAKE A PHONE CALL- I WON'T BE GONE FIVE MINUTES-
O.K., "DADDY"- SANDY AND I'LL STAY RIGHT HERE-

GEE, THIS IS TH' SWELLEST HOTEL IN TOWN-AT LEAST IT'S TH' MOST 'S PENSIVE- SH-H-H- HERE COME SOME BIG SOCIETY FOLKS-

OH, THIS IS PRECIOUS- IT'S REALLY KILLING- I MUST TELL YOU, BUT NEVER REPEAT THIS TO A SOUL-IT'S ABOUT THAT MR. JONES-
NOT J. PIERPONT JONES?

YES- OH IT'S A SCREAM- HE'LL NEVER LIVE THIS DOWN- IT WILL RUIN HIM IF IT GETS OUT- I JUST HAPPENED TO OVER-HEAR A CONVERSATION-
YES-YES! WHAT WAS IT?

SH-H-- THAT LITTLE WRETCH IS LISTENING! HMPH!!! OF ALL THINGS!
SUCH ILL-BRED CONDUCT-
THE VERY IDEA!

IMAGINE! SUCH LACK OF MANNERS- WHAT ARE MODERN CHILDREN COMING TO? HUH!!! EAVES DROPPER!

WELL- WELL- WELL- NICE, CHARITABLE OLD SOULS! SO SHE HATES EAVES DROPPERS, EH? THAT'S A LAUGH- SHE'S HAD HER EAR TO KEY-HOLES SO LONG SHE'S LOP-SIDED-

YEAH- SHE SAID SHE OVERHEARD SOMETHIN' ABOUT A MR. JONES THAT WOULD RUIN HIM IF IT GOT OUT-
YES- I KNOW- HE'S A FINE CHAP, TOO- STRAIGHT AS A STRING- BUILT UP A WONDERFUL REPUTATION-

BUT SCANDAL PEDDLERS LIKE THAT CAN TEAR DOWN IN FIVE MINUTES WHAT IT HAS TAKEN A LIFE TIME TO BUILD-

WELL, LOOK AT THAT- JUST A COUPLE OF SLEEPING BEAUTIES- HEY!

HOME, CHARLEY, AND I HOPE YOU ARE QUITE REFRESHED BY YOUR NAP-
YES, SIR- NO, SIR- ER-ER- THAT IS, YES, SIR--

GOSSIP- IT ALWAYS HURTS- IT NEVER DOES ANY GOOD- BUT IT'S ALL SOME PEOPLE EVER SEEM TO TAKE ANY INTEREST IN-
WELL, I GUESS IF THERE WAS NO GOSSIPING A LOT OF FOLKS WOULD GET MIGHTY LITTLE USE OF THEIR TONGUES-

November 30, 1930

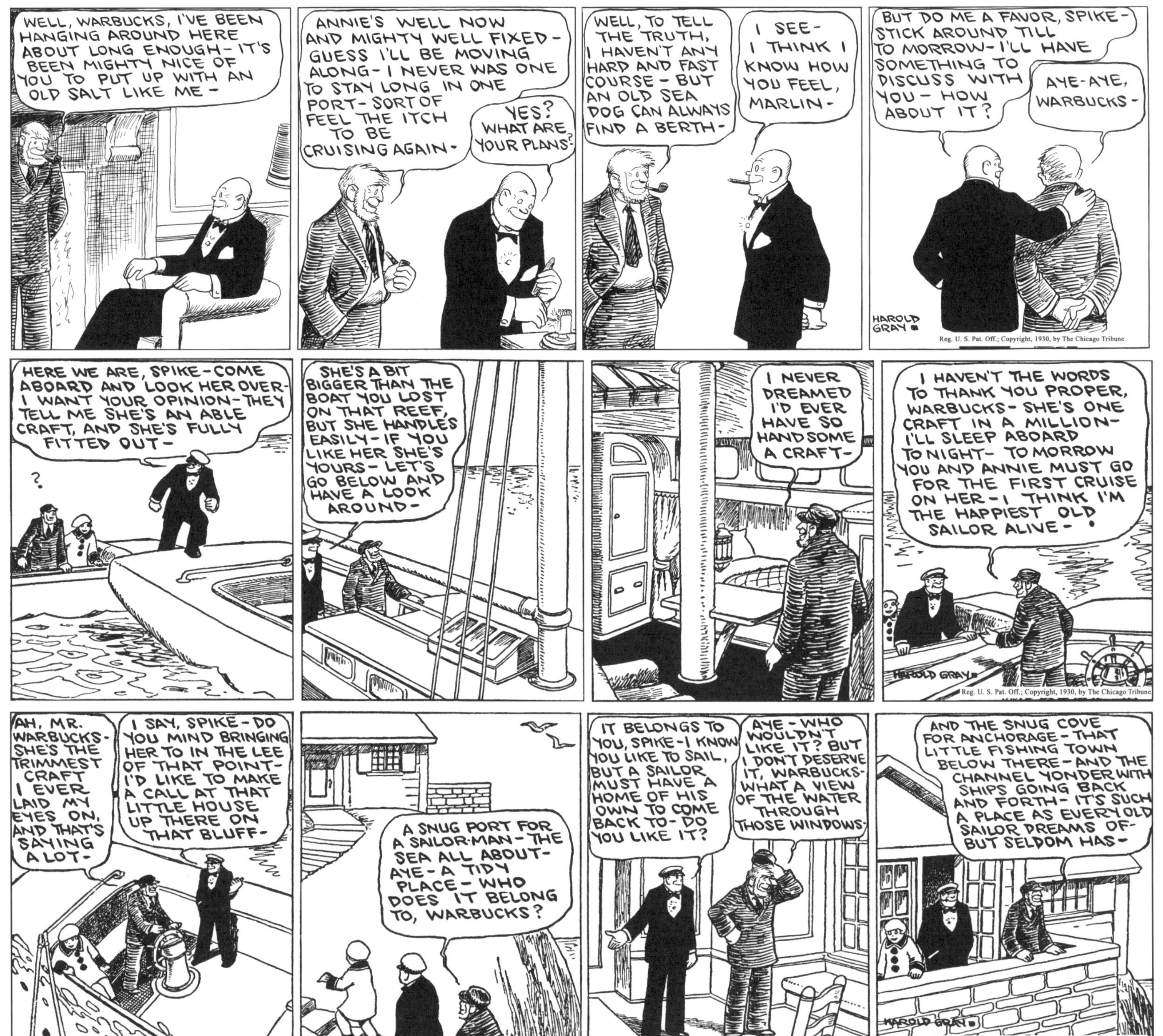
WELL, WARBUCKS, I'VE BEEN HANGING AROUND HERE ABOUT LONG ENOUGH - IT'S BEEN MIGHTY NICE OF YOU TO PUT UP WITH AN OLD SALT LIKE ME -
ANNIE'S WELL NOW AND MIGHTY WELL FIXED - GUESS I'LL BE MOVING ALONG - I NEVER WAS ONE TO STAY LONG IN ONE PORT - SORT OF FEEL THE ITCH TO BE CRUISING AGAIN -
YES? WHAT ARE YOUR PLANS?
WELL, TO TELL THE TRUTH, I HAVEN'T ANY HARD AND FAST COURSE - BUT AN OLD SEA DOG CAN ALWAYS FIND A BERTH -
I SEE - I THINK I KNOW HOW YOU FEEL, MARLIN -
BUT DO ME A FAVOR, SPIKE - STICK AROUND TILL TO MORROW - I'LL HAVE SOMETHING TO DISCUSS WITH YOU - HOW ABOUT IT?
AYE-AYE, WARBUCKS -
HAROLD GRAY
Reg. U. S. Pat. Off.; Copyright, 1930, by The Chicago Tribune.
HERE WE ARE, SPIKE - COME ABOARD AND LOOK HER OVER - I WANT YOUR OPINION - THEY TELL ME SHE'S AN ABLE CRAFT, AND SHE'S FULLY FITTED OUT -
?
SHE'S A BIT BIGGER THAN THE BOAT YOU LOST ON THAT REEF, BUT SHE HANDLES EASILY - IF YOU LIKE HER SHE'S YOURS - LET'S GO BELOW AND HAVE A LOOK AROUND -
I NEVER DREAMED I'D EVER HAVE SO HANDSOME A CRAFT -
I HAVEN'T THE WORDS TO THANK YOU PROPER, WARBUCKS - SHE'S ONE CRAFT IN A MILLION - I'LL SLEEP ABOARD TO NIGHT - TO MORROW YOU AND ANNIE MUST GO FOR THE FIRST CRUISE ON HER - I THINK I'M THE HAPPIEST OLD SAILOR ALIVE - !
HAROLD GRAY
Reg. U. S. Pat. Off.; Copyright, 1930, by The Chicago Tribune
AH, MR. WARBUCKS - SHE'S THE TRIMMEST CRAFT I EVER LAID MY EYES ON, AND THAT'S SAYING A LOT -
I SAY, SPIKE - DO YOU MIND BRINGING HER TO IN THE LEE OF THAT POINT - I'D LIKE TO MAKE A CALL AT THAT LITTLE HOUSE UP THERE ON THAT BLUFF -
A SNUG PORT FOR A SAILOR-MAN - THE SEA ALL ABOUT - AYE - A TIDY PLACE - WHO DOES IT BELONG TO, WARBUCKS?
IT BELONGS TO YOU, SPIKE - I KNOW YOU LIKE TO SAIL, BUT A SAILOR MUST HAVE A HOME OF HIS OWN TO COME BACK TO - DO YOU LIKE IT?
AYE - WHO WOULDN'T LIKE IT? BUT I DON'T DESERVE IT, WARBUCKS - WHAT A VIEW OF THE WATER THROUGH THOSE WINDOWS -
AND THE SNUG COVE FOR ANCHORAGE - THAT LITTLE FISHING TOWN BELOW THERE - AND THE CHANNEL YONDER WITH SHIPS GOING BACK AND FORTH - IT'S SUCH A PLACE AS EVERY OLD SAILOR DREAMS OF - BUT SELDOM HAS -
HAROLD GRAY
Reg. U. S. Pat. Off.; Copyright, 1930, by The Chicago Tribune.

GEE, "DADDY"- SPIKE SURE WAS TICKLED WITH THE BOAT AND THE HOUSE, WASN'T HE?
YES- HE'S A SIMPLE OLD SOUL BUT SIMPLE SOULS ARE THE FINEST- I'VE SEEN TO IT HE'LL ALWAYS BE CARED FOR-
YOU BLOODY MURDERER- SUCH ORFUL LANGUAGE- HI'LL FIX YOU!!!
AW, BATTEN YER HATCH, YUH !!! !!!-- !!!!! SON OF A SALAMANDER!
HI SAY, MISS ANNIE- LOOK OUT FOR 'IM- 'E'S A VILLAINOUS IMP OF SATAN, THAT 'E IS-
OH, WE'RE OLD PALS, AREN'T WE, DEACON-
HELLO, KID!
SAY, "DADDY"- OLD SPIKE WILL GET LONESOME UP THERE IN HIS HOUSE ALL ALONE- WHY NOT TAKE DEACON UP TO HIM FOR COMPANY?
THAT'S A GOOD IDEA, ANNIE- DEACON WILL LIKE THAT, TOO-
HAROLD GRAY
Reg. U. S. Pat. Off.; Copyright, 1930, by The Chicago Tribune.
JUST LOOK AT THOSE SEA-GULLS, DEACON- AREN'T THEY PRETTY?
HUH! SEA-GOIN' BUZZARDS!
HELLO, CAP'N- LOOKIE- I BROUGHT YOU A BOARDER- GOT ROOM FOR HIM?
WELL, WELL- COME IN- I'VE BEEN WANTING SOMEBODY TO TALK TO-
DEACON WILL SURE BE A HEAP OF COMPANY- HE'S NO FOOL- HE'LL BE SOMEBODY TO TALK TO- AND IF HE TALKS BACK TOO MUCH I CAN PUT A SACK OVER HIS HEAD-
HA! HA! HELLO, CAP'N- WHERE'S MY BUNK?
LOOK AT HIM- RIGHT AT HOME- HAD HIS DINNER AND NOW HE WANTS TO GO TO SLEEP-
PIPE DOWN, YOU FOG-HORN- PIPE DOWN- ------- -- Z-Z-Z.
Z-Z- Z-Z
HAROLD GRAY
Reg. U. S. Pat. Off.; Copyright, 1930, by The Chicago Tribune.
WELL, SANDY, THIS ISN'T MUCH LIKE THE ISLAND, IS IT? GORGEOUS HOUSE- SOFT CUSHIONS AND THOUSANDS O' PRETTY AND EXPENSIVE THINGS-
CARPETS TWO INCHES THICK- NOTHIN' TO DO- PLENTY TO EAT- IF YUH WANT ANY THING AT ALL JUST PUSH A BUTTON AND ASK FOR IT-
AND LOOK AT THAT VIEW- THE SEA WITH BREAKERS AND SHIPS WAY OUT BEYOND- AND LIGHT-HOUSES- GEE, SANDY- DIDJA EVER SEE SUCH A PRETTY PITCHER?
AND ALL WE'VE GOT TO DO IS JUST SIT HERE AND SOAK UP THE VIEW- THIS SURE BEATS A HEAP O' SPOTS WE'VE BEEN, SANDY- YEP, PRETTY SOFT- PRETTY SOFT!
HAROLD GRAY
Reg. U. S. Pat. Off.; Copyright, 1930, by The Chicago Tribune.

December 4–6, 1930

Little Orphan
Annie

NOW, IF YOU BOYS PROMISE TO BE REAL GOOD, I'LL MENTION YUH IN THIS LETTER I'M WRITIN' TO SANTA CLAUS -
HAROLD GRAY

YESSIR, WILLIE, YOU'RE GETTIN' TO BE A BIG BEAR - LE'SSEE - HOW OLD ARE YOU, NOW, ANYWAY? WHEN I FIRST SAW YOU, YOU WERE JUST A LITTLE FELLER - THAT WAS LAST CHRISTMAS!

SAY!!! THAT JUST REMINDS ME - WHAT DAY OF THE MONTH IS THIS?

SUNDAY, DECEMBER SEVENTH - LEAPIN' LIZARDS - ONLY EIGHTEEN DAYS TILL CHRISTMAS!!!

GEE - WHAT DO I WANT SANTA TO BRING ME THIS YEAR? I'VE GOT EVER'THING I CAN THINK OF - THERE'S NOTHIN' I REALLY WANT VERY MUCH -

SANTA'S AN AWFUL BUSY GUY RIGHT NOW - NO SENSE IN WRITIN' TO HIM AN' TAKIN' UP HIS TIME WHEN THERE'S SO MANY POOR KIDS NEED THINGS SO MUCH -

SAY, "DADDY" - I BET YOU DON'T KNOW WHAT I KNOW - IT'S ONLY EIGHTEEN DAYS TILL CHRISTMAS!
WELL, WELL - THAT'S RIGHT - SO IT IS - ARE YOU WRITING TO SANTA CLAUS?

NO - I'VE GOT EVER'THING - I FIGGER HE OUGHT TO BE SPENDIN' ALL HIS TIME TAKIN' CARE O' POOR KIDS -
SAY - THAT'S A GOOD IDEA - WELL - HOW WOULD YOU LIKE TO HELP HIM?

GEE, THAT WOULD BE SWELL, IF I COULD - I KNOW WHERE THERE'S HUNDREDS O' FOLKS IN TH' CITY THAT SANTA DOESN'T EVER GET AROUND TO -

YES - HE'S A MIGHTY BUSY MAN - HE'S SURE TO MISS A LOT OF THEM - BUT I THINK I KNOW HOW YOU CAN HELP HIM OUT A LOT -

I'LL LEAVE IT TO YOU - JUST USE THIS CHECK-BOOK AND BUY THE THINGS YOU THINK SANTA WOULD LIKE TO GIVE - YOU'LL BE HIS ASSISTANT - AND YOU'LL HANDLE DELIVERIES TOO - AND EVERYTHING CAN BE MARKED "FROM SANTA" -

OH, "DADDY"
SMACK!!!

A LOT OF SMUG PEOPLE CLAIM THAT A HARD LIFE MAKES ONE HARD - HUH - HARD KNOCKS HAVE TAUGHT HER TO THINK OF OTHERS - I GUESS HARD CONTACTS DO MAR CHEAP STONES OR PEOPLE, BUT ONLY ADD LUSTER TO A DIAMOND -

December 7, 1930

OH, BOY - AM I GOIN' TO BE BUSY FROM NOW TILL CHRISTMAS !!! THERE ARE A MILLION THINGS TO DO - I HAVEN'T A SECOND TO LOSE -

SORRY, SANDY - I WON'T HAVE TIME TO PLAY WITH YOU TO-DAY - I'VE GOT A JOB ON MY HANDS -

AH - THERE IT IS - THERE'S TH' CHECKBOOK "DADDY" GAVE ME YESTERDAY - HE SAID I COULD BUY THINGS FOR ALL TH' POOR KIDS - ANYTHING I WANTED TO GIVE 'EM, AND THE SKY'S TH' LIMIT -
HAROLD GRAY

COURSE EVER'THING WILL HAVE A CARD SAYIN', "FROM SANTA CLAUS" - I'M JUST HELPIN' HIM OUT - NOW, LET ME SEE - WHERE SHALL I BEGIN ?

LE'SSEE, NOW - WHAT DO POOR KIDS LIKE BEST - CANDY, AND ALL KINDS O' TOYS - DOLLS - TRAINS - DRUMS - FIRE ENGINES - AIRPLANES - GAMES - FOOTBALLS - -

BUT WAIT A MINUTE - I'M FORGETTIN' - NO KID THAT'S HUNGRY CAN GET MUCH KICK OUT OF TOYS - I'VE GOTTA GIVE 'EM FOOD AN' LOTS OF IT - TURKEYS AN' ALL TH' FIXINS FRUIT - AND MILK, EGGS, BREAD AN' BUTTER AN' POTATOES, TOO -

AND FOLKS THAT ARE COLD CAN'T BE HAPPY OR ENJOY THEIR MEALS - THERE'S GOTTA BE WARM CLOTHES FOR 'EM - AND COAL, WHERE THEY HAVE STOVES - AND MONEY, TOO, FOR OTHER THINGS I'M SURE TO FORGET -
HAROLD GRAY

LEAPIN' LIZARDS! THIS SURE IS A BIGGER JOB THAN IT LOOKED LIKE AT FIRST - BUT I'VE STARTED IT AND I'LL FINISH IT - NOW LET'S SEE - WHAT ELSE DO POOR FOLKS NEED MOST ?

GEE - THERE ARE SOME SWELL LITTLE SUITS FOR KIDS, AND SWEATERS THAT LOOK WARM - BUT HOW MANY SHALL I BUY, AND WHAT SIZES ?
BUY XMAS SEALS
THERE'S A SWELL DOLL HOUSE - EVERY KIND OF TOY IN THIS STORE - BUT I'VE GOTTA DOPE OUT WHO THEY'RE GOIN' TO, AND JUST WHAT THEY'D LIKE MOST -

EVER'BODY ELSE SEEMS TO KNOW WHAT TO BUY - BUT I'M DARNED IF I'M NOT STUCK - I DON'T KNOW WHERE TO START -

C'MON, JOE - I'M GOIN' HOME - TH' STORES ARE CLOSED - AND, ANYWAY, I'VE GOTTA THINK - THIS JOB IS GETTIN' TOUGHER EVERY SECOND, BUT I'M NOT GOIN' TO LET IT LICK ME -
HAROLD GRAY

December 8–10, 1930

HEY! CUT THAT OUT! WHAT'SAMATTER WITH YOU, SANDY? HAVEN'T I TOLD YOU NOT TO CHASE THOSE RABBITS?
AW, I DIDN'T MEAN TO BE CROSS, SANDY- I KNOW YOU WERE JUST PLAYIN'- YOU WOULDN'T HURT TH' RABBITS- I'M JUST UPSET TO-DAY- THAT'S ALL-
DOG GONE IT ALL- I THOUGHT MAYBE I COULD THINK BETTER IF I TOOK A WALK- BUT I'M NOT GETTIN' ANYWHERE-
HAROLD GRAY
I GUESS I'VE BEEN GOIN' AT THIS THING BACKWARDS - WHAT I'LL HAVE TO DO IS PICK OUT TH' POOR FOLKS I'M GOIN' TO BUY THINGS FOR- THEN I'LL KNOW JUST WHAT TO BUY-
Reg. U. S. Pat. Off.; Copyright, 1930, by The Chicago Tribune.
POOR- POOR- POOR- HUNDREDS OF 'EM- THOUSANDS OF 'EM- NO MATTER HOW HARD YUH TRY, HOW CAN YUH HELP ALL OF 'EM?
BUY XMAS SEALS
I'D SORTA FORGOTTEN HOW BAD OFF SO MANY FOLKS ARE- HOW AM I EVER GOIN' TO MAKE A LIST OF ALL TH' POOR FOLKS IN THIS TOWN?
IT DOESN'T SEEM FAIR TO HELP SOME AND NOT HELP OTHERS- BUT NO MATTER HOW HARD YUH TRY YOU'RE BOUND TO MISS A LOT-
STILL I GUESS IT'S BETTER TO HELP SOME THAN NONE AT ALL- ALL YUH CAN DO IS MAKE AS MANY FOLKS AS YUH CAN HAPPY- I'LL START MAKIN' OUT A LIST TO-MORROW-
HAROLD GRAY
Reg. U. S. Pat. Off.; Copyright, 1930, by The Chicago Tribune.
I'VE SPOTTED ABOUT A DOZEN POOR FAMILIES ALREADY- BUT THAT'S NOT EVEN A START- THERE MUST BE A HUNDRED IN THIS BLOCK ALONE-
BUY XMAS SEALS
AW, DERE AIN'T NUTTIN' IN DIS ONE, SIS-
HOW KIN YUH TELL 'LESS YUH DIG AROUND? YUH GIVE UP TOO EASY-
AW, LET ME LOOK, WON'TCHA?
?
GEE- IMAGINE KIDS SO POOR AND COLD AND HUNGRY- CHRISTMAS DOESN'T MEAN MUCH TO KIDS LIKE THAT, 'LESS FOLKS WITH DOUGH GET BUSY-
BUT NO WONDER SANTA CLAUS MISSES SO MANY EVERY YEAR- I DON'T SEE HOW HE FINDS AS MANY AS HE DOES- I NEVER RE'LIZED BEFORE WHAT A TOUGH JOB OLD SANTA HAS-
HAROLD GRAY
Reg. U. S. Pat. Off.; Copyright, 1930, by The Chicago Tribune.

December 11–13, 1930

Little Orphan Annie
HAROLD GRAY

HEY! JUST LISTEN TO THIS - IT'S A RADIOGRAM FROM SANTA CLAUS! HE SAYS!- "DEAR ANNIE;— HAVE JUST HEARD OF THE WONDERFUL HELP YOU ARE GIVING ME THIS CHRISTMAS- IF THERE WERE MORE THOUGHTFUL AND GENEROUS YOUNGSTERS LIKE YOU, AND GROWN-UPS TOO, IT WOULD MAKE MY JOB MUCH EASIER- I THANK YOU SINCERELY - SANTA CLAUS"- LEAPIN' LIZARDS! BUSY AS HE IS NOW, AND YET HE TAKES TIME TO SEND THIS TO ME- SANTA SURE IS A SWELL GUY-

I'VE GOT PLENTY OF MONEY TO HELP A LOT OF POOR FOLKS- BUT WHERE SHALL I BEGIN?

WAIT HERE, WILL YUH, CHARLEY? I'M GOIN' FOR A LITTLE WALK-
QUITE RIGHT, MISS ANNIE-

EVERYBODY'S AWFUL POOR DOWN IN THIS PART OF TOWN- THOUSANDS O' FOLKS HERE THAT HAVEN'T HAD A SQUARE MEAL FOR YEARS-

GEE- A WHOLE FAMILY LIVIN' DOWN IN THAT DARK, DIRTY BASEMENT- THAT'S NO PLACE FOR HUMANS-

BEIN' AWAY FOR SO LONG MYSELF I'D SORTA FORGOTTEN HOW MANY POOR PEOPLE THERE ARE-

GUESS WHEN YOU'RE DOIN' WELL YERSELF IT'S SORTA EASY TO FORGET 'BOUT THE FOLKS WHO NEVER SEEM TO GET A BREAK- LOOK AT THOSE RAGGED KIDS-

POOR PEOPLE, IS IT? SURE THERE'S NOTHING ELSE HEREABOUTS - ONE AS POOR AS THE NEXT- STILL, SOME ARE SICK, AND SOME ARE CRIPPLED- YES- I COULD TIP YOU OFF TO WHO'S WHO IN THIS WARD-

I'LL BE MAKIN' A LIST OF THE ONES THAT ARE WORST OFF FOR YOU- IT'S A KIND HEART YE HAVE, LITTLE GIRL-

JUST LOOK AT TH' SWELL CARS ON THIS STREET- HARDLY SEEMS FAIR THAT SOME SHOULD BE SO RICH AND OTHERS SO POOR- STILL, IT'S ALWAYS THAT WAY- MUST BE A REASON- BRAINS OR LUCK OR MAYBE BOTH- I DUNNO-

WELL, HOW'S OUR LITTLE LADY OF CHARITY GETTING ALONG?

OH, "DADDY"- I'M STUCK - I DON'T KNOW WHERE TO START- I THOUGHT IT'D BE EASY, WITH SO MUCH TO SPEND- BUT THERE ARE SO MANY POOR FOLKS- IT'S NOT FAIR TO HELP SOME AND MISS OTHERS- BUT HOW CAN YUH HELP 'EM ALL?

IT'S TOO BIG A JOB FOR ANY ONE PERSON, ANNIE - IF EVERYONE WHO WAS ABLE WOULD GIVE, THIS WOULD BE A MUCH HAPPIER WORLD - BUT SO FEW PEOPLE REALIZE HOW MUCH FUN IT IS TO BE GENEROUS - AS LONG AS WE DO OUR BEST TO HELP OTHERS, THAT'S ALL ANYONE CAN DO-

December 14, 1930

GEE-TH' CATTLE DOWN ON MR. SILO'S FARM USED TO HAVE A LOTS BETTER HOME THAN MOST OF TH' FOLKS IN THIS PART O' TOWN-
I'M GETTIN' A FEW FOLKS ON MY LIST, BUT IT'S SLOW WORK-BUYIN' TH' STUFF TO GIVE 'EM IS EASY ENOUGH-BUT YUH'VE GOTTA KNOW WHAT TO BUY-
OUGHT TO HAVE TH' NAME O' EVERY KID-OUGHT TO KNOW A LOT ABOUT EACH FAMILY, TOO-THEN I'D KNOW JUST TH' RIGHT THINGS TO GIVE-
I'VE GOT TO TALK TO 'EM-BUT FOLKS IN THIS END O' TOWN DON'T PAL UP WITH STRANGERS QUICK-I OUGHT TO HAVE STARTED THIS JOB A LOT EARLIER-
BUY XMAS SEALS
HAROLD GRAY
Reg. U. S. Pat. Off.; Copyright, 1930, by The Chicago Tribune.
GOOD MORNING-YOU LIVE NEAR HERE AND MUST KNOW A LOT O' FOLKS IN YOUR BLOCK-COULD YOU TELL ME......
NO SPIK ENGLISH-
SHE SPEAKS ENGLISH O.K.-SHE'S JUST GIVIN' ME TH' ICE-WELL, YUH CAN'T BLAME HER-SHE'S GOT PLENTY O' TROUBLES, I S'POSE-NO WONDER SHE'S SORTA HARD-BOILED-
BUY XMAS SEALS
HELLO, THERE-WHAT'S YOUR NAME? IS THAT YOUR LITTLE BROTHER? DO YOU LIVE NEAR HERE? HOW OLD ARE YOU?
NO SALE! THEY JUST LOOK AT ME AND WALK AWAY-GUESS IT'S 'CAUSE I LOOK LIKE A RICH KID-GEE-FUNNY HOW HARD IT IS TO GET CHUMMY WITH ANYBODY 'ROUND HERE-
HAROLD GRAY
Reg. U. S. Pat. Off.; Copyright, 1930, by The Chicago Tribune.
I'M STUMPED, SANDY-I CAN'T GET ANY OF TH' POOR FOLKS I WANT TO HELP TO TALK TO ME-AND I'VE GOTTA TALK TO 'EM IF I'M GOIN' TO FIND OUT WHAT THEY NEED MOST, AN' ALL ABOUT 'EM-
I NEVER USED TO HAVE ANY TROUBLE PICKIN' UP FRIENDS-BUT THEN I WAS JUST A POOR ORPHAN KID-AS POOR AS TH' POOREST OF 'EM-
HM-M-M-YUH KNOW, SANDY, I'M SORTA BEGINNIN' TO GET AN IDEA-MAYBE IT'LL WORK, AND MAYBE IT WON'T-BUT IT'S WORTH TRYIN' ANYWAY-
YESSIR-I'M GOIN' BACK DOWN INTO THAT POOR END O' TOWN TO-MORROW AND I THINK THIS TIME I'LL GET SOME PLACE-
Reg. U. S. Pat. Off.; Copyright, 1930, by The Chicago Tribune.
HAROLD GRAY

December 15–17, 1930

ALL RIGHT, JOE- TAKE ME DOWN TO THAT SIDE STREET WHERE YOU ALWAYS LET ME OUT- I'VE GOT LOTS TO DO TO DAY-
HUMPH! NOW WHAT IS SHE HUP TO? A SUITCASE- AND THE SHADES HALL DRAWN- BUT HI AM TO KEEP AN EYE ON HER AND DO ANYTHING SHE HORDERS- HIT'S THE MARSTER'S HORDERS, AND 'E'S MOST STRICT-
HOW DO I LOOK, JOE? D'YUH THINK ANYBODY'D TAKE ME FOR A RICH KID IN THIS RIG?
?
'ORRORS! HIT'S DISGRACEFUL! WHY, SHE LOOKS LIKE THE WORST LITTLE RAGAMUFFIN ON THE STREET- HI DON'T KNOW WHAT TO DO- HI MUST HINFORM THE MARSTER OF THIS-
HAROLD GRAY
Reg. U. S. Pat. Off.; Copyright, 1930, by The Chicago Tribune.
HIT WAS 'ORRIBLE, SIR- SHE HOB-NOBBING WITH ALL THOSE COMMON PERSONS- AND THOSE ORFUL CLOTHES!
YEAH? CLOTHES? WHAT CLOTHES?
SHE CHANGED IN THE CAR, SIR- HI 'ARDLY KNEW HER- HI FOLLOWED HER LIKE YOU ORDERED AND SHE HACTUALLY SEEMED ONE OF THEM, SIR- SAID SHE WANTED THEM TO TALK TO HER- E-MAGINE THAT, SIR-
GREAT!!! SO SHE DISGUISED HERSELF TILL THEY THOUGHT SHE WAS ONE OF 'EM, EH? DON'T YOU WORRY, JOE- SHE KNOWS WHAT SHE'S DOING-
BOY! THAT DOES ME GOOD- TALK ABOUT A RESOURCEFUL LITTLE IMP! SHE KNOWS HOW TO GET WHAT SHE WANTS- WHAT A GIRL!
HAROLD GRAY
Reg. U. S. Pat. Off.; Copyright, 1930, by The Chicago Tribune.
HOORAY!!! NOW! HAVE I GOT A LIST O' FOLKS NOW! WAIT TILL "DADDY" SEES THIS-
O-O-OO!!! WHY! EET EES ANN-EE!
HELLO! WHAT'S TH' MATTER?
OH, I FORGOT- I LEFT MY GOOD CLOTHES IN THE CAR- BUT I'VE GOT TH' DOPE I WENT AFTER- FOLKS WEREN'T AFRAID TO TALK TO ME IN THIS MAKE-UP- NOW TO MAKE DELIVERIES- THAT'S GOIN' TO BE A BIGGER JOB 'N I'D FIGGERED-
BUT "DADDY" 'LL KNOW HOW TO HANDLE THAT END- "DADDY" CAN DO ANYTHING-
HAROLD GRAY
Reg. U. S. Pat. Off.; Copyright, 1930, by The Chicago Tribune.

December 18–20, 1930

Little Orphan Annie
WHAT SORT OF A TRIP DID YOU HAVE?
WHAT IS YOUR OPINION OF THE UN-EMPLOYMENT SITUATION?
JUST A LITTLE SMILE, NOW-
HOW DO YOU LIKE THE AMERICAN GIRLS?
HEY!
HAROLD GRAY

LEAPIN' LIZARDS! I'VE GOT A LIST O' POOR FOLKS SEVEN MILES LONG- BUT IT'S ALMOST CHRISTMAS- I COULD NEVER GET ALL TH' PRESENTS TO 'EM IN TIME- I'LL ASK "DADDY" WHAT TO DO- HE'LL FIGGER OUT A WAY- HE CAN DO ANYTHING!

SEE, I'VE GOT ALL TH' NAMES AND ADDRESSES AND WHAT THEY NEED- FOOD AND CLOTHES AND TOYS AND CANDY-
HM-M-M-- YOU CERTAINLY HAVE BEEN BUSY- YES- YOU'VE DONE A MIGHTY GOOD JOB- NOW THE PROBLEM IS TO GET THEM DELIVERY ON THIS STUFF, EH?

HELLO, SPIKE? THIS IS WARBUCKS- YEAH- I WANT TO BORROW YOUR PLACE TILL CHRISTMAS- YEAH- GARAGE, TRUCKS, WAREHOUSE, THE WHOLE WORKS- AND SEND ABOUT TWENTY OF YOUR MEN AROUND- I'LL MEET 'EM THERE RIGHT AWAY- THANKS-

BRING THE LIST, ANNIE- WE HAVE NO TIME TO LOSE- HERE'S THE CAR-

THE TROUBLE WITH SO MUCH CHARITY IS THAT THOSE WHO GIVE ARE TOO LAZY TO REALLY GIVE INTELLIGENTLY- I SEE YOU'VE DISCOVERED CASES THAT MOST PEOPLE WOULD MISS- THOSE TOO HOPELESS TO COMPLAIN-

GEE- THIS IS RIGHT IN THE MIDDLE OF THE POOREST PART OF TOWN-
YES- THIS GARAGE AND WAREHOUSE WILL BE HANDY TO ALL THOSE FOLKS ON YOUR LIST-

HELLO- IS THIS THE MANAGER OF THE GIGANTIC DEPARTMENT STORE? THIS IS WARBUCKS- I WANT YOU TO OPEN YOUR STORE TONIGHT AND PUT ON A SPECIAL SHIFT- I'LL EXPLAIN LATER- THANKS-

WELL, BOYS- SPIKE SENT YOU OVER, EH? FIRST I WANT TO TALK TO THE TRUCK DRIVERS- GOT A JOB FOR YOU-

YOU'LL GO TO THE GIGANTIC DEPARTMENT STORE THIS EVENING, LOAD UP AND BRING EVERYTHING HERE- ANNIE'LL BE IN CHARGE OF EVERYTHING-

NOW, YOU MEN- TAKE THIS LIST TO THE GIGANTIC DEPARTMENT STORE- FILL EACH ORDER HERE AND BRING ALL THE STUFF HERE TO THE WAREHOUSE ON OUR TRUCKS- WE'LL MAKE DELIVERIES FROM HERE- IS THAT CLEAR?

FINDING WHO TO GIVE TO AND KNOWING WHAT TO GIVE WAS THE BIG JOB, ANNIE, AND YOU DID THAT-
SHUX- THAT WAS EASY- IT WAS GETTIN' TH' STUFF TO FOLKS THAT HAD ME STOPPED-

NOW YOU REALIZE WHAT AN ORGANIZATION SANTA CLAUS MUST HAVE TO CARE FOR ALL HIS CUSTOMERS-
GEE- AND WE'RE JUST HELPIN' HIM OUT WITH A FEW POOR FOLKS- HE'S GOT MILLIONS TO LOOK OUT FOR, AND NEW ONES EVERY YEAR- NO WONDER HE MISSES A FEW FOLKS NOW AND THEN-

December 21, 1930

GEE, "DADDY", IF YOU HADN'T GOT TH' TRUCKS AN' TH' MEN AN' ORG'NIZED EVER'THING I'D HAVE BEEN STUCK AFTER ALL-
YOU GOT THE NAMES AND ALL THE DOPE ON THE PEOPLE WHO NEED HELP MOST- THAT WAS THE IMPORTANT PART- WITH THAT INFORMATION THE REST WAS EASY-
WELL, THERE GOES THE FIRST LOAD- THEY'LL BE BUSY DELIVERING RIGHT UP TO CHRISTMAS- HELPING SANTA CLAUS IS A LOT OF FUN- EH, ANNIE?
YOU BET-
NOW WITH TH' LIST O' POOR FOLKS WE'VE GOT WE CAN KEEP RIGHT ON TAKIN' CARE OF 'EM AFTER CHRISTMAS, CAN'T WE?
RIGHT YOU ARE, ANNIE- PEOPLE GET JUST AS COLD AND HUNGRY AFTER CHRISTMAS AS BEFORE- BUT WE WON'T FORGET TO KEEP UP THIS WORK AS LONG AS IT'S NEEDED-
HAROLD GRAY
Reg. U. S. Pat. Off.; Copyright, 1930, by The Chicago Tribune.
WAIT A MINUTE, "DADDY"- ONE OF OUR TRUCKS IS DELIVERIN' THINGS TO THAT WIDOW WITH SEVEN LITTLE KIDS- I WANTA SEE WHAT HAPPENS-
WHAT'S GOING ON, ANNIE? CAN YOU SEE?
GEE- TH' KIDS' EYES ARE BIG AS SAUCERS- SHE'S PUT TH' NEW CLOTHES ON TH' BABY AND SHE'S CRYIN'- NOW SHE'S LAUGHIN'- NOW SHE'S CRYIN' AGAIN- AND TH' KIDS ACT 'BOUT HALF CRAZY- HEAR 'EM YELLIN'- EACH ONE IS FINDIN' SOMETHIN' WITH HIS OR HER NAME ON IT-
WHY, ANNIE! WHAT'S THE MATTER? HERE! HERE! YOU MUSTN'T CRY LIKE THAT- THERE'S NOTHING TO FEEL BAD ABOUT-
BOO! HOO!! HOO!!! I CAN'T HELP IT-
IT'S NOT 'CAUSE I FEEL BAD- IT'S 'CAUSE I FEEL SO GOOD- I NEVER KNEW MAKIN' OTHER FOLKS HAPPY COULD MAKE YUH FEEL SO GLAD!!!
HM-M-M- I SEE-
HAROLD GRAY
Reg. U. S. Pat. Off.; Copyright, 1930, by The Chicago Tribune.
WELL, ANNIE- EVERY BASKET AND EVERY PRESENT IS DELIVERED- YOU CAN GO TO SLEEP TO NIGHT KNOWING YOU'VE MADE A LOT OF PEOPLE HAPPY-
IT'S PRETTY LATE, ANNIE- THIS IS CHRISTMAS EVE- AREN'T YOU GOING TO HANG UP YOUR STOCKINGS?
YES, "DADDY"- I JUST WANT TO SIT HERE AND REST A MINUTE- I'M SORTA SLEEPY- THAT'S ALL-
PST-... CELESTE- ANNIE'S SOUND ASLEEP- BETTER PUT HER TO BED, BUT BE CAREFUL AND DON'T WAKE HER UP-
THE DEAR LITTLE TYKE- ALL WORN OUT CARING FOR OTHERS- SANTA CLAUS MAY NOT COME- STILL, I DON'T THINK HE'LL FORGET A GIRL AS GOOD AS ANNIE-
HAROLD GRAY
Reg. U. S. Pat. Off.; Copyright, 1930, by The Chicago Tribune.

December 22–24, 1930

DAYLIGHT! WOW!!! DID I SLEEP! AND HOW DID I GET TO BED? TH' LAST I REMEMBER IS SITTIN' IN FRONT OF TH' FIRE LAST NIGHT- GEE- CHRISTMAS! AND I NEVER EVEN HUNG UP MY STOCKINGS-
IF SANTA DID COME AN' DIDN'T SEE ANY STOCKINGS HE'D FIGGER THERE WASN'T ANY KID HERE AND WOULD GO AWAY WITHOUT LEAVIN' ANYTHING, MOST LIKELY- STILL, THERE'S NO HARM IN LOOKIN'-
I'M PRETTY WELL FIXED, O' COURSE- IF HE DID MISS ME, I'LL HUSTLE BACK TO BED AN' SAY NOTHING AND PRETEND I'M NOT DIS'POINTED- IF HE'S ONLY LEFT ME SOMETHIN'-
Reg. U. S. Pat. Off.; Copyright, 1930, by The Chicago Tribune.
OO-OH! LOOK! WHAT A TREE!!! AND ALL THOSE PRESENTS! "DADDY"!!! COME QUICK AND SEE WHAT SANTA CLAUS BROUGHT!
HAROLD GRAY
GEE- A REAL LITTLE TYPE WRITER JUST MY SIZE- AND THE FIRST LETTER I'M GOIN' TO WRITE ON IT IS TO SANTA CLAUS THANKIN' HIM FOR ALL TH' SWELL PRESENTS HE BROUGHT ME- GEE- WHERE'LL I START?
OH, BOY- I WONDER HOW SANTA CLAUS KNEW JUST TH' KIND OF A WRIST-WATCH I WANTED- THAT'D COST A LOT O' DOUGH IF YUH HAD TO GO OUT AN' BUY IT-
AN' ALL TH' NEW CLOTHES- AN EVENIN' WRAP, TOO, AND NEW HATS AND GLOVES AND SHOES- ALL TH' LATEST STUFF- WONDERFUL HOW SANTA KNOWS JUST TH' RIGHT THINGS ALWAYS-
AND A DOLL- GEE, IT'S BEEN A LONG TIME SINCE I'VE HAD A DOLL- S'POSE MAYBE IT'S SORTA SILLY FOR A KID AS BIG AS I AM TO STILL LIKE DOLLS- BUT I'M CRAZY 'BOUT THIS ONE- LISTEN, SANDY- HEAR THAT?
MA-MA!
ARF!
HAROLD GRAY
Reg. U. S. Pat. Off.; Copyright, 1930, by The Chicago Tribune.
GEE, YOU'RE A SWELL DOLL- FIRST, YOU'VE GOTTA HAVE A NAME- I THINK I'LL CALL YOU VIRGINIA- GINNY FOR SHORT- AND NEXT YOU'VE GOTTA HAVE SOME SWELL NEW CLOTHES-
LE'SSEE, NOW- THIS MAGAZINE JUST CAME YESTERDAY AND IT SURE IS FULL O' NEW STYLES- THERE'S A CLASSY LOOKIN' DRESS, ALL RIGHT- SIMPLE, TOO- HM-M-M...
SANTA CLAUS THOUGHT O' EVER'THING- HE EVEN BROUGHT ME THIS LITTLE SEWIN' MACHINE AND A LOT O' DRESS GOODS AND THREAD AND EVER'THING- YESSIR, GINNY, I'M GOIN' TO MAKE YOU TH' BEST DRESSED DOLL IN TOWN- JUST WAIT AND SEE-
OH, HERE YOU ARE- I WONDERED WHERE YOU WERE-
LOOKIE, "DADDY"- TH' NEW DRESS I MADE FOR GINNY- S'POSE I'M PRETTY BIG, BUT I GUESS GIRLS NEVER GET TOO BIG TO LIKE DOLLS-
HAROLD GRAY
Reg. U. S. Pat. Off.; Copyright, 1930, by The Chicago Tribune.

December 25–27, 1930

Little Orphan Annie
HELLO, FEWCLOTHES! GEE- IF THAT'S YOUR IDEA OF WHAT TO WEAR ON A SLEIGH-RIDE, YOU MUST BE EVEN TOUGHER 'N 1930 WAS-
OH, YEAH?
1931
HAROLD GRAY

HEIGH, HO! ANOTHER YEAR ALMOST GONE - AND WHAT A YEAR!!! WOW! TALK ABOUT HARD KNOCKS- BUT EVERYTHING'S WORKED OUT FINE- IT'S ALWAYS THAT WAY IF YUH JUST KEEP TRYIN' AN' DON'T GIVE UP-

ONE THING I KNOW- 1931 IS GOIN' TO BE LOTS BETTER'N 1930- THAT'S MY FIRST NEW YEAR RES'LUTION, SANDY, AND YUH CAN COUNT ON IT-

AND I'M NOT GOIN' TO GET TANGLED UP WITH ANY MORE CROOKS - NO SIR-EE!! NO MORE JAMS FOR YOU AN' ME SANDY- I'VE HAD MY LESSON-

AN' I'M GOIN' TO SEE TO IT THAT WE DODGE FLOODS - THAT TRIP ON TH' RAFT JUST ABOUT CURED ME O' RIVERS-

AN' NO MORE ISLANDS- THEY'RE O.K. IN STORIES, BUT FROM NOW ON WE STICK WHERE IT'S HEALTHY - AN' I'M NOT GOIN' TO BE MEAN TO ANYBODY - I'M GOIN' TO BE KIND AN' GEN'ROUS AN' P'LITE----

SH-H-H--- HERE COMES THAT STIFF-NECKED OLD BUTLER- HUH! WHAT A WALKIN' ICE-BOX HE IS- BET HE HASN'T SMILED FOR FORTY YEARS-

GEE- IF HE'D JUST LOSE HIS DIGNITY ONCE I COULD STAND HIM- BUT I HATE FOLKS THAT ARE SO DARNED PERFECT-

O-OO-OH! ZOWIE!!!

!!!!! !!! !!!
TCH! TCH! TCH!

OH, WHAT TERRIBLY NAUGHTY TALK - COME AWAY, SANDY - DON'T LISTEN TO HIM -

THERE'S A RES'LUTION MADE TO ORDER - NO MATTER WHAT TERRIBLE THING HAPPENS, WE'LL ALWAYS TRY TO SMILE, SANDY - SEE THE BRIGHT SIDE OF EVERY CLOUD - THAT'S US! HAW! HAW! HAW!
ARF!
Reg. U. S. Pat. Off.; Copyright, 1930, by The Chicago Tribune.

December 28, 1930

C'MON, SANDY- SPIKE MARLIN'S BOAT IS TIED UP DOWN HERE AT THE PIER- LOOKS LIKE HE'S FIXIN TO TAKE A TRIP-
AHOY THERE, ANNIE- WELL, WELL- MIGHTY GLAD TO SEE YOU- COME ABOARD-
HELLO, CAP'N--- WHAT'S GOIN' ON HERE? ARE YOU FIGGERIN' ON LEAVIN' US?
I'M JUST AN OLD SEA ROVER, ANNIE- IT'S IN MY BLOOD- WE'LL BE HAVING HEAVY WEATHER FROM NOW TILL SPRING- SO, SAYS I, WHY NOT DROP DOWN THE COAST TO WARM WEATHER AND CLEAR SKIES-
THE RICH BUGS ARE PULLING OUT WITH THEIR BIG YACHTS- I'M BETTER OFF THAN ANY OF 'EM- AYE- THAT I AM- AND WHEN SUMMER COMES BACK I'LL SAIL HOME TO THE LITTLE HOUSE ON THE POINT.
HAROLD GRAY
Reg. U. S. Pat. Off.; Copyright, 1930, by The Chicago Tribune.
THERE HE GOES, SANDY- THAT'S OLD SPIKE MARLIN ALL RIGHT-
WONDER IF HE SAW ME WAVIN'- HE'S A GOOD SAILOR AND DOESN'T MISS MUCH- YEP- HE'S LOOKIN' THIS WAY WITH HIS SPY-GLASS- NOW HE SEES US AND HE'S WAVIN'-
WHEE- GOOD-BYE, CAP'N, AND GOOD-LUCK- HE'LL BE BACK IN THE SPRING, BUT WE'LL MISS HIM, EH SANDY?
ARF!
WELL, I'M GLAD WE WENT OUT TO SEE HIM OFF- IT'LL CHEER HIM TO KNOW SOMEBODY CARES WHEN HE GOES AWAY-
HAROLD GRAY
Reg. U. S. Pat. Off.; Copyright, 1930, by The Chicago Tribune.
JUST A MOMENT, FOLKS- WHEN THE MUSICAL GONG STRIKES IT WILL BE EXACTLY TWELVE, MIDNIGHT, EASTERN STANDARD TIME- BONG!!! WHEE!!!
YEOW!!! HONK! HONK! HONK!
I JUST WANTED TO HEAR THE NEW YEAR IN- SH-H-H-- LISTEN--
IN JUST A MOMENT YOU WILL HEAR THE MUSICAL NOTE--- BING!!! WOWIE!!! YIP! YIP! YIP! BANG! BANG! BANG! HAPPY NEW YEAR, FOLKS- THERE'S A BIG, HAPPY CROWD HERE TO-NIGHT.
SH-H-H-H--- IT'S BEEN JUST AN HOUR- NOW IT'S NEW YEAR'S IN CHICAGO-
IN JUST A MOMENT, FOLKS, WHEN YOU HEAR THE MUSICAL CHIMES IT WILL BE EXACTLY MID-NIGHT, MOUNTAIN TIME--- DING-- DONG! WHEE! HAPPY NEW YEAR! TOOT! TOOT!
ANOTHER HOUR- LISTEN, SANDY-
IT IS NOW EXACTLY TWELVE, MIDNIGHT, PACIFIC COAST TIME, FOLKS, AND A FIRE ENGINE IS GOING BY---- HEAR IT?--- WHE-E-E-E-E-E! HAPPY NEW YEAR, EVERYBODY-
WELL, WE'VE BEEN WAITIN' THREE HOURS, BUT IT'S WORTH IT, EH, SANDY?
ARF!
HAROLD GRAY
Reg. U. S. Pat. Off.; Copyright, 1930, by The Chicago Tribune.

December 29–31, 1930

YESSIR, WILLIE - YOU SURE HAVE GROWN A LOT IN A YEAR - AND YOU'VE DONE A HEAP OF TRAVELIN' FOR ONE BEAR - GEE - TH' PLACES WE'VE BEEN AND TH' SIGHTS WE'VE SEEN SINCE LAST NEW YEAR'S DAY -
I LIKE TO JUST SORTA SIT IN A QUIET CORNER ON NEW YEAR'S AND THINK OF THE PAST YEAR - THIS LAST YEAR HASN'T BEEN SUCH A KNOCKOUT IN SOME WAYS - BUT IT COULD HAVE BEEN LOTS WORSE -
WE'RE ALIVE AND GETTIN' ALONG GREAT - IT STARTED OUT BAD - BUT IT'S NOT SO MUCH HOW YUH START THAT COUNTS - IT'S HOW YUH FINISH -
HAROLD GRAY
AND I'VE GOT A HUNCH THIS YEAR, 1931, IS GOIN' TO BE A HUMDINGER, FULL OF ALL SORTS O' THINGS - WELL, NO MATTER WHAT COMES, WE'LL MEET IT HALF-WAY - EH, SANDY?
ARF!
Reg. U. S. Pat. Off.; Copyright, 1931, by The Chicago Tribune.
WONDER WHAT'S UP - "DADDY" SAID HE WANTS TO SEE ME -
WELL, ANNIE, THE HOLIDAYS ARE ABOUT OVER AND IT'S TIME TO GET DOWN TO BUSINESS AGAIN - NOW, IN YOUR CASE, THAT MEANS SCHOOL, SO I'VE HIRED A TUTOR FOR YOU -
NOW THE PUBLIC SCHOOL IS THE BEST PLACE FOR ANY YOUNGSTER BUT YOUR CASE IS A BIT UNUSUAL - THIS TUTOR WILL HELP YOU CATCH UP ON YOUR SCHOOLING A BIT FASTER THAN YOU'D GO IN A CLASS-ROOM -
WHEN YOU'RE CAUGHT UP ON ARITHMETIC AND SPELLING, OR WHATEVER THEY TEACH YOUNGSTERS NOW-DAYS, YOU CAN ENTER SCHOOL IN A CLASS OF YOUR OWN AGE - SEE?
HAROLD GRAY
Reg. U. S. Pat. Off.; Copyright, 1931, by The Chicago Tribune
ANNIE, THIS IS YOUR NEW TUTOR, PROFESSOR FLIBBERGIBBET - I THOUGHT YOU'D WANT TO GET ACQUAINTED BEFORE STARTING IN ON YOUR STUDIES MONDAY -
WELL, WELL, WELL - ER -- AHEM -- NOW THEN, MISS ANNIE, I FEEL SURE WE ARE GOING TO GET ALONG JUST SWIMMINGLY -
ER, YES SIR -
WE WON'T START ON OUR LESSONS TO-DAY - TIME ENOUGH FOR THAT NEXT WEEK - SO I WILL SEE YOU, BRIGHT AND EARLY MONDAY MORNING - SHALL WE SAY NINE O'CLOCK?
O. K. PROFESSOR -
WELL! SO THAT'S TEACHER, EH? WOW, WHAT WHISKERS! HE'S FUNNY-LOOKING BUT HE SEEMS LIKE A HARMLESS SORT O' GUY AND HE OUGHTA BE GOOD FOR A FEW LAUGHS, ANYWAY -
HAROLD GRAY
Reg. U. S. Pat. Off.; Copyright, 1931, by The Chicago Tribune.

January 1–3, 1931

Little Orphan Annie
WHADDYUH SAY WE GO CALL ON OLD SPIKE MARLIN TO-DAY, SANDY?

GEE, HE'LL SURE BE S'PRISED TO SEE US- I'LL BET HE GETS LONESOME, ALL BY HIMSELF, IN HIS LITTLE HOUSE UP THERE ON THE POINT-

HE'S HOME- HIS BOAT IS ANCHORED DOWN IN THE COVE BACK OF THE POINT- SURE GET A VIEW FROM UP HERE-

AHOY THERE, MATES- I MADE YOU OUT FROM MY LOOKOUT- COME IN-
HELLO, CAP'N- SANDY AN' I JUST CAME OVER TO SAY HELLO AN' SEE HOW YOU ARE GETTIN' ALONG-

IT'S A SNUG CABIN, ANNIE AND EVERY WINDOW LOOKS OUT TO SEA- BEEN GOIN' TO TAKE A CRUISE, BUT I'VE BEEN PRETTY BUSY-

GOT MY SHOP BACK HERE-MAKIN' A MODEL OF THE OLD WIND-JAMMER I WAS SKIPPER OF ONCE-

HELLO, DEACON- HOW'S TH' OLD KID?
WELL, WELL! I'LL BE A ✶!!!✶✶! ANNIE AND SANDY!!! HOWAREYUH? HOWAREYUH?
ARF!

OLD TIMERS FROM THE COVE COME UP OFTEN AND WE WATCH THE CRAFT PASSING UP AND DOWN THE CHANNEL YONDER-

I GO FOR A LITTLE CRUISE NOW AND THEN AROUND THE SOUND-BUT IT'S SNUG HERE- NEVER THOUGHT I'D BE CONTENTED ASHORE, BUT SOMEHOW THIS IS DIFFERENT-

G-BYE, CAP'N! WE'LL BE BACK AGAIN, OFTEN- GEE, HE'S SURE HAPPY UP THERE IN HIS LITTLE HOUSE-

AND THERE'S THE LITTLE FISHIN' TOWN RIGHT NEARBY FULL O' HIS CRONIES- YEP- HE'S EASY TO PLEASE- HE DOESN'T NEED A LOT O' MONEY OR EXCITEMENT-

I GUESS DIFFERENT FOLKS GET A KICK OUT O' DIFFERENT THINGS- BUT TH' PEOPLE WHO GET HAPPINESS FROM THE SIMPLEST THINGS ARE THE HAPPIEST PEOPLE- EH, SANDY?
ARF!
HAROLD GRAY
Reg. U. S. Pat. Off.; Copyright, 1931, by The Chicago Tribune.

January 4, 1931

WELL, ANNIE, OUR FIRST STEP WILL BE TO HAVE AN EXAMINATION AND SEE HOW MUCH YOU KNOW- THEN WE WILL KNOW WHERE TO START-

O. K., PROFESSOR- C'MON IN HERE WHERE WE WON'T BE BOTHERED AND LET'S GET GOIN'-

HAROLD GRAY
Reg. U. S. Pat. Off.; Copyright, 1931, by The Chicago Tribune.

?
?

HM-M-M--- THIS SURE IS DEEP STUFF- AND I'VE GOTTA WADE THROUGH TEN PAGES FOR MY FIRST LESSON- WELL, I GUESS TH' QUICKEST WAY IS TO JUST DIG RIGHT IN AND KEEP GOIN' TILL IT'S DONE-

THERE'S A YOUNGSTER FOR YOU- NOT MANY OF HER AGE NOW DAYS WHO'D BE WILLING TO SIT DOWN QUIETLY WITH A SCHOOL-BOOK AND TRY TO LEARN SOMETHING-

HAROLD GRAY

IT'S ALL RIGHT, BOYS- DON'T YOU WORRY ABOUT ANNIE- SHE'S NOT SICK- JUST MIGHTY BUSY CATCHING UP ON THE BACK SCHOOL-WORK SHE'S MISSED- SEE?
Reg. U. S. Pat. Off.; Copyright, 1931, by The Chicago Tribune.

THERE- THREE-THIRTY- SCHOOL'S OUT FOR TO-DAY- NOW I CAN GO OUT AND PLAY WITH SANDY AND WILLIE TILL DARK-

SHE'S BEEN HARD AT IT STUDYING ALL DAY- SHE'S EARNED A LITTLE TIME OFF- WONDER WHAT SORT OF SUBJECTS THAT TUTOR HAS HER WORKING ON NOW-

HUH! A LOT OF TRICK STUFF- SHORT-CUTS TO LEARNING, I SUPPOSE THEY'RE CALLED- WHERE'S HER ARITHMETIC AND READER AND SPELLING BOOK?

A LOT OF NEW-FANGLED WAYS TO GET A SO-CALLED EDUCATION WITHOUT HAVING TO KNOW A THING- I'M GOING TO HAVE A TALK WITH THAT PROFESSOR TO-MORROW-
HAROLD GRAY
Reg. U. S. Pat. Off.; Copyright, 1931, by The Chicago Tribune.

January 5–7, 1931

SAY, PROFESSOR- I HAVE A FEW THINGS TO TAKE UP WITH YOU- I WAS LOOKING OVER THOSE TEXT BOOKS YOU ARE HAVING ANNIE READ-

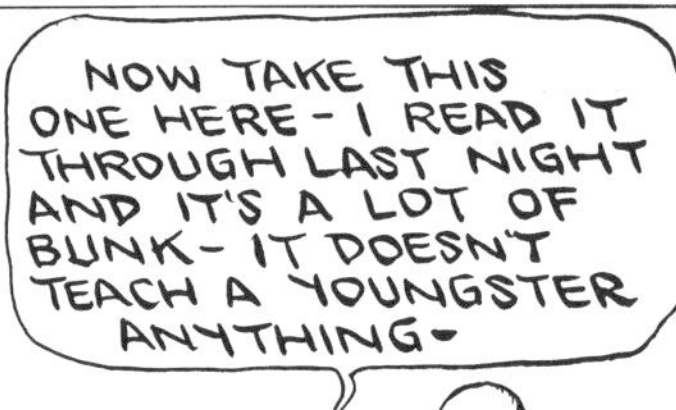
NOW TAKE THIS ONE HERE- I READ IT THROUGH LAST NIGHT AND IT'S A LOT OF BUNK- IT DOESN'T TEACH A YOUNGSTER ANYTHING-

B-BUT MR. WARBUCKS- YOU KNOW THE MODERN METHOD OF TEACHING...
"BUT" NOTHING! I DON'T CARE WHAT ANYONE SAYS- THE OLD FASHIONED METHOD SUITS ME- I WANT ANNIE TO LEARN SOMETHING-
Reg. U. S. Pat. Off.: Copyright, 1931, by The Chicago Tribune.

TEACH HER TO READ, WRITE AND KNOW SOMETHING ABOUT ARITHMETIC- AND I WANT HER TO BE ABLE TO SPELL AND USE GOOD GRAMMAR- THAT'S WHAT I WANT- YOU FOLLOW MY ORDERS AND NO "BUTS"-
YES, SIR-
HAROLD GRAY

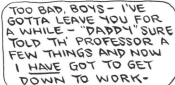

TOO BAD, BOYS- I'VE GOTTA LEAVE YOU FOR A WHILE- "DADDY" SURE TOLD TH' PROFESSOR A FEW THINGS AND NOW I HAVE GOT TO GET DOWN TO WORK-

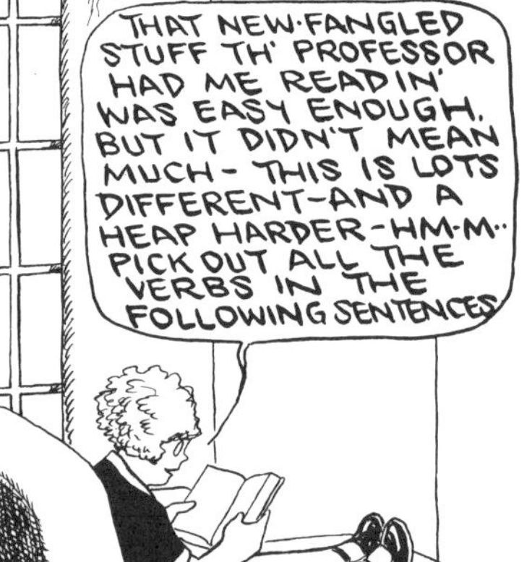
THAT NEW-FANGLED STUFF TH' PROFESSOR HAD ME READIN' WAS EASY ENOUGH, BUT IT DIDN'T MEAN MUCH- THIS IS LOTS DIFFERENT-AND A HEAP HARDER-HM-M.. PICK OUT ALL THE VERBS IN THE FOLLOWING SENTENCES

AND 'RITHMETIC- GUESS I'M GOIN' TO HAVE TO WORK FROM NOW ON- IF FOUR MEN CAN DO A PIECE OF WORK IN TWELVE DAYS, IN HOW MANY DAYS CAN THREE MEN DO THE SAME WORK? HM-M-M....

SPELLING ALWAYS WAS TOUGH FOR ME- BUT I'LL SHOW "DADDY" I CAN LEARN- Y-A-C-H-T-- GEE- THAT'S "YACHT"- BUT I'D NEVER HAVE SPELLED IT LIKE THAT- I'LL LEARN TH' FIRST TEN WORDS IN THIS BOOK TO DAY- AN' TEN MORE EACH DAY- WONDER HOW MANY WORDS THERE ARE, ANYWAY-
HAROLD GRAY

GOOD MORNING, MISS ANNIE- WELL, WELL- ARE YOU ALL READY TO RECITE YOUR HISTORY LESSON?

SAY !!! WHAT'S TH' BIG IDEA?

SEE THAT? DOES THAT MEAN ANYTHING TO YOU? IT SAYS SATURDAY !!! AND THERE'S NO SCHOOL ON SATURDAY-
SAT JAN 10

TODDLE ALONG, BIG BOY- ROLL YER HOOP- MONDAY I'LL BE ALL SET FOR SOME MORE SCHOOL- BUT SATURDAY IS MY DAY OFF, AND DON'T YOU FORGET IT-

CAN YOU 'MAGINE THAT GUY? I WONDER IF HE DIDN'T KNOW SATURDAY IS A HOLIDAY, OR IF HE JUST FIGGERED I WAS DUMB-
HAROLD GRAY
Reg. U. S. Pat. Off.; Copyright, 1931, by The Chicago Tribune.

Little Orphan Annie
C'MON, SANDY- HURRY- NOBODY'S LOOKIN'- NOW'S OUR CHANCE-

'ORRORS! GONE - SHE WAS THERE HONLY A MOMENT AGO- THERE'S 'ER BOOK- HI HONLY TURNED MY BACK FOR AN HINSTANT-

HIT'S THE MARSTER'S ORDERS SHE MUST NOT GET OUT OF MY SIGHT- IF SHE GETS LOST 'E'LL SKIN ME HALIVE - 'E PROMISED AS MUCH -

WELL, THAT'S ONCE WE DUCKED THAT BUTLER- HE'S NOT A BAD OLD DUFFER, BUT HE DRIVES ME TWITTERY, ALWAYS FOLLOWIN' ME AROUND-

I HOPE THIS ICE IS O. K. THE BUTLER SAID IT WAS THIN AND THE THAWING HAD MADE IT SOFT AND DANGEROUS-

BUT THEN HE DIDN'T WANT ME TO GO SKATIN'- GEE! THIS IS GREAT-

NOW 'WATCH, SANDY- I'LL SHOW YUH A COUPLE O' TRICKS YOU WON'T SEE EVERY DAY, I BETCHA-

OOP!

YEOW!

LEAPIN' LIZARDS!!! AN' I DIDN'T EVEN PUT A DENT IN THE ICE - ONLY A FUNNY LITTLE STAR-

HI 'AVE LOOKED ALL OVER AND 'ERE YOU ARE - BUT YOU MUSTN'T SKATE THERE, MISS - THE HICE IS THIN AND SOFT - HIT MIGHT BREAK AT ANY MOMENT-
OH, YEAH?

THAT SHOWS HOW MUCH YOU KNOW 'BOUT ICE - IT'S TWO FEET THICK AND HARD ALL THE WAY THROUGH- I KNOW!
HAROLD GRAY
Reg. U. S. Pat. Off., Copyright, 1931, by The Chicago Tribune

January 11, 1931
BUSTED!

HI BEG YOUR PARDON, SIR, BUT YOUR PRIVATE SECRETARY IS CALLING OVER THE PRIVATE WIRE, SIR- HE SAYS IT IS MOST URGENT-
THANKS, PHILIP-

WHAT? ARE YOU SURE ABOUT THAT? THERE MUST BE SOME MISTAKE- YOU SAY YOU CABLED? HM-M-M- LISTEN- I'LL BE DOWN IN THE MORNING - YEAH - I'LL FIGURE OUT SOMETHING - HAVE ALL THE DATA READY - O.K.-

HE MUST BE WRONG - STILL, HE'S ALWAYS BEEN RIGHT BEFORE - AND HE'S CHECKED UP, HE SAYS - I'VE GOT TO THINK FAST - WOW - NO TELLING WHAT THIS WILL MEAN -

NO - NO - THERE'S NOTHING WRONG, ANNIE - JUST A LITTLE BUSINESS MATTER - THAT'S ALL - NOTHING SERIOUS - DON'T YOU WORRY ABOUT ANYTHING AT ALL -
HAROLD GRAY
Reg. U. S. Pat. Off.; Copyright, 1931, by The Chicago Tribune.

THINGS SURE ARE IN AN AWFUL MESS - I KNEW BUSINESS HAD BEEN BAD, BUT I HAD NO IDEA HOW BAD - MY SECRETARY WAS RIGHT - BUT I'VE BEEN IN TIGHT PLACES BEFORE - I'M NOT LICKED AND I WON'T BE - GOTTA THINK THIS THING OUT ALONE -

YOU HAD TH' DOOR LOCKED, "DADDY" - WILL IT BOTHER YOU IF I COME IN?
NOT AT ALL, ANNIE - COME RIGHT IN - DON'T KNOW HOW THAT DOOR GOT LOCKED -

LOOKIE, "DADDY" - I WANTA SHOW YOU HOW WELL I'M GETTIN' ALONG WITH MY LESSONS - I'M WAY TO HERE IN MY 'RITHMETIC, AN' WAIT'LL I SHOW YOU MY SPELLIN' BOOK -
MY! THAT'S FINE, ANNIE - YOU SURE ARE GETTING ALONG GREAT - YOU'VE BEEN WORKING HARD - I CAN SEE THAT -

THAT YOUNGSTER! I MUSTN'T LET HER SEE I'M WORRIED - NO USE LETTING HER KNOW EVERYTHING ISN'T ALL RIGHT - TIME ENOUGH TO TELL HER WHEN I HAVE MY BUSINESS BACK ON IT'S FEET AGAIN -
HAROLD GRAY
Reg. U. S. Pat. Off.; Copyright, 1931, by The Chicago Tribune.

I AM TELLING YOU, MR. WARBUCKS, WE ARE NOT THE ONLY ONES IN THE SAME FIX - OVER-PRODUCTION AND BAD COLLECTIONS - THAT IS THE CAUSE OF ALL OUR TROUBLES -

WELL, WHY IN SAM HILL WASN'T I INFORMED OF ALL THIS BEFORE? I KNEW BUSINESS WAS BAD, BUT I FIGURED WE WERE BIG AND STRONG ENOUGH TO GO THROUGH ANY DEPRESSION - WHY WASN'T I TOLD?

TOLD? WE TOLD YOU AND TOLD YOU, MR. WARBUCKS - MYSELF I SENT YOU RADIOGRAMS WHILE YOU WERE ON YOUR YACHT - BUT YOU WOULD TAKE NOTHING SERIOUSLY - YOUR MIND WAS ELSE-WHERE -
HAROLD GRAY

GUESS YOU'RE RIGHT, SAM - BUT MY MIND'S SURE ON MY BUSINESS NOW - THE COUNTRY IS SOUND - GOOD TIMES ARE HERE - OUR BUSINESS MUST NOT BE TOO FAR GONE TO BE SAVED - I'LL FIND A WAY OUT YET -
I HOPE SO -
Reg. U. S. Pat. Off.; Copyright, 1931, by The Chicago Tribune.

January 12-14, 1931

EIGHT BILLION--- NINE BILLION--- HM-M-M--- TEN BILLION, ELEVEN MILLION AND---
LEAPIN' LIZARDS! IT'S AFTER TWELVE O'CLOCK AND "DADDY" IS STILL SITTIN' UP FIGGERIN'- HE ACTS AWFUL WORRIED 'BOUT SOMETHIN' LATELY-
IT CAN'T BE BUSINESS, SANDY, 'CAUSE "DADDY'S" GOT MORE MONEY'N HE COULD EVER SPEND- BUT HE'S FIGGERIN' AN' SORTA TALKIN' TO HIMSELF-
HE'S BEEN ALL SMILES TO ME JUST LIKE HE WAS FEELIN' GREAT- BUT HE CAN'T FOOL ME- THERE'S SOMETHIN' MIGHTY WRONG- HE'S NOT HIMSELF-
HAROLD GRAY
Reg. U. S. Pat. Off.; Copyright, 1931, by The Chicago Tribune.
THERE COMES MY GENERAL MANAGER NOW- I TOLD HIM TO BRING ALL THE REPORTS OUT HERE WHERE WE COULD GO OVER THEM ALONE-
NOW THAT YOU HAVE DUG OUT ALL THE FACTS WHAT DO YOU THINK- IS IT AS BAD AS IT LOOKED AT FIRST?
WORSE-
HM-M-M--- NOT SO GOOD- ACCORDING TO THIS WE'RE PRACTICALLY DONE FOR RIGHT NOW-
YES- IT'S VERY BAD- EVERYTHING IS THERE- BAD COLLECTIONS- OVER-PRODUCTION- PERSONALLY I SEE NO WAY OUT-
HAROLD GRAY
I KNEW WE WERE SLIPPING, BUT I WAS SURE BUSINESS WAS COMING BACK- IT IS- BUSINESS IS PICKING UP AGAIN BY LEAPS AND BOUNDS- BUT ARE WE TOO FAR GONE TO BE HELPED? WELL, THE NEXT FEW DAYS WILL ANSWER THAT-
Reg. U. S. Pat. Off.; Copyright, 1931, by The Chicago Tribune.
SAY, "DADDY"- WHAT'S TH' MATTER? THERE'S SOMETHING WRONG- I CAN TELL-
WHAT'S THAT? "WRONG"?
HA! HA! HA! WHY, THERE'S NOT A THING WRONG, ANNIE- WHAT EVER GAVE YOU SUCH AN IDEA? EVERYTHING'S DANDY- COULDN'T BE BETTER- "WRONG"? HA! HA! HA!
THE LITTLE IMP- YOU CAN'T FOOL A YOUNGSTER AS SMART AS ANNIE- BUT I CAN'T TELL HER- THERE'S STILL A CHANCE I CAN WIGGLE OUT OF THIS JAM AND SAVE MY FORTUNE- NO SENSE IN LETTING HER KNOW HOW CLOSE WE ARE TO BECOMING PAUPERS-
NOTHING WRONG, EH? WHY, IT'S WRITTEN ALL OVER "DADDY'S" FACE- HE'S WORRIED- HE CAN'T FOOL ME- HE JUST LAUGHS SO I WON'T GET WISE- I WISH I KNEW WHAT'S BOTHERIN' HIM-
HAROLD GRAY
Reg. U. S. Pat. Off.; Copyright, 1931, by The Chicago Tribune.

January 15–17, 1931

Little Orphan Annie
PRETTY TOUGH FOR BIRDS THIS KIND O' WEATHER, WITH SNOW ALL OVER EVERTHING-
I'M GOIN' IN AND GET TH' COOK TO GIVE ME SOME CRUMBS TO FEED 'EM- THEY MUST BE AWFUL HUNGRY AND THEY LOOK HALF FROZEN-
LOOK AT 'EM, SANDY- WOW, ARE THEY HUNGRY! AND TAME, TOO- THEY KNOW WE'RE THEIR FRIENDS-
WELL, THEY'LL BE ALL RIGHT NOW- I WOULDN'T HAVE ANY HARM COME TO THEM FOR THE WORLD-
?
PSSST
R-R-R
ARRUFF!
MEOW!
GR-R-R-R-R- YIPE!!!
PSST! PSST! REOW!!!
SANDY! TH' IDEA! CHASING POOR TOMMY- AREN'T YUH 'SHAMED?
E-YOW!
GEE- YOU ACT LIKE YOU HADN'T DONE ANYTHING WRONG- ARE YOU TRYIN' TO KID ME, OR WHAT?
?
WELL, I'LL SOON GET TO TH' BOTTOM O' THIS- I STILL CLAIM IT WAS VERY NAUGHTY TO CHASE POOR TOMMY- BUT WE'LL SEE WHAT THESE TRACKS TELL-
AH-HA! NOW I SEE IT ALL- THE WHOLE STORY IS WRITTEN ON THE SNOW- YOU SPOTTED TOMMY SNEAKIN' UP ON TH' BIRDS AND THAT'S HOW TH' ROW STARTED-
SANDY- I TAKE IT ALL BACK- I SHOULD HAVE KNOWN YOU HAD A GOOD REASON- IT WAS WRONG TO SCOLD YOU TILL I KNEW THE WHOLE STORY- WILL YOU FORGIVE ME?
ARF!
Reg. U. S. Pat. Off.; Copyright, 1931, by The Chicago Tribune.
HAROLD GRAY

January 18, 1931

YES - BUSINESS SURE IS PICKING UP FAST - IT WON'T BE LONG NOW TILL EVERY-ONE WILL HAVE FORGOTTEN ALL ABOUT 1930 - IF I CAN ONLY KEEP GOING FOR A FEW MORE MONTHS.
GOOD MORNING, ANNIE - WELL, WELL, WELL - YOU'RE UP BRIGHT AND EARLY -
MORNING, "DADDY" - WHERE ARE YOU GOING SO EARLY?
OH, I'M JUST GOING DOWN TOWN - GOTTA SEE A MAN - I'LL GET HOME AS SOON AS I CAN -
G'BYE, "DADDY" - GEE, I HATE TO HAVE YOU GO AWAY, EVEN FOR JUST A LITTLE WHILE -

IF TOM BULLION IS ONLY IN TOWN - I'VE SAVED HIM FROM RUIN TIME AND TIME AGAIN - HE'S HEAD OF A GREAT BANKING SYSTEM NOW - WITH HIS HELP I CAN PULL THROUGH - THREE MONTHS AND I'LL BE ON MY FEET AGAIN - LUCKY I HAVE A FRIEND LIKE TOM BULLION -
HAROLD GRAY

YOU SAY MR. BULLION WILL BE BACK TO-MORROW - GOOD - THIS IS WARBUCKS - MAKE A DATE FOR ME TO SEE HIM, WILL YOU? TWO O'CLOCK TO-MORROW AFTERNOON? FINE -

GOOD OLD TOM BULLION - HE'S THE ONLY ONE WHO CAN SAVE ME - BUT AFTER ALL I'VE DONE FOR HIM HE'LL BE GLAD TO HELP ME - IT WILL BE THE FIRST TIME I'VE EVER CALLED ON HIM FOR ANYTHING -

GEE, "DADDY", I'M GLAD YOU'RE CHEERFUL AGAIN AND HAVE QUIT WORRYIN' 'BOUT YOUR BUSINESS - I WAS 'FRAID YOU'D BE RUNNIN' AWAY TO CHINA OR SOME PLACE AGAIN AND LEAVE ME BEHIND -
NOT A CHANCE, ANNIE - MY BUSINESS IS STILL IN BAD SHAPE, BUT NO MATTER WHAT HAPPENS I'LL NEVER GO AWAY AND LEAVE YOU ALONE AGAIN - THAT'S A PROMISE -
HAROLD GRAY

YOU SEE, TOM, I'VE COME TO YOU AS A LAST RESORT - IF YOU DON'T HELP ME I'M RUINED - BUT I KNOW YOU ARE MY FRIEND -
AH, YES - I SEE - HM-M-M-M - QUITE SO - QUITE SO -

MY COLLEAGUES AND I COULD ACQUIRE YOUR BUSINESS FOR NEARLY NOTHING, MERELY BY FAILING TO LOAN YOU MONEY AT THIS TIME - OF COURSE THERE IS THE MATTER OF OUR FRIEND-SHIP - BUT, AS YOU KNOW, SENTIMENT SHOULD HAVE NO PLACE IN BUSINESS - REALLY, I AM AFRAID WE HAVE NO MONEY TO LOAN AT THIS TIME -

WHAT? DO YOU MEAN YOU INTEND TO SMASH ME? LET ME DOWN? ROB ME? IS THAT IT?
TUT-TUT-IT'S MERELY A MATTER OF BUSINESS - YOU MAKE IT MOST UNPLEASANT FOR ME - YOU ARE SO BLUNT -

THERE, YOU DOUBLE-CROSSER - THAT'S WHAT I THINK OF YOU - I MAY HAVE LOST IN BUSINESS BUT I'M NOT USED TO LOSING AND I DON'T LIKE IT - SEE?
HAROLD GRAY

January 19–21, 1931
BUSTED!

TO THINK A MAN LIKE TOM BULLION WOULD TURN ON ME- I BEFRIENDED HIM AND NOW, WHEN I'M DOWN, HE JOINS THE WOLVES AGAINST ME- OF COURSE THAT'S BUSINESS, BUT I NEVER PLAYED IT THAT WAY- MAYBE THAT'S WHY I'M MIGHTY NEAR A FAILURE NOW-
STILL, I'D RATHER BE HONEST AND SHOOT SQUARE WITH MY FRIENDS, THAN TO BE A JUDAS FOR ALL THE MONEY IN THE WORLD- I'M GLAD I PUNCHED BULLION'S FACE YESTERDAY-
POOR "DADDY"- HE WAS ALL SMILES A COUPLE O' DAYS AGO- SEEMED TO THINK HIS BUSINESS TROUBLES WERE ALL FIXED- THEN HE SAW SOME BIRD DOWN TOWN AND SINCE THEN HE'S BEEN ACTIN' TERRIBLE
I DON'T LIKE IT- HE DIDN'T GO TO BED AT ALL LAST NIGHT- JUST WALKED UP AND DOWN IN HIS LIBRARY- I HEARD HIM- AND IF A SERVANT BOTHERS HIM HE SWEARS AWFUL- SOMETHING'S MIGHTY WRONG-
HAROLD GRAY
Reg. U. S. Pat. Off.; Copyright, 1931, by The Chicago Tribune.
YI-I-I-!!! OW! NO! NO! HELP!
DID THE MARSTER STRIKE HIM?
HIT'S THE TUTOR- 'E WAS LOAFING IN THE MARSTER'S STUDY- PROWLING ABOUT IN HIS PAPERS, 'E WAS, WHEN THE MARSTER HENTERED HUNEXPECTEDLY-
ONLY A GLAWNCING BLOW- MY WORD- LOOK AT HIM GO-
GEE-
MY HOPINION IS THE MARSTER 'AS 'AD REVERSES- 'E IS NOT HIMSELF AT ALL- WE MUST BE MOST CAREFUL NOT TO IRRITATE HIM- 'E HAS A MOST 'ORRIBLE TEMPER WHEN 'E IS AROUSED-
HAROLD GRAY
Reg. U. S. Pat. Off.; Copyright, 1931, by The Chicago Tribune.
I'M NOT SEEING ANYONE- IF ANYBODY COMES TO SEE ME I'M NOT IN- DO YOU UNDERSTAND?
YES, SIR- YES, SIR- QUITE RIGHT, SIR-
CREDITORS- JACKALS WITH PAPERS TO SERVE- THE CUSTOMARY COLLECTION OF COYOTES- WELL, LET 'EM STAND AROUND OUTSIDE AND LOOK AT MY FRONT DOOR- THEY WON'T GET IN-
HELLO, "DADDY"- TH' BUTLER SAID YOU SAID FOR ME TO STAY IN THE HOUSE TO-DAY-
OH, HELLO, ANNIE- YES- STAY IN THE HOUSE TO-DAY-
LEAPIN' LIZARDS! THAT'S NOT LIKE "DADDY"- HE ALMOST SNAPPED AT ME- AND THERE IS A GANG OF CHEAP-LOOKIN' GUYS OUT IN FRONT LOOKIN' FOR HIM- I WISH I KNEW WHAT IT'S ALL ABOUT-
HAROLD GRAY
Reg. U. S. Pat. Off.; Copyright, 1931, by The Chicago Tribune.

January 22–24, 1931

Little Orphan Annie
I WONDER WHERE THAT BIG BULLY IS TO DAY- I WISH SANDY WAS WITH ME-
GUESS HE'S NOT AROUND- HE PROMISED HE'D WASH MY FACE AND STUFF SNOW DOWN MY BACK IF HE CAUGHT ME- HE'D DO IT, TOO- HE'S TOO BIG AND TOUGH FOR ME-
YEOW! THERE HE IS- IF I CAN JUST MAKE THAT CORNER-
SOCK!
LEAPIN' LIZARDS! CORNERED- NOT A CHANCE TO GET BY HIM- I'VE GOTTA DO SOMETHIN' QUICK-
I'VE GOTCHA NOW-
G'WAN! THROW IT- GIRLS CAN'T HIT NOTHIN'-
IS THAT SO? I'LL SHOW YUH!
SHUX! MISSED HIM-
HAW! HAW! TOO HIGH- OVER MY HEAD A MILE-
GREAT CAESAR'S SUSPENDERS! I HOPE HE'S NOT HURT BAD- I NEVER MEANT FOR THOSE BIG ICICLES TO FALL ON HIM- HONEST I DIDN'T-
OW!!! MY HEAD- WHAT HIT ME?
GOOD- HE'S COMIN' AROUND ALL RIGHT NOW-
YOU! DON'T HIT ME AGAIN- I'LL NEVER BOTHER YOU ANYMORE- HONEST!
HUH??? OH!
I NEVER EVEN SAW THAT SECOND SNOW-BALL COMIN' AT ALL-
AW, I JUST TOSSED THAT SECOND ONE- NEXT TIME I'LL REALLY SOCK YUH- SEE?
OH, HELLO, SANDY- GUESS I WON'T NEED YOU NOW- BUT YOU SHOULD HAVE BEEN AROUND TO SEE ME POLISH OFF THAT BIG YOKEL-
Reg. U. S. Pat. Off.; Copyright, 1931, by The Chicago Tribune.
HAROLD GRAY

January 25, 1931
BUSTED!

THINGS SURE ARE GOIN' FROM BAD TO WORSE- TH' HOUSE WAS COLD THIS MORNING- SOMEBODY LET THE FIRE GO OUT- THEY SAY A LOT OF THE SERVANTS QUIT LAST NIGHT- JUST WALKED OUT-
LOOKIE, SANDY- THERE GO THREE MORE OF 'EM WITH THEIR SUITCASES-
MY MAID QUIT A WEEK AGO- WOULDN'T TELL ME WHY- BUT I HEARD THEY ALL THINK "DADDY" IS GOIN' BROKE AND THEY'RE 'FRAID THEY WON'T GET PAID-
'MAGINE THAT? WHY, WITH ALL HIS MONEY, HOW COULD "DADDY" EVER GO BROKE? GEE- IT SURE IS DESERTED HERE- I'VE WALKED THROUGH TWENTY ROOMS AND HAVEN'T SEEN OR HEARD EVEN ONE SERVANT-
HAROLD GRAY
Reg. U. S. Pat. Off. Copyright 1931, by The Chicago Tribune
HI BEG YOUR PARDON, MR WARBUCKS- BUT IS HIT TRUE YOU ARE IN FINANCIAL DIFFICULTIES?
WHAT? MAYBE I AM AND MAYBE I'M NOT- WHAT'S IT TO YOU?
HONLY THIS, SIR- HI HAVE NEARLY NINE THOUSAND DOLLARS, MY LIFE'S SAVINGS, SIR- YOU 'AVE BEEN VERY KIND TO ME, IF I MAY SAY SO, AND IF YOU NEED A BIT OF HELP, SIR, HI WILL BE GLAD TO LET YOU HAVE IT, SIR-
YOUR LIFE'S SAVINGS- AND YOU'D TAKE A CHANCE ON LOANING IT ALL TO ME- YOU ARE A FRIEND, SIMPSON- I WOULDN'T THINK OF TAKING YOUR MONEY- YOU HANG ON TO IT- BUT I'LL SURE REMEMBER THAT YOU STOOD BY WHEN FRIENDS WERE SCARCE-
NINE THOUSAND!!! NINE MILLION WOULD HARDLY HELP ME MUCH RIGHT NOW- BUT IMAGINE THAT- WILLING TO HAND ME HIS LIFE'S SAVINGS EVEN WHEN HE KNOWS I'M SLIPPING- FOOLISH OF HIM, NO DOUBT, BUT TRUE FRIENDSHIP-
HAROLD GRAY
Reg. U. S. Pat. Off. Copyright 1931, by The Chicago Tribune
I CAN'T GET OVER SIMPSON, THE OLD BUTLER, OFFERING ME HIS NINE THOUSAND YESTERDAY- OF COURSE I WOULDN'T TAKE IT- HE'LL NEED IT- AND ANYWAY A HUNDRED TIMES THAT MUCH WOULDN'T GET ME OUT NOW-
BUT WHAT A GENEROUS OLD SOUL- ANY MAN CAN COUNT HIS REAL FRIENDS ON THE FINGERS OF ONE HAND, EVEN IF HE HAS A COUPLE OF FINGERS CUT OFF-
WHEN YOU'RE DOING WELL EVERY ONE IS YOUR PAL- IT'S WHEN HARD LUCK HITS YOU THAT YOU CAN REALLY TELL THE WHEAT FROM THE CHAFF- THE PLATINUM FROM THE TIN- THE SINCERE FRIENDS FROM THE SYCOPHANTS-
OH, WELL- IT'S EASY TO BE A FRIEND TO SOME ONE WHO IS DOING WELL AND WHO PAYS THE BILLS- IT'S NOT SO EASY TO BE A FRIEND WHEN IT'S EXPENSIVE-
HAROLD GRAY
Reg. U. S. Pat. Off.; Copyright, 1931, by The Chicago Tribune.

January 26–28, 1931

THERE'S SOME BIRD DOWN IN FRONT HAVIN' AN ARGUMENT WITH SIMPSON- SAYS HE'S GOT TO SEE "DADDY" WARBUCKS-
HE HAD A BADGE AND SIMPSON LET HIM IN- C'MON, SANDY- LET'S SEE WHAT HE WANTS-
HE SAYS HE'S FROM SOME LAWYER AND HE'S HANDIN' "DADDY" A LEGAL-LOOKIN' PAPER- "DADDY" DOESN'T ACT LIKE HE WANTED THE PAPER VERY MUCH BUT HE'S TAKIN' IT-
DOG-GONE IT- I WISH I WAS OLDER AND KNEW MORE- THEN MAYBE I COULD DO SOMETHIN' TO HELP- "DADDY'S" SURE IN TROUBLE, BUT IT'S ALL WAY OVER MY HEAD-
HAROLD GRAY
Reg. U. S. Pat. Off., Copyright, 1931, by The Chicago Tribune
HEY! LOOK! THERE'S A COUPLE O' BOZOS TRYIN' TO GET AWAY WITH TH' CARS-
THAT'S A NERVE- STEALIN' 'EM RIGHT OUT OF OUR GARAGE WITH US LOOKIN'- C'MON-
BUST INTO PRIVATE GROUNDS AND TRY LIFTIN' A CAR, WILL YUH? NOT WHILE I'M A CHAUFFEUR ON THIS JOB, YUH WON'T- WOT A CRUST YOU GOT!
WAIT! WAIT! OW!
LOOK! HE'S SOME KIND OF A COP-
HERE- THERE ARE THE ATTACHMENT PAPERS- I HAVE THE POWER BY LAW TO SIEZE THESE CARS- YOU CAN'T RESIST-
WELL, I'LL BE---- HUH! - WELL, I'M GLAD WE SOCKED 'EM, ANYWAY- THE BOSS MUST BE IN BAD SHAPE WHEN THEY CAN TAKE HIS CARS- LOOKS LIKE WE'RE OUT OF A JOB NOW-
HAROLD GRAY
Reg. U. S. Pat. Off., Copyright, 1931, by The Chicago Tribune
LEAPIN' LIZARDS!!! ALL TH' CARS GONE SLICK AS A WHISTLE- MUST HAVE BEEN STOLEN!
"DADDY"- I WAS JUST OUT TO THE GARAGE AND EVERY CAR IS GONE-
YES, I KNOW, ANNIE- THEY WERE ALL TAKEN DOWN TOWN YESTERDAY-
OH, THEN YOU KNEW ABOUT IT- I THOUGHT THEY HAD BEEN STOLEN-
STOLEN? ER- WELL, NOT EXACTLY- DON'T YOU WORRY ABOUT IT, ANNIE- IT'S A LONG STORY- I'LL EXPLAIN IT ALL TO YOU SOME TIME-
Reg. U. S. Pat. Off.; Copyright, 1931, by The Chicago Tribune.
YOU MARK MY WORDS, SANDY- THINGS ARE GETTIN' WORSE AND WORSE AND WORSE!!! "DADDY" ACTS SORTA STUNNED- NOT LIKE HIMSELF AT ALL- HE JUST SITS AND LOOKS AT NOTHIN'- SOMETHING'S GOTTA BE DONE-
HAROLD GRAY

January 29–31, 1931

Little Orphan Annie

SOMETHING MUST BE DONE ABOUT WILLIE - HE'S NOT HIMSELF - TAKES NO INTEREST IN ANYTHING -

WE'LL TAKE HIM TO TH' ZOO - MAYBE HE'LL GET A KICK OUT O' SEEING THE OTHER BEARS - IT'S WORTH TRYING -

C'MON, WILLIE - DON'T LOOK SO DROOPY - SNAP OUT OF IT - COME ON IN AND MEET SOME OF YOUR DISTANT COUSINS -

TO THE ZOO

WE BROUGHT LITTLE WILLIE - THOUGHT MAYBE HE'D LIKE TO SEE SOME OTHER BEARS, IF YOU'LL LET HIM IN -

WELL, ANNIE, I DON'T KNOW OF ANY RULE AGAINST LETTIN' BEARS INTO THE ZOO -

?

THAT BIG BRUTE! WILLIE! LOOK OUT!!!

WHY, WILLIE! ARE YOU TRYING TO TELL ME YOU'RE OLD FRIENDS? THAT'S IMPOSSIBLE -

BOUF! BOUF!

DON'T SEEM LIKELY THEY EVER MET BEFORE - SHE WAS CAPTURED 'BOUT A YEAR AGO NEAR A LITTLE BACK-WOODS TOWN CALLED BLUNDERVILLE -

WHAT? BLUNDERVILLE! WHY, THAT'S WHERE I WAS LIVIN' WHEN WILLIE CAME 'BOUT A YEAR AGO - SHE MUST BE WILLIE'S MAMA -

'MAGINE THAT! NO WONDER THEY SEEM SO TICKLED TO SEE EACH OTHER -

BOUF!

HAROLD GRAY

IT WOULD BE GOOD FOR BOTH OF THEM IF YOU'D LET WILLIE STAY HERE - I KNOW HE'D BE VERY HAPPY -

GEE - I NEVER FIGGERED ON ANYTHING LIKE THIS - STILL, HE WOULD HAVE A SWELL HOME HERE, AND HE WOULDN'T BE LONESOME -

WE'RE GOIN' TO MISS WILLIE - BUT HE SURE WAS TICKLED TO SEE HIS MAMA AGAIN - HE'LL REALLY BE LOTS HAPPIER AT THE ZOO - AND, AFTER ALL, IF WE REALLY CARE FOR A FRIEND, OUR FIRST THOUGHT SHOULD BE FOR HIS HAPPINESS - EH, SANDY?

ARF!

February 1, 1931

LEAPIN' LIZARDS! JUST LOOK AT TH' TOP O' THAT CABINET- DUST, DUST- DUST!
SAY - WE SHOULD HAVE HAD DINNER AN HOUR AGO- WONDER WHAT'S THE MATTER WITH THE COOK- I'M GOIN' BACK TO THE KITCHEN AND SEE WHAT'S WRONG- I'M HUNGRY-

TH' WHOLE HOUSE IS LIKE THAT- JUST ABOUT ALL TH' SERVANTS HAVE PULLED OUT- SEEM TO BE SCARED THEY WOULDN'T GET THEIR PAY-

WHAT ARE YOU LOOKIN' AT? IS THERE SOMEBODY OUT IN FRONT?
HAROLD GRAY

DOZENS OF TRADES·PERSONS- BILL·COLLECTORS HAND CLERKS FROM SOLICITORS' HOFFICES WITH LEGAL DOCUMENTS - THE MARSTER SAYS NOT TO HADMIT ANYONE- HIT'S HAWFUL, MISS ANNIE- HI DON'T LIKE IT HAT ALL-
Reg. U. S. Pat. Off., Copyright, 1931, by The Chicago Tribune

HM-M-M----THAT'S FUNNY- NOT A SOUL IN THE BUTLER'S PANTRY- AND NO SIGN OF ANYONE HERE IN THE KITCHEN-

HERE'S SOME STUFF LEFT OVER FROM LAST NIGHT- COLD BEANS AND A DRUM-STICK- AND SOME MILK- AND I KNOW WHERE THE BREAD IS-
Reg. U. S. Pat. Off.; Copyright, 1931, by The Chicago Tribune.

WELL, YOU AND I AREN'T FUSSY, SANDY- FOOD IS FOOD- WE'LL GET ALONG, NO MATTER WHAT HAPPENS - BUT THIS PLACE SURE IS GOIN' TO TH' DOGS A MILE A MINUTE- EH, SANDY?
ARF!
HAROLD GRAY

HELLO! HELLO! OPERATOR!!! HELLO, CENTRAL! HELLO!!!
CLICK!
CLICK!

HEY! WHAT'S THE MATTER WITH THE PHONE? I CAN'T EVEN GET THE OPERATOR-

HI MEANT TO TELL YOU- THERE WAS A NOTICE SOME TIME AGO- HIT WAS ABOUT THE BILL NOT BEING PAID, SIR- HI FANCY THEY HAVE DISCONTINUED THE SERVICE, SIR-

POOR "DADDY"- I NEVER SAW HIM THIS WAY BEFORE- IT CAN'T BE MONEY, SANDY. WHY, HE'S GOT MILLIONS- IT MUST BE SOMETHING ELSE-
HAROLD GRAY
Reg. U. S. Pat. Off., Copyright, 1931, by The Chicago Tribune

February 2–4, 1931

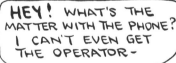

I KNOW- YOU'RE FROM BULLION'S LAWYERS- WELL, HAND ME THE PAPER AND GET IT OVER WITH-

ER, I WAS INSTRUCTED TO SAY, SIR, THAT YOU HAVE UNTIL ONE WEEK FROM TO DAY TO VACATE THE HOUSE- THAT WILL BE THURSDAY, FEBRUARY 12- AND OF COURSE YOU MAY TAKE YOUR CLOTHING AND PERSONAL EFFECTS-

WELL, IT'S COME AT LAST- EVICTED! THROWN OUT OF MY OWN HOUSE- PENNILESS- BROKEN- I NEVER THOUGHT IT WAS POSSIBLE- I FIGURED SOME MIRACLE MUST INTERVENE- HUH! WHAT A CHUMP I'VE BEEN- THINK OF IT- WARBUCKS BROKE!!!
HAROLD GRAY
Reg. U. S. Pat. Off.; Copyright, 1931, by The Chicago Tribune.

BROKEN! BUSTED FLAT! NOT EVEN A HOUSE- NO JOB- NOTHING- AND AT MY AGE TO START ALL OVER AGAIN- THAT'S FATE FOR YOU- OVER-PRODUCTION- BAD COLLECTIONS- AND FOR ONCE I FAILED TO PAY ATTENTION TO BUSINESS-

COME HERE, SANDY- YOU'VE GOT TO HELP ME- I'M IN TROUBLE, OLD BOY- I DON'T MIND, FOR MYSELF- I HAVE HEALTH AND MY TWO HANDS- I CAN ALWAYS GET ALONG; BUT ANNIE!
?

I'VE GOT TO TELL HER- I CAN'T DO THAT, SANDY- SHE HAS SUCH FAITH IN ME- AND NOW SHE'LL FIND I'VE BEEN JUST A COMMON SAP- IT'S NOT FAIR TO HER- SHE'S HAD ENOUGH HARD TIMES IN HER LIFE-

AND NOW, JUST AS IT SEEMED SHE'D HAVE RICHES, AND ALL THE ADVANTAGES AND PLEASURES THEY BUY, WHY, SHE'LL FIND HERSELF PENNILESS AGAIN- HOW CAN I EVER TELL HER THAT, SANDY? BUT I MUST TELL HER- SANDY, I'VE BEEN A WEAK, FUMBLING OLD FOOL-
HAROLD GRAY

WELL, I'VE GOT TO TELL ANNIE THAT I'M A PAUPER, AND ALL THAT IT MEANS, EVEN IF THE WORDS CHOKE ME- BUT HOW AM I GOING TO TELL HER? AND HOW WILL SHE TAKE IT? HOW CAN SHE HELP LOSING HER RESPECT FOR ME?

OH, ER, HELLO, ANNIE-
HELLO, "DADDY"- THE BUTLER SAID YOU WANTED TO SEE ME- WHAT IS IT, "DADDY"?

OH-- ER-- THAT IS---- NOTHING, RIGHT NOW, ANNIE- I DID HAVE SOMETHING I WAS GOING TO TELL YOU, BUT NOT RIGHT NOW- I'M VERY BUSY RIGHT NOW- SEE YOU A LITTLE LATER-

I COULDN'T- IT WOULD BE LIKE SLAPPING HER IN THE FACE TO TELL HER- IF I DIDN'T LOVE HER SO MUCH IT WOULDN'T BE SO BAD- BUT ANNIE!!! THE BRAVE, CHEERFUL LITTLE TYKE- TELL HER WE'VE LOST OUR LAST CENT? I CAN'T- NOT YET-
HAROLD GRAY
Reg. U. S. Pat. Off.; Copyright, 1931, by The Chicago Tribune.

February 5–7, 1931

Little Orphan Annie
GEE, THIS IS A SWELL NECKLACE "DADDY" GAVE ME - I'VE HARDLY WORN IT AT ALL -

"DADDY" SAYS IT'S NOT SAFE TO GO AROUND WITH A LOT O' JEWELRY SHOWIN' - BUT SHUX - IT'S BROAD DAYLIGHT - I'M NOT SCARED -

WOT A BREAK - A FUR COAT, EASY WORT' A GRAND - AN' DAT BRAT'S WEARIN' A FORTUNE IN DIAMONDS - JUST ONE O' DEM DUMB RICH KIDS, TOO -

NOBODY IN SIGHT - A DESOITED STREET - I'LL CATCH UP WIT' HER DOWN BY DAT NEW HOUSE THEY'RE BUILDIN' - A TAP ON TH' COCO TO STOP HER SQUAWKIN' - AND EASY STREET TH' REST OF MY LIFE -

FUNNY, BUT I FEEL SORTA NERVOUS - S'POSE IT'S 'CAUSE I'M WEARIN' ALL THIS VALUABLE STUFF -- SH-H-H-H!!! WHAT'S THAT?

YI!!!

HE'S GAININ' EVERY JUMP AND I'M GETTIN' FARTHER FROM HOME EVERY SECOND -

I CAN'T RUN MUCH FARTHER - I FEEL LIKE I'M GOING UP-HILL -

?

THERE!!! HOW D'YUH LIKE THAT? WANT ME TO FEED YUH SOME MORE O' THIS PLANK? YUH WON'T ANSWER ME, EH?

I'LL TEACH YUH TO PICK ON A DEFENSELESS, HELPLESS LITTLE GIRL AND TRY TO STEAL HER JOOLS, I WILL -

HUH! GUESS I MADE AN HONEST GUY OUTA THAT BIRD FOR A FEW MINUTES - 'MAGINE HIM THINKIN' HE COULD ROB ME - BUT THEN MOST CROOKS ARE SAPS - THAT'S WHY THEY'RE CROOKS -
Reg. U. S. Pat. Off., Copyright, 1931, by The Chicago Tribune.
HAROLD GRAY

February 8, 1931
BUSTED!

THIS HOME, WITH ALL IT CONTAINS - MY FORTUNE - MY CARS - MY YACHT - EVERYTHING I HAD - GONE!!! LOST!!! TAKEN FROM ME - IT'S GOING TO BE HARD TO LEAVE IT ALL -
BUT THE HARDEST PART IS TO TELL ANNIE - SHE DOESN'T SUSPECT - THURSDAY IS ALMOST HERE; THE DAY WE MUST LEAVE - SHE MUST HAVE A LITTLE WARNING - THE POOR LITTLE TYKE -
I HARDLY DARE TO TELL HER - SHE WON'T BE ABLE TO HELP LOSING ALL RESPECT FOR HER OLD "DADDY" - A FAILURE - SHE LOVED ME WHEN I WAS RICH - IT'S A LOT HARDER TO CARE FOR SOME ONE WHO IS PENNILESS -
IT WILL BE A TERRIBLE DISAPPOINTMENT TO HER - IT'S ALMOST SURE TO KILL HER LOVE FOR ME - SHE'LL DESPISE ME - BUT I MUST TELL HER - I'LL DO IT TO-MORROW -
HAROLD GRAY
Reg. U. S. Pat. Off.; Copyright, 1931, by The Chicago Tribune.
OVER-PRODUCTION AND POOR COLLECTIONS, ANNIE - YOU WON'T UNDERSTAND IT ALL - BUT THE FACT IS I'VE LOST EVERY CENT I'VE EVER HAD - THE HOUSE HERE ISN'T OURS - WE HAVE TO GET OUT THURSDAY - WE'LL HAVE NOTHING BUT WHAT WE WEAR -
I'M A FAILURE, ANNIE - I DID THE BEST I KNEW HOW - I WAS NOT DISHONEST - BUT I HAVE LOST EVERYTHING - EVEN LOST YOU, I SUPPOSE - WHY, YOU CAN'T CARE FOR AN OLD DUFFER LIKE ME ANY MORE NOW - I DESERVE IT, ANNIE, BUT IT'S BEEN MIGHTY HARD TO TELL YOU -
"DADDY" - IS THAT ALL? I KNEW SOMETHIN' WAS WRONG, BUT I FIGGERED IT MUST BE SOMETHIN' REAL BAD - SHUX! WHAT'S LOSIN' YER DOUGH? LOTS O' FOLKS GO BUST -
HAROLD GRAY
I COULD SEE YOU WERE ALL UPSET 'BOUT SOMETHIN' AND I WAS WORRIED SICK - LEAPIN' LIZARDS!!! YOU WON'T BE GOIN' AWAY WITHOUT ME NOW - AND I'VE BEEN POOR BEFORE - IT'S NOT SO BAD - YUH SAY WE LEAVE HERE THURSDAY, EH? THAT'S DAY AFTER TO-MORROW -
Reg. U. S. Pat. Off.; Copyright, 1931, by The Chicago Tribune.
GEE - I DON'T FEEL SLEEPY - THIS IS TH' LAST NIGHT IN THIS SWELL HOUSE - TO-MORROW WE'VE GOTTA GET OUT - OH, WELL - WE'LL GET ALONG - SNIFF - SNIFF - WHAT'S THAT? SMELLS LIKE SMOKE - SNIFF - - -
IT IS SMOKE!!! THIS PLACE IS ON FIRE!!! RUN, SANDY - CALL "DADDY"! WE'VE GOTTA GET OUTA HERE QUICK! LEAPIN' LIZARDS!
ARF! ARF!
HERE, ANNIE - GIVE ME YOUR HAND -
"DADDY" - WHERE ARE YOU? DON'T STOP FOR ANYTHING - THIS SMOKE - - - KER-CHOO!
Reg. U. S. Pat. Off.; Copyright, 1931, by The Chicago Tribune.
COME ON, ANNIE - WE'RE OUTSIDE - BUT NONE TOO SOON -
HAROLD GRAY

February 9–11, 1931

GEE- IT'S STILL BURNIN'-
WHEW!!! WE DIDN'T GET OUT A SECOND TOO SOON- WISH WE'D HAD TIME TO GRAB SOME MORE CLOTHES, STEAD O' JUST GRABBIN' TH' FIRST THINGS THAT CAME HANDY-
WONDER HOW THAT FIRE STARTED? OH, WELL, WE SHOULD WORRY- IT WASN'T OUR HOUSE ANY MORE, AND WE WERE LEAVIN' TO-DAY ANYWAY- EH, "DADDY"?
YES- AND IF WE'RE SEEN AROUND HERE WE MAY BE SUSPECTED OF STARTING THAT FIRE- JUST AS WELL TO MOVE ALONG AND KEEP AWAY FROM THE MAIN ROAD FOR A SPELL, TOO-
HAROLD GRAY
Reg. U. S. Pat. Off.; Copyright, 1931, by The Chicago Tribune.
GEE, I TORE OUTA TH' HOUSE SO FAST, AND TH' SMOKE WAS SO THICK I LEFT ALL MY JEWELRY AND MONEY- YOU GOT ANY DOUGH, "DADDY"?
ONLY A FEW DOLLARS THAT HAPPENED TO BE IN THESE CLOTHES- WE'D BETTER SAVE WHAT WE HAVE AS LONG AS POSSIBLE-
HEY!!! GOIN' TO TH' CITY? WELL, HOP IN BEHIND- PLENTY O' ROOM- HURRY UP-
GEE! THANKS, MISTER-
WELL, THIS IS LOTS BETTER THAN WALKING. MIGHTY DECENT OF THAT TRUCK DRIVER TO OFFER US A RIDE-
POOR FOLKS ARE MOST ALWAYS PRETTY GOOD-HEARTED-
HAROLD GRAY
AND, AS NIGHT COMES ON, THE TRUCK ROLLS THROUGH THE SUBURBS, OVER A LONG BRIDGE AND PLUNGES INTO THE HEART OF THE CITY-
Reg. U. S. Pat. Off.; Copyright, 1931, by The Chicago Tribune.
YES, I SEE THE SIGN- "FURNISHED ROOMS"- BUT WHAT A DIRTY OLD BUILDING- AND WHAT A NEIGHBORHOOD!!! NO-NO, ANNIE- WE'LL FIND A BETTER PLACE THAN THAT-
BUT, "DADDY"- WE HAVEN'T MUCH MONEY- ANY BETTER PLACE WILL COST TOO MUCH- WE OUGHTA GET A CHEAP ROOM AN' HAVE A LITTLE DOUGH LEFT FOR EATS- AT LEAST TILL YOU GET A JOB-
WELL, MAYBE YOU'RE RIGHT, ANNIE- STILL, I CAN'T BRING MYSELF TO LET YOU LIVE IN A CHEAP ROOMING HOUSE IF WE CAN HELP IT-
AW, DON'T WORRY 'BOUT ME, "DADDY"- I'VE NOT ALWAYS HAD IT SO SWELL,- YUH KNOW- AND SOME O' THESE CHEAP DUMPS AREN'T SO BAD- LET'S GO IN AND LOOK AT SOME OF 'EM, ANYWAY-
HAROLD GRAY
Reg. U. S. Pat. Off.; Copyright, 1931, by The Chicago Tribune.

February 12–14, 1931

AW, WHAT'S GETTIN' INTO ME? WHAT DO I CARE WHAT HAPPENS TO ANY OF 'EM? HUH - I MUST BE GETTIN' TO BE AN OLD SOFTIE -

CHAPTER FIVE

GOOD NEIGHBOR POLICY

IN WHICH ANNIE

AND HER "DADDY" FIND GREEN PASTURES AMIDST HARD TIMES

GAINS TWO TRIED-AND-TRUE FRIENDS AMONG THEIR LOWLY SURROUNDINGS

AND MAY VERY WELL END UP AN ORPHAN FOR A SECOND TIME...

Little Orphan Annie
FURNISHED ROOM
LOOK, "DADDY,"- THERE'S A PLACE FOR RENT-

WE'RE LOOKIN' FOR A ONE-ROOM APARTMENT- SOMETHIN' WITH A KITCHENETTE IF YOU HAVE IT-
I'LL SHOW YOU WHAT I'VE GOT-

ONLY THING VACANT NOW IS THE FOURTH FLOOR BACK- YOU CAN LOOK AT IT, BUT YOU WON'T LIKE IT-

HM-M- ONE WINDOW- BUT BEIN' UP ON TH' FOURTH FLOOR IT LETS IN SOME LIGHT-
WELL, THIS IS ALL I'VE GOT- LOOK IT OVER-

NOT MUCH OF A KITCHENETTE- JUST A CLOSET WITH A GAS PLATE- BUT IT COULD BE WORSE- WE CAN GET BY HERE O. K.-

YUH SEE, WE HAVEN'T MUCH DOUGH- BUT "DADDY'S" GOIN' TO GET A JOB RIGHT AWAY- HE HAD MILLIONS BUT HE LOST EVERY CENT-
OH, YEAH? WELL, THE RENT'LL BE TWENTY BUCKS A MONTH, IN ADVANCE- D'YUH WANT THE ROOM, OR DON'TCHA?

WE'LL TAKE IT FOR A MONTH- THERE Y'ARE- A TEN AND TWO FIVES-
SAY! IS THAT YOUR DOG?

GIT OUTA HERE! I'LL HAVE NO MUTTS IN MY HOUSE DRAGGIN' IN BONES AN.......
HEY!

DON'T YOU DARE TOUCH SANDY- IF HE CAN'T STAY HERE TH' DEAL'S OFF- C'MON- GIMME BACK MY DOUGH- HURRY UP- WE'RE GOIN'-

HM-M---- SPUNKY, AREN'T YUH? HA-HA-HA--- REG'LAR LITTLE WILD-CAT- I LIKE A KID WITH GINGER-

OH, THANKS! BUT WHY GIVE ME BACK FIVE DOLLARS?
AW, DON'T THANK ME! TH' RENT'S FIFTEEN TO YOU- THAT'S ALL- AND YUH CAN KEEP YER DOG- HUH! I MUST BE GETTIN' SOFT-
HAROLD GRAY

I KNOW IT WAS AN AWFUL JOLT LOSIN' EVER'THING SO SUDDEN, "DADDY"- BUT DON'T YOU WORRY- LOOKIE- SHE GAVE ME BACK FIVE BUCKS- WE CAN LIVE ON THAT FOR A WEEK DOWN HERE- AND YOU'LL GET A SWELL JOB IN NO TIME, SURE- WE'RE SITTIN' PRETTY-
Reg. U. S. Pat. Off.; Copyright, 1931, by The Chicago Tribune

February 15, 1931
GOOD NEIGHBOR POLICY

HERE'S TH' LINEN THAT GOES WITH THIS ROOM- BETTER KEEP THESE TOWELS IN HERE- IF YOU LEAVE 'EM IN THE BATH-ROOM SOME O' THE OTHER ROOMERS ARE LIABLE TO TAKE 'EM, BY MISTAKE-
THANKS-
HUH! TWO RAGGED OLD TOWELS- HAVE TO USE ONE FOR A DISH TOWEL- SEE TH' HOLES- MORE HOLES 'N A PIECE OF LACE-
THAT'S AN OUTRAGE- SO THAT'S OUR "LINEN"- WHERE ARE THE NAPKINS AND TABLE CLOTH AND EXTRA SHEETS?
AW, NEVER MIND- WE'VE GOT A WARM ROOM- A BED AND A COT- A GAS STOVE AND DISHES AND A TABLE AND TWO CHAIRS- WE'LL GET BY TILL YOU GET A JOB- DO YOU SEE ANYTHING IN THE PAPER THAT LOOKS GOOD?
WELL, HERE ARE A FEW POSITIONS OPEN FOR EXECUTIVES- THEY DON'T SOUND VERY GOOD, BUT YOU NEVER CAN TELL-
HAROLD GRAY
Reg. U. S. Pat. Off.; Copyright, 1931, by The Chicago Tribune.
"UNLESS YOU ARE WORTH FIFTY THOUSAND A YEAR DO NOT APPLY FOR THIS POSITION": GEE-
HM-M- THAT SOUNDS LIKE IT MIGHT BE ALL RIGHT- I'LL GO DOWN THERE RIGHT AWAY AND LOOK INTO THAT-
FIFTY THOUSAND A YEAR- NOT MUCH, AFTER WHAT WE'VE HAD, BUT IT WOULD GET US OUT OF HERE AND BE A STEPPING STONE TO SOMETHING BETTER-
WELL, SO LONG, ANNIE- IF THAT JOB IS HALF AS GOOD AS IT SOUNDS, I'LL TAKE IT-
GOOD LUCK, "DADDY"-
GEE- FIFTY THOUSAND A YEAR- IF HE GETS THAT JOB, WE WON'T BE HERE LONG- BUT I MIGHT AS WELL CLEAN UP TH' PLACE- NO USE LIVIN' IN A DIRTY ROOM, EVEN FOR A COUPLE O' DAYS-
HAROLD GRAY
Reg. U. S. Pat. Off., Copyright, 1931, by The Chicago Tribune.
GEE- WHAT A DIRTY NEIGHBORHOOD- NOBODY ELSE 'ROUND HERE EVER SEEMS TO WASH THEIR WINDOWS-
IT ISN'T THAT THERE'S SO MUCH TO SEE IF YUH DO LOOK OUT- BUT I WANT TO LET A LITTLE SUN-LIGHT IN- THIS ROOM CAN STAND A LITTLE LIGHT, NOW THAT I'VE GOT IT HALF-WAY CLEAN-
OH, HELLO, "DADDY"- DIDJA HAVE ANY LUCK TO-DAY?
NOPE- I ANSWERED ADS AT A COUPLE OF PLACES, BUT THE JOBS WEREN'T WHAT I WANT- ANYWAY THEY WERE TAKEN BEFORE I GOT THERE- I'D RATHER TAKE MY TIME AND GET A GOOD JOB, THAN TO JUST GRAB THE FIRST THING THAT TURNS UP-
HAROLD GRAY
Reg. U. S. Pat. Off.; Copyright, 1931, by The Chicago Tribune.

February 16–18, 1931

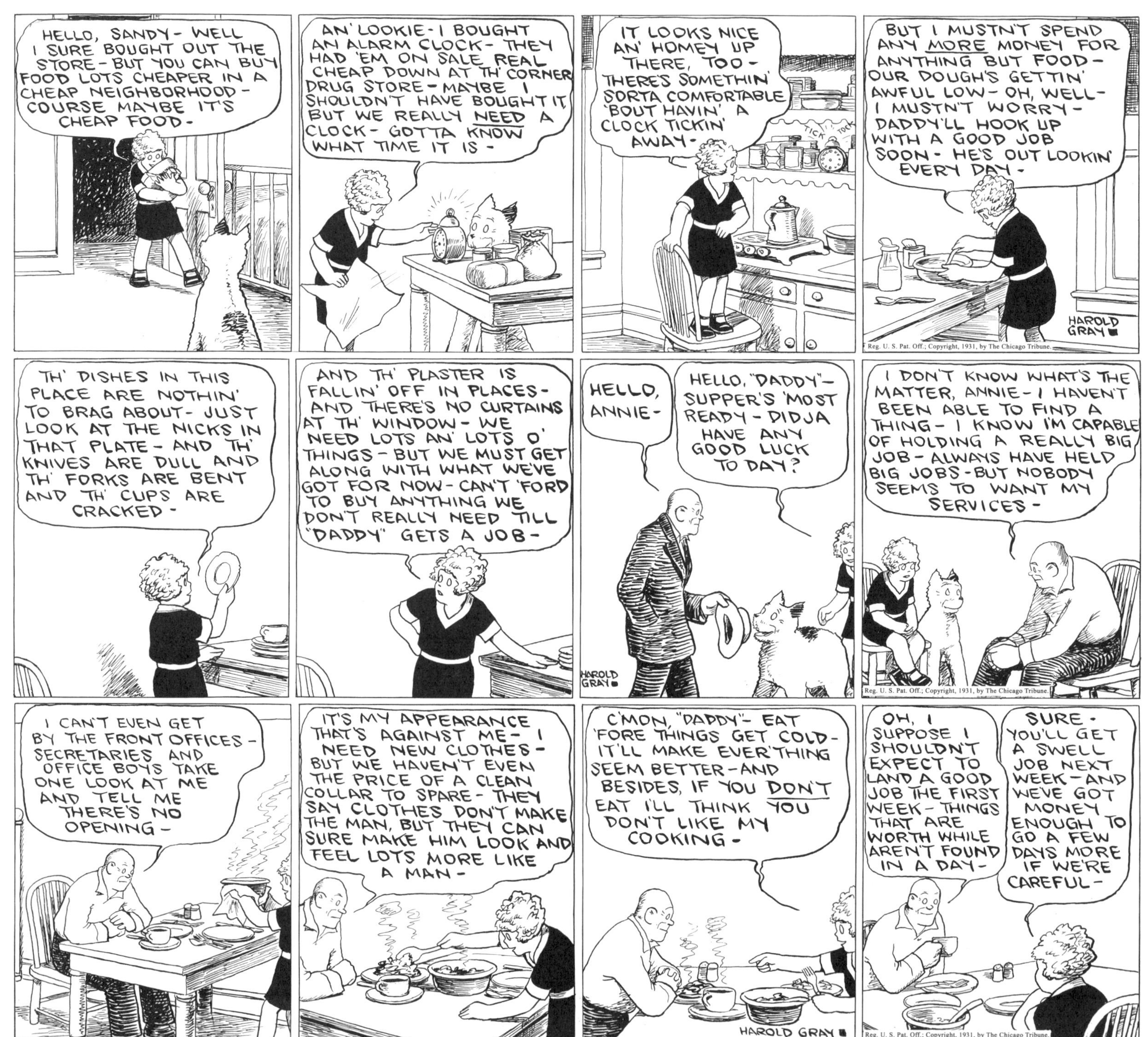

HELLO, SANDY - WELL I SURE BOUGHT OUT THE STORE - BUT YOU CAN BUY FOOD LOTS CHEAPER IN A CHEAP NEIGHBORHOOD - COURSE MAYBE IT'S CHEAP FOOD -
AN' LOOKIE - I BOUGHT AN ALARM CLOCK - THEY HAD 'EM ON SALE REAL CHEAP DOWN AT TH' CORNER DRUG STORE - MAYBE I SHOULDN'T HAVE BOUGHT IT BUT WE REALLY NEED A CLOCK - GOTTA KNOW WHAT TIME IT IS -
IT LOOKS NICE AN' HOMEY UP THERE, TOO - THERE'S SOMETHIN' SORTA COMFORTABLE 'BOUT HAVIN' A CLOCK TICKIN' AWAY -
TICK TOCK
BUT I MUSTN'T SPEND ANY MORE MONEY FOR ANYTHING BUT FOOD - OUR DOUGH'S GETTIN' AWFUL LOW - OH, WELL - I MUSTN'T WORRY - DADDY'LL HOOK UP WITH A GOOD JOB SOON - HE'S OUT LOOKIN' EVERY DAY -
HAROLD GRAY
Reg. U. S. Pat. Off.; Copyright, 1931, by The Chicago Tribune.
TH' DISHES IN THIS PLACE ARE NOTHIN' TO BRAG ABOUT - JUST LOOK AT THE NICKS IN THAT PLATE - AND TH' KNIVES ARE DULL AND TH' FORKS ARE BENT AND TH' CUPS ARE CRACKED -
AND TH' PLASTER IS FALLIN' OFF IN PLACES - AND THERE'S NO CURTAINS AT TH' WINDOW - WE NEED LOTS AN' LOTS O' THINGS - BUT WE MUST GET ALONG WITH WHAT WE'VE GOT FOR NOW - CAN'T 'FORD TO BUY ANYTHING WE DON'T REALLY NEED TILL "DADDY" GETS A JOB -
HELLO, ANNIE -
HELLO, "DADDY" - SUPPER'S 'MOST READY - DIDJA HAVE ANY GOOD LUCK TO DAY?
HAROLD GRAY
I DON'T KNOW WHAT'S THE MATTER, ANNIE - I HAVEN'T BEEN ABLE TO FIND A THING - I KNOW I'M CAPABLE OF HOLDING A REALLY BIG JOB - ALWAYS HAVE HELD BIG JOBS - BUT NOBODY SEEMS TO WANT MY SERVICES -
Reg. U. S. Pat. Off.; Copyright, 1931, by The Chicago Tribune.
I CAN'T EVEN GET BY THE FRONT OFFICES - SECRETARIES AND OFFICE BOYS TAKE ONE LOOK AT ME AND TELL ME THERE'S NO OPENING -
IT'S MY APPEARANCE THAT'S AGAINST ME - I NEED NEW CLOTHES - BUT WE HAVEN'T EVEN THE PRICE OF A CLEAN COLLAR TO SPARE - THEY SAY CLOTHES DON'T MAKE THE MAN, BUT THEY CAN SURE MAKE HIM LOOK AND FEEL LOTS MORE LIKE A MAN -
C'MON, "DADDY" - EAT 'FORE THINGS GET COLD - IT'LL MAKE EVER'THING SEEM BETTER - AND BESIDES, IF YOU DON'T EAT I'LL THINK YOU DON'T LIKE MY COOKING -
HAROLD GRAY
OH, I SUPPOSE I SHOULDN'T EXPECT TO LAND A GOOD JOB THE FIRST WEEK - THINGS THAT ARE WORTH WHILE AREN'T FOUND IN A DAY -
SURE - YOU'LL GET A SWELL JOB NEXT WEEK - AND WE'VE GOT MONEY ENOUGH TO GO A FEW DAYS MORE IF WE'RE CAREFUL -
Reg. U. S. Pat. Off.; Copyright, 1931, by The Chicago Tribune.

February 19–21, 1931

Little Orphan Annie
WELL, SANDY, LET'S CLEAN UP THE PLACE 'FORE "DADDY" GETS HOME-

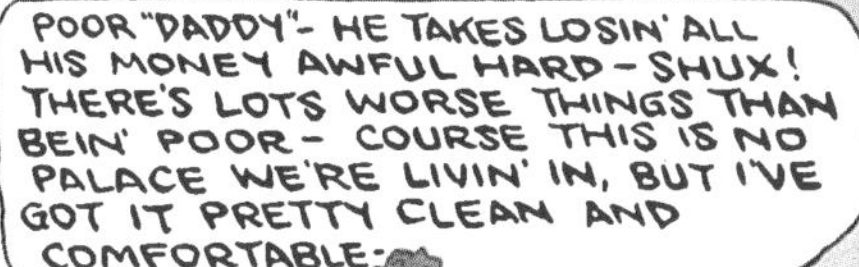
POOR "DADDY"- HE TAKES LOSIN' ALL HIS MONEY AWFUL HARD-SHUX! THERE'S LOTS WORSE THINGS THAN BEIN' POOR- COURSE THIS IS NO PALACE WE'RE LIVIN' IN, BUT I'VE GOT IT PRETTY CLEAN AND COMFORTABLE-

AND WE'VE BEEN EATIN' REG'LAR SO FAR- COURSE OUR MONEY'S 'BOUT ALL GONE AND "DADDY" HASN'T BEEN ABLE TO LAND A JOB YET- BUT HE'LL GET ONE IN A DAY OR TWO, SURE- THEN WE'LL BE O.K.-
HELLO, "DADDY"- AW, DON'T LOOK SO WORRIED- WHAT IF YOU HAVEN'T GOT A JOB YET? YOU CAN'T EXPECT TO GRAB OFF SOMETHIN' GOOD ALL AT ONCE-

HELP WANTED- HERE WE ARE- AUTOMOBILE MECHANICS- BAKERS- BARBERS- BUTCHERS- CARPENTERS- CHAUFFEURS- DELIVERY-MEN- - HM-M-M- BUT I DON'T KNOW ANY TRADE-
AW, YOU COULD BE ANY OF THOSE THINGS IF THEY'D JUST GIVE YOU A CHANCE-

WHAT ARE YOU CUTTING OUT THERE, "DADDY"?
UN SKILLED LABOR- THEY'RE ADVERTISING FOR FIFTY MEN- I'LL GO AROUND IN THE MORNING- THERE'S JUST A CHANCE-

I'VE BEEN HANDLING MEN ALL MY LIFE- BUT THEY'RE NOT HIRING EXECUTIVES- AT LEAST NOT ONE WHO HAS MADE A FLOP OF HIS OWN BUSINESS-

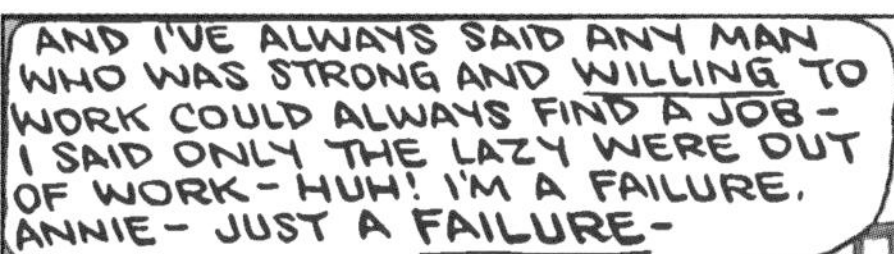
AND I'VE ALWAYS SAID ANY MAN WHO WAS STRONG AND WILLING TO WORK COULD ALWAYS FIND A JOB- I SAID ONLY THE LAZY WERE OUT OF WORK- HUH! I'M A FAILURE, ANNIE- JUST A FAILURE-

SHUX! DON'T MAKE ME LAUGH- YOU? A FAILURE? THAT'S FUNNY- JUST A LITTLE BAD LUCK AND YOU'RE READY TO QUIT? NOT IF I KNOW YOU-

LEAPIN' LIZARDS! I ALMOST LET TH' BEANS BURN UP- PUT TH' DISHES ON TH' TABLE, WILL YOU, "DADDY"- I'LL HAVE DINNER ON IN NO TIME-

YIPE!
LOOK OUT, SANDY !!! THIS IS HOT!
S. Pat. Off.; Copyright, 1931, by The Chicago Tribune.

NOTHIN' FANCY, BUT IT SURE TASTES GOOD EH? EAT A LOT, "DADDY", OR I'LL THINK YOU DON'T LIKE MY COOKIN'- I'VE NOTICED EVER'THING ALWAYS LOOKS A LOT BRIGHTER AFTER A GOOD SQUARE MEAL-
HAROLD GRAY

February 22, 1931
GOOD NEIGHBOR POLICY

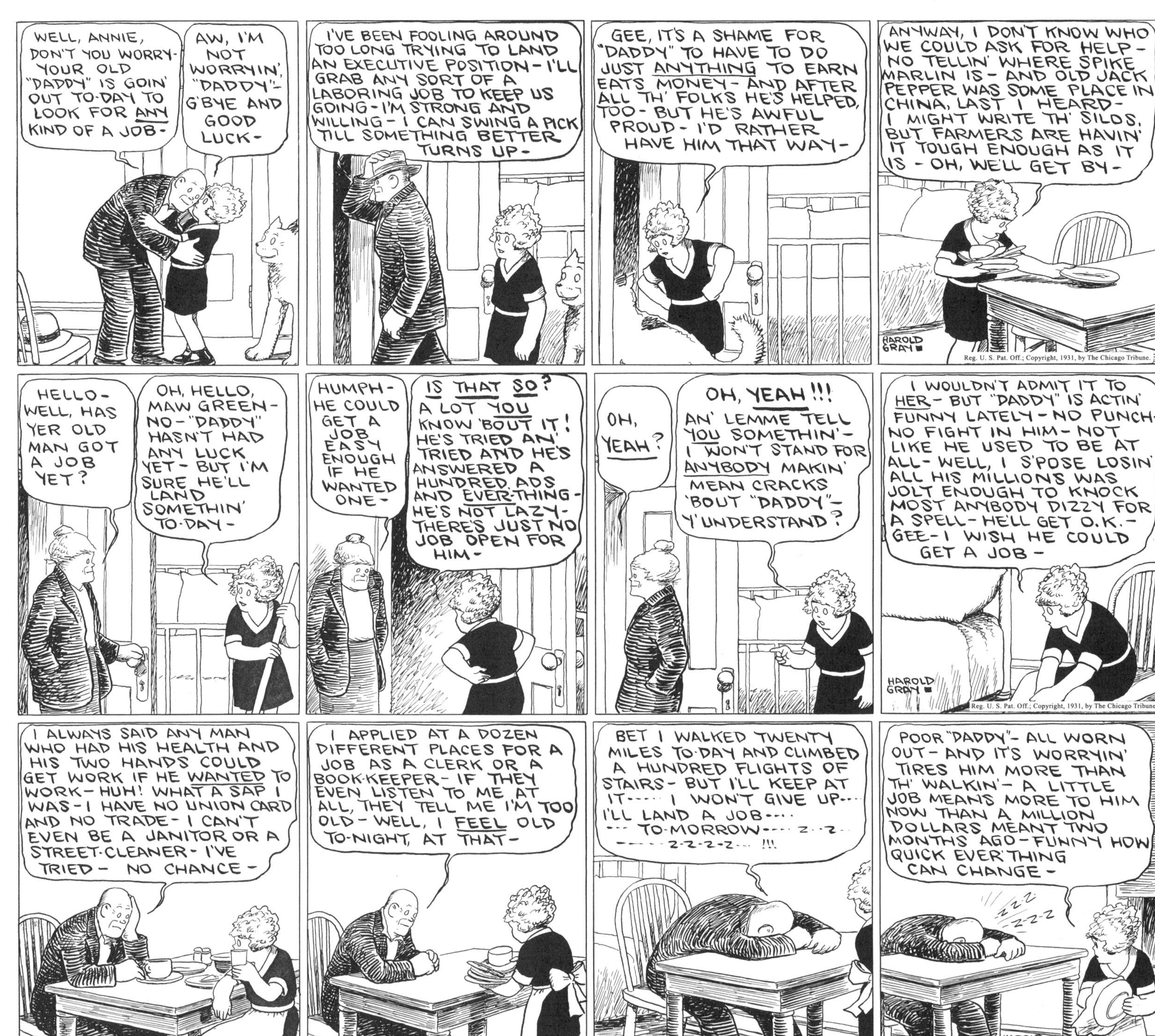
WELL, ANNIE, DON'T YOU WORRY- YOUR OLD "DADDY" IS GOIN' OUT TO-DAY TO LOOK FOR ANY KIND OF A JOB-
AW, I'M NOT WORRYIN', "DADDY"- G'BYE AND GOOD LUCK-
I'VE BEEN FOOLING AROUND TOO LONG TRYING TO LAND AN EXECUTIVE POSITION- I'LL GRAB ANY SORT OF A LABORING JOB TO KEEP US GOING- I'M STRONG AND WILLING- I CAN SWING A PICK TILL SOMETHING BETTER TURNS UP-
GEE, IT'S A SHAME FOR "DADDY" TO HAVE TO DO JUST ANYTHING TO EARN EATS MONEY- AND AFTER ALL TH' FOLKS HE'S HELPED, TOO- BUT HE'S AWFUL PROUD- I'D RATHER HAVE HIM THAT WAY-
ANYWAY, I DON'T KNOW WHO WE COULD ASK FOR HELP- NO TELLIN' WHERE SPIKE MARLIN IS- AND OLD JACK PEPPER WAS SOME PLACE IN CHINA, LAST I HEARD- I MIGHT WRITE TH' SILOS, BUT FARMERS ARE HAVIN' IT TOUGH ENOUGH AS IT IS- OH, WE'LL GET BY-
HAROLD GRAY
Reg. U. S. Pat. Off.; Copyright, 1931, by The Chicago Tribune.
HELLO- WELL, HAS YER OLD MAN GOT A JOB YET?
OH, HELLO, MAW GREEN- NO- "DADDY" HASN'T HAD ANY LUCK YET- BUT I'M SURE HE'LL LAND SOMETHIN' TO-DAY-
HUMPH- HE COULD GET A JOB EASY ENOUGH IF HE WANTED ONE-
IS THAT SO? A LOT YOU KNOW 'BOUT IT! HE'S TRIED AN' TRIED AND HE'S ANSWERED A HUNDRED ADS AND EVER-THING- HE'S NOT LAZY- THERE'S JUST NO JOB OPEN FOR HIM-
OH, YEAH?
OH, YEAH!!! AN' LEMME TELL YOU SOMETHIN'- I WON'T STAND FOR ANYBODY MAKIN' MEAN CRACKS 'BOUT "DADDY"- Y'UNDERSTAND?
I WOULDN'T ADMIT IT TO HER- BUT "DADDY" IS ACTIN' FUNNY LATELY- NO PUNCH- NO FIGHT IN HIM- NOT LIKE HE USED TO BE AT ALL- WELL, I S'POSE LOSIN' ALL HIS MILLIONS WAS JOLT ENOUGH TO KNOCK MOST ANYBODY DIZZY FOR A SPELL- HE'LL GET O.K.- GEE- I WISH HE COULD GET A JOB-
HAROLD GRAY
Reg. U. S. Pat. Off.; Copyright, 1931, by The Chicago Tribune.
I ALWAYS SAID ANY MAN WHO HAD HIS HEALTH AND HIS TWO HANDS COULD GET WORK IF HE WANTED TO WORK- HUH! WHAT A SAP I WAS- I HAVE NO UNION CARD AND NO TRADE- I CAN'T EVEN BE A JANITOR OR A STREET-CLEANER- I'VE TRIED- NO CHANCE-
I APPLIED AT A DOZEN DIFFERENT PLACES FOR A JOB AS A CLERK OR A BOOK-KEEPER- IF THEY EVEN LISTEN TO ME AT ALL, THEY TELL ME I'M TOO OLD- WELL, I FEEL OLD TO-NIGHT, AT THAT-
BET I WALKED TWENTY MILES TO-DAY AND CLIMBED A HUNDRED FLIGHTS OF STAIRS- BUT I'LL KEEP AT IT---- I WON'T GIVE UP--- I'LL LAND A JOB--- --- TO-MORROW---- Z-Z- ------ Z-Z-Z-Z--- !!!
POOR "DADDY"- ALL WORN OUT- AND IT'S WORRYIN' TIRES HIM MORE THAN TH' WALKIN'- A LITTLE JOB MEANS MORE TO HIM NOW THAN A MILLION DOLLARS MEANT TWO MONTHS AGO- FUNNY HOW QUICK EVER'THING CAN CHANGE-
Z-Z-Z Z-Z-Z
HAROLD GRAY
Reg. U. S. Pat. Off.; Copyright, 1931, by The Chicago Tribune.

February 23–25, 1931

DON'T YOU WORRY, "DADDY"- YOU'RE BOUND TO HIT SOMETHIN' GOOD TO-DAY- AN' EVEN IF YUH DON'T, WE'VE GOT PLENTY TO EAT AND A PLACE TO SLEEP-
YEAH - I DIDN'T TELL ANYTHING BUT TH' TRUTH - WE HAVE PLENTY TO EAT FOR TO-DAY- BUT WE CAN'T GO MUCH LONGER LIKE THIS IF "DADDY" DOESN'T GET SOME KIND O' JOB -
WAIT A MINUTE - I'M GOIN' TO FIND OUT JUST HOW WE STAND - BEEN SORTA SCARED TO LOOK CLOSE LATELY - BUT THERE'S NO USE PUTTIN' OFF TH' BAD NEWS ANY LONGER-
LEAPIN' LIZARDS! THERE'S EVEN LESS'N I THOUGHT - JUST ENOUGH TO BUY GRUB FOR ONE MORE DAY, IF I'M CAREFUL - BUT LISTEN, SANDY, WE MUSTN'T LET "DADDY" KNOW HOW NEAR BUSTED WE ARE - GOTTA KEEP HIM CHEERFUL-SEE?
ARF!
HAROLD GRAY
Reg. U. S. Pat. Off.; Copyright, 1931, by The Chicago Tribune.
WELL, IS THE OLD DUFFER STILL OUT OF A JOB?
ER- WELL, HE HASN'T CONNECTED YET- BUT I EXPECT HIM TO FIND SOMETHING TO-DAY-
HUH- HE'S AN OLD BUM- WHAT IF HE DID HAVE HEAVY DOUGH? HE HASN'T GOT IT NOW, AN' THAT'S WHAT COUNTS- S'POSE IT IS HARD FOR HIM TO FIND WORK- DO HIM GOOD TO HAVE TO GET OUT AND HUSTLE FOR A CHANGE-
BUT THAT RED-HEADED KID- SHE'S A LITTLE SPIT-FIRE- AND HOW SHE STICKS UP FOR TH' OLD BIRD- SHE'S WITH YUH OR AGAINST YUH - I LIKE A KID LIKE THAT- I'VE GOTTA KEEP AN EYE ON HER AND SEE TO IT SHE DOESN'T GO HUNGRY OR NOTHIN'-
AW, WHAT'S GETTIN' INTO ME? WHAT DO I CARE WHAT HAPPENS TO ANY OF 'EM? HUH - I MUST BE GETTIN' TO BE AN OLD SOFTIE -
HAROLD GRAY
Reg. U. S. Pat. Off.; Copyright, 1931, by The Chicago Tribune.
I'LL HANG UP YER COAT AND HAT- SIT DOWN, "DADDY"- SUPPER'S ALL READY-
I THOUGHT SURE I HAD A JOB TO-DAY - BUT IT FELL THROUGH -
AW, NEVER MIND NOW, "DADDY"- WAIT'LL YUH GET WRAPPED AROUND SOME O' THIS STEW - THEN THINGS WON'T SEEM SO BAD -
I HATE TO TELL YOU, "DADDY", BUT I MIGHT AS WELL COME RIGHT OUT WITH IT- WE'RE BUSTED - I HAD TO SPEND OUR LAST MONEY TO-DAY FOR WHAT WE'RE EATIN' TO-NIGHT- THERE MAY BE ENOUGH LEFT TO KEEP US GOIN' OVER SUNDAY -
WELL, I'LL GET A JOB MONDAY- I'LL HAVE TO GET ONE - THAT'S ALL THERE IS TO IT-
SURE YOU WILL - I'M NOT WORRYIN', "DADDY"- YOU'VE ALWAYS MADE GOOD - YOU'LL DO IT THIS TIME, TOO -
HAROLD GRAY
Reg. U. S. Pat. Off.; Copyright, 1931, by The Chicago Tribune.

February 26–28, 1931
GOOD NEIGHBOR POLICY

Little Orphan Annie
EMPTY! GEE, SANDY- WE'RE SURE UP AGAINST IT-

NOT A THING LEFT TO EAT, AND NOT A CENT TO BUY GRUB WITH- I'VE DONE MY BEST, BUT YUH CAN MAKE FOOD GO ONLY JUST SO FAR- AND "DADDY'S" TRIED AND TRIED- BUT HE JUST CAN'T SEEM TO FIND A JOB-

OH, HELLO, MAW GREEN- WHEN I HEARD YUH COMIN' UP TH' STAIRS I THOUGHT IT WAS "DADDY" WARBUCKS-

NOT A CRUMB IN THE PLACE- I THOUGHT SO- I'VE BEEN WATCHIN' AND THERE'S NOT MUCH OLD MAW GREEN MISSES- WHY DOESN'T YER "DADDY" BUY SOME FOOD?

HE CAN'T, MAW- HE HASN'T A CENT O' MONEY-
WELL, THEN, WHY DOESN'T THE OLD GOOD-FOR-NOTHIN' GET A JOB?

LISTEN HERE, YOU! DON'T YOU CALL MY "DADDY" NAMES- 'TISN'T HIS FAULT- HE'S TRIED AND TRIED AND HE'S STILL TRYIN'-
HUMPH!

EVERY PLACE THEY SAY HE'S TOO OLD, OR THEY WANT A UNION MAN, BUT HE HASN'T ANY TRADE AND HE CAN'T WAIT TO LEARN ONE NOW- HE'S GOTTA GET SOME SORT OF A JOB QUICK- DON'T YOU DARE KNOCK HIM TO ME AGAIN-

HUH! THAT HARD-BOILED OLD RHINOCEROS- SHE'S GOT HER NERVE TALKIN' LIKE THAT 'BOUT "DADDY"- SHE DOESN'T KNOW HIM LIKE WE DO, SANDY- GEE! I JUST WISH SHE'D COME BACK- I THOUGHT OF A COUPLE MORE THINGS TO TELL HER!

OH-- ER-- WHAT?

WHAT'S THAT? IS THAT FOR US? THE PIE, TOO?
YEAH- NOW KEEP THIS STEW HOT TILL YER "DADDY" SHOWS UP- SEE? IT'S GOOD- I MADE IT MYSELF-
HAROLD GRAY

AW, NIX- DON'T THANK ME- I CAN'T HAVE FOLKS STARVIN' IN MY HOUSE, CAN I? YUH DON'T DESERVE IT- GUESS I'M JUST GETTIN' SOFT-HEADED-
OH, GEE- THANKS!

SOFT-HEADED, NOTHIN'- SOFT-HEARTED! SHE'S EVEN FOOLED HERSELF INTO THINKIN' SHE'S HARD-BOILED- BUT SHE CAN'T FOOL ME ANY MORE- UM-M-M- JUST SMELL THAT STEW, SANDY-
ARF!
Reg. U.S. Pat. Off.: Copyright, 1931, by The Chicago Tribune.

March 1, 1931
GOOD NEIGHBOR POLICY

NOT EVEN A CRUMB IN THE PLACE TO EAT- DON'T KNOW WHAT WE'RE GOIN' TO DO- "DADDY" OUGHTA BE HOME- HE'S SO DISCOURAGED- IF HE COULD ONLY FIND A JOB- HUSH, SANDY- WHAT'S THAT? SOMEBODY RUNNING UP TH' STAIRS-

HELLO, ANNIE! HELLO, SANDY! I'D HAVE BEEN HOME SOONER, BUT I STOPPED AT THE STORE-
"DADDY"! WHY- YOU MUST HAVE GOT A JOB-

BREAD AN' MEAT AN' BUTTER AN' CANNED SOUP- EVER'THING! OH, "DADDY"- I KNEW YOU'D FIND WORK-
YEP- NOT MUCH OF A JOB- DAY LABOR- ONLY MADE THREE DOLLARS TO-DAY AND I BLEW IT ALL ON GROCERIES- BUT WE CAN EAT NOW, ANYWAY-
Reg. U. S. Pat. Off.; Copyright, 1931, by The Chicago Tribune

AND OF COURSE IT'S A TEMPORARY JOB- I MAY BE LAID OFF ANY DAY- BUT WE CAN GET BY ON IT WHILE IT LASTS- SOMETHIN' ELSE IS BOUND TO TURN UP SOON-
HAROLD GRAY

DON'T FORGET YOUR LUNCH, "DADDY"- I PUT IN LOTS O' SANDWICHES AND DOUGHNUTS AND SOME OTHER THINGS-

G-BYE, ANNIE- I'LL BE HOME AS QUICK AS I CAN GET HERE AFTER WORK TO-NIGHT-
G-BYE, "DADDY"- I'LL HAVE SUPPER ALL READY- HURRY, NOW, OR YOU'LL BE LATE TO WORK-

GOOD BYE-

GEE, IT SURE IS LOTS MORE CHEERFUL WITH "DADDY" WORKIN'- HE'S NOT DISCOURAGED ANY MORE- BUT HE SAYS OF COURSE HE MAY BE LAID OFF ANY DAY- HM-M-M- WISH I COULD THINK O' SOME WAY I COULD MAKE A LITTLE SIDE MONEY-
HAROLD GRAY
Reg. U. S. Pat. Off.; Copyright, 1931, by The Chicago Tribune

I WILL TAKE THE ROOM- HERE IS A MONTH'S RENT- MY TRUNK IS OUT IN FRONT- IN A CAB- I'LL HAVE THE MAN BRING IT UP-
O.K.

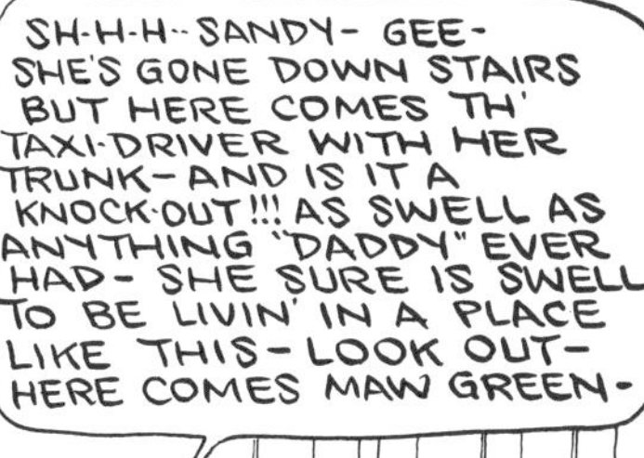
SH-H-H- SANDY- GEE- SHE'S GONE DOWN STAIRS BUT HERE COMES TH' TAXI-DRIVER WITH HER TRUNK- AND IS IT A KNOCK-OUT!!! AS SWELL AS ANYTHING "DADDY" EVER HAD- SHE SURE IS SWELL TO BE LIVIN' IN A PLACE LIKE THIS- LOOK OUT- HERE COMES MAW GREEN-

WELL, I SAW YUH RUBBERIN'- GOT A GOOD LOOK AT HER- NAME'S MISS GILT- WHAT DO YOU THINK OF HER?
ER- I WAS PEEKIN'- BUT I DIDN'T KNOW ANYBODY SAW ME- WHY, I DUNNO- SHE LOOKED AWFUL CLASSY TO BE LIVIN' HERE-
HAROLD GRAY
Reg. U. S. Pat. Off.; Copyright, 1931, by The Chicago Tribune.

YEAH! YOU SAID IT- TOO CLASSY- WHY DOES SHE WANT TO LIVE IN A GRUBBY NEIGHBORHOOD LIKE THIS? SAYS SHE'S WORKIN' IN A SHOP ON THE AVENUE- MAYBE- I'M GOIN' TO KEEP AN EYE ON HER TILL I FIND OUT WHAT HER RACKET IS-

March 2–4, 1931

GOOD MORNING- AREN'T YOU THE LITTLE GIRL WHO LIVES RIGHT ACROSS THE HALL FROM MY ROOM- MY NAME IS MISS GILT-
YESSUM- HOWDY DO, MISS GILT- MY NAME IS ANNIE-
WELL, I'M VERY GLAD TO MAKE YOUR ACQUAINTANCE, ANNIE- SINCE WE ARE SUCH CLOSE NEIGHBORS WE MUST BE GOOD FRIENDS-
YESSUM-
GEE- SHE'S NICE- SORTA HARD LOOKIN', MAYBE- BUT I DON'T S'POSE SHE CAN HELP THAT-
HUMPH! MAKIN' A BIG FUSS OVER ANNIE- COURSE SHE MAY BE ON TH' LEVEL- BUT I'VE GOT A HUNCH SHE'S WORKIN' SOME RACKET- SHE'D BETTER LEAVE ANNIE OUT OF IT, IF SHE IS- I'LL KEEP MY EYE ON THAT DAME-
HAROLD GRAY
Reg. U. S. Pat. Off.; Copyright, 1931, by The Chicago Tribune.
SEVEN DOLLARS AN' TWENTY-TWO CENTS- COURSE I'VE GOTTA BUY A FEW GROCERIES OUTA THAT FOR SUPPER- BUT EVEN SO WE'RE GETTIN' AHEAD- "DADDY" BRINGS HOME EVERY CENT HE MAKES, 'CEPT HIS CARFARE-
HE HAS TO WORK AWFUL HARD AND THEY DON'T PAY MUCH FOR DAY LABOR- BUT IT DOESN'T COST US MUCH TO LIVE EITHER- IF HE CAN JUST HOLD HIS JOB WE'LL GET ALONG GREAT-
"DADDY" SAYS HE DOESN'T MIND HARD WORK AT ALL- HE'S AWFUL STRONG- STILL HE DOES GET PRETTY TIRED AND TH' FIRST COUPLE O' DAYS HE GOT SOME WHOPPIN' BIG BLISTERS ON HIS HANDS- I WISH HE DIDN'T HAVE TO WORK SO HARD-
IF I COULD ONLY FIGGER OUT SOME WAY TO MAKE SOME DOUGH TOO- I OUGHTA BE ABLE TO HELP OUT SOME- MAYBE SOMETHIN' WILL TURN UP-
HAROLD GRAY
Reg. U. S. Pat. Off., Copyright, 1931, by The Chicago Tribune
HELLO, ANNIE- MAY I COME IN?
OH, HELLO, MISS GILT- SURE- COME IN- HAVE A CHAIR-
THANKS- I JUST THOUGHT I'D DROP OVER AND CALL- PRETTY LONESOME OVER IN MY ROOM- YOU'VE GOT YOUR PLACE FIXED UP VERY NICE-
WELL- I'VE DONE TH' BEST I CAN- GOT IT CLEAN, BUT I WOULD LIKE TO HAVE SOME CURTAINS AN' THINGS-
CURTAINS? WHY DON'T YOU BUY THEM, IF YOU WANT THEM?
AW, I CAN'T 'FORD 'EM- COURSE "DADDY" IS WORKIN' NOW- BUT HE DOESN'T MAKE MUCH- ANYWAY I HATE TO SPEND TH' HOUSE MONEY FOR EXTRAS LIKE THAT- IF I COULD ONLY MAKE SOME SIDE MONEY-
OH, I SEE- YOU'D LIKE TO MAKE SOME MONEY OF YOUR VERY OWN- NATURALLY- THAT HADN'T OUGHT TO BE SO HARD- HM-M-M-- YOU'RE A BRIGHT GIRL- YOU LET ME THINK ABOUT IT- I MAY BE ABLE TO HELP YOU-
HAROLD GRAY
Reg. U. S. Pat. Off.; Copyright, 1931, by The Chicago Tribune.

March 5–7, 1931

Little Orphan Annie
GEE! THERE'S THAT GANG WAITIN' FOR ME-

I SPENT OUR LAST CENT FOR THIS GRUB- I HOPE THOSE TOUGH BIRDS DON'T GET WISE THAT THERE'S EGGS IN THIS BAG- ANYWAY, I DON'T WANT ANY TROUBLE- MAW GREEN SAYS I'M A LITTLE LADY- WHAT'D SHE THINK?

HEY, YOUSE GUYS- HERE COMES DAT NEW GIRL- TINKS SHE'S SOME-BODY-
GOT A LOAF O' BREAD, BUT WHAT'S IN DE PAPER BAG?
GRAB IT- MAYBE IT'S DOUGH NUTS-

?

HEY, YOU! JUST A MINUTE- WOT'S IN DAT BAG?

CUT THAT OUT!!!
DAT'S DE STUFF- SPILL 'ER ON 'ER NOSE-

NEVER MIND KICKIN' DAT BREAD AROUND, GUYS- DERE'S EGGS IN DE BAG- C'MON- LET'S BUST 'EM-

? ? ? ?
WANTA BUST SOMETHIN', DO YUH? WELL, BUST YER KISSER ON THAT!

LOOKIN' FER TROUBLE, EH? I'LL GIVE YUH A STUMMICK-FULL, I WILL-

OUGHTA BE 'SHAMED O' YERSELVES, PICKIN' ON A LITTLE GIRL-

WELL, WE CAN STILL USE TH' BREAD- AND NOT ONE O' TH' EGGS EVEN GOT CRACKED- WOW!!! LUCKY MAW GREEN DIDN'T SEE THAT- SHE'D NEVER CALL ME A LITTLE LADY AGAIN-
Reg. U. S. Pat. Off., Copyright, 1931, by The Chicago Tribune

ZOWIE- THE WAY THAT LITTLE WILD-CAT WORKED ON THOSE YOUNG HOODLUMS! SHE'S GOT SPUNK- SCARED O' NOTHIN' AND GAME ALL THE WAY THROUGH- CLASS I CALLS IT- YEP- SHE'S A REAL LITTLE LADY-
HAROLD GRAY

March 8, 1931
GOOD NEIGHBOR POLICY

HUMPH- I HEARD THAT MISS GILT CHEWIN' TH' RAG WITH ANNIE JUST NOW- I WON'T REST EASY TILL I KNOW MORE ABOUT THAT DAME-
WELL, ANNIE, HOW DO YOU LIKE YOUR NEW NEIGHBOR? SHE'S BEEN ACROSS TH' HALL TO SEE YOU- FRIENDLY, AIN'T SHE?
YESSUM- SHE SAYS MAYBE SHE CAN THINK OF A WAY FOR ME TO MAKE SOME EASY MONEY-
"EASY MONEY," EH? WELL, YOUNG LADY- WHEN ANYBODY SAYS "EASY MONEY" TO YOU, LOOK OUT! MOST GENERALLY "EASY MONEY" ISN'T HONEST MONEY- JUST REMEMBER THAT-
YESSUM-
HAROLD GRAY
Reg. U. S. Pat. Off.; Copyright, 1931, by The Chicago Tribune.
HEY, SPEED- DON'T LOOK JUST YET- BUT THERE SHE IS- THE KID WITH THE RED HAIR- SHE'S SMART IN A WAY- BUT I DON'T THINK SHE'D GET WISE TO OUR GAME- SHE'S PERFECT FOR WHAT WE WANT-
YEAH- SHE LOOKS ALL RIGHT- NO BODY'D PICK HER OFF ON SIGHT- BUT HOW DO YOU KNOW SHE WOULDN'T TALK?
SAY! LEAVE HER TO ME CANTCHA? I'LL TELL HER SOME FAIRY STORY THAT'LL THROW HER OFF THE TRACK-
O.K.- I'M LEAVING THAT TO YOU- BUT IT WOULD BE TOUGH IF SHE'S NOT AS DUMB AS YOU THINK-
HUMPH- NOW WHO'S THAT SHIFTY EYED BIRD WITH MISS GILT- LOOKIN' AT ANNIE- WISH I COULD HAVE HEARD MORE OF WHAT THEY WERE TALKIN' ABOUT-
HAROLD GRAY
Reg. U. S. Pat. Off.; Copyright, 1931, by The Chicago Tribune.
LISTEN- I DON'T GO 'ROUND STICKIN' MY BILL INTO OTHER FOLKS' BUSINESS- BUT I'M SORTA LOOKIN' OUT FOR ANNIE, SEE? JUST HOW COME YOU'RE GETTIN' SO FRIENDLY WITH HER ALL OF A SUDDEN-
WHAT DO YOU MEAN BY SPEAKING LIKE THAT TO ME? ANNIE IS A VERY NICE LITTLE GIRL AND SEEMED LONESOME- I'VE BEEN TRYING TO CHEER HER UP- ANY CRIME IN THAT?
SO YOU DON'T STICK YOUR BILL INTO OTHER FOLKS' BUSINESS, EH? THAT'S A HOT ONE- HAW! HAW! HAW!
HUMPH! GUESS I FUMBLED THAT TIME- STILL, THAT DAME IS HARD-BOILED, FOR ALL HER SWELL AIRS- HUH- JUST FOR THAT I WILL STICK MY BILL IN HER BUSINESS FROM NOW ON-
HAROLD GRAY
Reg. U. S. Pat. Off.; Copyright, 1931, by The Chicago Tribune.

March 9–11, 1931

IF YOU CAN KEEP A SECRET, ANNIE, I'M GOING TO HELP YOU MAKE FIVE DOLLARS — CAN YOU KEEP A SECRET, EVEN FROM YOUR "DADDY" AND FROM MAW GREEN?
SURE - I CAN KEEP A SECRET - MISS GILT -
WELL, YOU SEE I WANT TO PLAY A JOKE ON A FRIEND OF MINE - I CAN'T TELL YOU ANY MORE THAN THAT NOW - BUT HERE'S ALL YOU'LL HAVE TO DO, PROBABLY ON MONDAY -
YOU'LL BE STANDING IN A DOOR-WAY - A MAN WILL COME ALONG AND HAND YOU A PACKAGE AND WALK RIGHT ON - YOU STICK THE PACKAGE IN YOUR DRESS AND WALK BACK HOME HERE - THAT'S ALL - CAN YOU DO THAT?
SURE - BUT...
THAT'S ALL THERE'LL BE TO IT - IT'S JUST A LITTLE JOKE - I'LL TELL YOU ALL ABOUT IT LATER - BUT, REMEMBER - NOT A WORD - PROMISE?
SURE - I PROMISE -
HAROLD GRAY
Reg. U. S. Pat. Off.; Copyright, 1931, by The Chicago Tribune.
WELL, I SEE YER "DADDY" GOIN' OUT - HE'S WORKIN' STEADY NOW, EH?
YESSUM - HE'S GETTIN' ALONG REAL GOOD - IT'S AWFUL HARD WORK, BUT HE SAYS HE DOESN'T MIND -
SAY, WHAT'S THIS GILT DAME GOT UP HER SLEEVE? WHAT WAS SHE IN HERE WHISPERIN' TO YOU ABOUT YESTERDAY?
WELL - ER - AW - IT WAS NOTHIN' - JUST A LITTLE JOKE ON SOME FRIEND O' HERS - I PROMISED NOT TO TELL ANYBODY -
JOKE, EH? AND YOU PROMISED NOT TO TELL - SECRETS!!! IF YOU WAS MY KID I'D SWEAT ANY SECRETS YOU HAD OUT O' YOU WITH A SLIPPER -
AW, GEE - IT WAS NOTHIN' - HONEST - ONLY I SAID I WOULDN'T TELL - I CAN'T GO BACK ON MY WORD -
JOKE ON SOMEBODY! TELLS TH' KID IT'S ALL A SECRET - THAT DAME ISN'T SPENDIN' HER TIME PLAYIN' JOKES - SHE'S PLAYIN' THAT KID FOR A SUCKER - THAT'S PLAIN TO ME AND IT'S NO JOKE -
HAROLD GRAY
Reg. U. S. Pat. Off.; Copyright, 1931, by The Chicago Tribune.
BE READY MONDAY, ANNIE - I'LL GIVE YOU ALL THE DOPE THEN - REMEMBER - NOT A WORD TO ANYBODY - THIS SURE IS GOING TO BE A BIG JOKE AND YOU'LL BE IN ON IT -
YESSUM - I WON'T SAY A WORD -
GEE - MONDAY - I CAN HARDLY WAIT - I'M TO STAND IN A DOORWAY AND A GUY IS TO HAND ME A PACKAGE - I'M TO HIDE IT AND JUST WALK HOME HERE AND MISS GILT WILL GIVE ME FIVE DOLLARS -
NOTHIN' WRONG WITH THAT, FAR AS I CAN SEE - COURSE IT DOES SOUND SORTA FUNNY - BUT, SHUX - SHE SAID IT'S ALL A BIG JOKE ON A FRIEND O' HERS - IF SHE WANTS TO PAY ME FIVE DOLLARS WHY SHOULD I ASK A LOT OF SILLY QUESTIONS?
Reg. U. S. Pat. Off.; Copyright, 1931, by The Chicago Tribune.
GEE - WON'T "DADDY" BE S'PRISED WHEN I GET A LOT O' NEW DISHES AN' THINGS AND HE FINDS OUT I EARNED TH' MONEY FOR 'EM MYSELF?
HAROLD GRAY

March 12–14, 1931
GOOD NEIGHBOR POLICY

Little Orphan Annie
NOW WHO COULD THAT BE?
NOK! NOK! NOK!

WELL, YER MONTH'S UP- HOW ABOUT THE RENT? I HEAR THE OLD MAN'S WORKIN', AT LAST-ABOUT TIME-
OH, COME IN, MAW GREEN- I'LL GET YOU TH' MONEY-

THIRTEEN--- ---FOURTEEN- FIFTEEN- THERE YOU ARE-NOW WE'RE PAID UP FOR ANOTHER MONTH-
HUMPH- YOU DID HAVE IT ALL, EH? WELL, NOW I'VE GOT SOME NEWS FOR YOU-

THE OTHER TENANTS HAVE BEEN KICKIN'- THAT DOG'S GOTTA GO- I WON'T HAVE THAT VARMINT IN MY HOUSE ANY LONGER- I RUN A HIGH GRADE PLACE HERE- YOU CAN STAY, LONG AS YOU PAY YER RENT- BUT OUT HE GOES-

WELL? WHO ARE YOU, AND WHADDYUH WANT?

UP WIT' 'EM, AND NOT A PEEP OUTA EITHER OF YUH- I FIGGERED YUH'D BE COLLECTIN', SO I FOLLERED YUH-

C'MON- GIMME DAT- AN' NO SQUAWKS, IF YUH WANTA STAY HEALTHY- SEE?

'AT A BOY, SANDY- TAKE HIM!
BAM!!!

NIX! NIX! I'LL GIVE YER MONEY BACK- HELP!!!
OW!
C'MON! DROP IT! R-R-R-R-!!!!

AH HA!

ARE YEZ GOIN' PEACEFUL, OR SHALL I LET 'EM AT YEZ AGAIN?
KEEP 'EM OFF ME-
HAROLD GRAY

YOU'RE A PAL- I DON'T CARE IF EVERY LOW-LIFE ROOMER I'VE GOT KICKS- LET 'EM MOVE OUT- YOU'RE GOIN' TO STAY- D'YUH UNDERSTAND THAT, SANDY?
GEE!
ARF!

March 15, 1931
GOOD NEIGHBOR POLICY

MISS GILT TOLD ME TO WAIT HERE TILL SOME GUY COMES BY AND HANDS ME A PACKAGE - I'M TO TAKE IT HOME - WONDER HOW MUCH LONGER 'FORE HE COMES -
IT'S ALL OFF FOR TO-DAY, ANNIE - SORRY - BE HERE SAME PLACE SAME TIME TO-MORROW -
DON'T LET ON WE EVEN KNOW EACH OTHER - IF WE'RE SEEN TOGETHER IT MAY SPOIL EVERYTHING - I'LL SEE YOU AT THE FLAT -
WELL, I CAN'T FIGGER THIS ALL OUT - STILL, I CAN FOLLOW ORDERS - IT MUST BE AN AWFUL FUNNY JOKE IF SHE'S WILLING TO GO TO SO MUCH TROUBLE AN' PAY ME FIVE DOLLARS BESIDES TO PUT IT OVER -
HAROLD GRAY
Reg. U. S. Pat. Off.; Copyright, 1931, by The Chicago Tribune.
GEE - WHAT A SWELL ST. PATRICK'S DAY PARADE - WISH I COULD SEE IT BETTER - BUT I'VE GOTTA WAIT HERE LIKE MISS GILT TOLD ME - WOW - JUST LOOK AT THAT BIG CROWD -
HERE COMES A GUY, NOW - 'MAGINE HIM LEAVIN' 'FORE TH' PARADE'S OVER - BUT HE CAN'T BE TH' BIRD WITH TH' PACKAGE - HE'S NOT EVEN LOOKIN' MY WAY -
ALL RIGHT, YOU - QUICK, NOW - MIX WITH THAT CROWD ON THE AVENUE -
HAROLD GRAY
LOOK OUT, KID - THERE HE GOES, JERRY - GRAB HIM -
COPS -
Reg. U. S. Pat. Off.; Copyright, 1931, by The Chicago Tribune.
HM-M-M! HUNDRED THOUSAND DOLLAR NECKLACE STOLEN ON AVENUE YESTERDAY - THIEF ESCAPED IN PARADE CROWD - HERE'S A PICTURE OF A GUY TH' COPS GRABBED BUT TURNED LOOSE FOR LACK OF EVIDENCE - WHY, THAT'S TH' BIRD I SAW WITH THAT GILT DAME - HM-M-M---
IS IT SAFE FOR YOU TO COME HERE SO SOON, SPEED -
SURE - THEY GRABBED ME AND FRISKED ME - BUT MY REFERENCES WERE PERFECT - THEY HAVEN'T A THING ON ME - WHERE'S TH' STUFF?
TH' KID STILL HAS TH' STUFF - SHE'S TOO DUMB TO UNWRAP IT - IT'S SAFER WITH HER - SUPPOSIN' YOU WERE FOLLOWED HERE - I'M NOT GOIN' TO GET CAUGHT WITH TH' STUFF ON ME - WE'LL GET IT TO-MORROW JUST AS WE LEAVE FOR THE BOAT -
O. K. NO ONE CAN PIN A THING ON US -
NOW YOU'VE GOT TH' WHOLE STORY, CLANCY - I'M NOT SO CRAZY TO HELP TH' COPS - BUT I WON'T SEE ANNIE IN TROUBLE - WHEN I GIVE YUH TH' TIP-OFF YOU DO YER STUFF - I DON'T WANT ANY THANKS - YER CAPTAIN WILL GRAB ALL TH' CREDIT ANYWAY -
HAROLD GRAY
Reg. U. S. Pat. Off.; Copyright, 1931, by The Chicago Tribune.

March 16–18, 1931

FIVE BUCKS - THAT WAS SURE EASY MONEY - WONDER WHAT TH' JOKE WAS? MISS GILT WAS GOIN' TO TELL ME WHEN I GAVE HER THAT PACKAGE, BUT THAT GUY WHO HANDED IT TO ME WAS THERE TOO - MAYBE SHE DIDN'T WANT TO SPILL IT IN FRONT OF HIM -
LOOK OUT!
UP WITH 'EM!
NO YUH DON'T!
ALL RIGHT, CLANCY I'VE GOT HIM -
HERE'S TH' STUFF ALL RIGHT, BOYS!
WHAT TH'--- ?
I TELL YUH I'VE BEEN FRAMED -
I'LL GET SOMEBODY FOR THIS -
OH, YEAH?
WHY, THEY'RE PUTTIN' MISS GILT AND THAT SWELL GUY INTO A PATROL WAGON - WHAT'LL MAW GREEN THINK WHEN SHE HEARS 'BOUT THIS?
HAROLD GRAY
Reg. U. S. Pat. Off. Copyright, 1931, by The Chicago Tribune.
WELL, I S'POSE YOU SAW WHAT'S HAPPENED TO YER PALS - THIEVES - GREAT FOLKS YOU TIE UP WITH - HAVIN' SECRETS WITH A DAME LIKE MISS GILT - HUH!!!
BUT I DIDN'T KNOW - HONEST I DIDN'T -
DIDN'T KNOW, EH? OF COURSE YOU DIDN'T - YOU LET 'EM PLAY YOU FOR A SUCKER - LUCKY FOR YOU TH' COPS DIDN'T GRAB YOU WITH THOSE JEWELS - FOLKS HAVE MORE USE FOR A SMART CROOK THAN THEY HAVE FOR A DUMMY -
SECRETS - IF YUH'D TOLD ME, OR TOLD YER "DADDY" YUH'D NOT HAVE GOT MIXED UP IN THIS THING - IF A DEAL IS HONEST IT CAN BE TALKED ABOUT IN TH' OPEN - AFTER THIS STAY OUT OF ANYTHING YUH DON'T UNDERSTAND - KEEP TH' FIVE BUCKS THEY SLIPPED YUH - YOU EARNED IT FAIR - BUT, FROM NOW ON, WATCH YER STEP -
YESSUM -
LEAPIN' LIZARDS!!! I MIGHT HAVE BEEN IN JAIL - HOW WAS I TO KNOW? BUT SHE KNEW - SHE KNOWS EVER'THING - EVEN 'BOUT TH' FIVE BUCKS - B'LIEVE ME, I'M GOIN' TO ASK HER FROM NOW ON 'FORE I DO ANYTHING -
HAROLD GRAY
Reg. U. S. Pat. Off.; Copyright, 1931, by The Chicago Tribune.
WELL, I GUESS MISS GILT WON'T BE NEEDIN' THAT ROOM FOR TWENTY YEARS OR SO - SHE WAS A SLICK ONE - IF SHE'D LEFT ANNIE OUT OF IT SHE'D HAVE GOT AWAY WITH IT, TOO - BUT THEY ALL MAKE MISTAKES -
FURNISHED ROOM FOR RENT
'LO, CLANCY -
'LO, MAW GREEN -
FURNISHED ROOM FOR RENT
HELLO, ANNIE - SO YOU'RE LIVING AT MAW GREEN'S - SHE SEEMS TO THINK QUITE A LOT OF YOU -
ER, YES SIR, CLANCY - MAW GREEN SURE HAS BEEN MIGHTY SWELL TO ME -
NOW I WONDER HOW MUCH CLANCY KNOWS - PLENTY, I'LL BET - 'MAGINE TRYIN' TO KEEP A SECRET FROM HIM, OR FROM MAW GREEN - FROM NOW ON I'M TELLIN' THEM EVER'THING I EVEN THINK -
HAROLD GRAY
Reg. U. S. Pat. Off.; Copyright, 1931, by The Chicago Tribune.

March 19–21, 1931

Little Orphan Annie
HOW MUCH MONEY HAVE WE, "DADDY"?

WELL, NOT VERY MUCH, ANNIE, BUT ENOUGH TO LIVE ON FOR THE NEXT WEEK IF WE'RE CAREFUL, AND MAYBE A DOLLAR OR TWO OVER-
SAY, "DADDY"- I'VE BEEN THINKIN'- CAN I HAVE A QUARTER TO SPEND JUST AS I PLEASE AND NO QUESTIONS ASKED?

WHY, IT'S ALL YOURS, ANNIE, AS MUCH AS IT IS MINE- GO AHEAD- HELP YOURSELF-
THANKS- JUST A QUARTER- THAT'S ALL I WANT-

THAT'S WHERE YUH GET TH' KICK OUTA MONEY- BEIN' ABLE TO SPEND A LITTLE, NOW AND THEN, MAKIN' SOMEBODY HAPPY-

GEE, JOE- DO I GET ALL THOSE VIOLETS FOR ONLY A QUARTER-
ONLY A QUARTER TO YOU, MEES ANNIE-

SNIFF-SNIFF--- UM-M-M-M-- DO THEY SMELL SWELL?!!! AND AM I GOIN' TO PULL A S'PRISE WHEN I SHOW UP WITH THESE? JUST WAIT-

WELL, WHADDYUH WANT?
ER, HELLO, MAW GREEN- I DIDN'T MEAN TO BOTHER YOU BY KNOCKIN'- BUT I'VE GOT SOMETHIN' FOR YOU- THAT IS--- ER--- ER--

VIOLETS-
HERE- TAKE 'EM-

THESE? FOR ME? WASTING YER MONEY ON STUFF LIKE THIS, 'STEAD O' SAVIN' IT, EH? HUH!
B-B-BUT, I THOUGHT YOU'D LIKE 'EM-

LIKE 'EM! SURE I LIKE 'EM-

TH' LITTLE ANGEL- GIVIN' AN OLD BATTLE-AXE LIKE ME VIOLETS- WHY, IT'S BEEN THIRTY YEARS SINCE ANYBODY GAVE ME A BOUQUET- DOG GONE THAT KID- SHE'S MAKIN' A SOFTIE OUTA ME, BLESS HER HEART-

WHY, WHY- MAW GREEN'S CRYIN' AND SORTA GRINNIN', TOO- SHE DOES LIKE 'EM- GEE- LOTS O' FOLKS WOULD THINK SHE'S HARD AS NAILS, BUT, SHUX! SHE CAN'T FOOL ME- I KNOW HER TOO WELL-
HAROLD GRAY
Reg. U. S. Pat. Off., Copyright, 1931, by The Chicago Tribune.

March 22, 1931
GOOD NEIGHBOR POLICY

WHAT? FIFTEEN CENTS FOR THAT DINKEY LITTLE SOUP BONE? WHY, IT ISN'T WORTH A NICKEL-
HA! HA! YOU ARE JOKING- AT FIFTEEN CENTS I AM LOSING MONEY- TO ANYONE ELSE IT WOULD BE TWENTY CENTS
ALL RIGHT- IF YOU DON'T WANT MY BUSINESS I'LL GO ACROSS TH' STREET WHERE THEY 'PRECIATE A CASH CUSTOMER-
SUIT YOURSELF- FIFTEEN CENTS IS MY BOTTOM PRICE- TAKE IT OR LEAVE IT-
I'LL GIVE YUH SEVEN CENTS!
TWELVE CENTS! NOT A PENNY LESS-
WELL, TEN CENTS IS FAIR ENOUGH FOR THIS SOUP-BONE- THERE'S LOTS O' GOOD MEAT ON IT- 'MAGINE JAKE TRYIN' TO STICK ME FIFTEEN CENTS- HE MUST THINK I DON'T KNOW WHAT STUFF'S WORTH- BUT HE'S A GOOD GUY- I LIKE TO TRADE AT JAKE'S-
HAROLD GRAY
Reg. U. S. Pat. Off.; Copyright, 1931, by The Chicago Tribune.
IT WAS NICE O' MAW GREEN TO LOAN ME HER TUB AND RUB-BOARD SO I CAN DO TH' WASHIN' EASY- IF "DADDY" KEEPS HIS JOB I'LL HAVE A TUB OF OUR OWN 'FORE ANOTHER WEEK-
I S'POSE SOME KIDS WOULD FIGGER THEY WERE BEIN' ABUSED IF THEY WERE IN MY PLACE- SHUX- I'M JUST AS HAPPY AS IF I HAD A MILLION DOLLARS AND LIVED IN A PALACE-
HAPPIER, I GUESS, 'CAUSE THEN I'D HAVE NOTHIN' TO DO, 'CEPT FIGGER WAYS TO KILL TIME- YER HAPPIER WHEN YUH'VE GOT A REAL JOB TO DO- AND I'VE GOT EVER'THING- PLENTY TO EAT- A GOOD ROOM-
I'VE GOT A "DADDY" WHO LOVES ME- I'VE GOT YOU, SANDY- AND WE'RE ALL HEALTHY- WHAT ELSE IS THERE, ANYWAY?
HAROLD GRAY
Reg. U. S. Pat. Off.; Copyright, 1931, by The Chicago Tribune.
YOU'RE TH' MOST STUBBORN GUY I EVER SAW- I'VE BEEN HERE 'MOST AN HOUR- I HAVEN'T ANY MORE TIME TO WASTE ARGUIN'- TEN CENTS IS MY LAST OFFER-
WELL, I AM LOSING MONEY, BUT THIS ONCE I GIVE IN- TEN CENTS TO YOU-
LEAPIN' LIZARDS! I MUSTA LOST MY MONEY- EITHER THAT, OR I FORGOT TO BRING IT WITH ME- GEE- I CAN'T TAKE TH' CABBAGE AFTER ALL-
I TRUST YOU- TAKE THE CABBAGE- YOU PAY ME WHEN YOU COME IN NEXT TIME-
GEE- THANKS, JAKE-
SHE IS A GOOD LITTLE GIRL, THAT ANNIE- AND WHAT A HEAD FOR BUSINESS- THERE'S NO PROFIT TRADING WITH HER- YI- YI- BUT LIFE IS NOT ALL RECKONED IN THE CASH BOOK-
HAROLD GRAY
Reg. U. S. Pat. Off.; Copyright, 1931, by The Chicago Tribune.

March 23–25, 1931

HELLO, CLANCY- HOW'S THINGS?
GREAT, ANNIE- HOW'S EVERYTHING WITH YOU? GREAT WEATHER WE'RE HAVING-
WELL, ANNIE, I SEE THEM FOLKS LIVIN' UP OVER FELDMAN'S SNEAKED OUT WITHOUT PAYIN' THEIR RENT-
YEAH- BUT FELDMAN HAS THAT FLAT RENTED AGAIN- FOLKS NAMED GARFINKEL- GOT SEVEN KIDS, I HEAR-
HE SURE IS A CUTE LITTLE FELLER, EDDIE- WHAT KIND OF A DOG IS HE?
I DUNNO- JUST DOG, I GUESS- FELLERS OVER AT TH' FIRE STATION GAVE HIM TO ME-
HUH- THEY SAY FOLKS IN TH' CITY ARE COLD AN' HARD TO GET 'QUAINTED WITH- WHY, I KNOW EVER'BODY ON THIS STREET- JUST LIKE A LITTLE COUNTRY TOWN- I GUESS YOU FIND PLENTY OF FRIENDLY FOLKS 'MOST ANY PLACE, IF YER FRIENDLY YOURSELF-
HAROLD GRAY
Reg. U. S. Pat. Off.; Copyright, 1931, by The Chicago Tribune.
HERE, JAKE- TAKE IT OUT OF THIS FIVE- I HAVEN'T ANYTHING SMALLER-
FIVE DOLLARS- I DON'T SEE MANY OF THOSE IN THIS STORE- ONE DOLLAR BILLS, YES- BUT NOT FIVES-
TO TELL YOU THE TRUTH, JAKE, THAT'S NOT ONLY THE SMALLEST I HAVE, BUT IT'S ALL I HAVE- BUT "DADDY'S" WORKIN' STEADY NOW-
WELL, ANYBODY IS LUCKY TO HAVE A JOB- STILL, THEY SAY BUSINESS IS GETTING BETTER EVERY DAY-
HA-HA!!! THAT'S A GOOD ONE ON YOU, JAKE- HERE- YOU GAVE ME BACK A QUARTER TOO MUCH CHANGE-
I DID? HM-M-M-M- I NEVER KNEW THAT TO HAPPEN BEFORE-
TWENTY-FIVE CENTS TOO MUCH I GIVE HER- YI-YI- SUCH A DUMB-HEAD- BUT SHE GAVE IT BACK- JUST LIKE I SAID, THAT ANNIE IS NOT ONLY SMART- SHE IS A GOOD KID AND HONEST-
Reg. U. S. Pat. Off.; Copyright, 1931, by The Chicago Tribune.
HAROLD GRAY
HUH! I HEARD ABOUT IT- OLD JAKE GIVES YER A QUARTER TOO MUCH CHANGE AND, LIKE A DUMMY, YER GIVE IT BACK TO HIM- CHEE- WHAT A SAP YOU ARE-
WHADDYUH MEAN, "SAP"? JUST 'CAUSE I WAS HONEST? IT WASN'T MY QUARTER, WAS IT? JAKE MADE A MISTAKE- IT'D HAVE BEEN JUST LIKE STEALIN' IF I'D KEPT IT-
BEIN' SHARP IS O.K. THAT'S GOOD BUSINESS- BUT BEIN' A CROOK IS SOMETHIN' ELSE AGAIN- SEE?
OH, YEAH?
THAT KID!!! PLENTY OF FOLKS WOULD HAVE KEPT TH' QUARTER AN' SAID NOTHIN'- BUT NOT HER- NO SIREE- SHE'S A STRAIGHTSHOOTER- THEY TALK ABOUT SMART CROOKS- HUH- THERE'S NO CROOK SMART ENOUGH TO GET AHEAD OF A SMART SQUARE-SHOOTER-
HAROLD GRAY
Reg. U. S. Pat. Off.; Copyright, 1931, by The Chicago Tribune.

March 26–28, 1931
GOOD NEIGHBOR POLICY

Little Orphan Annie
D'YUH RE'LIZE, SANDY, NEXT SUNDAY IS EASTER?

GEE! IS THAT NIFTY? $13.98 - COURSE THIS IS A SWELL SHOP ON TH' AVENUE - I'VE GOT NO BUSINESS EVEN BEIN' ON TH' AVENUE - STILL, THERE'S NO HARM IN JUST LOOKIN' -
13.98

C'MON SANDY - LET'S CROSS OVER TO OUR STREET - IT'S ONLY A BLOCK - HEY! AM I GOIN' CUCKOO, OR IS THAT REALLY A HALF A DOLLAR?

LEAPIN' LIZARDS! FIFTY CENTS! TALK ABOUT LUCK - C'MON - LET'S GET OUTA HERE 'FORE SOME SHARP-SHOOTER COMES UP AND CLAIMS HE DROPPED IT -

LOOK!!! THERE'S THAT SAME DRESS OVER HERE IN THIS CHEAP STORE FOR ONLY 49¢ -
GIGANTIC FIRE SALE
EVERYTHING MUST GO
49¢

THAT'S THE ONE AND IT'S JUST MY SIZE - I'LL TAKE IT, MISTER - WRAP IT UP -
I AM TELLING YOU, LITTLE GIRL, YOU ARE GETTING A BARGAIN -

JUST WAIT TILL I GET INTO THIS - OH, BOY - WILL I KNOCK 'EM BOW-LEGGED IN THIS MAKE-UP?

JUST SHOWS YOU WHAT YOU CAN DO IF YOU KNOW STYLE AND SHOP AROUND ENOUGH - COURSE IT'S NOT S'PENSIVE GOODS, BUT IT'S CLASSY - AND CLASS IS WHAT THEY CHARGE FOR ON TH' AVENUE -

WHO IS IT?
IT'S ANNIE - BUT DON'T BE S'PRISED IF YOU DON'T REC'NIZE ME RIGHT AT FIRST -

LOOKIE, MAW, GREEN - MY NEW EASTER GOWN - HOW DO YOU LIKE IT?
HUH! HARD UP AS YOU ARE AND WASTIN' YER JACK ON A MESS O' RUFFLES - I SAW ONE O' THOSE IN A WINDOW ON TH' AVENUE - WHERE DID YOU GET $13.90?

NIX - 49¢ JUST DOWN TH' BLOCK HERE WHERE THEY'RE HAVIN' THAT FIRE SALE - AND FOUND FIFTY CENTS, SO I GOT TH' DRESS AND HAD A PENNY LEFT OVER -
OH, YEAH?

TRUST THAT YOUNGSTER - SHE'S A SMART ONE - I DON'T BLAME HER FOR WANTIN' A FLUFFY DRESS - HUMPH - I USED TO BE TH' BEST DRESSED DAME ON OUR STREET MYSELF - HEIGH HO - JUST SEEING HER MAKES ME FEEL LIKE A KID AGAIN -
HAROLD GRAY

March 29, 1931

HURRY UP, SANDY - "DADDY'LL" BE COMIN' HOME FROM WORK PRETTY SOON AND I WANT TO HAVE SUPPER READY WHEN HE GETS HERE -

WHY, "DADDY"- HOW COME YOU ARE HOME SO EARLY?
HELLO, ANNIE - THE JOB I WAS ON IS FINISHED AND ALL THE HELP WAS LAID OFF- SO I'M OUT OF A JOB AGAIN -

OH, "DADDY"- I'M AWFUL SORRY- BUT WHY WORRY? YOU'VE DONE SO MUCH FOR EVERYONE- WHY NOT LET OTHERS HELP YOU FOR A CHANGE?
NO! SPIKE MARLIN WOULD HELP US IF HE WERE HOME-WE COULD USE HIS HOUSE ANYWAY- BUT I CAN'T DO THAT, ANNIE- NOT WHILE I HAVE MY HEALTH- BUT MAYBE YOU'D BE BETTER OFF THERE WITH HIM.

"DADDY" KNOWS I WOULDN'T LEAVE HIM JUST 'CAUSE HE'S BUSTED- SHUX- WHY, WHEN HE'S UP AGAINST IT IS WHEN HE NEEDS ME MOST- AND, AFTER ALL, WHY SHOULD WE LEAN ON SPIKE, OR THE SILOS OR ANYONE? WE'RE GETTIN' BY ALL RIGHT -
HAROLD GRAY
Reg. U. S. Pat. Off.; Copyright, 1931, by The Chicago Tribune.

SOME FINE BANANAS, ANNIE? YES? A BARGAIN- COULD I SELL YOU A DOZEN MAYBE?
NO SALE, JAKE- I'VE GOTTA MAKE MY DOUGH GO A LONG WAY-"DADDY'S" LOST HIS JOB AND NO TELLIN' WHEN HE'LL GET ANOTHER ONE.

SO-O-O? HE IS OUT OF WORK? TCH! TCH! THAT IS TOO BAD-
OH, HE'LL FIND SOMETHIN' IN A DAY OR SO- I'VE JUST GOTTA BUY CHEAP FOR A SPELL- THAT'S ALL- HOW MUCH FOR A BIG HEAD O' CABBAGE TO-DAY?

YEP- THAT'S ALL THIS TIME, JAKE- GEE- THINGS ARE CHEAP TO-DAY- HOW DOES THAT HAPPEN?
SH-H-H!!! I WAS LUCKY- I BOUGHT CHEAP, SO I SELL CHEAP, TO YOU - BUT DON'T TELL ANYBODY-

TCH-TCH! WHAT IF I DID LET HER HAVE EVERYTHING UNDER COST? BAD BUSINESS, MAYBE- BUT MY BUSINESS- I WILL MAKE IT UP ON THE NEXT CUSTOMER- I WONDER WHY I LIKE THAT KID SO MUCH-
HAROLD GRAY
Reg. U. S. Pat. Off.; Copyright, 1931, by The Chicago Tribune.

GOOD MORNING, ANNIE- COME INTO MY STORE- I WOULDN'T TRY TO SELL YOU SOMETHING- I WANT TO TALK TO YOU- A BUSINESS PROPOSITION YOU COULDN'T REFUSE-

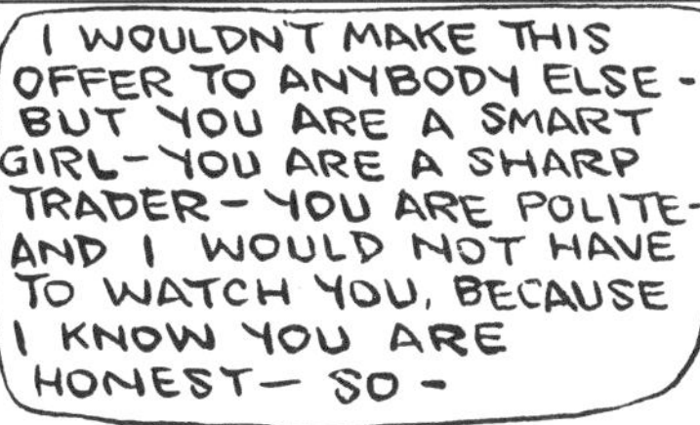
I WOULDN'T MAKE THIS OFFER TO ANYBODY ELSE- BUT YOU ARE A SMART GIRL- YOU ARE A SHARP TRADER- YOU ARE POLITE- AND I WOULD NOT HAVE TO WATCH YOU, BECAUSE I KNOW YOU ARE HONEST- SO-

NOW FOR HELPING OUT IN RUSH HOURS I COULDN'T AFFORD TO HIRE A CLERK- BUT I WILL GIVE YOU ALL THE MEAT AND GROCERIES YOU NEED AT YOUR PLACE- EGGS, MILK, FRUIT- YOU WOULDN'T HAVE TO BUY ANOTHER THING-
HAROLD GRAY
GEE, JAKE- YOU'RE A REAL PAL- SURE, I'LL TAKE THE JOB- IT'S A GO- SHAKE-
TCH-TCH! DON'T TALK ABOUT IT- I AM GETTING THE BEST OF THIS BARGAIN- YOU BEGIN NOW- YES?
Reg. U. S. Pat. Off.; Copyright, 1931, by The Chicago Tribune.

March 30–April 1, 1931
GOOD NEIGHBOR POLICY

HUMPH! LIVIN' PRETTY HIGH, AIN'TCHA, WITH YER "DADDY" OUT OF A JOB AGAIN?
OH, I'M WORKIN' FOR JAKE - I GET ALL WE CAN EAT FOR NOTHIN', JUST FOR HELPIN' OUT IN HIS STORE IN RUSH HOURS -
AIN'T SHE A CORKER? HOW MANY KIDS WOULD GRAB A JOB LIKE THAT IF THEY COULD— AND HOW MANY COULD? SHE'S GOT TH' STUFF, THAT KID -
BUT IMAGINE JAKE GIVING HER THE JOB - THAT OLD SKIN-FLINT - HE DOESN'T NEED ANY HELP - BUT HE MUST HAVE A HEART AFTER ALL -
HAROLD GRAY
GUESS YOU AIN'T SUCH A BAD GUY AS I THOUGHT - SO YOU HELPED ANNIE OUT WITH A JOB, EH?
WELL, IS THERE A LAW I SHOULDN'T? ANYWAY, I GET THE BEST OF THE BARGAIN -
Reg. U. S. Pat. Off.; Copyright, 1931, by The Chicago Tribune.
OH, I COULDN'T AFFORD TO BUY ANY APPLES TO-DAY -
AT THE PRICE, MRS. GOLDBLATT, YOU COULDN'T AFFORD NOT TO - ON SALE, TO-DAY ONLY -
YOU SURE GOT SOME GREAT BARGAINS TO-DAY, MRS. GOLDBLATT - HERE'S YOUR CHANGE - THANK YOU - CALL AGAIN -
WELL, I DIDN'T THINK I WOULD BUY SO MUCH JUST YET - BUT AT THE PRICES I SHOULD TAKE ADVANTAGE, LIKE YOU SAID -
YI-YI -- THAT MRS. GOLDBLATT - SHE COMES IN ALWAYS JUST TO HANDLE EVERYTHING AND SPEND MAYBE FIVE CENTS - AND ANNIE SELLS HER FOR TWO DOLLARS AND EIGHTY CENTS - I STAY AWAY AND LET HER HANDLE THE TRADE I MAKE MONEY -
NO LOAFER, NEITHER - EVERY MINUTE WORKING - WITHOUT BEING TOLD SHE IS RE-ARRANGING THE STOCK - WHAT A HEAD FOR BUSINESS, AND WITH RED HAIR, TOO -
HAROLD GRAY
Reg. U. S. Pat. Off.; Copyright, 1931, by The Chicago Tribune.
WHAT? YOU GET ALL OUR FOOD FOR WORKING IN JAKE'S STORE?
SURE - IT'S A CINCH - I ONLY HELP OUT IN RUSH HOURS AND I CAN BRING HOME ANYTHING I WANT - THE BEST IN THE STORE, FREE - I'VE GOTTA GO, NOW -
GREAT SCOTT! HAS IT COME TO THIS? WARBUCKS PRACTICALLY SUPPORTED BY A LITTLE GIRL? WHAT'S THE MATTER WITH ME? WHY CAN'T I GET GOING? I'VE HANDLED THE BIGGEST PROJECTS IN THE WORLD - PUT OVER TREMENDOUS DEALS -
MAYBE THAT'S IT - I'VE LOST THE KNACK OF SMALL AFFAIRS - I WAS ALWAYS A LONE WOLF - STILL, I HAD SOME BUSINESS FRIENDS - BUT THEY HAVE NO PLACE FOR A FAILURE - DON'T WANT ME AROUND - I DON'T WANT THEIR CHARITY ANYWAY -
BUT I CAN'T SEEM TO GET OR HOLD EVEN THE SIMPLEST KIND OF JOB - AND NOW ANNIE, WHOM I SHOULD BE TAKING CARE OF, IS EARNING THE VERY FOOD WE EAT - I'M JUST A FUMBLING OLD MISFIT -
HAROLD GRAY
Reg. U. S. Pat. Off.; Copyright, 1931, by The Chicago Tribune.

April 2–4, 1931

Little Orphan Annie
IS THIS A BREAK? A NICE, WARM DAY-ALMOST LIKE SUMMER-
C'MON, SANDY- LET'S GO OVER AN' WALK UP AN' DOWN TH' AVENUE WITH TH' REST OF TH' SWELLS- IT'S WHAT EVER'BODY DOES ON EASTER, IF THEY HAVE ANY NEW CLOTHES-
GEE- THERE'S CLASS FOR YUH, SANDY- HOT DAWG!
DIDJA EVER SEE SO MANY SWELLS AT ONCE BEFORE IN YER LIFE?
OH, LOOKIE, SANDY- PHOTOGRAPHERS- THEY'RE TAKIN' PITCHERS OF ALL TH' BIG SHOTS FOR TH' PAPERS- SAY, I'VE GOT AN IDEA, IF IT WORKS-
HEY, GUYS- GET SET- HERE COME MR. AND MRS. VAN BILLION- WE'VE GOTTA GET THEM-
YEAH- MISS THEM AND WE'D LOSE OUR JOBS-
ALL SET- HERE THEY COME, ALL ALONE-
AH, THERE ARE THE BOYS FROM THE PRESS-
WELL, IT'S ABOUT TIME- WE'VE WALKED MILES- I HOPE THEY GET A GOOD PICTURE THIS TIME-
WELL, JUST ONE PICTURE, BOYS, IF YOU INSIST-
CLICK
CLICK
WELL, WE WERE IN TH' EASTER PARADE- WE STARED AT FOLKS- FOLKS STARED AT US- AND WE GOT MUGGED BY PHOTOGRAPHERS- MIGHT AS WELL GO BACK HOME NOW-
LOOKIE- WONDER WHAT ALL TH' 'CITEMENT'S ABOUT- MUST BE SOMETHING BIG- JUST LOOK AT TH' CROWD-
HAROLD GRAY
YOUR PICTURE, ANNIE- LOOK- RIGHT ON TH' FRONT PAGE-
YEAH- I SAW IT FIRST- IT'S YOU, ALL RIGHT- LOOK-
C'MON- HERE SHE IS- ONE O' OUR GANG ON TH' FRONT PAGE O' TH' "REFLECTOR"-
HM-M-GOOD PICTURE OF ANNIE- SHOWS UP FINE- WHO IS THE OLD FAT DAME BACK OF HER?
WHY- THAT'S FAME-
AW, THAT'S OLD LADY VAN BILLION, WHOEVER SHE IS-
YEAH- DAT'S ANNIE-
GEE!
Reg. U. S. Pat. Off.: Copyright 1931 by The Chicago Tribune

April 5, 1931

HOORAY, ANNIE! I'VE LANDED A JOB!!!
OH, "DADDY"- THAT'S GREAT! WHAT KIND OF A JOB?
IT'S A BIG CONSTRUCTION JOB- I GOT IT THROUGH AN EMPLOYMENT AGENCY- I'LL JUST BE ONE OF A GANG, BUT IT'S A JOB- I'LL LEAVE TO-MORROW-
OH, ARE YOU GOING TO HAVE TO GO AWAY? THEN I'LL GO WITH YOU-
NO, ANNIE- YOU SEE THERE'LL BE JUST A LOT OF MEN- A ROUGH LOT- WE'LL LIVE IN A CAMP- BUT THIS WON'T BE LIKE OTHER TIMES I'VE GONE AWAY- I'LL ONLY BE A FEW MILES OUT OF TOWN- AND I'LL WRITE EVERY WEEK AND SEND MONEY FOR THE RENT-
ANYTHING IS LIABLE TO HAPPEN ON A BIG JOB LIKE THAT- IT MIGHT BE MY CHANCE- THEN WE COULD MOVE OUT OF THIS BUM PART OF TOWN-
AW, THIS PLACE ISN'T SO BAD, "DADDY"- IT'S JUST LIKE HOME HERE WHEN YOU'RE AROUND- I HOPE YOU CAN COME BACK SOON-
HAROLD GRAY
Reg. U. S. Pat. Off.; Copyright, 1931, by The Chicago Tribune.
NOW DON'T YOU WORRY, ANNIE- MAW GREEN WILL KEEP AN EYE ON YOU- YOU'LL BE ALL RIGHT HERE- I'LL WRITE EVERY WEEK AND I'LL BE BACK BEFORE YOU KNOW IT-
WRITE NICE LONG LETTERS, WON'T YOU, "DADDY"? AND BE AWFUL CAREFUL-
GOOD-BYE, ANNIE- I'LL SEND YOU MY ADDRESS SO YOU CAN WRITE TO ME- GOOD-BYE-
GOOD-BYE, "DADDY"- GOOD LUCK-
WELL- HE'S GONE- BUT HE'LL BE BACK SOON AND HE'LL WRITE- IT WON'T BE LIKE OTHER TIMES- I'LL KNOW WHERE HE IS AND CAN WRITE TO HIM- I WISH HE DIDN'T HAVE TO LEAVE, BUT HE'S GOT TO GO WHERE HE CAN GET A JOB-
GEE- IT'S PRETTY NEAR TIME FOR ME TO SHOW UP AT TH' STORE TO HELP JAKE- WELL, KEEPIN' GOOD AN' BUSY WILL HELP SOME TO MAKE ME FORGET "DADDY'S" AWAY-
HAROLD GRAY
Reg. U. S. Pat. Off.; Copyright, 1931, by The Chicago Tribune.
GOOD MORNING- COULD I SHOW YOU SOMETHING?
YEAH- YOU COULD SHOW ME TH' BOSS O' THIS JOINT, SISTER, AND MAKE IT SNAPPY- I'VE GOT BUSINESS WIT' HIM- SEE?
YES? COULD I SHOW YOU SOMETHING? SOME NICE FRESH FRUIT, MAYBE?
NAW- I'LL MAKE IT SHORT- I'M HERE TO SELL YOU A MEMBERSHIP IN A SWELL NEW PROTECTIVE ASSOCIATION WE'RE ORGANIZIN'- THE DUES TO YOU IS TWENTY-FIVE BUCKS A WEEK-
BUT, MISTER- I DON'T NEED PROTECTION- I'VE GOT INSURANCE- BESIDES, TWENTY-FIVE DOLLARS A WEEK I COULDN'T AFFORD-
YEAH? MAYBE YOU COULDN'T AFFORD NOT TO JOIN- WHADDA YUH THINK O' THAT? BETTER BE MIGHTY SURE BEFORE YOU SAY NO-
WHEN WE GIVE YUH PROTECTION WE PROTECT YUH- SEE? FROM ANY ACCIDENTS TO YER STORE, OR ANYTHING- GET ME? THINK IT OVER- I'LL BE BACK SATURDAY TO COLLECT TH' DUES-
HAROLD GRAY
Reg. U. S. Pat. Off.; Copyright, 1931, by The Chicago Tribune.

April 6–8, 1931

GEE, THAT BIRD THAT WAS IN HERE YESTERDAY SURE GOT JAKE AWFUL WORRIED - I DON'T SEE ANYTHING TO GET ALL WORKED UP ABOUT -
WHAT'S THE MATTER, JAKE? STILL WORRYING 'BOUT THAT FRESH GUY? WHY DON'T YOU FORGET HIM?
YI -- YI -- IF I ONLY COULD - BUT WHAT AM I GOING TO DO? TWENTY-FIVE DOLLARS A WEEK TO THAT BLOOD-SUCKER!
I AM LUCKY TO MAKE SO MUCH IN A WEEK - AND I SHOULD GIVE IT ALL TO HIM, OR ELSE! IT IS A RACKET - IF I DON'T PAY ANYTHING MIGHT HAPPEN - THE POLICE ARE NO GOOD - ANYWAY HOW CAN ONE POLICEMAN BE EVERY PLACE ON HIS BEAT AT ONCE?
POOR JAKE - HE IS IN A TOUGH SPOT - BUT THE POLICE CAN HELP - I'LL SEE CLANCY ABOUT THIS - HE'LL FIX THAT SMART GUY IN SHORT ORDER -
HAROLD GRAY
Reg U S Pat Off, Copyright, 1931, by The Chicago Tribune
OH, CLANCY - I'VE BEEN WAITIN' FOR YOU TO COME BY - IVE GOTTA TALK TO YOU -
HELLO, ANNIE - O.K. - WHAT'S ON YOUR MIND - LET'S HAVE IT -
SO THEN THIS BIRD GOES AWAY, BUT HE'S COMIN' BACK TO-MORROW TO COLLECT THAT TWENTY-FIVE - NOW YOU CAN MAKE HIM LAY OFF, CAN'T YOU, CLANCY?
I WISH I COULD, ANNIE - NOTHIN' WOULD SUIT ME BETTER THAN TO FEED ME NIGHT-STICK TO THAT HOODLUM - BUT IT'D BE ME JOB, SURE, I'M THINKIN' -
I CAN'T EXPLAIN IT ALL TO YOU, ANNIE, BUT IT'S A TOUGH JOB I HAVE - I'LL SEE THE CAPTAIN ABOUT IT, BUT UNLESS I MISTAKE NOT, HE KNOWS ALL ABOUT IT ALREADY, ELSE HOW WOULD THIS BIRD DARE BE WORKIN' HIS GAME - BUT FOR YOU, ANNIE, I'LL DO ME BEST - SAY NOTHING OF THIS TO A SOUL -
GEE - IT LOOKS LIKE JAKE WAS RIGHT AFTER ALL - TH' COPS DON'T SEEM TO HELP YUH MUCH IN A JAM LIKE THIS - BUT I KNOW CLANCY IS O.K. - IF HE CAN DO ANYTHING TO HELP, HE WILL -
Reg. U. S. Pat. Off.; Copyright, 1931, by The Chicago Tribune.
HAROLD GRAY
WELL, THIS IS SATURDAY - I'M HERE FOR THAT TWENTY-FIVE BUCKS -
BUT, MISTER - I AM A POOR MAN - TEN, MAYBE, BUT NOT TWENTY-FIVE -
NIX-NIX! TWENTY-FIVE OR NOTHIN' - ARE YUH COMIN' THROUGH?
NO! NOT ONE DIME!!! AND YOU COULD GET OUT OF MY STORE - AND IT WOULDN'T BE ANY USE YOU COMING BACK -
O.K. IF YOU FEEL THAT WAY ABOUT IT - BUT REMEMBER - YOU MAY WISH YOU'D JOINED THAT PROTECTIVE ASSOCIATION - IN FACT I THINK YOU'RE GOING TO CHANGE YOUR MIND - YOU MAY FIND IT CHEAPER TO JOIN - AND HEALTHIER!
HAROLD GRAY
GEE! YOU SURE STOOD UP TO HIM, JAKE - WHAT DO YOU THINK HE'LL DO NOW?
I WOULDN'T TRY TO GUESS - I DIDN'T LIKE THAT LAST CRACK HE MADE - BUT I AM AN HONEST BUSINESS MAN - I WILL NOT PAY BLOOD-MONEY, NO MATTER WHAT HAPPENS -
Reg. U. S. Pat. Off.; Copyright, 1931, by The Chicago Tribune.

April 9–11, 1931

Little Orphan Annie
WELL, I GOT A SUNDAY PAPER, ALL RIGHT-

GOT IT FOR HALF PRICE 'CAUSE PART OF IT WAS MISSIN'- BUT IT'S GOT EVERYTHING IN IT I WANTA SEE- BUT I CAN'T WASTE TIME LOOKIN' AT IT NOW- GOTTA GET THESE GROCERIES PUT AWAY FIRST- WE'VE GOT PLENTY TO EAT NOW, ANYWAY-

TH' WORK IS EASY DOWN AT JAKE'S STORE AND HE GIVES ME ALL OUR GRUB FOR WORKIN', 'STEAD O' PAYIN' ME WAGES - THAT'S FAIR ENOUGH-

COURSE THERE'S TH' RENT COMIN' DUE AGAIN PRETTY SOON- THAT'LL BE FIFTEEN BUCKS- BUT "DADDY'LL" HAVE THAT EARNED WHEN TH' TIME COMES-

HEY! LOOK OUT YUH DON'T SINGE YER WHISKERS THERE, SANDY- I KNOW IT SMELLS GOOD, BUT TAKE IT EASY-

HERE Y'ARE- HALF FOR YOU AND HALF FOR ME- BUT YOU'D BETTER GIVE IT TIME TO COOL SOME, IF YUH KNOW WHAT'S GOOD FOR YOU-

SORTA LONESOME WITH "DADDY" AWAY- BUT HE'LL BE BACK SOON- AND A JOB'S A JOB, WHEN YOU'RE AS POOR AS WE ARE-

THAT 'PLOYMENT AGENCY GOT HIM WORK WITH A CONSTRUCTION GANG- THAT MEANT GOIN' OUT OF TOWN FOR A SPELL-

COURSE HE WON'T GET MUCH FOR A WHILE, TILL HE GETS TH' 'PLOYMENT AGENCY PAID UP FOR GETTIN' HIM TH' JOB- BUT AFTER THAT, WE'LL BE SITTIN' PRETTY-

I CAN'T SEE THAT BEIN' POOR IS SO TERRIBLE- PLENTY TO EAT- A COMFORTABLE PLACE TO SLEEP- CLOTHES ENOUGH TO BE 'SPECTABLE- AND OUR HEALTH- WHAT ELSE IS THERE, ANYWAY- I'M SATISFIED-

IF I WAS RICH I'D BE OUT RIDIN' AROUND IN AN AUTOMOBILE TODAY, MAYBE- OR TRYIN' TO FIGGER OUT SOME 'SPENSIVE WAY TO KILL TIME- 'STEAD O' THAT, HERE I AM AT HOME READIN' TH' PAPER- AND I'M JUST AS HAPPY-

GUESS IT'S EASIER FOR POOR FOLKS TO BE HAPPY- THEY'VE GOT SO MUCH LESS THAN RICH FOLKS TO WORRY 'BOUT-
HAROLD GRAY
Reg. U. S. Pat. Off., Copyright, 1931, by The Chicago Tribune

April 12, 1931
GOOD NEIGHBOR POLICY

WOW! THAT WAS AN AWFUL LOUD S'PLOSION - THEN THERE WERE FOUR OR FIVE LITTLE ONES LIKE SHOTS OR MAYBE BACK-FIRIN' - THERE'S A BUNCH O' FOLKS RUNNIN' - WHY, THEY'RE ALL STOPPIN' IN FRONT O' JAKE'S STORE -
LEAPIN' LIZARDS! SOMEBODY BOMBED JAKE'S STORE -
OH, CLANCY - I HEARD IT WAY UP TO MY PLACE - SO IT WAS SHOOTIN' AND THEY HIT YOU -
AW, JUST WINGED ME, ANNIE - IT'S ONLY A SCRATCH - I WAS OFF DUTY AND DROPPED BY FOR A LOOK - RAN RIGHT INTO 'EM - BUT THEY WERE IN A FAST CAR AND GOT AWAY -
HERE COMES TH' CAPTAIN NOW, AND A SQUAD FROM THE STATION -
YI-YI - TWENTY MINUTES AFTER IT HAPPENED THEY COME, THE LOAFERS - BUT I SAW THE HOODLUMS FROM MY WINDOW OVER THE STORE - I CAN GIVE A GOOD DESCRIPTION OF THEM AND THEIR CAR - THAT SHOULD HELP -
HAROLD GRAY
Reg. U. S. Pat. Off.; Copyright, 1931, by The Chicago Tribune.
HELLO, ANNIE - HERE'S A LETTER FOR YOU -
FOR ME? THANKS - IT MUST BE FROM "DADDY" -
GEE, HE SAYS THEY HELD OUT HIS FIRST WEEK'S WAGES TO PAY THE 'PLOYMENT AGENCY FOR GETTIN' HIM TH' JOB - SO HE CAN'T SEND ANY MONEY TILL NEXT WEEK - AND OUR RENT IS DUE - I'LL HAVE TO STALL MAW GREEN SOME WAY - OH, WELL -
YI - SUCH A BUSINESS - THE INSURANCE COMPANY WOULDN'T GIVE ME A DIME AND THEY CANCELED MY INSURANCE - THEY SAY I'M A BAD RISK - AND ALL THE REPAIRS TO THE STORE I HAVE TO PAY FOR MYSELF -
POOR JAKE - AND LOTS O' FOLKS WILL BE SCARED TO TRADE HERE NOW, JUST 'CAUSE A BOMB HAS GONE OFF IN THIS PLACE - IF HE WAS SOME CROOK IT'D BE DIFFERENT - BUT HE'S AN HONEST BUSINESS MAN - SEEMS LIKE TH' MORE HONEST YUH ARE TH' MORE CROOKS PICK ON YUH -
HAROLD GRAY
Reg. U. S. Pat. Off.; Copyright, 1931, by The Chicago Tribune.
WELL - WELL - I SEE YOU HAD A LITTLE ACCIDENT - TOO BAD - NOW IF YOU'D JOINED OUR PROTECTIVE ASSOCIATION THAT COULDN'T HAVE HAPPENED - I HEAR THE INSURANCE COMPANY DROPPED YOU - A BAD FIRE WOULD HIT YOU HARD NOW - BUT WE'LL STILL TAKE YOU IN FOR $25.00 A WEEK -
QUICK, CLANCY - THAT CROOK IS IN THERE NOW - GRAB HIM - IT'S PLAIN AS DAY HE'S THE GUY THAT GOT JAKE'S STORE BLOWN UP -
SURE, ANNIE - BUT NO ONE CAN PROVE IT ON HIM -
AH HA! CLANCY! THE WISE COP - I SUPPOSE YOU FIGGER ON GETTIN' PROMOTED FOR STICKIN' YER BILL INTO OTHER FOLKS' BUSINESS - YEAH? WELL, A SMART BULL SEES LITTLE AND SAYS NOTHIN' - SEE? BUT YOU'LL LEARN - I'M HAVIN' DINNER WITH YER CAPTAIN TO-NIGHT -
CLANCY - WHY CAN'T YUH SOCK HIM ONE, EVEN IF YUH CAN'T ARREST HIM? YOU KNOW HE'S TO BLAME FOR ALL OUR TROUBLE -
A COPPER HAS TO FOLLOW ORDERS, ANNIE - IT'S NO PLEASANT JOB AT TIMES FOR AN HONEST MAN -
Reg. U. S. Pat. Off., Copyright, 1931, by The Chicago Tribune
HAROLD GRAY

April 13–15, 1931

IF YOU'RE GOIN' TO STAY IN BUSINESS YOU'VE GOT TO HAVE PROTECTION - THAT LITTLE ACCIDENT THE OTHER NIGHT OUGHTA SHOW YUH THAT- NOTHIN' LIKE THAT COULD HAVE HAPPENED IF YUH'D BEEN IN WITH US -
WHY, THAT WAS NOTHIN'- JUST A SHOW-WINDOW- SUPPOSIN' YER WHOLE STORE CAUGHT FIRE - YOU CAN'T GET ANY INSURANCE SINCE THAT ACCIDENT- YOU'D LOSE THE WHOLE WORKS-
ALL RIGHT, MISTER- I COULDN'T SAY NO ANY LONGER- I HAVE TO LIVE - I WILL HAVE TWENTY-FIVE DOLLARS FOR YOU SATURDAY-
THAT'S TH' TICKET, JAKE - NOW YER TALKIN' SENSE - YOU GO ALONG WITH US AND YOU'LL BE O.K. - YOU'D BE A SAP TO TRY TO DO WITHOUT US- WELL, I'LL DROP IN SATURDAY-
Reg. U. S. Pat. Off.; Copyright, 1931, by The Chicago Tribune.
OH, JAKE- DID YOU HAVE TO GIVE IN TO THAT CROOK?
I HAVE TO STAY IN BUSINESS, ANNIE - I AM JUST A POOR MAN- WHAT CAN I DO? THEY ARE THE PIRATES WHO LEVY TRIBUTE ON HELPLESS MERCHANTS- THE BIG MERCHANTS CAN FIGHT THEM OFF- BUT THE LITTLE FELLOWS LIKE ME, WE ARE HELPLESS -
HAROLD GRAY
YES, WE ARE DOING A GOOD BUSINESS, BUT WHAT'S THE USE, WHEN WE HAVE TO GIVE ALL THE PROFITS TO THAT BLOOD-SUCKER- BUT IT IS EITHER THAT, OR GO OUT OF BUSINESS - AND WE MUST LIVE-
HELLO, CLANCY- YER HAND IS GETTIN' WELL O.K., EH? I SEE YOU HAVE YER GLOVE ON AGAIN-
I JUST DROPPED IN TO TELL YOU GOOD-BYE - THE CAPTAIN CALLED ME ON THE CARPET THIS MORNING AND NOW I'M TRANSFERRED OUT TO THE STICKS - GUESS MAYBE I WAS TOO NOSEY TO SUIT SOME O' THE BIG SHOTS IN THIS DISTRICT-
HE SAID I WAS BEIN' SENT AWAY FOR THE GOOD OF THE DEPARTMENT - IT'S TOUGH- BUT I'M NOT WORRYIN' - ALL COPS AREN'T CROOKS BY A LONG SHOT IN SPITE OF ALL YOU HEAR AND SEE- MOST OF US ARE ON THE LEVEL- BUT ONE CROOK CAN MAKE THE WHOLE DEPARTMENT LOOK BAD-
HAROLD GRAY
Reg. U. S. Pat. Off.; Copyright, 1931, by The Chicago Tribune.
TWENTY-FIVE BUCKS! O.K. - NOW YOU'RE ONE OF US - YOU DON'T NEED TO WORRY ABOUT A THING, AS LONG AS YOU KEEP YOUR DUES PAID UP-
PRETTY CHEAP PROTECTION, I CALLS IT, WHEN YUH FIGGER TH' THINGS THAT MIGHT HAPPEN IF YUH DIDN'T HAVE A CROWD LIKE US LOOKIN' OUT FOR YOU-
WELL, JAKE, YOU'VE GOT MY NUMBER- ANYTHING YUH WANT ANY TIME JUST GIVE ME A BUZZ - I'LL BE SEEIN' YOU AGAIN NEXT SATURDAY- SO LONG -
YI- YI--- NOT ONLY TWENTY-FIVE DOLLARS A WEEK HE ROBS ME OF, BUT HE STEALS THE BEST FRUIT IN THE SHOP- ANYTHING HE WANTS HE FILLS HIS POCKETS WITH, AND I COULDN'T SAY A WORD-
HAROLD GRAY
Reg. U. S. Pat. Off.; Copyright, 1931, by The Chicago Tribune.

April 16–18, 1931

Little Orphan Annie
OH, GEE- A BASE BALL GAME-

I'VE GOT IT-
AW, SHUX-
HAW' HAW' GIT A BASKET-

OUT!
SMACK
?!

I'M DE UMPIRE- WHEN I SAY HE WAS OUT, HE WAS OUT!
BUT SHE'S A GIRL- SHE'S NOT ON OUR TEAM- WHY, SHE'S NO BALL PLAYER- SHE HASN'T EVEN GOT A GLOVE-

SAY! WHATYER TRYIN' TO DO? TROW TH' GAME? IT TAKES MORE'N A GLOVE TO MAKE A BALL-PLAYER- YOU'RE FIRED AN' SHE'S DE NEW SHORT-STOP- SEE?
HE'S DE MANAGER- WHAT HE SAYS GOES-

AN' DAT OUT BRINGS OUR SIDE TO BAT- ALL RIGHT, SIS- YOU'RE UP- LET'S SEE HOW YUH ARE WIT' DE STICK-
WE'LL FAN HER EASY-

WOW! A TWO-BAGGER--- A TRIPLE--- A HOMER--- THERE IT GOES OVER TH' FENCE--- LOOK OUT FER THAT WINDOW-

C'MON, YOUSE GUYS- LAM OUTA HERE- THAT'S OLD ANVIL-JAW'S WINDOW- IF WE DON'T MAKE DAT GATE WE'LL BE CORNERED-

YEAH- WEREN'T QUITE FAST ENOUGH, WERE YUH? NOW THEN- WHO SMACKED DAT BALL TRU MY WINDER? SPEAK UP- QUICK! WHO DID IT?

SHE DID IT MISTER- I SEEN HER SOCK IT I THINK SHE MEANT TO BUST YER WINDOW-
OH, YEAH?

WELL, I THINK YOU DID IT- NO GIRL COULD LAM A BALL THAT HARD- AN' YOU PIPED UP TOO QUICK, TRYIN' TO PASS TH' BUCK- THAT'S SURE PROOF YOU DID IT- YUH CAN'T FOOL ME!

WHEW- THAT WAS A CLOSE ONE FOR ME- WELL, I GUESS A TATTLE-TALE EARNS ALL HE GETS, AND GETS ALL HE EARNS, TOO, 'MOST ALWAYS-
Reg. U.S. Pat. Off.; Copyright, 1931, by The Chicago Tribune
HAROLD GRAY

April 19, 1931
GOOD NEIGHBOR POLICY

BUT, MAW GREEN - I CAN'T PAY YOU TH' RENT JUST YET - I SHOWED YOU TH' LETTER I GOT FROM "DADDY" - HE'LL SEND MONEY NEXT WEEK SURE - THEN I'LL PAY YOU -
HUMPH! SO I'M SUPPOSED TO HOLD TH' BAG, EH? WELL, I'LL GIVE YOU JUST ONE MORE WEEK -
HOW'S JAKE GETTIN' ALONG NOW? AFTER THEY SHOT OFF THAT FIRE-CRACKER I HEAR HE FOLDED UP AND IS PAYIN' 'EM 25 BUCKS A WEEK TO LAY OFF -
WELL, GEE WHIZ - WHAT ELSE COULD HE DO? TH' P'LICE WON'T HELP HIM - AN' JAKE'S NO GUN-MAN - HE'D RATHER PAY THAN GET BLOWN UP -
HOW CAN YUH PITCH A KID LIKE THAT OUT JUST FOR NOT PAYIN' HER RENT? I BET IF JAKE HAD HER SPUNK HE'D FIND A WAY TO GET OUT O' PAYIN' BLOOD MONEY TO THOSE RACKETEERS -
BUT ANNIE'S RIGHT - WHAT CAN JAKE DO? HE'S JUST A POOR, HONEST LITTLE STORE-KEEPER - HE CAN'T FIGHT OFF A GANG OF TOUGHS HOOKED UP WITH CROOKED POLITICIANS AND A FEW CROOKED COPS AND JUDGES - THE SHARKS ALWAYS LIVE OFF THE POOR LITTLE FISH -
HAROLD GRAY
Reg. U. S. Pat. Off.; Copyright, 1931, by The Chicago Tribune.
HEY, SANDY - LOOKIE - WE KNOW THAT MAN - THAT'S MR. WALSH, TH' CIRC'LATION MANAGER OF THE "REFLECTOR" 'MEMBER? I USED TO WORK FOR HIM WHEN I WAS RUNNIN' A NEWS STAND THREE YEARS AGO -
HELLO, MR. WALSH - DO YOU 'MEMBER ME? I USED TO WORK FOR YOU - I HAD A NEWS STAND -
WELL, WELL, ANNIE - I SURE DO 'MEMBER YOU - HOW ARE THINGS WITH YOU? WANT A JOB?
NO, THANKS - I'VE GOT A JOB WORKIN' FOR JAKE OVER THERE IN HIS STORE - SANDY AND I ARE GETTIN' ALONG O.K. NOW -
GLAD TO HEAR IT, ANNIE - WELL, ANYTHING I CAN DO FOR YOU ANY TIME, JUST LET ME KNOW -
THERE'S A SWELL GUY - ANYTHING HE CAN DO FOR ME JUST LET HIM KNOW - I WONDER, NOW - COULD HE? WOULD HE? I'M GOIN' TO SEE HIM TO-MORROW AND ASK HIM -
HAROLD GRAY
Reg. U. S. Pat. Off.; Copyright, 1931, by The Chicago Tribune.
YEAH - YOU HEARD ME - JUST TELL MR. WALSH IT'S ANNIE - HE'LL UNDERSTAND - AN' TELL HIM IT'S 'PORTANT - SEE?
WELL, JAKE SAID HE WOULDN'T JOIN THIS PROTECTIVE 'SOCIATION - SO SOMEBODY BLOWS OUT TH' FRONT OF HIS STORE - CLANCY TRIED TO GRAB 'EM AND GOT SHOT AT - THEY NICKED HIM, TOO - WELL, WHAT HAPPENS THEN?
CLANCY GETS A BAWLIN' OUT AND GETS SENT AWAY TO TH' BUSHES - AN' YUH CAN'T PROVE A THING ON THOSE GUYS - THIS HOODLUM IS THICK WITH THE POLICE CAPTAIN - SO JAKE'S GOTTA GIVE HIM TWENTY-FIVE BUCKS A WEEK - NOW CAN'T YOU DO SOMETHIN'? JAKE'S A SWELL GUY AND HE'S BEEN A PAL TO ME -
WELL, ANNIE - IT'S ALL OUT OF MY LINE - BUT IT SOUNDS LIKE A DIRTY PIECE OF BUSINESS - I'LL LOOK INTO IT - YOU'RE A RIGHT YOUNGSTER AND FOR YOU I'LL SEE WHAT CAN BE DONE -
THANKS, MR. WALSH - I KNEW YOU'D HELP -
HAROLD GRAY
Reg. U. S. Pat. Off.; Copyright, 1931, by The Chicago Tribune.

April 20–22, 1931

IT'S A DIRTY RACKET- NONE OF MY BUSINESS, MAYBE- BUT ANY RACKET THAT HURTS HONEST BUSINESS HURTS A NEWSPAPER- WHEN A STORE-KEEPER HAS TO PAY ALL HE CAN MAKE TO SOME RACKETEER HE HASN'T ANYTHING LEFT TO SPEND FOR ADVERTISING-
HELLO, CLANCY- I HEARD YOU WERE OUT HERE- I ALWAYS THOUGHT YOU WERE A SQUARE COP- LET'S HEAR ALL ABOUT IT-
NOT MUCH TO TELL, MR. WALSH, THAT I GUESS YOU DON'T KNOW- I GOT A LITTLE TOO NOSEY FOR MY OWN GOOD AND THEY PUT ME WHERE I'D BE LESS TROUBLE TO 'EM- THAT'S ALL-
THIS JAKE- HE'S A SQUARE SHOOTIN' LITTLE STORE-KEEPER, ISN'T HE? NO REASON WHY THEY SHOULD PICK ON HIM, IS THERE?
THAT'S JUST IT- HE'S A DECENT CHAP- HONEST- NO CROOK PALS- JUST A SET-UP FOR THOSE BIRDS- HE CAN'T FIGHT THAT CROWD- HE HASN'T THE PULL, OR THE MONEY TO BUY IT-
HM-M-M-- FUNNY WALSH RIDIN' WAY OUT HERE JUST TO SEE ME- HE'S A BIG SHOT- BIGGER THAN THE COMMISSIONER, THEY SAY- AND HE'S HONEST- FUNNY HIM TAKIN' AN INTEREST IN A LITTLE GUY LIKE JAKE- WELL, IT'S NOTHIN' TO ME- I'M JUST A COPPER-
HAROLD GRAY
Reg. U. S. Pat. Off.; Copyright, 1931, by The Chicago Tribune.
PS-S-T- HEY, ANNIE-
HUH? NOW WHO COULD THAT BE CALLIN' TO ME?
SH-H-- I DON'T WANT ANYBODY TO SEE ME AROUND HERE- BUT LISTEN- WHEN IS THAT BIRD DUE TO COLLECT FROM JAKE?
ER- OH, MR. WALSH- IT'S YOU- WHY, THAT GUY WILL BE IN TO-MORROW
LISTEN- DON'T SAY A WORD TO JAKE OR ANYONE ABOUT THIS, NOW OR LATER, BUT WHEN THAT GUY COMES IN YOU JUST WALK OUT AND WAVE TO ME- I'LL BE DOWN THERE IN THAT DOOR-WAY- AND DON'T LET ON YOU EVER SAW ME BEFORE- SEE?
YES, SIR-
WOW! I HOPED MR. WALSH WOULD DO SOMETHING, BUT I NEVER FIGGERED HE'D START SO QUICK- WISH I KNEW WHAT HE'S FIGGERIN' ON DOIN'- BUT I'VE GOTTA BE CAREFUL AND KEEP MY LIP BUTTONED LIKE HE SAID- GEE- HE'S A REAL GUY-
HAROLD GRAY
Reg. U. S. Pat. Off.; Copyright, 1931, by The Chicago Tribune.
WELL, I SEE BUSINESS IS PRETTY GOOD- SOME O' TH' BOYS WAS FOR RAISIN' YER DUES- BUT I SAID NIX- WE STICK TO OUR AGREEMENT- 25 BUCKS A WEEK- YER LUCKY TO BE IN WIT' AN HONEST OUTFIT LIKE US-
JUST A MINUTE- I WANT A WORD WITH YOU-
OH, YEAH? WHO ARE YOU? WOT'S YER GAME? IF YER A COP YUH'D BETTER GO ROLL YER HOOP- I STAND IN WIT' DE BIG BOIDS- SEE?
YOU DON'T STAND IN WITH ME- HERE HE IS, BOYS- MAKE HIM COMFORTABLE- BETTER TAKE THAT POP-GUN OUT OF HIS POCKET BEFORE HE HURTS HIMSELF WITH IT- COME ON- LET'S GO-
YI- YI- WHAT DOES IT MEAN? THIS HOODLUM WHO IS SO TOUGH- LOOK WHAT THAT MAN DID TO HIM, JUST LIKE HE WAS A SACK OF POTATOES- WHO WAS THAT MAN?
THAT MAN? HOW SHOULD I KNOW? BUT I WILL SAY HE'S ONE GUY WHO IS TEN TIMES AS HARD AS ANY HOODLUM IN THIS TOWN- IN HIS BUSINESS HE HAS TO BE-
HAROLD GRAY
Reg. U. S. Pat. Off.; Copyright, 1931, by The Chicago Tribune.

April 23–25, 1931
GOOD NEIGHBOR POLICY

Little Orphan Annie
OH, SANDY- ISN'T IT BEAUTIFUL ?

GEE- FLOWERS!!! IT'S SPRING, SANDY, BUT 'CEPT FOR IT BEIN' WARMER, YOU'D HARDLY KNOW IT HERE IN TH' CITY - NO BUDS OR GREEN LEAVES AND MIGHTY LITTLE GRASS IN THIS PART O' TOWN-

SNIFF-SNIFF- AH-H-H-H!!! BOY-DON'T THEY SMELL SWELL?
THEY ISS VERY NICE, MISS ANNIE - COULD I SELL YOU SOME? YES?

TELL YOU WHAT I WANTA GET, GUS- A BOX 'BOUT THAT SIZE, FULL O' DIRT. AN' ALL TH' FLOWERS IN IT I CAN GET FOR A QUARTER-
I FIX CHUST VAT YOU WANT- VAIT-

GEE- OLD GUS IS A REAL PAL- I'LL HAVE A GARDEN YET, EVEN IF WE DO LIVE IN TH' CITY AND HAVEN'T EVEN A YARD-

THERE WE ARE- LOTS O' SUN COMES IN THAT WINDOW- ISN'T IT WONDERFUL HOW A FEW FLOWERS CAN BRIGHTEN UP A ROOM?

NOW LESSEE- LETTUCE, BEETS, ONIONS AND RADISHES- CAN'T 'FORD TO HAVE ALL MY GARDEN IN FLOWERS- WISH I HAD ROOM FOR SOME SWEET CORN-

THERE NOW- THE EAST FORTY IN RADISHES AND THE SOUTH EIGHTY IN LETTUCE - IT WON'T BE LONG NOW TILL WE'LL BE HAVIN' GARDEN SASS RIGHT OUT OF OUR OWN GARDEN-

HM-M-M- THAT DIRT LOOKS RICH ENOUGH, BUT IT'S AWFUL DRY- THOSE SEEDS'LL NEVER EVEN SPROUT LESS IT RAINS- I OUGHTA HAVE A HOSE OR A SPRINKLIN' CAN-

NOW LET ME SEE- WHAT CAN I USE FOR A SPRINKLIN' CAN? COURSE I COULD PUNCH HOLES IN A TIN CAN- NOPE- I KNOW WHAT I'LL DO-
THIS OLD SALT SHAKER IS JUST THE THING- YESSIR, SANDY- A COUPLE O' DAYS NOW AND SOME O' THAT STUFF OUGHTA BE COMIN' UP- I CAN HARDLY WAIT-

DIGGIN' IN A GARDEN AND SEEIN' GREEN STUFF GROWIN' SURE MAKES IT SEEM A LOT MORE LIKE SPRING- EH, SANDY?
ARF!
HAROLD GRAY

April 26, 1931

POOR "DADDY"- HE SURE HAS HAD HARD LUCK- HE GOT PAID, BUT SOMEBODY PICKED HIS POCKET- THE WHOLE GANG HE'S WORKIN' WITH IS A BUNCH O' TOUGH CROOKS- I WISH HE HADN'T TAKEN THAT JOB-
GEE- I'M SORRY FOR "DADDY"- HE MUST FEEL TERRIBLE 'BOUT LOSIN' THAT MONEY- BUT SHUX-- WE DON'T NEED IT- THAT IS NOT VERY BAD- WE CAN STALL OFF MAW GREEN ANOTHER WEEK ON TH' RENT- WE'LL HAVE TO-
I WONDER WHAT HAPPENED SATURDAY AFTER MR. WALSH TOOK THAT RACKETEER AWAY IN HIS CAR- THOUGHT MAYBE WE'D HEAR SOMETHIN' TO-DAY, BUT NOT A WORD-
JAKE CAN'T FIGGER IT OUT AT ALL- COURSE HE NEVER HEARD O' MR. WALSH AN' NEVER EVEN SAW HIM BEFORE, AN' I CAN'T TELL HIM A THING- GEE- WISH I KNEW WHAT'S GOIN' TO HAPPEN NEXT MYSELF-
HAROLD GRAY
LEAPIN' LIZARDS! HERE COMES THAT TOUGH RACKETEER- AN', JAKE! JUST LOOK AT HIS FACE- AND HIS ARM'S IN A SLING, TOO-
YI- YI- HE HAS HAD AN ACCIDENT- I HOPE HE DOESN'T BLAME ME FOR IT-
HERE- THERE'S ALL TH' DOUGH I COLLECTED FROM YUH- AND A COUPLE O' HUNDRED FOR FIXIN' UP AFTER DAT BOMB- AND THERE WON'T BE NO MORE COLLECTIONS-
BUT, MISTER! I WANT TO KEEP ON BEING PROTECTED- SOMETHING ELSE MIGHT HAPPEN TO MY STORE-
DON'T YOUSE WORRY- YOU'VE GOT TH' BEST PROTECTION THERE IS- SEE? THERE AIN'T NOTHIN' GOIN' TO HAPPEN TO DIS JOINT EVER AGAIN- HOW DO I KNOW? MAYBE A LITTLE BOIDY TOLD ME- SO LONG- I GOTTA CATCH A TRAIN- I'VE HAD ENOUGH O' DIS TOWN-
BUT, ANNIE- WHAT DOES IT MEAN? MY MONEY BACK- EVERY CENT-
HAW! HAW! A LITTLE BIRD TOLD HIM, EH? THAT'S A CORKER- AW, HOW SHOULD I KNOW ANYTHING ABOUT IT? DIDJA SEE HIS FACE? A LITTLE "BOIDY," HE SAYS- WHAT A TOUGH BIRD THAT MUST HAVE BEEN- WOW!
HAROLD GRAY
Reg. U. S. Pat. Off.; Copyright, 1931, by The Chicago Tribune.
BUT WHY SHOULD THAT TOUGH HOODLUM GIVE BACK ALL MY MONEY? AND HOW DID HE GET SO BANGED UP, DO YOU SUPPOSE?
HOW SHOULD I KNOW? MAYBE HE FELL OVER A CHAIR OR SOMETHIN' AN' IT MADE HIM SOFT-HEARTED-
SOFT-HEARTED THAT GANGSTER WOULD NEVER BE- SCARED MAYBE- YES- WHO WAS THAT MAN WHO GRABBED HIM AND TOOK HIM AWAY IN THAT CAR SATURDAY- MAYBE HE TOLD HIM SOMETHING- BUT WHAT? AND WHY?
THAT MAN IN THE BIG CAR LAST SATURDAY- YOU DON'T KNOW WHO HE WAS, EH? THINK NOW, ANNIE- MAYBE YOU SAW HIM SOME PLACE-
ER- WELL, MAYBE- I DIDN'T SAY NO AND I DON'T SAY YES-
THAT KID- SHE KNOWS MORE ABOUT THIS THAN SHE IS TELLING- I BET SHE HAD A HAND IN IT- EVERY TIME SHE THINKS OF THAT HOODLUM, AND HOW SCARED HE LOOKED, SHE LAUGHS- BUT SHE WON'T TALK- YI- SHE IS A SMART ONE-
HAROLD GRAY
Reg. U. S. Pat. Off.; Copyright, 1931, by The Chicago Tribune.

April 27–29, 1931
GOOD NEIGHBOR POLICY

YEAH - SHE'S HALF A MONTH BEHIND WITH HER RENT - BUT I CAN'T BE TOO HARD ON THAT KID -
MIND YOU - I'M NOT PROMISING - BUT YOU WAIT - MAYBE I FIX IT SO ANNIE CAN PAY HER RENT - GIVE HER TILL SATURDAY -
WELL, IF IT ISN'T CLANCY - BACK ON YER OLD BEAT, EH?
BACK ON ME OLD BEAT, NOTHIN' - IT'S A SERGEANT I AM NOW - AND ME EX-BOSS, THAT CAPTAIN, HE GOT BUSTED AND IS WALKING A BEAT TEN MILES OUT IN THE COUNTRY -
IT'S ALL THE DOINGS OF THAT MR. WALSH, THE CIRCULATION MANAGER OF THE "REFLECTOR" - BUT WHAT I CAN'T FIGGER IS WHY HE WENT TO ALL THE TROUBLE, A BIG GUY LIKE HIM - AND HOW DID HE KNOW SO MUCH - SOMEBODY MUST HAVE TOLD HIM PLENTY -
SH--H-- IF YOU ASK ME, THAT LITTLE LADY KNOWS A LOT MORE THAN SHE'S TELLING -
ANNIE? HM-M-M--- I NEVER THOUGHT OF HER - YOU MIGHT BE RIGHT, AT THAT -
YES - SHE MIGHT KNOW THIS MR. WALSH - SHE USED TO SELL PAPERS -
HAROLD GRAY
Reg. U. S. Pat. Off.; Copyright, 1931, by The Chicago Tribune.
WELL, I PUT AN ADVERTISEMENT IN THE "REFLECTOR" FOR TO MORROW MORNING - MAYBE IT WILL BRING US SOME BUSINESS -
GEE - THAT'S A SWELL IDEA, JAKE -
WELL, WHY SHOULDN'T I ADVERTISE ONCE, ANYWAY? I AM SAVING TWENTY-FIVE DOLLARS A WEEK FROM THAT RACKETEER - AND IT WAS MR. WALSH OF THE REFLECTOR SAVED IT FOR ME - PART OF IT ANYWAY I COULD SPEND ON THE "REFLECTOR" I GUESS -
I SEE A LETTER THAT SHE LEFT IN HER ROOM FROM THAT OLD BIRD, WARBUCKS - NOW HE SAYS HE'S BEEN ROBBED - SO I GUESS SHE'LL BE BROKE FOR SOME TIME -
SO? THAT IS TOO BAD - WELL, LIKE I SAID, GIVE HER TILL SATURDAY - MAYBE SHE WOULD HAVE THE RENT AFTER ALL -
HAROLD GRAY
BILLS - BILLS - BILLS - ALWAYS I HAVE BILLS TO PAY - BUT WITH BUSINESS SO ROTTEN WHAT SHOULD I USE FOR MONEY? WELL, WE SHALL SEE - MAYBE THAT AD BRINGS A COUPLE NEW CUSTOMERS - ANYWAY, ANNIE MUST BE LOOKED OUT FOR -
Reg. U. S. Pat. Off.; Copyright, 1931, by The Chicago Tribune.
I NEVER INTENDED TO BUY SO MUCH, BUT EVERYTHING LOOKS SO GOOD - YOU HAVE A WONDERFUL STORE -
MY - MY - EVERYTHING IS SO REASONABLE HERE AND SO FRESH - AND TO THINK I NEVER KNEW OF THIS PLACE BEFORE -
IS THERE ANYTHING ELSE? WE HAVE SOME WONDERFUL STRAWBERRIES JUST FRESH THIS MORNING - I'M SURE YOU'LL LIKE 'EM -
NOR DID I TILL I READ HIS AD IN THIS MORNING'S "REFLECTOR" -
NOT A WORD, NOW - YOU EARNED IT AND A LOT MORE - TWENTY FIVE DOLLARS - WHAT IS THAT AFTER ALL I HAVE BEEN SAVED FROM AND AFTER THE WAY BUSINESS IS PICKING UP? NOW YOU CAN PAY YOUR RENT UP TO DATE - AND FROM NOW, ANNIE, I AM GIVING YOU ALL YOUR FOOD FROM THE STORE THE SAME AS BEFORE, AND FIVE DOLLARS A WEEK - NO-NO DON'T THANK ME -
OH, JAKE - YOU'RE WONDERFUL -
HEH - HEH - I KNEW YOU'D PAY TH' RENT AS SOON AS YOU GOT TH' DOUGH - BUT HERE'S FIVE BACK - IT'S ONLY TEN TO YOU FROM NOW ON, ANNIE - WHAT WITH THE OLD GENT AWAY MOST OF THE TIME AND YOU A STEADY ROOMER - NIX-NIX - DON'T THANK ME -
GEE! THANKS, MAW GREEN -
HAROLD GRAY
WHOOPIE!!! SANDY! WE'RE ON EASY STREET - TH' RENT'S PAID - I'VE GOT MONEY OVER - WE GET ALL OUR GRUB AN' I GET FIVE DOLLARS A WEEK FROM NOW ON - WHADDYUH THINK O' THAT?
ARF!
Reg. U. S. Pat. Off.; Copyright, 1931, by The Chicago Tribune.

April 30–
May 2, 1931

Little Orphan Annie
GEE- I WISH I HAD A NICKEL FOR A HOT DOG-

GEE- LISTEN TO THAT KID HOLLER- WHAT ON EARTH DO YUH S'POSE IS TH' MATTER WITH HIM? HE DOESN'T SEEM TO BE HURT-

HEY! WHAT'S TH' MATTER WITH YOU, BUDDY?
WAH! HOO! HOO! HOO! TH' DIME MAW GIMME TO GO TO TH' STORE- I DROPPED IT AND IT ROLLED DOWN THERE-

YEAH? WELL, I GUESS IT'S A GONER, ALL RIGHT-
I SEEN IT GO RIGHT DOWN THERE- IF I TELL MAW I LOST IT SHE'LL WHALE TH' STUFFIN' OUT O' ME-

HM-M-M- DON'T S'POSE YOU COULD TELL YER MAW THERE WAS A HOLE IN YER POCKET-
AW, WHEN SHE'S SORE YUH CAN'T TELL HER NOTHIN'-

WELL, QUIT BAWLIN' FOR A MINUTE- I'VE GOT AN IDEA- NO USE HOLLERIN' ANY MORE TILL WE SEE IF IT WORKS-

WHAT YER GOIN' TO DO NOW?
WELL, YUH SEE I'LL STICK THIS GUM ON TH' END O' THIS STICK- SORTA LIKE RIGGIN' UP A FISHIN' POLE- THEN WE'LL GO FISHIN' FOR THAT DIME-

GEE- ALL SORTS O' THINGS DOWN HERE- OLD PAPERS AN' RUBBISH- HEY- THAT LOOKS LIKE SOMETHIN' SHINY- STEADY, NOW- DON'T JIGGLE ME-
THAT'S RIGHT WHERE IT ROLLED-

WHY- I THOUGHT YOU SAID A DIME- THIS IS HALF A DOLLAR-
YEAH? BUT I ONLY LOST A DIME-- HOW-- WHAT---- ?

HERE, MISTER- GIVE US THREE HOT DOGS WITH LOTS O' MUSTARD ON 'EM, WILL YUH, PLEASE? TAKE IT OUT O' THIS HALF A DOLLAR-

NOW, THEN- YOU LOST A DIME- WELL, HERE'S YER DIME- AND I'M TREATIN' YUH TO A SWELL HOT-DOG- HOW'S THAT?
CHEE- THANKS!

FIFTEEN CENTS FOR HOT DOGS AND A DIME TO TH' KID FOR TH' ONE HE LOST AND A WHOLE QUARTER OVER- GUESS THAT JUST PROVES IT ALWAYS PAYS TO HELP FOLKS WHENEVER YOU CAN- EH, SANDY?
ARF!
HAROLD GRAY
Reg. U. S. Pat. Off.; Copyright, 1931, by The Chicago Tribune

May 3, 1931
GOOD NEIGHBOR POLICY

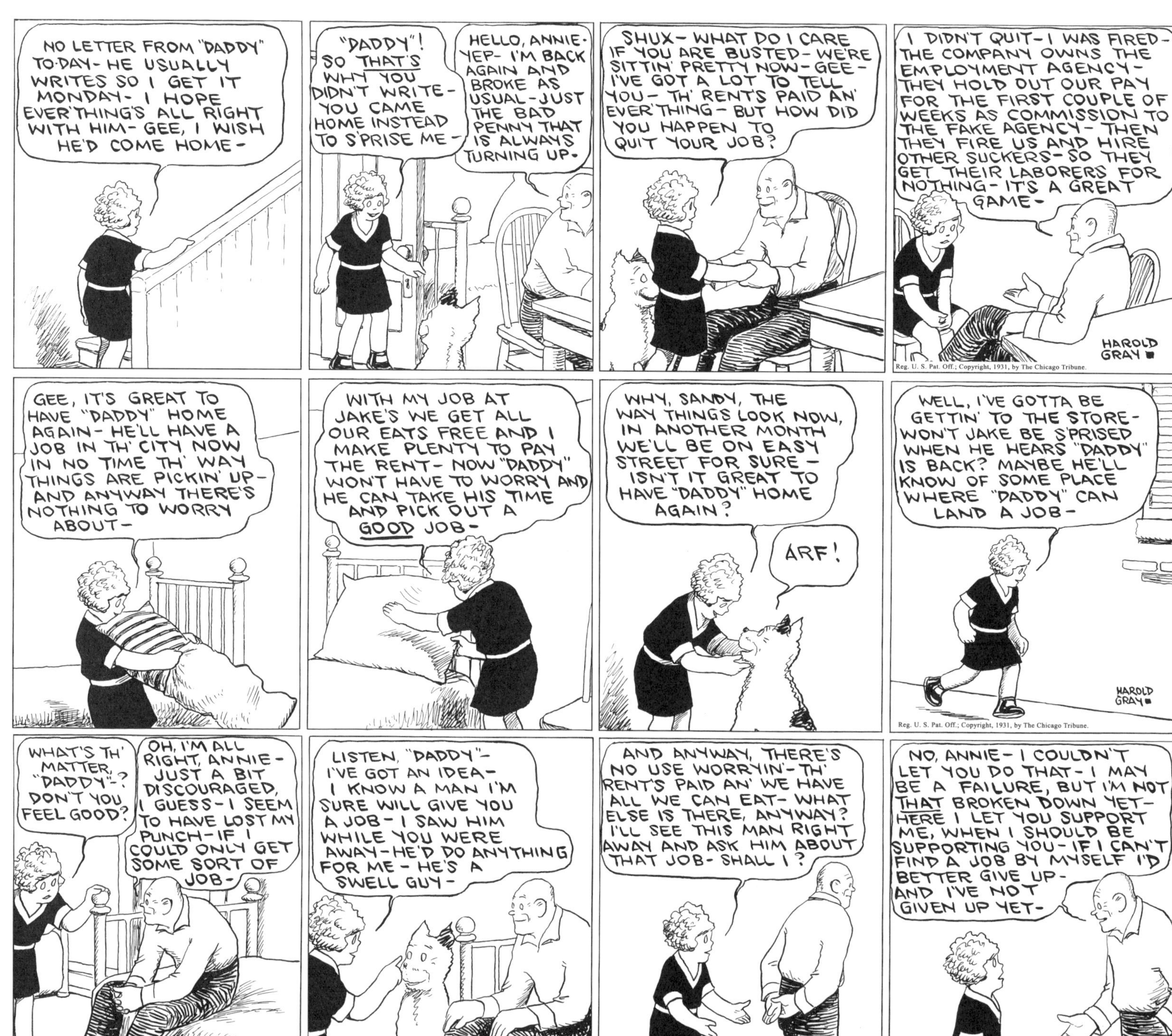
NO LETTER FROM "DADDY" TO-DAY- HE USUALLY WRITES SO I GET IT MONDAY- I HOPE EVER'THING'S ALL RIGHT WITH HIM- GEE, I WISH HE'D COME HOME-
"DADDY"! SO THAT'S WHY YOU DIDN'T WRITE- YOU CAME HOME INSTEAD TO S'PRISE ME-
HELLO, ANNIE- YEP- I'M BACK AGAIN AND BROKE AS USUAL-JUST THE BAD PENNY THAT IS ALWAYS TURNING UP.
SHUX- WHAT DO I CARE IF YOU ARE BUSTED- WE'RE SITTIN' PRETTY NOW- GEE- I'VE GOT A LOT TO TELL YOU- TH' RENT'S PAID AN' EVER'THING- BUT HOW DID YOU HAPPEN TO QUIT YOUR JOB?
I DIDN'T QUIT- I WAS FIRED- THE COMPANY OWNS THE EMPLOYMENT AGENCY- THEY HOLD OUT OUR PAY FOR THE FIRST COUPLE OF WEEKS AS COMMISSION TO THE FAKE AGENCY- THEN THEY FIRE US AND HIRE OTHER SUCKERS- SO THEY GET THEIR LABORERS FOR NOTHING- IT'S A GREAT GAME-
HAROLD GRAY
Reg. U. S. Pat. Off.; Copyright, 1931, by The Chicago Tribune.
GEE, IT'S GREAT TO HAVE "DADDY" HOME AGAIN- HE'LL HAVE A JOB IN TH' CITY NOW IN NO TIME TH' WAY THINGS ARE PICKIN' UP- AND ANYWAY THERE'S NOTHING TO WORRY ABOUT-
WITH MY JOB AT JAKE'S WE GET ALL OUR EATS FREE AND I MAKE PLENTY TO PAY THE RENT- NOW "DADDY" WON'T HAVE TO WORRY AND HE CAN TAKE HIS TIME AND PICK OUT A GOOD JOB-
WHY, SANDY, THE WAY THINGS LOOK NOW, IN ANOTHER MONTH WE'LL BE ON EASY STREET FOR SURE- ISN'T IT GREAT TO HAVE "DADDY" HOME AGAIN?
ARF!
WELL, I'VE GOTTA BE GETTIN' TO THE STORE- WON'T JAKE BE S'PRISED WHEN HE HEARS "DADDY" IS BACK? MAYBE HE'LL KNOW OF SOME PLACE WHERE "DADDY" CAN LAND A JOB-
HAROLD GRAY
Reg. U. S. Pat. Off.; Copyright, 1931, by The Chicago Tribune.
WHAT'S TH' MATTER, "DADDY"-? DON'T YOU FEEL GOOD?
OH, I'M ALL RIGHT, ANNIE- JUST A BIT DISCOURAGED, I GUESS- I SEEM TO HAVE LOST MY PUNCH- IF I COULD ONLY GET SOME SORT OF JOB-
LISTEN, "DADDY"- I'VE GOT AN IDEA- I KNOW A MAN I'M SURE WILL GIVE YOU A JOB- I SAW HIM WHILE YOU WERE AWAY- HE'D DO ANYTHING FOR ME- HE'S A SWELL GUY-
AND ANYWAY, THERE'S NO USE WORRYIN'- TH' RENT'S PAID AN' WE HAVE ALL WE CAN EAT- WHAT ELSE IS THERE, ANYWAY? I'LL SEE THIS MAN RIGHT AWAY AND ASK HIM ABOUT THAT JOB- SHALL I?
NO, ANNIE- I COULDN'T LET YOU DO THAT- I MAY BE A FAILURE, BUT I'M NOT THAT BROKEN DOWN YET- HERE I LET YOU SUPPORT ME, WHEN I SHOULD BE SUPPORTING YOU- IF I CAN'T FIND A JOB BY MYSELF I'D BETTER GIVE UP- AND I'VE NOT GIVEN UP YET-
HAROLD GRAY
Reg. U. S. Pat. Off.; Copyright, 1931, by The Chicago Tribune.

May 4–6, 1931

THERE'S MR. WALSH,- THE CIRCULATION MANAGER OF THE REFLECTOR- JUST TH' MAN I WANT TO SEE- YOO--HOO!!! OH, MR. WALSH-

GEE, I'M GLAD TO SEE YOU- I'VE BEEN HOPIN' I'D RUN INTO YOU- MY "DADDY'S" BACK AND HE NEEDS A JOB- YOU KNOW I TOLD YOU 'BOUT HIM- CAN YOU DO ANYTHING FOR HIM?
WHY, I SHOULD THINK THAT WOULD BE EASY, ANNIE-

WARBUCKS- WHY, A MAN LIKE THAT CAN HANDLE ANY JOB- I HAVEN'T ANY JOB BIG ENOUGH FOR HIM- BUT I CAN GIVE HIM SOMETHING TILL HE LANDS A BETTER JOB- WHERE CAN I SEE HIM?
THAT'S IT- WE'VE GOTTA BE CAREFUL- YUH SEE, "DADDY'S" AWFUL PROUD- HE WON'T TAKE A JOB IF HE THINKS I GOT IT FOR HIM- HE'S GOTTA GET IT HIMSELF-

I GET YOU- ALL RIGHT- I'LL DROP IN AT YOUR PLACE TO-MORROW NIGHT WHEN HE'LL BE HOME- SAY I'VE BEEN LOOKING FOR HIM- OFFER HIM A JOB- WON'T LET ON I KNOW YOU- HOW'S THAT?
GREAT- GEE, MR. WALSH- YOU SURE ARE A PAL- THANKS-
HAROLD GRAY
Reg. U. S. Pat. Off.; Copyright, 1931, by The Chicago Tribune.

MR. WALSH WILL BE OVER THIS EVENIN' TO GIVE "DADDY" A JOB- I MUSTN'T LET ON I KNOW A THING ABOUT IT OR "DADDY" WON'T TAKE IT- GEE- WON'T "DADDY" BE TICKLED, AFTER TRYIN' SO HARD TO LAND WORK-

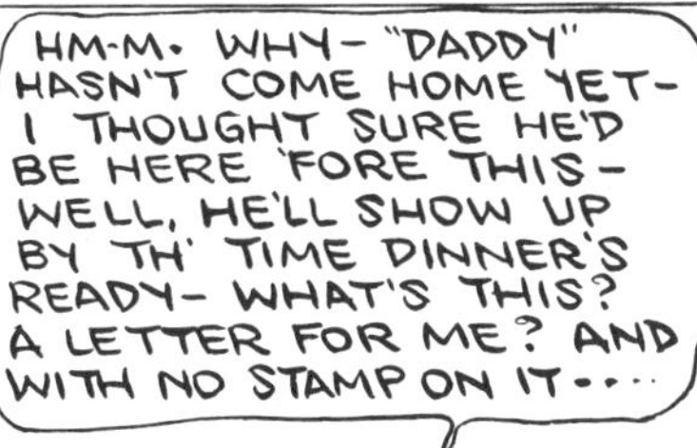

HM-M- WHY- "DADDY" HASN'T COME HOME YET- I THOUGHT SURE HE'D BE HERE 'FORE THIS- WELL, HE'LL SHOW UP BY TH' TIME DINNER'S READY- WHAT'S THIS? A LETTER FOR ME? AND WITH NO STAMP ON IT-...

IT'S FROM "DADDY"- HE SAYS IT'S HIS PLACE TO CARE FOR ME- IF HE CAN'T DO THAT, HE'LL CLEAR OUT AND NOT BE DEPENDENT ON ME- WHEN HE HAS MADE GOOD HE'LL BE BACK, BUT NOT BEFORE-

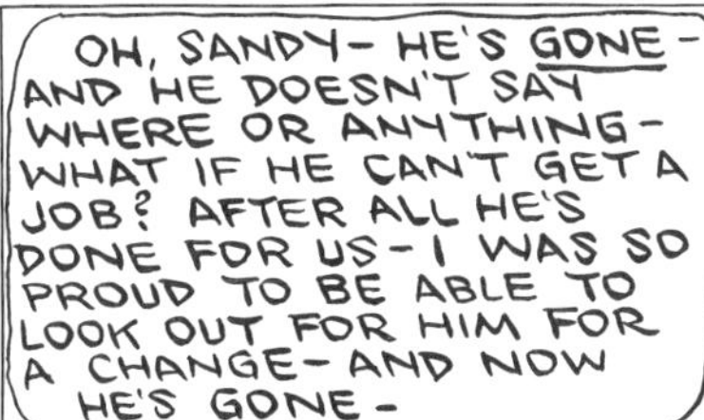

OH, SANDY- HE'S GONE- AND HE DOESN'T SAY WHERE OR ANYTHING- WHAT IF HE CAN'T GET A JOB? AFTER ALL HE'S DONE FOR US- I WAS SO PROUD TO BE ABLE TO LOOK OUT FOR HIM FOR A CHANGE- AND NOW HE'S GONE-
HAROLD GRAY
Reg. U. S. Pat. Off.; Copyright, 1931, by The Chicago Tribune.

YEAH- THE OLD NUT IS GONE AGAIN- SAID HE COULDN'T LIVE OFF TH' KID- SHE'D FIXED IT UP FOR HIM TO GET A JOB, TOO- OLD FOOLS ARE TH' WORST, ALL RIGHT-
STILL, HE WAS AN AWFUL BIG SHOT 'FORE HE WENT BROKE- IT MUST HAVE BEEN A TOUGH JOLT, LOSIN' ALL HIS DOUGH-

IF I ONLY KNEW WHERE "DADDY" WENT- THEN I COULD TELL MR. WALSH AND HE COULD GO AND GIVE HIM THAT JOB- THEN "DADDY'D" COME BACK- BUT HOW CAN I FIND HIM?

GEE, JAKE- HE WAS ALWAYS SO GOOD TO ME- AN' NOW, WHEN HE'S HAVIN' TOUGH LUCK- TH' FIRST TIME I'VE HAD A CHANCE TO DO SOMETHIN' FOR HIM- WHY WON'T HE LET ME HELP HIM?
HE IS A PROUD MAN, ANNIE- BUT DON'T YOU FRET- HE WILL MAKE GOOD SOON AND HE WILL BE BACK-

SO- HE IS NOT SO WEAK THAT HE LETS HER SUPPORT HIM, ANYWAY- MILLIONS HE LOST- I SHOULD LOSE SO MUCH I WOULD BE CRAZY- IT HURTS ANNIE THAT HE SHOULD GO AWAY- BUT I THINK MORE OF HIM- HE IS PROUD- HE HAS SPIRIT- SO THERE IS STILL HOPE FOR HIM-
HAROLD GRAY
Reg. U. S. Pat. Off.; Copyright, 1931, by The Chicago Tribune.

May 7–9, 1931

Little Orphan Annie
THERE GOES "DUD" RUNNIN' A MILE A MINUTE— BEEN UP TO ANOTHER OF HIS JOKES, I'LL BET— THE OVERGROWN LOUT—

HA! HA! DIDJA SEE THAT? "DUD" PUT A BANANA PEEL ON TH' WALK AND THAT OLD GEEZER CAME LIMPIN' ALONG AND PUT HIS CANE RIGHT ON IT— HE LOOKED LIKE A PIN-WHEEL—
YEAH? I DON'T THINK THAT WAS SO AWFUL FUNNY— TH' POOR OLD GUY—

THERE GOES "DUD" WITH ANOTHER OF HIS PRACTICAL JOKES— POOR OLD BIRD READIN' HIS PAPER AND NEVER SAW THAT ROPE— SUPPOSE THAT'S FUNNY, TOO—
HA! HA!! HA!!!

MAYBE I'VE GOT NO SENSE O' HUMOR, BUT I'LL BE SWITCHED IF I CAN SEE ANYTHING FUNNY IN NEARLY KILLIN' POOR OLD CRIPPLES— BUT "DUD" GETS A BIG KICK OUT O' SEEING FOLKS FALL AN' HURT THEMSELVES— JUST A REGULAR FUNNY GUY, HE IS— THERE HE GOES, NOW—

TH' LAME-BRAINED GOOF— HE NEVER PLAYED ANY OF HIS JOKES ON ME YET— I NEVER GAVE HIM A CHANCE—

SH-H-H... DON'T LOOK, SANDY— "DUD'S" SORTA WATCHIN' US FROM BEHIND THAT POST OVER THERE—

MY— MY— JUST LOOK AT THAT, SANDY— A WATER-PIPE MUST HAVE BUSTED AND NOW THAT BASEMENT THEY WERE DIGGIN' IS ALMOST HALF FULL O' MUD AN' WATER—

UH-HUH— I SORTA S'PECTED SOMETHIN' LIKE THAT—

WELL, WELL, WELL! IF IT ISN'T THE FUNNY GUY HIMSELF— HE'LL GET A BIG KICK OUT OF THIS, I BETCHA—

HA! HA! HA! HO! HO! HO! OH, BOY! ISN'T THAT FUNNY?

YOU— BLUB— BLUB— I'LL FIX YOU FOR THIS— HELP ME UP— I CAN'T GET OUT O' HERE 'LESS YOU HELP ME— IT'S TOO DEEP—

AW, WASH YER NECK! FIXIN' TO SHOVE ME IN THERE— THAT'D HAVE BEEN FUNNY— WELL, IT'S TH' SAME JOKE, ONLY YOU'RE IT— GO ON— LAUGH, CLOWN! LAUGH!

AW, LET HIM STAY THERE TILL HE COOLS OFF— HE'S LIKE MOST FUNNY GUYS— THEY'VE ALL GOT A GREAT SENSE O' HUMOR TILL TH' JOKE IS ON THEM FOR A CHANGE—
HAROLD GRAY
Reg. U. S. Pat. Off.; Copyright, 1931, by The Chicago Tribune.

May 10, 1931
GOOD NEIGHBOR POLICY

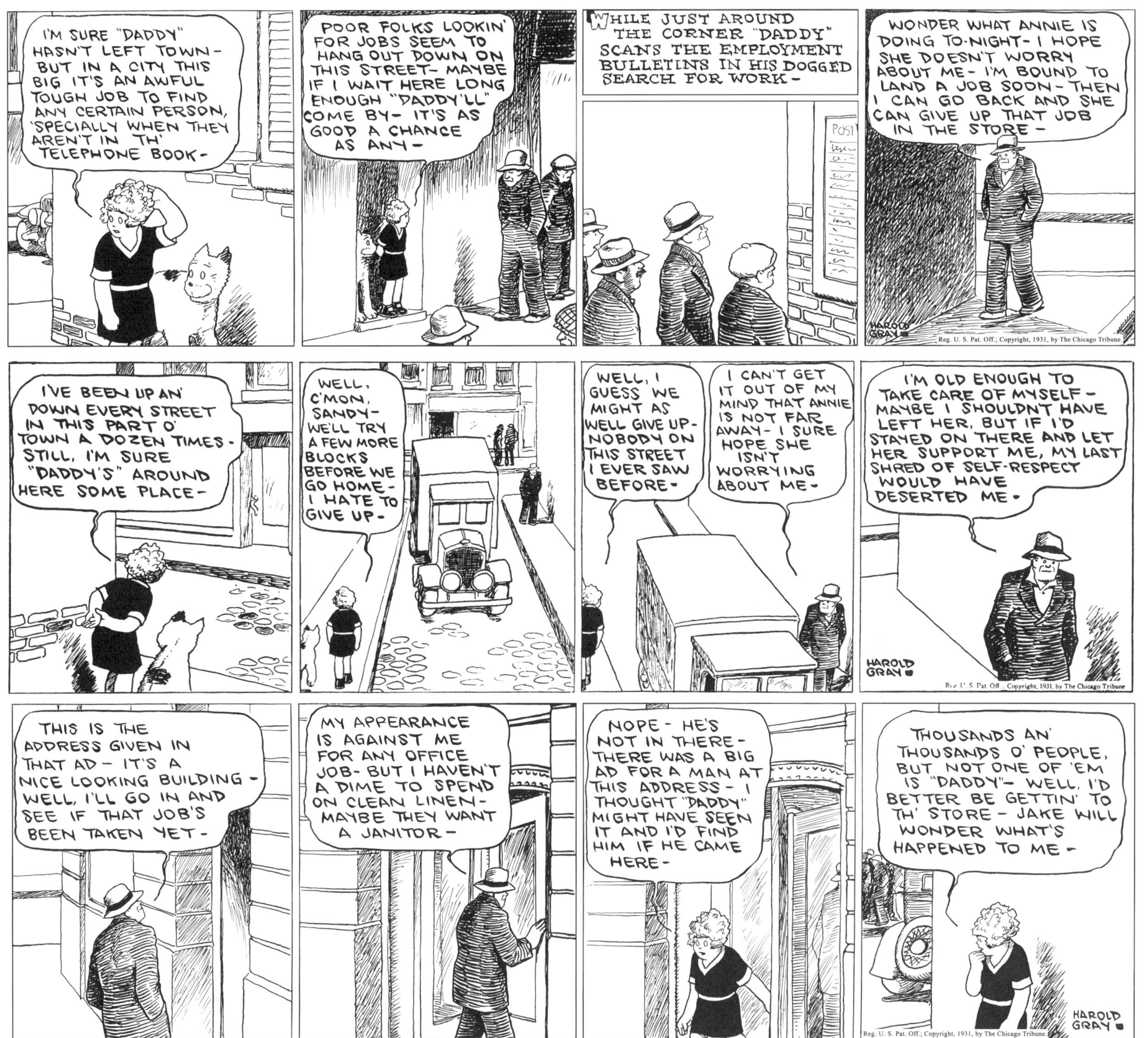
I'M SURE "DADDY" HASN'T LEFT TOWN- BUT IN A CITY THIS BIG IT'S AN AWFUL TOUGH JOB TO FIND ANY CERTAIN PERSON, 'SPECIALLY WHEN THEY AREN'T IN TH' TELEPHONE BOOK-
POOR FOLKS LOOKIN' FOR JOBS SEEM TO HANG OUT DOWN ON THIS STREET- MAYBE IF I WAIT HERE LONG ENOUGH "DADDY'LL" COME BY- IT'S AS GOOD A CHANCE AS ANY-
WHILE JUST AROUND THE CORNER "DADDY" SCANS THE EMPLOYMENT BULLETINS IN HIS DOGGED SEARCH FOR WORK-
WONDER WHAT ANNIE IS DOING TO-NIGHT- I HOPE SHE DOESN'T WORRY ABOUT ME- I'M BOUND TO LAND A JOB SOON- THEN I CAN GO BACK AND SHE CAN GIVE UP THAT JOB IN THE STORE-
HAROLD GRAY
Reg. U. S. Pat. Off.; Copyright, 1931, by The Chicago Tribune.
I'VE BEEN UP AN' DOWN EVERY STREET IN THIS PART O' TOWN A DOZEN TIMES- STILL, I'M SURE "DADDY'S" AROUND HERE SOME PLACE-
WELL, C'MON, SANDY- WE'LL TRY A FEW MORE BLOCKS BEFORE WE GO HOME- I HATE TO GIVE UP-
WELL, I GUESS WE MIGHT AS WELL GIVE UP- NOBODY ON THIS STREET I EVER SAW BEFORE-
I CAN'T GET IT OUT OF MY MIND THAT ANNIE IS NOT FAR AWAY- I SURE HOPE SHE ISN'T WORRYING ABOUT ME-
I'M OLD ENOUGH TO TAKE CARE OF MYSELF- MAYBE I SHOULDN'T HAVE LEFT HER, BUT IF I'D STAYED ON THERE AND LET HER SUPPORT ME, MY LAST SHRED OF SELF-RESPECT WOULD HAVE DESERTED ME-
HAROLD GRAY
Reg. U. S. Pat. Off.; Copyright, 1931, by The Chicago Tribune
THIS IS THE ADDRESS GIVEN IN THAT AD- IT'S A NICE LOOKING BUILDING- WELL, I'LL GO IN AND SEE IF THAT JOB'S BEEN TAKEN YET-
MY APPEARANCE IS AGAINST ME FOR ANY OFFICE JOB- BUT I HAVEN'T A DIME TO SPEND ON CLEAN LINEN- MAYBE THEY WANT A JANITOR-
NOPE- HE'S NOT IN THERE- THERE WAS A BIG AD FOR A MAN AT THIS ADDRESS- I THOUGHT "DADDY" MIGHT HAVE SEEN IT AND I'D FIND HIM IF HE CAME HERE-
THOUSANDS AN' THOUSANDS O' PEOPLE, BUT NOT ONE OF 'EM IS "DADDY"- WELL, I'D BETTER BE GETTIN' TO TH' STORE- JAKE WILL WONDER WHAT'S HAPPENED TO ME-
HAROLD GRAY
Reg. U. S. Pat. Off.; Copyright, 1931, by The Chicago Tribune.

May 11–13, 1931

SO YUH WANT A JOB, EH? CAN YUH DRIVE A TRUCK?
YES-
HEY! DUD!
TAKE THIS BIRD OUT AN' SEE IF HE CAN DRIVE A TRUCK LIKE HE CLAIMS- IF HE CAN, PUT HIM TO WORK—SEE?
O.K. BOSS.
YOU'RE O.K.- THERE'S NOTHIN' TO DRIVIN' A TRUCK DIS BIG- EVEN DE TAXICABS GETS OUTA YER WAY- TH' BOSS'LL FIX YUH UP WITH A DRIVIN' LICENSE AN' YUH CAN START IN TH' MORNING-
HAROLD GRAY
Reg. U. S. Pat. Off.; Copyright, 1931, by The Chicago Tribune.
IF HE'D ONLY WRITE SO I'D KNOW HE WAS WELL I WOULDN'T BE SO WORRIED-
AW, DON'T YOU FRET, ANNIE - THAT OLD GENT WILL TAKE CARE OF HIMSELF ALL RIGHT-
WARBUCKS KNEW ANNIE'D BE O.K. HERE OR HE WOULDN'T HAVE PULLED OUT- I GOTTA HAND IT TO THAT OLD COOT. FROM ONE O' TH' RICHEST GUYS IN TH' WORLD TO ONE O' TH' POOREST- IT'S EASY TO BE A GENTLEMAN WHEN YOU'RE RICH, BUT HE DOESN'T FORGET HOW TO BE ONE WHEN HE'S POOR- HE HAD CLASS. I'LL SAY THAT FOR HIM-
GEE, CLANCY, I THOUGHT TH' COPS COULD FIND ANYBODY IF THEY LOOKED FOR HIM-
AND SO THEY CAN, ANNIE- BUT IT'LL TAKE A BIT O' TIME- DON'T YOU WORRY- WE'LL FIND HIM FOR YOU-
IT'S NOT SO EASY PUTTIN' TH' FINGER ON ONE BIRD AMONG MILLIONS - STILL, WARBUCKS OUGHT TO BE EASY TO SPOT- BUT SUPPOSIN' I DO TURN HIM UP- IF HE DON'T WANT HER TO KNOW WHERE HE IS, WHY SHOULD I STICK MY BILL INTO HIS BUSINESS?
HAROLD GRAY
Reg. U. S. Pat. Off.; Copyright, 1931, by The Chicago Tribune.
HOW ARE THE PRUNES TO-DAY, ANNIE?
THE FINEST WE'VE HAD FOR MONTHS, MRS. GLOTZ- AND AT A SPECIAL LOW PRICE TO-DAY, IF YOU'D CARE TO LAY IN A SUPPLY-
YI, WHAT A DAY- TILL AFTER MIDNIGHT WE ARE BUSY EVERY SECOND- NOW I GUESS THERE WILL BE NO MORE CUSTOMERS SO I LOCK UP BEFORE SOME HOLD-UP MAN COMES IN- ADVERTISING! THE BIGGER THE AD I RUN THE MORE CUSTOMERS I GET- I SHOULD SOON HAVE TO GET A BIGGER STORE-
POOR ANNIE- ALL DAY SHE HAS BEEN WAITING ON CUSTOMERS- SHE MUST BE ALL WORN OUT- YOU SHOULD RUN ALONG HOME NOW, ANNIE, AND GET SOME SLEEP- I WILL SWEEP UP THE STORE-
OH, THAT'S ALL RIGHT, JAKE- I'M NOT TIRED- ANYWAY TO-MORROW IS SUNDAY AND I CAN SLEEP LATE-
I SHOULD NOT LET HER WORK SO HARD- AND YET, MAYBE IT IS BEST SHE KEEPS BUSY- THEN SHE DOES NOT THINK SO MUCH OF HER "DADDY"- AND WHEN SHE GOES HOME IF SHE IS VERY TIRED SHE GOES RIGHT TO SLEEP -
Reg. U. S. Pat. Off.; Copyright, 1931, by The Chicago Tribune.
HAROLD GRAY

May 14–16, 1931

Little Orphan Annie
C'MON, SANDY- LET'S SEE WHAT ALL TH' LOUD TALKIN' IS ABOUT-

MY OLD MAN WAS TH' GREATEST SOLDIER IN TH' WAR- TH' GENERAL TOLD HIM IF HE HAD A HUNDRED MORE GUYS LIKE DAD HE COULD HAVE LET TH' REST OF TH' ARMY GO HOME AND HAVE WON TH' WAR IN A MONTH-

SHUX! THAT'S NOTHIN' - TALKIN' OF BEIN' BRAVE - MY UNCLE WAS HUNTIN' ONE TIME IN AFRICA WHEN A DOZEN LIONS AND TWENTY TIGERS AND 'LEVEN ELEPHANTS ATTACKED HIM ALL AT ONCE - HIS GUN WAS EMPTY SO HE JUST PULLED OUT HIS HUNTIN' KNIFE AND KILLED 'EM ALL-

THAT'S NOT SO MUCH - MY COUSIN WAS ON A BIG LINER THAT SANK IN TH' MIDDLE O' TH' OCEAN WHERE THERE WUZ HUNDREDS O' SHARKS AN' HE JUMPED IN AN' SAVED A HUNDRED AN' TWENTY FOLKS AN' KILLED FORTY SHARKS WITH JUST HIS POCKET KNIFE-

AW, THAT WAS EASY - WHEN MY GRAN'DAD WAS A FIREMAN ONCE AN' EIGHTEEN HUNDRED WOMEN AN' CHILDREN WUZ TRAPPED IN A BURNIN' THEATRE HE RUSHED IN AN' BUSTED DOWN TH' DOORS AN' SAVED EVERY ONE WITHOUT EVEN GETTIN' SINGED-

HUH - GUESS YUH NEVER HEARD 'BOUT MY DAD WHEN HE WAS A COP - HE RUSHED INTO A PLACE WHERE THERE WUZ FIFTY OF TH' MOST DESP'RIT CRIM'NALS - AN' HE CAPTURED EVERY ONE OF 'EM - AFTER THAT THEY DIDN'T NEED COPS SO HE QUIT AN' WENT INTO TH' JUNK BUSINESS-

HELLO, ANNIE - WHAT DID YOUR FOLKS EVER DO?
YEAH - DIDN'T ANY O' YOUR PEOPLE EVER AMOUNT TO NOTHIN'?

AW, HOW COULD THEY? ANNIE'S AN ORPHAN - SHE NEVER HAD ANY FOLKS-
WELL, SHE MUST HAVE HAD PEOPLE SOME TIME - MY MAW SAYS SO-

SURE I HAD PEOPLE - LOTS OF 'EM - AN' THEY DID THINGS THAT'D MAKE THOSE BIRDS YOU'VE BEEN TELLIN' 'BOUT LOOK LIKE FOUR-YEAR-OLD KIDS THAT WEREN'T QUITE BRIGHT-

OH, YEAH? WELL, IF YOU HAD ANY FOLKS, AN' THEY WERE SUCH BIG SHOTS, WHY DON'T YUH TELL WHAT THEY DID AN' PROVE IT-

HUH - 'CAUSE IN MY FAMILY FOLKS NEVER BRAGGED - THEY DID THINGS THAT WERE SO BIG OTHER FOLKS DID THEIR BRAGGIN' FOR 'EM - SEE?

GEE - I WONDER IF I EVER DID HAVE ANY FOLKS OF MY REALLY OWN - WELL, THAT'S ONE THING 'BOUT BEIN' AN ORPHAN - YUH CAN MAKE UP AS BIG WHOPPERS AS YUH WANT TO 'BOUT YER FOLKS AN' WHAT THEY DID AN' NOBODY CAN PROVE IT ISN'T TRUE -
HAROLD GRAY
Reg. U. S. Pat. Off., Copyright, 1931, by The Chicago Tribune.

May 17, 1931
GOOD NEIGHBOR POLICY

ALL RIGHT, OLIVER - GET THIS SIGNED WHEN YOU DELIVER THIS LOAD O' BOXES THEN HUSTLE OVER TO THE FREIGHT HOUSE AND PICK UP A LOAD COMIN' BACK-
"OLIVER"- MY FIRST NAME WELL, THAT'S THE WAY I SIGNED ON HERE - NO NEED LETTING ANYONE KNOW MY LAST NAME - NO ONE AROUND HERE CARES WHO YOU WERE, SO LONG AS YOU CAN DRIVE A TRUCK-
WON'T ANNIE BE GLAD WHEN I TELL HER ABOUT THIS JOB? IT PAYS FAIRLY WELL, TOO - PLENTY FOR US BOTH TO LIVE ON AND MOVE TO A BETTER FLAT RIGHT AWAY - AND IT'S THE SORT OF JOB THAT MIGHT LEAD TO ANYTHING-
Reg. U. S. Pat. Off.; Copyright, 1931, by The Chicago Tribune.
BUT I WON'T TELL ANNIE TILL PAY DAY - THEN I'LL JUST WALK IN AND THROW MY PAY ENVELOPE ON THE TABLE - NOT THAT SHE CARES ABOUT THE MONEY - BUT IT WILL PROVE THAT AT LAST I'VE MADE A START - WON'T HER EYES SHINE?
HAROLD GRAY
CRASH!
GEE, IT LOOKS LIKE THERE'D BEEN A BIG ACCIDENT - WHAT HAPPENED DOWN THERE, MISTER-
AW, JUST A TRUCK RAN INTO AN L POST - THE DRIVER GOT BANGED UP A LITTLE, I GUESS - SERVED HIM RIGHT. TH' WAY THOSE TRUCK DRIVERS THINK EVERYTHING'S GOTTA GET OUT OF THEIR WAY-
THAT MUST BE TH' GUY WHO WAS DRIVIN' TH' TRUCK - WISH WE HAD TIME TO GO BACK AN' LOOK AT THE WRECK, BUT I'VE GOTTA BE GETTIN' TO TH' STORE-
BONG! BONG!
AMBULANCE
HAROLD GRAY
Reg. U. S. Pat. Off.; Copyright, 1931, by The Chicago Tribune.
AND WHAT ELSE TO-DAY, MRS. FINKLEDORFER? WE JUST GOT IN SOME VERY FINE PARSNIPS-
NOPE - THAT WILL BE ALL THIS TIME-
SO YOU HAVE NOT HEARD FROM YOUR "DADDY" YET SINCE HE WENT AWAY, EH?
NOT A WORD, JAKE - BUT HE SAID HE'D BE BACK AS SOON AS HE GOT A JOB, SO I FIGGER HE'LL SHOW UP 'MOST ANY TIME-
DOG GONE IT - HE COULD WRITE, SO I'D KNOW HE WAS O.K. - BUT HE'S MOST LIKELY TOO BUSY GETTIN' A JOB - GEE - WOULDN'T IT BE GREAT IF HE'D BE HOME WHEN I GET THERE?
WHILE, ON A COT IN THE EMERGENCY WARD AT THE HOSPITAL, LIES THE TORN AND BATTERED FORM OF A "MR. OLIVER", TRUCK-DRIVER - TO THE STAFF HE IS JUST ANOTHER CASE - HE SEEMED HARDLY WORTH PATCHING UP, BUT THE INTERNES DID THEIR BEST - IF HE LASTS TILL MORNING THE CHIEF SURGEON MAY LOOK AT HIM-
HAROLD GRAY
Reg. U. S. Pat. Off.; Copyright, 1931, by The Chicago Tribune.

May 18–20, 1931

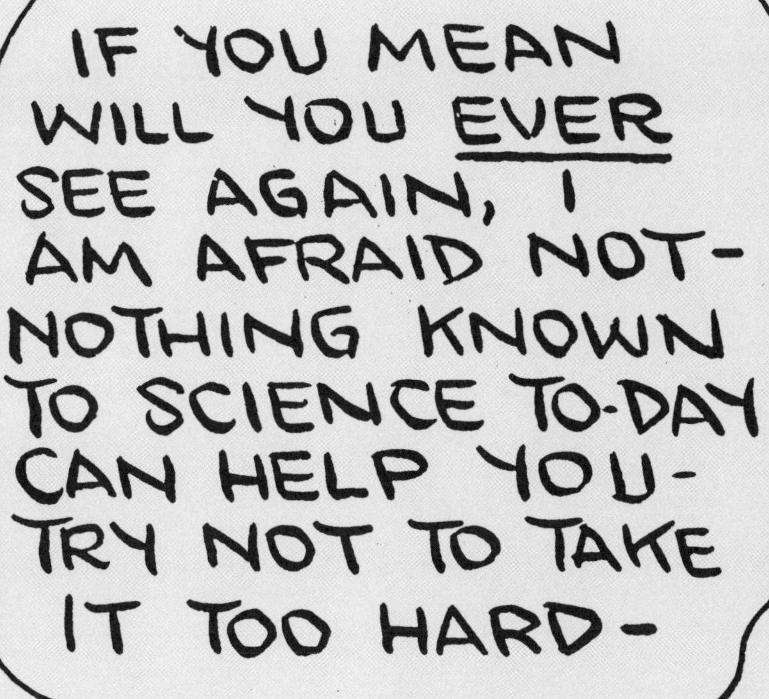
IF YOU MEAN WILL YOU EVER SEE AGAIN, I AM AFRAID NOT- NOTHING KNOWN TO SCIENCE TO-DAY CAN HELP YOU- TRY NOT TO TAKE IT TOO HARD-
ALL RIGHT, DOCTOR- THANKS FOR TELLING ME-

CHAPTER SIX

DOWN, BUT NOT OUT

IN WHICH ANNIE

ON HER OWN AGAIN, PROVES THAT HARD WORK PAYS OFF

UNSUCCESSFULLY REACHES OUT TO FRIENDS FAR AND WIDE

WOULD BE FRIGHTENED TO LEARN THAT "DADDY" IS UNDERGOING THE TRIAL OF HIS LIFE...

HAROLD GRAY

HM-M-M... A VERY INTERESTING CASE, DOCTOR- VERY INTERESTING INDEED-
HM-M-M- YES, DOCTOR- MOST RARE- HE SEEMS TO HAVE GREAT VITALITY- I BELIEVE HE WILL PULL THROUGH WITHOUT MUCH DOUBT- UNUSUAL- SO NEAR THE BRAIN-
ABOUT HIS EYES, DOCTOR- WHAT CHANCE WOULD YOU SAY HE HAS TO SEE AGAIN?
OH, NONE AT ALL, DOCTOR- NONE AT ALL- QUITE IMPOSSIBLE- HE WILL BE TOTALLY BLIND- BUT OTHERWISE HE WILL BE QUITE AS GOOD AS NEW AGAIN VERY SHORTLY-
I KNOW WHAT YOU ARE THINKING- A VERY SAD THING, DOCTOR- VERY SAD- OF COURSE IN OUR PROFESSION WE SEE SO MUCH SADNESS WE HAVE TO HARDEN OURSELVES- STILL, A THING LIKE THAT- IT'S A SHAME- A STRONG MAN- THE APPEARANCE OF A GENTLEMAN- A TRUCK-DRIVER I BELIEVE THEY SAID- HM-M-M-- BUT BLINDNESS IS AS BAD FOR THE POOR AS FOR THE RICH- WORSE IN FACT-
WELL, DOCTOR- WE MUST HURRY- WE HAVE MANY MORE PATIENTS AWAITING US- TRY TO FORGET THAT CASE, DOCTOR- PATHETIC; TERRIBLE- VERY TRUE- BUT JUST ONE OF THOSE THINGS THAT HAPPENS-
HAROLD GRAY
Reg. U. S. Pat. Off.; Copyright, 1931, by The Chicago Tribune.
GEE- THAT GUY- THE STREET SWEEPER- IS THAT "DADDY"?
OH- S'CUSE ME- ER-- ER-- THAT IS I THOUGHT YOU WERE SOMEBODY ELSE-
?
LEAPIN' LIZARDS! 'MAGINE ME TAKIN' THAT BIRD FOR "DADDY"- I MUST BE GOIN' GOOFY- STILL, FROM BEHIND- THE WAY HE STOOD AN' ALL- IT DID LOOK A LITTLE LIKE HIM-
AND THERE'S NO TELLIN' WHAT SORT O' JOB "DADDY'LL" GET- HE SAID HE'D DO ALMOST ANYTHING- OH, WELL- IF I KEEP LOOKIN' I'M BOUND TO FIND HIM SOON-
HAROLD GRAY
Reg. U. S. Pat. Off.; Copyright, 1931, by The Chicago Tribune.
WHEN I SAW THIS GANG AT WORK I THOUGHT MAYBE "DADDY" WOULD BE ONE OF 'EM- BUT HE'S NOT HERE- HE OUGHTA HAVE A BETTER JOB THAN THIS, ANYWAY-
MAYBE HE'S WORKIN' ON A BUILDIN' SOME PLACE- LOTS O' NEW BUILDINGS GOIN' UP ALL OVER TOWN- BUT NONE OF THOSE GUYS UP THERE IS "DADDY"-
HERE'S A STREET I HAVEN'T BEEN ON BEFORE- ALL THESE WHOLESALE PLACES HIRE A LOT O' LABORERS- HE MIGHT BE AROUND HERE-
POOR ANNIE- HOW CAN SHE KNOW THAT "DADDY" LIES ON A HOSPITAL COT- THAT HE IS DOOMED TO BE BLIND FOREVER MORE- EVEN HE HAS NOT BEEN TOLD THAT YET-
GOOD MORNING, MR. OLIVER- FEELING BETTER THIS MORNING?
GOOD MORNING, NURSE- OH, I'M ALL RIGHT- JUST BANGED UP A LITTLE- HOW SOON CAN I GET OUT OF THIS PLACE?
HAROLD GRAY
Reg. U. S. Pat. Off.; Copyright, 1931, by The Chicago Tribune.

May 21–23, 1931

Little Orphan Annie
SH-H-H--- ISN'T THAT A LITTLE DOG CRYIN'?

OH- ISN'T THAT A DIRTY SHAME, SANDY? TH' POOR LITTLE FELLER WITH THAT BIG TIN-CAN TIED TO HIS TAIL-
YI! YI! YI!

HUH! BIG BUSINESS! SCARIN' A POOR, DEFENSELESS LITTLE DOG HALF TO DEATH- YOU'RE OLD ENOUGH TO KNOW BETTER-

AW, PIPE DOWN- WOT'S IT TO YOU?

GO STICKIN' YER DIRTY PAW IN MY FACE, WILL YUH- UGH!
OOF!
PLUNK!

OW! MY STUMMICK!
C'MON, YOU- GIMME THAT STICK!
ER- YESSUM-

I'LL BURN SOME IDEAS INTO YUH 'BOUT BEIN' KIND TO DUMB ANIMALS, I WILL-

NOW LAM OUT O' HERE, AN' IF I EVER CATCH YUH ON THIS STREET AGAIN I'LL NAIL YER HIDE TO A FENCE-

YOU POOR LITTLE RASCAL- ALL ALONE AN' NOBODY TO LOOK OUT FOR YOU- WISH I COULD TAKE CARE OF YOU- BUT DON'T WORRY- I'LL GET YOU A SWELL HOME- YOU JUST LEAVE IT TO ME-

LOOKIE WHAT I BROUGHT YOU, MAW GREEN- A SWELL LITTLE DOG- ALL HE NEEDS IS A BATH AND A SQUARE MEAL- ISN'T HE A CUTE LITTLE RASCAL?
HUH! YOU KNOW I'VE GOT NO USE FOR DOGS-

NEVER DID LIKE MUTTS- THEY'VE MOST ALWAYS GOT FLEAS- ALWAYS YELPIN' AND TRACKIN' UP TH' FLOORS AND STICKIN' THEIR WET, SNIFFLY NOSES ON YER HAND- BUT ANNIE'S LEFT YUH HERE- I CAN'T PITCH YUH OUT-
?

IF ANYBODY'D SEE ME NOW THEY'D THINK I'D GONE SOFTY- BUT SHUX- DON'T YOU BE SCARED O' OLD MAW GREEN- HEH- HEH- HEH! YOU ARE A PERKY LITTLE RASCAL-
HAROLD GRAY

May 24, 1931
DOWN, BUT NOT OUT

WELL, YOU ARE COMING ALONG FINE - HOW DO YOU FEEL THIS MORNING?
OH, I FEEL ALL RIGHT - JUST STILL BRUISED A BIT - HOW LONG AM I GOING TO HAVE TO STAY IN THIS HOSPITAL? THERE'S NOTHING MUCH WRONG WITH ME, IS THERE?
OH, DON'T WORRY - YOU'RE COMING ALONG VERY FAST - I GUARANTEE YOU'LL BE ON YOUR FEET AGAIN IN A COUPLE OF WEEKS -
THAT'S GREAT - IF I COULD GET RID OF THIS BANDAGE AROUND MY HEAD AND SEE WHAT'S GOING ON IT WOULDN'T BE SO BAD -
DO YOU THINK HE SUSPECTS ABOUT HIS EYES YET, DOCTOR? DOES HE GUESS THAT HE'S BLIND?
WHO CAN TELL? HE'S NOT THE TYPE THAT WHINES - HE MAY SUSPECT, BUT HE CAN'T BE SURE YET, AND THERE'S NO USE IN TELLING HIM TILL I HAVE TO -
TELLING HIM THAT HE'S DOOMED TO WALK IN DARKNESS! WHAT A TERRIBLE SENTENCE TO PASS ON A STRONG MAN LIKE THAT - AND I'LL HAVE TO TELL HIM SOON - IT'S THE HARDEST KIND OF A JOB FOR A DOCTOR - THE BREAKING OF DREADFUL NEWS - BUT I'LL WAIT TILL HE'S STRONGER - HE'LL NEED ALL HIS STRENGTH TO STAND SUCH A BLOW -
HAROLD GRAY
Reg. U. S. Pat. Off.; Copyright, 1931, by The Chicago Tribune.
GEE, IT MUST BE GREAT OUT AT SILOS NOW - CORN PLANTIN' TIME ON TH' FARM - THE OATS AND WHEAT FIELDS ARE GREEN - THE LEAVES ARE OUT AND THE RAINS HAVE BROUGHT UP THE GRASS IN THE PASTURES - I'LL WRITE 'EM A LETTER - THEY'LL BE GLAD TO HEAR FROM ME -
LE'SSEE NOW - I'LL TELL 'EM ALL ABOUT WHAT WE'RE DOIN' - ABOUT JAKE 'AN' TH' STORE - ABOUT MAW GREEN - AND I'LL TELL 'EM 'BOUT "DADDY" LOSIN' HIS FORTUNE AN' TRYIN' SO HARD TO GET A JOB AN' ABOUT HOW HE'S OUT LOOKIN' FOR WORK NOW - MAYBE MR. SILO COULD USE HIM TO HELP ON TH' FARM -
I DIDN'T ASK ABOUT COMIN' OUT THERE, BUT THE SILOS ARE SWELL FOLKS - I BET THEY'LL WRITE AS SOON AS THEY GET THIS AND INVITE US ALL OUT TO TH' FARM -
LOOK, SANDY - TH' MOON - YOU DON'T SEE IT VERY OFTEN IN TH' CITY - AND WHEN YOU DO IT'S SORT OF DIRTY AND SOOTY - CAN'T YOU JUST 'MAGINE IT COMIN' UP OVER TH' WOODS DOWN ON TH' SILO FARM?
HAROLD GRAY
Reg. U. S. Pat. Off.; Copyright, 1931, by The Chicago Tribune.
POOR "DADDY" WARBUCKS, OR MR. OLIVER AS HE IS KNOWN AT THE HOSPITAL - QUIETLY HE LIES AND PLANS FOR THE TIME AHEAD, WHAT HE WILL DO WHEN HE IS WELL - DOES HE KNOW THE FATE AHEAD? THAT THE DAYS AND NIGHTS WILL ALL BE ONE LONG NIGHT OF DARKNESS FOR HIM -
THE DOCTOR SAID TWO OR THREE WEEKS - IF THEY'D ONLY LET ME READ TO PASS THE TIME -
COURSE THIS IS A GOOD JOB - IT'S PLEASANT HERE IN THE STORE - JAKE'S A SWELL GUY - TH' WORK'S EASY AN' SANDY AND I HAVE PLENTY TO EAT AND A GOOD ROOM -
STILL, IT'S NOTHIN' LIKE THE FARM - GEE, I CAN JUST SEE TH' SILOS WHEN THEY GET MY LETTER - MR. SILO'LL BE COMIN' IN TO DINNER WHEN TH' MAIL CARRIER BRINGS MY LETTER -
CLICKETY-CLICK! CLICKETY-CLICK! IN THE SWAYING MAIL CAR ANNIE'S LETTER HAS GONE INTO THE BAG FOR SIMMONS CORNERS -
U.S. MAIL
HAROLD GRAY

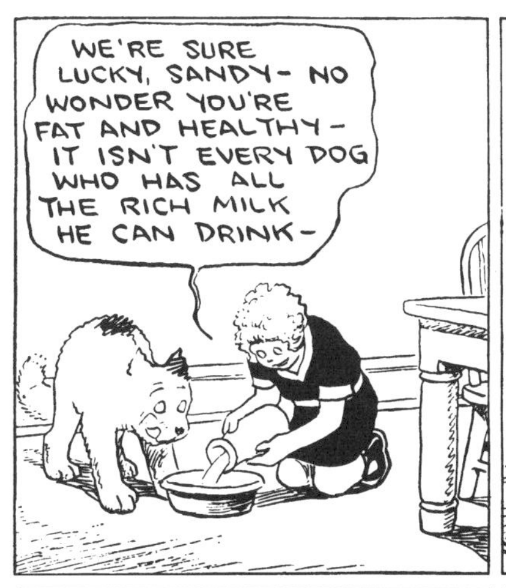
WE'RE SURE LUCKY, SANDY- NO WONDER YOU'RE FAT AND HEALTHY- IT ISN'T EVERY DOG WHO HAS ALL THE RICH MILK HE CAN DRINK-

IT ISN'T EVERY KID, EITHER IN THESE PARTS- IF I ONLY KNEW WHERE "DADDY" IS I'D BE HAPPY- BUT I'LL FIND HIM 'FORE LONG- BOUND TO-

THEN WHEN I GET AN ANSWER TO THAT LETTER I WROTE THE SILOS WE CAN HOP A TRAIN OUT THERE- IT'LL BE GOOD FOR "DADDY" TO GET OUT ON THE FARM FOR A SPELL-

WITH A CRASH AND ROAR THE LIMITED THUNDERS THROUGH SIMMONS CORNERS AND A MAIL-BAG, WITH ANNIE'S LETTER TO THE SILOS, BOUNCES AND ROLLS ALONG THE STATION PLATFORM-
NS CORNERS
HAROLD GRAY
Reg. U. S. Pat. Off.; Copyright, 1931, by The Chicago Tribune.

WELL, SANDY, IT WON'T BE LONG, NOW- I FIGGER THAT LETTER OUGHTA GET TO SILOS TO-DAY SURE- THEN BY THE FIRST OF THE WEEK WE OUGHTA HAVE AN ANSWER-
FRI-MAY-29

THE MOON-LIGHT SHINES ON SLEEPING SIMMONS CORNERS- ALL IS PEACEFUL- BUT WHAT IS THAT CURL OF SMOKE? IT SEEMS TO COME FROM THE POST OFFICE-
MEATS
POST OFFICE
HARD

SHE'S A GONER, SURE-
BRING AN AXE, ZEKE-
Reg. U. S. Pat. Off.; Copyright, 1931, by The Chicago Tribune.

HAROLD GRAY
MORNING- BY HEROIC EFFORT THE NEIGHBORING STORES ARE SAVED- BUT THE POST OFFICE IS A PILE OF ASHES- ONE ASH IS ANNIE'S LETTER- BUT WHO WILL EVER KNOW-

FOR WHY ALL THE POUNDING AND NOISE, ANNIE?
THERE WERE NO CUSTOMERS- I THOUGHT I'D OPEN UP THESE CRATES THAT CAME YESTERDAY AND PUT TH' STUFF ON TH' SHELVES-

ALWAYS BUSY- BUT NO NEED YOU SHOULD DO SUCH ROUGH WORK, A LITTLE LADY LIKE YOU- LET OLD JAKE GET THE SLIVERS IN HIS FINGERS-

AW, I DON'T MIND A LITTLE WORK, JAKE- I LIKE TO KEEP BUSY-

WHILE, AT THE HOSPITAL, THE DAY DRAWS NEAR WHEN WARBUCKS MUST BE TOLD THE WORST-

ARE YOU COMFORTABLE? ANYTHING YOU'D LIKE ME TO DO FOR YOU, MR. OLIVER?

I'M ALL RIGHT- ALL I WISH IS YOU'D TAKE THIS BANDAGE OFF MY FACE AS SOON AS YOU CAN- THEN I COULD READ-

Reg. U. S. Pat. Off.; Copyright, 1931, by The Chicago Tribune.

HM-M-M- NOT JUST YET- BUT BEFORE LONG NOW- LET'S SEE- THIS IS SATURDAY- WE'LL SEE ABOUT IT MONDAY- HOW'S THAT?
O.K., DOCTOR- I'M TRUSTING YOU-
HAROLD GRAY

May 28–30, 1931

Little Orphan Annie
HEY! HE'S GRABBED IT - LOOKIE - THERE HE GOES -
LOOK OUT - HE DOESN'T STEAL TH' BAIT - SET YER HOOK -

SH-H-H--- THERE'S A BIG ONE SWIMMIN' AROUND DOWN THERE SEE HIM?
YEAH - BUT IT WON'T DO YUH ANY GOOD IF YUH DO CATCH HIM -

THAT TOUGH GUY SAYS ALL TH' FISH CAUGHT FROM THIS PIER ARE HIS, NO MATTER WHO CATCHES 'EM - THAT'S WHY NOBODY ELSE IS FISHIN' HERE.

GOT HIM!
YEAH! YOU HOOKED HIM - BUT HE ISN'T LANDED YET -

IS THAT SO? THERE HE IS - ISN'T HE A BEAUTY? WONDER WHAT KIND HE IS?
GEE - HE'S A WHOPPER, ALL RIGHT -

HEY! NO YUH DON'T - WHEN I CATCH 'EM THEY STAY CAUGHT - WHAT KIND IS HE?
GRAB HIM, ANNIE - DON'T LET HIM GET AWAY -

NEVER MIND, KID - I'LL GET HIM OUT FROM BACK O' DAT BOX -

I FISHES DIS PIER AN' HE'S MY FISH, SEE? HE LOOKED LIKE A GOOD ONE, TOO - THANKS FOR CATCHIN' HIM FOR ME -
AW, YUH BIG BULLY!

?
?

WHAT TH' -----
IT MUST HAVE BEEN A CAT-FISH!!!

YOU'RE WELCOME, WISE GUY - YOU CAN HAVE THAT FISH - I HOPE EVER'THING YOU STEAL DOES YOU AS MUCH GOOD -
HAROLD GRAY
Reg. U. S. Pat. Off.; Copyright, 1931, by The Chicago Tribune.

May 31, 1931
DOWN, BUT NOT OUT

GAD - HOW I DREAD THIS - BUT HE MUST BE TOLD AND IT'S MY JOB TO TELL HIM - WELL, NO USE BEATING ABOUT THE BUSH - MIGHT AS WELL COME RIGHT OUT WITH IT AND HAVE IT OVER WITH -
MR. OLIVER, I HAVE VERY BAD NEWS FOR YOU - WE HAVE DONE ALL WE CAN, BUT THERE IS NO HOPE - YOU ARE TOTALLY BLIND -
BLIND, EH? WELL, I HAD BEGUN TO SUSPECT IT - ANY HOPE FOR THE FUTURE?
IF YOU MEAN WILL YOU EVER SEE AGAIN, I AM AFRAID NOT - NOTHING KNOWN TO SCIENCE TO-DAY CAN HELP YOU - TRY NOT TO TAKE IT TOO HARD -
ALL RIGHT, DOCTOR - THANKS FOR TELLING ME -
BUT, MAN! DO YOU REALIZE THE GRAVITY OF WHAT I HAVE JUST TOLD YOU?
OH, I REALIZE, ALL RIGHT - RUN ALONG, NOW, IF YOU DON'T MIND - I HAVE SOME THINKING TO DO -
HAROLD GRAY
Reg. U. S. Pat. Off.; Copyright, 1931, by The Chicago Tribune.
DID YOU TELL HIM HE WOULD ALWAYS BE BLIND?
YES - AND DO YOU KNOW, DOCTOR, AT FIRST I DIDN'T THINK HE UNDERSTOOD ME? IT MUST HAVE BEEN A TERRIBLE BLOW, BUT WHAT A GAME CHAP HE IS !!!
HIS RECORD SAYS HIS NAME IS OLIVER - MY GUESS IS HIS NAME IS NOT OLIVER - NO TELLING WHO HE REALLY IS - A TRUCK DRIVER - WELL, MANY GOOD MEN ARE FOUND DOING STRANGE THINGS THESE DAYS -
MEANWHILE ANNIE HOPEFULLY AWAITS AN ANSWER FROM THE SILOS - ALAS - HOW CAN SHE KNOW HER LETTER TO THEM WAS LOST FOREVER IN THE POST-OFFICE FIRE AT SIMMONS CORNERS?
NOPE - NO LETTER TO-DAY - WERE YOU EXPECTIN' ONE?
WELL, ER - YES AN' NO - MAYBE IT'LL COME TO-MORROW -
HAROLD GRAY
LE'SSEE - I MAILED THAT LETTER A WEEK AGO TO-NIGHT - EVEN IF THEY DIDN'T ANSWER IT RIGHT AWAY, STILL I SHOULD HAVE AN ANSWER BY NOW - COURSE, WITH SPRING WORK NOW, MR. SILO'S AWFUL BUSY - OH, WELL - WE'LL HEAR IN A DAY OR TWO, I BETCHA -
Reg. U. S. Pat. Off.; Copyright, 1931, by The Chicago Tribune.
YEP - ANOTHER DAY, SANDY - GET UP, GET BREAKFAST, GO TO WORK, COME HOME, GET SUPPER, GO TO BED - GET UP, AND DO IT ALL OVER AGAIN -
AH-H-H HUM -
WELL, WHAT OF IT? I LIKE THE WORK AT JAKE'S STORE - AND WHEN I'M BUSY I DON'T HAVE TIME TO WORRY 'BOUT WHERE "DADDY" IS, OR NOTHIN' -
DOG GONE IT - I HOPE I GET A LETTER FROM TH' SILOS TO-DAY - BEFORE I WROTE 'EM THEY HAD NO WAY O' KNOWIN' WHERE I WAS - BUT NOW THEY'RE SURE TO WRITE TO ME - WISH THEY'D HURRY -
HAROLD GRAY
GEE WHIZ - IT'S TIME I WAS DOWN AT THE STORE - JAKE WILL BE WONDERING WHATEVER HAS HAPPENED TO ME -
Reg. U. S. Pat. Off.; Copyright, 1931, by The Chicago Tribune.

June 1–3, 1931

SPIKE MARLIN MUST BE BACK AT HIS PLACE BY NOW- HE'LL FIND OUT WE'VE GONE AND WON'T KNOW WHERE TO FIND US- I'LL JUST DROP HIM A LINE AND GIVE HIM THIS ADDRESS- MAYBE HE'LL BE ABLE TO HELP ME FIND "DADDY"-

SPIKE WILL KNOW WHAT TO DO- AND, BESIDES, HE'LL BE WORRIED 'BOUT US, SOON AS HE HEARS 'BOUT "DADDY" GOIN' BROKE AND THE HOUSE BURNIN' DOWN AND ALL-

BUT SPIKE MARLIN IS STILL THOUSANDS OF MILES AWAY, LOAFING AROUND THE WORLD, NEVER EVEN DREAMING OF THE DISASTER THAT HAS OVERTAKEN WARBUCKS AND ANNIE-

AYE, MATES- I'VE BEEN OUT OF TOUCH WITH AMERICA FOR MONTHS- JUST AN OLD VAGABOND- THAT'S ME- A YEAR OR SO AND I'LL BE SAILIN' BACK TO THE LITTLE COTTAGE ON THE HILL- I MAY GO BACK SOONER- I GET LONESOME FOR LITTLE ANNIE- BUT SHE'S BUSY AND RICH- NEVER MISS AN OLD SALT LIKE ME-
HAROLD GRAY
Reg. U. S. Pat. Off.; Copyright, 1931, by The Chicago Tribune.

DON'T YOU THINK IT'S SORTA FUNNY TH' SILOS DON'T WRITE? YOU DON'T S'POSE MY LETTER NEVER GOT THERE, DO YOU?
WELL, YOU PUT A STAMP ON IT, DIDN'TCHA? AND YOU PUT THE NAME AND ADDRESS ON IT, DIDN'TCHA? I DON'T SEE HOW IT COULD MISS GETTIN' TO 'EM-

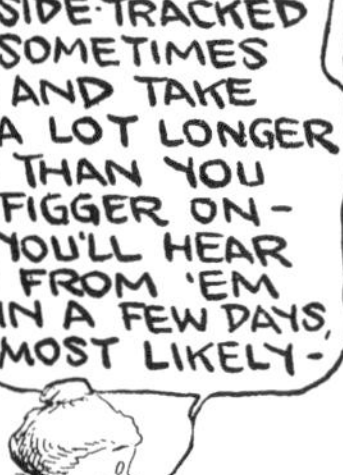
STILL, LETTERS GET SIDE-TRACKED SOMETIMES AND TAKE A LOT LONGER THAN YOU FIGGER ON- YOU'LL HEAR FROM 'EM IN A FEW DAYS, MOST LIKELY-
GEE, I HOPE SO- I'VE SORTA COUNTED ON HEARIN' FROM TH' SILOS- COURSE THEY'RE AWFUL BUSY RIGHT NOW, WHAT WITH SPRING WORK AND ALL-

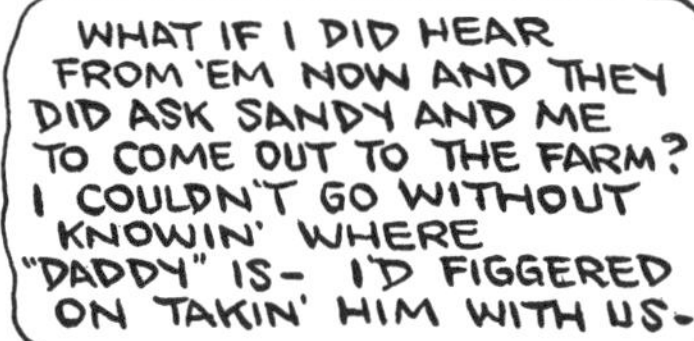
WHAT IF I DID HEAR FROM 'EM NOW AND THEY DID ASK SANDY AND ME TO COME OUT TO THE FARM? I COULDN'T GO WITHOUT KNOWIN' WHERE "DADDY" IS- I'D FIGGERED ON TAKIN' HIM WITH US-

HAROLD GRAY

WELL, SANDY, IT LOOKS LIKE YOU AND I ARE ALL ALONE FOR SURE- NO ANSWER TO MY LETTER TO SILOS- "DADDY" GONE- BUT WE'VE HAD LOTS OF S'PERIENCE GETTIN' ALONG BY OURSELVES- WE'LL MAKE OUT- STILL, IT'S SORTA LONESOME LOSIN' ALL YER OLD FRIENDS-
Reg. U. S. Pat. Off.; Copyright, 1931, by The Chicago Tribune.

WE SURE HAD A BIG DAY- WELL, GOOD-NIGHT, JAKE- SEE YOU EARLY MONDAY MORNING-
GOOD-NIGHT, ANNIE- I GO OVER THE BOOKS BEFORE I TURN IN-

BUSINESS- BUSINESS- YI- HOW IT PICKS UP- NEVER HAVE I SEEN IT BETTER- AND ANNIE I HAVE TO THANK FOR IT- SHE IT WAS GAVE ME THE IDEA- ADVERTISING- THE BIGGER THE AD THE MORE CUSTOMERS I HAVE IN THE STORE-

I COULD RUN EVEN BIGGER ADS- BUT HOW COULD I HANDLE THE CUSTOMERS? ANOTHER CLERK, MAYBE; OR TWO OR THREE CLERKS- HM-M-M··· MAYBE THIS WOULDN'T LAST- BUT EVERY DAY THE OLD CUSTOMERS COME BACK AND MORE NEW ONES- THEY READ THE ADS AND THEY COME-

NEXT DOOR WHERE THE POOL ROOM WAS IS NOW VACANT- I COULD MAYBE RENT IT CHEAP ON A LONG LEASE- I HAVE MONEY IN THE BANK- AND THE FIXTURES AND REMODELING I COULD MAYBE GET ON CREDIT- HM-M-M-- AM I SO BIG A GAMBLER I SHOULD TAKE THE CHANCE?
HAROLD GRAY
Reg. U. S. Pat. Off.; Copyright, 1931, by The Chicago Tribune.

June 4–6, 1931

Little Orphan Annie
JEALOUSY

LISTEN, SANDY - WHERE'S THAT CAT? SOUNDS LIKE IT'S IN THAT BARREL AND HE'S SO WEAK HE CAN HARDLY YOWL -
MEOW!

POOR KITTY - JUST LOOK AT HIM, SANDY - HE MUST BE ALMOST STARVED - HE'S SO WEAK AND THIN - BUT DON'T YOU WORRY, KITTY - I KNOW WHAT'LL FIX YOU UP -

YOU JUST COME WITH ME - IT'S A SHAME, A NICE KITTY LIKE YOU WITH NOBODY TO LOOK OUT FOR YOU - GEE - 'TISN'T FAIR - IF YOU WERE FED UP FAT YOU'D BE A SWELL CAT -

WHAT YOU NEED IS A REAL HOME - PLENTY TO EAT - A NICE PLACE TO SLEEP AND SOMEBODY TO PET YOU -

BREAD AND MILK - I GUESS THAT DOESN'T TASTE SO BAD, EH? GET AWAY, SANDY! BEAT IT - DON'T BOTHER KITTY WHEN HE'S EATING -

YES SIR - YOU'RE LOOKIN' BETTER ALREADY - A GOOD, SQUARE MEAL WAS ALL YOU NEEDED TO MAKE YOU GOOD AS NEW -

WELL, KITTY - WE'VE GOT A FULL HOUSE HERE OR I MIGHT TAKE YOU IN FOR A STEADY BOARDER - BUT YOU'LL BE LOTS BETTER OFF OUTSIDE ANYWAY NOW THAT YOU'RE FED -

A STREET CAT LIKE THAT WOULD NEVER BE HAPPY AS A HOUSE-CAT - IT'D CRAMP HIS STYLE - WHY, WHAT'S THE MATTER WITH SANDY?

SANDY! WHAT ON EARTH IS THE MATTER WITH YOU? YOU DON'T MEAN TO TELL ME YOU'RE JEALOUS OF AN OLD STREET CAT -

WHY, YOU OLD SILLY - AS IF I COULD EVER EVEN LOOK AT ANY OLD CAT A SECOND TIME, WHEN I HAVE YOU - YOU OUGHTA KNOW ME BETTER'N THAT -
HAROLD GRAY

SAY - I JUST THOUGHT O' SOMETHIN' - I'VE GOT SOME SWELL COOKIES HERE I'VE BEEN SAVIN' FOR YOU - DOES THAT PROVE I STILL LOVE YOU?
ARF!

June 7, 1931
DOWN, BUT NOT OUT

I AM GLAD YOU CAME EARLY BEFORE THE CUSTOMERS - LISTEN - ALL DAY YESTERDAY I HAVE BEEN THINKING - THE MORE ADVERTISING WE DO THE MORE BUSINESS WE GET - BUT WE CAN HANDLE NO MORE BUSINESS IN THIS STORE - NEXT DOOR IS VACANT - SHOULD I RENT IT AND MAKE A BIGGER STORE?

C'MON - LET'S GO OUT IN FRONT AND HAVE A LOOK - THAT WAS AN OLD POOL ROOM NEXT DOOR -

YES - AND NOW IT IS EMPTY - VACANT STORES IN A BLOCK DO NOT HELP BUSINESS - AND THIS IS A GOOD BUILDING.

YEP - IT'S THE OTHER HALF OF THE BUILDING - RENT IT AND YOU'D HAVE TH' WHOLE BUILDING - SURE - WHY NOT?

FOR RENT

I DO IT - MAYBE IT IS TAKING A CHANCE - BUT, AS YOU SAY, WHY NOT? YES - I SEE THE AGENT RIGHT AWAY -

HAROLD GRAY

WHILE WARBUCKS, SITTING UP FOR THE FIRST TIME SINCE HIS ACCIDENT, SEEMS STUNNED BY ALL THE MISFORTUNE THAT HAS BEEN HEAPED UPON HIM -

BLIND - AND I DON'T SEEM TO CARE MUCH - WHAT CAN BE THE MATTER WITH ME? HAVE I FORGOTTEN HOW TO FIGHT?

AND YOUR FIXTURES? I COULD GET YOU A NICE PRICE ON SOME SECOND HAND ONES.

YOU SHOULD NEVER MIND THE FIXTURES - THOSE I BUY NEW AND OF THE BEST - BY YOU I WANT THIS ROOM REMODELED AND REDECORATED - I TELL YOU JUST WHAT I WANT -

AND NOW THE FRONT - BOTH STORES I WANT SHOULD HAVE ONE NEW FRONT - NOT FLASHY BUT GENTEEL - FINE SHOW WINDOWS, LIKE THE BIG STORES ON THE AVENUE - SUCH A STORE I WANT THAT ANYBODY WOULD BE PROUD TO BE SEEN COMING OUT, BUT NOT SO FANCY ANYBODY WOULD BE SCARED TO GO IN -

I GET YOU, JAKE -

POOR WARBUCKS - EVEN IN THE DARKNESS HIS FIRST THOUGHT IS ALWAYS OF ANNIE AND HER WELFARE -

YES - IT'S A PRETTY TOUGH JOLT - MY FORTUNE SWEPT AWAY - EVERYTHING GONE - AND NOW EVEN MY EYESIGHT GONE - NO USE TELLING MYSELF EVERYTHING WILL WORK OUT ALL RIGHT - I KNOW IT NEVER CAN -

BUT THERE'S ONE LUCKY THING ABOUT IT ALL - ANNIE WILL NEVER KNOW - I'M SORRY IF I'VE MADE HER UNHAPPY BY LEAVING HER, BUT SHE NEED NEVER FIND OUT ABOUT MY BLINDNESS - IT WOULD HURT HER TOO MUCH - LUCKY THEY ONLY KNOW ME AS MR. OLIVER HERE - NO WAY SHE CAN EVER TRACE ME -

HAROLD GRAY

I WONDER IF I MADE A MISTAKE, ENLARGING MY STORE - WELL, IT IS TOO LATE NOW TO TURN BACK - YI - HOW SLOW THEY WORK, AND AT SUCH WAGES, TOO -

WELL, ANNIE, ALREADY THEY HAVE ALL THE PARTITIONS OUT NEXT DOOR - THE CONTRACTOR PROMISES BY SATURDAY TO HAVE EVERYTHING READY - EVEN THE WALL BETWEEN THE STORES OUT - ALL ONE BIG STORE -

GEE, THAT'S GREAT - THEN WE CAN HAVE A SWELL BIG OPENING ON MONDAY - GUESS THAT'LL BE GOOD FOR A BIG AD IN TH' PAPERS - EH, JAKE?

WHILE, AT THE HOSPITAL, WARBUCKS SUDDENLY FINDS REASON TO ASSERT HIMSELF -

YOU'RE THE BARBER, EH? WELL, BEAT IT - YES - THAT'S WHAT I SAID - GET OUT - SCRAM! NO SHAVE TO-DAY, OR ANY DAY - SEE?

HM-M-M-- WHISKERS - THEY'LL CHANGE MY LOOKS A LOT - AND A PAIR OF THOSE GREEN GLASSES - I'LL BE OUT OF HERE BEFORE LONG - IT WOULD NEVER DO FOR ANNIE TO RECOGNIZE ME - AND WITHOUT MY EYE-SIGHT I'D NOT BE ABLE TO DODGE HER - COME ON, WHISKERS - HIDE ME!

HAROLD GRAY

June 8–10, 1931

GREAT ACTIVITY PREVAILS ABOUT JAKE'S STORE- SOON ALL WILL BE READY FOR THE GRAND OPENING OF THE ENLARGED AND REJUVENATED ESTABLISHMENT-

JAKE SURE IS SPREADING OUT— WELL, HE'S BOUND TO SUCCEED- HE'S SO HONEST AND SO OBLIGING-
BUSINESS AS USUAL

WHILE IN THE CHARITY WARD AT THE HOSPITAL-

SO YOUR NAME'S OLIVER, EH? YOU KNOW, IT'S A FUNNY THING, BUT YOU LOOK A LOT LIKE A GUY NAMED WARBUCKS- YOU'VE HEARD OF HIM, MOST LIKELY- MILLIONAIRE, BUT HE LOST ALL HIS DOUGH- YEP- RESEMBLANCE THERE ALL RIGHT-
ABSURD! DID YOU EVER SEE THIS CHAP, WARBUCKS, CLOSE?
SURE, I SEEN HIM, NOT TEN FEET AWAY- FELLER POINTED HIM OUT TO ME- I GOT A GOOD LOOK AT HIM- WELL, OF COURSE WARBUCKS WAS A LEETLE STOUTER AND HE STOOD UP A BIT STRAIGHTER, TOO-

BUT YOU LOOK A LOT LIKE HIM- SHAVE OFF THOSE WHISKERS OF YOURS AND YOU'D SURE BE HARD TO TELL APART- FUNNY, AIN'T IT? ABOUT DOUBLES, I MEAN- ONE GUY LOOKIN' LIKE ANOTHER GUY, AND ALL THAT-
YEAH- IT SURE IS-
HAROLD GRAY

Reg. U. S. Pat. Off.; Copyright, 1931, by The Chicago Tribune.

HUMPH- SO I LOOK LIKE WARBUCKS, DO I? THAT'S A HOT ONE- WHO HAS A BETTER RIGHT? I SURE WISH THIS BEARD WOULD HURRY UP AND AMOUNT TO SOMETHING-

IF THAT YOKEL SAW A RESEMBLANCE ANNIE'D BE SURE TO SPOT ME ON SIGHT- THAT WOULD NEVER DO- BLIND, I COULD NEVER HOPE TO AVOID HER-

MY DISGUISE MUST BE COMPLETE WHEN I LEAVE THIS HOSPITAL- WELL, IT WILL BE- AND SHE'LL NEVER THINK OF LOOKING FOR A BLIND MAN- I SURE WISH I COULD GET SOME WORD FROM HER- FIND OUT HOW SHE'S MAKING OUT-

LATE AT NIGHT ANNIE AND JAKE WANDER ABOUT THE UNFINISHED STORE, ADMIRING, PLANNING, DREAMING-

GEE, JAKE- IT'S GOIN' TO LOOK SWELL- WITH THAT PARTITION OUT THIS'LL BE A BIG STORE, TOO-
ALWAYS, ANNIE, I HAVE DREAMED THAT SOME DAY I MIGHT BE A BIG MERCHANT- MAYBE THIS IS THE BEGINNING- WHO CAN TELL?
HAROLD GRAY

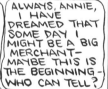

Reg. U. S. Pat. Off.; Copyright, 1931, by The Chicago Tribune.

THAT SURE IS A BIG HOSPITAL- EH, SANDY? THEY SAY IT'S AN AWFUL GOOD ONE, TOO- IF THERE IS SUCH A THING AS A GOOD HOSPITAL- BR-R-R-- I HOPE I NEVER HAVE TO GO TO ANY HOSPITAL-

THANK GOODNESS WE HAVE OUR HEALTH- HUNDREDS O' FOLKS IN THERE- MOST O' TH' PEOPLE IN THAT HOSPITAL ARE POOR, TOO- GEE, I FEEL SORRY FOR POOR PEOPLE WHO GET SICK- RICH FOLKS GET JUST AS SICK, I S'POSE, BUT THEY CAN HIRE LOTS O' NURSES AND DOCTORS AND SPECIAL ROOMS- IT DOESN'T SEEM SO BAD FOR RICH FOLKS-

BUT THERE'LL ALWAYS BE POOR FOLKS AND SICK FOLKS- MIGHTY LITTLE WE CAN DO ABOUT IT- WONDER WHERE "DADDY" IS- GEE, IT'S BEEN A LONG TIME SINCE HE WENT AWAY- I SURE HOPE HE'S ALL RIGHT-

WHILE, UNKNOWN TO ANNIE, WARBUCKS SITS IN THAT VERY HOSPITAL, WAITING FOR THE DAY WHEN THEY TELL HIM HE CAN GO FORTH— —TO WHAT? THAT IS THE QUESTION HE SPENDS THE ENDLESS HOURS IN A FUTILE EFFORT TO ANSWER-

Reg. U. S. Pat. Off.; Copyright, 1931, by The Chicago Tribune

June 11–13, 1931
DOWN, BUT NOT OUT

Little Orphan Annie
LISTEN TO THIS, SANDY-

IT SAYS HERE ELEVEN KIDS WERE HIT BY AUTOMOBILES YESTERDAY - SOME OF 'EM WERE HURT AWFUL BAD, TOO - SOME OF 'EM WILL BE CRIPPLED FOR LIFE, EVEN IF THEY LIVE -

THAT'S TERRIBLE - I'VE HEARD WISE GUYS SAY KIDS OUGHTA STAY OFF TH' STREETS - THAT'S O.K. FOR KIDS WHERE THERE ARE PLAY-GROUNDS OR FRONT YARDS - BUT WHAT'S A KID GOIN' TO DO IN THIS PART O' TOWN? SIT ON A FIRE-ESCAPE ALL TH' TIME -

LOOK AT THAT - LITTLE CHARLIE NEARLY GOT HIS THAT TIME - THAT GUY'S GOT GOOD BRAKES -

MOST FOLKS WITH CARS ARE PRETTY CAREFUL - BUT KIDS ARE KIDS - CHASIN' A BALL, OR PLAYIN' TAG OR ROLLER-SKATIN' THEY FORGET TO LOOK, AND BLOOIE! NOBODY'S REALLY TO BLAME, I S'POSE -

STILL, THERE OUGHTA BE SOME WAY O' FIXIN' IT - KIDS CAN'T STAY INSIDE ALL TH' TIME IN HOT WEATHER - AND FOR POOR KIDS TH' STREET'S TH' ONLY PLACE TO PLAY -

HM-M -- ALL TH' JUNK THOSE STREET REPAIR GUYS PILED IN HERE - ALL SORTS O' THINGS -

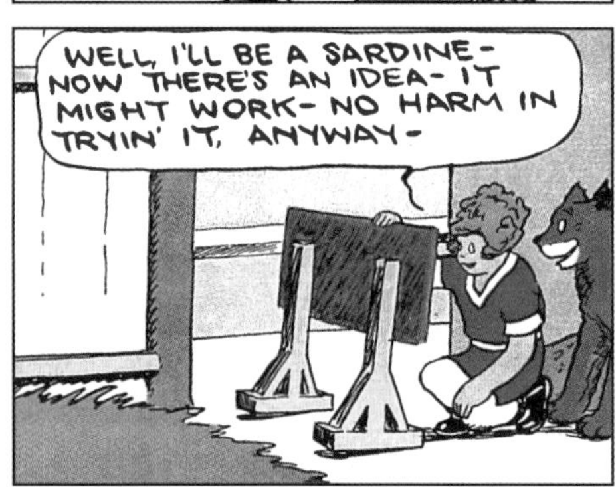
WELL, I'LL BE A SARDINE - NOW THERE'S AN IDEA - IT MIGHT WORK - NO HARM IN TRYIN' IT, ANYWAY -

IT'S A WONDER I NEVER THOUGHT O' THIS BEFORE - HOPE NOBODY NOTICES WHAT I'M DOIN' - BUT MOST FOLKS MIND THEIR OWN BUSINESS PRETTY MUCH AROUND HERE -

THERE, NOW! ONLY ONE SIGN, BUT THIS IS A ONE-WAY STREET - DON'T NEED ANY AT THE OTHER END - NOW WE'LL JUST HANG AROUND AND SEE WHAT HAPPENS -
STREET CLOSED
Reg. U.S. Pat. Off.; Copyright, 1931, by The Chicago Tribune

HEY - WE CAN'T TURN HERE - THE STREET'S CLOSED -
YEAH - MIGHT HAVE EXPECTED IT - ALWAYS DIGGIN' UP TH' STREETS - TOO MUCH POLITICS, IF YUH ASK ME -
HAROLD GRAY

NOW WHAT WOULD THEY BE CLOSIN' THIS STREET FOR? OH, WELL - IT'S THE DOINGS OF THIM STREET DEPARTMENT GUYS, AND NOTHIN' TO ME -
SH-H - DON'T LET ON YUH SEE HIM, SANDY, OR HE MAY GET NOSEY -

June 14, 1931
DOWN, BUT NOT OUT

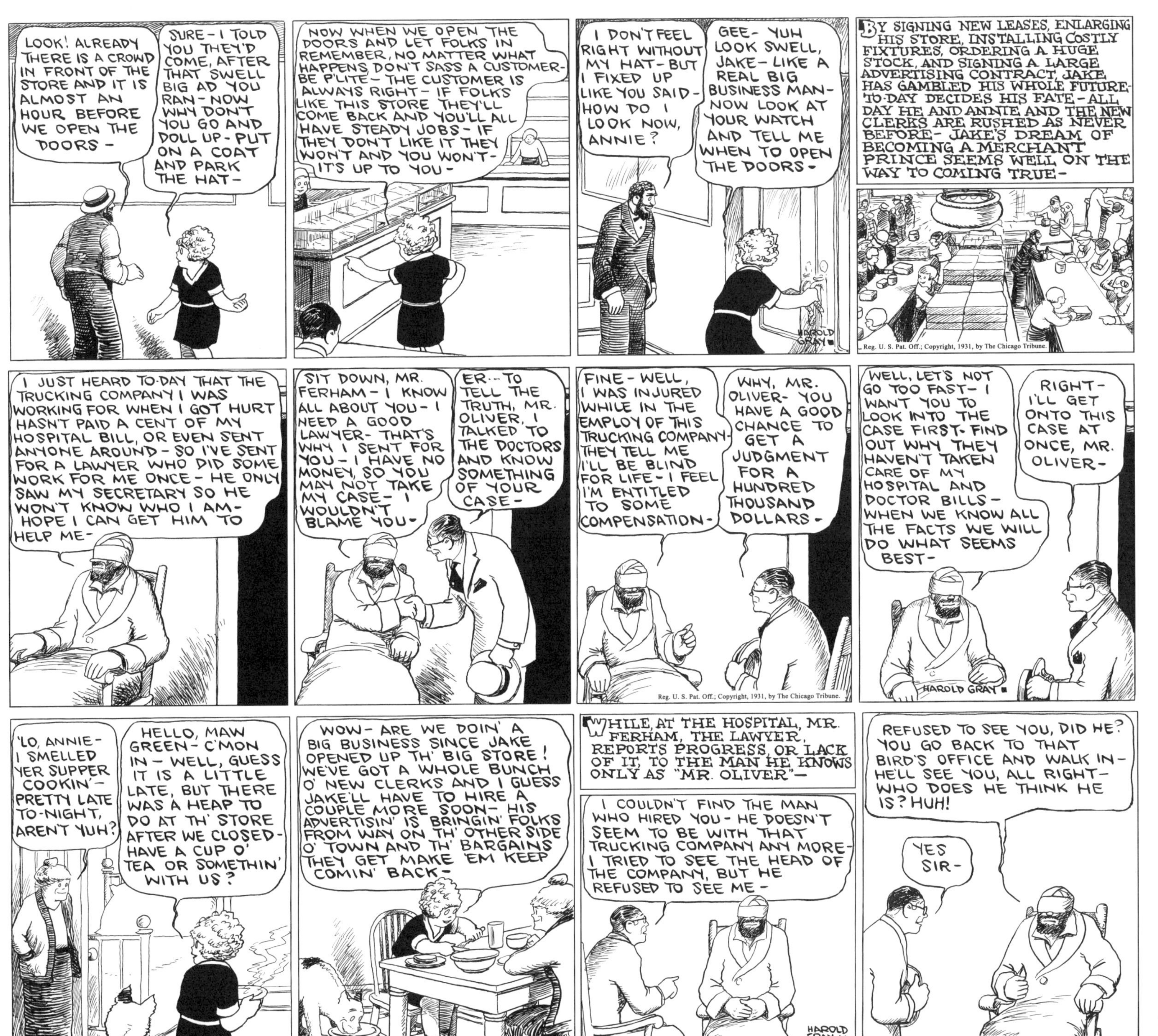
LOOK! ALREADY THERE IS A CROWD IN FRONT OF THE STORE AND IT IS ALMOST AN HOUR BEFORE WE OPEN THE DOORS-
SURE-I TOLD YOU THEY'D COME, AFTER THAT SWELL BIG AD YOU RAN-NOW WHY DON'T YOU GO AND DOLL UP-PUT ON A COAT AND PARK THE HAT-
NOW WHEN WE OPEN THE DOORS AND LET FOLKS IN REMEMBER, NO MATTER WHAT HAPPENS, DON'T SASS A CUSTOMER-BE P'LITE-THE CUSTOMER IS ALWAYS RIGHT-IF FOLKS LIKE THIS STORE THEY'LL COME BACK AND YOU'LL ALL HAVE STEADY JOBS-IF THEY DON'T LIKE IT THEY WON'T AND YOU WON'T-IT'S UP TO YOU-
I DON'T FEEL RIGHT WITHOUT MY HAT-BUT I FIXED UP LIKE YOU SAID-HOW DO I LOOK NOW, ANNIE?
GEE-YUH LOOK SWELL, JAKE-LIKE A REAL BIG BUSINESS MAN-NOW LOOK AT YOUR WATCH AND TELL ME WHEN TO OPEN THE DOORS-
HAROLD GRAY
BY SIGNING NEW LEASES, ENLARGING HIS STORE, INSTALLING COSTLY FIXTURES, ORDERING A HUGE STOCK, AND SIGNING A LARGE ADVERTISING CONTRACT, JAKE HAS GAMBLED HIS WHOLE FUTURE-TO-DAY DECIDES HIS FATE-ALL DAY HE AND ANNIE AND THE NEW CLERKS ARE RUSHED AS NEVER BEFORE-JAKE'S DREAM OF BECOMING A MERCHANT PRINCE SEEMS WELL ON THE WAY TO COMING TRUE-
Reg. U. S. Pat. Off.; Copyright, 1931, by The Chicago Tribune.
I JUST HEARD TO-DAY THAT THE TRUCKING COMPANY I WAS WORKING FOR WHEN I GOT HURT HASN'T PAID A CENT OF MY HOSPITAL BILL, OR EVEN SENT ANYONE AROUND-SO I'VE SENT FOR A LAWYER WHO DID SOME WORK FOR ME ONCE-HE ONLY SAW MY SECRETARY SO HE WON'T KNOW WHO I AM-HOPE I CAN GET HIM TO HELP ME-
SIT DOWN, MR. FERHAM-I KNOW ALL ABOUT YOU-I NEED A GOOD LAWYER-THAT'S WHY I SENT FOR YOU-I HAVE NO MONEY, SO YOU MAY NOT TAKE MY CASE-I WOULDN'T BLAME YOU-
ER--TO TELL THE TRUTH, MR. OLIVER, I TALKED TO THE DOCTORS AND KNOW SOMETHING OF YOUR CASE-
FINE-WELL, I WAS INJURED WHILE IN THE EMPLOY OF THIS TRUCKING COMPANY-THEY TELL ME I'LL BE BLIND FOR LIFE-I FEEL I'M ENTITLED TO SOME COMPENSATION-
WHY, MR. OLIVER-YOU HAVE A GOOD CHANCE TO GET A JUDGMENT FOR A HUNDRED THOUSAND DOLLARS-
Reg. U. S. Pat. Off.; Copyright, 1931, by The Chicago Tribune.
WELL, LET'S NOT GO TOO FAST-I WANT YOU TO LOOK INTO THE CASE FIRST-FIND OUT WHY THEY HAVEN'T TAKEN CARE OF MY HOSPITAL AND DOCTOR BILLS-WHEN WE KNOW ALL THE FACTS WE WILL DO WHAT SEEMS BEST-
RIGHT-I'LL GET ONTO THIS CASE AT ONCE, MR. OLIVER-
HAROLD GRAY
'LO, ANNIE-I SMELLED YER SUPPER COOKIN'-PRETTY LATE TO-NIGHT, AREN'T YUH?
HELLO, MAW GREEN-C'MON IN-WELL, GUESS IT IS A LITTLE LATE, BUT THERE WAS A HEAP TO DO AT TH' STORE AFTER WE CLOSED-HAVE A CUP O' TEA OR SOMETHIN' WITH US?
WOW-ARE WE DOIN' A BIG BUSINESS SINCE JAKE OPENED UP TH' BIG STORE! WE'VE GOT A WHOLE BUNCH O' NEW CLERKS AND I GUESS JAKE'LL HAVE TO HIRE A COUPLE MORE SOON-HIS ADVERTISIN' IS BRINGIN' FOLKS FROM WAY ON TH' OTHER SIDE O' TOWN AND TH' BARGAINS THEY GET MAKE 'EM KEEP COMIN' BACK-
WHILE, AT THE HOSPITAL, MR. FERHAM, THE LAWYER, REPORTS PROGRESS, OR LACK OF IT, TO THE MAN HE KNOWS ONLY AS "MR. OLIVER"-
I COULDN'T FIND THE MAN WHO HIRED YOU-HE DOESN'T SEEM TO BE WITH THAT TRUCKING COMPANY ANY MORE-I TRIED TO SEE THE HEAD OF THE COMPANY, BUT HE REFUSED TO SEE ME-
HAROLD GRAY
REFUSED TO SEE YOU, DID HE? YOU GO BACK TO THAT BIRD'S OFFICE AND WALK IN-HE'LL SEE YOU, ALL RIGHT-WHO DOES HE THINK HE IS? HUH!
YES SIR-
Reg. U. S. Pat. Off.; Copyright, 1931, by The Chicago Tribune.

June 15–17, 1931
DOWN, BUT NOT OUT

DAY BY DAY ANNIE'S FORTUNES ARE IMPROVING-
WITHOUT ANNIE I NEVER WOULD HAVE HAD THE NERVE TO ENLARGE MY STORE - AND NOW SHE IT IS WHO WATCHES EVERYTHING - A RAISE SHE HAS EARNED AND A RAISE I WILL GIVE HER-
WHILE "DADDY" WARBUCKS FINDS THE ROAD EVER STEEPER AND THE ODDS AGAINST HIM EVER GREATER-
THE HEAD OF THE TRUCKING COMPANY SAYS WHAT?
HE SAYS THEY HAVE NO RECORD THAT YOU WERE EVER EMPLOYED BY THEM AT ALL-
IF HE CLAIMS I NEVER WORKED FOR THEM HE'S A LIAR-
I BELIEVE YOU, MR. OLIVER - I'M ONLY TELLING YOU WHAT HE SAYS- HE CALLED ME AN AMBULANCE-CHASING SHYSTER AND THREATENED TO PREFER CHARGES AGAINST ME IF I PRESSED THIS CASE-
Reg. U. S. Pat. Off.; Copyright, 1931, by The Chicago Tribune.
YEAH? WE'LL SEE ABOUT THAT - YOU HUSTLE OUT AND ROUND UP WITNESSES - A DOZEN PEOPLE MUST HAVE SEEN THAT ACCIDENT - GET THE KID WHO RAN IN FRONT OF MY TRUCK - AND THE KID'S PARENTS - AND THE COP ON THE CORNER-
YES SIR- I'LL GET BUSY RIGHT AWAY-
HAROLD GRAY
DO YOU MEAN TO TELL ME YOU CAN'T FIND A SINGLE WITNESS WHO SAW ME SMASH THAT TRUCK TO SAVE THAT LITTLE KID?
THAT'S EXACTLY WHAT IT AMOUNTS TO, MR. OLIVER-
OH, I FOUND ENOUGH EVIDENCE TO SATISFY ME, BUT NO WITNESSES TO BRING INTO COURT- THE KID IS GONE COMPLETELY- HIS PARENTS HAVE MOVED AND NOBODY KNOWS WHERE- EVIDENTLY THEY WERE WELL PAID TO GO AWAY-
THERE'S A NEW POLICEMAN ON THE CORNER- I FINALLY LOCATED THE COP WHO SAW THE ACCIDENT- HE SAID HE'D TESTIFY TO WHAT HE SAW, BUT IF HE DOES IT WILL MEAN HE'LL LOSE HIS JOB, HE SAYS-
Reg. U. S. Pat. Off.; Copyright, 1931, by The Chicago Tribune.
EVERYWHERE IT WAS THE SAME - I FOUND HALF A DOZEN WITNESSES, BUT EVERY ONE HAS BEEN BOUGHT UP BY THE TRUCKING COMPANY - THEY'D ALL SWEAR THERE WAS NO KID IN THE STREET - THAT IT WAS CARELESSNESS ON YOUR PART, OR INTENT TO WRECK THE TRUCK - WE'RE UP AGAINST A TOUGH GAME-
HAROLD GRAY
WELL, I HATE TO DROP A CASE AS RAW AS YOURS, MR. OLIVER - SO I TOOK ANOTHER CRACK AT THE OWNER OF THAT TRUCKING COMPANY - I TOLD HIM WE WERE GOING TO SUE HIM FOR $100,000.00
WHAT DID HE SAY?
HE SAID IF WE DIDN'T DROP THE CASE COMPLETELY HE'D PROVE IN COURT THAT YOU STOLE THAT TRUCK AND WRECKED IT IN YOUR EFFORT TO GET AWAY- HE HAD THE NERVE TO ADD THAT HE'D NOT PRESS THAT CHARGE, HOWEVER, IF WE'D DROP OUR CLAIM FOR DAMAGES-
I'VE NEVER BEEN UP AGAINST SUCH A CROOK IN MY LIFE - IT BURNS ME UP - I HAVE SOME MONEY OF MY OWN AND I'M GOING AFTER THAT BIRD - I'LL SEND HIM TO JAIL, IF IT'S THE LAST THING I DO-
NIX, FERHAM - YOU'RE A FINE LAD AND MEAN WELL - BUT WE'RE LICKED - I'M JUST AN EX-TRUCK-DRIVER, BROKE AND BLIND - WE HAVE NO CHANCE AGAINST THOSE WOLVES - THEY'D CONTINUE THE CASE FOR YEARS AND MOST LIKELY BEAT US - LET IT GO - NO USE BUTTING YOUR HEAD AGAINST A WALL-
HAROLD GRAY
Reg. U. S. Pat. Off.; Copyright, 1931, by The Chicago Tribune.

June 18–20, 1931

Little Orphan Annie
GEE! ANOTHER LITTLE KID CRIPPLED BY A HIT-AND-RUN DRIVER-

STOP! LOOK OUT FOR THAT KID!!!
CHEE!!! THAT WAS TOO CLOSE TO SUIT ME-

THAT'S THE THIRD CLOSE CALL THIS WEEK IN FRONT OF MY GARAGE- THOSE KIDS WILL DRIVE ME CRAZY- WHY DON'T THE DUMB PARENTS KEEP THEIR BRATS OFF THE STREETS?
YEAH? AND WHERE WOULD THEY KEEP 'EM? HANG 'EM ON A FIRE ESCAPE? TH' STREET'S TH' ONLY PLACE 'ROUND HERE THAT KIDS CAN GO; UNLESS-----

UNLESS WHAT?
UNLESS TH' FOLKS AROUND HERE THAT HAVE PLENTY O' ROOM WILL LET TH' KIDS USE IT- THERE'S LOTS O' ROOM GOIN' TO WASTE RIGHT IN THIS BLOCK-

ROOM AROUND HERE GOIN' TO WASTE? WHY, EVERY INCH O' GROUND HAS A BUILDING ON IT.
SURE! BUT HOW ABOUT TH' ROOF ON A BUILDING, SAY LIKE YOUR GARAGE? IF YOU'D ONLY LET TH' KIDS PLAY UP THERE THEY'D BE OFF TH' STREET-

YEAH- AND HAVE 'EM KICKIN' HOLES IN TH' ROOF- NOTHING DOING-
SHUX- IT WOULDN'T COST MUCH TO FIX IT SO THEY COULDN'T SCUFF HOLES IN IT- COME ON UP AND LET ME SHOW YUH, WONTCHA?

ALL RIGHT, ANNIE- I ADMIT IT'S AN IDEA- BUT IT WON'T WORK- DON'T FALL NOW-

JUST LOOK- THIS ROOF IS ALMOST FLAT AND IT'S BIG ENOUGH TO PLAY BASE-BALL ON, WITH ROOM TO SPARE-
YEAH-

BUT WHAT'S TO KEEP TH' KIDS FROM FALLIN' OVER TH' EDGE? IF THERE'S ANY WAY TO GET HURT THEY'LL FIND IT-
WELL, WHY NOT PUT A GOOD HIGH FENCE ALL AROUND? THIS ROOF'S STRONG AND SOLID- IT COULD EASY BE COVERED WITH SOMETHING THAT WOULD STAND WALKIN' ON-

THERE COULD BE SWINGS AND SLIDES AND MERRY-GO-ROUNDS AND A BIG SAND-BOX- EVERYBODY'D BE GLAD TO CHIP IN-
HM-M-M--- SAY, THAT'S NOT A BAD HUNCH-

WELL, I'LL DO MY PART- I'LL START PUTTING UP THAT FENCE TO-MORROW-
AND IT WOULDN'T BE MUCH OF A JOB TO PUT STAIRS HERE, 'STEAD O' THIS LADDER-

LEAPIN' LIZARDS! I NEVER THOUGHT HE'D GO FOR THAT IDEA- HE'S A SWELL GUY- NOW WITH THAT START IT OUGHTA BE EASY TO GET THE OTHER BUSINESS MEN AND PARENTS 'ROUND HERE TO HELP BY GIVIN' SOMETHIN'- IF WE WORK FAST NEXT SUNDAY OUGHTA FIND US WITH A REAL PLAY-GROUND-
HAROLD GRAY

June 21, 1931
DOWN, BUT NOT OUT

I'VE BEEN WATCHING YOU, OLIVER—YOU'RE LEARNING TO GET AROUND FINE—AFTER ALL, EYES AREN'T SO IMPORTANT—NOWADAYS THERE ARE MANY ORGANIZATIONS TEACHING THE BLIND TO DO WONDERFUL THINGS—THEY'LL TEACH YOU TO READ AND WRITE AND ALMOST ANY TRADE, FREE OF CHARGE—

FREE OF CHARGE—MORE CHARITY—HERE I'VE BEEN IN THIS HOSPITAL OVER A MONTH AND UNABLE TO PAY A CENT—YET I'VE BEEN TREATED WITH EVERY CONSIDERATION—NO—ONCE OUT OF THIS PLACE I'LL ACCEPT NO MORE CHARITY

WHILE ANNIE, AT HER BREAKFAST, SKIMS THROUGH THE MORNING PAPER—

I LIKE TO READ "THE VOICE OF THE PEOPLE"—I'VE ALWAYS WONDERED WHAT THIS GUY "ANONYMOUS" LOOKS LIKE—HERE HE'S GOT A ROAST FOR MY FAVORITE FUNNY—

HE CLAIMS IT'S TOO SAD—YEAH—AND IF IT WAS JUST A STALE GAG EACH DAY THIS SAME BIRD WOULD BE YAMMERING THAT IT ISN'T TRUE TO LIFE—ME, I LIKE STORIES TRUE TO LIFE—SHUX—LIFE ISN'T ALL FUNNY—YUH GET SICK OF A BIRD WHO'S ALWAYS TRYIN' TO BE FUNNY—BUT WHY TRY TO PLEASE A BIRD NAMED "ANONYMOUS"?
HAROLD GRAY
Reg. U. S. Pat. Off.; Copyright, 1931, by The Chicago Tribune.

THE MISTAKES I'VE MADE AND THE FOOL I'VE BEEN—THAT TRUST FUND I SET UP FOR ANNIE FOR INSTANCE—I HAD IT ALL ARRANGED BY RADIO—ALL IT NEEDED WAS MY SIGNATURE ON THE PAPERS—THERE SEEMED TO BE NO HURRY—THEN SUDDENLY IT WAS TOO LATE FOR ANYTHING BUT REGRET—

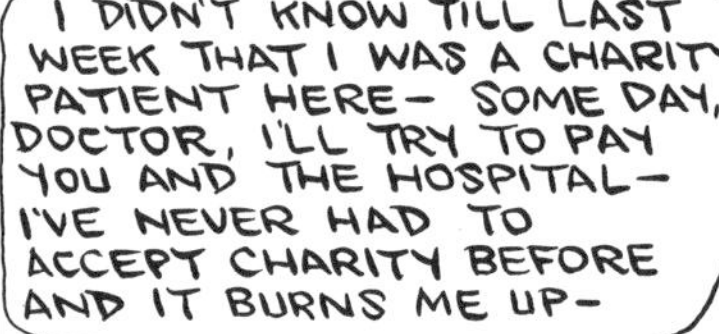
I DIDN'T KNOW TILL LAST WEEK THAT I WAS A CHARITY PATIENT HERE—SOME DAY, DOCTOR, I'LL TRY TO PAY YOU AND THE HOSPITAL—I'VE NEVER HAD TO ACCEPT CHARITY BEFORE AND IT BURNS ME UP—

FORGET IT, OLIVER—SOME DOCTORS BRAG ABOUT ALL THE CHARITY WORK THEY DO—THOSE WHO DO THE MOST BRAG THE LEAST—PERSONALLY I ALWAYS CHARGE THE RICH DOUBLE—IF I DIDN'T DO THIS SO-CALLED CHARITY WORK I'D FEEL I WAS A CHEAT—
Reg. U. S. Pat. Off.; Copyright, 1931, by The Chicago Tribune.

WHILE LITTLE ANNIE, CHEERFUL AND CONTENTED, CONSIDERS HER BLESSINGS—

LEAPIN' LIZARDS! WE SURE HAVE IT SOFT—TH' WORK AT JAKE'S IS JUST PLAY—AND I GET ALL I CAN EAT FREE, EVEN CANDY AN' CAKE AN' ICE CREAM—ANYTHING I WANT. YESSIR, SANDY—WE SURE ARE SITTIN' PRETTY—
ARF!
HAROLD GRAY

'LO, JERRY—JUST HEARD YOU WERE IN HERE AND THOUGHT I'D DROP IN AND SAY HELLO—HOW THEY TREATIN' YOU?
HELLO, BILL—GEE, YER SURE A GOOD SIGHT FOR SORE EYES—

SPEAKIN' OF EYES, WHO IS THAT BIRD WITH TH' BANDAGE OVER HIS LAMPS? BLIND, AIN'T HE?
HIM? YEAH—BLIND AS A BAT—SAYS HIS NAME IS OLIVER—I DUNNO—HE WAS DRIVIN' A TRUCK WHEN HE GOT HURT—

WHOEVER HE IS, HE'S A SWELL GUY—AN' WHAT A DIRTY DEAL HE GOT—TH' COMPANY HE WAS DRIVIN' FOR CLAIMS THEY NEVER HEARD OF HIM—TOO CHEAP TO PAY FOR HIS EYES—BUT WHAT CAN HE DO? NOTHIN'—HOW'S THAT FOR A TOUGH BREAK?
Reg. U. S. Pat. Off.; Copyright, 1931, by The Chicago Tribune.

A TOUGH BREAK! HUH! ONLY HIS EYES—ME, A MIDGET—SOMETHING TO BE POINTED AT AND LAUGHED AT—THEY DON'T RIDICULE A BLIND MAN—CURSED FOR LIFE WITH THESE BANDY LEGS—GREAT SCOTT—AND THEY THINK HE'S HAD A TOUGH BREAK—
HAROLD GRAY

June 22–24, 1931

DOWN, BUT NOT OUT

WELL, DOG GONE - GOT TH' BANDAGE OFF, EH? SAY, THOSE SPECS ARE TH' CLASS - AND YER GETTIN' SO YUH CAN USE THAT CANE GREAT - YOU'LL BE OUT O' HERE PRETTY QUICK NOW - I'VE GOTTA STAY A MONTH LONGER - YOU'RE LUCKY -
YES, SIR - LUCKY - SAY, I WAS TALKIN' TO FLOP-HOUSE BILL ABOUT YOU YESTERDAY - NOW THERE'S A BIRD YOU OUGHTA MEET - HE'S ONLY ABOUT UP TO YER BELT - SOMETHIN' WRONG WITH HIS LEGS - THEY NEVER GREW ANY - ALWAYS BEEN THAT WAY -
BUT WHAT A GUY - THEY DON'T LAUGH AT HIM NONE IN HIS END O' TOWN - NOTHIN' HE WON'T DO FOR A GUY HE LIKES - HE TOOK A SHINE TO YOU RIGHT OFF - NEXT TIME HE COMES IN I'LL HAVE YUH MEET HIM -
SO I'M LUCKY, AM I? WELL, THERE MIGHT BE SOMETHING TO WHAT JERRY SAYS - I HAVE ALL MY ARMS AND LEGS - IF THIS FLOP-HOUSE BILL IS ANY WORSE OFF THAN I AM - - - WELL, I'D LIKE TO MEET HIM - THAT'S ALL -
HAROLD GRAY
Reg. U. S. Pat. Off.; Copyright, 1931, by The Chicago Tribune.
WELL, OLIVER - YOU'LL BE GETTIN' OUT O' THIS JOINT SOON - WHAT DO YOU FIGGER ON DOIN'?
I HAVEN'T BEEN ABLE TO DECIDE YET, BILL - YOU SEE BLINDNESS RATHER HANDICAPS ME TILL I GET USED TO IT -
HANDICAP! THAT'S A GOOD ONE - IF YOU COULD GET A GOOD SLANT AT ME YOU'D KNOW WHAT A REAL HANDICAP IS - BUT IT AIN'T STOPPED ME - NO SIR - WHY, THERE'S NOTHIN' WRONG WITH YOU -
HERE - TAKE MY CARD - YOU MAY FIND TOUGH GOING AT FIRST - IF YOU SHOULD WANT A GOOD PLACE TO BUNK JUST SHOW THIS CARD TO ANYBODY - THEY'LL SEND YOU TO ME -
THANKS, BILL - THAT'S MIGHTY DECENT OF YOU -
WHAT A MAN! IF I ONLY HAD A PAIR O' LEGS LIKE THAT - TH' LUCKY STIFF!
HAROLD GRAY
I SEE THEY PRINTED MY LETTER TO THE "VOICE OF THE PEOPLE" - BY GOLLY, I SURE TOLD 'EM - I SEZ, AIN'T THERE PLENTY SADNESS AND BAD TIMES NOW, WITHOUT YOU SHOULD MAKE THE COMICS SAD TOO? IF YOU DON'T CUT OUT THE SADNESS I WILL QUIT READING YOUR DIRTY SHEET FOR GOOD -
I SAW THAT LETTER, BUT I DIDN'T KNOW YOU WROTE IT -
SURE - I SIGNED IT "ANONYMOUS" - THAT WAY NOBODY CAN GET BACK AT ME -
YI - A MAN SO CLEVER SHOULD BE A BIG SUCCESS IN HIS OWN BUSINESS - THAT WAS A GOOD ONE ABOUT QUITTING THE PAPER - HOW CAN THEY KNOW YOU NEVER BUY A PAPER ANYWAY?
PHOOIE! THAT LOW-LIFE! THAT SNAKE-IN-THE-GRASS! AFRAID TO SIGN HIS NAME TO A LETTER - MAYBE THAT COMIC IS SAD SOMETIMES - IT IS ANYWAY TRUE TO LIFE - BUT SUCH A SMART FELLER HE IS, FOR THREE YEARS NOW HIS WIFE SUPPORTS HIM - FOR WHAT?
YEAH - HIS KIND MAKE ANY TIME A HARD TIME FOR THEMSELVES - SHUX! WE'RE GETTIN' ALONG O. K. -
WHILE AT THE HOSPITAL - - - - - -
WELL, OLIVER, ASIDE FROM THE EYES, YOU'RE AS GOOD AS NEW - AND YOU'RE LEARNING TO GET AROUND GREAT WITH THAT CANE - I'M GOING TO LET YOU LEAVE THE HOSPITAL MONDAY -
THANKS, DOCTOR - I'LL BE GLAD TO GET OUT -
HAROLD GRAY
Reg. U. S. Pat. Off.; Copyright, 1931, by The Chicago Tribune.

June 25–27, 1931
DOWN, BUT NOT OUT

Little Orphan Annie
HM-M-M- I HAVEN'T SEEN A KID PLAYIN' IN TH' STREET FOR TH' LAST THREE BLOCKS- THAT'S SURE UNUSUAL-

GEE- YOU'VE GOT THE STAIRS ALL DONE AND EVERYTHING- CAN I GO UP?
SURE- AND YOU HAVEN'T SEEN ANYTHING YET- JUST WAIT TILL YOU SEE THE ROOF-

LEAPIN' LIZARDS! WHY, IT DOESN'T EVEN LOOK LIKE A ROOF ANY MORE-
AS SOON AS FOLKS HEARD WHAT WAS GOING ON THEY ALL HELPED- CARPENTERS AND PAINTERS WORKED FREE- STORE KEEPERS GAVE ALL KINDS OF THINGS-

THE SPORTING GOODS STORES DID THE MOST- BUT EVERYBODY AROUND HERE DID THEIR BEST-
NO WONDER THERE'S NO KIDS DOWN IN OUR STREET TO-DAY WITH A PLACE LIKE THIS TO COME TO-
STRIKE!
YER CRAZY!
HEY! SHOOT IT THOID!
SLIDE! SLIDE!

GEE! A REAL LITTLE PLAY-HOUSE-
JUST A COUPLE OF OLD PIANO BOXES WITH WINDOWS- BUT THE LITTLE GIRLS GET A LOT OF FUN OUT OF IT-

WHERE DID YOU GET ALL THE SWELL SAND?
ONE OF THE BOYS WHO KEEPS HIS TRUCK IN MY GARAGE GOT THE SAND LAST NIGHT- HE DIDN'T SAY WHERE HE GOT IT AND I DIDN'T ASK HIM- THE KIDS SURE ENJOY IT-

WHERE DO THOSE STAIRS GO?
OH, THEY GO UP ONTO THE BUILDING NEXT DOOR- COME ON- THAT'S A SURPRISE FOR YOU-

WHEE! A REAL SWIMMIN' POOL-
YEP- NOT FANCY- JUST AN OLD TANK- BUT WE CLEANED IT AND PAINTED IT AND BUILT A PLATFORM AROUND IT AND PIPED IT SO THE WATER WILL ALWAYS BE FRESH- IT DOESN'T MAKE SUCH A BAD POOL-

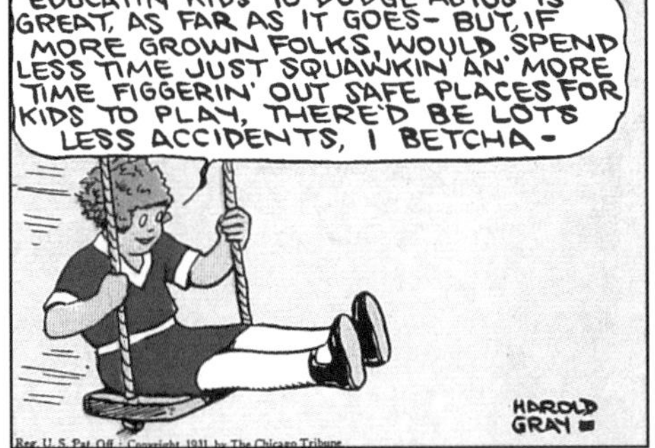
EDUCATIN' KIDS TO DODGE AUTOS IS GREAT, AS FAR AS IT GOES- BUT, IF MORE GROWN FOLKS WOULD SPEND LESS TIME JUST SQUAWKIN' AN' MORE TIME FIGGERIN' OUT SAFE PLACES FOR KIDS TO PLAY, THERE'D BE LOTS LESS ACCIDENTS, I BETCHA-
HAROLD GRAY

June 28, 1931

WELL, OLIVER, GOOD BYE AND GOOD LUCK- IF THERE'S EVER ANYTHING I CAN DO FOR YOU DON'T HESITATE TO LET ME KNOW- THINK OVER THOSE SCHOOLS FOR THE BLIND- THEY'D HELP YOU GET STARTED-
THANKS, DOCTOR- GOOD-BYE-
HE MEANS WELL, BUT I'M THROUGH TAKING CHARITY- I HAVE MY BRAINS- I'LL FIND SOME WAY TO GET ALONG- I WANT NO MORE CHARITY AND NO SYMPATHY-
GLAD I HAVE THIS BEARD TO HIDE BEHIND AND THESE DARK GLASSES- ANNIE'D NEVER RECOGNIZE ME NOW- NOW TO FIND A PLACE TO BOARD AND FIGURE OUT HOW TO GET A START- I'VE COME THREE BLOCKS- LET'S SEE- I TURN RIGHT AT THE NEXT CORNER-
IF YOU'LL STEER ME ACROSS THIS STREET I'LL BE O.K.- YOU SEE THIS IS MY FIRST DAY OUT OF THE HOSPITAL- I'LL GET ALONG ONCE I GET USED TO IT-
SAINTS ABOVE! YOUR FIRST DAY LIKE THAT, AND WALKIN' IN THESE PARTS- YE SURE HAVE YER NERVE-
HAROLD GRAY
Reg. U. S. Pat. Off.; Copyright, 1931, by The Chicago Tribune.
GUESS I'M LOST- I MUST HAVE MISSED A TURN SOME PLACE- BUT WHAT DIFFERENCE DOES IT MAKE WHERE I AM- ONE PLACE IS ABOUT AS GOOD AS ANOTHER- BUT I'VE GOT TO GET SET SOME PLACE SOON-
THAT DOCTOR WAS A FINE CHAP- HE GAVE ME A FEW DOLLARS TO EAT ON, BUT THAT'S ABOUT GONE NOW- I WONDER ABOUT THAT CHAP, FLOP-HOUSE BILL- HE SOUNDED LIKE A MAN WHO COULD GIVE ME SOME SOUND ADVICE-
I SEE YUH STANDIN' HERE- FIGGERED MAYBE SOMETHIN' WAS BOTHERIN' YUH- ANYTHING I COULD DO FOR YUH?
YES- I HAVE A CARD HERE SOME PLACE- THERE'S AN ADDRESS ON IT- MAYBE YOU COULD TELL ME HOW TO GET TO THIS PLACE-
FLOP-HOUSE BILL!!! YOU A FRIEND O' HIS? SAY! I WOULDN'T TELL YUH HOW TO GET TO HIS PLACE, PAL- I'LL TAKE YUH THERE MYSELF AND PROUD TO DO IT-
THANKS- THAT'S SURE NICE OF YOU-
HAROLD GRAY
Reg. U. S. Pat. Off.; Copyright, 1931, by The Chicago Tribune.
HELLO, BILL- WELL, YOU SEE I ACCEPTED YOUR INVITATION- I WANT A PLACE TO SLEEP AND I NEED YOUR ADVICE-
HELLO, OLIVER- GLAD YOU CAME AROUND- GOT PLENTY O' BEDS- I'LL PICK YOU OUT A GOOD ONE-
HERE WE ARE- THE BEST FLOP-HOUSE IN TOWN- CLEAN BLANKETS- GOOD COTS- NICE, QUIET PLACE- HM-M- WAIT- HM-M-
AH, THAT'S NO PLACE FOR TH' LIKES O' YOU- THAT'S FOR BUMS- HERE- YOU COME THIS WAY-
THAT'S O.K. BILL- I'M JUST A BUM MYSELF-
HAROLD GRAY
YOU? A BUM? SAY! YOU CAN'T FOOL ME- I'VE SEEN TOO MANY- HERE- THIS IS MY ROOM, BUT THERE'S AN EXTRA COT AND IT'S YOURS AS LONG AS YOU WANT IT-
Reg. U. S. Pat. Off.; Copyright, 1931, by The Chicago Tribune.

June 29–
July 1, 1931
DOWN, BUT NOT OUT

TAKE ME, F'RINSTANCE- I'VE BEEN A RUNT EVER SINCE I WAS A KID- TH' LEGS NEVER GROWED RIGHT- I WAS SCARED TO GO OUT O' MY OLD MAN'S HOUSE- ALL TH' GANG LAUGHED AT ME AN' MADE FUN O' ME- IT WAS AWFUL-
THEN I WAS LEFT ON ME OWN- I HAD TO GO OUT- WELL, NO NEED GOIN' INTO ALL THAT- BUT THEY DON'T LAUGH AT ME ANY MORE- I MADE GOOD- I'VE GOT A STRING O' FLOP-HOUSES ALL OVER TOWN- I'M IN THIS AND IN THAT- I'M TH' BOSS O' THIS WARD- AND ALL IN SPITE O' BEIN' A DWARF- I'M TELLIN' YUH, OLIVER, IT'S FIGHT THAT COUNTS-
SAY, I KNOW HOW YUH FEEL- ALWAYS BEEN STRONG AN' BIG- BUT DON'T FOLD UP- YOU'VE GOT A GREAT CHANCE- THOUSANDS O' THINGS YOU CAN DO- EYES AREN'T SO MUCH- I KNOW GUYS THAT NEVER SAW THAT ARE GETTIN' ALONG EVEN BETTER'N I AM- BUCK UP- YOU'LL BE GOIN' GREAT 'FORE YOU KNOW IT-
I CAN'T BLAME HIM FOR FEELIN' LOW- HE'LL COME OUT OF IT- IF HE'D NEVER SEEN, IT WOULDN'T BE SO TOUGH- IT'S LOSIN' SOMETHIN' HE'S HAD THAT HURTS- JUST TALKIN' TO HIM MAKES ME FEEL GOOD- HE'S TH' FIRST GUY I EVER KNEW THAT I FIGGERED WAS WORSE OFF THAN ME-
HAROLD GRAY
Reg. U. S. Pat. Off.; Copyright, 1931, by The Chicago Tribune.
SHUX- WHAT'S WRONG WITH BEGGIN'? I'LL BET YOU GAVE PLENTY TO BEGGARS WHEN YOU HAD IT- LET A FEW GUYS GIVE SOMETHIN' TO YOU FOR A CHANGE- I'LL FIX YUH UP WITH A GOOD SPOT, GIVE YUH A DOZEN PENCILS, TAKE CARE O' EVERYTHING, GIVE YUH ROOM AND BOARD AND WE SPLIT 50-50-
I HATE THE VERY IDEA OF BEGGING- BUT WHAT AM I TO DO? BILL IS FEEDING ME AND GIVING ME A COT IN HIS OWN ROOM- IT'S LITTLE ENOUGH TO ASK ME TO DO- I OWE HIM A LOT- WELL, I'LL DO IT, JUST TILL I GET BILL PAID OFF AND TILL SOMETHING TURNS UP- AND HE CAN HAVE ALL I TAKE IN- IT DOESN'T MATTER MUCH WHAT I DO NOW-
WHILE ANNIE'S THOUGHTS ARE OFTEN OF "DADDY WARBUCKS," YET LITTLE DOES SHE SUSPECT HIS REAL PLIGHT-
GEE, HERE'S A LIST O' SAILINGS- YOU KNOW, SANDY, BIG BOATS PULLIN' OUT- HERE'S ONE FOR BUENOS AIRES, AND A COUPLE FOR CHINA, AND ONE FOR SINGAPORE AND A WHOLE BUNCH OF 'EM FOR ENGLAND AN' FRANCE AN' ITALY-
IT WOULDN'T S'PRISE ME IF "DADDY" HAD GONE TO SOME FOREIGN COUNTRY- HE USED TO GO ALL OVER TH' WORLD- HE COULD GET A JOB ON SOME SHIP MOST LIKELY- THAT WOULD S'PLAIN WHY I HAVEN'T HEARD FROM HIM FOR SO LONG- HO, HUM! GEE, I'M SLEEPY- WELL, SANDY, I'M GOIN' TO TURN IN-
HAROLD GRAY
Reg. U. S. Pat. Off.; Copyright, 1931, by The Chicago Tribune.
C'MON, MAW GREEN- I'VE GOT TH' DEVILED EGGS AN' TH' JAM- HAVE YOU GOT TH' TABLE-CLOTH?
WE WANT TO GO TO THE PARK AND WE DON'T CARE HOW QUICK YOU GET US THERE-
GEE, WHIZ- ISN'T THAT STOP-LIGHT EVER GOIN' TO TURN GREEN? WE'VE BEEN SITTIN' HERE FOR TEN MINUTES, I BETCHA-
WE ARE NEARLY THERE- I CAN SEE THE TREES AT THE END OF THIS STREET- COULDN'T YOU MAYBE HURRY A LITTLE, MISTER?
AW, IF YUH WAS IN SUCH A HURRY WHY DIDN'TCHA TAKE A AIRY-PLANE?
I SEE A SPOT- C'MON- HURRY UP AN' LET'S GRAB IT 'FORE SOMEBODY BEATS US TO IT-
Reg. U. S. Pat. Off.; Copyright, 1931, by The Chicago Tribune.
YEAH- IT SURE IS GREAT TO GET OUT IN TH' COUNTRY AWAY FROM THE CROWDS, EH, JAKE?
YES- TREES AND GRASS- THIS IS MY FIRST PICNIC, AND, BELIEVE ME, I LOVE IT-
HERE, SANDY- THIS IS SOMETHIN' YOU'LL LIKE-
HAROLD GRAY

July 2–4, 1931

Little Orphan Annie
WELL, TH' BED'S MADE AND TH' DISHES ARE WASHED- I'M ALL THROUGH FOR TH' DAY-

NOT MUCH OF A VIEW- BACK WINDOWS AND FIRE ESCAPES AND WASHING HANGIN' OUT TO DRY, STILL IT'S SORTA INTERESTIN'- WONDER WHERE "DADDY" IS, AND OLD SPIKE MARLIN- AND WHY DON'T THE SILOS ANSWER THE LETTER I WROTE TO 'EM SIX WEEKS AGO-

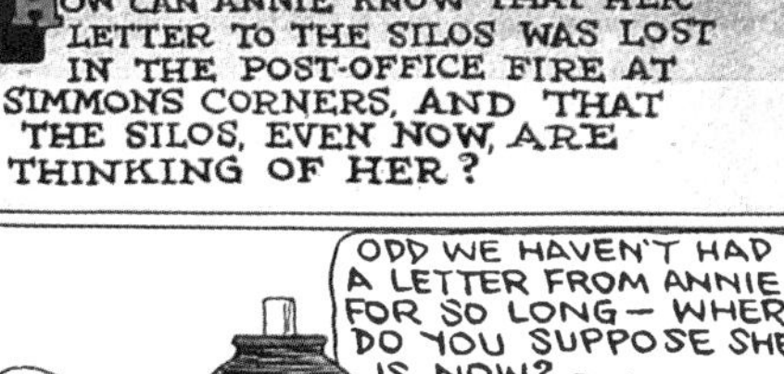
HOW CAN ANNIE KNOW THAT HER LETTER TO THE SILOS WAS LOST IN THE POST-OFFICE FIRE AT SIMMONS CORNERS, AND THAT THE SILOS, EVEN NOW, ARE THINKING OF HER?
ODD WE HAVEN'T HAD A LETTER FROM ANNIE FOR SO LONG- WHERE DO YOU SUPPOSE SHE IS NOW?

OH, MOST LIKELY SHE'S OFF ON A LONG CRUISE WITH MR. WARBUCKS ON HIS YACHT- WE KNOW SHE'S HAPPY AND SAFE WITH SUCH A GUARDIAN- THAT'S THE MAIN THING-
YES, BYRON- I GUESS YOU'RE RIGHT- SILLY OF ME TO WORRY ABOUT HER-

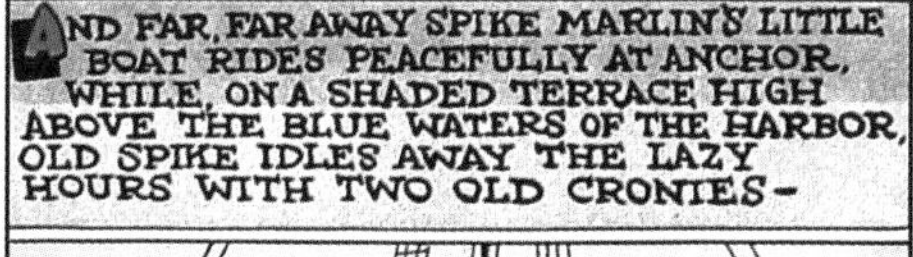
AND FAR, FAR AWAY SPIKE MARLIN'S LITTLE BOAT RIDES PEACEFULLY AT ANCHOR, WHILE, ON A SHADED TERRACE HIGH ABOVE THE BLUE WATERS OF THE HARBOR, OLD SPIKE IDLES AWAY THE LAZY HOURS WITH TWO OLD CRONIES-

AYE, MATES, SHE'S A LITTLE CORKER, THIS ANNIE I'VE BEEN TELLIN' YOU ABOUT- AND ALL OF WARBUCKS' MILLIONS WILL NEVER SPOIL THAT LITTLE LADY- NO SIREE!

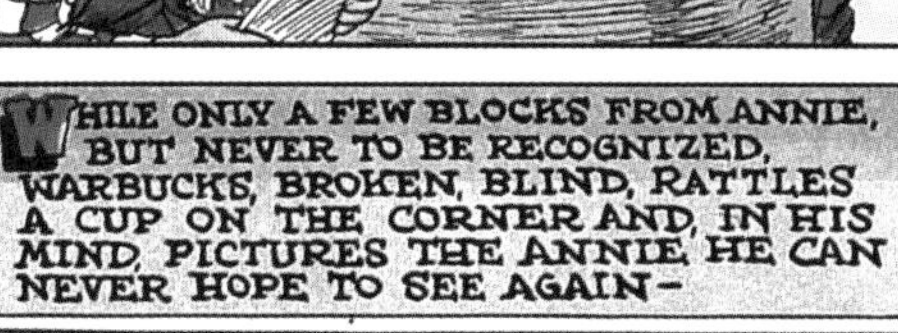
WHILE ONLY A FEW BLOCKS FROM ANNIE, BUT NEVER TO BE RECOGNIZED, WARBUCKS, BROKEN, BLIND, RATTLES A CUP ON THE CORNER AND, IN HIS MIND, PICTURES THE ANNIE HE CAN NEVER HOPE TO SEE AGAIN-

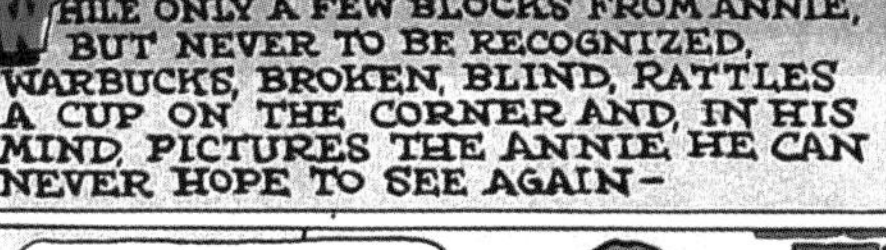

WELL, I GUESS ANNIE WOULD NEVER RECOGNIZE ME NOW- THE POOR LITTLE TYKE- I WONDER HOW SHE'S GETTING ON-

ALL I HOPE IS SHE NEVER DISCOVERS WHAT'S HAPPENED TO ME- SHE HAD SO MUCH FAITH IN ME AND NOW I'M A COMPLETE FAILURE-

BUT ALL THIS IS HIDDEN FROM LITTLE ANNIE- SHE ONLY KNOWS THAT SHE AND SANDY ARE ALONE- BUT WITH THE COURAGE OF YOUTH SHE TAKES EACH DAY AS IT COMES, AND BOLDLY FACES WHATEVER IT MAY BRING-
OH, WELL- NO USE HANGIN' AROUND THE ROOM ALL DAY, SANDY-

LET'S GO FOR A LITTLE WALK- WE COULD GO OVER TO THE RIVER AND WATCH TH' BOATS, OR OVER TO TH' AVENUE, OR UP TO TH' PARK- LOTS O' PLACES TO GO-

I'VE GOT AN IDEA, SANDY- LET'S YOU AN' I GO DOWN TO ANGELO'S AN' GET TWO ICE CREAM CONES- DO YOU THINK YOU COULD FIND ROOM FOR AN ICE CREAM CONE, SANDY?
ARF!

NOT BAD, EH? I TELL YUH, SANDY, WE'RE SITTIN' PRETTY- ME WITH A GOOD JOB AT JAKE'S STORE- PLENTY TO EAT- NOTHIN' TO WORRY ABOUT- YESSIR- WE'RE DOG-GONED LUCKY-
HAROLD GRAY

July 5, 1931
DOWN, BUT NOT OUT

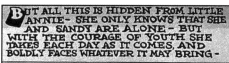

YESSIR, OLIVER- THERE'S MY IDEA OF A REAL GUY- I'VE GOT EVERY PICTURE OF HIM I EVER SAW- CUT 'EM OUT OF TH' PAPERS AND TACKED 'EM UP HERE ON TH' WALL- WHAT A GO-GETTER HE IS!
WHO ARE YOU TALKING ABOUT, BILL?

WHY, THIS CHAP, WARBUCKS- YOU'VE HEARD OF HIM- STARTED FROM NOTHIN', THEY SAY- BUT MONEY NEVER SPOILED A GUY LIKE HIM- YUH KNOW IT'S A SAP IDEA, I S'POSE, BUT I'VE ALWAYS WISHED I COULD BE LIKE THAT GUY- I STARTED FROM NOTHIN', TOO, BUT THAT'S AS FAR AS I GOT BEIN' LIKE HIM- WHAT'S TH' MATTER?

MATTER?

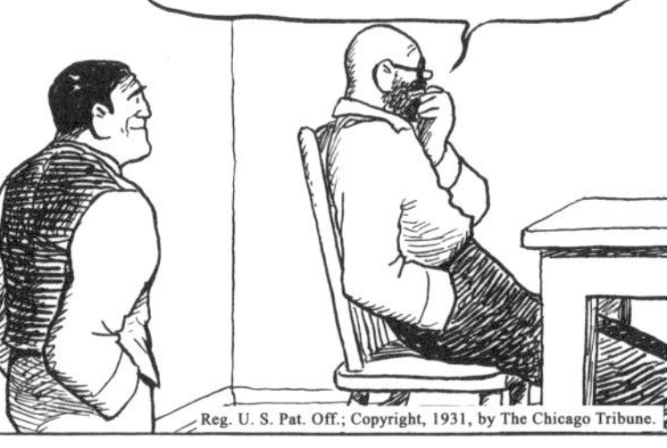
OH, NOTHING- NOTHING AT ALL- HA! HA! SO YOU THINK THAT BIRD WARBUCKS IS QUITE A GUY, EH? I SUPPOSE YOU KNOW HE WENT BROKE A WHILE BACK- LOST EVERY DIME HE HAD- WHERE DO YOU SUPPOSE HE IS NOW?

SURE- I HEARD THAT STORY- BUT I DON'T BELIEVE IT- PROPOGANDA- THOSE RICH BIRDS LIKE WARBUCKS ARE SMART- BET HE STARTED THAT STORY HIMSELF- NO TELLING WHERE HE IS, BUT WHEREVER IT IS, HE'S GETTIN' ALONG O.K.- YOU CAN BET ON THAT-

YEAH? YOU THINK SO, EH?

HAROLD GRAY

YESSIR- I'VE ALWAYS ADMIRED THAT BIRD, WARBUCKS, MORE'N ANY OTHER GUY IN TH' WORLD- NEVER SAW HIM PERSONALLY, BUT HIS PICTURES TELL TH' STORY- WHAT A FACE- HE'S A SCRAPPER- NONE O' YER PUSSY-FOOTIN' SLICK SNOBS, ROBBIN' WIDOWS AN' ORPHANS- HE TOOK HIS AWAY FROM GUYS THAT COULD GIVE HIM A BATTLE-

YUH KNOW, OLIVER, YOU HAVE A LOT TH' SAME BUILD AS WARBUCKS- AND WITHOUT THOSE WHISKERS AND TH' GLASSES, YOU'D LOOK SOMETHIN' LIKE HIM, TOO- FUNNY I NEVER NOTICED THAT BEFORE- DRESSED LIKE HIM YOU'D LOOK A LOT LIKE HIM-
HUH! THAT'S A CRAZY IDEA-

I'VE WATCHED PEOPLE A LOT- I FIGGER THAT FOLKS THAT LOOK ALIKE MOST ALWAYS ARE ALIKE- ACT ALIKE- THINK ALIKE- ALL THAT STUFF- WHY, WITH TH' SAME BREAKS THIS GUY WARBUCKS HAS HAD, YOU MIGHT HAVE BEEN AS BIG A GUY AS HIM- YOU CAN'T TELL-
POPPYCOCK!

WHILE ANNIE, HAVING HEARD NOTHING FROM "DADDY" WARBUCKS, IS FIRMLY CONVINCED HE HAS GONE TO A FAR COUNTRY-

YEAH- I'VE BEEN THINKIN' IT OVER AND I'M SURE OF IT- IF "DADDY" WAS ANYWHERE 'ROUND HERE I'D HAVE HEARD FROM HIM LONG 'FORE THIS- HE MUST HAVE LIT OUT FOR CHINA OR AFRICA OR SOME PLACE WITHOUT HAVIN' A CHANCE TO TELL ME GOOD-BYE-
HAROLD GRAY

SO YOU THINK MR. WARBUCKS WENT MAYBE TO CHINA OR AFRICA, EH?
SURE- NO TELLIN' WHERE- BUT IT'S A CINCH HE'S TAKEN A LONG TRIP OR WE'D HAVE FOUND HIM 'FORE THIS- HE'S ALWAYS BEEN THAT WAY- THINKS NO MORE O' GOIN' HALF WAY 'ROUND TH' WORLD THAN YOU DO O' CROSSIN' TH' STREET- BUT I'LL BE GETTIN' A LETTER 'FORE LONG, I BETCHA-

WHILE FLOP-HOUSE BILL, UNWITTINGLY SHOWS WARBUCKS WHAT A STUMBLE-BUM HE HAS BECOME- THE OLD CHAMPION IS DOWN- WILL HE GET UP?

YEAH! I'VE HEARD ABOUT THIS BIRD, WARBUCKS YOU'VE BEEN RAVING ABOUT- LOST EVERY DIME HE EVER HAD- COULDN'T EVEN GET A JOB- JUST A DOWN-AND-OUTER- A BUM, THEY SAY-

BALONEY! HE MAY HAVE LOST SOME DOUGH, BUT THAT BIRD COULDN'T EVER BE A BUM- HE'S TOO GOOD A FIGHTIN' MAN- HE MIGHT LOSE HIS MONEY BUT NOTHIN' COULD MAKE HIM FOLD UP- NEVER- UP AN' AT 'EM- THAT'S HIM-
SO NOTHING COULD EVER MAKE THIS GUY WARBUCKS FOLD UP, EH? HOW DO YOU KNOW THAT?

HUH! HOW DO I KNOW? WHY, GUYS LIKE WARBUCKS JUST DON'T KNOW TH' MEANING OF THE WORD "QUIT"- THAT'S ALL-
?
HAROLD GRAY

July 6–8, 1931
DOWN, BUT NOT OUT

AM I SO BAD OFF? LOOK AT BILL - LOOK AT THE HANDICAP HE'S ALWAYS HAD - HE'S LAUGHED IT OFF AND MADE GOOD - I'VE LOST MY SIGHT - WELL, WHAT OF IT? SYMPATHIZING WITH MYSELF WON'T BRING IT BACK - IT'S GONE - I'LL GET BY - I'LL BE BIGGER THAN I EVER WAS BEFORE -
BILL DOESN'T RECOGNIZE ME - HOW COULD HE? HE THINKS I'M JUST A BUM - BUT HE IDOLIZES THE MAN I WAS - WELL, WHY NOT BE THAT MAN AGAIN? AM I GOING TO BE A CRY-BABY - A QUITTER? AM I GOING TO LET A LITTLE MISFORTUNE MAKE ME FOLD UP? AM I YELLOW?
NOT BY A LONG SHOT!!! I'LL SHOW 'EM! I'VE BEEN DOWN LONG ENOUGH - NOBODY EVER COUNTED TEN OVER ME YET -
Reg. U. S. Pat. Off.; Copyright, 1931, by The Chicago Tribune.
HEY! WHAT'S TH' BIG NOISE? WHAT HAPPENED? WHY! WHAT TH- - - - - GREAT SAINTS!!! WHY - YOU ARE WARBUCKS!!!
HAROLD GRAY
BUT I CAN'T GET OVER IT - HOW COULD I MISS RECOGNIZIN' YUH? YOU ARE REALLY MR. WARBUCKS -
WELL, WHAT OF IT? SURE - I'M WARBUCKS AGAIN ALL RIGHT - BUT NOBODY MUST KNOW IT - SEE?
NOT A SOUL MUST KNOW WHERE I AM - YOU CALL ME OLIVER - IT'S MY FIRST NAME, ANYWAY - IF I'VE GOT TO WORK IN THE DARK I'LL KEEP MY ENEMIES IN THE DARK, TOO -
CHEE! ME CALLIN' YOU BY YOUR FIRST NAME - BUT ANYTHING YOU SAY GOES - LET ME BE YER EYES, WON'T YER? I CAN KEEP MY LIP BUTTONED AND FOLLOW ORDERS -
BILL - YOU'RE GOING TO BE MY PARTNER - YOU AND I TO-GETHER WILL WHIP THE WORLD AND I'LL SHOW YOU HOW IT'S DONE -
YOUR PARTNER!!! YOUR BRAINS AND MY EYES! WHAT A TEAM!!! WHAT A TEAM!!!
Reg. U. S. Pat. Off.; Copyright, 1931, by The Chicago Tribune.
ALL RIGHT, BILL - FIRST YOU MAKE A LIST OF THINGS WE NEED - WE MUST HAVE A SMALL OFFICE, BUT ONE THAT'S ABSOLUTELY PRIVATE -
YEAH - AND YOU'VE GOTTA HAVE SOME NEW CLOTHES, TOO -
HAROLD GRAY
IF I'D SEARCHED THE WORLD OVER I COULDN'T HAVE FOUND A MORE LOYAL PARTNER THAN BILL - HE HAS A FEW THOUSAND SAVED UP AND IS PUTTING EVERY CENT IN AS A STAKE - THAT'S FAITH FOR YOU - WELL, I'LL NEVER LET HIM DOWN - HE'S DONE ME THE GREATEST GOOD TURN BY MAKING ME SNAP OUT OF IT, AND FORGET MY TROUBLES -
WHEE! THAT'S TH' STUFF - NOW YOU'RE BEGINNIN' TO LOOK LIKE YERSELF - HERE'S TH' DUDS I BROUGHT YUH - GOT AN IDEA O' WHAT YUH LIKE, FROM THOSE PICTURES - HOPE THEY FIT O. K. -
THANKS, BILL - FRESH CLOTHES WILL HELP ME FEEL A LOT LESS LIKE A BUM -
I COULDN'T MAKE TH' GRADE ON A BIG SPARKLER LIKE YOU USED TO WEAR - TH' REAL ONES RUN INTO BIG DOUGH, AND I KNEW YOU WOULDN'T WANT ANY GLASSY -
O. K., BILL - WE'LL HAVE PLENTY FOR DIAMONDS BEFORE LONG - DON'T YOU WORRY -
CHEE! MY PARTNER!
CLOTHES MAY NOT MAKE THE MAN, BUT THEY SURE MAKE HIM FEEL A LOT MORE LIKE ONE - NOW TO GET DOWN TO BUSINESS -
HAROLD GRAY
Reg. U. S. Pat. Off.; Copyright, 1931, by The Chicago Tribune.

July 9–11, 1931
DOWN, BUT NOT OUT

OOPS!
WHAT'S THIS? WHAT'S THIS???
Z-Z-Z
HAROLD GRAY
Chicago Tribune.

CHAPTER SEVEN

AND A BLIND MAN SHALL LEAD THEM

IN WHICH ANNIE

PLAYS THE "QUEEN OF SHEBA" TO CLEOPATRA

RECEIVES A MYSTERIOUS MESSAGE FROM THE ORIENT

AND LEARNS THAT BANKING HER PAYCHECK CAN HAVE AN UNEXPECTED BONUS...

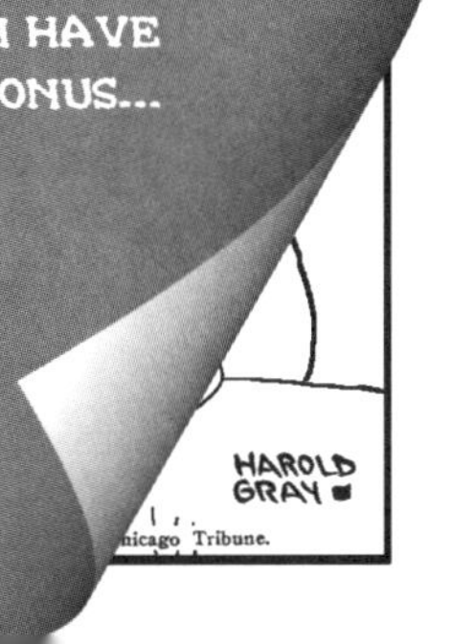

Little Orphan Annie
I'LL BE WITH YOU IN A MINUTE, SANDY-

ARF! ARF!
SH-H-H- DO BE QUIET, SANDY!!! I KNOW I PROMISED TO TAKE YOU FOR A WALK AND GET YOU AN ICE CREAM CONE-

BUT I JUST NOTICED THIS STORY IN TH' MAGZINE SECTION- GOTTA READ THIS FIRST- KEEP AWAY, I TELL YUH- I WON'T BUDGE A STEP TILL I'M DONE WITH THIS STORY-

IDEA

SANDY!

NOW LOOK WHAT YOU DID!!! AND JUST AS I GOT TO TH' MOST 'CITING PART OF TH' STORY, TOO- NOW I NEVER WILL KNOW HOW IT ENDED-

OF ALL TH' CLUMSY YOKELS! WITH ALL TH' FURNITURE IN THIS ROOM TO FALL OVER, YOU HAD TO PICK OUT THAT PARTICULAR CHAIR-

WELL, I HOPE YER SATISFIED! SPOIL MY PAPER AN' MAKE ME ALL KINDS O' WORK CLEANIN' UP THAT BATTER- YOU'D BETTER LOOK SCARED-

THE OLD FRAUD! I'VE HALF A HUNCH HE FIGGERED THAT ALL OUT-

SO ALL DOGS ARE DUMB ANIMALS, EH? HUH! I BET SANDY'S NOT HALF AS DUMB AS THE BIRD WHO MADE THAT CRACK-
HAROLD GRAY
Reg. U. S. Pat. Off.; Copyright, 1931, by The Chicago Tribune.

July 12, 1931
AND A BLIND MAN SHALL LEAD THEM

WELL, HERE IT IS MONDAY- NOW WHAT DO YOU WANT ME TO DO FIRST, MR. WARBUCKS?
FIRST, I'VE GOT TO BREAK YOU O' CALLING ME WARBUCKS! I TOLD YOU ABOUT THAT BEFORE- CALL ME OLIVER!
IF YOU CALL ME WARBUCKS HERE, YOU'LL SLIP AND MENTION MY NAME TO OTHERS- THAT WOULD BE FATAL- IF THE MEN WHO RUINED ME HAD ANY IDEA I WAS TRYING TO COME BACK WE'D NEVER HAVE A CHANCE TO GET SET- SEE?
I MUST WORK FROM THE DARK, IN MORE WAYS THAN ONE- THE MEN WHO STAND BETWEEN US AND SUCCESS MUST NOT EVEN GUESS THAT I'M ALIVE- GIVE ME A MONTH AND I'LL BE IN SHAPE TO PUT UP A BATTLE- TWO MONTHS AND I'LL PICK A BATTLE- BUT NOT YET, BILL-
NOW GET US AN OFFICE- YOU KNOW WHAT WE NEED-
O.K., OLIVER- I'M ON MY WAY- I KNOW JUST TH' SPOT- I OWN TH' OLD BUILDING- IT'S VACANT NOW- NOBODY'D EVER GUESS THAT YOU'D HAVE AN OFFICE THERE-
HAROLD GRAY
Reg. U. S. Pat. Off.; Copyright, 1931, by The Chicago Tribune.
WELL, PUT ON MORE MEN- THIS JOB'S GOTTA BE DONE TO-MORROW- WHAT DO I CARE IF YUH WORK ALL NIGHT? GETTIN' PAID, AIN'TCHA?
O.K. IF YOU SAY SO- SURE GOIN' TO BE ABOUT TH' SWELLEST OFFICE IN TOWN-
AND HERE'S TH' BACK ROOM JUST TH' SPOT FOR OLIVER- NEXT TO MY OFFICE AND WITH A PRIVATE DOOR TO THE BACK STAIRS SO HE CAN SLIP IN OR OUT AN' NOBODY TH' WISER- AND WE'LL HAVE FROSTED GLASS IN ALL TH' WINDOWS SO NO NOSEY BIRDS CAN SEE WHO'S INSIDE-
CHEE! WHAT A CARPET- AN INCH AN' A HALF THICK- BUT IT'S JUST WHAT OLIVER ORDERED- DIGNIFIED, BUT RICH, HE SAYS- AND HE KNOWS WHAT'S WHAT.
Reg. U. S. Pat. Off.; Copyright, 1931, by The Chicago Tribune.
WELL, TH' PLACE IS JUST ABOUT ALL SET- THEY'RE MOVIN' IN TH' FURNITURE- NOW WHAT ELSE DO WE NEED-
GOOD- NOW GET THE 'PHONE IN- A TRUNK LINE AND SWITCHBOARD, BUT AN UNLISTED NUMBER- KEEP IT PRIVATE- SEE? AND I WANT TO ROUND UP A FEW OF MY OLD EMPLOYEES WHO WERE FAITHFUL AND CLOSE-MOUTHED- THAT'LL START OUR ORGANIZATION
HAROLD GRAY
EVER'THING JUST LIKE YOU SAID, OLIVER- THIS IS MY OFFICE WHERE I'LL SIT BACK O' TH' BIG DESK AND TRY TO LOOK SMART-
IT ALL FEELS FINE- THICK CARPET- BIG, EASY CHAIRS- PANELED WALLS, YOU SAY?
YES- AND THIS PANEL SLIDES- AND RIGHT IN HERE IS YOUR OFFICE- YOU'LL BE SITTIN' RIGHT BACK O' ME ALL TH' TIME, BUT NOBODY IN MY OFFICE WILL EVEN GUESS IT- BUT I'VE GOT IT ALL FIXED UP SWELL- I'LL SHOW YUH-
MY OFFICE IS WIRED- HERE'S A SOUND BOX- YOU CAN HEAR EVERY WORD THAT'S SAID OUT THERE- YOU'LL HEAR EVERYTHING BUT WON'T SHOW- I'LL BE OUT THERE LIKE A DUMMY- YOU'LL PULL THE STRINGS.
FINE, BILL- BUT YOU'RE NO DUMMY- YOU'RE MY PARTNER- WE'RE GOING TO WHIP THE WORLD AND NOW WE'RE READY TO STRIKE THE FIRST BLOW-
QUEER, IN A WAY, BEING BLIND- THERE'S ADVANTAGE IN IT, AT THAT- I'LL HAVE ALL MY TIME TO PLAN AND THINK AND OUT-GUESS 'EM ALL- THEY THINK I'M DONE FOR- HUH- LET 'EM KEEP ON THINKING SO- THE UNSEEN POWER BEHIND THE THRONE- WELL, I WILL BE A POWER AGAIN- NOW FOR MY FIRST MOVE-
HAROLD GRAY
Reg. U. S. Pat. Off.; Copyright, 1931, by The Chicago Tribune.

July 13–15, 1931

WHEW - I DIDN'T RE'LIZE HOW LATE IT WAS GETTIN' - NEARLY ONE A.M. - BUT ALL TH' STOCK HAD TO BE RE'RANGED AN' I COULDN'T LET JAKE DO IT ALL ALONE - AND NONE O' THOSE NEW CLERKS KNOW ANYTHING 'BOUT IT - WELL, I'M 'MOST HOME NOW -
OOPS! WHAT'S THIS? WHAT'S THIS???
Z-Z-Z
HEY! WAKE UP, SIS - WHO ARE YOU, ANYWAY? WHERE DIDJA COME FROM? WHO ARE YER FOLKS? HOW DIDJA GET HERE? GEE - CAN'TCHA TALK? D'YUH KNOW IT'S DARN NEAR ONE IN TH' MORNIN'? YOU OUGHTA BE HOME IN BED -
SH, SANDY - SHE'S ASLEEP AGAIN - I DON'T BLAME YUH FOR BEIN' S'PRISED - I WASN'T S'PECTIN' COMPANY MYSELF - BUT WE CAN'T LEAVE THIS KID DOWN IN TH' HALL ALL NIGHT - HER FOLKS WILL SHOW UP IN TH' MORNING -
HAROLD GRAY
Reg. U. S. Pat. Off.; Copyright, 1931, by The Chicago Tribune.
WHADDYUH FIGGER ON DOIN' WITH HER, ANNIE?
OH, I'LL KEEP HER, TILL HER FOLKS SHOW UP - THEY'RE SURE TO BE AROUND LOOKIN' FOR HER SOON -
HER FOLKS! HUH! IT'S MY GUESS YOU WON'T BE SEEING ANY OF THEM - SHE'S ABANDONED - THAT'S ABOUT TH' SIZE OF IT -
ABANDONED NOTHIN' - A CUTE LITTLE KID LIKE THAT? NOT MUCH -
WELL, LOOK AT TH' WAY SHE'S DRESSED - NOT FANCY, BUT LOTS BETTER'N ANY OF TH' BRATS AROUND HERE - AND SHE'S TOO LITTLE TO DO MUCH MORE'N TODDLE - IT'S A CINCH SHE DIDN'T HOOF IT HERE FROM THE OTHER END O' TOWN - NOPE - SHE WAS PLANTED DOWN THERE IN TH' HALL AND WHOEVER PLANTED HER THERE WON'T BE BACK -
HAROLD GRAY
YEAH? GEE - I NEVER THOUGHT O' THAT - WHAT A MEAN TRICK! STILL, I GUESS MAYBE IT WAS A GOOD BREAK FOR TH' KID, IF SHE HAD FOLKS WHO'D PULL A DIRTY TRICK LIKE THAT - HERE, SIS - BETTER NOT BE EATIN' THAT BOX - THIS COOKIE'LL DO YUH LOTS MORE GOOD -
Reg. U. S. Pat. Off.; Copyright, 1931, by The Chicago Tribune.
TCH! TCH! SHE'S JUST A BABY - WHAT WILL EVER BECOME OF HER?
OH, I CAN TAKE CARE OF HER ALL RIGHT -
ONE OF US COULD ADOPT HER, I SUPPOSE -
IT'S OUR DUTY -
OH, BUT THAT'S SILLY - YOU! WHY, YOU'RE FAR TOO YOUNG TO KNOW HOW TO RAISE A CHILD PROPER - YOU CAN'T KEEP HER -
OH, YEAH? WHO SAYS I CAN'T KEEP HER? I'D JUST LIKE TO SEE ANYBODY TRY TO TAKE HER AWAY FROM ME - THAT'S ALL -
YEAH! WHAT'S IT TO YOU BIRDS? I HEARD EVERY WORD - ANNIE'LL RAISE TH' KID BETTER'N ANY O' YOU - MOTHERS, ARE YUH? HUH! WHERE ARE YER OWN KIDS NOW? OUT IN TH' STREET SOME PLACE - YOU DON'T CARE SO LONG AS THEY'RE OUT OF YOUR SIGHT - A FINE BUNCH YOU ARE TO BE GIVIN' ADVICE -
LOOKIE, MAW GREEN - SHE'S TAKING A BIG SHINE TO YOU - SHE KNOWS WHO HER FRIENDS ARE -
YEAH - SHE'S A SMART KID - RAISIN' HER MAY BE A BIG JOB, BUT BETWEEN YOU AN' ME AN' SANDY I GUESS WE CAN MANAGE IT - GOOD NATURED, AIN'T SHE - BUT I GUESS MY OLD FUNNY-FACE IS ENOUGH TO MAKE ANYBODY LAUGH -
HAROLD GRAY
Reg. U. S. Pat. Off.; Copyright, 1931, by The Chicago Tribune.

July 16–18, 1931

Little Orphan
Annie
ARF!
SH-H-H- NOT SO LOUD, SANDY- SIS IS TAKIN' HER NAP-

AW, YUH WOKE HER UP- OH, WELL- SHE'S BEEN SLEEPIN' ALL AFTERNOON-
UMPH

WELL, SIS, HOW DO YOU FEEL NOW? HOW WOULD YOU LIKE SOME SWELL CRACKERS AND MILK?
EAT? UH-HUH-

THERE YOU ARE, SIS- AND WHILE YOU'RE CLEANIN' THAT UP I'LL SLIP DOWN TO TH' CORNER AND GET A PINT OF ICE CREAM- D'YUH LIKE ICE CREAM?
ITH CREAM- GOOD!

GEE- I'VE ALWAYS WANTED A KID SISTER- WHAT A BREAK, FINDIN' HER IN OUR HALL LIKE WE DID- SHE'S TOO LITTLE TO 'MEMBER HER NAME, OR WHO HER FOLKS ARE- BUT IF THEY WANTED HER VERY BAD THEY WOULDN'T HAVE LET HER GET LEFT IN OUR HALL- WELL, I WANT HER AND I'LL KEEP HER- NIX, SANDY- YOU STAY HERE AND LOOK OUT FOR SIS TILL I GET BACK-

?

!

WELL, I'LL BE A SARDINE! WHAT A KID- CLEANED UP HER CRACKERS AND MILK AND WENT RIGHT BACK TO SLEEP- LUCKY SHE'S NOT THE KIND THAT HAS TO BE WATCHED-

HUH! I THOUGHT I TOLD YOU TO LOOK OUT FOR SIS- HERE I COME HOME AND FIND YOU ALMOST ASLEEP- WHAT IF SHE'D TRIED TO CLIMB OUT A WINDOW, OR SOMETHIN'?
HAROLD GRAY

July 19, 1931
AND A BLIND MAN SHALL LEAD THEM

WELL, I GUESS YOU WERE RIGHT MAW GREEN, ABOUT HER FOLKS LEAVIN' HER HERE ON PURPOSE - AT LEAST NOBODY'S BEEN AROUND FOR HER YET -
YOU MIGHT PUT AN AD IN THE PAPERS ABOUT HER -
UM - GOOD -
AN AD TELLIN' ABOUT ME FINDIN' HER IN TH' HALL? SAY! ARE YOU TRYIN' TO KID ME, OR WHAT?
-WELL, MAYBE HER FOLKS WOULD BE SHAMED INTO TAKING HER BACK - THEY'D BE ALMOST SURE TO SEE YER AD IN TH' PAPER -
YEAH - AN' THEY'RE NOT TH' ONLY ONES THAT'D SEE IT - IF HER FOLKS WERE MEAN AND LOW-DOWN ENOUGH TO WANT TO LOSE HER, THEY'D NEVER PEEP - BUT THERE'D BE A BUNCH O' NOSEY UP-LIFT BIRDS HERE IN NO TIME - THEY'D POP TH' KID INTO SOME OLD ORPHANAGE AN' FIGGER THEY'D DONE SOMETHIN' REAL NOBLE -
COURSE SOME ORPHAN HOMES ARE O.K., I S'POSE - BUT NO ORPHANAGE FOR HER - SHE'LL BE NO FACTORY PRODUCT - THIS KID'LL BE HAND RAISED, AND BY ME, OR I'LL KNOW TH' REASON WHY -
GOOD FOR YOU, ANNIE -
HAROLD GRAY
Reg. U. S. Pat. Off.; Copyright, 1931, by The Chicago Tribune.
GEE, JAKE - I'M AWFUL SORRY I'M SO LATE THIS MORNIN' - BUT I WAS SO BUSY GETTIN' TH' KID DRESSED AND FED THAT I DIDN'T NOTICE HOW LATE IT WAS GETTIN' -
THAT'S ALL RIGHT, ANNIE - BUT I DON'T UNDERSTAND - THIS KID - WHAT KID IS THAT?
OH, GEE - I FORGOT - I WASN'T GOIN' TO TELL ANYBODY 'BOUT HER - BUT I CAN TELL YOU - YOU WON'T BLAB - SHE'S JUST A LITTLE BABY, 'BOUT A YEAR AND A HALF OLD - SOMEBODY LEFT HER IN OUR HALL AND I'M RAISIN' HER -
BUT WHO WILL TAKE CARE OF HER WHILE YOU ARE HERE AT THE STORE?
OH, SHE'LL BE O.K. - SANDY'S THERE WITH HER - AND MAW GREEN LOOKS IN NOW AND THEN - SHE'S A SWELL KID - HARDLY YELPS AT ALL AND EATS ANYTHING - Y'OUGHTA SEE HER GO FOR BANANAS - COURSE I DON'T LET HER HAVE TOO MANY - AND IS SHE CUTE! CURLY HAIR - I CAN'T FIGGER ANY FOLKS WANTIN' TO GET RID OF A KID LIKE THAT - BUT IT'LL BE A BREAK FOR HER, 'CAUSE I'M GOIN' TO GIVE HER A REAL HOME - SEE?
YI - SUCH A GIRL - NOW SHE TAKES IN A LITTLE WAIF TO RAISE - SHE IS YOUNG IN YEARS - YES - BUT SHE WILL RAISE THAT KID FINE - MAYBE IF I WORK IT RIGHT ANNIE WILL LET OLD JAKE BE GOD-FATHER TO THIS LITTLE ONE - I THINK I COULD BE A GOOD GOD-FATHER -
HAROLD GRAY
Reg. U. S. Pat. Off.; Copyright, 1931, by The Chicago Tribune.
POOR SANDY - HE LIKES TH' KID ALL RIGHT, BUT HAVIN' TO STAY IN AND LOOK OUT FOR HER BORES HIM SILLY - BUT I DON'T NEED TO WORRY 'BOUT HER WHEN HE'S HERE - NOW I'LL GET HOME AS EARLY AS I CAN, SANDY - YOU TAKE GOOD CARE OF HER - UNDERSTAND?
ARF!
YIPE!
HA - HA -
ME CATCH!
?
?
HAROLD GRAY
Reg. U. S. Pat. Off.; Copyright, 1931, by The Chicago Tribune.

July 20–22, 1931

AND A BLIND MAN SHALL LEAD THEM

BUT YOU MUST HAVE A NAME - CAN'T YOU REMEMBER? WHAT DID THEY CALL YOU? THINK HARD - WAS IT HELEN? OR DOROTHY, MAYBE - OR HAZEL - SURE IT WASN'T HAZEL? OR LORETTA - OR MARY - OR WAS IT GENEVIEVE? NO?

BABY - THAT'S NO REAL NAME - CHARLOTTE OR CATHERINE OR JANE - NOPE? ALL WRONG NUMBERS, EH? LOUISE, MAYBE - BESSIE - ELSIE - FRANCES - CLARA - EMMA - NO? HM-M-M--- GEORGIA - CAROLINE - GEE WHIZ - HAVEN'T YOU ANY NAME?
BABY!

ROSE OR VIOLET OR PANSY OR JUNE OR MAY - ALL MISSES, EH? HOW ABOUT CYNTHIA OR ZOLA OR PEARL OR RUBY? LEAPIN' LIZARDS! LISTEN TO ME, KID - SPEAK UP - YOU MUST HAVE SOME NAME -
KID -

WELL, I GIVE UP - I'VE TRIED ALL TH' NAMES I CAN THINK OF ON HER, BUT NOT ONE OF 'EM GETS TH' SLIGHTEST RISE OUT OF HER - MAYBE IT'LL COME TO HER LATER - I DON'T KNOW WHAT ELSE WE CAN DO, 'CEPT JUST WAIT -
HAROLD GRAY
Reg. U. S. Pat. Off.; Copyright, 1931, by The Chicago Tribune.

?
WAH! HOO! HOO! HOO!

YEOW! OW! WOW! WOW!

ULP!

HA! HA! HA! BALL -
HAROLD GRAY
Reg. U. S. Pat. Off.; Copyright, 1931, by The Chicago Tribune.

NAMES - NAMES - NAMES - I NEVER KNEW THERE WERE SO MANY - AS LONG AS TH' KID CAN'T REMEMBER WHAT HER OWN NAME IS, I'M GOIN' TO GIVE HER ONE - BUT IT'S GOTTA BE SOMETHIN' DIFFERENT -

WHAT IF I DO GIVE HER A DIFFERENT NAME FROM TH' ONE SHE STARTED WITH? IT WAS A BUM START SHE HAD, ANYWAY - NOW SHE'S GETTIN' A NEW START AND SHE OUGHTA HAVE A NEW NAME - LET ME SEE - I KNOW - CLEOPATRA!

SAY, SANDY, I THINK WE'VE GOT IT - YES, SIR - CLEOPATRA - IT'S A GOOD NAME, ANY WAY YOU LOOK AT IT - WE CAN CALL HER PAT, WHEN SHE'S LITTLE - AND WHEN SHE GROWS UP TO BE A GREAT LADY, CLEOPATRA WILL BE A SWELL, HIGH-TONED NAME -

GEE - TH' LITTLE DARLIN' - NOT A WORRY IN TH' WORLD - WHAT A LONG WAY SHE'S GOT TO GO! AND WHAT A LOT O' BUMPS AHEAD FOR HER - AN ORPHAN KID, SAME AS I'VE ALWAYS BEEN BUT I'LL DO ALL I CAN TO MAKE THINGS EASIER FOR HER - I'LL ALWAYS GIVE HER A REAL HOME, BUT I CAN'T SHIELD HER FROM EVER'THING - OH, IF SHE COULD ALWAYS STAY JUST LIKE SHE IS NOW AND NEVER GROW UP -
HAROLD GRAY
Reg. U. S. Pat. Off.; Copyright, 1931, by The Chicago Tribune.

July 23–25, 1931

Little Orphan Annie
OH, HELLO, MAW GREEN - COME RIGHT ON IN -

"SIS" IS NO NAME FOR THE KID - SHE'S GOT TO HAVE A REAL NAME - HAVEN'T YOU THOUGHT OF ONE YET?
ONE NAME! HUH! I'VE THOUGHT OF A HUNDRED NAMES, BUT NOT ONE OF 'EM SEEMS JUST RIGHT -

HERE'S A LIST I MADE LAST NIGHT - ESTHER - HELEN - MARY - JANE - LOUISE - DOROTHY - VIRGINIA - CHARLOTTE - AGNES - OTTILIE - ROSE -
HM-M-M--- NOPE - ALL PRETTY NAMES, BUT NONE OF 'EM JUST RIGHT FOR THE KID -

SAY! I JUST THOUGHT OF A RING-TAILED KNOCKOUT OF A NAME - PERFECT ANY WAY YOU LOOK AT IT -
YEAH? WHAT IS IT?

CLEOPATRA!
!

WHAT? CLEOPATRA!!! ARE YOU CRAZY? SAY! I READ ABOUT THAT DAME - SHE WAS A WILD ONE, ACCORDING TO THAT STORY - THAT'D BE A SWELL NAME TO HANG ONTO A POOR LITTLE KID, WOULDN'T IT?

AW, IT'S A GOOD NAME - I'LL BET THOSE STORIES ABOUT CLEOPATRA ARE THE BUNK - HUH! D'YUH FALL FOR EVERYTHING YOU READ?
NO! BUT CLEOPATRA! THAT'S NO NAME FOR A REAL KID -

WHAT'LL THEY BE CALLIN' HER? CLEO! SUFFERIN' CATS! D'YUH WANT A "CLEO" IN TH' FAMILY? PIN THAT SAPPY NAME ONTO HER AND, AS SOON AS SHE GETS BIG ENOUGH, SHE'LL BEAT YER BLOCK OFF -

OH, YEAH? WELL, IF IT'S ANY NEWS TO YOU, TH' NICKNAME FOR CLEOPATRA ISN'T CLEO - IT'S PAT!
PAT?

HM-M-M - PAT, IS IT? WELL, THAT'S NOT SO BAD - PAT'S A GOOD, SOLID, HONEST NAME, FOR A BOY - AND, FOR A GIRL, IT'S SORTA CUTE, AIN'T IT? HM-M - PAT -

YEAH - AND IT JUST FITS THE LITTLE TYKE - DON'T YOU THINK SO?
YEAH - IT DOES, AT THAT - D'YUH KNOW, I LIKE THAT NAME -
HAROLD GRAY

AND WHEN SHE GROWS UP TO BE A GREAT LADY CLEOPATRA WILL SOUND GRAND - ANY WAY YOU LOOK AT IT, IT'S A FINE NAME -
HERE, PAT - COME TO OLD MAW GREEN - WHADDYUH SAY?
PAT -
Reg. U. S. Pat. Off.; Copyright, 1931, by The Chicago Tribune.

July 26, 1931
AND A BLIND MAN SHALL LEAD THEM

WHEN YOU FIRST SAID "CLEOPATRA" I THOUGHT IT WAS A TERRIBLE NAME - BUT, LIKE YOU SAID, EVERYBODY'LL CALL HER PAT - AND THERE'S SURE NOTHIN' WRONG WITH THAT - DOES SHE KNOW HER NEW NAME YET?
HEY, PAT, WHAT'S YER NAME?
PAT-

WELL, PAT, ANNIE'S GOTTA BE GETTIN' TO TH' STORE - BUT I'LL BE HOME EARLY AND SANDY'LL STAY HERE WITH YOU, SO YOU'LL BE O. K. - NOW WHADDYUH SAY TO ANNIE?

G-BYE, ANNIE-

WHAT A KID! SHARP AS A TACK - KNOWS HER NEW NAME ALREADY - GLAD MAW GREEN LIKES TH' NAME - I KNOW "PAT" WOULD BE A HIT WITH HER - WAIT'LL I TELL JAKE ABOUT THIS -

SO - CLEOPATRA IT IS - I HAD THOUGHT MAYBE YOU WOULD CALL HER REBECCA - I WOULD HAVE LIKED TO BE GOD-FATHER TO A LITTLE BECKY - BUT PAT IS A GOOD NAME TOO-
WELL, YOU CAN BE HER GOD-FATHER, EVEN IF HER NAME IS PAT, CAN'TCHA, JAKE?
HAROLD GRAY

BY GOLLY, OLIVER, YOU SURE KNOW YOUR STUFF - GUESS WHAT YOU'VE RUN THAT TEN THOUSAND WE STARTED WITH UP TO - WELL, I'LL TELL YOU - FIVE HUNDRED THOUSAND BERRIES!!!

HALF A MILLION DOLLARS!!! THINK OF IT - WE'RE RICH, OLIVER! RICH!
RICH? HALF A MILLION?

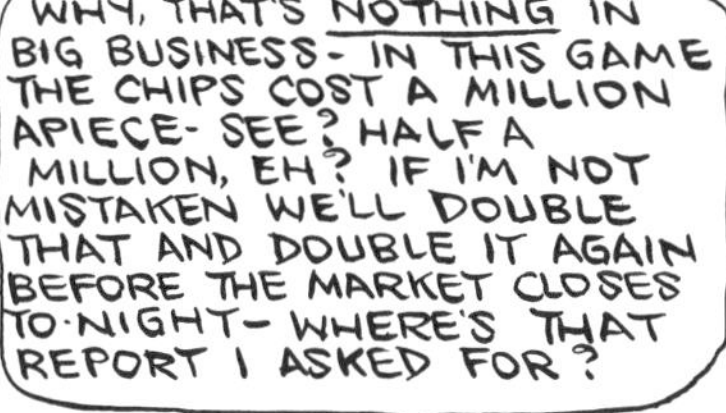
WHY, THAT'S NOTHING IN BIG BUSINESS - IN THIS GAME THE CHIPS COST A MILLION APIECE - SEE? HALF A MILLION, EH? IF I'M NOT MISTAKEN WE'LL DOUBLE THAT AND DOUBLE IT AGAIN BEFORE THE MARKET CLOSES TO-NIGHT - WHERE'S THAT REPORT I ASKED FOR?

IF I COULD ONLY SEE - BUT AT LEAST I CAN HEAR - SO READ, BILL - LET'S FIND OUT WHAT THAT CROWD'S UP TO NOW - THEN WE'LL FIGURE WHERE TO SET OUR TRAP AND HOW TO BAIT IT -
HAROLD GRAY

SAY, OLIVER - WASN'T IT THIS BIRD, BULLION, TH' BANKER, THAT PUT TH' SKIDS UNDER YOU? HE'S TH' GUY WE'RE AFTER, ISN'T HE?
BULLION? OH, HE LET ME DOWN ALL RIGHT - BUT HE WAS ONLY FOLLOWING HIS ORDERS - I REALIZE THAT NOW -

HE'S A BIG BANKER, BUT, EVEN SO, HE'S JUST A FLUNKY FOR THE BIG BOY - THE REAL HEAD OF THE RING IS J. J. SHARK AND HE'S WELL-NAMED - YOU NEVER HEAR MUCH ABOUT HIM - HE LETS OTHERS, LIKE BULLION, DO HIS DIRTY WORK AND TAKE THE DOUBTFUL GLORY - BUT HE GIVES THE ORDERS AND HE TAKES THE LION'S SHARE OF THE LOOT -

WHILE, IN THE MEANTIME, J. J. SHARK HIMSELF PREPARES TO TAKE THE PUBLIC FOR A FEW MORE MILLIONS -

WELL, GENTLEMEN, I BELIEVE THE TIME HAS ARRIVED TO SHEAR US A FEW LAMBS - AS YOU KNOW, MILLIONS OF SMALL STOCK HOLDERS NOW HOLD SHARES OF OUR VARIOUS COMPANIES, MOSTLY ON MARGIN -

OUR COURSE IS CLEAR - BY DUMPING A FEW THOUSAND SHARES ON THE MARKET CONFIDENCE WILL BE DESTROYED AND THE POOR SUCKERS WILL ALL TRY TO SELL AT ONCE - WE SELL AT THE TOP, THEN BUY AT THE BOTTOM AND BE READY TO DO IT ALL OVER AGAIN, AS SOON AS THE POOR PUBLIC HAS FORGOTTEN AND THE SUCKERS HAVE SAVED ENOUGH OF THEIR WAGES TO MAKE IT WORTH OUR WHILE -
HAROLD GRAY

July 27–29, 1931

QUICK, OLIVER- WHAT SHALL I DO? THE BOTTOM'S DROPPED OUT- SOMEBODY IS DUMPING STOCKS RIGHT AND LEFT- IT LOOKS LIKE THAT GUY, SHARK, STARTED IT- BUT IF WE DON'T DO SOMETHING QUICK WE'LL BE CLEANED OUT- SHOULD I TRY TO SELL EVERYTHING WE HAVE AND GET OUT WHILE THERE'S TIME?
SELL? GREAT SCOTT, NO! THIS MAY BE OUR CHANCE- WHEN I WAS IN THE GAME SHARK WAS CAREFUL- BUT HE'S BEEN GETTING CARELESS LATELY- LET HIM SELL, SELL, SELL!!! WE CAN'T COVER ALL HIS STOCKS- WE'LL CONCENTRATE WHERE WE CAN DAMAGE HIM THE MOST-
BUT BUY CAREFULLY, BILL- WE MUSTN'T SHOW OUR HAND- BUT, IF I KNOW SHARK, HE'LL SELL SHORT- THEN IT'LL BE OUR TURN- WHEN HE WANTS TO BUY HE'LL HAVE TO BUY FROM US SEE? WHERE'S THE TELEPHONE?
HAROLD GRAY
WE CAN'T HOPE TO FIGHT HIM ON A REALLY BIG SCALE- BUT IF WE PUT THIS OVER WE'LL PUT A DENT IN HIM AND MAKE ENOUGH TO PUT US IN THE GAME AT THE SAME TIME- HERE- YOU'VE GOT THE PHONE- NOW DO JUST AS I TELL YOU-..
Reg. U. S. Pat. Off.; Copyright, 1931, by The Chicago Tribune.
YOU'LL GET A COOKIE WHEN SUPPER'S READY, PAT, AND NOT BEFORE-
COOKIE?
IF YOU EAT COOKIES NOW YOU WON'T HAVE ANY APPETITE FOR SUPPER-
LEAPIN' LIZARDS!!! HOW DID YOU EVER GET THAT COOKIE? OH, I SAW YOU POP IT INTO YOUR MOUTH- BUT HOW DIDJA REACH IT?
WHILE "DADDY" WARBUCKS STARTS SOFTLY AND QUIETLY BACK UP THE LADDER OF FORTUNE FROM WHICH HE WAS PUSHED SO RUTHLESSLY-
SHARK'S STILL SELLING, EH? IF HE JUST KEEPS THAT UP A LITTLE LONGER WE'LL HAVE HIM- AND SO FAR HE DOESN'T EVEN SUSPECT WE'RE IN THIS GAME- WHAT A SHOCK WHEN WE CALL FOR DELIVERY AND HE FINDS HE CAN'T DELIVER-
HAROLD GRAY
Reg. U. S. Pat. Off.; Copyright, 1931, by The Chicago Tribune.
IF YOU BIRDS WANT ANY O' THIS YOU'LL HAVE TO SPEAK QUICK- I'LL BET YOU DON'T KNOW WHAT THIS IS, ANYWAY, DO YOU, PAT?
ARF!
ITH KEEM!
HEY! WHAT IS THIS? A RACE? LISTEN! TH' FIRST ONE DONE HAS TO TAKE A NAP FOR AN HOUR- THERE- I THOUGHT THAT'D SLOW YUH DOWN-
WHILE WARBUCKS AND BILL GO INTO CONFERENCE-
WELL, AS NEAR AS I CAN MAKE IT, WE HAVE FORTY-EIGHT PERCENT OF THE STOCK WE NEED-
YES- AND SHARK STILL ISN'T WISE TO US-
Reg. U. S. Pat. Off.; Copyright, 1931, by The Chicago Tribune.
HE'S BOUND TO SELL A LOT MORE MONDAY- THEN WE CAN PICK UP ENOUGH TO CONTROL- AND IF HE DOESN'T WE HAVE AS GOOD A CHANCE AS HE TO GRAB WHAT WE NEED IN THE OPEN MARKET FOR HE CAN'T BE HOLDING MUCH OF IT NOW- YEP, BILL- IT BEGINS TO LOOK LIKE SHARK IS DUE FOR A BIG SURPRISE SOON-
HAROLD GRAY

July 30–
August 1, 1931

Little Orphan Annie

PAT'S SOUND ASLEEP AT LAST— NOW, SANDY, I'VE GOT TO GO OUT, BUT I WON'T BE GONE LONG— MOST LIKELY SHE WON'T WAKE UP, BUT YOU STAY HERE, JUST IN CASE— IT'LL BE AN EASY JOB FOR YOU, SANDY—

AN-NIE!
BANG!
?

AN-NIE! BOO-HOO!!!
? ? ? ?

WAH! WAH!

YEOW!

?

BLAH!

?

HA!
YI!

HA! HA! HA! HA! HA-HA- HA!
Reg. U. S. Pat. Off.; Copyright, 1931, by The Chicago Tribune.

WELL, WELL— HAVIN' A HIGH OLD TIME— EH, SANDY? I HEARD YOU TWO WHOOPIN' IT UP AS I CAME UP-STAIRS— I'LL BET YOU WOKE PAT UP ON PURPOSE, SO SHE'D PLAY WITH YOU—
HAROLD GRAY

August 2, 1931
AND A BLIND MAN SHALL LEAD THEM

SHARK AND HIS CROWD DON'T SEEM TO SUSPECT WE'RE OUT AFTER THEM YET, DO THEY?
NOPE - THEY'RE STILL SELLING AND WE HAVE ALL WE NEED TO SQUEEZE THEM - ALL WE HAVE TO DO NOW IS SIT TIGHT AND WAIT FOR THE BLOW-OFF.
SAY, BILL - I'M WORRIED ABOUT LITTLE ANNIE - I'VE BEEN WORRIED RIGHT ALONG, BUT I CAN'T FIGURE HOW TO GET IN TOUCH WITH HER WITHOUT HER FINDING OUT I'M BLIND -
LITTLE ANNIE? OH YES - I REMEMBER - THAT'S THE ORPHAN KID YOU WERE TELLING ME ABOUT -
HERE'S WHAT I'VE BEEN THINKING - WHY CAN'T YOU DO A LITTLE DETECTIVE WORK? I'LL GIVE YOU HER ADDRESS - SEE HOW SHE'S GETTING ON - I'VE GOT TO KNOW THAT SHE'S ALL RIGHT -
SURE - WHAT'S THAT ADDRESS AGAIN?
JUST LEAVE IT TO ME, OLIVER - I'LL FIND OUT ALL ABOUT HER - I'LL CHECK UP ON MAW GREEN AND JAKE AND TH' WHOLE OUTFIT - IT'S A CINCH -
HAROLD GRAY
Reg. U. S. Pat. Off.; Copyright, 1931, by The Chicago Tribune.
SO YOU WANT TO LOOK AT ROOMS, EH? WELL, I'VE GOT A COUPLE OF VACANT ROOMS, BUT I DON'T THINK THEY'D SUIT YUH -
OH, I'M NOT PARTICULAR - MAYBE I COULD TAKE ONE AND CHANGE LATER WHEN SOME ONE MOVES OUT - I'M JUST LOOKING TO-DAY, ANYWAY -
SURE, YOU CAN LOOK AT THAT ROOM - BUT IT'S OCCUPIED AND IT WON'T BE VACANT - SPECIAL FRIEND O' MINE HAS IT - LITTLE ORPHAN GIRL - WORKS IN A STORE NEAR HERE - ONE OF THE SWEETEST KIDS YOU EVER SAW -
THAT'S CLEOPATRA - CALL HER PAT - ANNIE FOUND HER IN TH' HALL ONE NIGHT AND IS RAISIN' HER - CUTE LITTLE TRICK, AIN'T SHE?
HELLO, PAT -
'LO
WELL, DIDJA SEE ANY ROOM YOU'D LIKE TO RENT? IF YOU DID I COULD HOLD IT FOR YOU -
THANKS - BUT I'LL LOOK A LITTLE FARTHER - THEY'RE ALL FINE ROOMS - I MAY BE BACK -
HAROLD GRAY
Reg. U. S. Pat. Off.; Copyright, 1931, by The Chicago Tribune.
YOU SEE WE DON'T GET MUCH CALL FOR IT, SO WE DON'T STOCK IT - BUT I'LL CALL JAKE - HE'S THE BOSS AND I'M SURE HE'LL BE GLAD TO ORDER IT FOR YOU -
I WILL BE GLAD TO ORDER ANYTHING YOU WANT, MISTER -
YES, THAT'S WHAT THE LITTLE GIRL SAID - SAY, SHE'S A SMART KID, ALL RIGHT - KNOWS HER BUSINESS - DOES SHE WORK HERE RIGHT ALONG? SHE SEEMS PRETTY YOUNG TO BE A REGULAR CLERK -
ANNIE? HA - SHE IS NO REGULAR CLERK - LIKE MY OWN DAUGHTER IF I HAD ONE, ONLY SMARTER - SHE IT IS WHO GOT ME TO ENLARGE MY STORE - SUCH A HEAD FOR BUSINESS - AND ALWAYS POLITE - ANYTHING IN MY STORE SHE COULD HAVE FREE - SO MUCH I THINK OF HER -
WELL, I GUESS NOBODY NEED WORRY A WHOLE LOT ABOUT THAT KID - BEIN' AN ORPHAN IS TOUGH IN PLENTY O' WAYS, BUT BEIN' ON YER OWN SURE TEACHES YOU TO TAKE CARE OF YOURSELF - NO WONDER WARBUCKS THINKS A LOT OF HER - WHO WOULDN'T LOVE AN INDEPENDENT KID LIKE THAT -
HAROLD GRAY
Reg. U. S. Pat. Off.; Copyright, 1931, by The Chicago Tribune.

August 3–5, 1931

I WISH BILL WOULD SHOW UP- HE OUGHT TO HAVE ALL THE DOPE ON ANNIE BY THIS TIME- WONDER WHAT'S KEEPING HIM- AH, HERE HE COMES NOW- I CAN TELL HIS STEP-
WELL, OLIVER, YOU DON'T NEED TO WORRY ABOUT THAT KID- SHE'S O. K.- BETWEEN MAW GREEN AND JAKE SHE'S LIVIN' SWELL- PLENTY TO EAT AND A GOOD HOME- THOSE TWO THINK A LOT OF HER- SHE'S RAISIN' A KID NOW-
WHAT?

SURE- ANNIE FOUND A LITTLE GIRL IN TH' HALL- JUST OLD ENOUGH TO TALK A LITTLE- CUTE AS A BUG- SHE'S NAMED TH' KID CLEOPATRA, OR PAT FOR SHORT- OH, YES- I ALMOST FORGOT- ANNIE IS SURE YOU'VE GONE TO SOME FOREIGN COUNTRY, PROBABLY CHINA-

SO ANNIE THINKS I'VE GONE TO CHINA, EH? HM-M-M-

HAROLD GRAY
Reg. U. S. Pat. Off.; Copyright, 1931, by The Chicago Tribune.
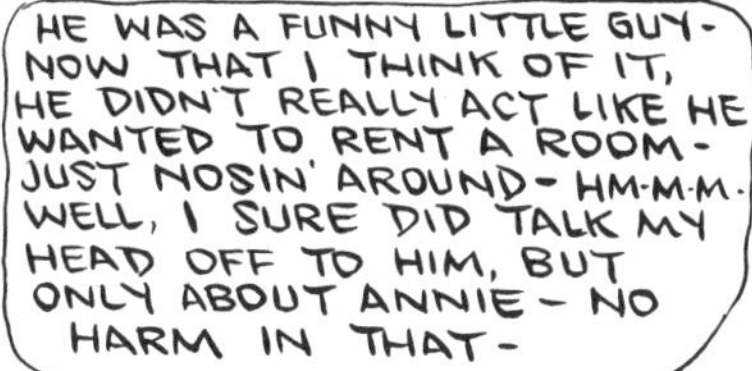
SO THAT GUY WITH THE LITTLE LEGS WAS INTO TH' STORE, WAS HE? WHAT WAS HE TALKIN' TO JAKE ABOUT?
OH, HE WANTED SOMETHIN' WE DIDN'T HAVE AND HE JUST GOT TO CHEWIN' TH' RAG WITH JAKE ABOUT THIS 'N' THAT- HE STAYED ABOUT AN HOUR-
HE WAS A FUNNY LITTLE GUY- NOW THAT I THINK OF IT, HE DIDN'T REALLY ACT LIKE HE WANTED TO RENT A ROOM- JUST NOSIN' AROUND- HM-M-M- WELL, I SURE DID TALK MY HEAD OFF TO HIM, BUT ONLY ABOUT ANNIE- NO HARM IN THAT-

WHILE, A FEW BLOCKS AWAY, "DADDY" WARBUCKS AND BILL GO INTO CONFERENCE-
I COULD SEND HER A LOT OF MONEY- BUT I WONDER IF SHE ISN'T BETTER OFF FOR THE PRESENT AS SHE IS- SHE'S HAPPY THINKING I'M IN CHINA- IF SHE LEARNS I'M HERE SHE'LL EXPECT ME TO COME BACK TO HER- AND I CAN'T- NOT BLIND-

I'D LIKE TO SEND HER A LETTER- BUT HOW AM I GOING TO MAKE HER BELIEVE I'M IN CHINA?
LEAVE IT TO ME, OLIVER- I'VE GOT A PLAN THAT'LL WORK PERFECT AND I KNOW JUST TH' GUY WHO CAN PUT IT OVER-

HAROLD GRAY
Reg. U. S. Pat. Off.; Copyright, 1931, by The Chicago Tribune.

I'LL ENCLOSE A HUNDRED DOLLARS TO PROVE I'M WORKING- HAVE YOU GOT THAT LETTER DONE, BILL?
CHEE! I SURE WASN'T CUT OUT TO BE A STENOGRAPHER- BUT I GUESS ANNIE CAN READ THIS- I DATED THIS A MONTH AGO FROM HONGKONG-
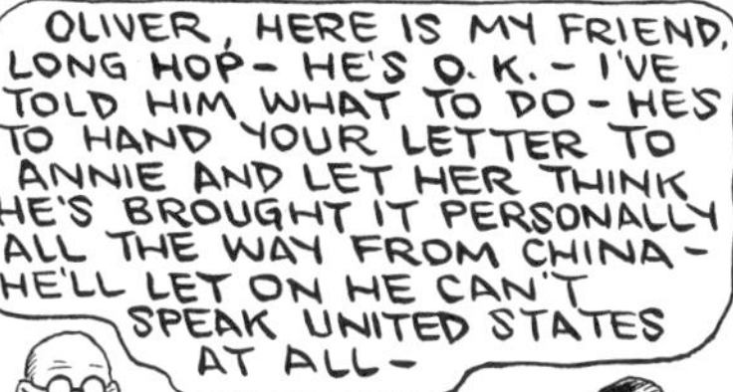
OLIVER, HERE IS MY FRIEND, LONG HOP- HE'S O. K.- I'VE TOLD HIM WHAT TO DO- HE'S TO HAND YOUR LETTER TO ANNIE AND LET HER THINK HE'S BROUGHT IT PERSONALLY ALL THE WAY FROM CHINA- HE'LL LET ON HE CAN'T SPEAK UNITED STATES AT ALL-

LOOK, BILL- TELL ME IF THIS IS THE RIGHT PLACE FOR MY NAME- I'LL JUST SCRIBBLE "DADDY"- GUESS I CAN DO THAT IN THE DARK ALL RIGHT-
FINE- THAT'LL PROVE IT'S FROM YOU, ALL RIGHT-

NOW YOU KNOW WHAT YOU'RE TO DO, LONG HOP- REMEMBER, NOT A WORD TO HER- YOU CAN'T ANSWER ANY OF HER QUESTIONS-
QUITE SO- AND I WILL ATTIRE MYSELF AS MOST HUMBLE COOLIE TO COMPLETE THE ILLUSION- I HAND HER THIS LETTER AND GO AWAY QUICKLY-
HAROLD GRAY
Reg. U. S. Pat. Off.; Copyright, 1931, by The Chicago Tribune.

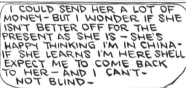

August 6–8, 1931
AND A BLIND MAN SHALL LEAD THEM

Little Orphan Annie
OW!

EAT!

oOOH!

COOKIES!

HEY! WHAT'S THIS? TH' COOKIE CAN! HOW DID YOU EVER GET HOLD OF THAT?

IT'S HALF EMPTY, TOO - BUT NO CRUMBS ON YOUR WHISKERS, SANDY - THAT LETS YOU OUT - BUT, PAT - HOW COULD YOU EVER REACH WAY UP HERE? AND I KNOW I LEFT THIS CAN UP HERE WHERE I WAS SURE IT WOULD BE SAFE -

NO CHAIR NEAR ENOUGH TO CLIMB ON, EITHER - YET YOU DID GET TH' COOKIES - NOW LET ME THINK - I'LL GET TO TH' BOTTOM O' THIS YET - ONE OF YOU FOUND SOME WAY TO REACH THOSE COOKIES --

NOW, I WONDER! HM-M-M--- SANDY! YOU LOOK ME IN THE EYE!
HAROLD GRAY
Reg. U. S. Pat. Off.; Copyright, 1931, by The Chicago Tribune

August 9, 1931
AND A BLIND MAN SHALL LEAD THEM

DID YOU CALL ME, MAW GREEN?
YEAH! COME DOWN HERE, ANNIE, AND SEE WHAT THIS BIRD WANTS - I THINK HE'S GOT SOME KIND OF A LETTER FOR YOU -
FOR ME? WHAT IS IT? WHO'S IT FROM?
IT'S FROM "DADDY" - I KNEW IT. I TOLD YOU SO - LOOK! HONGKONG - THAT'S WAY OVER IN CHINA - AND HE SAYS HE'S GOT A GOOD JOB AND IS DOIN' FINE - LOOK - HE SENT ME A HUNDRED DOLLARS - THAT PROVES IT - SAYS HE WON'T SEE ME FOR A LONG TIME, MAYBE, BUT HE'LL WRITE TO ME -
HEY! WHERE DID THAT GUY GO? I WANT TO ASK HIM A LOT O' QUESTIONS - HE MUST HAVE BROUGHT THIS LETTER FROM "DADDY" - HE'D KNOW WHERE "DADDY" IS AND ALL ABOUT HIM - GEE WHIZ - WHERE DID HE GO?
HE WAS HERE A SECOND AGO - NOW HE'S GONE SLICK AS A WHISTLE - WELL, HE COULDN'T TALK U. S. ANYWAY -
HAROLD GRAY
Reg. U. S. Pat. Off., Copyright, 1931, by The Chicago Tribune.
A HUNDRED DOLLARS FROM "DADDY" - GEE - IT'S NOT SO MUCH TH' MONEY THAT MATTERS, BUT IT'S KNOWIN' "DADDY'S" DOIN' WELL - WISH I KNEW WHERE TO WRITE TO HIM - BUT HE'LL BE BACK SOME TIME 'FORE VERY LONG -
WELL, HOW'S MY RICH ROOMER THIS MORNING? S'PECTED TO SEE YOU ALL DOLLED UP, NOW THAT YOU'VE COME INTO MONEY -
NIX - NOT ME - ANYWAY, I'M NOT VERY RICH - OF COURSE A HUNDRED DOLLARS IS A LOT OF MONEY -
YOU BET YER LIFE A HUNDRED DOLLARS IS A LOT O' MONEY - IT'S MORE'N A LOT O' FOLKS EVER HAVE AT ONCE IN A WHOLE LIFETIME - WHAT DO YOU FIGGER ON SPENDIN' IT FOR?
HAROLD GRAY
SPEND IT, NOTHIN'!!! NOT MUCH - THAT HUNDRED GOES INTO A GOOD BANK - NEVER KNOW WHEN YOU'LL NEED DOUGH BAD FOR SOMETHIN' - I'M GOIN' TO SAVE THAT FOR 'MERGENCIES -
Reg. U. S. Pat. Off.; Copyright, 1931, by The Chicago Tribune.
YOU DON'T NEED TO WORRY ABOUT THAT KID, ANNIE - SHE'S SURE A CORKER - I'VE BEEN CHECKIN' UP ON HER LIKE YOU SAID - FOUND OUT EVERY MOVE SHE'S MADE - GUESS WHAT SHE DID WITH THAT HUNDRED DOLLARS -
WHAT?
PUT IT IN TH' BANK - YES SIR - EVERY CENT OF IT - AND IT'S THE SAME ONE YOU USE - IS SHE A GOOD PICKER, OR NOT?
WHAT A GIRL! SO SHE PICKED THE SAME BANK I DID, EH? HM-M-M - A HUNDRED DOLLARS - SHE OUGHT TO HAVE MORE THAN THAT - BUT I MUSTN'T JUST SEND IT TO HER - SHE'D GET SUSPICIOUS - FIGURE MAYBE I WASN'T SO FAR AWAY AFTER ALL -
I HAVE IT - I'LL SEND $5,000.00 TO THE BANK TO BE PLACED TO HER ACCOUNT - CHANCES ARE SHE WON'T KNOW ANYTHING ABOUT IT UNLESS SHE NEEDS MONEY, AND, IF SHE SHOULD NEED IT BADLY, SHE'LL HAVE IT - TAKE CARE OF IT, WILL YOU, BILL? HERE'S THE CHECK BOOK -
HAROLD GRAY
Reg. U. S. Pat. Off.; Copyright, 1931, by The Chicago Tribune.

August 10–12, 1931

AND A BLIND MAN SHALL LEAD THEM

GEE, YUH CAN'T BE TOO CAREFUL IN PICKIN' A BANK THESE DAYS- I DON'T WANT TO PUT MY DOUGH IN ANY BANK THAT'S LIKELY TO FOLD UP-HM-M- THAT LOOKS LIKE A GOOD SOLID ONE-
BANK
YEP- IT'S A NICE ONE, TOO- AND LOTS O' OTHER FOLKS ARE PUTTIN' THEIR MONEY IN- THAT'S A GOOD SIGN- AND THERE'S A COP TO SEE THERE'S NO CROOKED WORK OR HOLD-UPS- I GUESS I'LL TAKE A CHANCE ON THIS PLACE-
HERE, MISTER- I WANT TO PUT A HUNDRED DOLLARS IN YOUR BANK WHERE I WON'T LOSE IT- IT'LL BE SAFE HERE, WON'T IT? AND I CAN GET IT ANY TIME I WANT IT?
YES- IT WILL BE SAFE AND YOU CAN DRAW IT OUT ANY TIME- YOU'LL BE PAID INTEREST ON IT, TOO-
RECEIVING TELLER
GEE- WHAT A CUTE LITTLE BOOK HE GAVE ME- AND HERE IT IS- $100.00 UNDER "DEPOSITS"- THAT SHOWS I'VE GOT IT IN THE BANK AND NO-BODY CAN STEAL IT- SURE MAKES YUH FEEL IMPORTANT TO KNOW YUH HAVE MONEY IN TH' BANK-
HAROLD GRAY
Reg. U. S. Pat. Off.; Copyright, 1931, by The Chicago Tribune.
LONG AS I'VE GOT A BANK ACCOUNT THERE'S NO USE KEEPIN' DOUGH AROUND TH' ROOM- I'M GOIN' TO PUT THIS SEVEN DOLLARS IN WITH THAT HUNDRED-
HERE'S SEVEN DOLLARS MORE TO KEEP FOR ME- HOW MUCH DOES THAT MAKE THAT I HAVE IN THE BANK NOW?
ELLER
LET'S SEE- ONE HUNDRED- AND FIVE THOUSAND- AND SEVEN- THAT MAKES FIVE THOUSAND ONE HUNDRED AND SEVEN DOLLARS-
WHAT? ALREADY? THANKS!
LEAPIN' LIZARDS!!! WHAT A BANK! WHEW!!! I FEEL SORTA DIZZY!!!
HAROLD GRAY
Reg. U. S. Pat. Off.; Copyright, 1931, by The Chicago Tribune.
WHAT A BANK! I PUT ONE HUNDRED BUCKS IN LAST WEDNESDAY AND WHEN I WENT IN YESTERDAY I HAD $5,100.00- THE MAN TOLD ME SO AND HE WROTE IT IN MY BOOK, TOO- IT'S NO MISTAKE, JAKE- BANKS DON'T MAKE MISTAKES LIKE THAT-
YES, YOU PICKED THE BEST BANK IN TOWN- BUT YI!!! $5,000.00 EXTRA- IT COULDN'T GROW ON TREES- MAYBE THIS "DADDY" WARBUCKS DID IT- HE COULD HAVE DEPOSITED IT TO YOUR CREDIT, MAYBE- THAT IS THE ONLY ANSWER-
NIX, JAKE- USE YER HEAD- HOW COULD HE FROM HONGKONG WAY OVER IN CHINA? HE'S THERE- YOU SAW HIS LETTER- AND EVEN IF HE COULD SEND THE MONEY, HOW COULD HE KNOW WHAT BANK I HAD MY DOUGH IN? NO SIR-
YI! I GIVE UP- IT IS TOO DEEP FOR ME-
HM-M-M-- I WONDER, NOW- HE COULDN'T KNOW WHAT BANK I WENT TO, EVEN IF HE WASN'T IN CHINA- STILL, "DADDY" ALWAYS DID HAVE WAYS OF FINDING OUT ALMOST EVERYTHING- GEE- I WONDER- WELL, NO USE TRYIN' TO FIGGER IT OUT- GEE, I'M RICH- BUT I'M NOT GOIN' TO LET IT SWELL ME UP-
HAROLD GRAY
Reg. U. S. Pat. Off.; Copyright, 1931, by The Chicago Tribune.

August 13–15, 1931

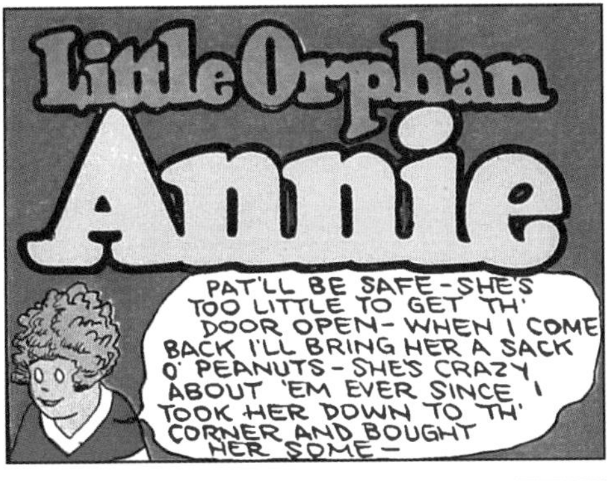
Little Orphan
Annie
PAT'LL BE SAFE - SHE'S TOO LITTLE TO GET TH' DOOR OPEN - WHEN I COME BACK I'LL BRING HER A SACK O' PEANUTS - SHE'S CRAZY ABOUT 'EM EVER SINCE I TOOK HER DOWN TO TH' CORNER AND BOUGHT HER SOME -

UM!

MONEY!
ONE DIME

?

WHY, SHE CAN'T BE MORE'N TWO YEARS OLD -

PEANUTS -
PEANUTS, IS IT? GREAT SCOTT!!! SO THERE YOU ARE - ARE YOU SURE YOU'RE BIG ENOUGH TO BE OUT ALONE?

KIDS START OUT YOUNG AROUND HERE - HM-M - GOOD DOG, THAT - GUESS HE'LL LOOK OUT FOR HER BETTER'N HER OLD LADY SEEMS TO -

OH, I FORGOT TO BRING PAT THOSE PEANUTS - WHAT TH...? LEAPIN' LIZARDS!!! SHE HAS PEANUTS!
HAROLD GRAY

PAT! YOU'LL DRIVE ME CUCKOO, YET! MAW GREEN'S AWAY - SHE NEVER BROUGHT YOU THOSE - AN' NOBODY ELSE AROUND HERE DID - AN' YOU COULDN'T GET OUT O' HERE - HOW TH' SAM HILL DIDJA DO IT? IT'S TOO DEEP FOR ME -
PEANUTS?
Reg. U. S. Pat. Off., Copyright, 1931, by The Chicago Tribune.

August 16, 1931
AND A BLIND MAN SHALL LEAD THEM

GENTLEMEN, WE'RE SUNK! WHILE WE'VE BEEN SELLING SHORT, SOME OTHER OUTFIT HAS BEEN BUYING AND HAS CAUGHT US SHORT- BUT WHO ARE WE UP AGAINST? IF WE KNEW, WE COULD FIGHT BACK- IT HAS ALL THE EAR-MARKS OF A WARBUCKS JOB- HE'S THE ONLY BIRD I KNOW OF WHO COULD PUT OVER ANYTHING THIS BIG WITHOUT SHOWING HIS HAND-

BUT IT CAN'T BE WARBUCKS- WHY, I CRUSHED HIM COMPLETELY-WHEN HE CAME TO ME FOR A LOAN LAST WINTER I HAD HIM AT MY MERCY- I TOOK EVERY CENT HE HAD- I CRUSHED HIM ABSOLUTELY- HE CAN NEVER RISE AGAIN-

BAH! SO YOU CRUSHED WARBUCKS, DID YOU? DON'T KID YOURSELF- A BIRD LIKE WARBUCKS IS NEVER BEATEN TOO FLAT TO COME BACK-

WHILE NEWS OF ANNIE'S AFFLUENCE BRINGS AN EARLY CALLER AND AN OPPORTUNITY FOR INVESTMENT-
THIS IS THE BEST CORNER LOT IN MARSH HEIGHTS FOR ONLY $4990. WHY, IT'LL BE WORTH TEN THOUSAND IN TWO WEEKS- ALL YOU HAVE TO DO IS SIGN THIS CONTRACT AND PAY A SMALL DEPOSIT-
NO!
HAROLD GRAY
Reg. U. S. Pat. Off.; Copyright, 1931, by The Chicago Tribune.

WE'VE GOT 'EM, OLIVER- THEY'RE TRYING TO COVER- OUR STOCK HAS DOUBLED TEN TIMES SINCE THE MARKET OPENED AND WE CAN DRIVE IT UP TO ANY PRICE- WE'RE WORTH MILLIONS! MILLIONS!

YES- WE'RE WORTH A FEW MILLIONS, BILL- BUT THAT'S ONLY CHICKEN-FEED IN THIS GAME- WAIT TILL WE GET A BILLION BEFORE CROWING TOO LOUD- A MILLION ISN'T SO MUCH-

WELL, MAYBE A MILLION ISN'T SO MUCH, BUT IT'S JUST NINE HUNDRED AND NINETY THOUSAND BUCKS MORE'N I EVER HAD BEFORE- IT MAY NOT BE MUCH TO YOU, OLIVER, BUT IT'S ENOUGH TO MAKE ME SORTA GOOFY JUST THINKIN' ABOUT IT-

WHILE ANNIE'S BANK BALANCE CONTINUES TO ATTRACT SALESMEN AS FLIES ARE DRAWN TO SUGAR-
BUT YOU MUST HAVE ACCIDENT INSURANCE- WHY, ONLY LAST WEEK MR. GAZOOKUS WOULDN'T TAKE ONE OF THESE POLICIES AND YESTERDAY HE WAS HIT BY A TAXICAB- NO TELLING WHAT WILL HAPPEN TO YOU ANY MINUTE- NOW WILL YOU JUST SIGN THIS APPLICATION?
NO!
HAROLD GRAY
Reg. U. S. Pat. Off.; Copyright, 1931, by The Chicago Tribune.

I TELL YOU, WHOEVER THIS IS WE'RE UP AGAINST, HE'S GOT TO BE STOPPED- DO YOU REALIZE IF WE DON'T STOP HIM, WE'LL ALL BE RUINED- I INSIST NO MAN BUT WARBUCKS COULD HAVE TRAPPED US SO COMPLETELY-

WHERE IS WARBUCKS? WHO KNOWS ANYTHING ABOUT HIM? TRACE HIM- FIND HIM- THEN AT LEAST WE'LL KNOW WHO WE'RE FIGHTING-

I AGREE WITH YOU, MR. SHARK- WE CAN'T FIGHT A SHADOW-
SHADOW!!! HUMPH! WELL, WHOEVER THIS BIRD IS, HE'S A MIGHTY SOLID SHADOW-
HAROLD GRAY

WHILE STILL ANOTHER GOLDEN OPPORTUNITY IS OFFERED TO ANNIE- THIS TIME IT'S A SURE-FIRE STOCK DEAL-

WE CAN LET IN ONLY A FEW OF OUR FRIENDS ON THIS STOCK- IT GUARANTEES THREE HUNDRED PER CENT.- SAY YOU INVEST FIVE THOUSAND- YOU'RE SURE TO GET BACK $20,000- YOU'RE NOT GOING TO LET A CHANCE LIKE THAT GET AWAY- YOU'RE TOO SMART- CAN I PUT YOU DOWN FOR $5,000.00?

NO!

Reg. U. S. Pat. Off.; Copyright, 1931, by The Chicago Tribune.

August 17–19, 1931
AND A BLIND MAN SHALL LEAD THEM

SHARK AND HIS CROWD STILL SEEM TO BE PLENTY STRONG- IF WE COULD ONLY THINK OF SOME WAY TO LAND A KNOCK-OUT WHILE WE'VE GOT 'EM GROGGY-
YES- WHAT'S HOLDING THEM UP? THEY MUST HAVE BIG RESOURCES WE DON'T KNOW ABOUT-

I'VE GOT IT- NOW I REMEMBER- SHARK CONTROLS A GIGANTIC SHIPPING COMPANY IN THE ORIENT- HE'D NEVER EXPECT AN ATTACK IN THAT QUARTER- SMASH HIS SHIPPING COMPANY AND HE'LL BE DONE FOR-

HE HAS A FLEET OF MERCHANT SHIPS, WHARVES, WARE-HOUSES- A BIG LAYOUT- BUT NOT TOO BIG FOR US TO TACKLE- GET IN TOUCH WITH OUR MEN IN CHINA- HURRY, BILL- TIME IS EVERYTHING NOW- IF WE'RE GOING TO GET SHARK WE'VE GOT TO NAIL HIM BEFORE HE HAS TIME TO GET SET AGAIN-

WHILE TO-DAY A BUSINESS OPPORTUNITY IS OFFERED TO OUR LITTLE CAPITALIST-
FOR FIVE THOUSAND DOLLARS I WOULD GIVE YOU A PARTNERSHIP IN MY FINE BUSINESS- YOU WOULD EASY MAKE A FORTUNE- IS IT A GO?
NO!
HAROLD GRAY

WELL- YOU'RE DETECTIVES- WHAT DID YOU FIND OUT? WHAT'S HAPPENED TO WARBUCKS? COME ON- LET'S HAVE YOUR REPORT-
WELL, ER, IT WAS HARD TO TRACE HIM, MR. SHARK- BUT HERE'S WHAT WE FOUND OUT-

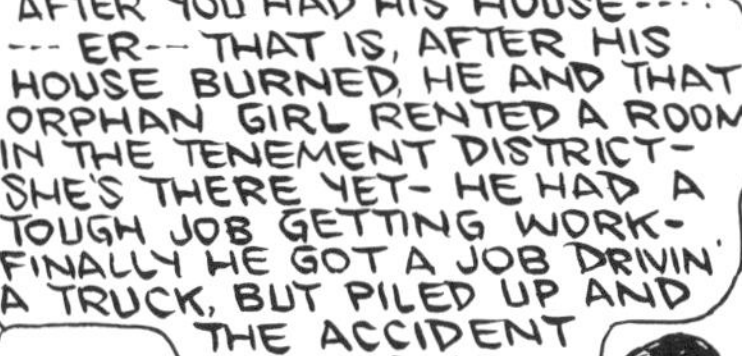

AFTER YOU HAD HIS HOUSE---- ---ER--- THAT IS, AFTER HIS HOUSE BURNED, HE AND THAT ORPHAN GIRL RENTED A ROOM IN THE TENEMENT DISTRICT- SHE'S THERE YET- HE HAD A TOUGH JOB GETTING WORK- FINALLY HE GOT A JOB DRIVIN' A TRUCK, BUT PILED UP AND THE ACCIDENT BLINDED HIM-
BLIND, EH?

YEAH- HE'S BLIND AS A BAT- THE TRUCK COMPANY DIDN'T PAY HIM A DIME- WE TRACED HIM TO THE HOSPITAL, BUT WHEN HE LEFT THERE HE JUST VANISHED- NOT A TRACE OF HIM SINCE- BUT IT'S A CINCH HE'S JUST A BLIND BUM, WHEREVER HE IS-

BROKE AND BLIND, EH? WELL, THAT'S A BREAK! NO GUY, NOT EVEN WARBUCKS, COULD BEAT A COMBINATION LIKE THAT- JUST THE SAME, I'D FEEL BETTER IF I KNEW WHERE THAT BIRD IS NOW-
HAROLD GRAY

HERE'S A BUNCH O' CABLES FROM HONG-KONG AND CANTON AND PEKIN- NOTHIN' MUCH IN ANY OF 'EM- HERE'S ONE FROM OUR MAN OVER IN SINGAPORE- MENTIONS A BIRD THERE CALLED SPIKE MARLIN-
SPIKE MARLIN! GREAT SCOTT! HE'S JUST THE MAN- HONEST- LOYAL- CAPABLE- AND HE KNOWS THE SEA AND SHIPS AND SAILORS-

SEND OUR MESSAGE IN CODE TO OUR MAN IN SINGAPORE- TELL HIM THE WHOLE STORY- WE'LL PUT MARLIN IN FULL CHARGE, GIVE HIM UNLIMITED CREDIT- HAVE HIM BUY OR LEASE A FLEET AND MAN IT- TELL HIM TO RUN THAT SHIPPING COMPANY OF SHARK'S OUT OF BUSINESS- HE'LL KNOW HOW-

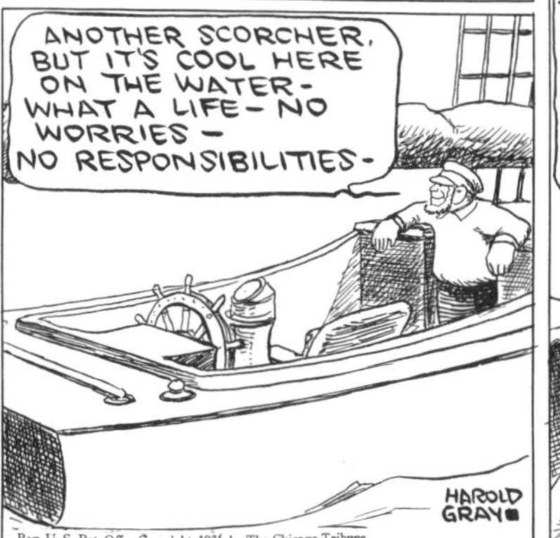

WHILE SPIKE MARLIN, IN FAR AWAY SINGAPORE, LITTLE SUSPECTS WHAT IS IN STORE FOR HIM-
ANOTHER SCORCHER, BUT IT'S COOL HERE ON THE WATER- WHAT A LIFE- NO WORRIES- NO RESPONSIBILITIES-
HAROLD GRAY

A SOUND CRAFT, PLENTY OF MONEY- I OUGHT TO BE SATISFIED, BUT MAYBE LIFE'S TOO EASY FOR AN OLD SALT THAT'S HAD A HARD LIFE FOR SO MANY YEARS- WISH SOMETHING IN MY LINE WOULD COME ALONG THAT I COULD TACKLE- BUT I'M SUPPOSED TO BE TOO OLD- HUH- I'M AS SOUND AS EVER-

August 20–22, 1931

Little Orphan Annie
THERE'VE BEEN A LOT O' FUNNY THINGS HAPPENIN' LATELY THAT I CAN'T FIGGER OUT- THEY THINK I'M MILES AWAY- NOW TO SEE WHAT GOES ON WHEN THEY THINK I'M GONE-

YI!

HA! HA! HA! SANDY FUNNY!

PAT DO IT AGAIN-

AH---

BLUB!

OW! WAH!

?
ULP!

NOW, NOT ANOTHER YELP OUT O' YOU- YOU ONLY GOT JUST WHAT YOU DESERVED- YOU DIDN'T KNOW IT BEFORE, BUT I'LL BET YOU KNOW NOW THAT STEPPIN' ON SANDY'S TAIL IS BAD-
OOO! BAD!!! MUSTN'T TOUCH-
ZIP

AND AS FOR YOU- YOU HAD NO BUSINESS PULLIN' A TRICK LIKE THAT ON PAT- BUT I'M LETTIN' YUH OFF THIS TIME- COME ON OUT O' THERE-

SHE DIDN'T MEAN ANY HARM, BUT THAT DIDN'T MAKE IT HURT SANDY'S TAIL ANY LESS- WELL, HE BROKE HER O' THAT TRICK, AND HOW! WISE OLD SANDY- AND TH' LOOK ON HIS FACE WHEN I CAME IN - WOW! I WOULDN'T HAVE MISSED THAT FOR A MILLION DOLLARS!
GOOD SANDY.
HAROLD GRAY
Reg. U. S. Pat. Off.; Copyright, 1931, by The Chicago Tribune

August 23, 1931
AND A BLIND MAN SHALL LEAD THEM

HEY, YOU LUBBER! SHEER OFF - IF YOU KNOCK ANY PAINT OFF O' THIS CRAFT I'LL BASH IN YER LIGHTS WITH A BELAYIN' PIN - Y'OUGHTA BE KEEL-HAULED FOR SPEEDIN' IN A CROWDED HARBOR - WATCH WHERE YER A'GOIN' -

WHAT? YOU HAVE A MESSAGE FROM WARBUCKS? WELL, QUIT LUFFIN' AN' HAULIN' ABOUT AN' LET'S HAVE IT -
MR. WARBUCKS WANTS YOU TO COME ASHORE AND TALK TO HIM BY RADIO TELEPHONE - HE WILL EXPLAIN EVERYTHING IN DETAIL, CAPTAIN - HE SAYS THERE ISN'T A MOMENT TO LOSE, SIR -

WARBUCKS ALWAYS WAS ONE TO MOVE FAST - HAVE YOU AN IDEE AS TO WHAT IT'S ALL ABOUT, SON?
YES, CAPTAIN - HE WANTS YOU TO ESTABLISH A BIG SHIP COMPANY - IT'S TO PUT MR. SHARK'S COMPANY OUT OF BUSINESS - HE'S CABLED YOU MILLIONS AND WANTS YOU TO TAKE FULL CHARGE -

AYE - IT'LL BE A FIGHT - BUT I KNOW THE SEA AND SHIPS AND SAILOR MEN - I'VE ALWAYS WONDERED HOW IT WOULD FEEL TO BE AN ADMIRAL - WHERE'S THAT TELEPHONE, SON?
HAROLD GRAY
Reg. U. S. Pat. Off.; Copyright, 1931, by The Chicago Tribune.

GREAT SCOTT! HOW DID THEY EVER KNOW I OWNED THAT SHIPPING COMPANY IN THE ORIENT - IT WAS THE ONE ENTERPRISE I WAS COUNTING ON TO CARRY ME THROUGH - NOW THIS CABLE FROM SINGAPORE - MY SHIPS TIED UP WITH INJUNCTIONS - MY BEST MEN DESERTING TO JOIN A BIG NEW SHIP COMPANY - WHO IS THIS CAPTAIN MARLIN? MUST BE ACTING FOR SOME ONE -
THEY'RE SMASHING OUR SHIP COMPANY - WHO IS CAPTAIN MARLIN? HE'S SPENDING MILLIONS TO BREAK US - WHO DOES HE REPRESENT? I TELL YOU WE MUST STOP AT NOTHING - BUT WHO IS THE BRAINS OF THIS OUTFIT WE ARE UP AGAINST? WE MUST FIND THE HEAD AND CRUSH IT -

WELL, MR. SHARK, OUR INVESTIGATORS SAY IT IS THAT MAN CALLED FLOP-HOUSE BILL - ALL THE ORDERS COME FROM HIM - YOU KNOW I TOLD YOU HE WAS SMARTER THAN YOU SAID - I KNEW FROM THE FIRST THAT HE WAS DANGEROUS -

FLOP-HOUSE BILL! THAT RUNT! BAH! HE NEVER HAD BUT A FEW THOUSAND AND NEVER THE BRAINS TO RUN IT UP - HE'S FRONTING FOR SOMEBODY AND I THINK I KNOW WHO IS BEHIND HIM - YES - AND I KNOW WHAT TO DO ABOUT IT, TOO - THIS IS NO TIME TO BE NICE AND DAINTY - IT'S WARBUCKS OR ME AND IT WON'T BE ME -
HAROLD GRAY
Reg. U. S. Pat. Off.; Copyright, 1931, by The Chicago Tribune.

YEAH, DAT'S DE JOINT WE'RE TO CASE - LOOKS LIKE A DUMP, BUT THEY SAY IT'S DOLLED UP SWELL INSIDE - IT OUGHTA BE EASY TO GET INSIDE -
YEAH - BUT IT DON'T PAY TO TAKE NO CHANCES - THOSE EASY LOOKIN' JOINTS IS OFTEN DE TOUGHEST - FLOP-HOUSE BILL HANGS OUT THERE - HE'S NO SAP -
WONDER WHAT IT'S ALL ABOUT - SHARK PAID US FIVE GRAND AND SAID THERE'D BE TEN GRAND MORE IF WE GOT ALL DE PAPERS - HE MUST WANT THEM PAPERS PRETTY BAD -
YEAH! HE SAID NOT TO WORRY NONE IF WE HAD TO BUMP SOME GUY - SAID HE'D TAKE CARE OF US NO MATTER WHAT - I GOT DE IDEA HE WANTS US TO RUB OUT SOME GUY -

SH-H-H -- DIS IS TH' BACK WAY INTO DE JOINT - CHEE - IT LOOKS TOO EASY - MAYBE IT'S A TRAP - C'MON - LET'S SCRAM OUT O' HERE WHERE WE CAN TALK -
IT'S A CINCH - TO-MORROW NIGHT IN WE GOES - WHATEVER THERE IS TO DO, WE DOES - THEN BACK TO SHARK AN' COLLECTS THAT TEN GRAND - DAT'S EASY -
YEAH - AN' IF WE BUMPS INTO ANY GUY IN DAT JOINT WE LETS 'IM HAVE IT LIKE SHARK SAID - THAT WAY THERE'LL BE NOBODY TALKIN' AFTERWARDS -
HAROLD GRAY
Reg. U. S. Pat. Off.; Copyright, 1931, by The Chicago Tribune.

August 24–26, 1931

NOW, IF WE RUN INTO ANYBODY, NO PALAVER- NO MATTER WHO HE IS, IT'LL BE JUST TOO BAD FOR HIM-
YUH DON'T TINK I'M YELLOW, DO YUH? FER FIFTEEN GRAND I'D RUB OUT ME OWN BRUDDER- C'MON - HERE WE GO-

CHEE!!! YUH KNOW WHO DAT IS, DON'TCHA? IF HE SAW US, WE AIN'T GOT A CHANCE- C'MON- SCRAM!
SURE- I KNOW DAT GUY- DAT'S WARBUCKS! I DON'T TINK HE SAW US, BUT NOBODY EVER CAN TELL ABOUT DAT BOID- HE'S TOO RICH FER MY BLOOD- LET'S GET GOIN'-
Reg. U. S. Pat. Off.; Copyright, 1931, by The Chicago Tribune.

DAT GUY, SHARK, NEVER TOLD US WARBUCKS WAS MIXED UP IN DIS DEAL- CHEE- WE MIGHT HAVE GOT MOIDERED!
I'D LIKE TO FIX DAT GUY, SHARK'S, CLOCK FER GETTIN' US INTO DIS, BUT WE AIN'T GOT TIME- I WON'T FEEL EASY TILL WE'RE A THOUSAND MILES FROM DIS TOWN-
HAROLD GRAY

OLIVER!!! LOOK!!! ER- THAT IS, FEEL OF THESE- TWO PISTOLS IN THE BACK HALL AND THE DOOR WIDE OPEN- SOMEBODY CAME TO ROB THIS PLACE- BUT NOT A THING'S BEEN TOUCHED- LOOKS LIKE WHOEVER IT WAS THREW AWAY THEIR GUNS AND LIT OUT FAST- WONDER WHAT SCARED 'EM-

HM-M-M- I REMEMBER, WHEN I WAS SITTING HERE LATE LAST NIGHT, I DID HEAR A LITTLE NOISE, BUT I DIDN'T THINK MUCH OF IT AT THE TIME- THEY COULD HAVE SHOT ME, EASY AS NOT- WONDER WHY THEY DIDN'T- SHARK MUST HAVE SENT THEM- NOW I SUPPOSE HE KNOWS I'M HERE- STILL, IF THOSE HOODLUMS FAILED THEY'D HARDLY GO BACK TO HIM- I WONDER-

WHILE, IN THE MEANTIME, THE HIRED HOODLUMS STILL FEEL THE URGE TO TRAVEL FAST AND FAR-
MAYBE WE OUGHTA HAVE TOOK A SHOT AT WARBUCKS- WE HAD TH' DROP ON HIM- SHARK SAID HE'D TAKE CARE O' US, NO MATTER WHAT-
YEAH! I HEARD ABOUT A BOID ONCE DAT THOUGHT HE HAD DE DROP ON WARBUCKS- DAT GUY IS POISON- SEE?

DE MORE I TINKS OF IT, DE SURER I AM SHARK WAS TRYIN' TO GET US INTO A JAM- DON'TCHA T'INK HE KNEW ALL DE TIME WARBUCKS WAS THERE?
AW, IF YUH WANTA KNOW GO BACK AND ASK HIM- ME, I'M KEEPIN' RIGHT ON AS LONG AS DIS BUS RUNS- A THOUSAND MILES AIN'T NOTHIN' IF DAT GUY, WARBUCKS, DID SPOT US LAST NIGHT-

HAROLD GRAY
Reg. U. S. Pat. Off.; Copyright, 1931, by The Chicago Tribune.

I TELL YOU IT MUST BE WARBUCKS- MEN SENT TO GET HIM ARE NEVER HEARD OF AGAIN- THE TWO BIRDS I SENT OVER TO SEE WHAT THEY COULD FIND OUT HAVE VANISHED- SUNK WITHOUT A TRACE- IF THEY HADN'T RUN INTO WARBUCKS THEY'D HAVE REPORTED BACK HERE TO ME BEFORE THIS-
YOU FUMBLER!
YOU HAVE RUINED US!
YOU MUST HAVE DOUBLE-CROSSED US-
IF WE HADN'T LISTENED TO YOU
YOU INCOMPETENT FAT-HEAD! YOU---YOU--

PULL HIM DOWN!
STAND BACK, YOU FOOLS- WE'RE ALL IN THIS TO-GETHER-
LET ME AT HIM!
HAROLD GRAY

IF THEY HAD STUCK BY ME, WE MIGHT STILL HAVE SAVED SOMETHING- WE EVEN MIGHT HAVE WON OUT- NOW WE'RE ALL RUINED- RUINED!!! BUT I'LL GET WARBUCKS FOR THIS, IF IT'S THE LAST THING I EVER DO-
Reg. U. S. Pat. Off.; Copyright, 1931, by The Chicago Tribune.

Little Orphan Annie
?
BOO! HOO! HOO!

OW! WOW! WOW!

?

UGH! NO! NO!
BOP!

?
YEOW!

BOO! HOO! HOO-HOO-HOO!

ULP?

BLAH!

WAH! WAH! HURT!!!

AH-H-H!

UM-M-- YUM-M-M--
HAROLD GRAY
Reg. U. S. Pat. Off.; Copyright, 1931, by The Chicago Tribune.

August 30, 1931
AND A BLIND MAN SHALL LEAD THEM

HEY! QUIT PLAYIN' WITH YER OAT MEAL AND EAT IT UP LIKE A GOOD GIRL - WHAT ON EARTH IS THE MATTER WITH YOU, PAT? AREN'T YOU HUNGRY THIS MORNING?
UGH!

HM-M-M-- PAT SURE ISN'T HERSELF TO-DAY - JUST OFF HER FEED A LITTLE, I GUESS - SORT OF UPSET - SOMETHIN' SHE ATE, MOST LIKELY - I'LL HAVE TO GIVE HER SOME CASTOR OIL - THAT'LL STRAIGHTEN HER OUT -

WHILE J. J. SHARK, DESERTED BY HIS ERSTWHILE PALS, OUT-WITTED AND BEATEN BY WARBUCKS IN THEIR FINANCIAL BATTLE, DECIDES TO TAKE A COWARDLY AND DASTARDLY VENGEANCE ON HIS BLIND FOE -

THAT'S HIS HANGOUT - IF THOSE BIRDS I SENT TO GET HIM HADN'T BEEN YELLOW I'D BE SITTING PRETTY NOW - BUT I'M STILL IN THIS GAME -

UP THOSE STAIRS IS THE BACK DOOR DIRECTLY INTO HIS PRIVATE OFFICE - HE'LL BE ALONE THERE TO-MORROW NIGHT - WITH HIM OUT OF THE WAY I CAN WIN BACK MY FORTUNE YET - THIS TIME I'LL DO THE JOB MYSELF - WHO WOULD SUSPECT ME? AND EVEN IF I AM SUSPECTED, WITH MY WEALTH AND POWER AGAIN I'LL BE TOO BIG FOR ANYONE TO TOUCH -
HAROLD GRAY

WHO IS IT? AH - I KNOW YOUR VOICE - SHARK!
YEAH! AND I'VE GOT YOU RIGHT WHERE I WANT YOU - THOUGHT YOU COULD BREAK ME AND GET AWAY WITH IT, EH? IF THAT IDIOT, BULLION, HADN'T FUMBLED, I'D HAVE HAD YOU SIX MONTHS AGO - BLIND, EH? HA! HA! HA! WELL, WHEN I GET DONE WITH YOU, YOU - ! - !

WHAT TH-- ? UGH!
BOOM!

CRASH!

I HEARD TH' SHOOTIN' AND GOT HERE AS QUICK AS I COULD, OLIVER - CHEE! I GUESS YOU DON'T NEED ANY HELP TO TAKE CARE OF YOURSELF - CHEE!
HAROLD GRAY

CHEE! I CAN'T GET OVER TH' WAY YOU OUT-SMARTED SHARK WHEN YOU TURNED OUT TH' LIGHT ON HIM SO HE COULDN'T SEE ANY BETTER'N YOU COULD - WOW, AND WHAT A BEATIN' YOU HANDED HIM! I'VE JUST BEEN DOWN TO CITY HALL LIKE YOU SAID AND IT'S ALL FIXED - SHARK'LL GET TWENTY YEARS, ANYWAY - HE'S DONE FOR - YOU DON'T HAVE TO WATCH OUT FOR HIM ANY MORE -

FINE, BILL - NOW I'VE GOT ANOTHER JOB FOR YOU - THIS OLD BUILDING IS A DUMP - THERE'S NO NEED FOR US TO HIDE OUT HERE ANY MORE - WE HAVE MILLIONS NOW AND WE'LL HAVE MORE - WE MIGHT AS WELL BE COMFORTABLE - LOOK AROUND AND FIND US A GOOD PLACE - THE TOP FLOORS OF A TALL BUILDING OVERLOOKING THE HARBOR - SOMETHING THAT WILL BE AIRY AND PRIVATE -

WHILE IN THE MEANTIME THINGS ARE NOT SO GOOD IN ANNIE'S LITTLE HOUSEHOLD -

GEE, SANDY - SOMETHING'S JUST GOTTA BE DONE - PAT HAS HARDLY EATEN A THING FOR TWO DAYS AND SHE'S HOT AS A STOVE - MAYBE THAT CASTOR OIL WASN'T SUCH A GOOD IDEA AFTER ALL -

HAROLD GRAY

AW, KIDS ARE ALWAYS GETTIN' UPSET - BUT THEY GET OVER IT IN A DAY OR TWO - QUIT WORRYIN' -
BUT I'M TELLIN' YUH, MAW GREEN - THIS IS BAD - I GAVE HER CASTOR OIL AND EVER'THING, BUT SHE'S GETTIN' WORSE AN' WORSE -

August 31–
September 2, 1931

LEAPIN' LIZARDS! I'VE GOTTA GET A DOC. QUICK- MAW GREEN SAYS ANY DOC. WOULD BE O.K.- BUT NO HORSE-DOCTORS FOR PAT- I'M GOIN' OVER ON TH' AVENOO AN' GET HER A SWELL DOC.- SHE'S GOTTA HAVE TH' BEST-
DR. LENS- HE MUST BE A REAL GOOD DOCTOR TO HAVE SUCH A RITZY PLACE- GEE- I HOPE HE'S IN- I'VE GOTTA FIND SOMEBODY RIGHT AWAY-
DR. LENS
SHE'S AWFUL SICK, DOCTOR- I DON'T KNOW WHAT'S TH' MATTER, BUT IT'S BAD, AND YOU MUST COME RIGHT AWAY, PLEASE-
HM-M-M-- WELL, REALLY- YOU SEE I NEVER MAKE CALLS-
TO TELL YOU THE TRUTH I RARELY TAKE ANY CASE- I'M A CONSULTING SPECIALIST- I HAVEN'T BEEN PRACTICING FOR SEVERAL YEARS-
THAT'S GREAT, DOC.- I DON'T WANT ANY BIRD THAT'S STILL PRACTICING- I WANT A GUY WHO KNOWS HIS BUSINESS- C'MON- IT'S ONLY A FEW MORE DOORS NOW-
HAROLD GRAY
Reg. U. S. Pat. Off.; Copyright, 1931, by The Chicago Tribune.
GEE, DOC., IS SHE VERY BAD?
HM-M-M--
HERE'S SOME MEDICINE, ANNIE- GIVE HER ONE TEA-SPOON FULL EVERY TWO HOURS- I'LL BE BACK IN THE MORNING-
HAROLD GRAY
GREAT SCOTT, ANNIE! DO YOU KNOW WHO THAT DOC. IS? THAT'S DOCTOR LENS- I SAW HIS PICTURE IN THE PAPERS THE OTHER DAY- HE'S RICH AS ALL GET OUT AND DOESN'T HAVE TO WORK, BUT THE PIECE IN THE PAPER SAID HE'S ONE OF THE SMARTEST DOCS IN THE WORLD- HOW'D YOU EVER GET HIM TO COME HERE?
Reg. U. S. Pat. Off.; Copyright, 1931, by The Chicago Tribune.
IS SHE ANY BETTER, DOC.? SHE SEEMS LOTS BETTER.
EH? OH, YES- SHE'S COMING ALONG VERY WELL, ANNIE- BY THE WAY- YOU'VE TOLD ME QUITE A BIT ABOUT YOURSELF, YOUR JOB AT THE STORE AND ALL-
AND YOU WISH TO RAISE THIS YOUNGSTER- I QUITE UNDERSTAND HOW YOU FEEL ABOUT IT- BUT PAT WILL NEVER GROW UP WELL AND STRONG HERE- NOT NEARLY ENOUGH FRESH AIR AND SUN-SHINE- ALSO HER DIET SHOULD BE CAREFULLY WATCHED-
I SEE- IT'LL MEAN THROWIN' UP MY JOB AT JAKE'S AND MOVIN' AWAY- ALL RIGHT- I'LL DO ANYTHING FOR PAT- I'VE GOT ENOUGH IN TH' BANK TO TAKE US ANYWHERE YOU SAY- I CAN GIVE HER ALL ANY "HOME" CAN GIVE HER, I BETCHA- AN' NO MATTER WHAT IT COSTS, SHE'S NEVER GOIN' TO KNOW WHAT IT MEANS TO BE AN ORPHAN KID-
WELL, WE'LL WAIT A COUPLE OF DAYS AND SEE HOW SHE COMES ALONG- THEN WE'LL DECIDE WHAT'S BEST-
HAROLD GRAY
Reg. U. S. Pat. Off.; Copyright, 1931, by The Chicago Tribune.

September 3–5, 1931

Little Orphan Annie
C'MON, PAT- WE'LL TAKE A NICE WALK- YOU KNOW TH' DOC. SAID YOU OUGHT TO GET OUT IN TH' OPEN MORE-

OH, LOOKIE! A WATER MAIN MUSTA BUSTED AND NOW THERE'S WATER ALL OVER THE STREET- I KNOW WHAT! WE'LL TAKE OFF OUR SHOES AND STOCKINGS AND GO WADING-

GO ON IN, PAT- I'LL BE RIGHT WITH YOU-

IT'S SORTA DIRTY- YOU CAN'T SEE TH' BOTTOM- BUT WE'RE ONLY GOING WADING- WHAT'S THE MATTER?
DEEP!

SHUX- IT CAN'T BE DEEP- USE YER HEAD- BUT, O' COURSE, YOU'RE TOO LITTLE TO FIGGER THINGS OUT LIKE I CAN- YUH SEE THAT'S JUST A REFLECTION OF TH' TALL BUILDINGS THAT MAKES IT LOOK SO DEEP- BUT IF IT WAS OVER A FEW INCHES DEEP IT'D BE OVER TH' SIDE-WALK-

YEOW!
SHUX! A LITTLE WATER WON'T HURT YOU- HUH! SCARED O' REFLECTIONS! TCH! TCH!

NO!
AW, DON'T BE SILLY, PAT- C'MON IN- SEE? IT'S NOT EVEN UP TO MY KNEES - DON'T BE A FRAIDY-CAT-

OOPS! WHAT TH'-----?

?
ULP!

WHOOF!

HA! HA!
PHOOIE! I THINK I SWALLOWED A TAD-POLE- UGH! SUCH MUCKY WATER! YUH CAN'T SEE TH' BOTTOM AT ALL- HOW COULD I TELL THERE WAS A GREAT BIG HOLE HERE IN TH' STREET?

YOU SURE HAD TH' RIGHT DOPE, PAT- AFTER THIS I'LL LISTEN TO YOU- THAT JUST PROVES YOU CAN KNOW TOO MUCH FOR YOUR OWN GOOD- AND IF YOU GO BLUNDERIN' ALONG, WITHOUT KNOWIN' WHERE YOU'RE GOIN', YOU'LL FIND YOURSELF IN DEEP WATER ALMOST EVERY TIME-
ANNIE ALL WET-
HAROLD GRAY
Reg. U. S. Pat. Off.; Copyright, 1931, by The Chicago Tribune.

September 6, 1931
AND A BLIND MAN SHALL LEAD THEM

SO YOU'RE GOIN' TO LEAVE ME, ARE YOU, ANNIE?
GEE- I HATE TO GO, MAW GREEN- BUT YOU SEE HOW IT IS- I'VE GOT TO DO WHAT'S BEST FOR PAT- AND DOCTOR LENS HAS OFFERED ME A JOB AT HIS PLACE AND THAT'LL MEAN PAT'LL HAVE EVERY CHANCE TO GROW UP HEALTHY-

DO YOU MEAN TO TELL ME DOCTOR LENS WANTS YOU AND PAT TO LIVE AT HIS HOUSE?
THAT'S IT- HE SAID THERE WAS PLENTY O' ROOM AND HE'S GOT A BIG YARD WHERE TH' SUN SHINES ALL DAY LONG- IT'LL BE JUST TH' PLACE FOR PAT- I COULDN'T SAY NO-

THAT'S GREAT, ANNIE- YOU GO RIGHT AHEAD- DOC IS A MIGHTY FINE GUY- IT'LL BE A GOOD HOME FOR YOU- AND I CAN ALWAYS GET ANOTHER ROOMER-
GEE, MAW- I KNEW YOU'D UNDERSTAND HOW 'TIS- YOU'VE BEEN MIGHTY SWELL TO US AND I HATE LIKE EVER'THING TO LEAVE- BUT WE'LL BE BACK TO VISIT YUH REAL OFTEN- EH, SANDY?
ARF!

HERE Y'ARE, PAT- TIME FOR YOUR MEDICINE- WHEN WE GET MOVED OVER TO DOC LENS' PLACE YOU'LL GET REAL STRONG AND WON'T HAVE TO TAKE ANY MORE MEDICINE-
HAROLD GRAY
Reg. U. S. Pat. Off.; Copyright, 1931, by The Chicago Tribune.

YUH SEE, JAKE, IT'LL MEAN EVER'THING TO PAT- AND I'VE GOTTA THINK OF HER FIRST- YOU'LL GET ALONG GREAT WITHOUT ME- BUSINESS IS GETTIN' BETTER EVERY DAY-
YI- I WILL MISS YOU, ANNIE- AND THE CUSTOMERS WILL MISS YOU- BUT IT IS A FINE CHANCE FOR YOU AND PAT- YOU MUST TAKE IT-

GEE, JAKE, YOU'VE BEEN A MIGHTY SWELL GUY TO ME- I'LL SURE HATE TO LEAVE- BUT I'LL COME AND SEE YOU REAL OFTEN-
GOOD LUCK, ANNIE- AND WHEN YOU GET IN THAT SWELL HOME, DON'T FORGET OLD JAKE- HE WILL ALWAYS BE THINKING OF YOU-

YI-YI- SUCH A GIRL- IT WILL BE LONESOME IN THE STORE WITHOUT HER- THE CLERKS! PHOOIE! WHAT ARE THEY TO ME? BUT ANNIE- LIKE MY OWN DAUGHTER, SHE WAS- AND LIKE A PARTNER, TOO- SUCH A PARTNER!

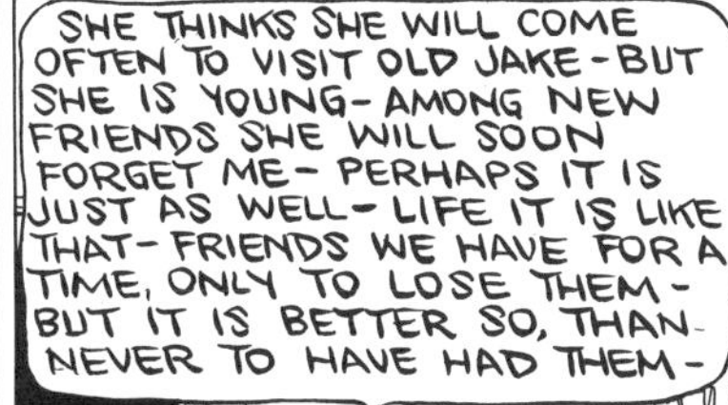
SHE THINKS SHE WILL COME OFTEN TO VISIT OLD JAKE- BUT SHE IS YOUNG- AMONG NEW FRIENDS SHE WILL SOON FORGET ME- PERHAPS IT IS JUST AS WELL- LIFE IT IS LIKE THAT- FRIENDS WE HAVE FOR A TIME, ONLY TO LOSE THEM- BUT IT IS BETTER SO, THAN NEVER TO HAVE HAD THEM-

HAROLD GRAY
Reg. U. S. Pat. Off.; Copyright, 1931, by The Chicago Tribune.

HEY- AREN'T YOU READY YET? HERE'S DOC LENS AND HE'S GOT HIS CAR WAITIN' DOWN IN FRONT-
HELLO, DOC.- I'LL BE WITH YUH IN JUST A SECOND- THIS IS TH' LAST I'VE GOT TO PACK-

WOW- YUH NEVER RE'LIZE HOW MUCH STUFF YUH'VE GOT TILL YUH START TO MOVE- COURSE MOST O' THIS JUNK IS PAT'S- I'M WEARIN' ABOUT ALL I'VE GOT-

HEY- LOOK OUT, SANDY- MOVE OVER- G'BYE, MAW GREEN- WE'LL BE SEEIN' YUH AGAIN REAL SOON-
WELL, DOC., YOU'RE STEALIN' TH' BEST ROOMER I EVER HAD- BUT YOU'LL GIVE HER A LOT FINER HOME, SO IT'S O.K. WITH ME- G'BYE, ANNIE-

TH' LITTLE DARLIN'- IT'S SURE GOIN' TO BE LONESOME AROUND HERE WITHOUT HER- SHE SEEMED ALMOST LIKE MY OWN KID- HUMPH! WHAT'S TH' MATTER WITH ME? I MUST BE GETTIN' TO BE A DRIVELIN' OLD SOFTIE-
HAROLD GRAY
Reg. U. S. Pat. Off.; Copyright, 1931, by The Chicago Tribune.

September 7–9, 1931

CHAPTER EIGHT

DISTANT RELA-TIONS

IN WHICH ANNIE

RELISHES HER NEW ROLE AS PAT'S PROTECTOR

SEES THE BENEFIT OF FAMILY FIRST HAND AS MAW GREEN DISCOVERS A LONG-LOST RELATIVE

SQUARES OFF AGAINST THE CUNNING DAME WHO THREATENS TO BRING IT ALL CRASHING DOWN...

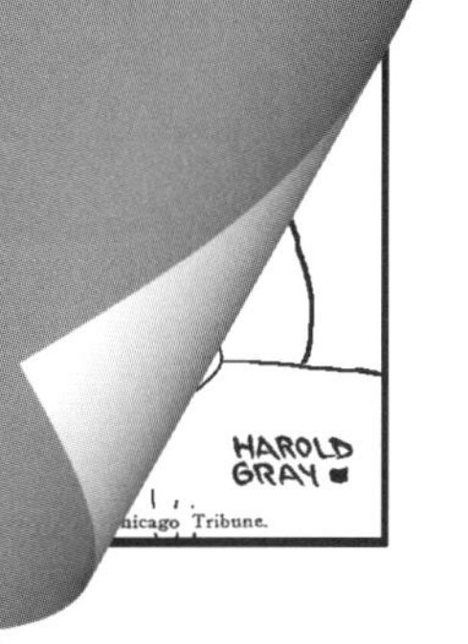

PAT DREAM-
DREAM NOTHIN'! C'MON- GET UP, PAT- IT'S MORNING- LOOK AT TH' SUNSHINE- AND THERE'S A BIRD OUT THERE SINGIN' IN A TREE- WOW! WHAT A JOINT! WHAT A JOINT!
HEY! COME IN HERE AND GET A LOAD O' THIS- BOY-OH-BOY! ARE WE GOIN' TO BE A COUPLE O' CLEAN KIDS! PAT! GET UP!!!
JUST LOOK AT THAT BACK YARD- A SWIMMIN' POOL AND A SAND BOX AND FLOWERS AND TREES AND SUNSHINE- AND A HIGH WALL ALL AROUND- IT'S AS GREEN AN' QUIET HERE AS IT IS OUT IN TH' COUNTRY-
HAROLD GRAY
GEE- I NEVER KNEW ANY PLACE IN A CITY COULD BE SO FRESH AND CLEAN AND PEACEFUL-
Reg. U. S. Pat. Off.; Copyright, 1931, by The Chicago Tribune.
CAN'T WEAR OLD CLOTHES IN A SWELL HOME LIKE THIS- HOW'S THIS NEW DRESS, PAT? SH-H-H- THERE'S TH' DOOR-BELL AND NOBODY ANSWERIN' IT- DOC. HAS PATIENTS TO-DAY- I'D BETTER GO-
HOW DO YOU DO- WON'T YOU COME RIGHT IN?
THANK YOU- I WISH TO SEE DOCTOR LENS- IS HE IN?
THE DOCTOR'S PRETTY BUSY- GUESS YOU'LL HAVE TO WAIT A FEW MINUTES- HAVE SOMETHIN' TO READ? SORRY ALL TH' MAGAZINES ARE SO OLD, BUT THERE'S A PRETTY GOOD STORY ABOUT TH' MAYOR IN THIS ONE, IF YOU'D CARE FOR IT-
THERE GOES TH' DOOR-BELL AGAIN- WELL, THEY'RE SMILIN' AN' FRIENDLY NOW, ANYWAY- NOT JUST SITTIN' AND STARIN' AT EACH OTHER- DOC'S GOTTA GET SOME NEW MAGAZINES IF HE S'PECTS FOLKS TO WAIT VERY LONG IN THERE- I'LL MENTION IT TO HIM TO-MORROW-
HAROLD GRAY
Reg. U. S. Pat. Off.; Copyright, 1931, by The Chicago Tribune.
WONDER WHAT'S IN THIS ROOM- GEE- THAT'S FUNNY- TH' DOOR'S LOCKED AND I KNOW THERE'S NO-BODY IN THERE-
SAY- HOW COME THAT DOOR'S LOCKED? WHAT'S IN THERE?
OH, YOU MUST NEVER GO IN THAT ROOM, MISS ANNIE- THE DOCTOR ALLOWS NO ONE IN THERE- NOT EVEN TO DUST-
YEAH? WHAT'S HE GOT IN THERE?
NO-BODY KNOWS- HE SPENDS HOURS IN THERE ALONE- SOME-TIMES HE STAYS IN THERE ALL NIGHT- I CAN SEE THE LIGHT UNDER THE DOOR- MAYBE HE READS-
READS- HUH! HE WOULDN'T LOCK HIMSELF UP IN A ROOM ALL NIGHT JUST TO READ- AND ANYWAY, IF IT WAS ONLY BOOKS IN THERE, HE'D LET 'EM DUST TH' PLACE- COURSE IT'S NONE O' MY BUSINESS, BUT I CAN'T HELP BEIN' CURIOUS 'BOUT THAT ROOM-
HAROLD GRAY
Reg. U. S. Pat. Off.; Copyright, 1931, by The Chicago Tribune.

September 10–12, 1931

Little Orphan Annie
IT SURE WAS SWELL OF DOCTOR LENS TO TAKE PAT AND SANDY AND ME INTO HIS SWELL HOME TO LIVE - NOW PAT'LL REALLY HAVE A CHANCE TO GROW UP HEALTHY -

GEE, SORTA GETTIN' UP IN TH' WORLD, EH PAT? PRETTY FANCY CHAIR YOU'VE GOT - BEATS PERCHIN' ON A PACKIN' BOX, EH?
PAT GET DOWN AND PLAY NOW?

REMEMBER, PAT- GOTTA BE REAL CAREFUL AND NOT BANG TH' FURNITURE - YOU'VE GOTTA BE A REAL LITTLE LADY WHEN YOU LIVE IN A SWELL PLACE LIKE THIS -

WELL, ANNIE, HOW IS OUR LITTLE PATIENT COMING ALONG?
FINE, DOCTOR - I WEIGHED HER THIS MORNING AND SHE'S GAINED THREE POUNDS - I'M GOIN' TO TAKE HER OUT IN TH' SUN NOW -

YOU'D BETTER BE PEELIN' OFF THAT DRESS, PAT - AND YOUR SHOES AN' STOCKINGS, TOO - AH - HERE WE ARE -

OH, BOY! WHAT A BACK YARD - GRASS, BUSHES, TREES, WATER, FLOWERS, AND SUNSHINE -

KICK - THAT'S TH' STUFF - DON'T MIND SWALLOWIN' A LITTLE WATER - IT WON'T HURT YOU - I'M GOIN' TO MAKE A BATHIN' BEAUTY OUT O' YOU YET - KEEP GOIN', NOW - I'M GOIN' TO TURN YOU LOOSE -

WELL, THAT'LL BE ABOUT ENOUGH FOR TO-DAY - NOW WE'LL LIE ON THE GRASS IN THE SUN AND BAKE - CAN'T GO TRACKIN' WATER INTO THE HOUSE - GOTTA GET REAL DRY.

DOC. SAYS SUNSHINE AND FRESH AIR AND EXERCISE ARE 'BOUT TH' BEST MEDICINES THERE ARE - AND THEY'RE FREE, TOO, FOR FOLKS THAT HAVE A CHANCE TO USE 'M - WHEE! I'M BEGINNIN' TO GET REAL TANNED ALREADY -

SANDY!!! COME OUT 'O THERE! YOU KNOW YOU'RE NOT S'POSED TO GO SWIMMIN' THERE - NOW YOU'RE TOO SOAKIN' WET TO GO INTO TH' HOUSE WHEN WE GO IN -

JUST LOOK AT YOURSELF! AND YOU KNOW WE'VE GOT TO BE ABSOLUTELY DRY 'FORE WE CAN GO INSIDE - DO YOU THINK WE'RE GOIN' TO WAIT OUT HERE WHILE YOU DRY? NOT A CHANCE -

Reg. U. S. Pat. Off.; Copyright, 1931, by The Chicago Tribune.
HAROLD GRAY

September 13, 1931

TELL ME HOW IT LOOKS, BILL-
CHEE! THIS SURE IS A NIFTY JOINT, OLIVER-
WELL, IT'S A WHOPPIN' BIG HOUSE WITH GARDENS ALL AROUND IT AND TH' WHOLE WORKS IS SITTIN' ON TOP OF ALMOST TH' TALLEST BUILDIN' IN TOWN-ONE CAN SEE FOR FIFTY MILES FROM ANY WINDOW-
IT'S WELL FURNISHED TOO, EH? LET'S STEP OUT INTO THE YARD AND SEE HOW THE AIR IS UP HERE-
BOY! WHAT A VIEW-AND FRESH AIR-TALK ABOUT YER CASTLE IN TH' SKY-THIS IS IT!
AND YOU SAY THERE IS GRASS IN THE YARD WAY UP HERE ON TOP OF THIS BUILDING? AND ISN'T THAT A FOUNTAIN I HEAR?
HAROLD GRAY
WELL, BILL, THIS WILL BE A GOOD HOME FOR US-QUIET AS THE COUNTRY, YET RIGHT IN THE MIDDLE OF THINGS-A PERFECT ARRANGEMENT-
YES-AND ALL OUR OFFICES ON TH' FLOORS JUST BELOW-PERFECT IS RIGHT-
Reg. U. S. Pat Off., Copyright, 1931,
OLD MAW GREEN-SHE WAS MIGHTY GOOD TO LITTLE ANNIE-SOMETHING OUGHT TO BE DONE FOR HER-SHE SHOULDN'T HAVE TO RUN A CHEAP ROOMING HOUSE THE REST OF HER LIFE-SHE'S GETTING ALONG IN YEARS-SHE SHOULD HAVE IT EASY AND NO WORRIES-
BUT I KNOW HER SORT-HAND HER MONEY AND SHE'D THROW IT IN YOUR FACE-PROUD-INDEPENDENT-LET ME THINK-HOW WOULD BE A TACTFUL WAY TO HELP HER? SHE MUST NEVER SUSPECT WHERE THE HELP COMES FROM-HM-M-M---
WHILE THE CLOSED DOOR TO THE SECRET ROOM INTRIGUES ANNIE BEYOND ALL HER POWERS OF RESISTANCE-
GEE-I WONDER WHAT CAN BE IN THAT ROOM-THE MAID SAID NO-BODY BUT DOC. LENS EVER GOES IN THERE AND THE DOOR'S ALWAYS LOCKED---ER--WHY, IT'S NOT LOCKED NOW-
HAROLD GRAY
Reg. U. S. Pat. Off.; Copyright, 1931, by The Chicago Tribune.
JUST LOOK AT ALL TH' JIGGERS AN' GADGETS AN' THINGS-AN' BOTTLES AN' BOXES ALL AROUND-LOOKS SORTA LIKE A WORKSHOP, ONLY MORE MYSTERIOUS-WHEW-I'D BETTER SCRAM 'FORE ANYBODY CATCHES ME PEEKIN'-
I HAVE IT, BILL-I KNOW HOW TO TAKE CARE OF OLD MAW GREEN AND MAKE HER COMFORTABLE FOR LIFE-GIVE HER A SMALL FORTUNE-AND SHE'LL ACCEPT IT, TOO, AND BE PROUD TO TAKE THE MONEY-
HOW WILL YOU WORK IT?
IT'S SIMPLE-HAVE A LAWYER GO TO HER AND TELL HER OF AN IMAGINARY RELATIVE IN THE OLD COUNTRY THAT'S LEFT ALL HIS MONEY TO HER-WE CAN MAKE IT PLAUSIBLE-SHE'LL BE SO PROUD IN THE BELIEF SHE'S HAD A RICH ANCESTOR THAT SHE WON'T QUESTION THE MATTER MUCH-
SAY-THAT'S GREAT, AND IT'LL WORK-
WHILE ANNIE OPENS HER MOUTH AND PUTS HER FOOT IN IT-
SAY, DOC.-DIDJA KNOW THAT DOOR THAT NOBODY'S S'POSED TO TOUCH WAS UNLOCKED YESTERDAY?
HOW DO YOU KNOW?
WHY--ER--THAT IS----
HAROLD GRAY
Reg. U. S. Pat. Off.; Copyright, 1931, by The Chicago Tribune.

September 14-16, 1931
DISTANT RELATIONS

NOW YOU HAVE THE DETAILS - MAW GREEN HAS HAD A DISTANT UNCLE - UNCLE JERRY, LET'S SAY - HE HAS LEFT HIS FORTUNE TO HER - MAKE AN AIR-TIGHT STORY, PAPERS AND ALL - LOOK UP HER FAMILY SO THERE'LL BE NO SLIPS -
YES, SIR - IT SHOULD BE QUITE A SIMPLE MATTER - A DAY OR TWO SHOULD SUFFICE TO COMPLETE THE DETAILS -
WHAT DID THE LAWYER SAY? CAN HE DO IT ALL RIGHT?
SURE - IT'S ALL SET - MAW GREEN WILL GET THE MONEY AND A RICH ANCESTOR NO ONE EVER HEARD OF THROWN IN FOR GOOD MEASURE -
WHILE ANNIE IS ALLOWED TO ENTER THE SECRET ROOM -
COME ON, ANNIE - IF YOU ARE STILL CURIOUS I'LL SHOW YOU WHAT'S IN THAT ROOM THAT'S ALMOST ALWAYS LOCKED -
GEE, DOC! I NEVER MEANT TO PEEK IN THERE YESTERDAY - HONEST -
HAROLD GRAY
LOOK AROUND ALL YOU WANT TO, ANNIE, BUT DON'T TOUCH ANYTHING - IF YOU ARE VERY CAREFUL I MAY FIND A WAY FOR YOU TO HELP ME HERE IN MY LABORATORY LATER ON -
GEE - THINGS LOOK BIG THROUGH THIS THING, DON'T THEY?
Reg. U. S. Pat. Off.; Copyright, 1931, by The Chicago Tribune.
DOC. SURE MUST FIGGER I'M CAREFUL TO TRUST ME IN HIS LAB-A-TORY - AND HE'S GIVEN ME A JOB IN HERE, TOO - EVERY DAY I'M TO WASH UP ALL TH' TEST-TUBES AN' BOTTLES HE LEAVES ON TH' TABLE FOR ME - BUT I MUSTN'T TOUCH TH' MIKER-SCOPES OR NOTHIN' -
HM-M - NOW I WONDER WHAT'S IN THIS CLOSET - I NEVER NOTICED THIS DOOR BEFORE - DOCTORS ARE LI'BLE TO HAVE MOST ANYTHING IN THEIR LAB-TORIES - NO TELLIN' - GEE - I S'POSE I SHOULDN'T LOOK, BUT WHO'LL KNOW IF I JUST PEEK?
YEOW!
LEAPIN' LIZARDS!!! AM I SWEATIN' BULLETS! HOW WAS I TO S'PECT THERE WERE BONES IN THERE? WHEW!!! GUESS THAT'S WHAT THEY MEAN BY "A SKELETON IN TH' CLOSET" -
HAROLD GRAY
Reg. U. S. Pat. Off., Copyright, 1931, by The Chicago Tribune
WE'LL JUST DROP IN ON MAW GREEN AND SAY HELLO - LOOK, SANDY - WHAT'S ALL THAT CROWD DOIN' ON HER FRONT STEPS?
WHO IS THAT KID?
THAT'S LITTLE ANNIE
YEAH - SHE KNOWS MAW GREEN REAL WELL -
HEY! MAW GREEN! IT'S ME - ANNIE - OPEN TH' DOOR AND LET ME IN, WON'TCHA?
GEE WHISKERS! WHY ALL TH' CROWD OUT IN FRONT? WHAT'S GOIN' ON HERE?
HAVEN'T YOU HEARD? I'M RICH - YES SIR; RICH!!! TH' LAWYER WAS HERE LAST NIGHT - AT FIRST I THOUGHT IT WAS SOME MISTAKE, BUT HE PROVED IT'S TRUE, ALL RIGHT -
SEE - I'VE GOT ALL TH' PAPERS - IT WAS ME SECOND UNCLE JERRY IN THE OLD COUNTRY, REST HIS SOUL - I CAN'T REMEMBER HIM, BUT HE TOOK A SHINE TO ME AS A BABY IT SEEMS - POOR OLD UNCLE JERRY, HE LEFT ALL HIS FORTUNE TO ME - THEY HAD AN AWFUL TIME FINDIN' ME, THIS LAWYER SAYS -
GEE, MAW GREEN - THAT'S SWELL -
HAROLD GRAY
Reg. U. S. Pat. Off.; Copyright, 1931, by The Chicago Tribune.

September 17–19, 1931
DISTANT RELATIONS

Little Orphan Annie
I GOT PAT ALL DRESSED UP AND SENT HER OUT IN THE YARD-NOW I WONDER WHAT SHE'S UP TO- SHE'S AWFUL QUIET-

MIGHT HAVE KNOWN IT- OUT THERE PLAYING WITH HER SAIL BOAT IN THE POOL, AND WITH THAT CLEAN DRESS ON, TOO-

SHE'LL BE FALLING IN SURE, IF I DON'T GET HER AWAY FROM THERE MIGHTY QUICK-

STILL, SANDY'S WITH HER- HE'S MIGHTY WATCHFUL- I GUESS HE WON'T LET HER GET WET- I'LL JUST WAIT HERE AND SEE WHAT HAPPENS-

GEE- THEY SURE UNDERSTAND EACH OTHER- LOOK AT THAT- SHE CAN'T REACH THE BOAT AND SHE WANTS SANDY TO HELP HER- NOW WHAT'LL HE DO?

WELL, OF ALL THINGS- HE'S GOIN' TO HOLD HER WHILE SHE REACHES OUT AND GRABS TH' BOAT- THERE'S A BRAINY DOG FOR YOU-

WELL, WELL- GUESS THERE'S NO NEED TO WORRY 'BOUT PAT WHEN YOU'RE AROUND- EH, SANDY?

ARF!

?
WHOOF!

LEAPIN' LIZARDS!!! OF ALL TH' CLUMSY TRICKS!

NOW JUST LOOK AT HER DRESS- SOAKIN' WET- GOTTA CHANGE EVERY STITCH- HUH! AND JUST AS I WAS COMPLIMENTIN' YUH, SANDY, ON TAKIN' SUCH GOOD CARE OF HER, TOO- BUT YOU HAD TO GO "ARFIN" AND DROP HER IN-

BUT THAT'S TH' WAY IT GOES- YOU'RE JUST LIKE A LOT O' FOLKS, SANDY- A LITTLE FLATTERY AND YOU LOSE YER HEAD-
HAROLD GRAY

September 20, 1931

BACK ON TOP OF THE HEAP- IT'S BEEN A TOUGH BATTLE, BUT IT'S BEEN WORTH IT- BILLIONS, AND I'LL NEVER LOSE THEM AGAIN- I'VE LEARNED MY LESSON - I'M RICHER AND STRONGER THAN EVER-

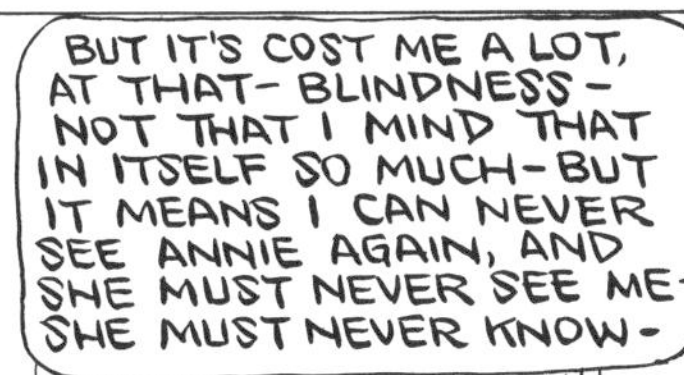
BUT IT'S COST ME A LOT, AT THAT- BLINDNESS - NOT THAT I MIND THAT IN ITSELF SO MUCH- BUT IT MEANS I CAN NEVER SEE ANNIE AGAIN, AND SHE MUST NEVER SEE ME- SHE MUST NEVER KNOW-

OF COURSE I KNOW SHE'S WELL AND HAPPY- IN A GOOD HOME- CONTENTED - THAT'S ALL THAT MATTERS, I SUPPOSE - BUT I'M JUST SELFISH ENOUGH TO WANT MORE THAN THAT- HER PICTURE-

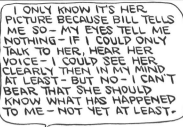

I ONLY KNOW IT'S HER PICTURE BECAUSE BILL TELLS ME SO - MY EYES TELL ME NOTHING - IF I COULD ONLY TALK TO HER, HEAR HER VOICE- I COULD SEE HER CLEARLY THEN IN MY MIND AT LEAST- BUT NO - I CAN'T BEAR THAT SHE SHOULD KNOW WHAT HAS HAPPENED TO ME - NOT YET AT LEAST-
HAROLD GRAY

BILL, HERE I AM WITH EVERYTHING IN THE WORLD, ALMOST- UNTOLD WEALTH- LEISURE TO ENJOY IT- A PARTNER I CAN TRUST- EVERYTHING, IN FACT, BUT THE ONE THING I MISS MOST- MY SIGHT-
SHUX! WHAT'S EYES, OLIVER? YOU WHIPPED 'EM ALL WITHOUT EYES, DIDN'TCHA?

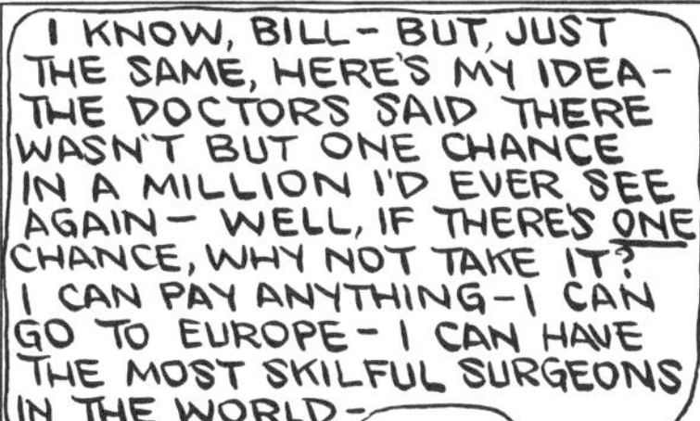
I KNOW, BILL- BUT, JUST THE SAME, HERE'S MY IDEA- THE DOCTORS SAID THERE WASN'T BUT ONE CHANCE IN A MILLION I'D EVER SEE AGAIN- WELL, IF THERE'S ONE CHANCE, WHY NOT TAKE IT? I CAN PAY ANYTHING - I CAN GO TO EUROPE - I CAN HAVE THE MOST SKILFUL SURGEONS IN THE WORLD-

SURE- WHY NOT?

WITH MONEY ANYTHING IS POSSIBLE-
IT'S A CINCH, OLIVER- YOUR NEW YACHT'S LYIN' IN TH' HARBOR COSTIN' A WAR-LOAN EVERY DAY- WHY NOT USE IT? AND ANY WAY YOU LOOK AT IT, TH' TRIP WOULD DO YOU GOOD-
HAROLD GRAY

DO YOU THINK YOU CAN HANDLE THINGS ALL RIGHT WHILE I'M GONE?
WITH WHAT I'VE LEARNED FROM YOU IT'LL BE A PIPE- ANYWAY I CAN CALL YUH UP ON THE RADIO TELEPHONE ANY TIME I GET STUCK- YOU JUST LEAVE IT TO ME, OLIVER-

I'VE JUST BEEN OUT TO THE YACHT- EVERYTHING IS ALL READY TO PULL OUT TOMORROW-

FINE- NOW LET'S GO OVER THOSE PAPERS AND GET EVERYTHING CLEANED UP-

A LITTLE LOWER DOWN- THERE- SIGN RIGHT THERE- THAT'S GREAT-
MAYBE WHEN I COME BACK FROM EUROPE I WON'T HAVE TO FUMBLE AROUND LIKE THIS ANY MORE- MAYBE I'LL BE ABLE TO SEE WHAT I'M DOING-

CHEE! I SURE WISH YOU ALL TH' LUCK IN TH' WORLD- I WANT YOU TO SEE AGAIN, EVEN IF IT WOULD MEAN YOU WOULDN'T NEED A LITTLE RUNT LIKE ME ANY MORE-

WHADDYUH MEAN, I WOULDN'T NEED YOU ANY MORE? DO YOU THINK IT'S ONLY BECAUSE I'M BLIND THAT YOU'RE MY PARTNER? BIRDS AS LOYAL AND SQUARE-SHOOTING AS YOU, ARE TOO RARE TO BE THROWN AWAY- I'LL ALWAYS NEED YOU FOR A PARTNER AND DON'T YOU FORGET IT-
HAROLD GRAY

September 21–23, 1931

GOOD-BYE, BILL- I'LL KEEP IN TOUCH WITH YOU ALL THE TIME- IF ANYTHING COMES UP LET ME KNOW-
GOOD-BYE, OLIVER, AND THE BEST OF LUCK-

WELL, WE'RE OFF- STARTED THE MOMENT I STEPPED ABOARD- A FEW MINUTES MORE AND WE'LL BE OUT TO SEA- WHEN WE COME HOME AGAIN PERHAPS I CAN SEE- BUT I MUSTN'T COUNT ON THAT TOO MUCH-

THE FAINT TINKLE OF BELLS BELOW - TRIM FIGURES MOVING ABOUT ON DECK - THE CHANNEL WIDENS - THE GREAT YACHT GATHERS SPEED AND SLIPS SWIFTLY OUT TO SEA, CARRYING WARBUCKS TO FOREIGN SHORES AND FAMOUS SURGEONS - HOW LONG BEFORE HE WILL RETURN? WHAT WILL BE THE OUT-COME OF THIS VOYAGE? TIME ALONE CAN ANSWER -
HAROLD GRAY

GEE! WHAT A SWELL NEW BOILER! AND A GUY TO DRIVE IT, TOO-
WELL, I FIGURE, AS LONG AS POOR UNCLE JERRY WANTED ME TO BE RICH AND LEFT ME HIS FORTUNE HE'D WANT ME TO LIVE UP TO ME NEW STATION-

DO YOU KNOW, MAW GREEN, I THINK THAT'S AN AWFUL PRETTY OUTFIT AND MIGHTY BECOMIN'-
THANKS, ANNIE- I WENT TO TH' SWELLEST JOINT IN TOWN AND TOLD 'EM TO DO THEIR BEST AND DRESS ME UP- THEY SAY FINE FEATHERS MAKE FINE BIRDS- BUT IT'S PRETTY HARD TO MAKE ANYTHING BEAUTIFUL OUT OF A TOUGH OLD BIRD LIKE ME-

HERE'S THE HOUSE I'VE BOUGHT- NOT SO BIG, BUT PLENTY OF ROOM FOR ME AND FOR MY FEW REAL FRIENDS- HOW DO YOU LIKE IT, ANNIE?
WHY, IT'S WONDERFUL- I WAS SCARED YOU'D GO AN' GET A BIG CASTLE OR SOMETHIN'-

NOPE- IN SPITE OF RICHES, ANNIE, I'LL NEVER BE A FINE LADY- I'M STILL JUST OLD MAW GREEN, AND I KNOW IT— SOCIETY! BAH! WHAT'S IN IT FOR THE LIKES O' ME? I PREFER THE SOCIETY OF A GOOD DOG, AND MAYBE A GOAT, TO THE SOCIETY OF A LOT OF MONEY-WORSHIPERS THAT'D SMIRK IN MY FACE AND SNEER AT MY BACK- I'LL HAVE CONTENTMENT- THAT'S MORE THAN LOTS OF RICH FOLKS-
HAROLD GRAY

ANNIE! YI! ONLY JUST NOW I WAS THINKING OF YOU- SO YOU COME TO VISIT OLD JAKE- WHAT A PRETTY DRESS-
WOW! AND ARE YOU ALL DRESSED UP! YOU LOOK LIKE A MILLION BUCKS-

HA! YOU SHOULD LOOK ME OVER ONCE- THE MERCHANT PRINCE, EH? ALL DRESSED UP LIKE A BROKEN ARM SO THE CUSTOMERS WILL KNOW WHAT A HIGH-CLASS STORE THIS IS- BUT COME BACK TO THE OFFICE WHERE WE CAN TALK-

PHOOIE- I COULDN'T FEEL RIGHT IN THAT FANCY COAT- AND WITHOUT ANY HAT I DON'T FEEL DRESSED- BUT THE PUBLIC DEMANDS I SHOULD BE DRESSED UP LIKE A TAILOR'S DUMMY, AND THE PUBLIC IS ALWAYS RIGHT-
BUSINESS SURE MUST BE GOOD- EH, JAKE-

THERE- THE SPATS AND THE STRIPED PANTS I WOULDN'T HAVE TO LOOK AT- NOW I FEEL BETTER- MORE LIKE OLD TIMES; EH, ANNIE? YES, BUSINESS I HAVE NEVER SEEN SO GOOD WITH ME- BEFORE LONG I WOULD HAVE TO MOVE TO A BIGGER STORE IF IT KEEPS UP- AND HOW IS EVERYTHING WITH YOU?
HAROLD GRAY

Little Orphan Annie
A NICE LONG WALK IS JUST WHAT WE NEED- EH, PAT?
LOOK- TOUGH BOYS-

WOT'S DIS? WHY, IF IT AIN'T LITTLE FLOSSIE, HERSELF, STRUTTIN' ALONG LIKE SHE OWNED DIS STREET-
YEAH! AN' GIT A LOAD OF DE FANCY MAKE-UP.
WHO DOES SHE TINK SHE IS? DE DRESSED UP SISSY-

AW, DON'T NOTICE 'EM, PAT- THEY'RE JUST A BUNCH O' WISE EGGS- OOOO-- LOOK AT ALL THAT OLD FRUIT- IF ONLY PAT WASN'T ALONG WHAT I'D DO TO THOSE BIRDS- BUT I'VE GOTTA BE A LADY IN FRONT O' PAT-

I KNEW IT- THEY'RE STOPPIN' BY THAT CAN- DON'T LOOK BACK, PAT- IF WE LOOK NOW, THEY'LL START THROWIN' STUFF SURE- AN' DON'T RUN- WALK- WE'RE ALMOST TO TH' CORNER-

THERE- SAFE FOR A MINUTE- I COULD LIGHT OUT AND MAKE IT HOME FROM HERE, BUT PAT'S TOO LITTLE TO RUN FAST- THEY'D CATCH UP WITH US IN HALF A BLOCK, SURE- GEE! WHAT'LL I DO? I DON'T WANT TO GET SOCKED WITH A TOMATO, OR EVEN AN OLD APPLE-

HM-M-M--- WHAT A TOUGH-LOOKIN' GUY- I'LL BET ANYBODY THAT PICKED ON THAT BIRD WOULD BE SORRY-

LISTEN, PAT- NO MATTER WHAT HAPPENS, YOU WAIT RIGHT THERE TILL I COME BACK- I WON'T BE GONE MORE'N A SECOND-

THERE SHE IS, GUYS-
LET 'ER HAVE IT-
YAH-H-H! PHOOIE!

SMACK!

GET 'EM, MISTER!!! I WOULDN'T STAND FOR THAT-

WOW! WHAT A MAN- HE DIDN'T LET A SINGLE ONE OF 'EM GET AWAY-

COURSE I COULD HAVE SAILED INTO 'EM AND TAUGHT 'EM SOME MANNERS- BUT I'D HAVE BEEN SURE TO GET MY DRESS ALL DIRTY- AND, BESIDES, IT'D HAVE BEEN A BAD Z'AMPLE FOR PAT-
HAROLD GRAY

September 27, 1931

YOU SURE ARE GETTING STRONGER AND HEALTHIER EVERY DAY, PAT- THESE WALKS IN TH' PARK WILL GIVE YOU AN APPETITE- WILL YOU BE READY FOR DINNER TO-NIGHT?
PAT READY FOR DINNER NOW-
KITTIES!
KITTIES, NOTHIN'! THOSE ARE SQUIRRELS-GEE- AREN'T THEY CUTE? AND TAME, TOO- SOME DAY WE'RE GOIN' TO HAVE TO TAKE YOU OUT TO THE COUNTRY, PAT-
THEN YOU'LL SEE HORSES AND COWS AND PIGS AND CHICKENS AND DUCKS AND GEESE AND TURKEYS AND ALL SORTS O' THINGS- YOU'LL BE CRAZY 'BOUT TH' FARM- ALL KIDS ARE- OH, I'VE GOT LOTS O' PLANS FOR YOU-
HAROLD GRAY
IT SURE IS FUN TO RAISE A KID- I NEVER HAD A VERY GOOD TIME MYSELF, BEIN' IN TH' "HOME" SO LONG- BUT PAT'LL NEVER HAVE TO GO THROUGH WHAT I DID- NO SIR-EE- SHE'S GOIN' TO HAVE EVER'THING I CAN GIVE HER-
Reg. U. S. Pat. Off., Copyright, 1931, by The Chicago Tribune.
STOP! STOP, I SAY! LET ME OUT- THERE'S TH' KID- I'D KNOW HER ANYWHERE- DON'T LET HER GET AWAY- STOP!!!
LEAPIN' LIZARDS! COME ON, PAT- LET'S SCRAM- THEY'RE COMING BACK-
THERE THEY GO- TURN AROUND- HURRY, YOU IDIOT- KEEP YOUR EYE ON 'EM-
GREAT CAESAR'S SUSPENDERS! WHO WAS THAT DAME? SHE POINTED RIGHT AT PAT- C'MON, PAT- WE HAVEN'T A SECOND TO LOSE- YOU'RE MY GIRL AND NO-BODY'S GOIN' TO TAKE YOU AWAY FROM ME-
STEP ON IT! THEY COULDN'T HAVE GOTTEN FAR- WHERE DID THEY GO?
SH-H-- KEEP YER HEAD DOWN-
HAROLD GRAY
Reg. U. S. Pat. Off.; Copyright, 1931, by The Chicago Tribune.
EVER SINCE THAT BIG DAME TRIED TO GRAB PAT YESTERDAY I'VE FELT ALL TWITTERY- I WOULDN'T TAKE HER OUT WALKIN' TO-DAY FOR A MILLION BUCKS- NO TELLIN' WHAT MIGHT HAPPEN-
GREAT SCOTT! I MIGHT HAVE KNOWN IT-
HEY! KEEP AWAY FROM THAT WINDOW! D'YUH WANT SOME-BODY TO SEE YOU? LEAPIN' LIZARDS! WE'VE GOTTA LIE LOW FOR A SPELL-
ANNIE TAKE PAT OUT FOR WALK?
NIX- NOT TO-DAY- IT ISN'T HEALTHY OUT IN THE STREET- SEE? AND DON'T EVEN LOOK OUT OF THE WINDOW ANY MORE-
HAROLD GRAY
Reg. U. S. Pat. Off.; Copyright, 1931, by The Chicago Tribune.

September 28–30, 1931

LEAVING HIS YACHT AT A FOREIGN SHORE, WARBUCKS BOARDS A WAITING PLANE- SOON HE WILL REACH THE MOST SKILLED SURGEONS OF ALL EUROPE-
AND NOW, FOR THE FIRST TIME, WE LOOK IN AT THE HOME OF MR. AND MRS. TERRACE, WELL-TO-DO SUBURBAN RESIDENTS- AN IMPORTANT DISCUSSION SEEMS IN PROGRESS- LET'S LISTEN IN----
TWO AND A HALF MONTHS AND NO WORD OF OUR BABY- I CAN'T STAND IT MUCH LONGER- WE MUST DO SOMETHING-
ER- THE POLICE---
NO-NO! YOU KNOW MRS. CUNNING SAYS THAT WOULD BE THE MOST TERRIBLE MISTAKE- WHOEVER TOOK OUR BABY MIGHT DO ANYTHING, IF THEY KNEW THE POLICE WERE AFTER THEM- MRS. CUNNING WAS SO FOND OF HER- SHE IS SEARCHING FOR HER NIGHT AND DAY- SHE WILL FIND HER- BUT HOW LONG? HOW LONG?
YOU ARE QUITE RIGHT, MRS. TERRACE- I AM SURE I'LL FIND THE DARLING SOON- IN FACT I HAVE TRACE OF HER- WE MUST BE PATIENT- ABOVE EVERYTHING, THE POLICE MUST BE KEPT OUT OF THIS-
SEE, GEORGE- HEAR WHAT MRS. CUNNING SAYS? I WAS RIGHT-
HUMPH-
HAROLD GRAY
Reg. U. S. Pat. Off.; Copyright, 1931, by The Chicago Tribune.
MAYBE I'M SILLY TO WORRY- THAT BIG DAME IN TH' TAXI MAY HAVE MADE A MISTAKE- ANYWAY I GOT PAT AWAY PRETTY SLICK- I DON'T GUESS THERE'S MUCH CHANCE SHE HAS ANY IDEA WHAT HOUSE WE LIVE IN-
LOOKIN' OUT TH' WINDOW AGAIN- OH, WELL- I GUESS IT'S SAFE ENOUGH- NOT ONE CHANCE IN A MILLION THAT ANYBODY THAT MATTERS WILL SEE HER- AND I CAN'T KEEP HER AWAY FROM TH' WINDOWS ALL TH' TIME-
THERE SHE IS, AL- SEE HER LOOKIN' OUT THAT WINDOW? I WASN'T HER NURSE FOR MONTHS WITHOUT KNOWIN' THAT BRAT WHEN I SEE HER- NOW WE'VE GOT TO DOPE OUT SOME WAY O' GRABBIN' HER WITHOUT A SCENE-
DOC. LENS LIVES THERE- HE'S A BIG SHOT- I DUNNO ABOUT TRYIN' ANYTHING THERE-
YOU ALWAYS WERE A YELLOW LITTLE RUNT- WHAT I EVER MARRIED YOU FOR BEATS ME- BUT YOU'RE GOING THROUGH WITH THIS- WHAT YUH SCARED OF? DOC. LENS IS OUT O' TOWN- IF WE ONCE GET HOLD OF THAT KID WE'RE RICH- AND WHO'S GOIN' TO STOP US?
ALL RIGHT- ALL RIGHT-
HAROLD GRAY
Reg. U. S. Pat. Off.; Copyright, 1931, by The Chicago Tribune.
DO YOU REALLY THINK YOU WILL FIND MY BABY SOON? I HAVE SUCH CONFIDENCE IN YOU-
I'M SURE OF IT, MA'M- BUT, ABOVE ALL, NOT A WORD TO THE POLICE, OR I'M AFRAID YOU'D NEVER SEE HER AGAIN- JUST LEAVE IT TO ME, MRS. TERRACE-
THAT DUMB-BELL- WELL, I KNOW WHERE HER KID IS, NOW- THAT'S THE MAIN THING- GETTIN' HER OUGHT TO BE EASY- IF SHE JUST LEAVES IT ALL TO ME, EVERYTHING WILL BE GREAT- BUT WE'VE GOT TO WORK FAST-
WELL, AL- I STALLED HER OFF FROM CALLIN' TH' COPS FOR A LITTLE LONGER- BUT WE'VE GOTTA WORK FAST- I'M GETTIN' SICK O' THAT MAID RACKET ANYWAY- NOW THAT WE KNOW WHERE TH' BRAT IS, THERE'S NO USE STALLIN' ANY MORE-
YEAH- THAT'S WHAT I SAY-
WE'VE TH' SAME AS GOT THE KID- YOU START WRITIN' THE LETTERS AND I'LL ADVISE THE TERRACES WHEN THEY GET 'EM SO THEY DON'T GO YELPIN' TO TH' COPS- WRITE THIS- "YOUR CHILD IS SAFE- IF YOU WANT TO SEE HER AGAIN KEEP YOUR MOUTH SHUT AND DO JUST WHAT YOU ARE TOLD"- THAT OUGHT TO HOLD 'EM FOR A DAY OR TWO-
HAROLD GRAY
Reg. U. S. Pat. Off.; Copyright, 1931, by The Chicago Tribune.

October 1–3, 1931

Little Orphan
Annie
WATCH ME, PAT- I'LL SHOW YUH HOW TO CLIMB A TREE-

IT'S A CINCH, WHEN YUH KNOW HOW- LOTS MORE FUN THAN PLAYIN' SEE-SAW-

SEE HOW HIGH I AM NOW- AND I'M NOT HALF STARTED- I'M GOIN' TO CLIMB WAY UP WHERE I CAN SEE ALL OVER TOWN-

THIS IS A SWELL TREE TO CLIMB, TOO-
WHOOP!

YIPE!

GEE!
WHEE!

WOW! WHAT A TRICK THAT WAS- JUST LIKE THEY DO IN TH' CIRCUS- SIMPLE, TOO, IF YUH DO IT JUST RIGHT-

SAY- YUH KNOW THAT'D MAKE A DOG-GONED GOOD ACT- COURSE I'D JUMP NEXT TIME, AND NOT FALL- C'MON- LET'S TRY THAT AGAIN-
SURE-
?

THERE- NOW YOU SIT THERE JUST LIKE YOU DID BEFORE AND I'LL CLIMB UP AND JUMP- AND WHEN I HIT THIS END OF TH' BOARD YOU'LL SAIL OVER MY HEAD-----

BUT WAIT A MINUTE- WHAT'S PAT GOIN' TO LIGHT ON? WE'RE NOT ALL HERE- WHERE DID SANDY GO?
HAROLD GRAY

HUH! WE SHOULD HAVE BEEN SITTIN' PRETTY TWO MONTHS AGO- BUT YOU HAD TO GO AND BUNGLE THE JOB-
YEAH? HOW COULD I HELP IT?
YOU PROBABLY COULDN'T- THERE I WORKED MY HEAD OFF FOR THOSE DUMB TERRACES AND GOT 'EM TO TRUST ME WITH TH' KID- THEN I FRAMED THE WHOLE THING- I SLIP TH' KID TO YOU AND TELL THEM SHE'D BEEN GRABBED- ALL YOU HAD TO DO WAS BRING HER IN YER CAB TO THIS HANGOUT-
THEN WRITE A FEW LETTERS AND, WITH ME ADVISIN' 'EM AND HANDLIN' THAT END, IT'D HAVE BEEN A CINCH TO CLEAN UP- BUT NO- YOU HAD TO LET THOSE PUNKS STEAL YER CAB, AND TH' KID IN IT, AND GUM UP TH' WORKS- WHAT A GUY YOU ARE!
AIN'T I TOLD YUH A THOUSAND TIMES- I LEFT TH' KID IN TH' TAXI TO GO IN AND 'PHONE- HOW WAS ANYBODY TO KNOW THOSE BIRDS WOULD STEAL MY CAB- WE FOUND IT ABANDONED TH' NEXT DAY, EMPTY- WHOEVER PINCHED TH' CAB MUST HAVE LEFT TH' KID IN SOME HALL WAY, AND TH' RED-HEAD FOUND HER- BUT WE'VE TH' SAME AS GOT HER AGAIN NOW, SO QUIT YAPPIN' ABOUT IT-
HAROLD GRAY
Reg. U. S. Pat. Off.; Copyright, 1931, by The Chicago Tribune.
THERE'S TH' HOUSE WHERE SHE IS- TOO BAD WE DIDN'T GRAB HER WHEN WE HAD A CHANCE-
YEAH- YOU FUMBLED, AS USUAL, OR WE'D HAVE CAUGHT HER THAT DAY- NOW TH' RED-HEAD IS SCARED TO TAKE HER OUT ANY MORE-
THAT RED-HEAD IS A CAGEY LITTLE BRAT- IF IT WASN'T FOR HER IT'D BE A CINCH TO GRAB TH' KID- WE'VE GOT TO FIGGER OUT SOMETHING THAT'LL WORK-
I HAVE IT, AL- WE'LL LET ON WE'RE TH' KID'S PARENTS- SEE? JUST WALK RIGHT IN AND TAKE HER-
YEAH? AND S'POSIN' SOMEBODY PUTS UP A SQUAWK AND MAKES US PROVE WE'RE HER FOLKS-
NOT A CHANCE IF WE WORK IT FAST- THEY KNOW TH' KID MUST HAVE FOLKS- ALL WE'VE GOT TO DO IS SPILL A COCK-AN-BULL STORY ABOUT LOSIN' HER- WE'LL HAVE HER AND BE GONE BEFORE THEY CAN GET ORGANIZED TO START ANY ARGUMENT-
HAROLD GRAY
Reg. U. S. Pat. Off.; Copyright, 1931, by The Chicago Tribune.
I S'POSE IT'S SILLY O' ME TO WORRY 'BOUT IT, BUT, EVER SINCE THAT BIG DAME IN TH' TAXI LIT OUT AFTER PAT A WEEK AGO, I'VE HAD A FEELIN' TH' HOUSE IS BEIN' WATCHED-
SHUX! I GOT PAT AWAY SLICK AS A WHISTLE- NOBODY SAW US COME HOME- HOW COULD THAT DAME KNOW WHERE WE LIVE? WE WERE BLOCKS FROM HERE WHEN SHE SAW US AND I RAN THE OTHER WAY WITH PAT, TOO- THAT'D FOOL HER-
MOST LIKELY SHE WAS JUST SOME NUT- PROBABLY SHE NEVER SAW PAT BEFORE- LIKE AS NOT SHE'S FORGOTTEN ALL ABOUT IT BY NOW- ANYWAY SHE'D BE WATCHIN' TH' PART O' TOWN WHERE SHE SAW US- ALL WE'D HAVE TO DO IS GO WALKIN' IN THE OTHER DIRECTION-
CAN'T KEEP PAT CAGED UP FOREVER- SHUX- IT'S SAFE ENOUGH- I'LL TAKE HER FOR A GOOD, LONG WALK TO-MORROW-
HAROLD GRAY
Reg. U. S. Pat. Off.; Copyright, 1931, by The Chicago Tribune.

October 5–7, 1931

C'MON, PAT- WE'LL TAKE A REAL, LONG WALK TO-DAY- CLEAR AROUND TH' PARK AND BACK- LET'S GET GOIN'-
WHAM!
CLICK
LEAPIN' LIZARDS! THAT WOMAN! WHAT A CLOSE CALL THAT WAS! WHEW!
HAROLD GRAY
Reg. U. S. Pat. Off.; Copyright, 1931, by The Chicago Tribune.
YOU SAY SHE'S YOUR CHILD AND YOU WISH TO ENTER THIS HOUSE AND REGAIN POSSESSION OF HER- HOW DID YOU LOSE HER IN THE FIRST PLACE?
LISTEN- YOU'RE A LAWYER AND WE'RE HIRIN' YOU TO DO WHAT YOU'RE TOLD- SEE? IT DOESN'T MAKE ANY DIFFERENCE HOW WE LOST TH' KID- WE WANT HER AND A LAWYER LIKE YOU CAN GET US INTO TH' HOUSE LEGAL-
HM-M... I SEE- WELL, WE WILL NEED A SEARCH WARRANT- I WILL TAKE CARE OF THAT AND YOU WILL MEET ME HERE TO-MORROW AT THIS TIME-
THAT MOUTH-PIECE WANTS TO KNOW TOO MUCH- IF HE GETS WISE HE'LL WANT TO CUT IN-
YEAH- BUT THERE'S NO NEED O' HIM GETTIN' WISE- AND WE NEED HIM TO MAKE IT LOOK LEGAL-
Reg. U. S. Pat. Off.; Copyright, 1931, by The Chicago Tribune.
HAROLD GRAY
I AM A LAWYER AND THIS IS A SEARCH-WARRANT WHICH EMPOWERS US TO SEARCH THIS HOUSE- WHERE IS DOCTOR LENS?
DR LENS IS OUT- BUT IF YOU WANT TO COME IN AND LOOK AROUND JUST HELP YOURSELF- IT'S O. K. WITH ME-
NOW YOU COME CLEAN- WHERE IS THAT CHILD?
ARE YOU ASKING ME? SHUX- YOU'RE A SMART GUY- MAYBE IT TELLS IN THAT SEARCH-WARRANT PAPER WHERE SHE IS- GO ON AND LOOK FOR HER- I'M BUSY-
WE'VE LOOKED EVERY PLACE- TH' KID ISN'T HERE- THAT'S SURE-
?
A LOT O' GOOD YER SEARCH WARRANT DID- AS A LAWYER YOU'RE A BUST-
WELL, I GOT YOU IN, DIDN'T I? IS IT MY FAULT IF THE CHILD ISN'T THERE?
HUH- SHE WAS THERE, ALL RIGHT- ONE LOOK AT THAT RED HEAD'S SMUG MAP WOULD TELL YOU SHE KNOWS A LOT- I'D LIKE TO LAY MY HANDS ON THAT SMARTY- SHE'D SING-
HAROLD GRAY
Reg U. S. Pat. Off., Copyright, 1931, by The Chicago Tribune

October 8–10, 1931
DISTANT RELATIONS

Little Orphan Annie
WHEW! I DON'T KNOW WHAT TO DO - I'M SCARED -

EVER SINCE THAT WOMAN TRIED TO GRAB PAT ON THE STREET I'VE BEEN AFRAID TO LET HER OUT OF MY SIGHT FOR A SECOND - THEY SEARCHED THE HOUSE YESTERDAY, BUT THEY'RE LIABLE TO COME BACK TO-DAY - I WON'T LET 'EM TAKE PAT AWAY FROM ME - I WON'T -

LEAPIN' LIZARDS!!! I KNEW IT - THERE'S THAT DETECTIVE AND THAT LAWYER AND A COP, AND THEY'RE COMIN' TO THE DOOR -

NO WAY TO KEEP 'EM OUT - THERE - TH' MAID IS LETTIN' 'EM IN - HERE THEY COME - NOW THEY'LL SEARCH TH' WHOLE PLACE - AND IF THEY FIND PAT THEY'LL TAKE HER AWAY -

WE HAVE A SEARCH WARRANT AND WE WANT THAT KID - IF YOU KNOW WHAT'S GOOD FOR YOU, YOU'LL TELL US WHERE SHE IS -
OH, YEAH? WELL, IF YUH'VE GOT A SEARCH WARRANT, GO AHEAD AND SEARCH, YUH BIG FLAT-FOOT - NO-BODY'S STOPPIN' YUH, ARE THEY?

AN' I HOPE YUH FALL IN TH' CISTERN!
C'MON - NO USE TRYING TO GET HER TO TALK - IF TH' KID'S HERE WE'LL FIND HER, EASY ENOUGH -

HUMPH! NOT A SIGN OF HER - THAT'S FUNNY - SHE MUST BE HERE -
THIS IS THE LAST ROOM IN THE HOUSE - I WISH WE COULD MAKE THAT RED-HEAD TALK -

HERE'S THE BACK YARD - WALLED IN TIGHT - YOU CAN SEE THERE'S NO ONE OUT HERE - THAT DOG LOOKS MEAN - I WONDER IF HE'S CHAINED -
GR-R-R!

NO! HE ISN'T -
LOOK OUT, YOU BIRDS - LET ME OUT O' HERE -
R-R-R-R

LET'S GO -
IF THAT BRAT WAS HERE WE'D HAVE FOUND HER -
I'D LIKE TO SUE SOMEBODY FOR THIS -

WELL, THEY WON'T BE BACK TO-DAY - I SURE WAS NERVOUS WHEN THEY CAME OUT HERE IN TH' YARD, BUT YOU HANDLED 'EM JUST RIGHT, SANDY -
HAROLD GRAY

IT'S O.K. NOW, PAT - COME ON OUT -
Reg. U. S. Pat. Off.; Copyright, 1931, by The Chicago Tribune.

October 11, 1931

WE AIN'T GETTIN' ANY PLACE- WHAT DO YOU THINK THAT RED-HEAD HAS DONE WITH TH' KID?
DONE WITH HER! HID HER- THAT'S ALL- AND RIGHT THERE UNDER ALL OUR NOSES, TOO-AR-R-R! WOULDN'T I LOVE TO GET MY HANDS ON THAT RED-HEAD'S NECK FOR JUST ONE MINUTE-
THAT RED-HEAD IS SMART-
SMART! SMART ALECK! THAT'S WHAT SHE IS- WE, WITH A SEARCH WARRANT, BREAKIN' OUR BACKS LOOKIN' UNDER BEDS AND IN CLOSETS- AND THERE SHE SITS AND LEERS AT US- SMART! BAH! I'D LIKE TO MAKE HER SMART-
WHILE THE SUBJECT OF ALL THIS CAUSTIC COMMENT REMAINS CALM, BUT ALERT-
WELL, SANDY, I GUESS THOSE CROOKS THAT ARE TRYIN' TO GRAB PAT WON'T BE BACK ANY MORE TO-DAY-
C'M'ON OUT, PAT- WHEN IT COMES TO PLAYIN' HIDE AN' SEEK WE SURE KNOW OUR HIDE-OUTS- EH, PAT?
PAT PLAY DOGGIE- WOOF! WOOF!
HAROLD GRAY
THERE- THAT LETTER WILL KEEP 'EM QUIET FOR A LITTLE LONGER- I'VE TOLD 'EM THEIR KID'S SAFE-
YEAH- THAT'LL HOLD 'EM FOR A WHILE- AND SAY- WE'VE BEEN SAPS-
WHY DO WE HAVE TO HAVE TH' KID BEFORE MAKIN' A PLAY FOR TH' MONEY? WHY DO WE HAVE TO HAVE TH' KID AT ALL? IF THEY THINK THEY'RE GOIN' TO GET TH' KID, THEY'LL PAY- WHAT DO WE CARE, AFTER THAT?
NOTHING DOING! THAT WOULDN'T BE HONEST AND YOU KNOW IT- IF WE CAN'T DELIVER TH' KID, WE'D HAVE NO RIGHT TO TAKE THEIR MONEY- I'M SURPRISED YOU'D SUGGEST A CROOKED TRICK LIKE THAT-
HUMPH! YOU ALWAYS WERE TOO HONEST FOR YOUR OWN GOOD- NO BUSINESS MAN- NO WONDER YOU NEVER GOT ANYWHERE. HUMPH!
HAROLD GRAY
Reg. U. S. Pat. Off.; Copyright, 1931, by The Chicago Tribune.
BUT LISTEN, ELSIE- WHY NOT TURN THAT LETTER OVER TO THE POLICE? MRS. CUNNING HAS BEEN TRYING TO FIND BABY FOR MONTHS AND HAS FAILED-
GEORGE! DON'T BE ABSURD- YOU KNOW SHE SAYS HERSELF THAT THE POLICE WOULD SPOIL EVERYTHING-
WHY, THEY MIGHT BUNGLE MATTERS SO WE'D NEVER SEE OUR BABY AGAIN- YOU KNOW HOW MRS. CUNNING LOVED THE BABY AND HOW UTTERLY BROKEN UP SHE IS- WE MUST GIVE HER A LITTLE MORE TIME- SHE WILL GET HER BACK FOR US-
WELL, ALL RIGHT, ELSIE- IF YOU HAVE SUCH FAITH IN THAT WOMAN- I ONLY HOPE YOU'RE RIGHT-
OH, GEORGE- I KNOW I'M RIGHT-
AIN'T IT WONDERFUL HOW DUMB AND TRUSTIN' SOME FOLKS CAN BE? IT'S SURE A BREAK FOR ME AND AL- IF SHE CAN JUST KEEP HER HUSBAND FROM CALLIN' IN TH' COPS! HE'S GETTIN' AWFUL FIDGETY-
HAROLD GRAY
Reg. U. S. Pat. Off.; Copyright, 1931, by The Chicago Tribune.

AW, CAN'T YUH SHUT UP ABOUT THAT? I KNOW I WAS WRONG TO LEAVE TH' KID IN TH' TAXI WHEN I WENT IN TO 'PHONE - BUT WHO'D FIGGER THOSE BIRDS WOULD PICK THAT TIME TO STEAL MY CAB?

AND I GOT MY CAB BACK AND WE'LL GET TH' KID BACK, TOO - LAY OFF O' ME, CAN'TCHA?

HOW MUCH CAN THIS DUMB BIRD, TERRACE, RAISE? THAT'S TH' QUESTION - HAVE YUH GOT ANY IDEA?

WELL, NOT EXACTLY - THEY'RE WELL FIXED - THEY OWN THEIR HOME AND HE'S GOT A GOOD INCOME - AND THEY HAVE RICH FRIENDS - THEY'D BE ABLE TO DIG UP A LOT FOR THAT BRAT -
HAROLD GRAY
Reg. U. S. Pat. Off.; Copyright, 1931, by The Chicago Tribune.

IF IT'S MONEY THEY WANT FOR OUR BABY, WHY DON'T THEY SAY SO? I'D PAY THEM ANY ANY AMOUNT - EVERY CENT WE COULD RAISE - TWENTY THOUSAND DOLLARS - ANYTHING TO GET HER BACK ALIVE AND UN-HARMED -

WHAT LUCK - IF I'D ASKED HIM RIGHT OUT, I COULDN'T HAVE GOT A BETTER ANSWER - TWENTY THOUSAND! WAIT'LL AL HEARS THIS -

AL, I JUST HEARD TERRACE TALKIN' TO HIS MISSUS - HE SAID HE'D PAY TWENTY THOUSAND TO GET TH' KID BACK -
TWENTY GRAND? THAT'S GREAT -

YEAH - AND IF HE SAYS HE CAN RAISE TWENTY GRAND HE CAN RAISE MORE -
SURE - BUT WE GOTTA BE CAREFUL - ASK TOO MUCH AND HE'S LIABLE TO BLOW UP - WE'LL MAKE IT TWENTY-FIVE THOUSAND - BUT WE'VE GOTTA GET TH' KID FIRST -
HAROLD GRAY

YOU HADN'T OUGHT TO LET FOLKS SEE US TO-GETHER ON TH' STREET - NO TELLIN' WHAT THAT TERRACE BIRD WOULD THINK IF HE SAW US TALKIN' -
AW, THAT DUMMY WOULD ONLY FIGGER I WAS ARGUIN' WITH A CAB DRIVER - DON'T HE THINK I'M WORKIN' TO GET TH' KID BACK FOR 'EM?
HAROLD GRAY

AN' THIS IS IMPORTANT - DOC. LENS IS BACK HOME - IF WE GO OVER THERE AGAIN, AND TELL HIM WE'RE TH' KID'S PARENTS, HE'LL MAKE TH' RED-HEAD TURN TH' BRAT OVER TO US -

TRUE ENOUGH, DOCTOR LENS HAS RETURNED AND ANNIE HAS JUST TOLD HIM OF THE ATTEMPT TO TAKE PAT FROM HER AND OF HER STRATEGY IN PREVENTING THIS SCHEME -

HM-M-M - SEARCHED THE HOUSE, DID THEY? I LIKE THEIR NERVE - BUT IF THEY ARE PAT'S PARENTS, ANNIE, THEY ARE ENTITLED TO HER -

I KNOW, DOC - BUT THEY AREN'T FIT TO RAISE PAT - THEY'RE A COUPLE O' CROOKS, I THINK -
STILL, IF THEY ARE HER PARENTS, THERE'S NOTHING YOU CAN DO BUT GIVE PAT UP TO THEM - THAT'S THE LAW -
Reg. U. S. Pat. Off.; Copyright, 1931, by The Chicago Tribune.

October 15–17, 1931

Little Orphan Annie
HERE'S THE PLACE-
YES- NOW, IF WE WORK THIS RIGHT AND GET THAT KID, OUR FORTUNE IS MADE-

LEAPIN' LIZARDS! HERE COMES THAT AWFUL WOMAN WHO HAS BEEN TRYING TO TAKE PAT AWAY FROM ME- NO USE TRYING TO HIDE PAT ANY LONGER- WE'VE GOTTA HAVE A SHOW-DOWN- BUT I WON'T GIVE UP PAT- I WON'T! I WON'T!

THIS IS MR. AND MRS. CUNNING- THEY SAY THEY ARE PAT'S PARENTS AND THAT SHE WAS STOLEN FROM THEM- OF COURSE PAT'S PARENTS HAVE THE FIRST CLAIM TO HER-
YES- WHERE IS MY DARLING BABY?
ALL RIGHT, DOC.

YEAH- I'LL GO AND GET HER- BUT WHAT SWELL PARENTS YOU MUST HAVE BEEN TO LEAVE HER OUT WHERE SHE COULD BE STOLEN - HUH!

WELL- HERE SHE IS-
OH, MY DARLING! COME TO YOUR MAMA- DON'T YOU REMEMBER ME, PRECIOUS?
THAT'S OUR BABY, ALL RIGHT-

WHAT? ISN'T THIS YOUR MAMA?
NO! NO! NO!
WHY, SHE DOESN'T KNOW WHAT SHE'S SAYING- OF COURSE I'M HER MOTHER-
OF COURSE WE'RE HER PARENTS-

JUST A MINUTE- IF YOU ARE HER FOLKS, YOU CAN PROVE IT EASY ENOUGH-
HUMPH- OF COURSE WE CAN PROVE IT-
CERTAINLY WE CAN PROVE IT-

ON WHICH SHOULDER IS THE SCAR WHERE SHE WAS BURNED WHEN SHE WAS TINY? RIGHT OR LEFT?
SCAR? OH, TO BE SURE- ER- IT'S ON THE LEFT-
ER- ER- NO- IT'S ON THE RIGHT SHOULDER-

BLAH!!! THERE ISN'T ANY SCAR ON HER- PARENTS, MY EYE! I THOUGHT YOU WERE A PAIR OF SHARP-SHOOTERS!
?
?

I DON'T KNOW WHAT YOUR GAME IS AND I DON'T WANT ANY EXPLANATIONS- GET OUT OF MY HOUSE AND STAY OUT-
YEAH! SCRAM!

ANNIE'S GIRL-
YOU BET YER LIFE YOU'RE ANNIE'S GIRL- AND NO BUNCH O' CROOKS ARE EVER GOIN' TO GET YOU AWAY FROM ME-

THERE ARE OTHER WAYS TO GET THAT KID- BAH- THE WAY YOU FELL FOR THAT OLD TRICK-
THE WAY I FELL- HOW ABOUT YOU? TO THINK OF IT!!! OUT-WITTED BY THAT LITTLE RED-HEAD!!! BUT WE'LL EVEN THAT SCORE- JUST WAIT!
HAROLD GRAY

October 18, 1931

THERE, WE AS GOOD AS HAD TH' KID IN OUR HANDS - THAT DOC. FELL FOR OUR LINE AND TOLD TH' RED-HEAD TO TURN TH' BRAT OVER TO US - THEN THAT LITTLE SMARTY SAYS - "ON WHICH SHOULDER HAS TH' KID GOT THAT SCAR WHERE SHE WAS BURNED?" AND YOU FELL FOR THAT OLD GAG -

WELL, HOW ABOUT YOU? I SUPPOSE YOU DIDN'T FALL FOR IT, TOO - YOU PIPED RIGHT UP AND SAID, "TH' LEFT" - SO I SAID, "NO, TH' RIGHT" - FIGGERIN' ONE OF US WAS SURE TO BE RIGHT - THEN SHE SAYS THERE WASN'T ANY SCAR AT ALL AND GIVES US A BRONX CHEER -

IF YOU'D KEPT YER YAP SHUT, I'D HAVE SEEN THROUGH HER TRICK - BUT WHEN YOU SAID "TH' LEFT SHOULDER" I FIGGERED THERE WAS A SCAR - YOU WERE TH' KID'S NURSE LONG ENOUGH - YOU SHOULD HAVE KNOWN -
HAROLD GRAY

HUH! DO YOU SUPPOSE I EVER PAID THAT MUCH ATTENTION TO TH' LITTLE BRAT? NOW DOC. LENS IS WISE TO US AND WE DON'T DARE GO BACK THERE - MAYBE I WAS AS BIG A SAP AS YOU ARE - BUT ADMITTIN' THAT DOESN'T GET US TH' KID, DOES IT?
Reg. U. S. Pat. Off.; Copyright, 1931, by The Chicago Tribune.

WELL, I GUESS MAYBE THOSE CROOKS HAVE HAD ENOUGH - ANYWAY, NO-BODY SEEMS TO BE WATCHING THE HOUSE ANY MORE - STILL, NO TELLIN' WHAT CROOKS LIKE THAT WILL TRY NEXT -

ANNIE, I CAN'T GET OVER THE WAY YOU SHOWED UP THOSE CROOKS - THAT WAS A MIGHTY CLEVER TRICK -
AW, THAT WASN'T SO SLICK O' ME - IT WAS JUST DUMB O' THEM TO FALL FOR THAT OLD ONE -

COURSE THAT TRICK DID WORK FINE - BUT CROOKS ARE 'MOST ALWAYS EASY TO FOOL - IF THEY WERE VERY SMART THEY WOULDN'T BE CROOKS -

WELL, PAT, I GUESS YOU WON'T HAVE TO HIDE IN TH' DOG HOUSE WITH SANDY ANY MORE - BUT YOU DIDN'T SEEM TO MIND THAT - DON'T YOU EVER WORRY 'BOUT ANYTHING?
PAT BUILD BIG DOG-HOUSE FOR PAT AND SANDY, AND ANNIE, TOO -
HAROLD GRAY
Reg. U. S. Pat. Off.; Copyright, 1931, by The Chicago Tribune.

OH, PLEASE LET ME HAVE JUST A LITTLE MORE TIME - I WAS SO SURE I WOULD HAVE THE LITTLE DARLING BACK SOON, AND THEN ALL MY PLANS WENT WRONG - BUT TRUST ME - I KNOW WHERE SHE IS AND SHE IS SAFE, FOR THE PRESENT -

YOU DON'T KNOW HOW TERRIBLE I FEEL - HOW I MISS THE LITTLE DARLING - I AM THE ONLY ONE WHO CAN GET HER BACK SAFELY - BUT IT TAKES SO LONG - AND IT WILL COST SO MUCH - MUCH MORE THAN I HAD THOUGHT - OH, BOO! HOO!

OH, MRS. CUNNING - DON'T CRY SO - WE BOTH KNOW HOW YOU FEEL - BUT WE TRUST YOU IMPLICITLY - WE KNOW YOU WILL GET BACK OUR DARLING FOR US - AND AS FOR MONEY, WE WILL PAY ANYTHING -
YES - YES - WE WILL PAY ANYTHING TO GET HER BACK SAFELY -

OH, BOY - DID I PUT THAT SCENE OVER - I ALWAYS SAID I SHOULD HAVE GONE ON THE STAGE - JUST WAIT TILL AL HEARS THIS - THEY'LL PAY ANYTHING - WELL, THEY'LL SURE GET A CHANCE TO SPEND THEIR MONEY -
HAROLD GRAY
Reg. U. S. Pat. Off.; Copyright, 1931, by The Chicago Tribune.

October 19–21, 1931

NOW WHERE CAN THAT LOAFER BE? I TOLD HIM TO MEET ME HERE- HE NEVER DOES ANY BUSINESS WITH THAT CAB- BUT TH' CAB MAY COME IN HANDY- IT'S A GOOD FRONT AND TH' COPS WON'T PICK HIM UP FOR VAGRANCY WHEN HE SEEMS TO BE WORKING- HERE HE COMES NOW-
TAXI STAND

BURNIN' UP GASOLINE RIDIN' AROUND, EH? BUT I HAVEN'T TIME TO WORRY ABOUT THAT NOW- C'MON- I'LL GET IN AND YOU DRIVE, SO NO-BODY'LL NOTICE US TALKIN' HERE-
VACANT

YES, MR. AND MRS. TERRACE BOTH SAID THEY'D PAY ANYTHING FOR TH' KID, TH' DUMMIES- WHY, THEY'D GO FOR ANOTHER FIVE GRAND, EASY AS NOT-
YEAH- A LOT O' GOOD THAT DOES, IF WE CAN'T GET TH' KID-
HAROLD GRAY

DIDN'T I TELL YUH WE DON'T NEED TH' KID AT ALL? AS LONG AS THEY DON'T KNOW WHO HAS HER THEY'LL PAY- THAT'S ALL WE CARE ABOUT, AIN'T IT?
AIN'T I TOLD YOU I WOULDN'T STAND FOR A CROOKED DEAL LIKE THAT? EITHER WE DELIVER TH' KID, OR WE DON'T COLLECT-
Reg. U. S. Pat. Off.; Copyright, 1931, by The Chicago Tribune.

HM-M-M-- IT SAYS HERE TH' COPS THINK TH' JOB WAS DONE BY HIRED HOODLUMS AND THERE IS NO CLUE AS TO WHO WAS BEHIND THE JOB- SAY, THAT GIVES ME AN IDEA-

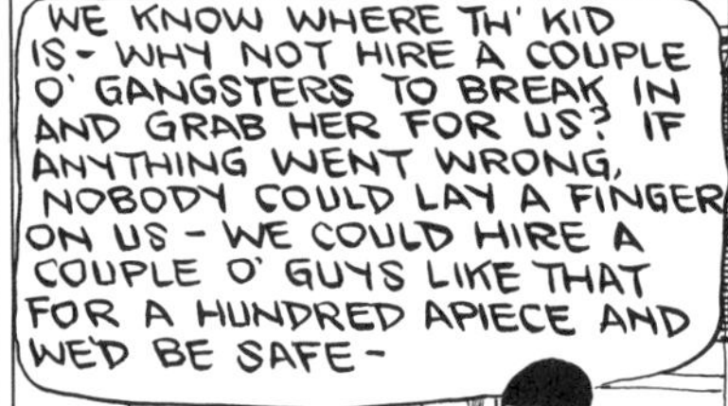
WE KNOW WHERE TH' KID IS- WHY NOT HIRE A COUPLE O' GANGSTERS TO BREAK IN AND GRAB HER FOR US? IF ANYTHING WENT WRONG, NOBODY COULD LAY A FINGER ON US- WE COULD HIRE A COUPLE O' GUYS LIKE THAT FOR A HUNDRED APIECE AND WE'D BE SAFE-

SAFE, MY EYE- NOTHING DOING! YOU MUST BE CRAZY- ONCE YOU LET A COUPLE O' BIRDS LIKE THAT MUSCLE IN ON US WE'D BE DONE FOR- THEY'D HAVE TH' KID- NOT US- AND THEY'D COLLECT, TOO, AND KEEP EVERY CENT-
Reg. U. S. Pat. Off.; Copyright, 1931, by The Chicago Tribune.

WHAT DO YOU THINK WE'D GET OUT OF IT? WE'D EITHER FADE AND KEEP QUIET, TOO, OR WE'D GET SOMETHIN' TO KEEP US QUIET- NOT ON YER LIFE- ONCE YUH MIX UP WITH GANGSTERS, YOU'RE DONE FOR-
HAROLD GRAY

SEE- THAT'S TH' KID'S BED-ROOM WINDOW- IT'D BE A CINCH TO SLIP IN AND GRAB HER- NOTHIN' TO IT-
YEAH! AND JUMP OUT RIGHT INTO THAT COP'S ARMS-

AW, YOU MAKE ME SICK- AIN'T I BEEN WATCHIN' THAT WINDOW EVERY NIGHT THIS WEEK? YOU CAN SET YER WATCH BY THAT COP- EVERY NIGHT HE GOES BY ON HIS BEAT AT THE SAME TIME- IT'S TWO HOURS BEFORE HE SHOWS AGAIN- I BOOST YOU IN AND STAND OUTSIDE- IF ANYBODY'S COMIN' I TIP YOU OFF AND WE BEAT IT IN PLENTY O' TIME-

IT WOULDN'T TAKE BUT A MINUTE- IN YUH GO- GRAB TH' KID- HAND HER OUT TO ME- WE HAVE TH' CAB IN TH' SIDE STREET- WE JUMP IN AND SCRAM- I TELL YUH THERE ISN'T A CHANCE TO MISS- WHERE'S YER NERVE?
Reg. U. S. Pat. Off.; Copyright, 1931, by The Chicago Tribune.

O.K.- I'LL DO IT- BUT GIMME TIME- I'VE GOTTA THINK THIS OVER A LITTLE, AIN'T I? COPS GIVE ME CHILLS AND YOU KNOW IT- I'VE GOTTA BE SURE YOU KNOW WHAT YOU'RE TALKIN' ABOUT, TOO- BUT I'LL DO IT- JUST DON'T SHOVE ME- SEE?
HAROLD GRAY

October 22–24, 1931

Little Orphan Annie
I S'POSE THERE'S NOTHING TO BE WORRIED 'BOUT-STILL, I FEEL ALL TWITTERY TO-NIGHT-

THOSE FOLKS WHO TRIED TO GET PAT AWAY FROM ME ARE STILL HANGIN' AROUND - I SAW 'EM WATCHIN' TH' HOUSE LAST NIGHT- NO TELLIN' WHAT THEY'LL TRY NEXT-

NOW YOU'RE NOT S'POSED TO STAY IN TH' HOUSE, SANDY - BUT IF YOU'RE REAL QUIET I'LL LET YOU SLEEP IN OUR ROOM TO-NIGHT- DOC. WOULDN'T MIND IF HE KNEW HOW REAL SCARED I AM-

SOUND ASLEEP ALL READY- OH, WELL- HE'LL HEAR TH' SLIGHTEST SOUND- I CAN GO TO SLEEP NOW WITHOUT WORRYIN'-

THE LIGHT'S BEEN OUT FOR AN HOUR AND THE WINDOW'S WIDE OPEN - I'LL WATCH UNDER THE WINDOW WHILE YOU GRAB THE KID AND HAND HER OUT- THEN WE'LL HOP INTO THE CAR AND SCRAM- IT'S A CINCH AND OUR FORTUNE WILL BE MADE-

HUMPH! IT'S DARK AS A POCKET IN HERE, BUT I DON'T DARE USE A LIGHT-

I CAN'T SEE A THING, BUT THIS IS THE RIGHT ROOM AND HERE'S A BED- NOW TO GRAB THAT KID AND GET OUT OF HERE QUIET-

OW!
R-R-R

NIX- NIX! NICE DOGGIE!

SO YUH WANT TO GET OUT, NOW, EH? WELL, THEN, GNAW YERSELF A HOLE IN THAT FLOOR-GWAN! ROOT RIGHT INTO IT- HOW D'YUH LIKE IT, EH?
LE'MME OUTA HERE-
R-R-R
R-R-R-

OOF!

BAD MAN WAKE PAT UP-
WHAT ARE YOU TALKIN' ABOUT? YOU MUST HAVE BEEN HAVIN' A BAD DREAM, PAT- THAT'S ALL- NOW YOU GO RIGHT BACK TO SLEEP AND FORGET ALL ABOUT HORRID DREAMS-
HAROLD GRAY

October 25, 1931
DISTANT RELATIONS

WELL, YOU DON'T GET A BIT OF SYMPATHY FROM ME- HUH- ANYBODY BUT YOU AND WE'D HAVE THE BRAT BY NOW- THERE YOU WERE, RIGHT IN THE ROOM- AND YOU LET THAT LITTLE RED-HEAD AND HER CUR-DOG RUIN YOU- WHAT A BUM! I SHOULD HAVE GONE IN MYSELF-
I WISH YOU HAD-
ALL YOU HAD TO DO WAS GRAB TH' KID AND PASS HER OUT TO ME- BUT YOU COULDN'T EVEN DO THAT-
OW-W! MY BACK!
HUMPH! YOU AND YOUR SPRUNG BACK, AND YER BENT NOSE AND CRACKED HEAD AND YOUR CHEWED HAND-
I'M TELLIN' YUH THAT DOG IS A WOLF- AND THAT RED-HEAD IS NOTHIN' SHORT OF A WILD-CAT- SHE BIT MY THUMB HALF OFF- ALL RIGHT- BE STIFF-NECKED ABOUT IT-
STIFF-NECKED! HOW ELSE COULD I BE? THERE I STOOD UNDER THAT WINDOW WITH ALL THAT DIN GOIN' ON INSIDE WAITIN' FOR YOU TO TOSS ME TH' KID, WHEN OUT YOU COME, LIKE A BIG MULE, AND LIGHT RIGHT ON MY HEAD- IT'S A WONDER MY NECK AIN'T BROKE!
HAROLD GRAY
Reg. U. S. Pat. Off.; Copyright, 1931, by The Chicago Tribune.
OW! MY NECK! I DON'T THINK IT'LL EVER BE RIGHT AGAIN- WHY DIDN'T YUH TELL ME YOU WERE GOIN' TO JUMP OUT THAT WINDOW-
YEAH! I SUPPOSE I HAD TIME TO WRITE YOU A LETTER, WITH THAT RED-HEADED LITTLE MANIAC AND HER DOG TRYIN' TO TEAR MY HEAD OFF-
I'VE GOT TO GO DOWN TO THE DRUG-STORE AND PHONE MRS. TERRACE WHY I HAVEN'T SHOWED UP FOR TWO DAYS- I'LL SAY I'VE BEEN SICK AND THAT WON'T BE ANY LIE-
YEAH- AND GET SOME MORE LINIMENT AND IODINE AND BANDAGES AND TAPE-
WHAT TH'--- WHY, THERE GOES THAT MRS. CUNNING INTO THAT DRUG-STORE- LUCKY I SPOTTED HER FIRST- MAYBE SHE LIVES NEAR HERE-
DRUGS
HM-M-M- SHE'S GONE INTO TH' 'PHONE BOOTH- I'D GIVE A NICKEL TO HEAR WHAT SHE'S SAYING- I'LL DUCK DOWN THE STREET AND KEEP AN EYE ON THIS DOOR-
DRUGS
HAROLD GRAY
Reg. U. S. Pat. Off.; Copyright, 1931, by The Chicago Tribune.
THERE SHE GOES- MRS. CUNNING- WONDER IF THAT'S WHERE SHE LIVES- WOW, WHAT A JOB I'VE HAD FOLLOWIN' HER- IN SPITE OF HER SIZE, SHE'S SLICK AS AN EEL-
GEE, THAT'S HER WINDOW, I BETCHA- YESSIR, AND THERE'S MR. CUNNING SITTIN' IN THAT ROOM- I'VE GOTTA BE CAREFUL HE DOESN'T LOOK OUT AND SPOT ME-
YEP- AND THERE MRS. CUNNING COMES IN- AND THAT'S HIS CAB SITTIN' OUT IN FRONT- THAT'S THEIR HANGOUT, ALL RIGHT- WHAT A BREAK TO HAVE FOUND WHERE THEY LIVE-
BUT I'D BETTER SCRAM OUT OF THIS NEIGHBORHOOD- IF THEY S'PECTED I KNEW WHERE THEY LIVE THEY'D MOVE AND I'D NEVER FIND 'EM AGAIN- BUT NOW IF PAT SHOULD GET GRABBED I'D KNOW WHERE TO PUT TH' FINGER ON THEM-
HAROLD GRAY
Reg. U. S. Pat. Off.; Copyright, 1931, by The Chicago Tribune.

October 26–28, 1931

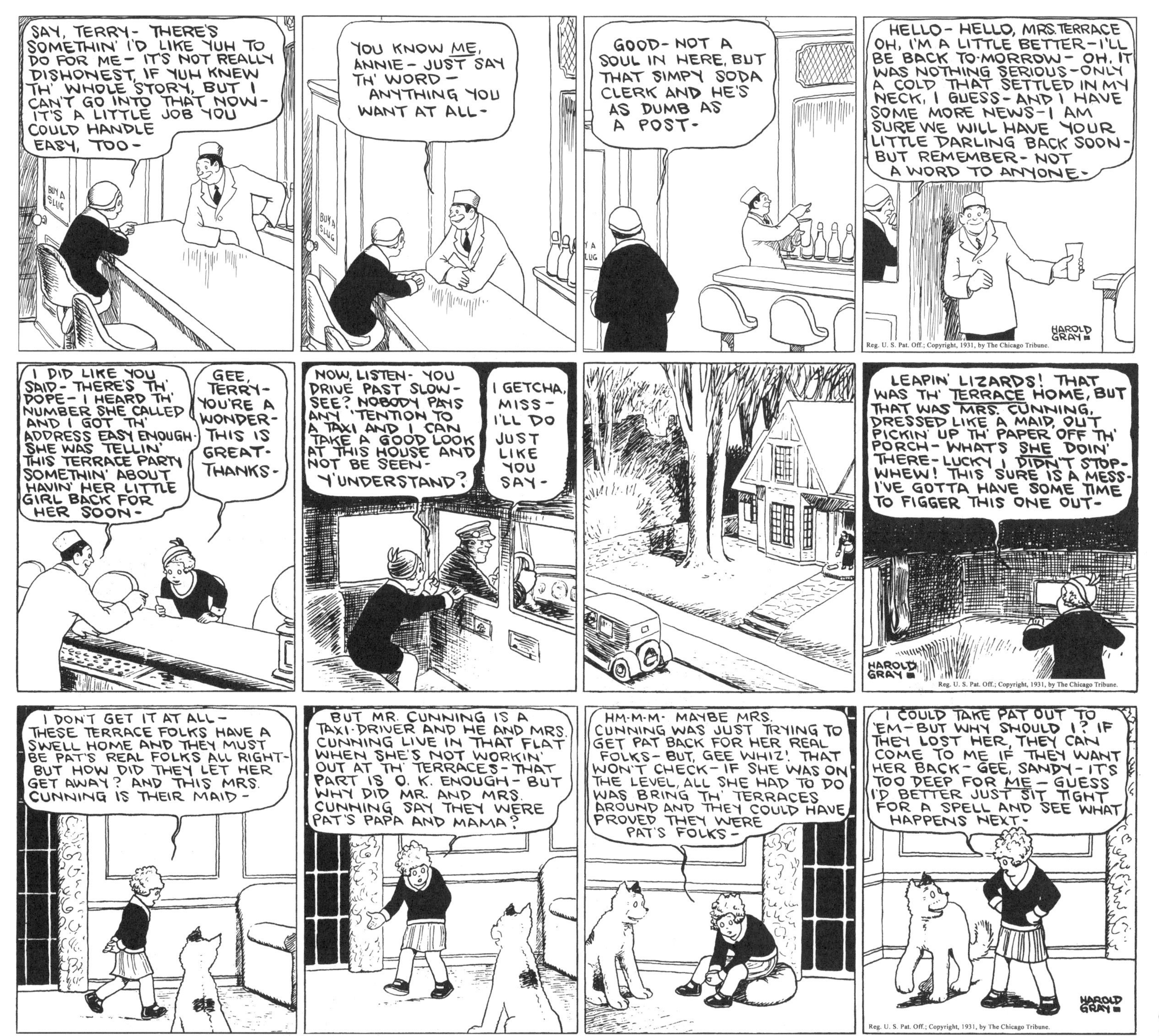
SAY, TERRY- THERE'S SOMETHIN' I'D LIKE YUH TO DO FOR ME- IT'S NOT REALLY DISHONEST, IF YUH KNEW TH' WHOLE STORY, BUT I CAN'T GO INTO THAT NOW- IT'S A LITTLE JOB YOU COULD HANDLE EASY, TOO-
BUY A SLUG
YOU KNOW ME, ANNIE- JUST SAY TH' WORD- ANYTHING YOU WANT AT ALL-
GOOD- NOT A SOUL IN HERE, BUT THAT SIMPY SODA CLERK AND HE'S AS DUMB AS A POST-
HELLO- HELLO, MRS. TERRACE OH, I'M A LITTLE BETTER- I'LL BE BACK TO-MORROW- OH, IT WAS NOTHING SERIOUS- ONLY A COLD THAT SETTLED IN MY NECK, I GUESS- AND I HAVE SOME MORE NEWS- I AM SURE WE WILL HAVE YOUR LITTLE DARLING BACK SOON- BUT REMEMBER- NOT A WORD TO ANYONE-
HAROLD GRAY
Reg. U. S. Pat. Off.; Copyright, 1931, by The Chicago Tribune.
I DID LIKE YOU SAID- THERE'S TH' DOPE- I HEARD TH' NUMBER SHE CALLED AND I GOT TH' ADDRESS EASY ENOUGH- SHE WAS TELLIN' THIS TERRACE PARTY SOMETHIN' ABOUT HAVIN' HER LITTLE GIRL BACK FOR HER SOON-
GEE, TERRY- YOU'RE A WONDER- THIS IS GREAT- THANKS-
NOW, LISTEN- YOU DRIVE PAST SLOW- SEE? NOBODY PAYS ANY 'TENTION TO A TAXI AND I CAN TAKE A GOOD LOOK AT THIS HOUSE AND NOT BE SEEN- Y'UNDERSTAND?
I GETCHA, MISS- I'LL DO JUST LIKE YOU SAY-
LEAPIN' LIZARDS! THAT WAS TH' TERRACE HOME, BUT THAT WAS MRS. CUNNING, DRESSED LIKE A MAID, OUT PICKIN' UP TH' PAPER OFF TH' PORCH- WHAT'S SHE DOIN' THERE- LUCKY I DIDN'T STOP- WHEW! THIS SURE IS A MESS- I'VE GOTTA HAVE SOME TIME TO FIGGER THIS ONE OUT-
HAROLD GRAY
Reg. U. S. Pat. Off.; Copyright, 1931, by The Chicago Tribune.
I DON'T GET IT AT ALL- THESE TERRACE FOLKS HAVE A SWELL HOME AND THEY MUST BE PAT'S REAL FOLKS ALL RIGHT- BUT HOW DID THEY LET HER GET AWAY? AND THIS MRS. CUNNING IS THEIR MAID-
BUT MR. CUNNING IS A TAXI-DRIVER AND HE AND MRS. CUNNING LIVE IN THAT FLAT WHEN SHE'S NOT WORKIN' OUT AT TH' TERRACES- THAT PART IS O. K. ENOUGH- BUT WHY DID MR. AND MRS. CUNNING SAY THEY WERE PAT'S PAPA AND MAMA?
HM-M-M- MAYBE MRS. CUNNING WAS JUST TRYING TO GET PAT BACK FOR HER REAL FOLKS- BUT, GEE WHIZ! THAT WON'T CHECK- IF SHE WAS ON THE LEVEL, ALL SHE HAD TO DO WAS BRING TH' TERRACES AROUND AND THEY COULD HAVE PROVED THEY WERE PAT'S FOLKS-
I COULD TAKE PAT OUT TO 'EM- BUT WHY SHOULD I? IF THEY LOST HER, THEY CAN COME TO ME IF THEY WANT HER BACK- GEE, SANDY- IT'S TOO DEEP FOR ME- GUESS I'D BETTER JUST SIT TIGHT FOR A SPELL AND SEE WHAT HAPPENS NEXT-
HAROLD GRAY
Reg. U. S. Pat. Off.; Copyright, 1931, by The Chicago Tribune.

October 29–31, 1931

Little Orphan Annie
I'LL PUT ALL THIS STUFF BACK IN TH' KITCHEN 'FORE TH' COOK GETS UP IN TH' MORNING-

LE'SSEE, NOW- FLAT IRON, ROLLIN' PIN, 'TATO MASHER, AND ALARM CLOCK- THAT OUGHTA BE ENOUGH- AND A TIN BUCKET AND A PIECE O' STRING-

COURSE THOSE CROOKS MAY HAVE HAD ENOUGH, AFTER WHAT SANDY AND I DID TO 'EM LAST SUNDAY- BUT YOU NEVER CAN TELL WHAT BIRDS LIKE THAT WILL TRY NEXT-

I'LL SLEEP LOTS BETTER IF I KNOW I'M SAFE- THIS BURGLAR 'LARM MAY NOT STOP ANYBODY, BUT IT'LL SURE S'PRISE 'EM A HEAP-

I'LL OPEN THIS WINDOW JUST SIX INCHES AND LOCK IT THERE- IT'LL LET IN PLENTY O' AIR, BUT THAT'S ALL IT'LL LET IN-

THERE- NOW FOR A GOOD NIGHT'S SLEEP-

OH, BOY! AND AM I TIRED TO-NIGHT- THAT BURGLAR 'LARM WAS A SWELL IDEA, IF I DO SAY SO- I WONDER IF THERE'S ANY CHANCE IT WOULDN'T WORK, IF THAT DOOR WAS OPENED-

LEAPIN' LIZARDS! I WONDER IF I FORGOT TO TURN OUT THAT LIGHT IN TH' KITCHEN, WHEN I WAS DOWN THERE GETTIN' THAT STUFF-

I BET I LEFT THAT LIGHT ON- IF I DID, TH' COOK, OR SOME-BODY, IS LI'BLE TO SEE IT AND START ASKIN' A LOT O' QUESTIONS-

I'D BETTER BE SURE- IT WON'T TAKE BUT A MINUTE TO TIP-TOE DOWN AND SEE, BUT I MUSTN'T MAKE A BIT OF NOISE-

WHAM!

WHEW! IT SURE WORKED, ALL RIGHT-
HAROLD GRAY

IT'S NICE OUT IN THE BACK YARD AND SAFE, TOO- YOU RUN ALONG, PAT, AND PLAY WITH SANDY- I'LL BE OUT IN JUST A FEW MINUTES-
WELL, HERE'S WHAT I KNOW- MR. CUNNING IS A TAXI DRIVER AND MRS. CUNNING IS TH' MAID AT TH' TERRACE'S- MRS. CUNNING STAYS AT HER OWN FLAT A LOT OF TH' TIME NOW- AND MRS. TERRACE IS MOST LIKELY PAT'S REAL MAMA-
BUT I'VE GOTTA BE SURE 'BOUT THAT- LE'SSEE- HERE'S TH' TERRACE NUMBER- YEP- THIS IS RIGHT, 'CAUSE TH' ADDRESS IS TH' ONE I WAS OUT TO SATURDAY, WHEN I SAW MRS. CUNNING ON TH' PORCH- I COULD CALL UP MRS. TERRACE AND ASK HER IF SHE LOST A LITTLE GIRL-
I S'POSE THAT'S TH' THING TO DO- BUT, GEE- I HATE TO DO IT- IT'LL MOST LIKELY MEAN LOSIN' PAT- AND I THINK I COULD RAISE HER BETTER'N ANY DAME DUMB ENOUGH TO KEEP A CROOK LIKE MRS. CUNNING FOR A MAID- I'LL WAIT AND CALL HER TOMORROW-
HAROLD GRAY
Reg. U. S. Pat. Off.; Copyright, 1931, by The Chicago Tribune.
HELLO- IS THIS MRS. TERRACE? DID YOU LOSE YOUR LITTLE GIRL 'LONG 'BOUT TH' MIDDLE O' LAST JULY?
YES- YES- MY LITTLE GIRL WAS STOLEN ON JULY 16TH- I'LL NEVER FORGET THAT AWFUL DAY- YES-YES- THAT IS HER DESCRIPTION- YOU SAY YOU HAVE HER? OH, WHAT SHALL I DO, MRS. CUNNING? I'M SO UPSET- WHAT SHALL I SAY?
I'LL HANDLE THAT, MRS. TERRACE- QUICK! GIVE ME THE PHONE-
HELLO! WHO IS THIS? HELLO! HELLO! HUMPH- THEY'VE HUNG UP-
CLICK!
HUH- SO THAT'S HOW IT IS, EH? WELL, MRS. TERRACE IS PAT'S MAMA, ALL RIGHT, ELSE SHE WOULDN'T KNOW IT WAS JULY 16TH I FOUND PAT- BUT THERE'S TOO MUCH MRS. CUNNING IN IT TO SUIT ME- I'D KNOW THAT DAME'S VOICE IN A BOILER FACTORY- IF SHE THINKS I'M GOIN' TO BREAK DOWN AN' TELL ALL TO HER SHE'S CRAZIER'N I THINK SHE IS-
HAROLD GRAY
Reg. U. S. Pat. Off.; Copyright, 1931, by The Chicago Tribune.
THERE'S A LOT TO THIS MIXUP THAT I CAN'T FIGGER OUT- F'RINSTANCE, WHERE DOES MR. CUNNING, TH' TAXI DRIVER, FIT IN TH' PICTURE? SOMETHIN' TELLS ME IF I KEEP A SHARP EYE ON TH' CUNNINGS FOR A SPELL I MAY FIND OUT A LOT- AH- THERE THEY BOTH GO AWAY IN TH' TAXI-
THIS IS MY CHANCE- THERE- THAT MUST BE TH' DOOR TO THEIR FLAT- MOST LIKELY IT'S LOCKED- AND THERE'S NO PLACE TO HIDE HERE IN THIS HALL- I'D BETTER BE GETTIN' OUT O' HERE 'FORE SOMEBODY SEES ME-
YEP- THEIR DOOR IS LOCKED- BUT WHAT'S THIS DOOR? JUST A CLOSET FULL O' MOPS AN' BROOMS AN' BUCKETS AN' OLD RUBBISH- WAIT A SECOND- WHAT'S THAT CRACK ON TH' OTHER SIDE O' TH' CLOSET?
HAROLD GRAY
GEE- IT'S ANOTHER DOOR RIGHT INTO THEIR FLAT- BUT IT'S NOT USED- THERE'S A BUREAU OR SOMETHIN' AGAINST IT- BUT I CAN SEE THROUGH THIS CRACK AND HEAR SWELL- WHAT A LUCKY BREAK THIS IS-
Reg. U. S. Pat. Off.; Copyright, 1931, by The Chicago Tribune.

November 2–4, 1931

WELL, I COPPED TH' KID AND YOU LOST HER - THEN I FOUND HER AGAIN, BUT YOU'VE MUFFED EVERY CHANCE WE'VE HAD TO GRAB HER - I COULD HANDLE TH' WHOLE THING BETTER ALONE -
AW, WHY KEEP HARPIN' ON TH' PAST? YOU'RE SORE BECAUSE I WON'T LET YUH COLLECT FROM TH' TERRACES 'LESS WE DELIVER TH' KID - I'M NO DOUBLE-CROSSER

BLAH! WHY BE A SAP? THEY'LL PAY 25 GRAND - IF WE HAD TH' BRAT, AND SOMETHIN' SLIPPED, WE'D BE IN A JAM - BUT LET THAT RED-HEAD KEEP HER AND NO-BODY CAN PROVE ANY KIDNAPIN' ON US - IT'S SAFE AS A CHURCH - AND WE CAN WRITE 'EM LATER WHERE TH' KID IS - THEY'LL GET HER BACK ALL RIGHT -

THEY PAY US FOR TH' KID AND THEY'LL GET TH' KID - ONLY WE WON'T BE HOLDIN' TH' BAG IF ANYTHING SLIPS - BUT THAT RED-HEAD WILL HAVE A LOT TO EXPLAIN -
YEAH? WELL, THAT MIGHT BE O. K. AS LONG AS TERRACES GET THEIR KID BACK - BUT I WON'T STAND FOR ANY CHEATIN' -
THE CRACK IN THE WALL

LEAPIN' LIZARDS! TALK ABOUT GETTIN' AN EAR-FULL - WOW! IF THEY EVER GUESSED I KNEW ALL I DO MY LIFE WOULDN'T BE WORTH A NICKEL IF THEY COULD CATCH ME - I DON'T FEEL SAFE CARRYIN' AROUND ALL I KNOW - I'VE GOTTA UNLOAD TO SOMEBODY -
HAROLD GRAY

THERE, NOW, CAPTAIN - THAT'S THE WHOLE STORY IN A COUPLE OF NUT-SHELLS - I FIGGERED YOU OUGHT TO KNOW 'BOUT IT -
HM-M... BUT WHY DIDN'T THE TERRACES CALL IN THE POLICE MONTHS AGO? DON'T THEY WANT THEIR CHILD BACK?

SURE THEY WANT HER BACK - BUT THEY'RE AWFUL DUMB, I GUESS - LEASTWISE THIS MRS. CUNNING KEEPS TELLIN' 'EM IF THEY TELL TH' COPS, THEY MAY NEVER SEE TH' KID AGAIN AND THEY BELIEVE EVERYTHING SHE SAYS - THEY NEVER EVEN S'PECTED HER OF STEALIN' PAT IN TH' FIRST PLACE - AND SHE'S SOLD 'EM TH' IDEA THAT TH' POLICE AREN'T TO BE TRUSTED - THEY'RE LEAVIN' IT ALL TO HER -

LET US HAVE A LITTLE TIME ON THIS, ANNIE - I WANT TO CHECK UP ON A FEW POINTS - DROP IN TO-MORROW AND WE'LL BE ABLE TO STRAIGHTEN IT ALL OUT, I'M SURE -
THANKS, CAPTAIN - I KNEW YOU'D KNOW HOW TO HANDLE IT -

GEE - I SHOULD HAVE GONE TO TH' POLICE IN TH' FIRST PLACE - BUT I FIGGERED I COULD TAKE CARE O' MYSELF, AND I WANTED TO KEEP PAT -
HAROLD GRAY

AH, ANNIE - COME RIGHT IN - I HAVE QUITE A LOT TO REPORT -

MY DETECTIVES HAVE GONE INTO THE CASE THOROUGHLY - BUT I MUST SAY THEY HAVE FOUND OUT NOTHING YOU DIDN'T TELL ME - YOU SHOULD BE ON THE FORCE, ANNIE - NOW, AS THINGS STAND, WE HAVE NO CASE AGAINST THE CUNNINGS - WE KNOW THEY ARE CRIMINALS, BUT WE CAN'T PROVE A THING -

HOWEVER, WE'LL GIVE THEM A BIT MORE ROPE AND, WITH YOUR HELP, I BELIEVE THEY WILL TRAP THEMSELVES - YOU WILL BE THE DETECTIVE, ANNIE, AND KEEP ME POSTED ON EVERY MOVE THE CUNNINGS MAKE - I'M DEPENDING ON YOU, ANNIE -

O. K. CAPTAIN -

THEY'RE UP THERE - THERE'S A LIGHT IN THEIR WINDOW - I'LL SLIP OVER AND TRY TO GET INTO THAT CLOSET WITHOUT GETTIN' CAUGHT - IT'S RISKY BUSINESS, BUT KNOWIN' THAT TH' POLICE DEPARTMENT IS BACKIN' YUH UP SURE MAKES YUH LOTS BRAVER -

HAROLD GRAY

November 5–7, 1931

Little Orphan Annie
GEE, IT'S GOING TO BE TOUGH TO GIVE UP PAT-

AND AFTER ALL THE WONDERFUL PLANS I HAD FOR HER, TOO- BUT, NOW THAT I KNOW WHO HER REAL FOLKS ARE, THERE'S NOTHING ELSE I CAN DO -

I STILL THINK I COULD RAISE HER A LOT BETTER'N THEY WILL- BUT I S'POSE LOTS O' PEOPLE FEEL TH' SAME WAY 'BOUT OTHER FOLKS' KIDS -

STILL, I'D NEVER LEAVE TH' RAISIN' OF A KID O' MINE TO ANY SERVANT- TH' WAY I LOOK AT IT, IF A KID'S WORTH HAVIN' IT'S WORTH RAISIN' PERSONALLY-

COURSE, MR. AND MRS. TERRACE ARE TOO TRUSTIN' TO RELIZE WHAT A CROOK MRS. CUNNING, THEIR MAID, IS - BUT DUMBNESS IS NO EXCUSE

MAYBE THEY'LL DO BETTER RAISIN' HER, AFTER LOSIN' HER FOR A SPELL- I HOPE SO, FOR PAT'S SAKE-

BUT THAT CROOKED MRS. CUNNING AND HER NO-GOOD HUSBAND, AL, AREN'T OUT OF THE WAY YET AND, TILL THEY'RE IN JAIL, THEY'RE LIABLE TO TRY ANYTHING- THEY'RE MOST LIKELY WATCHING THIS HOUSE RIGHT NOW-

OH, WELL, I'M NOT SCARED O' THOSE CROOKS OR OF ANYTHING- LUCKY FOR ME I'M NOT NAT-CHERLY NERVOUS - - - -

OOP!
WHANG!
SWISH!

YEOW!

WHEW! BET MY HEART'S BEATIN' ABOUT FOUR HUNDRED A MINUTE- THAT DOG-GONED OLD SHADE! MIGHT HAVE KNOWN WHAT IT WAS, IF I'D STOPPED TO THINK-

BIG NOISE ?
OH, THAT- HA- HA! NOTHING AT ALL, PAT- JUST THIS WINDOW-SHADE SNAPPED UP- NOTHING TO GET EXCITED ABOUT-
HAROLD GRAY

November 8, 1931

AW, QUIT WORRYIN', AL- IT'S IN TH' BAG, I TELL YUH- YOU WRITE THAT LETTER TO TH' TERRACES DEMANDIN' $25,000.00- I'LL BE THERE WHEN THEY GET IT AND OFFER TO HANDLE IT FOR 'EM- THEN THEY'LL GIVE ME TH' DOUGH- THEY'RE TOO DUMB TO GET WISE- LEAVE IT TO ME-
AFTER WE GET TH' COIN, WE'LL SCRAM- BUT JUST BEFORE WE LEAVE TOWN WE'LL CALL 'EM AND TELL 'EM WHERE THEIR BRAT IS- AND LET THAT SMART LITTLE RED-HEAD TRY TO EXPLAIN IT TO TH' COPS- WE GET TH' DOUGH- TERRACES GET THEIR KID- TH' RED-HEAD HOLDS TH' BAG- THAT'LL BE PERFECT-
PERFECT, MY NECK! WHEW! LUCKY I HEARD THAT- I'M SURE GLAD I WENT TO TH' POLICE WHEN I DID-
THERE'S AL MAILIN' THE LETTER TO THE TERRACES- NOW I'LL DROP IN AND SEE TH' CAPTAIN AND TELL HIM ALL I HEARD- MAYBE HE'LL FIGGER SOME WAY OUT O' THIS-
HAROLD GRAY
Reg. U. S. Pat. Off.; Copyright, 1931, by The Chicago Tribune.
DO YOU MEAN TO SIT THERE AN' TELL ME THERE'S NO WAY TO PROVE A THING ON THOSE TWO CROOKS?
THAT'S RIGHT, ANNIE- AS IT STANDS, WITH A SMART LAWYER THEY'D GO SCOT FREE-
BUT, WITH YOUR HELP, ANNIE, I BELIEVE I HAVE A PLAN THAT WILL WORK- IT MAY NOT BE EXACTLY ACCORDING TO HOYLE, BUT IT WILL BE ACCORDING TO JUSTICE- NOW WE BOTH KNOW THEY ARE CRIMINALS--- BUT COME INTO THE BACK ROOM WHERE WE WON'T BE OVER-HEARD-
NOW, ANNIE, THAT'S THE PLAN- DO YOU THINK YOU CAN CARRY OUT YOUR PART OF IT?
LEAVE IT TO ME, CAPTAIN- YOU JUST DO YOUR JOB AT TH' RIGHT TIME- THAT'S ALL- I'LL HANDLE MY END-
LEAPIN' LIZARDS! WHAT A MAN! THAT GUY'S SURE GOT A HEAD ON HIM- WOW! I'VE GOT PLENTY TO KEEP ME BUSY- WHAT A LOT OF REHEARSIN' PAT'S GOT TO DO-
HAROLD GRAY
Reg. U. S. Pat. Off.; Copyright, 1931, by The Chicago Tribune.
IT'S FROM THAT HORRID MAN- HE SAYS IF WE WANT TO SEE OUR CHILD AGAIN WE MUST PAY HIM $25,000.00 ON FRIDAY, OR ELSE--- - OH, WHAT DOES HE MEAN BY, "OR ELSE"?
OH, MRS. CUNNING- YOU MUST HELP US- YOU ARE THE ONLY ONE WE CAN TRUST-
HM-M-M--- $25,000.00, EH? AND IT MUST BE PLACED AT A CERTAIN SPOT- HM-M- AND NO ONE SHALL TRY TO WATCH FOR HIM- I'D BETTER HANDLE THIS FOR YOU-
OH, MRS. CUNNING- WE COULDN'T ASK YOU TO DO THAT- THE DANGER! NO- NO- ANYTHING MIGHT HAPPEN TO YOU-
WELL, O' COURSE, IT'S RISKY- BUT FOR THE LITTLE DARLING'S SAKE! AND I CAN DO IT BETTER'N YOU FOLKS- NOBODY'D HARM ME-
MRS. CUNNING- YOU'RE A BRICK- I'LL GO RIGHT DOWN TOWN AND GET THE CASH AND YOU SHALL TAKE IT TO THE PLACE FRIDAY- I DON'T KNOW HOW WE CAN EVER REWARD YOU FOR THE WAY YOU'VE STUCK BY US IN THIS TERRIBLE TROUBLE-
Reg. U. S. Pat. Off.; Copyright, 1931, by The Chicago Tribune.
HAROLD GRAY

November 9–11, 1931

BOO! HOO! HOO!
I H-H-HATE TO BE A BLAMED C-C-CRY BABY- BUT I CAN'T HELP IT - I'D C-C-COUNTED SO MUCH ON HAVING PAT TO RAISE-
BOO! HOO! HOO!

SNIFF-SNIFF! AW, BAWLIN' WON'T DO ANY GOOD- AND HER REAL FOLKS ARE NICE, EVEN IF THEY ARE AWFUL DUMB- AND THEY'LL GIVE HER A REAL HOME- I'VE GOT NO RIGHT TO KEEP HER FROM HER REAL PARENTS, NOW THAT I KNOW SHE HAS PARENTS-

BUT THOSE CROOKS, TH' CUNNINGS, HAVE GOTTA BE PUNISHED- AND, BY LUCIFER, THEY'RE GOIN' TO GET THEIRS, TOO, OR I MISS MY GUESS- BUT I'VE GOT A JOB TO DO FIRST-

NOW, PAT- WHEN YOU PLAY HIDE AN' SEEK, YOU'VE GOTTA LEARN TO KEEP AB-SO-LUTELY STILL FOR EVER SO LONG-SEE? NOT A SOUND- AND Y'GOTTA LEARN TO STAY IN TH' DARK ALONE, TOO- NOW LET'S SEE WHICH OF US CAN KEEP REAL STILL TH' LONGEST, JUST FOR PRACTICE-
O. K.
HAROLD GRAY
Reg. U. S. Pat. Off.; Copyright, 1931, by The Chicago Tribune.

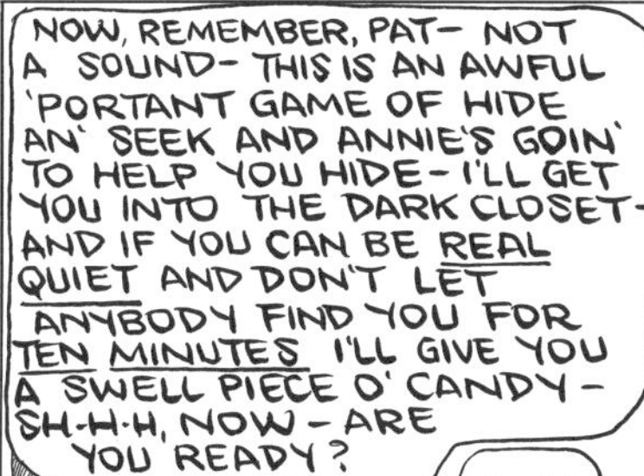

NOW, REMEMBER, PAT- NOT A SOUND- THIS IS AN AWFUL 'PORTANT GAME OF HIDE AN' SEEK AND ANNIE'S GOIN' TO HELP YOU HIDE- I'LL GET YOU INTO THE DARK CLOSET- AND IF YOU CAN BE REAL QUIET AND DON'T LET ANYBODY FIND YOU FOR TEN MINUTES I'LL GIVE YOU A SWELL PIECE O' CANDY- SH-H-H, NOW- ARE YOU READY?
O. K.

TAKE IT EASY- I ARREST YOU FOR KIDNAPING AND EXTORTION- BOYS, SNAP TH' CUFFS ON THEM-

KIDNAPIN', MY EYE! YOU MUST BE CRAZY- YOU CAN'T HANG ANY KIDNAPIN' ON US- YOU CAN'T PROVE A THING-
SO? BOYS, PULL OUT THAT DRESSER FROM IN FRONT OF THAT DOOR AND TAKE A LOOK IN THAT CLOSET-
Reg. U. S. Pat. Off.; Copyright, 1931, by The Chicago Tribune.
HAROLD GRAY

THERE'S THE CHILD, HID IN THE CLOSET, AS I SUSPECTED, AND WITH THE RANSOM MONEY ON THE TABLE, IT'S A CLEAR CASE-
I TELL YUH WE'VE BEEN FRAMED!
PAT GOT FOUND-
HUH!

MY BABY- MY PRECIOUS! SO IT WAS MRS CUNNING, WHOM WE TRUSTED SO, WHO STOLE HER FROM US- OH, WHAT FOOLS WE'VE BEEN- BUT WE'LL NEVER LET OUR BABY OUT OF OUR SIGHT AGAIN- OH, MY DARLING-
MAMA-

WELL, THAT'S OVER- I HEARD THEM OFFER TO REWARD YOU- WHAT DID YOU TELL THEM, ANNIE?
AW, I WAS POLITE AND JUST SAID, "NO THANKS"- HUH- I WONDER IF THEY THOUGHT ANYBODY COULD BUY PAT FROM ME-

WELL, SOME PEOPLE ARE THAT WAY- THEY WANTED TO DO SOMETHING FOR ME, TOO- I TOLD THEM, ALL I ASKED WAS THAT, IN FUTURE, THEY HAVE A LITTLE MORE FAITH IN THE ABILITY AND HONESTY OF THE POLICE- POLICE CAN'T DO MUCH WHEN THE PUBLIC MISTRUSTS AND HINDERS THEM-
P. D.
HAROLD GRAY

THE CUNNINGS WILL BE PUT WHERE THEY'LL NEVER HURT ANYONE ELSE- THEY'LL GET JUSTICE- AND PAT'S PARENTS HAVE LEARNED- NO MORE LEAVING THEIR CHILD TO THE CARE OF UN-KNOWN HELP- THEY'VE LEARNED THAT, IF KIDS ARE WORTH HAVING THEY'RE WORTH RAISING-
YES- I HATED TO GIVE UP PAT- BUT I GUESS EVER'THING'S WORKED OUT FOR THE BEST-
Reg. U. S. Pat. Off.; Copyright, 1931, by The Chicago Tribune.

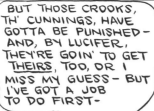

GIVE ME A SECOND--- THE LIGHT OR SOMETHING - MAYBE I'M AFRAID TO FIND OUT THE TRUTH---

CHAPTER NINE

A HUNDRED TO ONE

IN WHICH ANNIE

VISITS WITH SOME OLD AND DEAR FRIENDS

SEES THAT THE SOLUTION TO ALL HER TROUBLES MAY BE IN PLAIN SIGHT...

AND IS REMINDED YET AGAIN THAT WHERE THERE'S A WILL, THERE'S A WAY

HAROLD GRAY

Chicago Tribune.

Little Orphan Annie
IT'S SURE LONESOME AROUND HERE WITH PAT GONE- EH, SANDY?
ARF!

BUT SHE'LL BE LOTS BETTER OFF WITH HER OWN FOLKS- AND, AFTER LOSIN' HER ONCE, THEY'LL BE LOTS MORE CAREFUL NOW AND RAISE HER SWELL, I BETCHA-

AND THOSE CROOKS THAT WERE TRYIN' TO GRAB HER ARE IN JAIL, NOW, WHERE THEY CAN'T MAKE ANY MORE TROUBLE FOR ANYBODY-

IT'S AWFUL QUIET HERE SINCE PAT LEFT- C'MON, SANDY- LET'S GO FOR A WALK- WITH THOSE CROOKS LOCKED UP, IT'S SAFE NOW- WE CAN GO ANY-WHERE-

YEP- SAFE- NOTHIN' TO WATCH OUT FOR ANY MORE-

HEY!
YIPE!
3-N-52

WHAT'S TH' BIG IDEA? TRYIN' TO RUN OVER SANDY, ER WHAT? WATCH WHERE YOU'RE GOIN'- WHY DON'TCHA TOOT YER HORN, YUH BIG ----

YI!
HONK!

WHADDYUH T'INK Y'ARE, STANDIN' IN TH' STREET WAVIN' YER ARMS? A TRAFFIC COP? G'WAN! STAY ON DE SIDE-WALK, IF YUH DON'T WANT TO GET HIT-
TAXI

WHAT I'D LIKE TO TELL THAT BIG GORILLA! HUH! WHY, HE DIDN'T MISS ME AN INCH-

SAFE, MY EYE! YOU'RE NEVER SAFE, SANDY! ANYTHING'S LI'BLE TO HAPPEN ANY TIME- GOTTA WATCH EVERY SECOND IF YUH S'PECT TO GET HOME ALIVE-

STILL, I S'POSE THAT'S WHAT EYES ARE FOR- YUH NEED A GOOD SCARE 'BOUT EVERY SO OFTEN TO KEEP YUH WIDE AWAKE- WELL, FROM NOW ON, I'M WATCHIN' MY STEP-
HAROLD GRAY

November 15, 1931

WELL, HERE I AM IN EUROPE AND HERE I'VE BEEN FOR MONTHS - THEY'VE GIVEN ME EVERY TEST - X-RAYS BY THE HUNDREDS - DOZENS OF THE GREATEST DOCTORS HAVE CONSULTED - I'M TO GET THEIR FINAL VERDICT - I'M TO BE TOLD WHAT MY CHANCES ARE TO SEE AGAIN -

MR. WARBUCKS, WE HAVE GONE INTO YOUR CASE WITH GREATEST THOROUGHNESS - NOTHING KNOWN TO SURGERY HAS BEEN OVERLOOKED - BUT IT IS THE OPTIC NERVE - WE ARE POWERLESS TO AID YOU - I AM MOST SORRY -

IT IS MOST REGRETTABLE, SIR - OF COURSE, SOME DAY, PERHAPS, A NEW DISCOVERY WILL BE MADE - SOME SURGEON WILL GO ONE STEP FARTHER - BUT AT PRESENT WE ARE HELPLESS -
ETERNAL DARKNESS, EH? HM-M - I'D SORT OF HOPED MAYBE - - - BUT WHAT'S THE USE? THAT SETTLES IT -

AFTER ALL, MY FRIEND, ONE CAN BE VERY HAPPY WITHOUT EYES - ONE MAY NOT SEE THE BEAUTIFUL THINGS, BUT ALSO ONE IS SPARED THE UGLY SIGHTS - IT IS MOST DISAPPOINTING, THIS FAILURE - YOU ARE A STRONG MAN - YOU MUST, HOW DO YOU SAY, BRACE UP -
HAROLD GRAY
Reg. U. S. Pat. Off.; Copyright, 1931, by The Chicago Tribune.

SO THE BEST DOCS IN ALL EUROPE ADMIT THEY CAN DO NOTHING TO HELP ME - I'M TO BE BLIND FOREVER - I WAS SURE THEY COULD DO ANYTHING IF ONE HAD MONEY ENOUGH TO HIRE THEM - THIS IS THE GREATEST BLOW OF MY LIFE - TILL NOW I HAVE HAD HOPE AT LEAST -

OH, WELL - NO USE HANGING AROUND OVER HERE ANY MORE - IF I'M BLIND I'M BLIND - THE SOONER I GET BACK TO AMERICA THE BETTER I'LL FEEL - THAT'S HOME, AND I WANT TO BE HOME - WHERE TH' DICKENS ARE ALL THE SERVANTS?

PACK UP - TELL THE CAPTAIN TO HAVE THE YACHT READY - I'M GOING HOME - WE LEAVE AT ONCE - TO-NIGHT IF POSSIBLE - TO-MORROW CERTAINLY -
YES, SIR - QUITE SO, SIR -

HI TELL YOU IT'S A BLOODY SHAME - WHAT GOOD ARE THE BLINKIN' DOCTORS? 'IM BLIND AND NO 'OPE - IS THAT JUSTICE?
'OW DOES 'E TAKE IT?
THAT'S A SILLY QUESTION - "OW DOES 'E TAKE IT?" LIKE A MAN - 'OW ELSE WOULD WARBUCKS TAKE IT?
HAROLD GRAY
Reg. U. S. Pat. Off.; Copyright, 1931, by The Chicago Tribune.

ALL RIGHT, CAPTAIN - LET'S GET UNDER WAY - THIS WHOLE TRIP HAS BEEN A WILD GOOSE CHASE - WE CAN'T GET BACK HOME ANY TOO SOON TO SUIT ME -
AYE - AYE, SIR -

HOMEWARD BOUND - BACK TO AMERICA - NEAR TO LITTLE ANNIE AGAIN, EVEN IF I CAN'T SEE HER - WE'RE ONLY JUST STARTED HOME, BUT I FEEL BETTER ALREADY -

OPEN WATER - FULL SPEED AHEAD - THE YACHT FAIRLY LEAPS FORWARD, STREAKING ACROSS THE SEA FOR HOME - A FAST LINER IS OVERHAULED AND SLIPS BACK - SOON IT WILL BE ONLY A STREAK ON THE HORIZON - THEN NOTHING -
HAROLD GRAY
Reg. U. S. Pat. Off.; Copyright, 1931, by The Chicago Tribune.

November 16–18, 1931

IT'S SURE LONESOME AROUND HERE, SINCE PAT IS BACK WITH HER FOLKS - BUT I'VE GOT PLENTY TO DO TO KEEP ME BUSY HERE IN DOC. LENS' LAB-ER-TORY -
AND I'D BETTER KEEP MY MIND ON WHAT I'M DOIN' IN HERE, TOO - IT WOULDN'T DO TO BUST ANYTHING OR GO POKIN' INTO TH' WRONG JUGS AN' JARS AN' CASES -
STILL, THERE ISN'T SO MUCH TO DO AROUND HERE, WHEN I REALLY GET AT IT - I'LL HAVE LOTS O' TIME ON MY HANDS NOW - I'M GOIN' TO MISS PAT, BUT SHE'S BETTER OFF WITH HER FOLKS -
HAROLD GRAY
HELLO, SANDY - ARE YOU LONESOME, TOO? SAY, HOW ABOUT YOU AND I GOIN' OUT TO-MORROW AND CALL ON MAW GREEN AT HER NEW HOUSE AND SEE HOW SHE'S GETTIN' ALONG? SHE'S RICH NOW, YOU KNOW, BUT SHE'D STILL BE GLAD TO SEE US - WHADD'YUH SAY?
ARF!
Reg. U. S. Pat. Off.; Copyright, 1931, by The Chicago Tribune.
GEE - I HOPE MAW GREEN IS HOME -
HELLO, MAW GREEN - SANDY AND I JUST DROPPED IN TO SAY HELLO AND SEE HOW YOU'RE GETTIN' ON -
HELLO! WELL, ANNIE, AIN'T YOU AND SANDY A SIGHT FOR SORE EYES - COME ON IN BY THE FIRE -
YEAH - PAT'S BACK WITH HER FOLKS NOW - SANDY AND I ARE STILL WITH DR. LENS - HAVEN'T HEARD FROM "DADDY" FOR MONTHS -
HM-M - FUNNY HE DOESN'T WRITE TO YOU - HE LEFT OVER SIX MONTHS AGO - BACK IN MAY IT WAS - THEN YOU HAD THAT LETTER THAT THE CHINAMAN BROUGHT YOU -
YEAH - AND HE WAS DOIN' WELL, HE SAID, AND SENT ME MONEY - THAT'S TH' LAST I'VE HEARD - I SURE WISH HE'D WRITE AGAIN, OR COME BACK, EVEN IF HE IS BROKE AGAIN -
DON'T WORRY - HE'LL MOST LIKELY SHOW UP 'FORE LONG - HE SURE THOUGHT A LOT O' YOU -
HAROLD GRAY
Reg. U. S. Pat. Off.; Copyright, 1931, by The Chicago Tribune.
SAY, JAKE - THERE HASN'T BEEN ANY LETTER COME HERE FOR ME, HAS THERE? FROM CHINA, MAYBE?
NO, ANNIE - FROM MR. WARBUCKS YOU WERE EXPECTING ONE, MAYBE - NO - BUT YOU SHOULDN'T WORRY - YOU WOULD BE HEARING FROM HIM AGAIN SOON, MOST LIKELY -
IT'S ALL RIGHT FOR MAW GREEN AND JAKE TO TELL ME NOT TO WORRY 'BOUT "DADDY" - BUT I DO WORRY - IT'S NOT LIKE HIM TO BE AWAY SO LONG WITHOUT WRITIN' OR NOTHIN' - MAYBE HE'S ON HIS WAY BACK FROM CHINA AND IS GOIN' TO S'PRISE ME -
FUNNY HOW LITTLE I KNOW 'BOUT WHERE HE WENT OR ANYTHING - THERE HE WAS, BROKE AND COULDN'T GET A JOB - SAID HE WASN'T COMIN' BACK TILL HE GOT ONE - THEN TH' NEXT I HEARD WAS THAT LETTER TH' CHINAMAN BROUGHT FROM HIM -
THERE WAS SOMETHIN' SORT O' PHONEY 'BOUT THAT TOO - THE WAY THAT CHINAMAN GAVE ME TH' LETTER AN' THEN JUST DISAPPEARED - AND ALL THAT MONEY IN TH' BANK - I'VE GOT A HUNCH WE'RE GOIN' TO SEE "DADDY" AGAIN 'FORE LONG - DON'T YOU HOPE SO, SANDY?
ARF!
HAROLD GRAY
Reg. U. S. Pat. Off.; Copyright, 1931, by The Chicago Tribune.

November 19–21, 1931

Little Orphan Annie
HURRY UP, SANDY, IF YOU'RE GOIN' WITH ME-

MY, WHAT A SWELL DAY FOR A LONG WALK- IT'S A SHAME TO WASTE A MINUTE OF A SWELL DAY LIKE THIS INSIDE ANY OLD HOUSE- LET'S WALK PAST TH' STORES- WE HAVEN'T BEEN THAT WAY FOR A LONG TIME-

UM-M-M-- JUST LOOK AT ALL THAT SWELL CANDY- I'LL BET I COULD EAT THAT WHOLE FIVE-POUND BOX THERE- HOW WOULD YOU LIKE TO BE TURNED LOOSE IN THERE, SANDY?
ARF!

BUT CANDY'S PRETTY RICH- HADN'T OUGHTA EVER MAKE A PIG OF YERSELF OVER CANDY- AT LEAST, THAT'S WHAT THEY SAY- STILL, I'VE EATEN AN AWFUL LOT O' CANDY, AT TIMES, AND I NEVER FELT ANY TH' WORSE FOR IT-

GUESS IF IT'S GOOD CANDY, YOU CAN EAT AS MUCH AS YOU WANT- LEAPIN' LIZARDS! JUST LOOK HERE! MINCE PIES!!!
GEE- THEY MAKE ME HUNGRY- DON'T THEY LOOK GOOD-

COURSE THEY SAY HOME-MADE PIES ARE BEST- BUT, WHEN A BAKER USES GOOD STUFF, I DON'T SEE WHY HIS PIES SHOULDN'T BE JUST AS GOOD- LET'S YOU AND I SETTLE THAT QUESTION-

THAT ONE WILL DO FINE- NOW, PLEASE WILL YOU CUT IT FOUR WAYS AND WRAP IT UP, SO I CAN CARRY IT?

NOW FOR A NICE BENCH OUT HERE IN TH' PARK- WE'LL SOON KNOW IF THIS BAKERY PIE IS AS GOOD AS MRS. SILO USED TO MAKE-

C'MON, SANDY- GOTTA CLEAN THIS UP- WELL, I WON'T SAY ANY PIE COULD BE BETTER THAN MRS. SILO USED TO MAKE, BUT THIS ONE SURE IS JUST AS GOOD-

WHEW! THAT SURE FILLED ME UP- YESSIR, SANDY, AND I BET I COULD HELP YUH CHEW UP ANOTHER ONE, TOO- BUT I DON'T GUESS I COULD SWALLOW IT-

O-O-O-O-O! MY STUMMICK!!! I FEEL AWFUL!
OW!

IT ISN'T THAT PIE'S FAULT- IT'S 'CAUSE WE DIDN'T KNOW ENOUGH TO STOP WHEN WE'D HAD PLENTY- TOO MUCH OF EVEN TH' BEST OF ANYTHING WILL GET TH' BEST OF YOU-
HAROLD GRAY

November 22, 1931
A HUNDRED TO ONE

BUFFETED BY HEAVY STORMS, THE YACHT DRIVES EVER FORWARD - TOMORROW WARBUCKS WILL BE HOME -
CAN YOU MAKE OUT WHO IT IS, CAPTAIN?
NO, SIR - IT'S A FAST PLANE AND HE'S CIRCLING LOW ABOVE US - I THINK HE WANTS TO LAND AND COME ABOARD, SIR -

HELLO, OLIVER - THOUGHT I'D COME OUT AND MEET YOU - I GOT YOUR LOCATION FROM YOUR RADIO MAN BUT I PROMISED TO WRING HIS NECK IF HE TOLD YOU - I WANTED TO SURPRISE YOU -
HELLO, BILL - I'LL SAY YOU SURPRISED ME - THIS IS GREAT - I'VE NEVER BEEN SO LONESOME IN MY LIFE -

WELL, BILL - HOW IS LITTLE ANNIE? HAVE YOU ANY NEWS ABOUT HER FOR ME?
GHEE! YOU SHOULD HAVE BEEN THERE - A COUPLE O' SMART CROOKS TRIED TO PUT ONE OVER ON HER - I KEPT AN EYE ON TH' MATTER - BUT SHE DIDN'T NEED ANY HELP FROM ME - NOT THAT KID - I'LL TELL YOU THE WHOLE STORY - - - - - -
HAROLD GRAY

GEE - THINGS SURE ARE DEAD - DOC. LENS OUT O' TOWN - PAT BACK WITH HER FOLKS - NO TELLING WHERE "DADDY" IS - IN CHINA, MOST LIKELY - - - - -

SANDY! LOOK! IT'S DADDY!
ARF!

COME ON, SANDY! HELLO, "DADDY"! WHEN DIDJA GET BACK? DON'T YOU SEE ME?
IT'S LITTLE ANNIE -
YES - I KNOW HER VOICE -

IT'S O.K., BOYS - DRIVE ON -
DADDY! WHY, YOU'RE WEARING GLASSES! WHY ... WHY ... CAN'T YOU .... ARE YOU - - - OH, "DADDY" - MY DADDY!!!
ANNIE - SO YOU FOUND ME OUT -
HAROLD GRAY

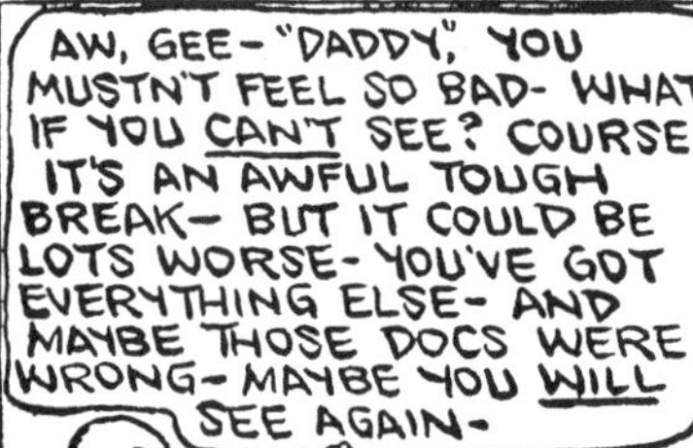
AW, GEE - "DADDY," YOU MUSTN'T FEEL SO BAD - WHAT IF YOU CAN'T SEE? COURSE IT'S AN AWFUL TOUGH BREAK - BUT IT COULD BE LOTS WORSE - YOU'VE GOT EVERYTHING ELSE - AND MAYBE THOSE DOCS WERE WRONG - MAYBE YOU WILL SEE AGAIN -

LEAPIN' LIZARDS! WHAT A VIEW, SANDY - TH' WHOLE CITY SPREAD OUT DOWN THERE LIKE A MAP - AND THIS SWELL HOUSE UP HERE ON TOP O' THIS SKY-SCRAPER - GORGEOUS PAINTINGS AND BEAUTIFUL FURNITURE - BUT POOR "DADDY" CAN'T SEE ANY OF IT?

HEY! THIS WILL NEVER DO, ANNIE - YOU MUSTN'T CRY LIKE THAT - WHAT'S WRONG? TELL OLD BILL ALL ABOUT IT -
OH, BOO! HOO! IT'S "DADDY" BEIN' BLIND - IT'S NOT FAIR, BILL - IT'S NOT FAIR!!!

SURE, ANNIE - I KNOW - BUT BAWLIN' NEVER HELPS - HE THINKS SO MUCH O' YOU HE WOULDN'T LET YOU SEE HIM BLIND FOR FEAR O' MAKIN' YOU SAD - NOW YOU'VE FOUND HIM, THOUGH - YOU CAN HELP HIM MORE THAN ANYONE ELSE - BUT YOU'VE GOT TO CHEER UP OR YOU CAN'T CHEER HIM UP - SEE?

I GUESS YOU'RE RIGHT, BILL -

HAROLD GRAY

YESSIR, "DADDY"– I SURE HAVE LOTS TO BE THANKFUL FOR– ALL MY FRIENDS ARE DOIN' PRETTY WELL, IN SPITE OF TH' HARD TIMES FOLKS TALK ABOUT– AND I HAVE YOU BACK– THAT'S THE BEST OF ALL–

WOW! WHAT A DINNER! TURKEY AN' DRESSIN' WITH OYSTERS IN IT, AN' CRANBERRY SAUCE AN' PUNKIN' PIE– DUNNO IF I SHOULD HAVE TAKEN THAT SECOND PIECE O' PIE OR NOT– I FEEL SORTA FUNNY–

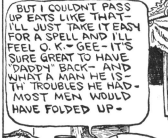

BUT I COULDN'T PASS UP EATS LIKE THAT– I'LL JUST TAKE IT EASY FOR A SPELL AND I'LL FEEL O. K.– GEE– IT'S SURE GREAT TO HAVE "DADDY" BACK– AND WHAT A MAN HE IS– TH' TROUBLES HE HAD– MOST MEN WOULD HAVE FOLDED UP–
Reg. U. S. Pat. Off.; Copyright, 1931, by The Chicago Tribune.

BUT NOT "DADDY"– HE NEVER GIVES UP– GUESS THAT'S WHY HE ALWAYS COMES OUT ON TOP– AND HE'S THE MOST GENEROUS GUY IN TH' WORLD, TOO– GEE– WITH HIM FOR OUR FRIEND WE'VE SURE GOT PLENTY TO BE THANKFUL FOR– EH, SANDY?
ARF!
HAROLD GRAY

SANDY– SOMETHING HAS GOTTA BE DONE 'BOUT "DADDY"– WE CAN'T JUST SIT QUIET AN' DO NOTHIN' WHEN HE'S BLIND– THERE MUST BE SOME WAY WE CAN HELP–

LEAPIN' LIZARDS! WITH ALL TH' THOUSANDS AN' THOUSANDS O' DOCTORS THERE MUST BE PLENTY OF 'EM WHO COULD MAKE HIM SEE AGAIN IF HE'D LET 'EM TRY–

BUT LISTEN, "DADDY"– WON'T YOU PLEASE JUST LET DOC. LENS SEE YOU AND TALK TO YOU? HE'S AN AWFUL GOOD DOCTOR– HE CURED PAT IN NO TIME–
Reg. U. S. Pat. Off.; Copyright, 1931, by The Chicago Tribune.

DON'T BE SILLY, ANNIE– WHY, I'VE SPENT MONTHS WITH THE VERY GREATEST DOCTORS OF ALL EUROPE– THEY'VE DONE EVERYTHING POSSIBLE, AND FAILED– IF THEY CAN'T HELP ME, WHAT CHANCE IS THERE THAT YOUR UN-KNOWN DOCTOR LENS COULD HELP– NO USE, ANNIE– FORGET IT–
HAROLD GRAY

WHAT'S THAT? YOU SAY YOU'VE LOOKED UP THIS DOCTOR LENS AS I ASKED YOU TO, EH? YES? HM-M-M. IS THAT SO? WELL-WELL- I SEE– YOU DON'T THINK SO– OH, YOU DO THINK SO– HM-M-M··· WELL, THANK YOU VERY MUCH–

HM-M··· WELL, DOC. LENS APPEARS TO BE A BETTER MAN THAN I REALIZED– SKILFUL SURGEON– BROAD EXPERIENCE– BRILLIANT DIAGNOSTICIAN– BUT HAS PRACTICALLY DROPPED ALL PRACTICE FOR THE PAST TWO YEARS– DOING SOME SORT OF RESEARCH WORK–

TURNED INTO A LABORATORY NUT, NO DOUBT– IF HE WAS SUCH A KNOCKOUT AS A SURGEON HE'D HARDLY DROP A WONDERFUL PRACTICE, WOULD HE? OR WOULD HE? WHAT DIFFERENCE DOES IT MAKE TO ME?
HAROLD GRAY

HE WAS MIGHTY GOOD TO ANNIE– I OUGHT TO MEET HIM AND THANK HIM FOR THAT– BUT AS FAR AS THIS CHAP HELPING ME ANY– THAT'S ABSURD– I'M BLIND AND WILL STAY BLIND AND THE SOONER I BECOME RESIGNED TO THAT THE BETTER OFF I'LL BE–

November 26–28, 1931

Little Orphan Annie
GEE, "DADDY" SURE HAS A SWELL PLACE UP HERE -

YOU'D NEVER GUESS THAT THIS GARDEN IS WAY UP ON TOP O' ONE OF THE TALLEST BUILDINGS IN TOWN -

LEAPIN' LIZARDS!

WHEW! WHAT A DROP! I FEEL GIDDY -

WHAT A SWELL VIEW FROM UP HERE - BUT POOR "DADDY" - VIEWS DON'T DO HIM ANY GOOD - HE CAN'T EVEN TELL IF IT'S DAY-LIGHT OR DARK -

SO YOU LIKE THE VIEW FROM UP HERE, EH? SIT DOWN AND TELL ME ABOUT IT, ANNIE -
OH, IT'S A KNOCK-OUT, "DADDY" - WHY, FROM THIS WINDOW I CAN SEE FOR OVER FIFTY MILES, I BETCHA -

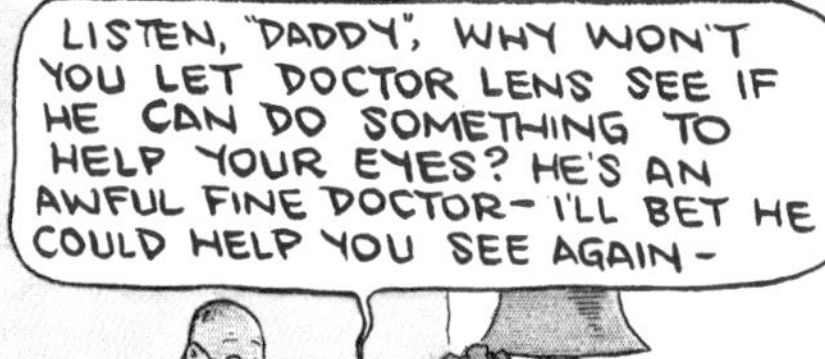
LISTEN, "DADDY", WHY WON'T YOU LET DOCTOR LENS SEE IF HE CAN DO SOMETHING TO HELP YOUR EYES? HE'S AN AWFUL FINE DOCTOR - I'LL BET HE COULD HELP YOU SEE AGAIN -

NONSENSE, ANNIE - WHAT CHANCE IS THERE THAT YOUR DOCTOR LENS COULD HELP IN MY CASE, WHEN THE GREATEST SPECIALISTS IN ALL EUROPE HAVE FAILED COMPLETELY?
BUT, "DADDY" - HE MIGHT BE ABLE TO HELP - YOU DON'T KNOW HE CAN'T, TILL HE'S HAD A CHANCE TO TRY - PLEASE, CAN'T I CALL HIM UP AND HAVE HIM COME OVER AND TALK TO YOU ABOUT IT, ANYWAY?

OH, ALL RIGHT - HE MUST BE A FINE CHAP AND WORTH TALKING TO - HAVE HIM OVER, IF YOU INSIST -
OH, "DADDY" - I'LL GO AND CALL HIM UP RIGHT AWAY -

OF COURSE THERE ISN'T A CHANCE - BUT IT WILL PLEASE ANNIE TO FEEL SHE IS DOING EVERYTHING SHE CAN TO HELP ME - AND DR. LENS HAS BEEN KIND TO ANNIE - HE MUST BE A GOOD SORT - MAYBE THERE'LL BE SOMETHING I CAN DO FOR HIM -

LEAPIN' LIZARDS! I WAS AFRAID "DADDY" WAS NEVER GOIN' TO SAY "YES" - MAYBE DOC. LENS CAN'T DO A THING - BUT IT'S SURE WORTH TRYIN' - HELLO! HELLO! IS THIS YOU, DOC? THIS IS ANNIE - - - -
HAROLD GRAY

November 29, 1931

WELL, DOCTOR LENS- YOU KNOW OF MY CASE-ANNIE HAS BEEN AFTER ME TO LET YOU TRY TO RESTORE MY SIGHT- I'LL BE FRANK WITH YOU-I HAVE NO IDEA YOU CAN HELP ME- BUT, TO PLEASE ANNIE, I'D LIKE YOU TO LOOK ME OVER-
I'D BE GLAD TO, MR. WARBUCKS-
AND I WANT TO TELL YOU, DOCTOR, YOU WERE MIGHTY NICE TO ANNIE, TAKING HER IN AS YOU DID- I WON'T FORGET THAT-
OH, THAT WAS NOTHING- ANNIE IS A WONDERFUL LITTLE GIRL- SHE MORE THAN EARNED HER WAY-
WELL, SANDY- THAT'S THAT- HE'LL X-RAY AND POKE AROUND AND ASK QUESTIONS AND MAKE A LONG REPORT- THEY ALL DO - NOTHING WILL COME OF IT- THEY'RE ALL ALIKE, THESE DOCTORS-
BUT IT WILL PLEASE ANNIE-NATURALLY SHE THINKS THIS CHAP IS A MARVEL- HE'S A FINE CHAP AT THAT, BUT IT DOESN'T STAND TO REASON HE CAN SUCCEED WHERE THE FINEST SURGEONS OF ALL EUROPE HAVE FAILED-
HAROLD GRAY
Reg. U. S. Pat. Off.; Copyright, 1931, by The Chicago Tribune.
WELL, DOC, ARE YOU ALL DONE WITH ME FOR TO-DAY?
YES, MR. WARBUCKS- I'LL GO OVER THESE PLATES AND I'LL HAVE A REPORT FOR YOU TO-MORROW.
WELL, YOUR DOCTOR SEEMS QUITE A THOROUGH CHAP- UNUSUAL, TOO- HE DIDN'T ASK ANY QUESTIONS AT ALL-
WHAT DID HE SAY, "DADDY"? IS HE GOING TO CURE YOU?
WELL, HE DIDN'T SAY MUCH, EITHER- SAID HE'D SEE ME TO-MORROW- AND AS TO CURING ME- NO, ANNIE- I WOULDN'T COUNT ON THAT- HE'S A FINE DOCTOR, NO DOUBT- BUT EVEN FINE DOCTORS CAN'T PERFORM MIRACLES-
BUT YOU'LL LET HIM TRY, WON'T YOU, "DADDY"? COURSE I LOVE YUH JUST AS MUCH, ANYWAY, BUT IT'D BE SO WONDERFUL FOR YOU IF YOU COULD SEE AGAIN-
WE'LL SEE, ANNIE- WE'LL SEE-
HAROLD GRAY
Reg. U. S. Pat. Off.; Copyright, 1931, by The Chicago Tribune.
SO YOU THINK YOU CAN CURE ME, EH? WELL, BEFORE WE GO INTO THAT I WANT TO SETTLE SOMETHING ELSE- I WANT TO DO SOMETHING FOR YOU- WHAT WOULD YOU SAY IF I BUILT YOU A HOSPITAL-FINE LABORATORIES- FIVE OR TEN MILLION- YOU COULD DO A LOT FOR HUMANITY WITH A PLANT LIKE THAT, EH?
THANKS- I APPRECIATE YOUR OFFER- BUT THE TRUTH IS I AM A WEALTHY MAN MYSELF- STILL, YOUR OFFER IS MOST GENEROUS- IT IS EVIDENT YOU ARE TRULY ANXIOUS TO DO SOMETHING OUTSTANDING TO ADVANCE SURGERY AND AID HUMANITY-
IF THAT IS THE CASE I HAVE A WAY WHICH I BELIEVE WILL AID MORE THAN MILLIONS- FOR TWO YEARS I HAVE BEEN EXPERIMENTING ON JUST SUCH A CASE AS YOURS- IT WOULD INVOLVE AN OPERATION ON THE OPTIC NERVE- IT WOULD BE SUCH AN OPERATION AS HAS NEVER YET BEEN SUCCESSFUL-
I BELIEVE NOW I AM READY TO PERFORM SUCH AN OPERATION SUCCESSFULLY- IF YOU WOULD LEND YOURSELF TO SUCH AN EXPERIMENT YOU MIGHT HELP TO ADVANCE SURGERY IMMENSELY-
HM-M- I WOULD BE SORT OF THE GUINEA PIG, OR WHITE RABBIT, EH? WELL, THAT'S AN IDEA, ANYWAY-
HAROLD GRAY
Reg. U. S. Pat. Off.; Copyright, 1931, by The Chicago Tribune.

November 30–
December 2, 1931

SAY, DOC.-YOU KNOW I'VE BEEN THINKING OVER YOUR PROPOSITION THAT I LET YOU TRY OUT YOUR NEW OPERATION ON ME-PRETTY DELICATE JOB, I SUPPOSE-WHAT WOULD YOU SAY WOULD BE THE PERCENTAGE? THAT IS, WHAT WOULD BE MY CHANCE TO COME OUT O.K.?
ANY OPERATION SO NEAR THE BRAIN HAS ITS RISKS-PERSONALLY I THINK I COULD SUCCEED - YOU HAVE A VERY STRONG CONSTITUTION- ALL THE CONDITIONS ARE IDEAL-
BUT THERE WOULD BE NO PARTIAL CURE, MR. WARBUCKS- FRANKLY YOU WOULD BE TAKING A VERY DECIDED GAMBLE-THE OPERATION WOULD MEAN ONE OF TWO THINGS-

EITHER YOU WOULD REGAIN YOUR SIGHT COMPLETELY, AS I HOPE--OR ELSE, YOU WOULD NEVER COME OUT OF THE OPERATION AT ALL-
HAROLD GRAY
Reg. U. S. Pat. Off.; Copyright, 1931, by The Chicago Tribune.

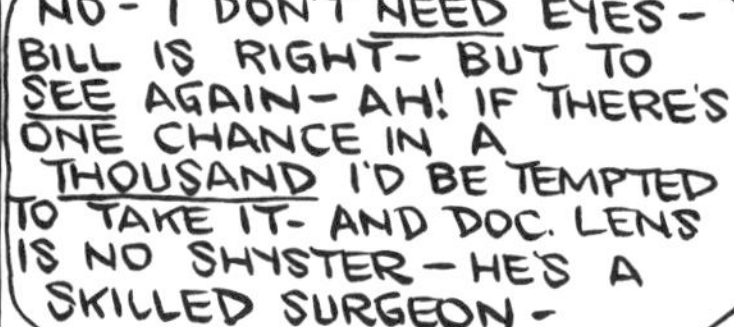
GREAT SCOTT! WHAT DO YOU WANT TO TAKE A CHANCE LIKE THAT FOR, OLIVER-IF THAT DOC. GUESSES RIGHT, YOU'LL SEE-IF HE'S WRONG, YOU'LL BE DEAD-YOU DON'T NEED YOUR EYE-SIGHT BAD ENOUGH TO TAKE ANY HUNDRED-TO-ONE SHOT LIKE THAT-
NO-I DON'T NEED EYES-BILL IS RIGHT- BUT TO SEE AGAIN-AH! IF THERE'S ONE CHANCE IN A THOUSAND I'D BE TEMPTED TO TAKE IT- AND DOC. LENS IS NO SHYSTER-HE'S A SKILLED SURGEON-

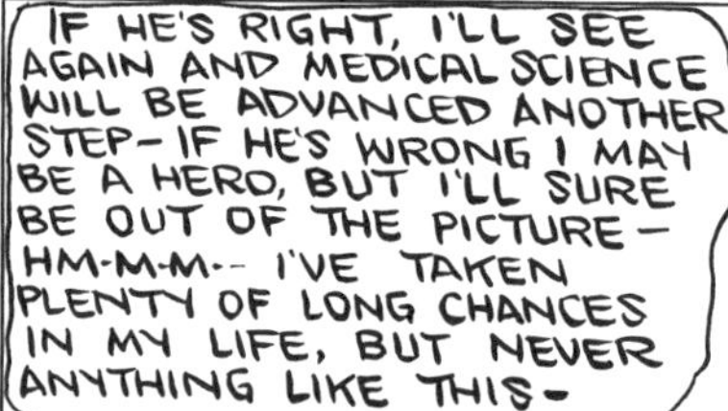
HE'S BEEN WORKING ON JUST SUCH AN OPERATION FOR TWO YEARS-TESTING, EXPERIMENTING, WORKING CONSTANTLY-NOW HE IS READY TO TRY OUT HIS THEORY- MY CASE GIVES HIM A PERFECT OPPORTUNITY TO PROVE WHETHER HE IS RIGHT OR WRONG-
IF HE'S RIGHT, I'LL SEE AGAIN AND MEDICAL SCIENCE WILL BE ADVANCED ANOTHER STEP-IF HE'S WRONG I MAY BE A HERO, BUT I'LL SURE BE OUT OF THE PICTURE-HM-M-M-- I'VE TAKEN PLENTY OF LONG CHANCES IN MY LIFE, BUT NEVER ANYTHING LIKE THIS-

HAROLD GRAY
Reg. U. S. Pat. Off.; Copyright, 1931, by The Chicago Tribune.

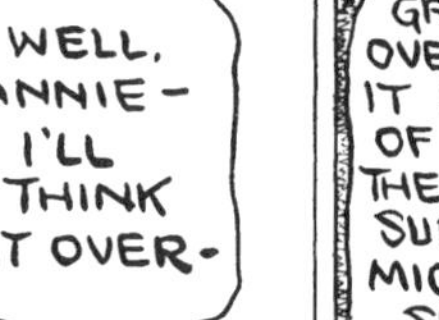
OH, PLEASE, "DADDY"- I JUST KNOW DOC. LENS CAN MAKE YOU SEE AGAIN- WON'T YOU PLEASE LET HIM TRY?
WELL, ANNIE-I'LL THINK IT OVER-
GREAT SCOTT! THINK IT OVER! I'VE BEEN THINKING IT OVER FOR THREE DAYS-OF COURSE ANNIE HASN'T THE SLIGHTEST IDEA WHAT SUCH AN OPERATION MIGHT MEAN-IS ALMOST SURE TO MEAN-

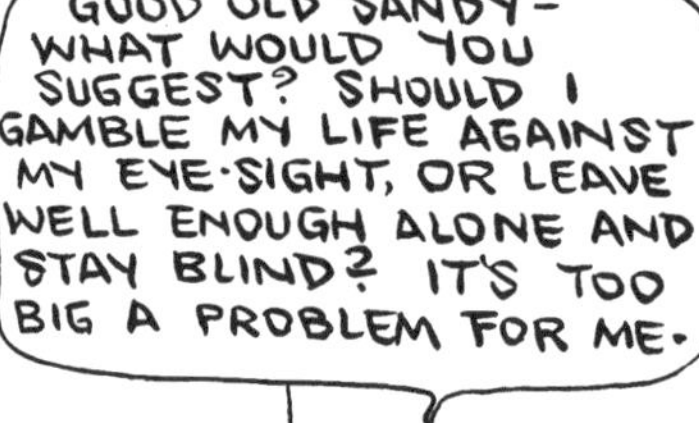
GOOD OLD SANDY-WHAT WOULD YOU SUGGEST? SHOULD I GAMBLE MY LIFE AGAINST MY EYE-SIGHT, OR LEAVE WELL ENOUGH ALONE AND STAY BLIND? IT'S TOO BIG A PROBLEM FOR ME-

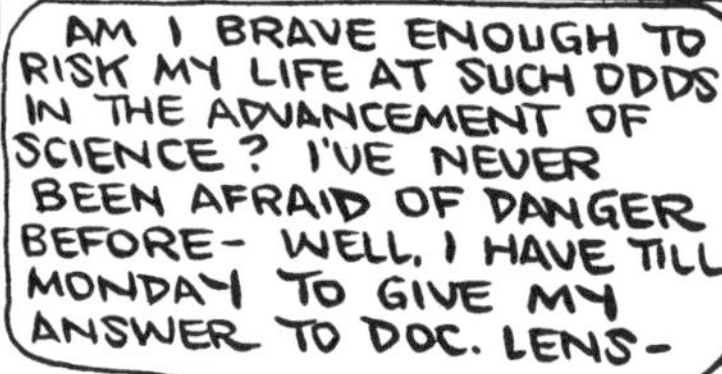
AM I BRAVE ENOUGH TO RISK MY LIFE AT SUCH ODDS IN THE ADVANCEMENT OF SCIENCE? I'VE NEVER BEEN AFRAID OF DANGER BEFORE- WELL, I HAVE TILL MONDAY TO GIVE MY ANSWER TO DOC. LENS-

HAROLD GRAY
Reg. U. S. Pat. Off.; Copyright, 1931, by The Chicago Tribune.

December 3–5, 1931
A HUNDRED TO ONE

Little Orphan Annie
"DADDY" SEEMS TO BE THINKIN' AWFUL HARD 'BOUT SOMETHIN' — GUESS WE'D BETTER NOT BOTHER HIM NOW —

WHEW! WHAT A DECISION TO HAVE TO MAKE — DOC. LENS WANTS TO TRY OUT HIS NEW OPERATION ON ME — SAYS EITHER MY SIGHT WILL BE COMPLETELY RESTORED, OR ELSE --- OR ELSE I WILL BE COMPLETELY DONE FOR —

SAYS IT'S A HUNDRED TO ONE HE'LL FAIL — THAT'S A LONG SHOT TO TAKE WITH ONE'S LIFE — BILL SAYS I'M A SAP EVEN TO CONSIDER IT — STILL I'VE ALWAYS TAKEN CHANCES — HM-M -- A HUNDRED TO ONE —

IS IT WORTH THE RISK? HERE I HAVE A TREMENDOUS FORTUNE — EVERY COMFORT — WHAT ARE EYES, AFTER ALL — I WHIPPED 'EM ALL WITHOUT 'EM —

OH, "DADDY" — SANDY AND I ARE GOIN' OUT FOR A LITTLE WALK — DON'TCHA WANT TO GO, TOO —
OH, I GUESS I WON'T GO THIS TIME, ANNIE — BE CAREFUL AND DON'T STAY OUT TOO LONG —

WE'LL BE CAREFUL — AND WE'LL BE BACK IN AN HOUR — G'BYE, "DADDY" —
SMACK!

THE LITTLE DARLING — WHAT A GIRL — AND I WAS AFRAID TO LET HER FIND OUT I WAS BLIND — AS IF THAT COULD MAKE ANY DIFFERENCE TO A KID LIKE ANNIE —

SHE'D MISS ME, IF THE OPERATION WENT WRONG — AND THE OPTIC NERVE IS A DANGEROUS THING TO TAMPER WITH — STILL, DOC. LENS IS A FINE SURGEON — AND ONE CHANCE EVEN IN A HUNDRED, IS ONE CHANCE —

TO SEE AGAIN! LET ME GET THIS THING STRAIGHT — IF I WIN, I'LL HAVE EVERYTHING — HEALTH, WEALTH AND EYE-SIGHT — BUT IF I LOSE — WHAT THEN?

WELL, IF I LOSE, I WON'T KNOW A THING ABOUT IT — AND AS FOR MY FORTUNE, I CAN HAVE THAT FIXED SO ANNIE WILL ALWAYS BE WELL CARED FOR — SHE'LL MISS ME — BUT SHE'S YOUNG AND WOULD SOON GET OVER IT —

IT COMES DOWN TO THIS — AM I GAMBLER ENOUGH TO RISK MY LIFE AGAINST THE CHANCE OF REGAINING MY SIGHT? IS MY EYE-SIGHT WORTH THAT MUCH TO ME?
HAROLD GRAY

YES! I'LL CALL DOC. LENS AND TELL HIM TO GO AHEAD — IT'S MY LIFE — IF I WANT TO RISK IT, THAT'S MY BUSINESS — IF IT WERE ONE CHANCE IN A THOUSAND, I'D BE A COWARD NOT TO TAKE IT — AND NO ONE YET EVER CALLED OLIVER WARBUCKS YELLOW —
WELL, FOLKS, THIS MAY BE WARBUCKS' LAST APPEARANCE IN THE FUNNY PAPER —

December 6, 1931
A HUNDRED TO ONE

HELLO! DOC LENS? THIS IS WARBUCKS - I'VE THOUGHT IT ALL OVER AND I'M GOING TO LET YOU GO AHEAD AND TRY OUT THAT OPERATION OF YOURS ON MY EYES - YEP - I'LL HAVE TO CLEAN UP MY AFFAIRS - I CAN GO TO THE HOSPITAL THURSDAY - O.K.? NEXT THURSDAY, THEN -
WELL, ANNIE - I'VE DECIDED TO LET YOUR DOCTOR LENS TRY HIS LUCK ON ME - OF COURSE I CAN'T SPARE THE TIME RIGHT NOW, BUT AS SOON AS I GET MY BUSINESS IN SHAPE I'LL TAKE A FEW DAYS OFF -
OH, "DADDY" - I KNOW HE'LL CURE YOU - I ONLY WISH YOU COULD GO RIGHT AWAY -
OF COURSE IT'S YOUR LIFE YOU'RE GAMBLING WITH, OLIVER - BUT I THINK YOU'RE CRAZY TO TAKE A CHANCE LIKE THAT -
PROBABLY YOU'RE RIGHT, BILL - BUT WHAT'S THE DIFFERENCE? I'LL FIX IT SO ANNIE'LL ALWAYS BE CARED FOR - JUST IN CASE -
WHAT A MAN! I'VE KNOWN SOME GREAT GAMBLERS, BUT THEY WERE ALL PIKERS COMPARED TO WARBUCKS - THEY RISKED MILLIONS AT EVEN ODDS - HE GAMBLES HIS LIFE AGAINST HIS EYE-SIGHT AT A THOUSAND TO ONE - FOOLISH - CRAZY, MAYBE - BUT I'VE GOT TO ADMIRE HIM -
HAROLD GRAY
Reg. U. S. Pat. Off.; Copyright, 1931, by The Chicago Tribune.
THEY'RE ALL HERE, OLIVER - SHALL I HAVE 'EM COME IN?
YES, BILL - I'LL SIGN EVERYTHING IN HERE -
YOU MEN KNOW WHAT I AM ABOUT TO DO, AND YOU ARE ALL BOUND TO SECRECY - BY SIGNING THESE PAPERS I DO NOT TURN OVER CONTROL IN ANY WAY, BUT IN CASE MY COMING OPERATION IS NOT A SUCCESS MY AFFAIRS WILL BE LEFT IN GOOD SHAPE AND MY WARD, MISS ANNIE, WILL BE PROVIDED FOR -
WELL, BILL, HOW'S THAT FOR WRITING IN THE DARK? WELL, I WON'T HAVE TO DO THAT MUCH LONGER - EITHER I'LL SEE WHAT I'M DOING, OR I WON'T BE WORRYING ABOUT IT, EH?
HAROLD GRAY
IMAGINE HIM JOKING ABOUT IT -
HE OUGHT TO BE RESTRAINED FROM TAKING SUCH A SUICIDAL CHANCE -
I BELIEVE NOW ALL I'VE ALWAYS HEARD OF HIS IRON NERVE -
IRON NERVE, NOTHING - HE HAS NO NERVES, IF YOU ASK ME -
HA! WHO IS THERE WHO HAS EVER BEEN ABLE TO RESTRAIN WARBUCKS -
GREAT SCOTT! LISTEN TO OLIVER LAUGH - HE AND ANNIE HAVE BEEN WHOOPING IT UP ALL EVENING - HE'S TOLD HER HE'S GOING OUT OF TOWN FOR A FEW DAYS ON BUSINESS, SO SHE WON'T WORRY ABOUT HIM IN THE HOSPITAL - LISTEN TO HIM - YOU'D THINK HE DIDN'T HAVE A WORRY IN THE WORLD -
HA! HA! HA! THAT'S A GOOD ONE, ANNIE - NOW RECITE THAT ONE ABOUT THE ORGAN GRINDER AND THE MONKEY -
GOOD-NIGHT, "DADDY" - AND YOU WON'T STAY AWAY LONG ON YOUR TRIP, WILL YOU?
NO, I'LL BE GONE FOR ONLY A FEW DAYS - GOTTA GET BACK AND SEE YOUR DOC, AS I PROMISED - GOOD-NIGHT, ANNIE -
WELL, TO-MORROW I TAKE THE BIG STEP - MAYBE I SHOULD TELL ANNIE, BUT SHE'LL KNOW SOON ENOUGH, AND THERE'S NO NEED TO CAUSE HER NEEDLESS WORRY.
HAROLD GRAY
Reg. U. S. Pat. Off.; Copyright, 1931, by The Chicago Tribune.

December 7–9, 1931
A HUNDRED TO ONE

WELL, OLIVER- GOOD-BYE AND GOOD LUCK-
GOOD-BYE, BILL- IF THINGS GO AS I HOPE, I'LL BE SEEING YOU SOON-

WELL, DOC- HERE I AM- WHEN DO WE START?
NOT RIGHT AWAY, MR. WARBUCKS- THERE ARE A FEW DETAILS TO ATTEND TO FIRST-

WELL, MY NOSE TELLS ME THIS IS A HOSPITAL EVEN IF MY EYES DON'T- ETHER- DISINFECTANT- WHEW- IT SMELLS LIKE A NICE CLEAN PLACE-
RIGHT IN HERE- THIS WILL BE YOUR ROOM-

WE WILL OPERATE EARLY TO-MORROW MORNING-
BUT LISTEN, DOC- I FEEL GREAT- I KNOW THE RULES, BUT WHAT'S THE SENSE OF PUTTING ME TO BED NOW LIKE I WAS ALREADY AN INVALID-
HAROLD GRAY

GEE, "DADDY'S" GONE AWAY FOR A FEW DAYS- SAID HE HAD TO TAKE A LITTLE TRIP ON BUSINESS- WHEN HE GETS BACK HE'S PROMISED TO LET DOC LENS TRY TO CURE HIS EYES- I JUST KNOW DOC LENS CAN MAKE HIM SEE- I WISH "DADDY'D" HURRY BACK SO DOC CAN MAKE HIM SEE SOON-

WHILE, UNSUSPECTED BY ANNIE, TENSE DRAMA FILLS A HUSHED OPERATING ROOM- SH-H-H--- ALL IS NOT GOING AS IT SHOULD-

AH, DOCTOR! IT WAS MAGNIFICENT! MARVELOUS- SUCH TECHNIQUE- SUCH COOLNESS- NOT ANOTHER SURGEON I HAVE KNOWN COULD COMPARE-
THANKS, DOCTOR-

NOT ANOTHER SURGEON HE HAS KNOWN COULD COMPARE, EH? HUH! NOT ANOTHER SURGEON I'VE EVER KNOWN WOULD HAVE BEEN SO BIG AN IDIOT AS TO TRY WHAT I TRIED- TO A CERTAIN POINT I WAS O.K.- THEN I WAS LOST- I DID WHAT I COULD- WHAT A FOOL I'VE BEEN-
HAROLD GRAY

HAVE YOU HEARD FROM "DADDY"? WHEN IS HE GOING TO GET BACK FROM HIS TRIP?
"DADDY"? OH, SURE, ANNIE- HE'LL BE BACK IN A FEW DAYS- THE FIRST OF THE WEEK, MAYBE-

WHEW! GOTTA KEEP HER THINKING HE'S ON A TRIP- GREAT SCOTT! I HOPE IT DOESN'T TURN OUT THAT HE IS ON A TRIP, ONE OF THOSE LONG TRIPS- THEY WON'T TELL ME A THING AT THE HOSPITAL- SOMETHING TELLS ME THINGS DIDN'T GO ANY TOO WELL-

BILL'S HUNCH IS RIGHT- THINGS DID NOT GO AT ALL AS EXPECTED- BUT WHILE THERE'S LIFE THERE'S HOPE- THE OLD WARRIOR IS NOT QUITE THROUGH YET-

YOU'VE HAD TWENTY-FOUR HOURS WITHOUT SLEEP, DOCTOR- LET ME WATCH WHILE YOU GET SOME REST-

REST! HUH! AS IF I COULD REST WITH THIS THING ON MY MIND- EVERYTHING WENT SO UNEXPECTEDLY- WHAT A NIGHTMARE- I'LL GET SOME COFFEE AND GET BACK IN THERE- I MAY NOT BE ABLE TO DO A THING TO SAVE HIM- BUT, AT LEAST, I'LL SEE THIS THING THROUGH-
HAROLD GRAY

December 10–12, 1931

Little Orphan Annie
LEAPIN' LIZARDS! ONLY TEN MORE SHOPPING DAYS BEFORE CHRISTMAS-

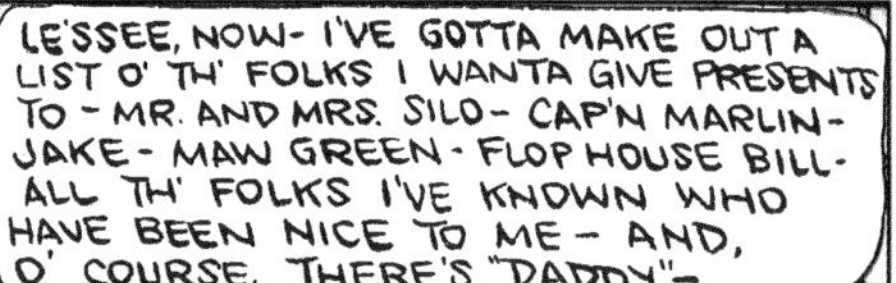
LE'SSEE, NOW- I'VE GOTTA MAKE OUT A LIST O' TH' FOLKS I WANTA GIVE PRESENTS TO - MR. AND MRS. SILO - CAP'N MARLIN - JAKE - MAW GREEN - FLOP HOUSE BILL - ALL TH' FOLKS I'VE KNOWN WHO HAVE BEEN NICE TO ME - AND, O' COURSE, THERE'S "DADDY"-

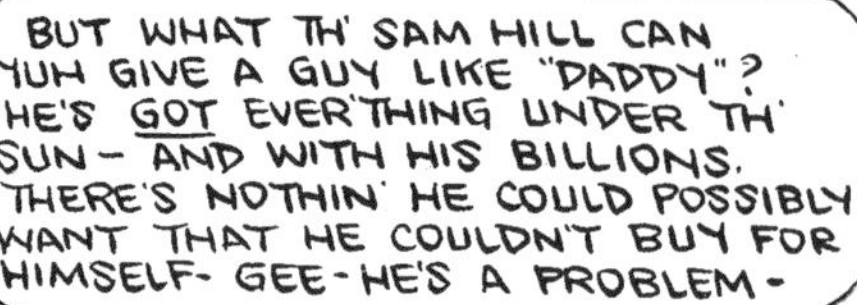
BUT WHAT TH' SAM HILL CAN YUH GIVE A GUY LIKE "DADDY"? HE'S GOT EVER'THING UNDER TH' SUN - AND WITH HIS BILLIONS. THERE'S NOTHIN' HE COULD POSSIBLY WANT THAT HE COULDN'T BUY FOR HIMSELF- GEE- HE'S A PROBLEM-

C'MON, SANDY- LET'S GO TAKE A LITTLE WALK AND LOOK IN TH' SHOP WINDOWS- MAYBE WE'LL SEE SOMETHIN' "DADDY'D" LIKE- THERE SURE ARE SOME SWELL THINGS IN TH' STORES THIS YEAR-

WHICH CAR DOES MISS ANNIE WISH TO-DAY?
NEVER MIND ANY CAR THIS TIME, HENRY- SANDY AND I ARE JUST GOIN' TO TAKE A LITTLE WALK-

IT'S SURE SWELL TO BE RICH, 'SPECIALLY 'ROUND CHRISTMAS TIME- THEY SAY TH' WAY TO BRING BACK GOOD TIMES IS TO SPEND- IF THAT'S TH' CASE, I'M SURE GOIN TO DO MY SHARE THIS YEAR-

THAT REMINDS ME- I MUST GET MY CHRISTMAS SEALS 'FORE I SEND OUT ANY PRESENTS OR LETTERS OR CHRISTMAS CARDS-
CHRISTMAS GREETINGS 1931

THERE, NOW- OUGHTA BE ABLE TO PICK OUT SOMETHIN' THERE THAT "DADDY'D" LIKE- IF HE HADN'T GONE OUT O' TOWN I'D GET HIM TO JUST WALK BY HERE WITH ME- MAYBE HE'D SAY SOMETHIN' THAT'D GIVE ME A TIP ON WHAT HE'D LIKE-

COURSE, IT'S LIKE "DADDY" WAS SAYIN' THE OTHER DAY- THIS YEAR FOLKS WHO HAVE DOUGH, SHOULD SPEND IT HELPIN' FOLKS WHO NEED HELP- I KNOW LOTS O' POOR FOLKS I'M GOIN' TO HELP- BUT I'VE GOT ENOUGH THIS YEAR TO TAKE CARE OF THEM AND STILL BUY "DADDY" SOMETHIN'- GEE- I WISH "DADDY'D" HURRY HOME-

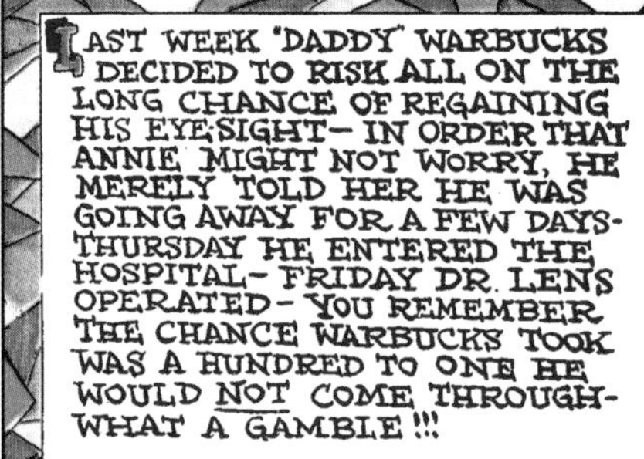
LAST WEEK 'DADDY' WARBUCKS DECIDED TO RISK ALL ON THE LONG CHANCE OF REGAINING HIS EYESIGHT- IN ORDER THAT ANNIE MIGHT NOT WORRY, HE MERELY TOLD HER HE WAS GOING AWAY FOR A FEW DAYS- THURSDAY HE ENTERED THE HOSPITAL- FRIDAY DR. LENS OPERATED- YOU REMEMBER THE CHANCE WARBUCKS TOOK WAS A HUNDRED TO ONE HE WOULD NOT COME THROUGH- WHAT A GAMBLE!!!

HM-M-M-
HAROLD GRAY

BUT, DOCTOR LENS - IT WAS ZE MAGNIFICENT OPERATION-
YES, DOCTOR - BUT WAS IT WORTH THE CHANCE? IF HE SHOULD FAIL TO RALLY I COULD NEVER FACE THE WORLD AGAIN-
WERE THE ODDS TOO GREAT? IF DOCTOR LENS HAS FAILED, IS HE TO BE BLAMED?

December 13, 1931
A HUNDRED TO ONE

HAVE I BEEN ASLEEP LONG, DOCTOR? WHAT DAY IS THIS?
WHAT DAY IS THIS? LET'S SEE- BLESSED IF I KNOW, MYSELF- BUT DON'T WORRY ABOUT THAT NOW- TRY TO GO BACK TO SLEEP, IF YOU CAN-
HE'S PULLED THROUGH- AT LEAST HE'LL LIVE- AND NOW HE'S SLEEPING NORMALLY, AT LAST-
YES, DOCTOR- AND IT'S TIME YOU HAD SOME NORMAL SLEEP- YOU'VE BEEN ON GUARD FOR THREE DAYS AND NIGHTS WITHOUT CLOSING YOUR EYES ONCE-
Z-Z-Z Z-Z-Z
HE'S SLEEPING NOW- HE'S RALLIED AND WILL LIVE- BUT I DOUBT VERY MUCH IF THE OPERATION WILL RESTORE HIS SIGHT-
HE'S PULLED THROUGH? THAT'S THE MAIN THING, DOC.- IF HE HADN'T-.....
I'LL UNDRESS IN A MINUTE- JUST WANT TO REST FOR A MINUTE FIRST- JUST-.. -REST Z-Z-Z-Z..
LEND A HAND, BOYS-WE MUST GET DOCTOR LENS PROPERLY TO BED- HE'S ALL IN-
HAROLD GRAY
Reg. U. S. Pat. Off.; Copyright, 1931, by The Chicago Tribune.
DON'T HOPE FOR TOO MUCH, MR. WARBUCKS- I THOUGHT I KNEW ALL THERE WAS TO KNOW ABOUT SUCH AN OPERATION- PERHAPS I WAS OVER-CONFIDENT- AT LEAST NEARLY EVERYTHING TURNED OUT DIFFERENTLY FROM WHAT I'D EXPECTED- I DID MY BEST, BUT-......
DON'T WORRY, DOC.- I KNOW YOU DID YOUR BEST- I KNEW THE CHANCE WE WERE TAKING- I WON'T BLAME YOU IF--- IF--
GIVE ME A SECOND--- THE LIGHT OR SOMETHING- MAYBE I'M AFRAID TO FIND OUT THE TRUTH---
WHY--- WHY!
Reg. U. S. Pat. Off.; Copyright, 1931, by The Chicago Tribune.
I CAN SEE! DO YOU HEAR? I CAN SEE!
HAROLD GRAY
HE SHOULD HAVE TOLD ME, SO I COULD HAVE BEEN AT THE HOSPITAL- WHEN WAS THE OPERATION? OH, BILL- YOU WON'T TELL ME A THING- BUT I KNOW IT WILL COME OUT RIGHT-
COME ON, BILL- AREN'T YOU COMING IN WITH ME TO SEE "DADDY"?
NO- NOT JUST YET- YOU GO ON IN, ANNIE- I'LL JUST WAIT HERE-
ANNIE! YOU WERE RIGHT- YOUR DOC LENS SURE IS A WONDER-
OH, "DADDY"! I KNEW IT- YOU CAN SEE!
Reg. U. S. Pat. Off.; Copyright, 1931, by The Chicago Tribune.
I AM GLAD- HOW COULD I WISH ANYTHING ELSE FOR A GUY AS SWELL AND REGULAR AS OLIVER WARBUCKS? CHEE! BUT NOW HE'LL SEE ME- THE LITTLE RUNT- IT WAS ALL RIGHT BEFORE- WE WERE PALS- HE'LL STILL TRY TO STICK TO ME- HE'S THAT KIND- BUT HE WON'T NEED ME ANY MORE- AND HOW CAN HE HAVE ANY RESPECT FOR A DWARF LIKE ME- IT'D BE BETTER IF I JUST FADED AWAY BEFORE HE EVER SEES ME-
HAROLD GRAY

December 14–16, 1931

GUESS I HAD DOC. LENS PRETTY BADLY WORRIED FOR A WHILE- BUT IT'S ALL OVER NOW AND I CAN SEE- I HATE TO GO TO SLEEP ANY MORE- I'M AFRAID I'LL MISS SOMETHING- IT'S ODD, BUT I SEE THINGS NOW THAT I NEVER NOTICED BEFORE I WAS BLIND-

BY THE WAY- WHERE'S BILL? WHY DOESN'T HE SHOW UP? ISN'T HE COMING TO VISIT ME?

HE'S OUT IN TH' HALL, "DADDY"- I CAN'T GET HIM TO COME IN- I DON'T KNOW WHAT AILS HIM-

HEY! BILL! WHY DON'T YOU COME ON IN HERE AND CONGRATULATE ME?
CHEE, OLIVER- IT'S GREAT- IT'S TH' BEST LUCK I COULD WISH YOU- BUT--- THAT IS--- AW--- CHEE- WHAT'S TH' USE? YOU WON'T BE WANTIN' ME MUCH MORE, NOW THAT YOU CAN SEE-
Reg. U. S. Pat. Off.; Copyright, 1931, by The Chicago Tribune.

WHY, YOU DOG-GONED SHRINKIN' VIOLET- WHAT DIFFERENCE CAN IT EVER MAKE BETWEEN US? PARTNERS, AREN'T WE? DO YOU THINK I'M TH' KIND OF BUZZARD THAT FORGETS A REAL FRIEND LIKE YOU, BILL?

CHEE! THEN WE'RE STILL PARTNERS- CHEE!

HAROLD GRAY

HOME AGAIN- AND THIS TIME I CAN SEE WHAT IT LOOKS LIKE- WELL, THIS ISN'T SUCH A BAD LAYOUT, IF I DO SAY SO- IT'S EVEN BETTER THAN I IMAGINED IT WAS-

WHAT A VIEW- AND THAT'S THE YACHT DOWN THERE IN THE RIVER, EH? YOU KNOW, I GET A LOT MORE KICK OUT OF A GOOD VIEW THAN I EVER DID BEFORE I WAS BLIND- THAT CHAP WHO SAID YOU NEVER APPRECIATE ANYTHING SO MUCH TILL AFTER YOU'VE LOST IT SURE KNEW HIS STUFF-

SAY, "DADDY"- WITH ALL TH' 'CITEMENT, I'LL BET YOU DON'T KNOW WHAT DAY THIS IS-
TO-DAY? WHY, THIS MUST BE FRIDAY- WHAT OF THAT?
Reg. U. S. Pat. Off.; Copyright, 1931, by The Chicago Tribune.

YES, IT'S FRIDAY, DECEMBER 18TH- AND THAT MEANS IT'S JUST ONE WEEK TILL CHRISTMAS!
GREAT SCOTT! SO IT IS-
HAROLD GRAY

NOW THAT I CAN SEE, IT'S SURPRISING HOW MANY PAPERS EVERYBODY SAYS IT IS ABSOLUTELY NECESSARY FOR ME TO READ- I'VE BEEN AT THIS FOR HOURS AND I'VE HARDLY MADE A DENT IN THIS STACK- WHAT DO I HIRE LAWYERS FOR? THEY'RE SUPPOSED TO PASS ON ALL THIS STUFF-

BAH! AN EXECUTIVE SHOULD KEEP HIS DESK CLEAR- BUSINESS WENT ALONG O.K. WHEN I COULDN'T SEE A THING- CONTRACTS- REPORTS- I'VE GOT MORE IMPORTANT THINGS TO THINK ABOUT-

BOY OH BOY! IT'S GREAT TO BE MYSELF AGAIN, AND TO BE ALONE WHERE I CAN HAVE A CHANCE TO THINK- WAS ANY MAN EVER SO LUCKY AS I? FROM RAGS TO RICHES- AND IF IT HADN'T BEEN FOR GOOD OLD BILL, I'D STILL BE A BUM- AND IF IT HADN'T BEEN FOR ANNIE, I'D NEVER HAVE MET DOC. LENS AND I'D STILL BE BLIND-

THAT SIGN OVER THERE- "WE HAVE SHARED"- WELL, I'VE SHARED, - WE SHOULD ALL SHARE- I'M GIVING AWAY A FORTUNE EVERY DAY- WHY SHOULDN'T I? WHAT'S MONEY? I HAVE MY HEALTH- THAT'S THE MAIN THING-
HAROLD GRAY
Reg. U. S. Pat. Off.; Copyright, 1931, by The Chicago Tribune.

Little Orphan
Annie
ARF! ARF! ARF!

HELLO, SANDY! IT SURE IS GOOD TO SEE YOU AGAIN-
ARF!

HELLO, "DADDY"-
WELL, WELL, ANNIE- HOW ARE YOU THIS MORNING?

GEE, "DADDY- IT'S SWELL TO HAVE YOU ALL WELL- HOW DOES IT FEEL TO BE ABLE TO SEE AGAIN AS GOOD AS EVER?

I NEVER VALUED MY SIGHT TILL I LOST IT- NOW I HATE TO SLEEP FOR FEAR I'LL MISS SOMETHING- JUST LOOK AT THAT VIEW- I WANT TO SPEND ALL MY TIME OUT HERE-JUST LOOKING-

I SEE THINGS NOW THAT I NEVER WOULD HAVE NOTICED BEFORE I WAS BLIND- HOW FOOLISH I WAS TO GO TO EUROPE LOOKING FOR A DOCTOR TO CURE ME, WHEN RIGHT HERE AT HOME WE HAVE THE FINEST DOCTORS IN THE WORLD- I CAN SEE THAT NOW-

SAY, "DADDY"- WITH SO MUCH 'CITEMENT AND EVER'THING I BET YOU DON'T KNOW WHAT'S ALMOST HERE- CHRISTMAS!- YES SIR- IT'S NEXT FRIDAY- AND I HAVEN'T GOT YOU ANY PRESENT YET- WHAT WOULD YOU LIKE, "DADDY"?

SAY! I'VE HAD MY CHRISTMAS PRESENT- I GOT MY EYE-SIGHT BACK, DIDN'T I? GUESS THAT'S ENOUGH CHRISTMAS PRESENT FOR ME- IF YOU WANT TO MAKE ME HAPPY, ANNIE, I TELL YOU WHAT YOU DO-

THE REGULAR CHARITY ORGANIZATIONS ARE FINE- I'VE SENT THEM MY CHECKS- BUT YOU KNOW A LOT OF FOLKS PERSONALLY WHO NEED HELP- YOU MAKE OUT A LIST OF EVERY ONE OF 'EM, AND YOU AND I'LL GET BUSY AND TAKE CARE OF THEM.

GEE, WITH ALL THAT'S HAPPENED TO "DADDY" YOU'D THINK HE'D SORT O' FORGET 'BOUT OTHER FOLKS- BUT HE NEVER FORGETS OTHERS- MAYBE THAT'S WHY HE'S SO SUCCESSFUL-

HE'S HAD PLENTY O' TOUGH BREAKS HIMSELF- I GUESS IT'S FOLKS WHO HAVE HAD ROUGH GOIN' THAT KNOW WHAT A HELPIN' HAND MEANS WHEN YOU'RE UP AGAINST IT- HE'S TH' MOST GENEROUS GUY IN TH' WORLD, BUT TH' MORE HE GIVES, TH' MORE HE SEEMS TO GET-

THEY SAY HEAVEN HELPS THOSE WHO HELP THEMSELVES, BUT DIDJA EVER STOP TO FIGGER HOW MUCH MORE IT MUST DO FOR THOSE WHO HELP TH' HELPLESS?
HAROLD GRAY

December 20, 1931

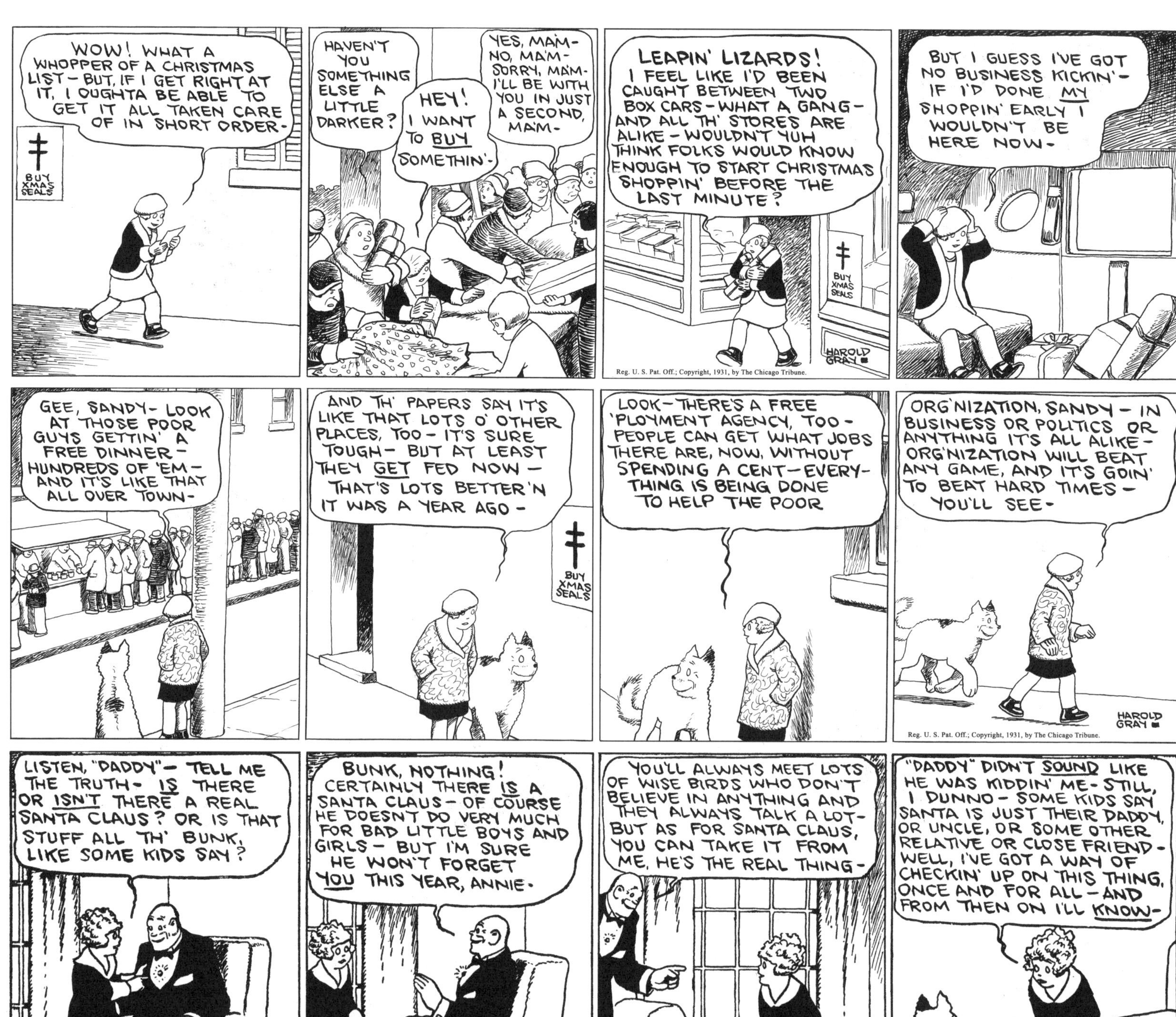
WOW! WHAT A WHOPPER OF A CHRISTMAS LIST - BUT, IF I GET RIGHT AT IT, I OUGHTA BE ABLE TO GET IT ALL TAKEN CARE OF IN SHORT ORDER -
BUY XMAS SEALS
HAVEN'T YOU SOMETHING ELSE A LITTLE DARKER?
HEY! I WANT TO BUY SOMETHIN'-
YES, MA'M - NO, MA'M - SORRY, MA'M - I'LL BE WITH YOU IN JUST A SECOND, MA'M -
LEAPIN' LIZARDS! I FEEL LIKE I'D BEEN CAUGHT BETWEEN TWO BOX CARS - WHAT A GANG - AND ALL TH' STORES ARE ALIKE - WOULDN'T YUH THINK FOLKS WOULD KNOW ENOUGH TO START CHRISTMAS SHOPPIN' BEFORE THE LAST MINUTE?
BUY XMAS SEALS
HAROLD GRAY
Reg. U. S. Pat. Off.; Copyright, 1931, by The Chicago Tribune.
BUT I GUESS I'VE GOT NO BUSINESS KICKIN' - IF I'D DONE MY SHOPPIN' EARLY I WOULDN'T BE HERE NOW -
GEE, SANDY - LOOK AT THOSE POOR GUYS GETTIN' A FREE DINNER - HUNDREDS OF 'EM - AND IT'S LIKE THAT ALL OVER TOWN -
AND TH' PAPERS SAY IT'S LIKE THAT LOTS O' OTHER PLACES, TOO - IT'S SURE TOUGH - BUT AT LEAST THEY GET FED NOW - THAT'S LOTS BETTER'N IT WAS A YEAR AGO -
BUY XMAS SEALS
LOOK - THERE'S A FREE 'PLOYMENT AGENCY, TOO - PEOPLE CAN GET WHAT JOBS THERE ARE, NOW, WITHOUT SPENDING A CENT - EVERYTHING IS BEING DONE TO HELP THE POOR
ORG'NIZATION, SANDY - IN BUSINESS OR POLITICS OR ANYTHING IT'S ALL ALIKE - ORG'NIZATION WILL BEAT ANY GAME, AND IT'S GOIN' TO BEAT HARD TIMES - YOU'LL SEE -
HAROLD GRAY
Reg. U. S. Pat. Off.; Copyright, 1931, by The Chicago Tribune.
LISTEN, "DADDY" - TELL ME THE TRUTH - IS THERE OR ISN'T THERE A REAL SANTA CLAUS? OR IS THAT STUFF ALL TH' BUNK, LIKE SOME KIDS SAY?
BUNK, NOTHING! CERTAINLY THERE IS A SANTA CLAUS - OF COURSE HE DOESN'T DO VERY MUCH FOR BAD LITTLE BOYS AND GIRLS - BUT I'M SURE HE WON'T FORGET YOU THIS YEAR, ANNIE.
YOU'LL ALWAYS MEET LOTS OF WISE BIRDS WHO DON'T BELIEVE IN ANYTHING AND THEY ALWAYS TALK A LOT - BUT AS FOR SANTA CLAUS, YOU CAN TAKE IT FROM ME, HE'S THE REAL THING -
"DADDY" DIDN'T SOUND LIKE HE WAS KIDDIN' ME - STILL, I DUNNO - SOME KIDS SAY SANTA IS JUST THEIR DADDY, OR UNCLE, OR SOME OTHER RELATIVE OR CLOSE FRIEND - WELL, I'VE GOT A WAY OF CHECKIN' UP ON THIS THING, ONCE AND FOR ALL - AND FROM THEN ON I'LL KNOW -
HAROLD GRAY
Reg. U. S. Pat. Off.; Copyright, 1931, by The Chicago Tribune.

December 21–23, 1931

THERE MAY BE A SANTA CLAUS, LIKE "DADDY" SAYS- BUT, IF HE'S BEEN KIDDIN' ME, I'LL KNOW BY MORNIN'- SH-H-- HEAR HIM SNORE- HE'S IN HIS ROOM ASLEEP- HIS DOOR IS SHUT- NOW'S MY CHANCE-

I KNOW SANTA HASN'T BEEN HERE YET- I JUST LOOKED, AND THERE'S NOTHIN' DOWN BY TH' FIRE-PLACE, 'CEPT MY SOCKS THAT I HUNG UP THERE-

NOW I'LL JUST PASTE THIS STICKER HERE ON "DADDY'S" DOOR- HE'LL NEVER NOTICE IT- BUT IN TH' MORNIN' I'LL LOOK- IF THIS STICKER IS BUSTED, I'LL KNOW HE'S BEEN OUT OF HIS ROOM-

I GUESS I'LL GET SOMETHIN' IN MY STOCKINGS ALL RIGHT- BUT I'M BETTIN' THAT IF SANTA CLAUS HAS BEEN HERE BY MORNING I'LL FIND THAT SEAL BUSTED ON "DADDY'S" DOOR, TOO- WE'LL SEE-
HAROLD GRAY

GEE! IT'S GETTIN' DAYLIGHT- IT'S CHRISTMAS MORNING! WOW! AND I ALMOST OVERSLEPT-

WELL, I'LL BE A SARDINE- THAT STICKER ON "DADDY'S" DOOR ISN'T BUSTED, SO HE CAN'T HAVE BEEN OUT OF HIS ROOM ALL NIGHT- GEE- MAYBE HE MEANT TO GET UP, BUT SLEPT TOO SOUND, OR SOMETHIN'-

SHUX! THERE WON'T BE ANYTHING IN MY SOCKS YET- BUT I'LL JUST LOOK, AND THEN SLIP BACK TO BED AND WAIT- "DADDY'S" BOUND TO WAKE UP SOON- AND I WON'T TELL HIM I WAS DOWN BEFORE- HE'LL NEVER KNOW I'M WISE TO HIM-
HAROLD GRAY

LEAPIN' LIZARDS! IT COULDN'T HAVE BEEN "DADDY"- THERE MUST BE A SANTA CLAUS AFTER ALL- HEY! "DADDY"- COME QUICK! MERRY CHRISTMAS! SANTA'S BEEN HERE-

GEE, "DADDY"- YOU GAVE ME SO MUCH FOR CHRISTMAS- AND SANTA GAVE ME SO MUCH- AND YOU GOT SO LITTLE-

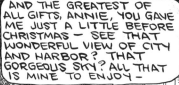

AND YOU'RE SO GOOD AND GENEROUS- I WANTED TO GIVE YOU SUCH NICE THINGS- BUT MY PRESENTS TO YOU SEEMED SO POOR-
WHY, YOU LITTLE DARLING- YOU GAVE ME WONDERFUL PRESENTS-

AND THE GREATEST OF ALL GIFTS, ANNIE, YOU GAVE ME JUST A LITTLE BEFORE CHRISTMAS- SEE THAT WONDERFUL VIEW OF CITY AND HARBOR? THAT GORGEOUS SKY? ALL THAT IS MINE TO ENJOY-
HAROLD GRAY

ALL THE BEAUTIFUL SIGHTS IN THE WORLD, ANNIE- YOU GAVE THEM ALL TO ME WHEN, THROUGH YOU, I MET DOCTOR LENS AND HE RESTORED MY SIGHT- VISION! THAT'S MY CHRISTMAS PRESENT FROM YOU, ANNIE- AND WHAT A GIFT TO GET-

December 24–26, 1931

Little Orphan Annie
DEC 27

WELL, SANDY, ANOTHER YEAR IS ALMOST GONE - AND WHAT A YEAR! "DADDY" GOIN' BROKE AND THEN HIS BIG HOUSE BURNIN' AND WE LIVIN' IN ONE LITTLE ROOM AT MAW GREEN'S - THEN ME GETTIN' A JOB -

BUT "DADDY" COULDN'T GET WORK AND HE PULLED OUT - COURSE I FIGGERED HE'D GONE TO CHINA OR SOME PLACE - GEE! IF I'D ONLY KNOWN HE WAS IN TH' HOSPITAL, BLIND FROM THAT AUTO SMASH-UP - AND 'CAUSE HE WAS SO POOR AND HELPLESS, NOBODY'D PAY HIM DAMAGES OR NOTHIN' -
ALL TH' TIME HE WAS SO CLOSE TO ME, BUT I NEVER S'PECTED - THEN I FOUND PAT, TH' LITTLE DARLIN' - AND THOSE CROOKS, MR. AND MRS. CUNNING, TRIED TO STEAL HER - BUT PAT'S REAL FOLKS GOT HER BACK SAFELY AT LAST -

THERE I WAS, LIVIN' AT DOC. LENS' PLACE, WHEN, ALL OF A SUDDEN, I FOUND "DADDY" - AND HE WAS AWFUL RICH AGAIN --- BUT BLIND -

AN' I TALKED AN' ARGUED AN' AT LAST HE LET DOC. LENS OP'RATE - GEE - THAT WAS A CLOSE ONE - BUT "DADDY" PULLED THROUGH - AND NOW HE'S AS GOOD AS EVER -

SH!
Z-Z-Z-Z
Z-Z-Z-Z

"DADDY'S" TAKIN' A LITTLE NAP - HE MUST BE AWFUL TIRED - HE WAS OUT TILL AFTER MIDNIGHT SEEIN' THAT POOR FOLKS WERE LOOKED AFTER RIGHT - YET A BUNCH O' WILD-EYED SOFT-HANDED BIRDS ARE FOREVER SOBBIN' THAT IT'S WRONG FOR ANYBODY TO BE RICH -

HUH - IF IT WASN'T FOR RICH AND GENEROUS FOLKS, LIKE "DADDY," A LOT O' THOSE ALL-TALK-AND-NO-WORK GUYS WOULD STARVE - HARD TIMES! HUH! "DADDY" WAS BROKE AND BLIND - LOST EVERYTHING - BUT DID THAT STOP HIM? NOT ON YER LIFE - UP AN' AT 'EM - THAT'S MY "DADDY" - AND THAT'S WHY NOTHIN' CAN LICK HIM -

SOME FOLKS SAY, WHAT'S TH' USE TO TRY? THEY SAY THERE'S NO USE LOOKIN' FOR WORK THESE TIMES - BALONEY! IT'S A CINCH THOSE WHO GIVE UP WILL NEVER GET ANYWHERE -

IT'S ALWAYS HARD TIMES FOR LAZY PEOPLE, OR FOLKS TOO WEAK OR SCARED TO GIVE TH' WORLD A FIGHT - BUT WHEN YUH SEE SOME OF THE DUMMIES THAT ARE GETTIN' BY, YOU CAN FEEL SURE YOU HAVE A CHANCE -

COURSE IT HAS BEEN A TOUGH YEAR - BUT WHAT'S TH' PAST? FORGET IT, I SAY - IT'S THE FUTURE THAT COUNTS - AND 1932 IS GOIN' TO BE A RING-TAILED HUMDINGER - YOU'LL SEE, SANDY - YOU'LL SEE -
HAROLD GRAY

December 27, 1931

HO! HUM!
GEE, I FEEL LAZY- THIS WEEK 'TWEEN CHRISTMAS AND NEW YEAR IS ALWAYS SORT O' DULL- THE OLD YEAR'S ALMOST OVER AND THE NEW ONE HASN'T BEGUN-

LOOKIE, SANDY- GUESS "DADDY" FEELS TH' SAME WAY I DO- HEY, "DADDY"! ARE YOU ASLEEP?

OH, I'M SORRY- I DIDN'T MEAN TO WAKE YOU UP, IF YOU WERE REALLY SLEEPIN'-
THAT'S ALL RIGHT, ANNIE- I WAS HAVING A BAD DREAM, ANYWAY- THIS PAST YEAR HAS HAD SPOTS IN IT THAT WOULD GIVE ANY ONE BAD DREAMS, I GUESS-

YEP- FIRST I LOST EVERY CENT- I WAS DOWN AND OUT- AND, AS IF THAT WASN'T BAD ENOUGH, THAT ACCIDENT BLINDED ME- THEN I MET FLOP-HOUSE BILL AND HE HELPED ME COME BACK- AND YOU HELPED ME GET BACK MY SIGHT- BAD LUCK AND GOOD- IT'S BEEN A HUMDINGER OF A YEAR- BUT IT'S ENDING FINE FOR US ALL- THAT'S WHAT COUNTS-

HAROLD GRAY
Reg. U. S. Pat. Off.; Copyright, 1931, by The Chicago Tribune.

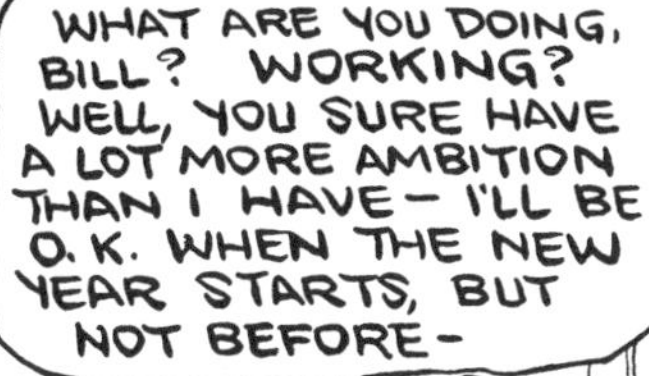
WHAT ARE YOU DOING, BILL? WORKING? WELL, YOU SURE HAVE A LOT MORE AMBITION THAN I HAVE- I'LL BE O.K. WHEN THE NEW YEAR STARTS, BUT NOT BEFORE-

SORT OF SEEING WHERE WE STAND, EH?
YES, I FIGURED THIS WAS A GOOD TIME TO CHECK UP- FROM NOTHING TO BILLIONS- WOW! WHAT A YEAR IT'S BEEN FOR US, OLIVER-

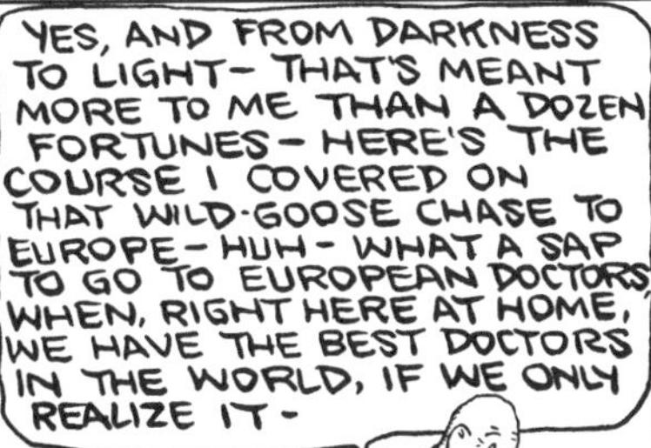
YES, AND FROM DARKNESS TO LIGHT- THAT'S MEANT MORE TO ME THAN A DOZEN FORTUNES- HERE'S THE COURSE I COVERED ON THAT WILD-GOOSE CHASE TO EUROPE- HUH- WHAT A SAP TO GO TO EUROPEAN DOCTORS, WHEN, RIGHT HERE AT HOME, WE HAVE THE BEST DOCTORS IN THE WORLD, IF WE ONLY REALIZE IT-

Reg. U S Pat. Off., Copyright, 1931, by The Chicago Tribune.

WELL, OLIVER- WE LIVE AND LEARN, EH?
YES, WE CERTAINLY DO. BUT SOME OF US HAVE TO LIVE A LONG, LONG TIME BEFORE WE LEARN VERY MUCH-
HAROLD GRAY

MY-MY- JUST LOOK, SANDY- JAKE'S TAKEN THE SECOND FLOOR AND HAS A WHOLE NEW FRONT ON HIS STORE- PRETTY SWELL, EH?

HELLO, JAKE- WE WERE JUST GOIN' BY AND THOUGHT WE'D DROP IN AND SAY HELLO- ARE YOU BUSY?
ANNIE! BUSY? OLD JAKE'S NEVER TOO BUSY TO SEE YOU- YOU MUST COME BACK TO THE OFFICE-

NOT HALF A DOZEN CUSTOMERS TO-DAY- BUT WE WORK HARDER THAN EVER- SEE? WE ARE GETTING READY FOR THE SALES- PRE-INVENTORY SALE! JANUARY CLEARANCE SALE! SALE! SALE! SALE!

HAROLD GRAY

WHAT A YEAR IT HAS BEEN FOR ME- AND I WILL NEVER FORGET WHO I SHOULD THANK- YOU IT WAS WHO HELPED ME- YOU MADE ME ADVERTISE- YI- WHAT A HEAD FOR BUSINESS- NOW OLD JAKE IS ESTABLISHED- AND NEXT YEAR IT SHOULD BE THREE TIMES SO GOOD-
GEE, JAKE- I'M GLAD-
Reg. U. S. Pat. Off.; Copyright, 1931, by The Chicago Tribune.

December 28–30, 1931

I GUESS IT WON'T HURT YOU TO SIT UP AND SEE THE OLD YEAR OUT, ANNIE- BUT YOU LOOK PRETTY SLEEPY TO ME- WELL, ANOTHER YEAR NEARLY GONE- ALMOST TIME TO PULL UP ONE'S BELT AND TIE INTO THIS BATTLE CALLED LIFE, WITH NEW VIM AND DETERMINATION-

THE DEAR LITTLE TYKE- SOUND ASLEEP- WELL, SHE STAYED AWAKE LONG AFTER HER REGULAR BED-TIME- IT'S NEARLY ELEVEN-

HERE, CELESTE- BE CAREFUL AND DON'T WAKE HER UP- SHE'S VERY TIRED- BETTER LET HER SLEEP TILL NEXT YEAR-

WHAT A KID- IF MORE OF US COULD ONLY BE LIKE HER- SIMPLE- DIRECT- HONEST- EXCEPT FOR LESSONS LEARNED FROM PAST MISTAKES, SHE NEVER LOOKS BACK- FACING EVER FORWARD, WITH FRESH HOPE AND FAITH, SHE FOLLOWS THE ONE COURSE THAT WILL ALWAYS BRING HAPPINESS TO HER AND TO THOSE ABOUT HER-
HAROLD GRAY
Reg. U. S. Pat. Off.; Copyright, 1931, by The Chicago Tribune.

WHAT'S THAT, ANNIE?
I SAY, "DADDY," WILL YOU HAVE TO BE GOIN' AWAY ON A LONG TRIP AGAIN 'FORE LONG? IT SEEMS LIKE MOST ALWAYS, WHEN EVER'THING IS GOIN' SWELL AND WE'RE SO HAPPY, YOU HAVE TO GO AWAY AND EVER'THING GOES WRONG-

DON'T YOU WORRY ABOUT THAT, ANNIE- I'VE BEEN A PRETTY BUM "DADDY" TO YOU LOTS OF TIMES IN THE PAST- BUT I'VE LEARNED MY LESSON-

GO AWAY AND LEAVE YOU, ANNIE? NEVER AGAIN, IF I CAN HELP IT, AND I THINK I CAN- YOU'RE A WITNESS TO THAT, BILL-

THIS IS MY NEW YEAR'S RESOLUTION- FROM NOW ON I WILL STICK TO ANNIE AND I WILL STAY AT HOME AND STICK TO BUSINESS, TOO-

GEE, "DADDY"- THAT'S SWELL-
YEAH! AND WE'LL HOLD YOU TO THAT ONE, OLIVER-
HAROLD GRAY
Reg. U. S. Pat. Off.; Copyright, 1932, by The Chicago Tribune.

THE PAPER, SIR-
OH, THANKS, ELBERT-

HM-M-M- I SEE HERE ANOTHER EX-CHAMP IS TRYING TO STAGE A COME-BACK- QUITE AN ARTICLE ABOUT IT- YEAH, AND, AS USUAL, SOME WISE GUY HERE DUSTS OFF THE OLD AXIOM THAT, "THEY NEVER COME BACK."-

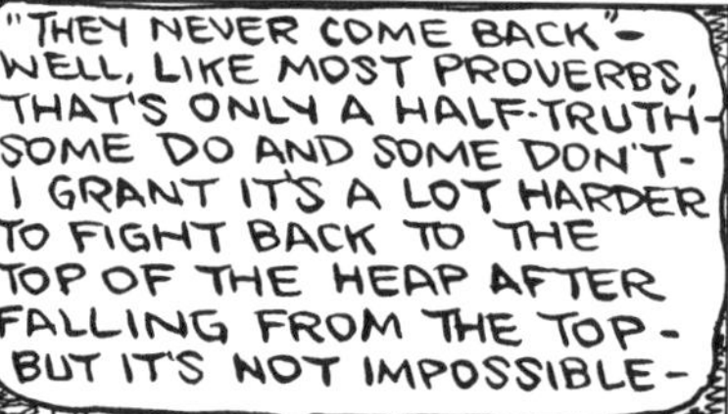
"THEY NEVER COME BACK"- WELL, LIKE MOST PROVERBS, THAT'S ONLY A HALF-TRUTH- SOME DO AND SOME DON'T- I GRANT IT'S A LOT HARDER TO FIGHT BACK TO THE TOP OF THE HEAP AFTER FALLING FROM THE TOP- BUT IT'S NOT IMPOSSIBLE-

Reg. U. S. Pat. Off.; Copyright, 1932, by The Chicago Tribune.

WHY, A YEAR AGO, I WAS ON TOP- THEN WAS ANY-ONE EVER LAID LOWER THAN I? EVEN MY SPIRIT WAS BROKEN, FOR A WHILE- BUT I FOUGHT BACK AND HERE I AM AT THE TOP AGAIN, TO STAY- SO "THEY NEVER COME BACK," EH? BALONEY-
HAROLD GRAY

December 31, 1931–
January 2, 1932

In Our Next Volume

Volume Four of The Complete Little Orphan Annie presents Harold Gray's spunky orphan in the midst of The Great Depression, while "Daddy" Warbucks finds a new love! With all Sunday pages in full color!

HERE THEY ARE-
PULL 'EM OUT O' THEIR CAR-
LET ME AT 'EM-
ALL RIGHT, PETE- LET'S GET 'EM INTO THE JAIL-
Harold Gray's
Little Orphan Annie
VOLUME FOUR
A HOUSE DIVIDED
INTRODUCING THE MYSTERIOUS WUN WEY
THE COMPLETE DAILIES AND COLOR SUNDAYS 1932 TO 1933
WITH A BIOGRAPHICAL ESSAY BY JEET HEER
Can America's Spunkiest Kid Trick Trixie and Save the Day?!

THE
LIBRARY OF
AMERICAN
COMICS

ACKNOWLEDGMENTS

We are indebted first and foremost to
THE HAROLD GRAY ARCHIVES AT THE HOWARD GOTLIEB ARCHIVAL RESEARCH CENTER
MUGAR LIBRARY, BOSTON UNIVERSITY
Sean Noel, Assistant Director; JC Johnson, Archivist; Alex Rankin, Assistant Director for Acquisitions
www.bu.edu/archives

The following people have been helpful in the preparation of this volume:
Stephen Tippie, Justin Eisinger, Beau Smith, Randy Scott, Richard Olson, John Province, Peter Maresca, Jon Merrill, Tony Raiola, Francis Olschafskie, Chris Stuart, Kim Thompson, Chris Ware, Mark Newgarden, Larry Shell, and David Allen.

In addition, for readers interested in exploring the breadth of comic strip and comic book history, we are fortunate to also have, among others, two comprehensive university library resources. We highly recommend them:

MICHIGAN STATE UNIVERSITY'S COMIC ART COLLECTION www.lib.msu.edu/comics
OHIO STATE UNIVERSITY'S CARTOON RESEARCH LIBRARY cartoons.osu.edu

Readers may also wish to seek out such books as *Terry and the Pirates, Dick Tracy, Scorchy Smith and the Art of Noel Sickles, Mary Perkins On Stage, The Heart of Juliet Jones, Little Sammy Sneeze, Krazy & Ignatz, Little Nemo in Slumberland*, *Popeye*, and *Peanuts*.

Index by RANDALL W. SCOTT, *Comic Art Bibliographer, Special Collections Division, Michigan State University, East Lansing, Michigan*

Index

Index

BACK ENDPAPERS:
Early Little Orphan Annie and Sandy cut-outs, circa 1925.

"SANDY"

—— CUT
- - - - FOLD
////// PASTE

PASTE DOUBLE
TAIL, EARS AND BACK LEGS